ALSO BY ALAN WALKER

Franz Liszt: Volume 1, The Virtuoso Years, 1811–1847
Franz Liszt: Volume 2, The Weimar Years, 1848–1861
Franz Liszt: Volume 3, The Final Years, 1861–1886
The Death of Franz Liszt
Reflections on Liszt
Hans von Bülow: A Life and Times

FRYDERYK
CHOPIN

FRYDERYK CHOPIN

A Life and Times

ALAN WALKER

Farrar, Straus and Giroux   New York

Farrar, Straus and Giroux
175 Varick Street, New York 10014

Library of Congress Cataloging-in-Publication Data
Names: Walker, Alan, 1930– author.
Title: Fryderyk Chopin : a life and times / Alan Walker.
Description: First edition. | New York : Farrar, Straus and Giroux, 2018. |
    Includes bibliographical references and index.
Identifiers: LCCN 2017046936 | ISBN 9780374159061 (hardcover)
Subjects: LCSH: Chopin, Frédéric, 1810–1849. | Composers—Biography.
Classification: LCC ML410.C54 W18 2018 | DDC 786.2092 [B]—dc23
LC record available at https://lccn.loc.gov/2017046936

Designed by Jonathan D. Lippincott

Our books may be purchased in bulk for promotional, educational, or business use.
Please contact your local bookseller or the Macmillan Corporate and Premium Sales
Department at 1-800-221-7945, extension 5442, or by e-mail at
MacmillanSpecialMarkets@macmillan.com.

www.fsgbooks.com
www.twitter.com/fsgbooks • www.facebook.com/fsgbooks

1   3   5   7   9   10   8   6   4   2

Frontispiece: Fryderyk Chopin; an oil painting by Teofil Kwiatkowski (1844)

To the memory of my grandfather
Edward Ernest Whitby,
wise counselor and best friend

CONTENTS

List of Illustrations   *xxi*
Acknowledgments   *xxv*
Chopin Family Tree   *xxxi*

Prologue   3

CHOPIN'S FAMILY BACKGROUND   21

*Mikołaj Chopin's French origins ~ his early years in Marainville, in the province of
Lorraine ~ he is brought up on the nearby estate of Polish-born Count Michał Jan Pác,
whose manager Adam Weydlich brings Mikołaj into his household, where the boy is
educated and learns Polish ~ in 1787, age sixteen, Mikołaj accompanies the Weydlich
family to Warsaw and becomes a French-language teacher in their newly opened boarding school ~ during the Kościuszko Uprising he joins the civilian militia (1794) and
takes part in the defense of Warsaw ~ he later finds a position as tutor to the children of
Countess Ludwika Skarbek in Żelazowa Wola, where he meets Justyna Krzyżanowska,
his future wife and the mother of Fryderyk Chopin ~ the marriage of Mikołaj and
Justyna (June 28, 1806) at the parish church of St. Roch in the village of Brochów ~ the
birth of Fryderyk, his three sisters, and their family life considered ~ Mikołaj is offered
a position as assistant master in French at the Warsaw Lyceum and settles in the Polish
capital.*

CHILDHOOD AND YOUTH IN WARSAW, 1810–1824   44

*On October 1, 1810, Mikołaj begins teaching at the Warsaw Lyceum, located in the
Saxon Palace ~ he opens a boarding school for boys to augment his income ~ the history
of the Lyceum and its academic curriculum outlined ~ Fryderyk overhears his sister*

playing the piano and finds his way to the keyboard ~ Mikołaj purchases a Buchholtz grand piano and Wojciech Żywny becomes Fryderyk's teacher ~ Żywny's eccentric personality drawn from contemporary descriptions ~ the boy publishes his first composition, a Polonaise in G minor, age seven ~ he makes his first public appearance on February 24, 1818, not yet eight years old ~ he is called "a Polish Mozart" and appears in the salons of the Warsaw aristocracy ~ the Tsarina of Russia visits Warsaw and Fryderyk presents her with two of his dances ~ he is summoned to the Brühl Palace to play for Grand Duke Constantine ~ Constantine's deranged personality described ~ Fryderyk's friendship with the Grand Duke's son Paul and Alexandrine de Moriolles ~ the soprano Angelica Catalani sings in Warsaw and after hearing Chopin play presents him with a gold watch ~ the boy gives concerts for Warsaw's Charitable Society ~ a holiday in Żelazowa Wola, summer of 1823, and a reminiscence from the octogenarian Antoni Krysiak ~ Fryderyk is admitted to Class IV of the Warsaw Lyceum ~ a description of his classmates and the rector, Dr. Samuel Linde ~ some schoolboy pranks ~ Fryderyk graduates at the end of the first year with a special prize.

EXPLORING POLAND: HOLIDAYS IN SZAFARNIA, 1824–1825   71

Chopin travels to the village of Szafarnia for a summer holiday, to the home of his friend "Domuś" Dziewanowski ~ the patriotism of the Dziewanowski family ~ Chopin's daily routine in Szafarnia ~ his failed attempts to ride a horse ~ a letter to his family ~ he issues a satirical journal called the Szafarnia Courier, and issues news bulletins ~ he explores the surrounding countryside of Mazovia and hears Polish peasant music for the first time ~ an early mazurka (the "Little Jew") ~ composes another mazurka, in A-flat major, and dedicates it to his friend Wilhelm Kolberg ~ harvesttime in Szafarnia ~ Tsar Alexander I arrives in Warsaw and opens the Polish Sejm, April 1825 ~ the fifteen-year-old Chopin is invited to play on the newly invented Aeolomelodikon for the tsar, who presents him with a diamond ring ~ two concerts in the Conservatory (May 27 and June 10).

Another holiday in Szafarnia (July 1825) ~ he roams across Mazovia and visits Toruń, the birthplace of Copernicus ~ some merrymaking during the harvest in Szafarnia ~ back in Warsaw the youth is appointed organist at the Church of the Nuns of the Visitation ~ descriptions of his playing ~ letters to his friend Jan Białobłocki ~ a Christmas visit to his birthplace, Żelazowa Wola.

THE DECEMBRIST REVOLT, 1825–1826   92

Tsar Alexander I dies of typhus ~ disaffected Russian army officers in Saint Petersburg refuse to acknowledge his brother Nicholas as his successor and the "Decembrist Revolt" breaks out ~ public hangings of the military in Petersburg ~ passive resistance grows in Poland ~ the Russian secret police arrest and torture dissenters in Warsaw ~ the death of the Polish statesman Stanisław Staszic (January 20, 1826) rallies the nation ~ Chopin's godfather, Fryderyk Skarbek, delivers an oration at the graveside of Staszic ~ Chopin receives a fragment of the Staszic burial shroud and treasures it as a relic ~ he becomes ill and is treated for tuberculosis by Dr. Wilhelm Malcz ~ some memories of Eugeniusz Skrodzki, including a skating accident on a frozen pond and a "tryst" in the botanical gardens ~ Justyna takes Chopin and his sister Emilia to the Reinerz (Duszniki) spa for a five-week "cure" ~ Chopin composes his Polonaise in B-flat minor ~ a description of Reinerz and Chopin's daily regimen ~ he gives two concerts in aid of Reinerz orphans and writes a letter to Elsner ~ visits Prince Radziwiłł on his return journey to Warsaw ~ a drawing of Chopin by Eliza Radziwiłł (1826).

AT THE WARSAW HIGH SCHOOL FOR MUSIC, 1826–1828   104

Chopin enrolls at Warsaw's High School for Music, whose rector is Józef Elsner ~ the complex connection between this institution and the Warsaw Conservatory, whose principal is Carlo Soliva ~ Chopin's curriculum of studies at the High School under Elsner ~ Elsner's early career reviewed, together with his maxims about music and musicians ~ Chopin's classmates at the High School ~ he comes across the music of John Field and composes his Nocturne in E minor (op. posth.) ~ the death and funeral of Emilia Chopin, age fourteen (April 10, 1827) ~ the Chopin family moves to the Krasiński Palace ~ Chopin completes his first year at the High School and accepts an invitation to join Count Ksewery Zboiński at his residence in Kowalewo, near Drobin ~ Chopin plans a journey across Pomerania to the northern port city of Gdańsk and begins work on his "Là ci darem" Variations ~ back in Warsaw he moves into his new home in the Krasiński Palace and plays in a concert to mark his father's name day, December 6, 1827 ~ his bosom friend "Jasio" Białobłocki dies from tuberculosis ~ Chopin composes his Sonata in C minor and dedicates it to Elsner ~ Hummel gives concerts in Warsaw and meets Chopin ~ after completing his second year at the High School, Chopin goes to Sanniki in Mazovia for another summer holiday.

FIRST TRIPS ABROAD: BERLIN AND VIENNA, 1828–1829   126

In September, Chopin attends an international science conference in Berlin in the company of the Warsaw zoologist Dr. Feliks Jarocki ~ Chopin meets Alexander von Humboldt and other famous scientists, but prefers to spend time at the Berlin opera ~ he hears performances of Weber's Der Freischütz, *Spontini's* Fernando Cortez, *and Cimarosa's* Il matrimonio segreto ~ *a performance of Handel's* Ode for Saint Cecilia's Day *at the Singakademie moves him deeply: "This is nearest to the ideal I have formed of great music" ~ returning to Warsaw, he stops at Züllichau and improvises on the piano at a local inn; it later becomes his Grand Fantasia on Polish Airs, op. 13 ~ at Poznań he visits Archbishop Wolicki and Prince Antoni Radziwiłł, who invites him to play at a concert that same day ~ the event is captured retrospectively in Henryk Siemiradzki's painting ~ Chopin dedicates his Piano Trio in G minor to Radziwiłł ~ Chopin's studies at the High School come to an end ~ Mikołaj Chopin appeals to the government for funds to allow his son to study abroad ~ the appeal is rejected: "Public funds should not be wasted for the encouragement of this type of artist."*

Tsar Nicholas I comes to Warsaw for his coronation as King of Poland (May 24, 1829) ~ the concerts of Paganini dominate the season ~ Chopin describes the Italian's playing as "absolute perfection" ~ a newspaper war breaks out between the supporters of Paganini and Karol Lipiński ~ Paganini and Chopin meet (July 16) ~ Chopin graduates from the High School for Music with flying colors (July 20); Elsner's report describes him as a "musical genius" ~ he sets out for Vienna (July 22), a journey subsidized by his father ~ an adventure in Ojców ~ he arrives in the imperial city on July 31 ~ Tobias Haslinger promises to publish the "Là ci darem" Variations ~ two concerts in the Kärntnertor Theater (August 11 and 18) ~ Czerny, Ignaz Schuppanzigh, and Count Dietrichstein are in attendance and urge him to stay in Vienna ~ trips to Prague, Teplitz, and Dresden, where he attends a performance of Goethe's Faust ~ back in Warsaw he begins work on some "exercises," the first versions of his Twelve Studies, op. 10.

KONSTANCJA GŁADKOWSKA: THE DISTANT BELOVED, 1829–1830   153
Chopin becomes infatuated with the singer Konstancja Gładkowska but does not declare his feelings ~ he unburdens himself instead to his best friend, Tytus Woyciechowski ~ the intimate nature of the friendship between Chopin and Tytus considered ~ Chopin receives an invitation to stay with Prince Antoni Radziwiłł at the latter's hunting lodge Antonin ~ a description of the lodge and Chopin's friendship with the Radziwiłł family ~ Konstancja becomes the inspiration for the Larghetto of the F minor Piano Concerto ~ the first performance of the Concerto in the Warsaw National Theater ~ he meets Konstancja for the first time (April 1830) ~ an encounter with the soprano Henrietta Sontag ~ he visits Tytus at the latter's estate at Poturzyn and presents him with the newly published "Là ci darem" Variations, which are dedicated to Tytus ~ Konstancja makes her debut in the Warsaw National Theater ~ Chopin prepares for a lengthy trip abroad, but procrastinates ~ he visits his birthplace, Żelazowa Wola, for the last time ~ civil unrest breaks out in Warsaw and many people are arrested ~ Chopin visits the military camp of General Piotr Szembek at Sochaczew and plays for him ~ in the midst of growing discontent against Russian rule Chopin gives a "farewell" concert in the National Theater (October 11) ~ before setting out on a tour that is supposed to take him to Austria and Italy, Chopin and Konstancja exchange rings ~ he leaves Warsaw on November 2, 1830, and Elsner and a group of Conservatory students serenade him as he departs the city ~ Tytus joins him at Kalisz and together they proceed to Vienna.

THE WARSAW UPRISING, 1830–1831   180
Chopin's route takes him through Wrocław, Dresden, and Prague ~ he and Tytus arrive in Vienna on November 25 and find an apartment on the Kohlmarkt ~ news reaches

*them of the Polish Uprising (November 29, 1830) ~ the Belvedere Palace is attacked by
Polish army cadets and Grand Duke Constantine flees the city ~ Tytus rushes back to
Warsaw and joins the army ~ Chopin heeds his parents' advice and stays in Vienna ~ a
description of Chopin's daily life in the imperial capital ~ he is visited by Hummel and
forms friendships with the Czech violinist Josef Slavík and Dr. Johann Malfatti,
Beethoven's old physician ~ an encounter with Thalberg: "he is not my man" ~ a homesick Christmas from which emerges the first version of the Scherzo in B minor ~ the
Poles remove Tsar Nicholas from the throne of Poland; he responds with a declaration
of war ~ an account of the first military battles ~ Chopin composes his Four Mazurkas,
op. 6, and Five Mazurkas, op. 7 ~ he visits the Vienna beer halls and hears the waltzes of
Strauss and Lanner ~ composes his Waltz in E-flat major, op. 18 ~ unable to secure
concert engagements, he runs out of money and his father makes good the loss ~ on
June 11, Chopin puts on his own concert in the Kärntnertor Theater but runs up more
debt ~ after several delays the Russians issue a passport that allows him to travel to
Munich ~ Chopin leaves Vienna in the company of the Polish scientist Alfons Kumelski and travels via Linz and Salzburg to Munich ~ Chopin stays in the Bavarian capital
for more than a month and gives a successful concert in the Odeon Theater (August 28)
~ at Stuttgart he hears of the fall of Warsaw ~ an account of the Warsaw bloodbath and
the capitulation of the city on September 8 ~ Chopin's "Stuttgart Diary" records his
reaction to the catastrophe ~ he composes his "Revolutionary" Study and travels via
Strasbourg to Paris, where he begins a new life as a Polish émigré.*

AN EXILE IN PARIS, 1831–1833   212

*Chopin arrives in Paris on October 5, 1831, and moves into an apartment on the fifth
floor of 27 Boulevard Poissonnière ~ his first impressions of Paris: "nothing but cries,
noise, din, and mud" ~ he confesses to an encounter with "Teresa," a prostitute in Austria
~ from his apartment's balcony Chopin witnesses street fighting against supporters of
the unpopular "citizen king," Louis-Philippe ~ General Girolamo Ramorino (who had
fought with Napoléon) moves into an apartment opposite Chopin's and his presence
attracts a demonstration ~ "Vive les Polonais!" ~ "You cannot imagine what impression
the menacing voice of the people made on me," Chopin writes.*

*The "Great Emigration" gets under way and thousands of Polish exiles arrive in Paris ~
among their number is Wojciech (Albert) Grzymała, who becomes Chopin's closest Polish
confidant ~ an account of Grzymała's storied career ~ Prince Adam Czartoryski arrives
in Paris and forms a de facto Polish government ~ Chopin becomes attached to the
Polish cause ~ he meets numerous musicians in Paris, including Franz Liszt and Friedrich Kalkbrenner ~ Chopin declines Kalkbrenner's offer to give him lessons ~ Kalkbrenner's personality considered ~ he is pilloried by Heine ~ short of money, Chopin
instructs his father to sell the diamond ring given to him by Tsar Alexander ~ Chopin
gives his first concert in Paris (February 26, 1832), which brings in no income but receives an excellent review from the critic F.-J. Fétis ~ Chopin is turned down for a concert*

*at the Paris Conservatoire ~ cholera returns to Paris: "a riot of the dead" ~ he moves to
a new address at 4 Cité Bergère ~ a description of his apartment by the critic Ernest
Legouvé ~ Chopin is chastised by his father for his cavalier attitude to money: "Let me
advise you to save what you can, so as not to find yourself without a penny" ~ Chopin
meets the Rothschilds, who open doors to the Paris aristocracy ~ "I have found my way
into the very best society" ~ he hears John Field play (December 25, 1832) but is not
impressed ~ an account of Field's stay in Paris ~ Chopin is elected to membership in
the Polish Literary Society ~ he moves into a new apartment at 5 rue de la Chaussée
d'Antin with his childhood friend Dr. Aleksander Hoffman ~ "How delighted I am that
you are together!" writes Mikołaj Chopin.*

CHOPIN AND THE KEYBOARD: THE RAPHAEL OF
THE PIANO   239
*The Paris Virtuoso School as "a theater of stunts" ~ Heine caricatures Kalkbrenner,
Dreyschock, Pixis, and others in his Musikalische Berichte aus Paris while eulogizing
Chopin as "the Raphael of the Piano" ~ the influence of the singing voice on Chopin's
compositions ~ Chopin as "the greatest contrapuntist since Mozart" ~ Chopin's "Sketches
Toward a Piano Method" ~ some views of Heinrich Neuhaus on Chopin considered ~
Chopin rejects the idea of "finger equalization" in favor of "finger individuation" ~ "The
third finger is a great singer" ~ Chopin's fingerings as prescribed for his pupils ~ Chopin's
pedaling observed by Antoine Marmontel ~ some special pedal effects in Chopin's music
~ Liszt and Chopin compared ~ Chopin and the Pleyel piano ~ its restricted compass
is turned to creative use by Chopin ~ his harmonic innovations arise from physical
contact with the keyboard ~ two techniques of composition considered: the "apotheosis
of themes" and "developing variation" ~ the demise of the Paris Virtuoso School as its
members go their separate ways.*

MARIA WODZIŃSKA: "MY MISFORTUNE," 1834–1837   279
*The Wodziński family invite Chopin to join them in Dresden ~ Chopin first visits the
Lower Rhine Music Festival in Aachen, where he meets Mendelssohn ~ Chopin takes
French citizenship (August 1, 1835) and travels via Carlsbad, where he is reunited with
his parents (August 15) ~ they spend an idyllic month together and visit Tetschen as
guests of the wealthy Thun-Hohenstein family ~ Chopin dedicates his Waltz in A-flat
major, op. 34, no. 1, to one of their daughters, Countess Josefina ~ he arrives in Dresden
on September 19 and becomes enamored of the sixteen-year-old Maria Wodzińska ~
they go for romantic strolls together along the banks of the Elbe ~ before departing
Dresden he dedicates his Waltz in A-flat major, op. 69, no. 1 ("L'Adieu") to Maria and
entertains hopes of an engagement ~ a letter to Chopin from Maria ~ he falls ill on the
way back to Paris and false reports of his death are circulated in Warsaw ~ he rejoins
the Wodziński family in Marienbad the following year and travels with them to Dresden
(August 1836) ~ he proposes to Maria at "the twilight hour" on September 9, 1836, and
is accepted ~ Mme Teresa Wodzińska insists that the engagement remain secret ~ she*

harbors doubts about Chopin's health and eventually withdraws her support ~ her letters to Chopin reveal her manipulative character ~ in early 1837 Chopin falls ill ~ he accepts an invitation from the Marquis de Custine to spend time at the latter's villa in Saint-Gratien ~ a description of this visit from the diary of Józef Brzowski ~ Chopin declines an invitation from Tsar Nicholas to become "Pianist to the Imperial Russian Court" ~ Chopin is caught up in the problems of Mme Wodzińska's son, Antoni, to whom he lends money that is not repaid ~ realizing that his ill-fated engagement to Maria is over, he bundles her letters into a package and labels it "My misfortune" ~ Maria's later life, her failed marriage to Józef Skarbek, and her final days considered.

AN ENGLISH INTERLUDE, JULY 1837 309

Camille Pleyel takes Chopin to England ~ some complications in Pleyel's private life ~ Chopin acquires a French passport (July 7, 1837) ~ the pair of travelers arrive in London on July 10 and stay at the Sablonnière Hotel ~ the Polish poet Stanisław Egbert Koźmian acts as their guide ~ Chopin insists on anonymity and is introduced as "Mr. Fritz from Paris" ~ he and Pleyel rent a carriage and in their quest "to spend money" they visit Richmond, Blackwall, and Windsor, among other places ~ at Arundel they observe the parliamentary election of Lord Dudley Stuart, the champion of the Polish cause in Britain ~ Chopin attends the opera and admires the singing of Pasta and Schröder-Devrient ~ he also attends a performance of Beethoven's "Emperor" Concerto played by Moscheles, which fails to impress him ~ Pleyel takes him to a soirée given by the piano manufacturer James Shudi Broadwood ~ Chopin is asked to play and the identity of "Mr. Fritz" is revealed ~ Chopin signs contracts with his English publisher, Christian Wessel, but objects to the nicknames that Wessel attaches to his works ~ at this time Pleyel probably meets the young Emma Osborn, who later becomes his common-law wife ~ Chopin visits Brighton Pavilion ~ he travels back to Paris from Dover and arrives in the French capital at the end of July.

BUFFETS AND REWARDS, 1833–1838 318

Chopin's position in the world of music has meanwhile been transformed ~ Fétis includes an entry on Chopin in his Biographical Dictionary *~ the Twenty-four Studies, opp. 10 and 25, considered, together with their respective dedications to Liszt and Marie d'Agoult ~ Ludwig Rellstab declares war on Chopin's music ("ear-splitting discords") in the columns of his journal* Iris *~ Charles Hallé's recollections of Chopin ~ Princess Cristina Belgiojoso-Trivulzio comes to the aid of the Italian refugees with a fund-raising concert ~ she arranges an "ivory duel" between Liszt and Thalberg and commissions* Hexaméron Variations, *based on a theme from Bellini's* I puritani, *to which Chopin makes a contribution ~ Bellini's premature death and funeral in Paris ~ his influence on Chopin considered ~ Chopin gives some important concerts in 1838, one of them in benefit of his friend Alkan (March 3, 1838) ~ a vituperative review of his Impromptu in A-flat major, op. 29, is published in* La Revue musicale *~ Chopin plays in Rouen (March 12, 1838) and receives a glowing tribute from Ernest Legouvé in the* Gazette musicale.

ENTER GEORGE SAND, 1836–1838   348

George Sand's Family Tree ~ George Sand takes up residence in the Hôtel de France, where she meets Chopin at a soirée on November 19, 1836 ~ the evening does not go well: "What an antipathetic woman that Sand is!" Chopin complains ~ he holds a soirée of his own on December 13, which goes much better, and his playing captures Sand's imagination ~ a backward glance at Sand's early life ~ her childhood home at Nohant, where she witnesses the death of her infant brother and her father ~ she is brought up by her grandmother, who places her in a convent school for young girls ~ through her rebellious behavior she becomes a "devil among the nuns" ~ at the age of seventeen she inherits Nohant and attracts several suitors ~ her marriage to Casimir Dudevant in 1822 produces two children, Maurice and Solange ~ the paternity of Solange questioned ~ Casimir and Sand separate and she moves to Paris ~ she meets the writer Jules Sandeau, the first syllable of whose name ("Sand") she adopts as her nom de plume ~ her novel Lélia (1833), with its approval of "free love," brings her notoriety ~ she dons men's apparel and smokes cigars to show equality with the opposite sex.

Sand makes several attempts to attract Chopin down to Nohant in 1837 ~ she finally meets him again in Paris in the summer of 1838, when they become lovers ~ her celebrated six-thousand-word letter to their friend Grzymała outlines the pros and cons of an affair with Chopin ~ she breaks with her current lover, Félicien Mallefille, who threatens her and Chopin with violence ~ Delacroix paints his well-known portrait of Sand and Chopin, which is cut into two separate images after the painter's death ~ Sand becomes concerned about Chopin's health and that of her son, Maurice ~ she accepts the advice of her friend Charlotte Marliani, the wife of the Spanish consul, and plans a trip to Majorca ~ a honeymoon in everything but name.

A WINTER IN MAJORCA, 1838–1839   372

Chopin and Sand leave France on November 1, 1838 ~ they journey through war-torn Spain to Barcelona and board the paddle steamer El Mallorquin for Majorca ~ a smooth voyage across the Mediterranean Sea to Palma ~ Sand rents a house called "So'n Vent" ("House of Winds"), where they stay for a month ~ the winter rains then begin to fall and he becomes ill ~ the local doctors diagnose tuberculosis and report his illness to the authorities ~ driven out of Palma by prejudice against the disease, Chopin and Sand move into a deserted Carthusian monastery in Valldemosa ~ Chopin likens his cell to an upright coffin ~ he cannot compose because his piano has not yet arrived from Paris ~ his illness worsens and a doctor is summoned ~ the piano finally arrives (mid-January 1839) and Chopin resumes work on the Preludes, the second Ballade, and the Third Scherzo ~ Sand's description of Chopin's disturbed mental state: "phantoms and terrors" ~ Chopin's money worries and his dealings with publishers considered ~ unable to tolerate the winter weather, Chopin and Sand return to Palma (February 13) and await passage back to Barcelona ~ during the sea voyage (shared with a hundred hogs) Chopin spits up "bowlfuls of blood" ~ the strange fate of Chopin's piano considered: a morality tale ~ he is treated in Marseille by Dr. Cauvière ~ the death of the tenor Adolphe Nourrit ~ Chopin plays the organ at the singer's funeral and Sand excoriates both the service and the poor condition of the instrument ~ Antoni Wodziński defaults on the repayment of money he owes Chopin ~ a sojourn in Genoa (May 5 to 16) and a rough sea passage back to Marseille ~ Chopin and Sand finally set out for Nohant ~ they travel along the Rhône River by ferryboat as far as Arles, and then transfer to a diligence, arriving on June 1.

AT NOHANT, 1839   398

Euphoric to be back at Nohant, Sand likens the place to "a Garden of Eden" ~ Sand and Chopin settle into their respective routines: she writes at night and sleeps during the day, he composes during the day and sleeps at night ~ Sand brings in a local physician, Dr. Gustave Papet, who examines Chopin and diagnoses an "inflammation of the larynx" ~ Sand comes to terms with her new responsibilities as Chopin's caregiver ~ she describes their relationship as "chaste," sustained by bonds of platonic friendship ~ Sand's insights into Chopin's complex personality outlined ~ her description of his tormented composing process: "He would spend six weeks on one page, only to return to . . . the first draft" ~ Chopin becomes frustrated with his rustic lifestyle at Nohant and invites Grzymała to join them ~ Grzymała is charged with the task of finding separate accommodations in Paris for Sand and Chopin ~ Chopin composes several works at Nohant, including the Sonata in B-flat minor, op. 35 ~ a description of the Sonata with some commentary on its unusual structural features ~ Schumann's criticism of the Sonata considered ~ Chopin and Sand leave Nohant and get back to Paris on October 11, 1839.

GROWING FAME, 1839–1843   420

Sand and Chopin move into separate apartments, hers at 16 rue Pigalle and his at nearby 5 rue Tronchet ~ Sand's new play, Cosima, is produced at the Comédie-Française on April 29, 1840, and is a failure ~ she loses 10,000 francs over the debacle, falls into debt, and is unable to return to Nohant in the summer of 1840 ~ Chopin, by contrast, is financially secure through his teaching and the publication of his latest pieces ~ Chopin as a teacher: his pupils include Friederike Müller, Georges Mathias, and Pauline Viardot-García ~ he meets Moscheles, and the two composers are invited to play at Saint-Cloud before the queen and her entourage, October 30, 1839 ~ Chopin composes his Trois Nouvelles Études for the Méthode des Méthodes, edited by Moscheles and Fétis ~ Sand works on two new novels, Consuelo and Horace, to help pay off her debts ~ her growing estrangement from Marie d'Agoult and her unflattering portrait of Marie in Horace ~ Balzac describes Sand's living quarters at the rue Pigalle ~ Paris is brought to a standstill by the state funeral of Napoléon Bonaparte, December 15, 1840 ~ an account of Napoléon's exhumation ~ Mickiewicz creates a stir with his lectures on the Slavs in the Collège de France, to which Sand "comes with the famous pianist Chopin and leaves in his carriage" ~ Chopin gives a recital in the

Salle Pleyel (April 26, 1841), which nets him 6,000 francs and is reviewed by Liszt for the Revue et Gazette ~ *Chopin reacts negatively to Liszt's article ~ the complex background to the review considered.*

Chopin and Sand return to Nohant for the summer of 1841 ~ an earthquake at Berry ~ his pupil Marie de Rozières has an affair with Antoni Wodziński ~ a hive of gossip ~ Chopin completes the Ballade in A-flat major, op. 47; the Two Nocturnes, op. 48; and the Fantaisie in F minor, op. 49 ~ back in Paris he plays for the Duke of Orléans in the Pavillon de Marsan, December 2 ~ he gives a second recital in the Salle Pleyel on February 21, 1842, which garners another 5,000 francs ~ Chopin's old teacher Adalbert Żywny dies that same night ~ Chopin's loyal following is likened to a congregation worshipping at "the Church of Chopin" ~ another summer at Nohant, where Sand and Chopin are joined by Delacroix ~ they move into new apartments in the Square d'Orléans (September 1842), where Chopin resumes his teaching ~ his pupils now include Wilhelm von Lenz, Mlle Laure Duperré, and the young Hungarian prodigy Károly Filtsch, perhaps his most gifted student ~ Meyerbeer drops in on a lesson and gets into an argument with Chopin about "tempo rubato" ~ Károly Filtsch's career considered in depth.

THE DEATH OF MIKOŁAJ CHOPIN, 1844   469
Chopin's father dies from tuberculosis on May 3, 1844, and is interred in Warsaw's Powązki Cemetery ~ the news reaches Chopin three weeks later and devastates him ~ the Warsaw Courier *publishes a panegyric to Mikołaj (May 12) ~ George Sand's letter of commiseration to Justyna Chopin: "He thinks only of you, his sisters, and all his family" ~ Chopin contacts his brother-in-law Antoni Barciński requesting a full account of his father's last days ~ Barciński reveals that Mikołaj wished that his body be cut open and the heart removed, "lest I be buried alive" ~ Professor Józef Bełza's influence in this matter ~ Chopin's sister Ludwika and her husband, Kalasanty, travel to France to spend a holiday with Chopin ~ he takes them sightseeing in Paris and brings them down to Nohant, where they are guests of Sand (August 1844) ~ family life in Nohant ~ Chopin completes his B minor Sonata, op. 58: the Sonata considered in detail ~ Kalasanty explores the countryside and Sand reads aloud from her new novel,* The Miller of Angibault ~ *Ludwika and Sand form bonds of attachment ~ Chopin returns to Paris with Ludwika and her husband, and arranges a farewell party for them on September 2, attended by a small audience, which listens to him and the cellist Auguste Franchomme play a short recital ~ the party does not break up until 2:00 a.m., when Chopin copies out his song "Wiosna" in Ludwika's album ~ a few hours later (September 3) Ludwika and Kalasanty return to Warsaw ~ after resting in Nohant for several weeks, Chopin returns to Paris (November 29), where he encounters the first of the winter snowstorms and falls ill ~ Sand arrives in the city and acts once more as his caregiver ~ during the Easter weekend they hear Mozart's* Requiem *and Haydn's* Creation *at the Conservatoire ~ the English actor William Macready visits Sand ~ an un-*

usual encounter with North American Indians ~ "I no longer have anything to do here, and I am bored," writes Sand ~ Chopin buys a new carriage and they depart for Nohant on June 12.

A HARVEST OF SORROWS, 1845–1847   495
The first fissures in the Chopin-Sand relationship appear ~ Nohant is swept by rainstorms and the Berry region is flooded ~ Chopin is marooned there, together with Pauline Viardot, who works on her vocal arrangements of Chopin's mazurkas with the composer's approval ~ Sand adopts the nineteen-year-old Augustine Brault and brings her to live at Nohant ~ Sand's daughter, Solange, objects to the presence of her new "sister" and roils the household with her rebellious behavior ~ a dark secret: Maurice Sand begins a clandestine affair with Pauline Viardot ~ in the midst of the turmoil Chopin brings his Three Mazurkas, op. 59, to fruition ~ Sand and Chopin return to Paris (November 1845), where he falls ill and once more becomes Sand's "resident patient" ~ Mickiewicz calls Chopin the "moral vampire" of Sand ~ after returning to Nohant (May 1846), Chopin resumes work on his Cello Sonata, op. 65, and completes his Polonaise-Fantaisie, op. 61 ~ a consideration of his "late style" ~ an account of Chopin's piano playing by Elisa Fournier: "an astonishing tour de force" ~ Sand's family circle begins to fall apart ~ Maurice and Solange at loggerheads ~ Sand works on her novel Lucrezia Floriani, *a thinly disguised account of her declining relationship with Chopin ~ Solange is seduced by the sculptor Auguste Clésinger and they marry in haste at Nohant (May 1847) ~ a squandered dowry and a violent quarrel between Clésinger and Sand, who exchange blows ~ Chopin, back in Paris, learns of the fiasco from Solange and takes her side ~ Sand accuses Chopin of "going over to the enemy" ~ he and Sand make a final break: "There is no point in ever discussing the rest."*

DEEPENING SHADOWS, 1847–1848   542
A bleak winter ~ Chopin plays for Baron James de Rothschild and Prince Czartoryski ~ Jane Stirling emerges as his chief caregiver ~ he visits the atelier of Louis-Auguste Bisson and sits for a daguerreotype (autumn of 1847) ~ friends persuade Chopin to give a concert in the Salle Pleyel (February 16, 1848), at which he plays the last three movements of his newly published Cello Sonata with Franchomme and his Barcarolle, op. 60 ~ a description of his playing by Charles Hallé and a revue in the Revue et Gazette musicale: *"The sylph has kept his word" ~ an unexpected encounter with Sand outside the home of Charlotte Marliani: "allow me to inform you that you are a grandmother" ~ revolution breaks out in Paris and King Louis-Philippe abdicates ~ rumors circulate that Chopin might return to Poland.*

TWILIGHT IN BRITAIN, 1848   556
Revolution and cholera bring Paris to a standstill ~ Chopin accepts an invitation from Jane Stirling to visit Britain ~ he arrives in London on April 20 and rents an apartment at 48 Dover Street ~ the artistic life of London ~ he is taken up by high society and

gives several concerts in private homes ~ he plays for Queen Victoria and Prince Albert at Stafford House ~ Pauline Viardot and her arrangements of the Chopin mazurkas considered ~ J. W. Davison's opposition to Chopin ~ Chopin's jaundiced views on the British aristocracy ~ Jane Stirling and Katherine Erskine loom large ~ he travels to Edinburgh and stays in Calder House as a guest of Lord Torphichen ~ Chopin suffers bruises when his carriage is overturned ~ a concert in Manchester (August 28) hosted by the industrialist Salis Schwabe ~ some mixed reviews ~ Chopin becomes a patient of the Polish homeopath Dr. Adam Łyszczyński ~ in the company of Jane Stirling he endures visits to Johnstone Castle, Strachur House, Milliken House, Keir House, and Hamilton Palace, among others ~ a concert in Merchants' Hall, Glasgow, September 27 ~ a description by the Scottish diarist Sir James Hedderwick ~ Chopin's letters to Grzymała ~ a concert in Edinburgh's Hopetoun Rooms, October 4 ~ Chopin lampoons the Scottish gentry ~ he returns to London on October 31 and plays at the Guildhall in aid of Polish refugees despite his illness: "a well-intentioned mistake" ~ Chopin returns to Paris and suffers a seizure during the channel crossing.

THE DEATH OF CHOPIN, 1849　　　　　　　　　　　　603

Chopin turns to three physicians for help: Dr. Pierre Louis, Dr. Jean Blache, and Dr. Jean-Baptiste Cruveilhier ~ cholera returns to Paris and Chopin moves to an expensive apartment in the suburb of Chaillot ~ Jane Stirling sends him an anonymous gift of 25,000 francs, which is mysteriously "lost" and traced with the help of the famous clairvoyant Alexis ~ Chopin's illness reaches a critical stage ~ he writes to his sister Ludwika asking her to come to Paris ~ she arrives with her husband, Kalasanty, and fourteen-year-old daughter, "Ludka" ~ among the friends who visit him at Chaillot are Jenny Lind, Franchomme, his pupil Gutmann, and Charles Gavard, who leaves a memoir of his visit ~ Chopin composes at Chaillot what some consider to be his last work, the Mazurka in G minor, op. 67, no. 2 ~ a visit from the poet Cyprien Norwid ~ in mid-August, Chopin moves into a new apartment at 12 Place Vendôme, where he is besieged by curiosity seekers ~ Delfina Potocka visits him and sings for him ~ the deathbed drawings of Teofil Kwiatkowski ~ Chopin is the unwilling recipient of extreme unction from the Polish cleric Jełowicki ~ Chopin dies on October 17 ~ a partial autopsy is carried out by Dr. Cruveilhier ~ Chopin's funeral service in the Madeleine Church ~ a committee is formed to raise a monument to his memory ~ Ludwika's "Confession" ~ Chopin's effects are auctioned ~ Ludwika returns to Poland carrying an urn containing Chopin's heart ~ the fate of George Sand's letters to Chopin.

EPILOGUE　　　　　　　　　　　　　　　　635

The Chopin family commissions Julian Fontana to bring out Chopin's unpublished manuscripts ~ Fontana's credentials as an editor ~ his problems, both financial and personal, considered ~ modern criticism of Fontana's posthumous edition of Chopin is rebuffed: "it is difficult to overestimate his contribution" ~ he refuses remuneration for his work, which he undertakes as a tribute to Chopin ~ Fontana's career considered in detail

~ he travels to Cuba, where he meets Camila Dalcour, his future wife ~ they marry in New York and move to Paris ~ Camila dies in childbirth ~ a distraught Fontana spends his final years facing illness and encroaching deafness ~ he commits suicide on December 23, 1869.

The search for a Chopin biographer ~ Grzymała and Fontana emerge as candidates, but their work founders ~ Liszt arrives on the scene with his book F. Chopin, a publication that incurs Jane Stirling's disapproval: "he spat on the plate to spoil the others' appetite" ~ the biography of Moritz Karasowski: "weaver of legends" ~ Frederick Niecks, Chopin's first modern biographer ~ the Polish scholar Ferdynand Hoesick takes command of the field ~ the spurious correspondence of Chopin and Delfina Potocka considered ~ the forged "Journal" of Chopin creates more pitfalls ~ "a lantern on the stern" ~ Chopin's heart is interred in Warsaw's Church of the Holy Cross ~ it is removed for safekeeping during World War II to the suburb of Milanówek ~ on October 17, 1945, the ninety-sixth anniversary of Chopin's death, the heart is returned to Warsaw via Żelazowa Wola and the nation pays homage ~ requests to take tissue samples from the heart to determine the cause of Chopin's death are denied by the Polish government.

Appendix: Liszt's Questionnaire Concerning His Life of Chopin   673

General Catalogue of Chopin's Works   679

List of Sources   695

Index   703

LIST OF ILLUSTRATIONS

Frontispiece: Fryderyk Chopin; an oil painting by Teofil Kwiatkowski (1844).

Page 7: Autograph page of the Prelude in G-sharp minor, op. 28, no. 12.

Page 33: Chopin's birthplace at Żelazowa Wola; a photograph (c. 1932).

Page 35: Mikołaj and Justyna Chopin; a drawing by Ambroży Mieroszewski (c. 1829).

Page 37: Ludwika Chopin; an oil painting by Ambroży Mieroszewski (1829).

Page 38: Izabella Chopin; an oil painting by Ambroży Mieroszewski (1829).

Page 40: Emilia Chopin; an anonymous watercolor on ivory.

Page 41: "Dear Papa," a name-day greeting to his father from the six-year-old Chopin, December 6, 1816.

Page 49: Wojciech Żywny; an oil painting by Ambroży Mieroszewski (1829).

Page 52: The first page of the Polonaise in G minor (1817); a lithograph by I. J. Cybulski.

Page 56: Grand Duke Constantine musters his troops on Saxon Square, 1825, to mark the passing of Tsar Alexander I; a lithograph by Jan Feliks Piwarski (1829).

Page 67: Dr. Samuel Linde; a chalk drawing by Chopin (c. 1825).

Page 85: A map of Chopin's Poland, 1815–1830.

Page 97: The front façade of the Casimir Palace, 1824; a lithograph by Lassalle, after a drawing by Jan Feliks Piwarski.

Page 102: Chopin; a pencil drawing by Princess Eliza Radziwiłł (1826).

Page 117: The Chopin family salon in the Krasiński Palace; a watercolor by Antoni Kolberg (1832).

Page 131: *Chopin Playing in the Salon of Prince Antoni Radziwiłł*, an oil painting by Henryk Siemiradzki (1887).

Page 160: Antonin, Prince Radziwiłł's hunting lodge.

Page 165: Konstancja Gładkowska; an anonymous pencil drawing made about ten years after Chopin had left Warsaw.

Page 206: *The Abduction of Polish Children by Russian Soldiers, September 1831*, a lithograph by Nicolaus Maurin, after a painting by M. Twarowski (c. 1832).

Page 210: A fragment from Chopin's "Stuttgart Diary," September 1831. "The enemy has reached my home."

Page 222: The Salle Pleyel, at 9 rue Cadet, Paris; a contemporary engraving.

Page 225: Chopin's first concert in Paris, February 26, 1832 (postponed from January 15).

Page 230: Fryderyk Chopin; a lithograph by Gottfried Engelmann, after a portrait by Pierre-Roch Vigneron (1833).

Page 251: Chopin's left hand; a marble cast by Auguste Clésinger (1849).

Page 264: Study in A minor, op. 10, no. 2. Chopin's corrected proof sheet.

Page 265: Chopin seated at the piano; a pencil drawing by Jakob Goetzenberger (October 1838).

Page 284: Maria Wodzińska; a self-portrait, undated.

Page 307: "My misfortune." Chopin's correspondence with Maria Wodzińska.

Page 311: Chopin's French passport, dated July 7, 1837.

Page 369: George Sand; an oil painting by Delacroix (1838).

Page 370: Chopin; an oil painting by Delacroix (1838).

Page 374: *El Mallorquin*, the paddle steamer on which Chopin and George Sand sailed to Majorca; a watercolor by Ramón Sampol Isern.

Page 379: The monastery at Valldemosa; a watercolor by Maurice Sand (1839).

Page 400: The Nohant château; a photograph taken from the garden side.

Page 407: Solange and Maurice Sand; a drawing by Nancy Mérienne (1836).

Page 412: Manuscript page of the Sonata in B-flat minor, op. 35, showing the opening measures. A copy in the hand of Adolf Gutmann.

Page 437: The lecture auditorium at the Collège de France (1844).

Page 465: Carl Filtsch; a lithograph by Franz Eybl (1841).

Page 472: Mikołaj Chopin's funeral announcement, Warsaw, May 5, 1844.

Page 474: Mikołaj Chopin's last words: "As this cough will suffocate me . . ."

Page 497: "That's the Listz [sic] way of playing." An ink drawing by Maurice Sand (June 1844).

Page 500: Solange Sand; a drawing by Auguste Clésinger (spring 1847).

Page 533: Auguste Clésinger; an undated engraving.

Page 553: Fryderyk Chopin; a daguerreotype by Louis-Auguste Bisson (1847).

Page 565: Chopin's concert at Lord Falmouth's house in St. James's Square, July 7, 1848.

Page 572: Jane Stirling; a portrait by Achille Devéria (c. 1842).

Page 574: A map: "Chopin Visits Britain: April–November 1848."

Page 578: Calder House near Edinburgh, the home of Jane Stirling's brother-in-law Lord Torphichen; a photograph (c. 1930).

Page 580: Chopin performs in the Gentlemen's Concert Hall, Manchester, August 28, 1848; a concert bill.

Page 609: "Mrs. Erskine left 15,000 francs." Chopin's diary entry for July 28, 1849.

Page 616: Chopin's last hours; an oil painting by Teofil Kwiatkowski (October 1849).

Page 621: An invitation to Chopin's funeral service.

Page 624: The Madeleine Church, where Chopin's funeral took place on October 30, 1849.

Pages 637–38: The letter authorizing Julian Fontana to be the sole editor of Chopin's posthumous works.

Page 669: The Reverend Leopold Petrzyk carries Chopin's heart past a guard of honor toward the birth house at Żelazowa Wola, October 17, 1945.

Page 676: A page of Jane Stirling's copy of Liszt's questionnaire.

ACKNOWLEDGMENTS

More than ten years have elapsed since I embarked on the writing of my life and times of Chopin. Many people helped me along the way and it is impossible to thank them all. Nonetheless, the following individuals must be acknowledged because without their assistance it is entirely possible that my work might have foundered and remained unfinished.

I received much help and encouragement from Polish scholars during my various visits to Warsaw and it is a pleasure to mention that fact here. For permission to work in the Chopin National Institute and the Chopin Museum in Warsaw I want to thank the director, Dr. Artur Szklener. The support I received from his staff, and especially from Dr. Marcin Konik, Iwona Łodzińska, and Izabella Butkiewicz of the institute's Photothèque, was exemplary. They showed much patience in dealing with the many questions I directed their way, and even served me with aromatic tea while doing so. I received similar warmth of treatment from the staff of the Chopin Museum, which houses many treasures on permanent display there. I am obliged to the curator of the museum, Maciej Janicki, for permission to work there, and I am especially grateful to Magdalena Kulig for introducing me to the museum's archives—where I was able to inspect a number of rare items at leisure, including Chopin's personal diaries, various music manuscripts, and the original copies of his youthful *Szafarnia Courier*, the journal he created and edited when he was fourteen years old. Nor must I forget to acknowledge the guidance of Mariola Wojtkiewicz, curator of Chopin's birthplace at Żelazowa Wola, who placed her knowledge of the history of the building and surrounding estate at my. disposal, and saved me from possible error and confusion. Paweł Kamiński, the co-editor of the Polish National Edition of Chopin's works, was more than generous in dealing with my questions and brought some instructive points of view to bear on a number of editorial matters connected with Chopin's texts. The many written exchanges that preceded our personal meetings in Warsaw were informative, and I am grateful for the interest that he showed in my work. I also owe thanks to Professor Tadeusz Dobosz, a member of the faculty of Wrocław's Medical University, who was present during the temporary exhumation of Chopin's heart from its resting place in Warsaw's Church of the Holy Cross, in April 2014, and shared some observations based on his visual inspection of the organ.

To Piotr Mysłakowski, one of Poland's leading Chopin scholars, it is hardly enough to say thank you. From the start he readily placed his knowledge of the minutiae of Chopin's daily life in Poland at my disposal, and dispensed erudition and hospitality in equal proportion. He not only answered with courtesy and kindness my countless questions about Chopin's Polish connections, however esoteric, but also acted as my guide on visits to such places as Szafarnia and Sanniki, where the adolescent Chopin spent his summer holidays, and to various locations in and around Warsaw associated with Chopin, including the historic Powązki Cemetery, where all the composer's immediate family members are buried and a number of his close friends and colleagues as well. Our journeys eventually extended to Antonin, Prince Antoni Radziwiłł's hunting lodge, where Chopin stayed as his guest and made music with the cello-playing prince and his family. These expeditions were a reminder of the importance of what I have elsewhere called "the geography of biography," the indispensable experience of visiting the places about which one writes, or risk losing the possibility of bringing them to life.

Gabriel Quetglas Olin, the director of the Chopin Museum in the Valldemosa Charterhouse, Majorca, helped me to clear up some complicated matters related to Chopin's stay on the island during the wretched winter of 1838–39. He also provided me with documentary evidence connected to the fate of the Pleyel piano sent to Chopin from Paris, which I have incorporated in the chapter titled "A Winter in Majorca," and I am grateful for his friendly assistance.

Much has changed at Nohant since Chopin's time and there are not many traces of his presence left. George Sand herself expunged many of them after her rupture with Chopin, and time did the rest. Still, there are ghosts that continue to haunt the Nohant estate for those who want to pursue them. It is a salutary experience to enter the small chapel just a stone's throw from the manor house, whose unyielding pews seated no more than a handful of worshippers. Here the local artisans and their families attended Sunday mass and were baptized, married, and eventually sent to their graves in the adjoining cemetery. It was in this chapel, in May 1847, that Sand gave away her daughter, Solange, in matrimony to the sculptor Auguste Clésinger and sowed the wind that ensured she would reap the whirlwind. The resulting storm tore her family apart and resulted in Sand's separation from Chopin as well. We have reserved for its proper place the telling of that dramatic story. For the moment it is enough to observe that buildings, too, reverberate with times past and may bear witness to the human condition.

To Lisa Yui, who gave me the benefit of her erudition whenever I appealed to it, I am particularly indebted. She was a part of the writing of this book almost from the beginning. She assisted me in dealing with myriad problems, both great and small, quietly prompted me toward their solutions, and treated my book with the same care as if it were her own. The Catalogue of Works, with its concordance tables, was particularly troublesome to bring into line with modern research, and Dr. Yui helped me to achieve its final form. To her I also owe some new information about the marriage of Camille Pleyel to the concert pianist Marie Moke, as well as its dissolution, which I have woven into the narrative of the chapter titled "An English Interlude." Professor Richard Zimdars and Professor Gábor Csepregi offered me welcome support in the early days when I most needed it, and their friendly inquiries across the years helped to keep the project moving.

The primary documents on which Chopin scholarship rests come to us in a variety of forms and languages. I received much help from Elizabeth Zabek and Anna Piotrowska with translations of Polish texts, some of which are to be found only in nineteenth-century newspapers in Warsaw or in the personal diaries and reminiscences of those who knew Chopin. Ms. Piotrowska also assisted me during the preliminary stages of my work, by addressing various inquiries to Polish archives and attending to their prompt resolution. Dominique Caplier went through the many French translations scattered throughout the book, and suggested better ones where it became evident that the old ones were no longer serviceable. She also provided an impressive array of secretarial services, read the entire typescript, and demonstrated yet again her uncanny ability to produce solutions before anyone knew that there was a problem. To Bridget Whittle of McMaster University Library's Research Collections, I also extend special thanks for help in preparing family trees, maps, and work lists, and for coming to my rescue in those areas where my lamentable lack of computer skills nearly brought the enterprise to a standstill. The fact that it was kept moving at all was due in no small measure to her colleague Beverly Bayzat, who provided emergency technical support whenever my chronic ineptitude with most things mechanical made further interventions a matter of urgent necessity. Alex Burtzos engraved the music examples and spent many hours preparing them for publication. He brought a composer's insight to bear on the task of reproducing Chopin's often idiosyncratic notation, and it is a pleasure to recognize the professional manner in which he carried out this work.

For permission to inspect the many original music manuscripts of Chopin in their possession, I want to extend my thanks to Nicolas Bell and the staff of the Manuscripts Department of the British Library, London; to David Plylar and the staff of the Music Division of the Library of Congress, Washington, D.C.; to Fran Barulich and the staff of the Morgan Library, New York; and to Jane Gottlieb and the staff of the Lila Acheson Library of the Juilliard School of Music, New York. Across the years I visited these libraries several times, and I acknowledge with thanks the friendly reception that was invariably extended to me and my work.

To the composer's long sojourn in Britain in 1848, and in particular to his eleven-week stay in Scotland, I have devoted more pages than one generally finds in biographies of Chopin. This trip was arranged and subsidized by his Scottish pupil Jane Stirling and her wealthy older sister, Katherine Erskine. In piecing together the details of the Scottish part of the journey, I received much help from the staffs of the General Register House and the National Library of Scotland in Edinburgh, and the Mitchell Library in Glasgow. I have made full use of their papers, including the last testaments of both Jane and Katherine, which throw fresh light on the Stirling family's wealth and explain the important benefactions that they were able to direct Chopin's way during his final, impoverished months.

This is the place, too, to recognize the assistance I received across the years from William Wright, who fielded with uncommon zeal a long series of obscure questions about Chopin's visit to Scotland and directed me to sources that I might otherwise have overlooked. On more than one occasion he rescued me from the blind alleys that always seemed to beckon, and set me on a better path. I came to regard him as "the Sage of Scotland"—a sobriquet that he would almost certainly wish to deny, but one that belongs to him by virtue of his exceptional knowledge of his native land.

It was my good fortune to have as my editor Ileene Smith, vice president at Farrar, Straus and Giroux. From the moment she saw the first drafts of my book she expressed enthusiasm for it, brought me into her fold of writers, and insisted on editing my work herself. It was the happiest of collaborations, free from many of the frictions that typify the relationship between writer and editor, and I learned much from her firm but friendly counsel. No author could have asked for more.

Alan Walker
London/Warsaw
Summer 2017

CHOPIN FAMILY TREE

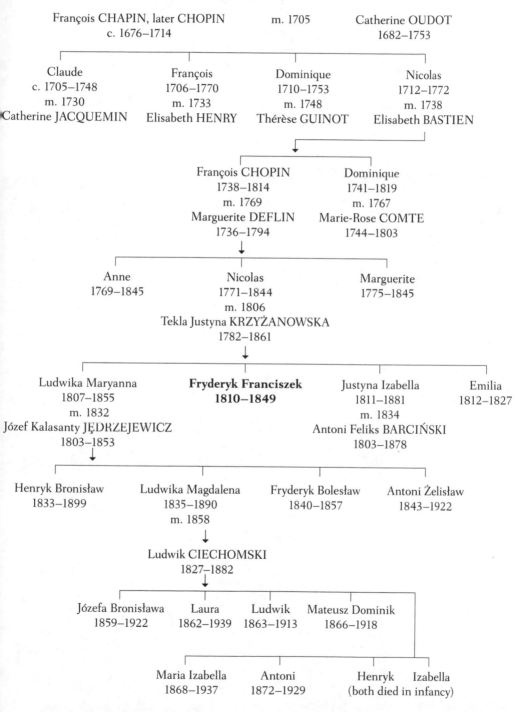

Antoine CHAPPEN
(died c. 1705)

François CHAPIN, later CHOPIN   m. 1705   Catherine OUDOT
c. 1676–1714   1682–1753

Claude   François   Dominique   Nicolas
c. 1705–1748   1706–1770   1710–1753   1712–1772
m. 1730   m. 1733   m. 1748   m. 1738
Catherine JACQUEMIN   Elisabeth HENRY   Thérèse GUINOT   Elisabeth BASTIEN

François CHOPIN   Dominique
1738–1814   1741–1819
m. 1769   m. 1767
Marguerite DEFLIN   Marie-Rose COMTE
1736–1794   1744–1803

Anne   Nicolas   Marguerite
1769–1845   1771–1844   1775–1845
              m. 1806
     Tekla Justyna KRZYŻANOWSKA
            1782–1861

Ludwika Maryanna   **Fryderyk Franciszek**   Justyna Izabella   Emilia
1807–1855   **1810–1849**   1811–1881   1812–1827
m. 1832   m. 1834
Józef Kalasanty JĘDRZEJEWICZ   Antoni Feliks BARCIŃSKI
1803–1853   1803–1878

Henryk Bronisław   Ludwika Magdalena   Fryderyk Bolesław   Antoni Żelisław
1833–1899   1835–1890   1840–1857   1843–1922
           m. 1858

Ludwik CIECHOMSKI
1827–1882

Józefa Bronisława   Laura   Ludwik   Mateusz Dominik
1859–1922   1862–1939   1863–1913   1866–1918

Maria Izabella   Antoni   Henryk   Izabella
1868–1937   1872–1929   (both died in infancy)

FRYDERYK
CHOPIN

PROLOGUE

When Alexander saw the breadth of his domain he wept, for there were no more worlds to conquer.

—Plutarch[1]

I

I would like to make an assertion that I cannot prove but am certain is true. Within a fifty-kilometer radius of where I am writing this Prologue, someone somewhere is either playing or listening to Chopin's music. Nor does it depend on the location of my writing desk—which happens to be situated near Toronto. Move it to New York, London, Berlin, Vienna, Moscow, or Beijing, and my proposition remains the same. Whatever the time zone, the sun never sets on Chopin's music. Millions of listeners are held in thrall to it. Radio stations across the world broadcast his compositions. The sale of Chopin recordings holds firm, even as others go into decline. The "Chopin recital" remains as popular as ever, a fixture in the concert hall. Chopin competitions continue to spring up across the globe. Finally, and most remarkably, Chopin has come to symbolize a nation. He is Poland's best-known son. Is there any other composer of whom similar things could reasonably be said?

Musicology devours its own children. Time was when Chopin was

---

1. *Lives*, VIII.

generally regarded as a "salon composer" of charming miniatures—
mazurkas, waltzes, nocturnes—unworthy of a place in the pantheon. It
never seemed to occur to our forefathers that a piece lasting just a couple
of minutes (witness some of the Preludes, op. 28) could contain more musical substance than an entire string quartet of Boccherini. One had to
compose symphonies, operas, and oratorios in order to be considered "great."
All that has changed, but it did not happen overnight, as we shall see.

II

Berlioz is said to have remarked that "Chopin was dying all his life,"[2] and
the image still haunts the literature. We cannot be sure when Chopin first
contracted tuberculosis, the wasting disease that eventually took his life,
but it must have been early. His sister Emilia died of the illness when she
was only fourteen years old. Years later his father, Mikołaj, succumbed to
the same malady. A number of Chopin's close Polish friends and associ-
ates were also carried off by the contagion, including his school friends
Jan Matuszyński and Jan Białobłocki. And we do not have to widen the
circle much further before finding that Ludwika Skarbek, on whose estate at Żelazowa Wola Chopin's parents met and conducted their court-
ship, and where Chopin himself was born, fell prey to the disease, as did
a number of Chopin's artistic colleagues in Warsaw with whom he came
into regular contact, including the conductor and organist Wilhelm Würfel and the poet Juliusz Słowacki. Tuberculosis was rampant in Poland during the first decades of the nineteenth century, and it has been estimated
that during Chopin's own lifetime a fifth of the entire population of central Europe succumbed to the disease, drawing tens of thousands of sufferers into its deadly folds.

The interesting question first raised by Esmond Long, an American expert on pulmonary illness, continues to lurk in the background: "How
many young people did Chopin infect by coughing during his lessons?"[3]
At least two of Chopin's pupils were carried off by "galloping consump-

2. These words, which have been widely quoted, were probably misconstrued from Berlioz's
obituary notice of Chopin ("Alas, Chopin was lost to music for quite a long time") published
in the *Journal des débats*, October 27, 1849.
3. LHT, p. 18.

tion" (the graphic description by which the final, accelerated form of the disease was popularly known) while they were still young. Paul Gunsberg was only twelve and Károly Filtsch barely fifteen when consumption claimed them—although it is impossible to prove a causal connection with their teacher.[4] In any case, mutual reinfection was a constant problem. But this in turn raises a further question. How was it possible that of the six people who comprised Mikołaj Chopin's household, three died of tuberculosis while the other three remained immune? Chopin's mother, Justyna, and his sisters Ludwika and Izabella showed no symptoms. We know that individuals differ in their disposition toward tuberculosis, and their resistance to infection can protect them for long periods of time. Moreover, even after being infected some sufferers may linger for years, showing hardly any symptoms, while others succumb quickly. Chopin and his young sister Emilia are textbook examples of such a difference. Emilia died within two years of first exhibiting symptoms of the disease; her brother struggled against it for more than twenty.

George Sand lived on terms of closest intimacy with Chopin for eight years, yet never contracted tuberculosis; and neither did her children, Solange and Maurice, who were his daily companions during the months they spent together in Majorca and later during his frequent sojourns at Sand's country home in Nohant, at the very time that the disease was increasing its deadly grip on him. Such puzzles preoccupied the medical fraternity and led to competing diagnoses. Sir James Clark, Queen Victoria's physician and Chopin's consultant in Britain in 1848, held the erroneous view that tuberculosis was not an infection at all, but a predisposition, harmless for those in contact with the sufferer, an opinion described elsewhere in this volume as inexplicable. By contrast, the Spanish doctors who treated Chopin during his ill-fated trip to Majorca in 1838 were adamant that it was contagious. Such divergent views led to equally divergent treatments. Sir James Clark and his followers prescribed rest, sunshine, a dry climate, and fresh air for their patients. "Go south" was their watchword. The response of Chopin's Spanish doctors was dramatically different. They reported his infection to the authorities, which led to his bedding being burned, his furniture destroyed, and Chopin himself coming close to being quarantined because they feared contagion. His bizarre journey through

---

4. SHC, p. 152.

the medical profession resulted in every conceivable remedy being prescribed to him along the way, including bleedings, leeches, and blisters, as well as an entire smorgasbord of diets and pharmaceutical products of dubious provenance. It continues to astonish us that Chopin consulted no fewer than thirty-three physicians during his short lifetime.[5] His intimate connection with doctors of every shade and hue cost him a small fortune across the years, and helps to explain why he was sometimes short of funds.

It remains to consider the effect that tuberculosis had on Chopin's creative output. We know that there were times when it was a simple inconvenience and he could go about his daily business with energy to spare. But there were others when his activities came to a virtual standstill, because the leaden weight of his symptoms—chronic tiredness, incessant coughing, inflammation of the larynx, breathlessness, and neuralgia— proved to be such a heavy burden that he could not function. On the dreadful journey from Majorca back to the Spanish mainland, George Sand tells us, Chopin coughed up "bowlfuls of blood." This was ten years before he died. We have to regard it as a marvel that it was precisely during this final decade that he composed such masterpieces as the sonatas in B-flat minor and B minor, the F minor Fantaisie, the Polonaise-Fantaisie, and the Barcarolle. During the last two or three years of his life, in fact, Chopin could not even climb the stairs and had to be carried by his manservant. And since the various medications prescribed for him by his doctors included opiates to suppress his other symptoms, the tranquilizing effect that this may have had on his will to work cannot be dismissed. Creativity, in brief, cost him dear.

Yet in the end it was creativity that consoled him, despite the struggle it entailed. Chopin's composing process was often slow and painful. A glance through his manuscripts reveals signs of serious conflict, with heavy corrections on many a page. He would sometimes scratch out a phrase half a dozen times in his search for the right construction—only to finish with the version he had originally started with. Meanwhile, the pleasure we take in viewing Chopin's manuscripts, even in facsimile, cannot be denied. It is an infinitely more rewarding experience than gazing at a cold, typeset

---

5. They are identified in SHC, pp. 153–54, which lists the name of every doctor who treated Chopin, and the approximate dates when he was under each one's care.

page of music, which purports to communicate the same information more readily. The manuscript discloses character. An entire world resides beneath the surface of what a more leisurely age used to call "penmanship." (How much more elegant is that word than the forbidding term "rastrology" with which musicology has lately been encumbered.) It is a world that contains an infinite variety of qualities—hope, joy, haste, languor, suffering, even ecstasy—all of which flow through the pen, jostle for expression on the written page, and quietly await their interpreter. A manuscript, in brief, is a companionable thing. When we confront it, we confront a portion of biography itself, for the images that come to mind are not easily dispelled. Isolated in his room, with a piano as his sole companion (Chopin invariably composed at the keyboard), it was not unusual for him to spend several weeks on a single page, pacing back and forth and breaking his pens in frustration. When Chopin corrected something, he made sure that the outside world would never know what his first thoughts had been. A

Autograph page of the Prelude in G-sharp minor, op. 28, no. 12.

single pen stroke through the offending bars would have sufficed for
most composers, but not for Chopin. Those bars had to be obliterated.

That his debilitating illness was in part to blame for the struggle cannot be doubted. But an infinitely more important factor was his quest for
perfection, a lifelong characteristic that happened to be one of his shining
virtues. And it produced a dividend. It can easily be shown that a greater
amount of Chopin's music is now alive and well in the concert hall, pro-
portionate to his relatively small output, than that of any other composer.

III

Much new information has flowed into the field of Chopin studies in recent years, and there would be no point in writing another biography of
the composer that did not reflect that fact. To give just a few examples:
No present-day account of Chopin's life can ignore the work of Georges
Lubin, whose magisterial edition of the letters of George Sand (in twenty-
six volumes) was brought to a conclusion in 1995 and brings her relations
with her contemporaries, and especially with Chopin, into sharper relief.
Equally indispensable is the work of George Sand's biographer-in-chief,
Curtis Cate, who left few stones unturned in his quest to uncover the veiled
complexities of her character. I have woven the work of both scholars into
my account of the Sand-Chopin *ménage* and have attempted to explore
aspects of the liaison that are often glossed over in the general rush to have
done with the story. Chopin's relationship with Sand was the most
intimate that he experienced with any human being—aside from the
members of his immediate family. His first meetings with Sand, their
"honeymoon" in Majorca, their subsequent shared life at Nohant and in
Paris for the next eight years, and the tumult that brought about their
final rupture are traced in somewhat greater detail than usual. In biographical work there is always a danger of "burying the hero beneath the
documents"—to use a telling phrase of André Maurois, one of Sand's
earlier biographers. Still, the transmission of sources is important, for
without them the chain of evidence is broken. The events in Sand's life
touched on those of Chopin at a hundred different points, and there
are times when the story of his life can hardly be told without reference
to hers.

As for Chopin's earlier years in Poland, the field has changed almost beyond recognition, making the provision of a fuller and more accurate account of his childhood and youth more necessary than ever. The work of Piotr Mysłakowski and Andrzej Sikorski has opened new vistas on the composer's early years in Warsaw, rendering much of what used to pass for the story of his life there redundant, filled as it was with fantasy and legend. Their book *Fryderyk Chopin: The Origins* (2010) rids the topic of much confusion and error. Based on a meticulous survey of church records of births, marriages, and burials; property mortgage deeds; bank accounts; and municipal archives in dozens of towns and villages across Poland and France, their research has become an indispensable source for Chopin scholars. Piotr Mysłakowski's later study *The Chopins' Warsaw* (2013) is also important, for it takes us into the heart of the Chopin family circle itself, offering new and unprecedented glimpses of their daily lives as they went about their business in the Polish capital. It is hardly possible to write a biography of Chopin that does not take these volumes into account, and the early chapters of my own narrative have been influenced by their texts.

The key players in the story of Chopin's life are easily recognized, for they turn up in all the standard biographies. Chopin's wide circle of Polish friends during his youth and adolescence in Poland included his classmates at the Warsaw Lyceum, Jan Matuszyński, Dominik ("Domuś") Dziewanowski, Jan ("Jasio") Białobłocki, Julian Fontana, and Tytus Woyciechowski, the dedicatee of his early "Là ci darem" Variations, op. 2. But how much do we actually know about these young men? Hardly anything, it seems, as we turn the pages of one Chopin biography after another. They make their entrances and their exits, but they never linger long enough for us to make their firm acquaintance; yet these friends were vitally important to Chopin. Then there were his teachers at the Lyceum, among them Professor Zygmunt Vogel, who taught drawing; Professor Józef Skrodzki, who taught chemistry; Professor Wacław Maciejowski, who taught history and classics; and above all its rector, Dr. Samuel Linde, an eminent philologist who produced Poland's first dictionary. And after the Lyceum came the High School for Music, with the founding director Józef Elsner as its chief luminary. These people, too, form part of the cavalcade of characters who regularly crowd their way into the story of Chopin's life. It is clear from comments that Chopin made in later life that he admired his mentors and was grateful for the superior education that they gave him. Yet we generally have to delve into arcane sources, beyond the reach of the average reader, to find out who they really were. For the rest, all history is biography. I have attempted to put a face on some of these personalities by offering them their own "cameos," so to speak, which may not only bring them to life but may put Chopin himself into sharper focus.

IV

Chopin's correspondence remains our primary source for understanding his life and work. In fact, it is impossible to produce a satisfactory chronology of his daily activities without constant reference to it. While his letters may lack the verbal polish of those of Schumann or Berlioz, both of whom were professional music critics, they nonetheless provide us with a trove of information unobtainable elsewhere. Chopin had no literary pretensions and he had no idea that his letters would one day be read by an international audience. Nor did he write with one eye on posterity (as Liszt sometimes did while revising his first drafts) but rather responded as best he could to the matters raised by his correspondents. Yet his epistolary style is engaging and it draws us into his world. To his family and to his Polish friends—Wojciech Grzymała, Julian Fontana, Józef Elsner, and others— he naturally wrote in Polish. To others he wrote in French, a language in which he was fluent from his youth. One notable exception to this rule was his correspondence with his father, Mikołaj Chopin, which was conducted in French despite the fact that Polish was the language of the home and French-born Mikołaj spoke it well, albeit with a marked accent. As a student at the Warsaw Lyceum, Chopin is known to have taken lessons in Italian, German, and English, although there are no letters from him in these last two languages. To his intimate friends he was always ready to reveal his deeper feelings. To others he was more guarded, preferring to wear a mask of polite civility rather than let his words betray him. Chopin was endowed with considerable powers of sarcasm, and he was ready to direct it against those whom he disliked, or whom he suspected of insincerity. Ever ready to puncture the vanity of these worthies, the cartoons that he occasionally sketched in the margins of his letters amount to a more powerful commentary on what he really thought than do his words. His sense of the absurd was never far from the surface. He was only fourteen years old when he created his satirical newspaper the *Szafarnia Courier*, a spoof on the conservative *Warsaw Courier*. Its madcap humor and comic "news stories," in which he reports on the rustic lifestyle of the Mazovian village of Szafarnia while on holiday there, belie his tender years. Chopin also had an abiding love of puns, which rarely deserted him, even when he was in physical discomfort and facing the end.

Closely connected to this firsthand material are the recollections of those who knew Chopin from his early childhood in Warsaw and grew up with him. The memoirs of Eugeniusz Skrodzki, Eustachy Marylski, and Józef Sikorski provide us with vignettes about him and his family that we cannot find elsewhere. Chopin's godfather, Fryderyk Skarbek, wrote an important autobiography in which there are references to the Chopin family beyond price to the biographer. I have drawn generously on these and other Polish sources in an attempt to create a somewhat fuller picture of Chopin's fledgling years than we are generally proffered.

It cannot be said that Chopin enjoyed writing letters. He often procrastinated and there were times when the writing of a single epistle would be spread across several days. The shorter ones amount to no more than a line or two, confirming an appointment here or a social engagement there. The longest letter to have survived runs to nearly six thousand words, took him a week to write, and was addressed to his family shortly after his arrival in Scotland, in mid-August 1848, giving them details of his sojourn in the British Isles. He entrusted this travelogue to his friend Woyciech Grzymała in Paris, asking him to treat it "as if it were one of my greatest works" and forward it to Warsaw.[6] There are approximately eight hundred letters by Chopin in existence, but this is considered to be a fraction of the number that he is thought to have written. Letters that at one time were in circulation disappeared, never to become part of the scholarly record. The European conflagrations that formed the backdrop to Chopin's story, together with the sheer indifference and neglect that his epistolary legacy endured at the hands of numerous individuals after his death, resulted in the loss of important documents and the creation of a void that has never been filled. Ferdynand Hoesick wrote about this lamentable state of affairs in the Preface to his influential *Chopiniana*.

---

6. CFC, vol. 3, p. 381; KFC, vol. 2, p. 262 (cited hereafter whenever Chopin's correspondence is written in Polish).

It is a strange thing that while the letters to such famous people as Adam Mickiewicz, Juliusz Słowacki, and Joachim Lelewel are reverently guarded as if they were some relics or family jewels, the letters of Chopin are treated very badly. Those who had them did not look after them very well, and precious letters were "borrowed," never to be returned. Thus, for instance, it is known that there was a whole collection of Chopin's letters addressed to Tomasz Nidecki [an older student who had studied at the Warsaw Lyceum], but only two letters survived. Why? Because the rest were "borrowed" or given away.[7]

Hoesick does not draw the depressing conclusion, so we will do it for him. So many documents on which a life story normally rests are missing, it is entirely possible that a definitive biography of Chopin may never be written. Scholarship abhors a vacuum, so speculation, hypothesis, and sheer fantasy have rushed in to fill it, and that has been Chopin's portion ever since the hour of his death.

The most complete collection of Chopin's letters on which we are still forced to rely remains the three-volume *Correspondance de Frédéric Chopin*, edited by the Polish scholar Bronisław Sydow and his collaborators, Suzanne and Denise Chainaye, published in the years 1953–60. This collection was actually a French translation of Chopin's original Polish texts, which had appeared in Sydow's own two-volume *Korespondencja Fryderyka Chopina* (1955). In the sixty years that have elapsed, no Chopin biographer has been able to dispense with these volumes, despite their known shortcomings. They are now being replaced by an annotated edition in Polish that will eventually run to three volumes, and is being published under the aegis of the University of Warsaw with a distinguished roster of Polish scholars at its head: Zofia Helman, Zbigniew Skowron, and Hanna Wróblewska-Straus. At the time of writing, only the first two volumes are available, covering the years 1816–39.

---

7. HFC, pp. iv–v.

V

A biography of Chopin, or of any composer for that matter, opens the door to an old topic. How important is a study of the life to an understanding of the music? There are two competing philosophies and they can hardly be reconciled. One is that the life and work are inseparable. Because the work could not have been brought into existence without the life, so the argument runs, it must bear traces of that life with all its joys and sorrows, its triumphs and its tragedies. The pursuit of such connections is therefore important, both to the player and to the listener.

The other argument maintains that music is a thing in itself, that it stands or falls without reference to the life that created it. Somewhat like a mathematical equation, it exists in splendid isolation, divorced from its creator. Indeed, we need not know who its creator is. Stripped of biography, yet continuing to function supremely well without it, a musical composition renders superfluous all attempts to reattach it to those mundane links that connect it to the outside world. Looked at this way, music becomes a solution in search of a problem. More to the point, a biography becomes a bridge to nowhere.

It is not difficult to see where Chopin stood in this debate. It is almost as if his life and music unfolded along parallel planes, with no point of intersection. His studies, preludes, nocturnes, mazurkas, and polonaises seem to exist in rarefied seclusion, unfettered by the human condition. Even the ballades, whose very title provokes the idea that they must be "about" something, have never yielded any secrets that the vast majority of us thinks worth knowing. Many attempts have been made to link them to the epic poetry of Poland's national bard, Adam Mickiewicz. But that dooms these unique musical structures to lie down on a Procrustean bed, in which they must be stretched out of shape to fit whatever story line the poet happens to be weaving.

Most of Chopin's contemporaries—including Berlioz, Liszt, Mendelssohn, and Schumann—attached pictures, poems, or storied titles to their music, in an attempt to "explain" it to their listeners. This was the age of program music, and the unity of the arts was the thing. By contrast, we could almost describe Chopin as a displaced person of musical history—a classical composer in word and deed, condemned to walk in silence among the chattering romantics. This is not a common view of someone who has been called the "Prince of Romantics," but it will bear contemplation. Chopin disdained program music, and his feelings are well illustrated by his reaction to Robert Schumann's celebrated review of his "Là ci darem" Variations ("An opus 2"), which even as it propelled him to fame provoked him to mirth.[8] Schumann thought he had identified in this music the *dramatis personae* of *Don Giovanni*, the opera from which the theme is drawn, with the Don making amorous advances to a coquettish Zerlina in the first variation, while in the second, "two lovers chase each other about, laughing all the while." The slow variation in B-flat minor was for Schumann a seduction scene. All this would have come as a surprise to Chopin, who had no such images in mind, but there was a sequel to the matter that is worth reporting here because it allows us to clear up a small mystery that lingers in the literature. Not long after Schumann's article appeared, Chopin wrote to his friend Tytus Woyciechowski, the dedicatee of the work, that he had received a review of the Variations that had sent him into peals of laughter.

> A few days ago I received a ten-page review from a German in Cassel who is full of enthusiasm for them. After a long-winded preface he proceeds to analyze them bar by bar, explaining that they are not ordinary variations, but a fantastic *tableau*. Speaking of the second variation he says that Don Giovanni runs around with Leporello; in the third he kisses Zerlina while Masetto's rage is pictured in the left hand—and in the fifth bar of the Adagio he declares that Don Giovanni kisses Zerlina *on the D-flat*. [Count Ludwik] Plater asked me yesterday where her D-flat was to be found? I could die of laughing at this German's imagination.[9]

It used to be thought that this "analysis" also came from Schumann's pen, because it is written in a similar vein to the one that he published. We now know that the "German in Cassel" was Friedrich Wieck, Schumann's future father-in-law, who happened to be passing through the city in the company of his prodigy daughter, Clara, basking in the reflected glory of her first tour as a concert pianist. Wieck himself sent the review to

8. *AmZ*, December 7, 1831.
9. CFC, vol. 2, p. 43; KFC, vol. 1, p. 201.

Chopin, having been swept off his feet by the Variations, which were now in Clara's repertoire. Later he would outrageously suggest that it was his daughter who had made them famous by including them in her concerts.[10] As for the scatological joke about kissing Zerlina "on the D-flat," which continues to make the rounds in the literature, it remains only to note Chopin's derision when faced with writing of this kind, and his lifelong resistance to it.

VI

Chopin's reputation as a concert pianist presents us with a paradox. It rested on fewer than twenty public concerts across his lifetime, in which with one or two exceptions he played only his own music. In earlier years he performed before large audiences in Warsaw, Vienna, Munich, and Paris; later on he played in Edinburgh, Manchester, and Glasgow. He faced his largest audience in Manchester during the closing months of his life, where twelve hundred people heard him play. Yet he was a reluctant virtuoso. He once admitted to Liszt, "I am not fitted to give concerts, the public frightens me; I feel suffocated by its panting breath, paralyzed by its curious glance, mute before those unknown faces."[11]

His sound was small and it often failed to carry in large halls. It would be a mistake, however, to suppose that this was the result of his weakened physical condition. Chopin despised the hard-hitting virtuosi of his time, and often likened their forced, rough sounds to those of a dog's mindless barking. His natural inclination was for infinite gradations of sound, and myriad colors. Heine called him "the Raphael of the piano," a happy phrase on which it is hard to improve. And it was on the silvery-toned Pleyel piano that he found his painter's palette waiting for him, with all the colors of the rainbow at his disposal. Once he had discovered this instrument he never abandoned it. It was in the salons of the aristocracy in Warsaw and

10. Wieck sent his review to Chopin prior to its publication, doubtless hoping for his approval, because the article had been rejected by the *AmZ*. It eventually appeared in the journal *Caecilia: Eine Zeitschrift für die musikalische Welt* (vol. 14, 1832). When Wieck tried to get it translated and published in *La Revue musicale*, Chopin protested and refused "to sacrifice my musical integrity for the sake of a bone-headed German." The matter has been adroitly summarized by Henry Pleasants in MWRS, pp. 17–18.
11. LC, p. 84.

Paris that Chopin came into his own, playing before a select audience of familiar faces, gathered around the keyboard in a charmed circle of admirers. Looking back on those times, Liszt described such assemblies, with a touch of mock solemnity, as "the Church of Chopin" and the audience as worshippers. These were nonetheless occasions to treasure and seasoned musicians such as Charles Hallé, Ferdinand Hiller, and Felix Mendelssohn went away enraptured by what they heard. But not everyone succumbed. After leaving a Chopin concert, Sigismond Thalberg, it was said, shouted all the way home because he needed some noise. He had heard nothing but *piano* all evening, he complained, "and now, for the sake of contrast, I want a little *forte*."[12] The critic of *Le Courrier français* put it well when he informed his readers, "The charms of [Chopin's] playing are simply microscopic. His talent is always best assessed by those seated next to the piano."[13]

VII

Chopin's indifference to the music of his contemporaries has often drawn comment. The music of Schumann and Mendelssohn might as well never have existed, for it left him cold. The music of Berlioz bewildered him. As for the music of Liszt, he came close to despising it, although he was always ready to acknowledge Liszt's sovereign position as a pianist. Beethoven he respected, but he never proffered the master that adulation so readily bestowed on him by practically every other musician of the nineteenth century. He is known to have played Beethoven's "Funeral March" Sonata, op. 26, and he taught one or two of the other sonatas to his pupils when they requested it. But his admission that he regarded the E-flat major Sonata, op. 31, no. 3, as "very vulgar" until he heard Hallé play it in Paris in the 1830s, speaks volumes.[14] When he received an invitation to attend the unveiling of a statue to Beethoven in Bonn, in 1845, marking the seventy-fifth anniversary of the composer's birth (an event attended by hundreds of his fellow musicians), his only comment was "You can guess

---

12. MMML, pp. 75–76.
13. Issue of March 10, 1841.
14. HLL, p. 35.

how likely I am to go!"[15] The two composers Chopin admired above all others were Bach and Mozart—although we must question just how much Bach he knew. The monumental edition of Bach's music, published by Breitkopf and Härtel, was not begun until after Chopin's death, and he probably never heard the cantatas and masses of the Protestant master in what was an overwhelmingly Catholic Poland. The one work of Bach with which we know Chopin to have been intimately acquainted was the 48 Preludes and Fugues—many of which he mastered during his youth and could still play from memory in later life. For that we must thank the encouragement he received, first from his only piano teacher, Wojciech Żywny, and later from his only composition teacher, Józef Elsner. Mozart was a different matter. Chopin was familiar with the piano sonatas and some of the chamber music (especially the E major Piano Trio, K. 542, which he played in public), and his love of the operas was unconditional. Perhaps his favorite Mozart opera was *Don Giovanni*, which he had known since his youth. But he adored as well the *Requiem*, which he is known to have heard twice in Paris, including the performance arranged for the reburial of Emperor Napoléon, in 1840. It appears to have been this latter performance that generated a desire within him to have the work played at his own funeral, a wish that was carried out by his friends, though not without difficulty.

What of Chopin's influence on the future? By common consent it has been enormous. Scriabin, Debussy, and Prokofiev all proclaimed a debt to him. Scriabin's famous Study in D-sharp minor, op. 8, would be unthinkable without Chopin's "Revolutionary" Study hovering in the inspired background. As for Debussy, the formal inscription on the title page of his Twelve Studies ("to the Memory of Frédéric Chopin") cannot veil their intimate attachment to the Polish composer's keyboard textures, which are audible on every page of this music. Prokofiev confessed that the Scherzo of his Third Symphony ("The Fiery Angel") was directly inspired by the Finale of the B-flat minor Piano Sonata. The barcarolles, nocturnes, and ballade of Gabriel Fauré could never have been written without Chopin's pioneering example before him. We know, too, that Ravel's admiration for Chopin was unbounded, as his centenary essay eulogizing the composer

15. CFC, vol. 2, p. 201; KFC, vol. 2, p. 137.

bears witness.[16] Nor should we forget to mourn those countless composers whose creative drive was so overwhelmed by Chopin's powerful personality that they ended up producing compositions cloned in the master's image. They are well represented by Felix Blumenfeld (the teacher of Heinrich Neuhaus and Vladimir Horowitz), whose music, which has its devoted followers, earned for him the title of "the Russian Chopin."

VIII

The difficulty of writing about Chopin's music has often been remarked. Arthur Rubinstein spoke for many when he said that when one hears Chopin's music it is like coming home—a phrase that seems to render further discussion pointless. The body of literature that has nonetheless emerged falls into two quite different categories, each one claiming to have roots in the "homeland" while moving in the opposite direction to the other. The school of perfumed poetry has had a long run and has attracted the pens of some notable writers, not all of them musicians. But however refined the poetry, it is generally autobiographical in nature, amounting to little more than a verbal response to the music's emotional "halo"—the main point of attraction in the first place. As for the school of "deep analysis," which has lately come to the fore in Chopin studies, but which was begun almost a century ago by Hugo Leichtentritt,[17] it is now so heavily burdened with specially minted terminology, aided by spreadsheets and graphs of uncommon complexity, that contact with the music it purports to describe cannot always be maintained. For the rest, any attempt to reveal the genius of Chopin's music by deconstructing it is bound to fail. One might as well try to understand the nature of time by dismantling a clock.

Given its immense diversity, even a casual review of the field raises concerns for the biographer: How best to structure a life of Chopin so that its narrative reflects the rich complexity of the subject, yet speaks effectively to the general reader? We draw much consolation from Somerset Maugham's droll observation, "There are three rules for writing biography, and nobody knows what they are." In electing to write a "Life and Times," I have

---

16. *Le Courrier musical*, January 1, 1910.
17. *Analyse von Chopin'schen Klavierwerke*, 2 vols. Berlin, 1921–22.

admittedly fallen back on an old formula, one that is not without its problems. But since the times are generally absent from the story of Chopin's life, the void was there, waiting to be filled. The political, military, and social turmoil against which Chopin lived out his daily existence, both in Poland and in France, did not leave him untouched. He lived through two revolutions—the first one in Poland in 1830–31, which he witnessed from foreign soil, and the second one in France in 1848, which he experienced at first hand. There were times when the battlefields of Europe were littered with the dead and dying, and the news was of nothing but carnage on an industrial scale. Then there were the upheavals brought about by the cholera epidemics that killed thousands of people and forced the ones who survived to flee European cities, including Paris, in large numbers. By any standards, these were cataclysmic events that are given short shrift in the many sanitized versions of Chopin's life to have come down to us.

One thing is beyond dispute and it is all that the biographer requires to keep his pen moving: Chopin's music everywhere keeps an interest in his life alive. Captivated by the boundless attractions of his ballades, scherzos, nocturnes, polonaises, and mazurkas—the entire cornucopia of his music, in fact—we are drawn to consider the time-honored questions that follow in its wake. What kind of person wrote it? When and where did he live, and with whom? What were the conditions that aroused the creative process from its slumbers, and what induced it to fall asleep again? It is in the clamor for answers that the biographer takes possession of his field. And in the case of Chopin it may lead to a fruitful discovery. Chopin's compositions are woven so closely into the fabric of his personality that the one becomes a seamless extension of the other. Without the music, the hollowed-out character that remained would contain little to interest us. In the pages that follow we have therefore allowed the life itself to usher in the music for review, although there are bound to be those for whom this principle of selection leaves something to be desired.

CHOPIN'S FAMILY BACKGROUND

The Child is father of the Man.
—William Wordsworth[1]

I

In 1787 a sixteen-year-old youth named Nicolas Chopin left his native France and journeyed a thousand miles across Europe—to Poland. Until modern times it was impossible to speculate about his reasons. The youth broke completely with his past and in later life he kept from his children all knowledge of their humble French relations. Nicolas Chopin embraced Poland as if it were his native land. He generated a powerful sense of patriotism that was to become the single most unifying influence in the life of his closely knit family. We now know that Nicolas was born in the village of Marainville, in the province of Lorraine, on April 15, 1771. This information and the attendant details of his lowly origins might never have come to light had it not been for the fact that he was forced to declare them when he retired as a professor of French at the School of Artillery and Military Engineering in Warsaw, the only way he could qualify for a pension. On this application he stated not only that he was born in Marainville, but also that his father was François Chopin (1738–1814) and

---

1. "Ode: Intimations of Immortality."

his mother was Marguerite Deflin (1736–94). The file was buried in Russian archives, Warsaw at that time being under Russian rule, and was only brought to light in 1925.[2] It was then but a short step to consult the register of births and deaths in Marainville to complete the rest of the story. We learn that Nicolas's father was a wheelwright by trade, whose marriage had produced two other children—Anne (1769–1845) and Marguerite (1775–1845). They were Fryderyk Chopin's aunts. It is one of the abiding puzzles of Chopin's family background that even as he enjoyed his greatest fame in Paris, these two elderly ladies lived less than three hundred kilometers away, unaware of their famous nephew, and he of them. After his retirement François Chopin abandoned his trade of wheelwright and became a vintner. By an odd coincidence Nicolas Chopin, at the moment of his own retirement, also took up the cultivation of grapes, in the somewhat more hostile climate of Poland, and proudly informed his famous son of the success he was having with his new pastime.

Marainville, where Nicolas was brought up, possessed strong Polish ties. Ever since Louis XV had conferred the title of Duke of Lorraine and Bar on his son-in-law, the deposed Polish king Stanislaw Leszczyński, in 1737, large numbers of exiled Polish aristocrats and their families had gravitated to the province. The Polish population of Lorraine grew even further after the First Partition of Poland in 1772 by the country's traditional enemies, Russia, Prussia, and Austria. Soon the province possessed a thriving community of Polish émigrés, where the language and customs of the mother country were everywhere to be found. In 1780 the château of Marainville was purchased by a Polish nobleman, Count Michał Jan Pac. It was here that the ten-year-old Nicolas caught the attention of the count's estate manager, a Pole named Adam Weydlich, whose sophisticated Paris-born wife, Françoise, took the boy under her wing, developed his social skills, and arranged for him to take lessons on the flute and violin—instruments on which he remained modestly proficient. He also discovered the works of Voltaire, whose writings he liked to quote in later life. It was a relatively privileged existence for Nicolas. By nature he was industrious, loyal, and thrifty, characteristics he exhibited all his life, and it is

2. By the Polish scholar Stanisław Pereświet-Sołtan. His discovery was given wide currency by Édouard Ganche, the president of the Paris Chopin Society, who published some additional findings in *La Pologne*, January 15, 1927.

possible that by his mid-teens he had already acquired a sound knowledge of the Polish language, which he heard spoken all around him. With the death of Count Pac in 1787, the château and its surrounding lands were sold off to pay the count's debts, and the Weydlichs, perhaps fearing the social upheavals of the approaching French Revolution, went back to Warsaw, taking young Nicolas with them. The youth lived for a time in the home of Weydlich's brother Franciszek, a teacher of German and Latin at Warsaw's so-called Knights' School for military cadets. It used to be thought that during these early years in Warsaw, Nicolas worked as an accountant in a tobacco factory formerly owned by Count Pac, a job for which his knowledge of bookkeeping and business transactions would certainly have fitted him—Weydlich had often entrusted him with matters concerning the Pac estate. But that idea has recently been jettisoned in favor of one that is better documented. On February 22, 1788, the Weydlichs announced in the *Warsaw Gazette* that they planned to open a boarding school for girls, promising proficiency in French. We detect the hand of Mme Françoise Weydlich in this enterprise, who saw in the seventeen-year-old Nicolas a potential language instructor whose fluent French was his (and their) greatest asset. His first two pupils were the children of Adam Weydlich—Henryka and Michał. We must also mention another pupil, ten-year-old Jan Dekert, who came along shortly afterward and with whose family Nicolas forged bonds of friendship. Dekert became a priest, and as Bishop Jan Dekert he delivered a moving funeral oration over the coffin of his old mentor, in May 1844, from which some important details of Nicolas's early years in Poland may be gleaned.[3]

What sort of city would have greeted Nicolas Chopin as he alighted from the stagecoach in that unsettled autumn of 1787? The English travel writer William Coxe left a graphic description of Warsaw at this time. It was populated by Ukrainians, Lithuanians, Russians, Jews, and of course Poles. Coxe marveled at "the prodigious number of foreigners" in a city of no more than seventy thousand inhabitants. This volatile mixture of solitudes has been memorably described as "a melting-pot that

---

3. The manuscript of Dekert's eulogy is preserved in the Chopin Museum, Warsaw, under the call number M/393.

never melted"—always simmering and ready to boil over at the slightest
provocation. And there were provocations aplenty at this moment in
Warsaw's turbulent history. Coxe wrote:

> The whole town has a melancholy appearance, exhibiting that strong
> contrast of wealth and poverty, luxury and distress, which pervade
> every part of this unhappy country. The streets are spacious, but
> ill-paved; the churches and public buildings are large and magnifi-
> cent; the palaces of the nobility are numerous and splendid; but the
> greatest part of the houses, particularly in the suburbs, are mean
> and ill-constructed wooden hovels.[4]

Nicolas was far from home and he gave serious thought to returning to
France; but he himself tells us that he fell ill and twice delayed the decision. And so he stayed, lived with the Weydlichs, and taught French at
their school for the next four years. It was a time of growing political unrest in Poland, and it coincided with the opening of the Great Sejm (or
Parliament), which promised fundamental freedoms for the Poles, enshrined in the celebrated Constitution of May 3, 1791, a document that
was modeled in part on the American Constitution of 1788. Caught up in
the rising tide of nationalism that was sweeping the country, Nicolas
adopted the Polish form of his name, Mikołaj, which he never abandoned,
and which we therefore propose to use throughout our narrative. His decision to remain in Poland rested on a practical consideration: he might
have faced military conscription in Napoléon's army had he returned to
Lorraine. In a solitary surviving letter to his parents Nicolas/Mikołaj told
them, "I would regret leaving here, only to become a soldier, even in my
own country."[5] When he penned these lines, he had no idea that within
three years he would join Warsaw's civilian militia, be placed in charge of
his own detachment of men, and fight alongside soldiers in the Polish army.

In 1793, Russia, under Catherine the Great, invaded Poland in an attempt to quell the threat of a growing movement for national independence,
and together with her Prussian ally partitioned the country for a second
time, virtually tearing Poland's new constitution to shreds. The Poles rose

4. CTP, vol. 1, p. 150.
5. CFC, vol. 1, p. xlix. Letter dated September 15, 1790.

up against their oppressors and won some impressive victories on the battlefield under the banner of the Polish national hero General Tadeusz Kościuszko. During the crucial Battle of Maciejowice (October 10, 1794), Kościuszko was wounded and taken prisoner.[6] The Poles fought a series of rearguard actions and fell back on the Warsaw suburb of Praga, on the right bank of the Vistula, where they took up defensive positions. On November 3, a Russian army of seventeen thousand soldiers under the command of General Alexander Suvorov reached the outskirts of Praga and began a fierce artillery barrage. This led the Poles to think that Suvorov planned a long siege, but under cover of darkness the Russians took the Polish defenders by surprise. The Battle of Praga began at three o'clock the following morning, November 4. Just before Russian troops overran the area, Mikołaj Chopin and the detachment of men under his command were ordered to take up a fresh position elsewhere in the city, which is how he survived the massacre that followed. In defiance of orders given by General Suvorov to his troops, the Russians went on a rampage, looting, burning, and raping as they went along, and by the time that Praga fell, upwards of twenty thousand men, women, and children had been slaughtered. This was carnage on an unprecedented scale, carried out against a civilian population, and it became seared in the memory of the nation. As General Suvorov was later to write, "The whole of Praga was strewn with dead bodies, blood was flowing in streams."[7] He reported his victory to the Russian empress, Catherine the Great, with three words: "Hurrah—Praga—Suvorov." Catherine replied with equal brevity: "Bravo Field Marshal, Catherine." His promotion to the rank of Field Marshal as a reward for what history recognizes as the "Massacre of Praga" stained his reputation and that of the Russian army he commanded. With Poland now surrounded on three sides by Russia, Prussia,

---

6. He was incarcerated in the Peter and Paul Fortress at Saint Petersburg. Perhaps because he was a U.S. citizen (an honor accorded him because of his participation in the American War of Independence), and because he also enjoyed honorary French citizenship, he was not executed. He recovered from his wounds, and following the death of Catherine the Great was granted clemency by her son, Tsar Paul I. He returned to the United States, where he pursued a long friendship with Thomas Jefferson. Kościuszko continued to work for Polish causes, went to live in France, and was even approached by Napoléon for help in the planning of his forthcoming campaign against Russia. When Kościuszko died in 1817, his remains were transported to Kraków, and in 1819 he was given the funeral of a national hero and buried in Kraków Cathedral among the tombs of the Polish kings.
7. MRCG, p. 446.

and Austria (a late arrival at the banquet table, gorging on the spoils of war), the uprising was doomed. The country was partitioned in 1795 for the third time, and sovereign Poland disappeared from the map. It was not restored until the Treaty of Versailles, in 1919. Napoléon made a small territorial adjustment in 1807 when he created the Duchy of Warsaw, into which Fryderyk Chopin was born. And after Napoléon's defeat the so-called Congress Kingdom was created by the victorious powers at the Congress of Vienna in 1815; but it was little more than a vassal state that lacked sovereignty, and it fell entirely under Russian dominion when Tsar Alexander I had himself crowned King of Poland a few years later. It is difficult to improve on the despairing but entirely appropriate description attached to the Poland of those times by one of its leading historians, Norman Davies, who dubbed it "God's Playground."

II

The catastrophic history of Poland, with its hundreds of thousands of dead, was an open wound that soaked the fabric of the nation with its blood. It is impossible to write a life of Chopin without taking these turbulent times into account, because throughout his childhood and adolescence there were countless families known to the young composer whose lives had been devastated by the conflicts that marked Poland's constant struggle for sovereignty. The soldiers who joined Napoléon's Polish Legion, and fought with his Grande Armée against Russia in 1812, were the stuff of legend while Chopin was growing up. A total of 98,000 of them fought with the French when Napoléon attacked and took Moscow. The Polish lancers of the Vistula region were the first troops to enter the city, and when he was forced to withdraw they protected Napoléon's flanks. Of the original 98,000 members of the Polish Legion, only 26,000 returned home.[8] For a generation or more these old campaigners—survivors of the battles of Maciejowice, Ostroleka, and Borodino—could be seen walking the streets of Warsaw, with missing limbs, and saber-scarred hands

---

8. Napoléon used to say that eight hundred Poles were the equivalent of eight thousand enemy soldiers, an observation based on his knowledge of their bravery on the field of battle. When he went into exile on the island of Elba, the only guards he took with him were the Polish lancers.

and faces, a daily reminder of the sufferings endured by the population at large. Like other Polish children of his generation, the young Chopin was utterly familiar with such sights. The most famous of these veterans was General Józef Sowiński, who lost a leg during the Napoléonic campaign of 1812, and now walked with the help of a prosthesis. This national hero was affectionately referred to as "the soldier with the wooden leg." He played a prominent role in the Polish Uprising of 1831, and was killed during the defense of Warsaw in September of that year. Chopin mourned his loss in his "Stuttgart Diary," referring to Sowiński as "that fine patriot."

After the Third Partition in 1795, and all the uncertainties that came in its wake, Mikołaj was thrown back on his own resources. Since the Weyd-lichs had closed their school he had led a peripatetic existence, earning a living as a French tutor to the children of several wealthy Polish families in Warsaw, before moving to the region of Kalisz in 1797. There his reputation as a reliable and trustworthy teacher flourished. The following year he moved to the village of Szafarnia, in the province of Mazovia, where he became the resident tutor of the wealthy Dziewanowski family, owners of the large estate there, forming lifelong bonds of friendship with them. (Many years later Fryderyk Chopin spent his summer holidays at Szafarnia in the company of his father.) Mikołaj then moved to the estate of Czerniewo as tutor to the young children of the wealthy Łączyński family, one of whose daughters was to find a place in history as the future Marie Walewska, the mistress of Napoléon and the mother of his son Alexandre Walewski. This early period of Mikołaj's career came to a close in 1802 when he gained a new position as tutor to the five children of Countess Ludwika Skarbek at her estate at Żelazowa Wola, which lay about sixty kilometers west of Warsaw.

III

In light of the central role that she and her children were to play in the lives of the Chopin family, a few words about Countess Ludwika Skarbek (1765–1827) are in order. She was the daughter of Jakub Fenger, one of the richest bankers in Toruń, the city where she was born. The family's wealth brought her an offer of marriage from Count Kacper Skarbek, who

emerges from the literature as a ne'er-do-well and a fortune hunter, someone who introduced much misery into Ludwika's life. Kacper arrived on
the scene with a checkered past and a mountain of debt. After abducting
a young girl, Justyna Dąmbska, from her family home and marrying her
when he was barely eighteen years old, he abandoned her a few years later,
leaving her with three young children and a line of creditors knocking at
the door. The marriage was annulled around 1789.[9] Kacper was not wrong
to see in Ludwika his possible salvation. On the day of the nuptials, in
1791, Kacper's new father-in-law, Jakub Fenger, paid off his debts, settled
a large dowry on the bride, and bought the pair the estate of Modzerowo
in western Poland as a wedding gift. For Kacper it was déjà vu all over
again. He proceeded to sire five children with Ludwika, squander a
second fortune through what was described as his "lordly and riotous" lifestyle, and then flee from his creditors, seeking sanctuary abroad and settling in the Grand Duchy of Poznań, where his pursuers had no leverage
over him.[10] The long-suffering Ludwika filed for a Protestant divorce (she
was brought up as a Lutheran), which was granted in 1806. She was
forty-one years old. Showing commendable resourcefulness, as well as
something of her father's business acumen, she began purchasing after the
latter's death in 1798 several properties in her own name, including the
estate at Żelazowa Wola in 1799, in order to protect herself from Kacper's
creditors.

All Ludwika's children were under ten years of age when they arrived
at their new home in Żelazowa Wola: Fryderyk Florian (1792–1866), Anna
Emilia (1793–1873), Anastazy-Teodor (1795–1812), Michał (1796–1834),
and Kazimierz (c. 1800–1805). They quickly fell under the spell of their
newly arrived French tutor, Mikołaj Chopin, the slender, self-assured gentle-

---

9. From the memoirs of Fryderyk Skarbek (Kacper's eldest son and Chopin's godfather) we
learn that this shotgun wedding was too much for the girl's mother, who placed a curse on her
daughter, uttering the fateful words, "May I be devoured by dogs if I set foot in my daughter's
home." Truth is sometimes stranger than fiction, for that is what happened in circumstances
that are beyond bizarre. About a year after the marriage the mother yielded to an invitation to
visit the young couple for the Easter festivities. During the journey by sleigh across the frozen
wastes of the surrounding countryside she fell ill, and by the time she arrived at the young
couple's house in Izbica she was dead. Her body was laid out in a frigid parlor where the Easter foods were also being preserved. In the middle of the night the dogs, attracted by the smell
of the hams, jumped through an open window and gnawed out the dead woman's cheeks.
SPFS, p. 30. See also MCW, p. 22.
10. SPFS, p. 8.

man with black hair and dark eyes who liked to quote Voltaire. He gained their affection with his quiet authority and his ability to arouse their curiosity in the world around them. After their lessons, conducted in both Polish and French, Mikołaj would sometimes take his pupils out of doors, where they would sit under the tall chestnut trees near the manor house, and regale them with stories about their country's history. Sometimes they would wander along the banks of the Utrata River, which ran through the estate, and explore the local geography, taking notes on ornithology and botany. A pause at the old water mill might lead to a spontaneous discussion on the magic of hydraulics, and how the power of water properly harnessed could transform the economy of an estate.

No topic was too abstruse for a question-and-answer session between the children and their young tutor. Mikołaj came to be regarded as a member of the family; he joined the countess and her fledglings for meals, and became a beloved authority figure. He treated his young charges not as children but as small adults, and for that they gave him their boundless respect. Mikołaj formed a special bond with Fryderyk Skarbek, Ludwika's eldest son, whose intellect he helped to shape, and who became not only a man of letters and a professor of economics at Warsaw University, but also Fryderyk Chopin's godfather.

Countess Ludwika liked to invite her Warsaw friends to visit Żelazowa Wola and join her for weekend house parties. Concerts were a regular feature of family life, as they were at most of the great Polish estates, and when the week's work was done friends and neighbors would gather in the drawing room of the manor house to enjoy whatever entertainment had been arranged. It may have been in response to one such invitation, in 1805, that Dr. Samuel Bogumił Linde, the rector of the recently established Warsaw Lyceum, turned up at Żelazowa Wola, where he formed a friendship with Mikołaj Chopin and took an interest in the latter's teenage pupil Fryderyk Skarbek. Years earlier Countess Ludwika had been Linde's pupil in Toruń and it was natural that she now wanted the education of her eldest son to be placed in the care of her former tutor. Within a few months, and with a bit of extra coaching from Mikołaj, young Skarbek passed the entrance examinations and became one of the first students at the Lyceum. Many years later, when he looked back on these halcyon days at Żelazowa Wola, Fryderyk Skarbek wrote a fine tribute to his old mentor, whose personality he enshrined in his memoirs.

Mikołaj Chopin, this tutor under whose care I lived in a strange
house, became my teacher, and after having spent several years with
me and my brothers, was then appointed French master at the
Warsaw Lyceum, where he taught until his old age, when he became
eligible for a pension. He was neither an emigrant nor a spoiled
priest, as were at that time most French tutors, who directed the
trend of education of our young people into paths so uncharacteristic of the Polish nation. Chopin came to Poland before the French
Revolution, as a clerk or accountant in a tobacco factory, established
in Warsaw by one of his countrymen.[11] He was not imbued either
with the principles of exaggerated Republican liberty, or with the
affected bigotry of the French emigrants; nor was he a Royalist infused with an idolatrous respect for the throne and the altar, but a
moral, honest man who, devoting himself to the upbringing of young
Poles, never attempted to turn them into Frenchmen or to incul-
cate in them the principles then reigning in France. With respect
for the Poles, and with gratitude towards the people in whose land
he had found a hospitable reception and a suitable way of earning
his living, he sincerely repaid his debt of gratitude by the conscientious upbringing of their offspring to be useful citizens. By his sojourn of many years in our country, through his amicable relations
with Polish homes, but chiefly through his marriage to a Polish lady,
and hence through the bonds of matrimony . . . he became a Pole
indeed . . . Under this revered teacher, who was until his death the
best friend of myself and of all my family, I received my first inclination towards learning, which at the time when I first went to
school, rested more on a general development of mental power than
on any training in particular subjects.[12]

The death of Ludwika's five-year-old son Kazimierz in 1805, following so hard on the heels of her abandonment by Kacper Skarbek, provided
her with an incentive to find someone to help her stabilize the household.
When she heard that Jakub Krzyżanowski, a longtime administrator of one
her estates, had died and left his daughter Justyna in impoverished cir-

---

11. Mikołaj Chopin lived in a house next to the tobacco factory, but as we learned on an earlier page he never worked there. The factory was both a workhouse and a jail, whose inmates
"earned money from their labour." MSFC, p. 160.
12. KCOL, p. 6. See also SPFS, pp. 8–11 and 87–88.

cumstances, Ludwika offered the young woman shelter and brought her to Żelazowa Wola as a housekeeper, where she met Mikołaj Chopin. Justyna Krzyżanowska was twenty-four years old and since she had no estate was probably considered (by the standards of the time) unmarriageable. Ludwika played the role of matchmaker and Justyna and Mikołaj, who was already thirty-five and regarded as a confirmed bachelor, were married within a year of their first meeting.

IV

Tekla Justyna Krzyżanowska, Chopin's mother, occupied a special place within Ludwika's family circle, where she was treated as an equal. It led to an unfounded assumption that the two families may have been related. Despite assiduous research by Polish scholars no such connection has ever been traced. Contrary to widespread assertions, Justyna's family had no blood ties with the Skarbeks.[13] It remains only to add that all the old virtues were present in Justyna's character. She was an excellent housekeeper, careful with money, and endowed with a kind and loving disposition. Contemporary observers describe her as having typical Polish features with flaxen hair and sapphire-blue eyes—which the only known portrait of her, painted when she was forty-seven years old, does nothing to contradict. She was musical, sang beautifully, and may have played the piano well enough to accompany Mikołaj on his flute. Her singing voice would have been among the first sounds that the infant Chopin heard. One of her favorite songs was the Polish melody "Już miesiąc zeszedł" ("The Moon Has Risen"), which Chopin later incorporated into his youthful "Fantasy on Polish Airs," op. 13.

Justyna was a devout Roman Catholic and a regular churchgoer, which provided the moral compass for her daily life, and incidentally for that of her children. She often took Chopin with her to the Catholic service in

---

13. MSFC, p. 68.

the Carmelite church on Krakowskie Przedmieście, where she had him kneel in front of her pew and read from his prayer book, "humble and repentant."[14] Chopin adored her. Many years later George Sand observed that Justyna was the only woman whom Chopin had ever truly loved. On his deathbed he is said to have cried out for her just hours before he died.

The marriage of Mikołaj and Justyna took place on June 28, 1806,[15] in the Roman Catholic Church of St. Roch and John the Baptist in the village of Brochów, the parish church of Żelazowa Wola. An entry in the church register runs:

> I, Ignatius Maryański, Curate of the Church, having called the banns on three Sundays in the presence of the congregation at divine service and having found no canonical impediment to the marriage between Mikołaj Chopin, gentleman, tutor at Żelazowa Wola, bachelor, and Justyna Krzyżanowska, spinster, have blessed and confirmed the contract legally according to the rites of the Church in the presence of Franciszek Grembecki, gentleman, and Karol Henke, gentleman.

After the wedding Mikołaj and Justyna moved into a modest tenement on the Skarbek estate that Ludwika made available for them. It resembled a bungalow with whitewashed walls shaded by trees, and lay not far from the manor house, where Justyna continued to supervise the running of the household and Mikołaj tutored the Skarbek children. It was in this simple dwelling that Chopin was born on March 1, 1810, at six o'clock in the evening. The place has meanwhile become a national shrine even though the infant spent only the first seven months of his life there.

Chopin was baptized in the Church of St. Roch in Brochów, where his parents had been married four years earlier. Owing to an inexplicable error, the curate registered the birth as "February 22." All his life, however, Chopin and his family insisted that March 1 was his birthday, and they celebrated it accordingly. His correspondence furnishes us with ample proof of that fact.[16] The baptism certificate reads:

---

14. MSFC, p. 38.
15. Correct. See MSFC, p. 166.
16. We need look no further than Chopin's letter of thanks on having been elected to membership in the Polish Literary Society in Paris in 1833, in which he declares that he was

Chopin's birthplace at Żelazowa Wola; a photograph (c. 1932). The obelisk in the foreground is a monument to Chopin's memory, unveiled in the presence of the Russian composer Mily Balakirev in 1894.

23 April, 1810. I, the aforesaid [Józef Morawski, curate of Brochów], have performed the ceremony of baptism over the infant baptized with water [*ex aqua*] by the two names Fryderyk Franciszek, born on February 22 of Mikołaj Choppen [*sic*], Frenchman, and Justyna *née* Krzyżanowska, his legal spouse. The godparents: Franciszek Grembecki, gentleman, from the village of Ciepliny, and Countess Anna Skarbek, spinster, of Żelazowa Wola.

---

born on March 1, 1810 (pp. 235–36). And that is also the date that Chopin sent to F.-J. Fétis, who incorporated it into his entry on the composer in his ongoing *Biographical Dictionary of Musicians* (1836). If corroborating evidence from members of Chopin's inner circle is required, it lies to hand. In a letter to his sister Ludwika, written after Chopin's death and dated March 1, 1851, Jane Stirling referred to this day as Chopin's birthday and made a pertinent observation: "He said to me one day, 'My mother, that is to say, my family, the mistress of the house [George Sand] and you, know the day of my birthday and you remember it.'" GSFC, p. 127.

The Latin words *ex aqua* draw attention. They refer to an earlier baptism carried out at home with ordinary water. Such "emergency baptisms" often took place where no priest was immediately available and the infant's life might be in danger. Any Christian could fulfill this ritual and no declaration was required until the "fulfillment baptism" took place in church. In Chopin's case, a comparison of his birth and baptismal certificates indicates a delay of several weeks, and carries the implication that his health was precarious from the start. Two of Countess Ludwika's children were Chopin's godparents, another indication of the closeness of the two families. Fryderyk Skarbek, after whom Chopin is named, was in Paris at the time of the ceremony, so Franciszek Grembecki acted as his proxy and it was from him that Chopin acquired his second name, Franciszek. Anna Skarbek, Chopin's godmother, was Countess Skarbek's seventeen-year-old daughter. The birth certificate, prepared on the same day, repeats the wrong date of birth.

In the year 1810, on April 23, at 3:00 p.m. Before me, the parish priest of Brochów, acting registrar of Brochów in the district of Sochaczew in the Department of Warsaw, there appeared Mikołaj Chopyn [sic], the father, aged forty domiciled in Żelazowa Wola, who showed me a male child which was born in his house on February 22 of this year at 6:00 o'clock in the evening, declaring that it was the child of himself and of Justyna born Krzyżanowska, aged twenty-eight, his spouse, and that it was his wish to give the child two names, Fryderyk Franciszek. After making this declaration, and showing me the child in the presence of Józef Wyrzykowski, bailiff, aged thirty-eight, and Fryderyk Geszt, aged forty, both domiciled in the village of Żelazowa Wola. The father and both witnesses after reading the present birth certificate declared that they could write. We have signed this document:

Fr. Jan Duchnowski,
parish priest of Brochów, acting registrar.
Mikołaj Chopin,
the father.

The signature of Mikołaj Chopin on a document bearing the wrong date of his son's birth is a puzzle that remains unresolved. It has been

Mikołaj and Justyna Chopin; a drawing by Ambroży Mieroszewski (c. 1829).

suggested that Mikołaj may have signed the certificate before the details themselves were written down—an idea supported by the incongruous position of the signature. Mikołaj's own name is misspelled twice, being rendered as "Chopyn" on the birth certificate and "Choppen" on the baptismal register, indicating some laxity on the part of the officiating clerics.[17]

V

There were three other children of the marriage, all of whom were girls. Ludwika Marianna (1807–55), the eldest of the four Chopin children, was named after Countess Ludwika Skarbek, her godparent. She was born not in Żelazowa Wola but in Warsaw, where the Skarbeks and the Chopins

---

17. It has been persuasively argued that these documents were entered into the church records several months after the ceremony they purport to describe, in an attempt perhaps to cover up the negligent bookkeeping at the Brochów church, which would make the actual year of Chopin's birth 1809. The pros and cons of the matter are far from settled, but have been ably summarized by Mariola Wojtkiewicz in WZW, pp. 57–62.

had sought temporary refuge during the years 1807–1808, "on account of the incessant passing of troops and the consequent unrest in the country," as Fryderyk Skarbek explained in his memoirs. She was the child who most closely resembled her father in manners and in the logical way she expressed her thoughts. Ludwika received her early education at a private school for girls run by Mme Bogumiła Wiłucka, on Warsaw's Nowy Świat Street, and she became an excellent linguist with a cultivated taste for the arts, especially poetry and music. She translated the *Life of Saint Veronika* from Italian into Polish. Her book *Józio's Journey*, a travelogue describing the Chopin family's sojourn in Duszniki-Zdrój (Bad Reinerz), as seen through the eyes of Countess Skarbek's grandchild, has become an indispensable source for the Chopin biographer. Ludwika was highly musical, played the piano, and also composed. Chopin was impressed with a mazurka that Ludwika wrote when she was just eighteen, which he described as "her *non plus ultra*, a mazurka to which Warsaw has not danced for a long time, and a *non plus ultra* of its kind."[18] It was toward Ludwika that he felt most closely drawn. During the last year of Chopin's life she traveled to Paris to sit by his bedside, became his major caregiver, and was with him when he passed away. It was Ludwika who brought the composer's heart back to Warsaw, where it was eventually placed in one of the pillars of the Church of the Holy Cross.

Ludwika was raised in the spirit of Polish patriotism. She was a "comrade" in the Polish Ladies Benevolent Society, one of whose directors was Katarzyna Sowińska (the wife of General Józef Sowiński, the defender of Warsaw during the uprising of 1830–31). The avowed purpose of the society was to dispense financial support to those who had been dispossessed by tsarist repression and were left with little more than the clothes on their backs. But the organization also had an unspoken agenda: namely, to keep the flame of passive resistance alive. Its premises were located on Warsaw's imposing Krakowskie Przedmieście Street, where the thirteen-year-old Fryderyk Chopin is known to have taken part in several of the society's fund-raising "soirées musicales." Ludwika also frequented the salon of the Luszczewski family, where the capital's literary elite used to meet, and from whose lively discussions politics would not have been excluded.

Ludwika's marriage to Dr. Józef Kalasanty Jędrzejewicz (1803–53), a

---

18. CFC, vol. 1, p. 44; KFC, vol. 1, p. 60.

Ludwika Chopin; an oil painting
by Ambroży Mieroszewski
(1829).

professor of administrative law at Marymont's Institute of Agriculture and
Forestry in Warsaw, took place in November 1832, at the Church of
St. Roch in Brochów, where her parents had been married and Chopin
baptized. There were four children of the union, Henryk, Ludwika, Fryderyk, and Antoni. As the years rolled by, it became clear that the marriage was not a happy one. Kalasanty appears to have been as demanding
in his domestic life as in his professional one. The very qualities that made
him an effective lawyer eventually turned him into a poor companion for
Ludwika, who worked hard to make the marriage work. Although the evidence is not abundant, it seems that Kalasanty found his connections to
the famous Chopin family a difficult burden to bear. His problematic behavior during Chopin's dying days, both toward his wife and his famous
brother-in-law, of whom he appeared to be unreasonably jealous, is a
wrenching story that is told on a later page.

Justyna Izabella (1811–81), the third of the Chopin children, was also

Izabella Chopin; an oil
painting by Ambroży
Mieroszewski (1829).

born in Warsaw after the family had taken up permanent residence there.
She was the sister who bore the greatest physical resemblance to Chopin,
a fact remarked on by Chopin himself in later years. Because she grew up
under the shadow of her older, more famous siblings, less attention has
been paid to her by Chopin scholars. We believe that she attended the
same school for girls as her older sister; and she may also have received
instruction from private tutors hired by Mikołaj Chopin to teach his
boarders, one of whom was Antoni Barciński (1803–78), a teacher of
mathematics and later an inspector of schools, whom Izabella married in
1834. There were no children of the marriage. Like her sister Ludwika,
Izabella belonged to the Polish Ladies Benevolent Society, and she worked
as well for the Orphans and Poor Children of the Warsaw Charitable
Society—established to look after the human flotsam left in the wake of
the failed November Uprising against Russia. Izabella showed an uncommon interest in literature, and in 1836 she published a two-volume work

for artisans titled *Mr. Wojciech, an Example of Work and Economy*, co-written with Ludwika. As the longest-lived and healthiest of all the Chopin children, Izabella came into possession of a large collection of Chopiniana acquired from family members who had passed away, and in later life she became a major source of biographical information about her famous brother. It fell to Izabella, as the family's sole survivor, to assume legal responsibility for Chopin's estate. She worked tirelessly to promote her brother's legacy, but always refused to benefit from it.

Emilia (1812–27), the fourth and youngest sibling, was so weak at the time of her birth that it was thought she might not survive. Just over three weeks after she was born in Warsaw, the infant was hurriedly baptized at home with ordinary water, like her brother before her. Emilia rallied but never enjoyed robust health. It was not until June 14, 1815, more than two and a half years after her birth, that she was formally baptized at the Church of the Holy Cross, Warsaw. She died of tuberculosis when she was fourteen years old. Of all the Chopin children, Emilia appears to have shown the greatest precocity. From Kazimierz Wóycicki's recollections of Emilia we learn that when she was only eleven years old she copied out the whole of Ignatius Humnicki's tragedy *Oedipus*. Two years later we find her helping Ludwika to translate from German a long novel by the children's author Christian Gotthilf Salzmann. Emilia consumed poetry and literature from an early age and wove her fantasies into short stories and plays. The stories generally took the form of morality tales, which showed the influence of the celebrated Polish children's writer Klementyna Tańska, and on warm summer days she would venture into the garden, sit near the flowers, and, with the Vistula River gleaming in the background, read aloud to groups of children gathered around her. One of her favorite books was *The Thousand and One Nights*, but her readings were often interrupted by bouts of coughing and the young girl, overcome by fatigue, would have to be carried indoors until she had recovered. Her pale face, her "luminous but angelic eyes," her flushed, high cheekbones, and her fragile demeanor already marked her for death. Together with Fryderyk she organized the make-believe Literary and Entertainment Society, with Fryderyk as president and herself as secretary. One of the plays was called *The Mistake, or The Presumed Joker*, a lighthearted farce written in rhyming verse, which she wrote with her brother and performed as a surprise for Mikołaj Chopin on his name day, December 6, 1824. Fryderyk played the unlikely part of

Emilia Chopin; an anonymous
watercolor on ivory.

a portly mayor, while Emilia took the role of his wraithlike daughter. The Chopin scholar André Clavier devoted an entire book to Emilia from which it is difficult to avoid the conclusion that he regarded her as a budding genius.[19]

Nothing better illustrates the loving atmosphere that prevailed in the Chopin household than the signed greetings that the children regularly addressed to their parents in careful copperplate handwriting, often on special parchment with decorated borders, to mark birthdays and name days. One of the most touching was written by the six-year-old Chopin to honor his father's name day.

> While the whole world gathers to celebrate your Name-day, my dear Papa, it also brings me joy to offer you my congratulations. May God

---

19. CEC.

"Dear Papa," a name-day greeting to his father from the six-year-old Chopin, December 6, 1816.

grant that you never experience any unhappiness and may good fortune always be your portion. These are my most ardent wishes.

F. Chopin

6 December 1816

This tradition was maintained across the years, culminating in a birthday poem from all four children to their father, presented to him on April 17, 1826, to mark his fifty-fifth birthday.[20] The original, in rhyming Polish, is given here in prose translation.

Dear Father,

Scarcely had the night flown, scarcely had the day dawned, when all your children were already fervently desiring to lay on your paternal knees the wishes with which their hearts are burning. But

---

20. Mikołaj believed that he was born on April 17, 1770. His real date of birth was April 15.

what, dear father, can we wish you once again today, if not what we repeat year after year? It is true that gratitude and knowledge increase with age, but love always remains the same through the centuries. Let us then omit these empty phrases, since all blessings come from God Almighty . . .

Emilia Chopin
Izabella Chopin
Fryderyk Chopin
Ludwika Chopin

On festive days there would invariably be a family concert, some poetry readings, or even a short play, giving the children a chance to exhibit their talents—a harvest of gratitude laid at the feet of the parents. Christmas and New Year celebrations were golden occasions, as in all Polish homes, when Justyna would prepare traditional dishes and the family would exchange presents and sing carols. Chopin would not have known the famous lines of Wordsworth, "Heaven lies about us in our infancy," but he would surely have recognized the realm from which they came. For it was from that realm that he drew comfort in later years, when he was far from home and needed solace and spiritual refreshment.

VI

Not long after the birth of Chopin, in 1810, we find Dr. Samuel Linde once more in Żelazowa Wola, this time on a special mission. The instructor in French at the Warsaw Lyceum, Charles Mahé, had fallen ill and was unlikely to get better. The new school year was looming and Linde needed to find a replacement. He remembered the French tutor of the Skarbek children, the teacher of his star pupil Count Fryderyk Skarbek, who had never ceased to sing his mentor's praises. Would Mikołaj be interested in accepting this position? At first there was some hesitation. Mikołaj was reluctant to uproot his young family from the relative security of Żelazowa Wola, especially since there was talk that the incumbent might recover. But when Linde assured him that the position was permanent and carried with it the promise of accommodation in the Saxon Palace, where the Lyceum itself was located, the lure of returning to Warsaw was too great to resist. Fifteen years had elapsed since Mikołaj had lived in the nation's capital (aside from brief visits), and he missed it. He was moreover aware of the many advantages that Warsaw could offer his family. So Mikołaj and Justyna spent the summer moving their possessions into the heart of the city, and by September everything was in place.

CHILDHOOD AND YOUTH
IN WARSAW, 1810–1824

*May you have constantly in your mind nationality, nationality,
and once more nationality.*

—*Stefan Witwicki to Chopin*[1]

I

On October 1, 1810, seven months after Chopin was born, Mikołaj took
up his duties as assistant master of French at the Warsaw Lyceum. Since
their rooms were not yet ready, the Chopin family lived for a time in Jan
Böhm House in Krakowskie Przedmieście Street.[2] That is where Izabella
was born, on July 9, 1811. It was not until the summer of 1812 that the
family was able to move into their own quarters in the Saxon Palace, where
Emilia, Chopin's youngest sister, was born on November 9. In order to supplement his meager income and support his growing family, Mikołaj
opened a boarding school for boys, offering them board and lodging in
rooms adjoining his apartment, while preparing them for a higher education within the Lyceum itself. The establishment was exceptionally well
managed and its reputation flourished. Soon the parents of the best families in Poland were competing for a place there, despite the fact that the

1. CFC, vol. 1, p. 269; KFC, vol. 1, p. 179.
2. MCW, p. 59.

fee was high—4,000 złotys per year. This was more than the annual salary of many Polish families.[3] For an exceptionally bright student the fee might be lowered if his parents could not afford the full amount. It was a great deal of money and accounts for the fact that the Chopin family in later years were able to afford the luxury of foreign trips to such places as Bad Reinerz in Silesia and Carlsbad in Bohemia. And Mikołaj had no difficulty in transferring large sums of money to Chopin after he had left Poland and settled abroad. He also made substantial loans to family friends such as Antoni Wodziński and Michał Skarbek—both of whom defaulted on their debts and the latter of whom still owed Mikołaj the large sum of nearly 23,000 złotys after committing suicide and failing to leave any provision for repayment in his will. By any reasonable measure, then, the Chopins were well-off.

Mikołaj was a devoted and conscientious teacher, and on June 1, 1814, he was promoted to the rank of full professor of French language and literature. He had in the meantime taken on the additional duties of lecturer in French at the Cadet School of Artillery and Engineering, a post he took up on January 1, 1812.

The driving force behind the creation and running of the Lyceum was its Prussian-born rector, Dr. Samuel Bogumił Linde, who remained as the head of the institution for its entire existence, 1804–31. Linde was a distinguished lexicographer and the compiler of the first Polish national dictionary, in six volumes. He came from the city of Toruń, and after studying theology at the University of Leipzig he settled in Warsaw. Although Linde became thoroughly Polonized, he never quite managed to shake off his Prussian accent, to the occasional (but always private) amusement of his Polish students. The curriculum he imposed on the Lyceum was comprehensive and included not only the humanities—with their emphasis on foreign languages, history, and the classics—but also the sciences and their related disciplines of arithmetic, geometry, chemistry, and botany. In a speech that he gave at the end of the academic year, 1822, Linde stressed that the aim of the school was "to shape character and heart" and to foster the conviction that education was "the greatest good in one's entire life," because "the better the man, the better the citizen."

---

3. Even after he had been promoted to the rank of full professor at the Lyceum, Mikołaj's salary was never more than 3,000 złotys per year.

The students had to wear a military-style uniform, consisting of a light blue knee-length frockcoat that was belted around the waist and adorned with epaulettes, matching trousers displaying white piping down the sides, black shoes, and a tall peaked cap. They were easily identified as they walked around the city in their marionette uniforms. In due course Chopin, too, was to don this unlikely apparel.

In 1817 the Saxon Palace was requisitioned by Grand Duke Constantine, commander in chief of the Polish army, who wanted it for his general headquarters and the spacious Saxon Square as a parade ground for his troops. Consequently the Lyceum was moved to the Casimir Palace, by which time it had grown into an academic body of six hundred students. The Chopin family were given rooms in the residential quarters of the palace, located on the second floor of the right annex, and they brought their boarders with them. There were never fewer than six boys boarding with the family, and the roll call sometimes rose to ten. Among them were Eustachy Marylski, Piotr Dziewanowski, Dominik ("Domuś") Dziewanowski, Julian Fontana, Jan ("Jasio") Białobłocki, and Tytus Woyciechowski, most of whom remained fast friends of Chopin's until death broke the link. Living in the same annex were professors from the Lyceum, together with faculty members and their families of the recently established University of Warsaw, which was located in an adjacent annex. An immediate neighbor of the Chopins was Professor Józef Skrodzki, whose son Eugeniusz (writing under the pen name "Wielisław") would later chronicle these times in loving detail. Directly beneath the Skrodzkis, on the first floor, was the apartment of Rector Linde, who lived there with his wife, Ludwika, and their two daughters. On the ground floor lived Professor Juliusz Kolberg and his family. Kolberg taught cartography and topography in the university's faculty of science, and his son Wilhelm ("Wiluś") became one of Chopin's intimate friends and the dedicatee of one of his early polonaises. Adjacent to the Kolbergs were the family of the poet Kazimierz Brodziński. Eugeniusz Skrodzki tells us that while living under the guidance of Mikołaj Chopin one was taught to be civilized, to be polite, and to develop good work habits: "The belief was that if one was not a good human being, whatever awards one possessed were worthless."[4] Fryderyk Skarbek echoed these sentiments in his memoirs, adding that those students who were

---

4. SRCY, *Bluszcz* (Ivy), no. 32, July 28 (August 8), 1882.

privileged to board with the Chopins invariably did something with their lives and were forever grateful.

Mikołaj's resources eventually stretched to the purchase of a Buchholtz grand piano, which remained Chopin's favorite instrument while he lived in Poland. Its keyboard was the first recipient of all his youthful compositions—from the juvenile polonaises in G minor and B-flat major right up to the two piano concertos, in E minor and F minor respectively. The instrument was destroyed by Russian soldiers during the uprising of 1863.

II

Fryderyk's piano playing had already begun to capture attention. He had a ready-made audience in the Casimir Palace, for Mikołaj and Justyna were never slow to invite their neighbors to private gatherings in which the child would show off his talents. According to tradition it was Justyna who started to give Chopin his first piano lessons when he was about four years old. The child is supposed to have broken into tears at the sound of the piano—as if he recognized his homeland—and we are told that he begged to be allowed to clamber onto the piano bench and sit next to his sister Ludwika during her lessons, in an attempt to gain access to the magic keyboard whose sounds so attracted him. It is one of those affecting legends that have become inseparable from his biography, one of a number of similar stories passed on by Chopin's family members to a later generation. Whatever the case, Fryderyk soon outstripped Ludwika, and by the time he was six years old he seemed to know in advance whatever Justyna tried to show him. That is when the parents decided to bring in a professional teacher.

Their choice fell on Wojciech (Adalbert) Żywny, a sixty-year-old musician from Bohemia, who had come to Poland years earlier as a violinist attached to the court of Prince Kazimierz Sapieha. With the collapse of Sapieha's court, after the First Partition of Poland, Żywny had moved to Warsaw, but because he was unable to find enough violin students to supplement his living he began to teach the piano as well. By the time he crossed Chopin's path he was a beloved music teacher, respected by many of the best families in Warsaw. Żywny already visited the Chopin household on a regular basis, because he also taught Ludwika and was employed by Mikołaj to teach music to the boarders as well.[5] He was a passionate disciple of Bach, and insisted on giving his pupils a solid grounding in the music of the great polyphonist. Chopin was forever grateful to him for that, and Bach's 48 Preludes and Fugues became his constant companions. Żywny himself was probably never more than a modest performer, either as a violinist or as a pianist, but he compensated for this by a true gift for teaching, and an ability to communicate his deep love of music to his young charges.

Żywny was an eccentric personality, of whom many colorful stories are told. Perhaps the best character sketch to come down to us, and one that forms the basis for most of the others, was provided by Eugeniusz Skrodzki, who used to spot Żywny going in and out of the Chopins' apartment.

> Żywny was one of those typical old-fashioned personalities of the past, whom one does not meet anymore today. His nose was of enormous proportions, colored purple since his early days, due to an excessive intake of snuff. Żywny was such an addict of snuff that his nose, chin, white tie, waistcoat, the lapels of his coat were covered with the powder. It covered even his Hungarian-style boots . . . and often fell on the keyboard of the piano. The hand of his pupil, boy or girl, when it was touched by Żywny smelled afterward abominably of cheap "Bernardine" tobacco. Apart from a huge snuff-box, holding half a pound of snuff, with a picture of Mozart or Haydn on its lid, Żywny carried with him a large square pencil, with which he made corrections on the page of music and not infrequently used it to rap the knuckles of his pupils . . .[6]

Żywny must have cut an unusual figure as he walked along the cobbled streets of Warsaw in his badly cut clothes, his yellow wig sometimes drooping at half-mast. Some observers claim that his favorite dress color was green, and that not only his coat but his trousers, too, were of this brilliant hue. He also sported a formidable collection of colorful waistcoats, which rumor held to have been made from the auctioned-off pantaloons

5. MFPC, pp. 19–20.
6. SRCY, *Bluszcz* (Ivy), no. 33, August 4 (16), 1882.

Wojciech Żywny; an oil
painting by Ambroży
Mieroszewski (1829).

of the former king, Stanisław August, who had abdicated the throne
after Poland's last partition, in 1795. This sartorial ensemble was set off
by a large and brightly colored handkerchief—the equivalent of a visual
sforzando—which he would pull out with a rainbow flourish whenever his
intake of snuff caused him to sneeze.[7]

The Chopin children could easily have found in Żywny a rather frightening caricature. Instead they became completely attached to him and

---

7. The fifteen-year-old Chopin left an affectionate pen sketch of Żywny in a letter to his
friend Jan Białobłocki, dated October 30, 1825. Żywny was giving a lesson to a young boarder
named Cajetan Górski, "who was on the point of falling asleep at the piano." Chopin, who was
sitting at a table writing his letter to Jan, decided to liven things up by reading part of the letter aloud to Żywny, wishing to impress him with the "musicality" of its prose. Żywny was so
pleased with what he heard that after adjusting his wig he "clapped his hands, took snuff,
wiped his nose, rolled his handkerchief into a trumpet, and put it into a pocket of his thickly
padded green jacket." Some words were intentionally misspelled in Polish by Chopin, to give
an idea of Żywny's bad accent. The boy's attempts to capture the sound of Żywny's laughter
between phrases—"hum, hum, ho, ho," rising to a crescendo in "hee, hee, hehehehe"—
remind us of his gift for parody. CFC, vol. 1, p. 40; KFC, vol. 1, pp. 58–59.

treated him like a member of the family. He often stayed for dinner after the lessons were over. These were occasions to treasure, especially on name days and birthdays, for which Justyna Chopin prepared some of her special dishes. Żywny liked to position himself next to the hostess and be the first to sample her culinary delights. The trouble was that he had lost most of his teeth, and the sight of him sampling meatballs and dumplings, to say nothing of Justyna's special breads, provoked the children to uncontrollable bouts of mirth.

Żywny was the only formal piano teacher that Chopin ever had. Their lessons were abandoned after six years, when Chopin was twelve years old. Thereafter the boy was left to find his own way at the keyboard, and he did so with such an instinctive feeling for the instrument that by the time he was nineteen he was a fully formed virtuoso, and had already begun to compose the first of his Twelve Studies, op. 10, in order to give himself new technical problems to solve. Żywny's great merit as a teacher is that he did not intervene, but allowed Chopin to develop in his own way. Żywny was also a composer, and while none of his compositions has survived, he brought a creator's outlook to bear on his lessons. It enabled him to provide Chopin with insights into the way music was constructed, especially the compositions of Hummel, Mozart, Ries, and early-period Beethoven, whose works, while not without controversy, were just starting to circulate in Warsaw. Żywny also provided the boy with some useful historical and biographical background to whatever repertoire they were studying.

III

Throughout Chopin's years of study with Żywny, the master encouraged the pupil to go on improvising at the piano and composing. The difference hardly existed for Chopin, because everything he composed began as an improvisation. He was never really able to compose away from the piano. By his seventh year he had produced a number of Polish dances and variations; these have not survived, but we know about them because they are mentioned in the Warsaw press. Chopin's first published composition appeared in 1817, a Polonaise in G minor. It bears the dedication "*à Son Excellence Mademoiselle la Comtesse Victoire Skarbek, par Frédéric Chopin, Musicien âgé de huit ans.*" The elegant French inscription and the fair copy of the manuscript itself were probably written out by Żywny, who played a role in persuading the private publishing house of the Reverend Izydor Cybulski to lithograph and distribute the work. The dedicatee, Wiktoria Skarbek, was Countess Ludwika's niece.[8] The Polonaise and its young composer were greeted by the Warsaw press with paeans of praise.

> The composer of this Polish dance, a boy only eight years old, is the son of Mr. Mikołaj Chopin, master of French language and literature at the Warsaw Lyceum, and a real musical genius. Not only does he play the most difficult piano pieces with the greatest facility and the most extraordinarily good taste, but he is already the composer of some dances and variations, over which musical connoisseurs cannot cease to wonder, especially considering the tender years of the composer. If this boy had been born in Germany or France, he would surely have attracted attention in every country; may the present remark serve as a hint that geniuses spring up in our country also, but the lack of publicity conceals them from the community at large.[9]

It is an exceptional composition for a child and can readily be compared with anything that Mozart was writing at a similar age. The stately character of Poland's national dance is captured from the opening bars. And in bar five the keyboard suddenly opens up with a sweeping arpeggio, four and a half octaves in compass, making the full range of the piano's sound vibrate beneath the fingers. The child here becomes father of the man. Observe as well the second half of the opening theme (five bars from the end), where the right hand boldly jumps over the left—a leap of three octaves—doubtless meant to capture the admiration of the boy's viewers. This early polonaise shows the influence of Prince Michał Ogiński (1765–1833), the military hero who liked to compose music when he was

---

8. And not her daughter, an error that has taken root in the literature. Wiktoria's parents had separated years earlier, and Countess Ludwika had given both mother and daughter sanctuary at Żelazowa Wola, where they got to know Mikołaj and Justyna Chopin. Wiktoria (1791–1828) was living there at the time of Chopin's birth, which may have given rise to the idea that she was one of Ludwika's children.

9. *Pamiętnik Warszawski* (Warsaw Album), vol. IV, book X, 1818.

The first page of the Polonaise in G minor (1817); a lithograph by I. J. Cybulski.

not on the battlefield fighting the Russians alongside General Tadeusz Kościusko, and doing so with such ferocity that Catherine the Great put a price on his head. To all young Poles of Chopin's generation, Ogiński was a national hero. He wrote at least twenty polonaises for piano, including the patriotic "Farewell to the Fatherland," through which there runs a deep vein of melancholy that finds an echo in Chopin's own music. The crossed-hands device, too, may be found in Ogiński's polonaises.

IV

Chopin made his first public appearance as a pianist on February 24, 1818, when he was not quite eight years old. Żywny may have had a hand in arranging this concert, for he was anxious to bring his young prodigy to the attention of Warsaw's nobility. The event was a charity concert, sponsored by Countess Zofia Zamoyska, a daughter of Prince Adam Czartoryski, and it was held in the Radziwiłł Palace, to which many of the most prominent families in Warsaw were invited. The countess had recently formed the

Warsaw Charitable Society, whose aim was to raise and disperse funds for the thousands of Poles who had been maimed and displaced as a result of the Napoléonic wars.[10] Its president that year was the poet and elder statesman Julian Ursyn Niemcewicz, one of the signatories to the Polish Constitution. The boy played a Concerto in E minor by Adalbert Gyrowetz, a fellow Bohemian of Żywny's, and a composer of thirty operas, nineteen masses, and sixty symphonies—one or two of which were good enough to have been mistakenly attributed to Haydn. The Concerto, a brilliant if superficial piece, was exactly the right choice for this audience, proffering them instant virtuosity while demanding little concentration in return. It was dispatched by the young virtuoso with such aplomb that he became an instant "lion" among the aristocrats of Warsaw. Several other musicians took part, but it is Chopin whom history remembers. We are told that Justyna had dressed Fryderyk somewhat like an English boy of fashion, with short knickerbockers and a large white lace collar over a dark velvet jacket. When Fryderyk got home and Justyna asked him what the audience had admired most, he is supposed to have replied, "My collar, Mamma!"[11] Before dismissing this well-worn anecdote as a branch of fiction, we should recognize that it chimes with everything we know about Chopin in later life. He was meticulous to the point of obsession about his personal grooming. His preconcert ritual often involved tailors, hairdressers, and personal valets, whose approval had to be met before he faced the scrutiny of an audience.

After the success of his debut, the Warsaw press began to refer to Fryderyk as "a Polish Mozart" and many doors were opened for him. Among the aristocratic families who invited the young wunderkind into their salons were the Zamoyskis, Sapiehas, Czetwertyńskis, Radziwiłłs, Czartoryskis, Lubeckis, Wolickis, and Pruszaks, names that were among the most illustrious in Poland. Aleksandra Tańska attended one such event and wrote in her diary, "Mme Grabowska invited me to her soirée—a large gathering. In the course of the evening young Chopin played the piano—a

---

10. An announcement in the *Warsaw Gazette* on February 21 informed its readers that "music, which touches our spirits with its tender melodies and delicately arouses our feelings, cannot help but contribute to the relief of human suffering." It identified the young virtuoso as "Schoppin," and added that tickets were on sale "at the usual price"—a euphemism for very expensive.

11. This was one of a number of family anecdotes that Chopin's sister Izabella passed on to Karasowski, who found a home for it in his pioneering biography. KCLB, p. 19.

child not yet eight years old, who, in the opinion of the connoisseurs of the art, promises to replace Mozart."[12] Chopin may not have "replaced Mozart," but, rather like the Austrian prodigy with whom he was now being openly compared, it was in the stately homes of the nobility that his artistic personality was formed. All of the boy's early concert experience was gained in the Warsaw salons, playing for Polish magnates and their aristocratic friends. With the Czetwertyński and Radziwiłł families Chopin was especially close. Princess Idalia Czetwertyńska had two sons—Kalikst and Borys—who later became schoolmates of Chopin's at the Warsaw Lyceum. His connection to the Radziwiłłs was even closer, and his visits to their family estate at Antonin in later years have been widely chronicled. Chopin was only five years old when the Congress Kingdom was created in 1815, following the upheavals of the Napoléonic wars, and the new order brought with it the necessary stability for culture to flourish in the nation's capital. For fifteen years the salons of the aristocracy were at the center of artistic life in Warsaw. Plays, poetry readings, art exhibitions, and chamber concerts all took place in these gilded residences, which in their way were as important to the cultural life of the capital as were the Polish National Theater and the Warsaw Conservatory, until everything was shut down after the failed uprising. This fifteen-year period coincided with Chopin's development as a musician, and when he left his native land shortly before the uprising broke out, in November 1830, he was fully formed.[13]

We do not know if the boy suffered from stage fright, but it appears unlikely, for he seemed to enjoy the attention lavished on him. The point is worth raising because it stands in marked contrast to the agonies Chopin endured in later life whenever he was preparing to give public concerts. His dislike of playing before large audiences set in early, and we already detect it getting in the way of his first appearances in Vienna, in 1830. Later on, after Chopin had settled in France, George Sand made fun of his almost pathological reluctance to play in public. She described the mood of panic that once took possession of him after he had agreed to give

---

12. Aleksandra Tarczewska (née Tańska), *Historia mego życie* (The Story of My Life), Warsaw, 1842, p. 243. Aleksandra was the older sister of Klementyna Tańska, the writer of Polish children's stories admired by Chopin's sisters.
13. One of the best accounts of artistic life in the salons of Warsaw has been given by Halina Goldberg in GCW, pp. 147–76.

a concert as "this Chopinesque nightmare."[14] None of this was evident in his childhood years. In the salons of the aristocracy, surrounded by a select and admiring audience able to appreciate the subtle nuances of his playing, he felt completely at ease. And this kind of intimate music making remained his preference for life. When he ventured onto the concert platform for what was to be his last concert in Paris (February 1848), Camille Pleyel had the stage of his three-hundred-seat concert hall bordered with flowers and covered with carpets, with chairs set out in a semicircle around the piano, reserved for the exclusive use of Chopin's inner circle of friends—re-creating the atmosphere of a salon to make him feel more at home.

In October 1818, Tsarina Maria Feodorovna, the mother of Tsar Alexander I, visited Warsaw as part of a royal tour of the Congress Kingdom—a piece of political window dressing meant to draw Poland more closely into Russia's embrace. Since the tour included an inspection of the fledgling University, the tsarina went across to the nearby Lyceum as well. The whole school turned out to greet her, and when she got to Mikołaj Chopin's class he introduced her to Fryderyk, who, although not yet a pupil, had been smuggled in among the other boys for the occasion. Fryderyk presented the tsarina with manuscripts of two of his dances, a brush with royalty that was almost certainly stage-managed by his father and was reported in the *Correspondents' Gazette* of October 6. Nothing more is known of these dances, which, like other juvenile compositions of Chopin, survived neither the passage of time nor, as in this particular case, the casual gaze of a monarch.

Not long after his encounter with the tsarina, and possibly because of it, Fryderyk was summoned to play at the Brühl Palace, the residence of the governor of the Congress Kingdom, Grand Duke Constantine Pavlovich Romanov. Constantine, a younger brother of Tsar Alexander, was so impressed by a military march the boy had composed that he had the piece scored and performed by his band on the parade ground in front of the Saxon Palace, where he regularly reviewed his troops. It was later published without Chopin's name and has meanwhile disappeared.

The Brühl Palace was the seat of Russian power, the place from where Constantine issued his political directives. He had exercised plenipotentiary authority over Poland ever since the Congress Kingdom had been

---

14. CGS, vol. V, p. 282.

Grand Duke Constantine musters his troops on Saxon Square, 1825, to mark the passing of Tsar Alexander I; a lithograph by Jan Feliks Piwarski (1829).

created and annexed to Russia. Constantine is generally described as a brutish figure, whose pug face revealed the coarseness of his character. His maltreatment of the Poles has earned for him a special place in infamy. One writer called him "eccentric, if not insane." His violent mood swings were unpredictable, and at the slightest provocation he would fall into an uncontrollable rage. As commander in chief of the Polish army, it was not unusual for him to drill his soldiers for twenty-four hours without respite until his rant had subsided, which frequently resulted in the deaths of men and their horses.[15] For this he was universally reviled by the army, which seethed with discontent under his erratic leadership. The high suicide rate among Polish soldiers was directly related to the degrading punishments that Constantine enjoyed inflicting on the rank and file, often

---

15. NFC, vol. 1, p. 33. These military parades took place on a weekly basis. Several hundred foot soldiers would be drawn up in tight formation, with officers astride their horses—part of a grand muster choreographed by the grand duke himself. They would have been witnessed by young Fryderyk on a regular basis from his coign of vantage in the Casimir Palace, and could not have failed to make a deep impression on his memory. MFPC, pp. 19–20.

out of sheer caprice.[16] The public flogging of his soldiers for minor infractions was not uncommon, and makes one wonder how his mutilated personality was brought into being.

V

For the answer we need only go back to Constantine's grandmother Catherine the Great, who provided the noxious atmosphere in which the boy was raised. It will do no harm to offer a brief account of the rigors that helped to form him, for they provide us with an explanation of the rigors that he in turn visited on an entire nation, to which Chopin was a daily witness.

Shortly after Constantine's birth Catherine removed him from the cradle, and over the objections of his parents—her son Grand Duke Paul and his wife, Grand Duchess Maria, who was still weak from the difficult labor—she took charge of his education herself, just as she had done with his older brother, the future Tsar Alexander I. The regimen was strict, even harsh. From infancy the boys endured a Spartan life. They were bathed in cold water and slept on flat hard beds. Their diet was plain, and the temperature of the room was never allowed to be higher than 15 degrees Celsius. No more than two candles were to be lit at the same time, in order to prevent the air in the room from becoming stale. They were even taught to till their own garden and grow their own vegetables. Catherine had something special in mind for Constantine. He was being prepared for a great responsibility. Once she had won her ongoing wars against Turkey and had annexed the Crimea, Constantine was destined to rule over Constantinople and a restored Byzantium empire, an aspect of the fantasy world she inhabited and into which Constantine was drawn. Even before his birth his name had been chosen for him by Catherine to fit him for this glorious role. Constantine was given a Greek nurse, specially imported from the island of Naxos, who taught him to speak fluent Greek. It would, after all, be unthinkable for a future emperor of Byzantium not to speak the language of the people.

One activity that Constantine loved above all others was playing soldiers. Entire regiments of toy soldiers, in their brightly painted uniforms,

---

16. CM, vol. 2, p. 309.

were on display in his room, and he became adept in textbook military drills as he maneuvered these inanimate objects from one position to another. The real-life parades that he choreographed in later life, watching real-life soldiers collapse through sheer exhaustion, were an extension of his childhood fantasies. Constantine's actual military record was not distinguished and he proved himself incompetent on the battlefield.

Throughout her grandsons' early childhood and adolescence Catherine's main thought was to find suitable wives for them, preferably from the German upper aristocracy from which she herself had been drawn, and thus not only secure the fragile Romanov succession but strengthen her political ties with Europe as well.[17] Her choice of a possible bride for Constantine was narrowed down to three princesses from the Saxe-Coburg family, who were summoned to Moscow so that she could parade them before the youth and allow him to make his choice. Princess Juliane was a girl of fourteen, and Constantine barely seventeen, when their arranged marriage took place in Saint Petersburg, in February 1796. Adam Czartoryski, who in 1831 became the leader of the Polish government in exile, and was present at the wedding ceremony, later wrote in his memoirs about the bizarre rituals surrounding the nuptials, and had some harsh words to say about Constantine.

The Princess [Juliane] was given to a youth barely entering manhood but with a violent temper and savage caprices which had already furnished many a topic of conversation . . . It was a mournful

---

17. And the succession was indeed fragile. Complicit in the assassination of her husband, Tsar Peter III, from whom she had seized the throne, Catherine had by that act usurped the claim of her son, the future Tsar Paul I. Admittedly the strength of Paul's claim to wear the Romanov crown is still a matter of conjecture. According to some historians he may have been the illegitimate offspring of one of Catherine's lovers, Sergei Saltykov, a serious shortcoming of her late husband, Tsar Peter III, having been the fact that he was impotent. Catherine's near-obsession with the future of her grandsons had much to do with this dark secret: they may not have had a drop of Romanov blood in them. Catherine's death was somewhat less spectacular than her life. After meeting with a group of court officials, she retired to her privy closet, where she suffered a massive stroke while sitting on her commode. Her aides had difficulty in moving the body, which had become wedged behind the door. Unable to lift her heavy frame, they dragged her across the floor on a mattress, where she lay unconscious for the next thirty-six hours. Her Scottish physician, Dr. John Rogerson, was summoned, and he bled her but failed to revive her. Every few hours her frightened entourage reentered the room to look at the body for signs of life. Catherine was finally pronounced dead at 9:45 on the evening of November 17, 1796.

spectacle, this handsome young princess, come from so far to adopt a foreign religion on foreign soil to be delivered up to the capricious will of a man who it was evident would never care for her happiness.

To which he adds the revealing comment: "What [Constantine] related to those with whom he was intimate about his honeymoon was marked by an unexampled want of delicacy towards his wife."[18]

After enduring three years of purgatory, Juliane fled the marriage and returned to her family in Germany, refusing all attempts at reconciliation.

VI

This was the situation that greeted the young Chopin when he first set foot inside the Brühl Palace. And it was shortly to become yet more bizarre. After many years of separation from Princess Juliane, Constantine secured the tsar's permission to divorce her and in 1820 he entered into a morganatic marriage with the Polish-born Joanna Grudzińska. Joanna was one of three stepdaughters of Adam Bronic, the grand marshal of the tsarist court in Poland, who lived with his family in the royal castle, and almost from the moment that Constantine set eyes on the golden-haired twenty-year-old girl, he had wanted her first as his mistress and then as his wife. She cast such a spell over him that in order to marry her he renounced his claim to the Russian Crown in favor of his younger brother Nicholas. On the eve of the wedding Tsar Alexander elevated Joanna to the ranks of the royals and gave her the title of Princess Łowicka. Because she so often intervened with her husband on Poland's behalf, she was dubbed "the guardian angel of Poland." That was her public image. What she endured in private after her marriage had bound her in perpetuity to Constantine can only be imagined because it happened behind closed doors and his mood swings became ever more unpredictable.

In 1822, Constantine and his large entourage of courtiers moved into the Belvedere Palace, the imposing castle on the outskirts of Warsaw that had just been made ready for him, and from where he continued his erratic

---

18. CM, vol. 1, pp. 103–104.

rule.[19] Visitors to Belvedere must have been confounded by the menagerie of household servants that roamed through the place, ranging in size from the massively built fighters drawn from the ranks of the armored cuirassiers down to the liveried dwarves, one of whom Constantine had brought back with him from his Turkish campaigns. Chopin was frequently invited to Belvedere by Princess Łowicka in order to play for Constantine and his guests. She was convinced that the boy's playing had a calming effect on her husband's unstable character. Constantine once observed the boy gazing up at the ceiling while improvising at the keyboard, and inquired if that was where he "found the notes." Perhaps the grand duke was being profound without knowing it, because even at this young age Chopin seemed to draw inspiration from a source that lay beyond the boundaries of the piano's keyboard. During these visits Chopin formed a friendship with Constantine's illegitimate son Paul, the product of an earlier liaison that Constantine had pursued with his French mistress Josephine Friedrichs, whom he had married off to a Russian colonel named Gustav Weiss at the time of his nuptials with Joanna Grudzińska, while arranging to keep his beloved son by his side. Paul was just two years older than Chopin, and he sometimes surprised the Chopin family by turning up at the Casimir Palace, accompanied by his French tutor Count Alexandre de Moriolles, in a coach drawn by a team of four horses—all abreast, Russian style, each of the outer ones mounted by a Cossack—come to bring Chopin back to Belvedere. Everyone knew what that meant. The grand duke was once more in a blind rage and Princess Łowicka, fearful of the consequences, wanted her young Orpheus to work his magic in the house of horrors.

Count de Moriolles had a daughter named Alexandrine, and after Chopin had played the piano for Constantine, the boy liked to escape into the palace gardens and relax with her and Paul. Alexandrine and Chopin formed an innocent attachment for each other, which on his side amounted to a teenage "crush" on a more mature woman. She was nine years older than Chopin and not the child that most of his biographers have mistaken her for. He turned her surname into the affectionate sobriquet "Moriolka," a name by which he refers to her in his correspondence. She in turn dubbed

---

19. None of Chopin's early childhood appearances took place at Belvedere, contrary to the literature. The palace had been purchased in 1818 by Tsar Alexander as a residence for Constantine, but in the years 1818–22 it was under reconstruction and Constantine did not live there. Chopin never played at Belvedere before 1822. MCW, pp. 74 and 76.

Chopin "a little devil," a reference perhaps to the playful kiss he occasionally stole from her. Chopin was probably one of the few persons with whom the young woman was able to enjoy a normal relationship. The stifling atmosphere that prevailed at Belvedere would have offered few opportunities for a regular existence. Chopin gave Moriolka some piano lessons and played duets with her, highlights of her cloistered existence. It must have brought her pleasure when Chopin placed her name on the dedication page of his Rondo à la Mazur, op. 5 (1826), which assured her a modest posterity. She always honored their friendship, which extended to the moment of Chopin's greatest triumph in Warsaw's National Theater, on March 22, 1830, when he played his *Krakowiak* Rondo and his F minor Concerto before a large and appreciative audience. Afterward she sent him a large laurel wreath to symbolize his musical conquest of the city.

VII

On November 21, 1819, the Italian soprano Angelica Catalani made her long-awaited appearance in Warsaw. She was one of the acknowledged stars of the art of *bel canto*, and gave four hugely successful concerts in the Town Hall. During her stay in the city she lived in the home of Konstanty Wolicki, one of her relatives, and it was in the elegant salon of the Wolicki family that the young Chopin heard La Catalani sing and she in turn asked him to play. She was so enchanted with his performance that she presented him with a gold watch, which he kept as a precious relic for the rest of his life. It bore the inscription

Mme Catalani
à Frédéric Chopin
âgé de 10 ans
à Varsovie
le 3 Janvier 1820

These encounters with the noble families of Warsaw helped mold the boy's character. The polish and refinement of his later years, which were often remarked in the salons of Paris and London, owed much to these early experiences. No matter how exalted the company, Chopin remained at ease, and he was able to fall back on the distinctive forms of address and old-world customs of the Polish aristocracy, suffused with pomp and circumstance, which went back to the eighteenth century and earlier. And in the salons of Paris, especially the ones peopled by Polish émigrés longing to reclaim their homeland, that was valued.

In February and March 1823, Chopin gave two further concerts for Warsaw's Charitable Society, this time in Countess Zofia Zamoyska's palace (known as the "Blue Palace" after the color of its roof). Because of the number of artists and prominent intellectuals who lived in the building's annexes, it was often called the "Polish Athens." On February 24, Chopin appeared there as soloist with the Conservatory orchestra in a performance of a piano concerto by Ferdinand Ries, conducted by Józef Jawurek, a Conservatory professor. And on March 17, the society invited him back again to appear in the ninth of its "Soirées Musicales," playing some solo items. These concerts revealed Fryderyk to be an artist mature beyond his years, and marked a turning point in his development as a pianist. On February 26, the *Kurier dla Płci Pięknej* (Courier for the Fair Sex) summed up the situation for its readers: "We can confidently state that we have never before heard a virtuoso in our capital who could, at such a tender age, overcome such remarkable difficulties with ease, and render the incomparable Adagio with both feeling and accuracy." And lest they failed to grasp the significance of what had happened, the *Kurier* turned the concert into a matter of national pride.

> The latest number of the Leipzig *Allgemeine musikalische Zeitung* reports, in an article from Vienna, that an equally young amateur by the name of List [sic] astonished everyone there by the precision, the self-assurance, and the strength of tone with which he executed a concerto by Hummel. After this musical evening we shall certainly not envy Vienna their Mr. List, as our capital possesses one equal to him, and perhaps even superior, in the person of the young Mr. Chopin.[20]

20. On December 1, 1822, the eleven-year-old Liszt had played Hummel's Concerto in A minor, which had created a sensation in Vienna. In its issue of January 1823 the *AmZ* had described the Hungarian prodigy in extravagant language as "a virtuoso fallen from the clouds," and as "a little Hercules."

It is the first known occasion on which a comparison between Liszt and Chopin had been made, the pros and cons of which have preoccupied the public's imagination ever since.

Chopin's lessons with Żywny were now becoming superfluous. The twelve-year-old boy had nothing more to learn from his teacher. The bonds of mutual affection remained strong, however, and even though the lessons were about to be terminated, Żywny stayed on as an irreplaceable presence in the Chopin household. He remained, in Chopin's words, "the soul of all our amusements."[21] Never again did Chopin take a formal piano lesson from anyone, the finest compliment that he could have paid to his old master. Chopin had already shown his gratitude by composing a Polonaise in A-flat major in honor of Żywny, which bore the inscription: *"Dédiée à Monsieur A. Żywny par Son élève Fryderyk Chopin à Varsovie, ce 23 Avril 1821."* April 23 was Żywny's name day, the feast of Saint Wojciech, and it was on that day that Fryderyk surprised and delighted his teacher with a performance of his new composition.

VIII

In the summer of 1823, the Chopins visited Żelazowa Wola for a short holiday as guests of the Skarbeks. After several months of hard work Chopin had passed the entrance examination to the Warsaw Lyceum and had been admitted to Class IV. He went to Żelazowa Wola to celebrate his success with his family, enjoy the bracing air of the Polish countryside, and build up his strength before the rigors of the new academic curriculum set in. Much had changed in the thirteen years since the Chopins had lived there. In 1814 the old manor house had been damaged by fire (possibly caused by a detachment of soldiers from Napoléon's retreating army), but the right annex had survived.[22] Although most of Countess Ludwika's possessions had gone up in flames, she had succeeded in reestablishing herself, and in 1818 had sold the estate to her son Fryderyk Skarbek while continuing to live there. On the warm summer nights that enveloped Żelazowa Wola, she had the servants push the piano out onto the lawn so that Chopin could

---

21. CFC, vol. 1, p. 81; KFC, vol. 1, p. 80.
22. H-BZW.

give impromptu concerts for the household, which also attracted a gathering of local villagers. The memory of these occasions might have been lost had it not been for the Russian composer Mily Balakirev, who, in 1894, made a widely publicized pilgrimage to Żelazowa Wola on the occasion of the unveiling of an obelisk to Chopin's memory, a project that Balakirev himself initiated, and he met there an old villager, an octogenarian named Antoni Krysiak, who had known the Chopin family and liked to reminisce about them.

> On beautiful starlit nights, the piano was hauled out of the house and placed under a spruce tree. Mr. Fryderyk often played under that tree . . . and with his improvisation he enchanted his listeners and brought tears to their eyes. The sounds wafted through the orchards and reached the ears of the villagers, who came to the house, and stood outside the palings to hear the young visitor from Warsaw . . . Fryderyk usually spent his summers at Mr. Skarbek's house."[23]

The venerable Krysiak, one of the few surviving witnesses to those far-away times, was given a new caftan with a sash around the waist, together with a fine sheepskin hat, to mark the occasion. A photograph of him wearing this sartorial outfit on the day of the unveiling still survives.[24] Krysiak's recollections carry the burden of uncertainty, for Balakirev tells us that the old villager sometimes confused the Skarbeks with the Chopins. Moreover, scholars of the topic like to point out that there are only two properly documented occasions when Chopin is known to have revisited his birthplace: one was on December 24, 1825, the start of winter, when an outdoor concert would have been impossible; and the other was during the summer of 1830 shortly before he left Poland for good, a visit with which Krysiak's recollection cannot easily be conflated. But Chopin would have gone back to his birthplace more often than that. Żelazowa Wola was a

---

23. Aleksander Poliński, "Co się dzieje z domkiem rodzinnym Chopina?" (What Is Happening to Chopin's Family Dwelling?), in *Wędrowiec* (Wanderer), November 1891, pp. 101–102. See also Aleksander Rajchman's article "Kolebka Chopina" (The Cradle of Chopin) in Warsaw's *Musical, Theatrical, and Artistic Echo,* November 2, 1891.
24. It is reproduced in KCOL, p. 98. For the reminiscences of Balakirev, see *Sovietskaya Muzyka,* no. 10, October 1949.

mere sixty kilometers from Warsaw and the journey could be accomplished in a single day by horse-drawn coach. The encounter between Balakirev and Antoni Krysiak is undeniable, and the firsthand testimony that it engendered concerning Chopin's visits to Żelazowa Wola may be confirmed from an independent source. In an interview that Ferdynand Hoesick conducted with Józefa Kościelska, a younger sister of Maria Wodzińska, Chopin's future fiancée, Józefa informed him that Chopin sometimes spent part of the summer holidays at Żelazowa Wola, and she had traveled with him there.[25]

On September 15, 1823, now back in Warsaw, Chopin donned the regulation Lyceum uniform (which he wore for the next three years), walked down the flight of stairs separating the family's apartment from the schoolrooms on the ground floor of the Casimir Palace, and joined his classmates in the Fourth Year. It was the first time that the newly teenaged Chopin had been taught in the formal setting of a classroom under the watchful eye of an instructor, and it might easily have been an intimidating experience. He had always been schooled at home by his father and the private tutors that Mikołaj had brought in to coach the boys who boarded with them. But from the moment that Chopin sat behind his desk he found himself among friends. Sitting in the same group were Julian Fontana, Dominik Dziewanowski, Jan Matuszyński, and Dominik Magnuszewski, who were all about his age. As for the teachers, some of them were his neighbors, colleagues of Mikołaj Chopin's. The faculty that Rector Samuel Linde had gathered around him since he had founded the Lyceum represented the cream of Warsaw's intelligentsia. They are barely mentioned in biographies of Chopin but we may introduce them here. Władysław Jasiński taught mathematics; Wacław Maciejowski taught classics; Józef Skrodzki taught chemistry and science; Tomasz Dziekoński conducted a course in Polish literature; and Sebastiano Ciampi gave instruction in classical philology and Greek. The revered painter Zygmunt Vogel, who was sixty years old and the country's finest master of oil paintings, offered a course in drawing and perspective. These mentors left a lasting impression on their students and provided one of the best educations in Poland.

Discipline was strict but tempered with kindness. Linde was popular

25. HSC, Part Two, pp. 287–88.

with the students, calling them "my children" as he peered at them through his rimless glasses and listening intently as they read their homework aloud.

> He often took the place of masters who on account of illness could not come to their lessons [wrote Eustachy Marylski, one of Mikołaj's young boarders]. Most often he analyzed Cicero's speeches . . . What an interesting class that was! What a wealth of knowledge he laid before us! . . . It sometimes happened that he came in place of the literature master . . . At such times we were always sorry that the hour had passed so quickly. Seeing this, if he had not finished a lesson, he called us to the classroom on a recreation day and discoursed to us for some hours. How unsatisfactory did the lessons of the other masters seem after his![26]

While Chopin's curriculum of studies is difficult to reconstruct, there is general agreement that he took modern languages, Polish history, classics (including some Latin), mathematics, and drawing. For this last subject he showed a special aptitude, and under the guidance of Zygmunt Vogel the boy's sketchbooks were soon filled with pencil drawings of scenes captured from various vantage points within Warsaw and its environs. The youth was adept at drawing portraits and he often produced amusing caricatures not only of his classmates but of his professors as well. When Samuel Linde got wind of the fact that Chopin had "honored" him with one such drawing, he confiscated it. There must have been some artistic merit in the image, for we are told that Linde returned it with the comment "Well done!" A more formal chalk drawing that the fifteen-year-old Fryderyk did of Linde has been preserved, and today hangs in the Municipal Museum at Radom.

Pranks, caricatures, and the telling of heroic tales of Poland's storied past were all part of Chopin's adolescent years. When the day was done, and schoolwork was set aside, the boys would sometimes gather around the piano in Chopin's apartment to hear about the legends of Polish history, or exchange frightening stories in the twilight hour, which Chopin would illustrate with background music. Eustachy Marylski recalled those

26. HSC, Part One, p. 91; KCOL, p. 64.

Samuel Bogumił Linde.

Dr. Samuel Linde; a chalk drawing by Chopin (c. 1825).

evenings: "At dusk, when we had a little time to ourselves, we told tales from Polish history, such as the death of King Warneńczyk, or of Żółkiewski, or the battles fought by our rulers, and young Chopin played it all on the piano. Sometimes this music made us cry, and Żywny was enchanted with his playing. Soon the name of Fryderyk resounded in Warsaw."[27]

According to Kazimierz Wodziński, who boarded with Mikołaj, the boys on one occasion became unruly and Antoni Barciński, the mathematics tutor who had been left in charge, was unable to control them. When Fryderyk entered the room and witnessed the disruption, Kazimierz tells us, he gathered the boys around the piano with a promise to tell them an adventure story about robbers intent on plundering a house at dead of night, a melodrama he accompanied with music. As the robbers mounted their ladders and were about to enter through the windows,

27. HSC, Part One, p. 90; KCOL, p. 68.

they were disturbed by a noise from within, which so frightened them that they ran away to hide in the darkness of the surrounding woods. So effective was the tale, to say nothing of the music that accompanied it, that the boys drifted off to sleep because the hour was late. Whereupon Fryderyk woke them up again with a loud crash on the piano. It is difficult to imagine the composer who was to become a standard bearer of "absolute" music improvising to illustrate a story, especially one so unlikely as this. It led Niecks to throw up his hands in despair and exclaim, "Those who think there is no salvation outside the pale of absolute music . . . will shake their heads sadly," before moving to what he called more important business.[28] Still, the anecdote offers a crumb of comfort to those "outside the pale" who continue to maintain that one or two of Chopin's later compositions might well be influenced by a program that simply remained unexpressed.

Fryderyk showed an unusual gift for mimicry. He had a quick eye for the ridiculous and could adapt his facial expressions and distort his body into almost any shape, depending on the character he wished to convey. In his youth his limbs were so flexible that he was able to put his feet around his neck whenever he wished to play the clown. He could move his spectators to laughter one moment and reduce them to tears the next. Sometimes he frightened them with uncanny personalities drawn from the repertory of characters he always seemed to have waiting in the wings—a pompous lecturer, a cringing beggar, a Jewish moneylender. And he could inflect his voice to fit these characters, from the stentorian to the whining, from the pleading to the cunning. Had he not been a musician Chopin could easily have become an actor, as George Sand confirmed years later when he used to entertain her guests at Nohant with his impersonations. Ferdinand Hiller never forgot the occasion when Chopin entered the salon of Countess Ludwika Plater in Paris, acting the part of Pierrot (one of the stock characters from the *commedia dell'arte*), and after darting and dancing around his Polish compatriots for more than an hour, he left without saying a word.[29]

There was a good deal of sympathy for Samuel Linde at this time

---

28. NFC, vol. 1, p. 50. The scene was memorialized in a painting by Andrew Carrick Gow, *A Musical Story by Chopin* (1879), which hangs in the Tate Gallery, London.
29. Ibid., p. 256.

because his wife, Ludwika, had recently passed away, leaving him with two young daughters, Ludka and Anna. He had always wanted a son and heir, but there had been a series of five stillbirths and he was now fifty-one years old. Undaunted, Linde took as his second wife a young woman less than half his age, Luiza Nussbaum, who went on to present him with four more daughters. Linde's family life, and his ever-expanding brood of girls, was a topic of gossip among the boys. When his new bride gave birth to their first child, the will was mistaken for the deed, and the rumor spread that it was a boy. "*Ecce homo!*" Fryderyk proclaimed in his best Latin. "Linde, yes Linde, has an heir." But later in that same letter to Jan Białobłocki, he had to correct himself when news of a different kind reached him. "Sorry! *Ecce femina, non homo.*"[30]

IX

As the summer of 1824 approached, Fryderyk's frail health and his emaciated appearance started to give cause for concern. He had worked diligently all year on a range of topics, some of which were new to him. Ever a perfectionist, he wanted to excel in them all. The family physician, Dr. François Girardot, was brought in and prescribed pills to stimulate the boy's appetite and have him put on a little weight. It was an unpleasant regimen because Girardot also required Fryderyk to drink half a decanter of herbal tea daily, plus six cups of roasted acorn coffee to help him digest his food, to sip sweet wine (which he disliked), and to eat plenty of ripe fruit. Girardot was an eminent physician who had earlier been a surgeon attached to the Polish light cavalry fighting under Napoléon, and in 1814 he had lost a leg to a Russian bullet. Many of the best families in Warsaw were his patients, so his homespun remedies were not to be treated lightly.

Dominik Dziewanowski, one of Fryderyk's classmates at the Lyceum, had boarded with the Chopins since 1822. His parents owned the village of Szafarnia in the province of Mazovia, about two hundred kilometers northwest of Warsaw, so when an invitation came for Fryderyk to accompany Domuś back to the family estate that summer, with its promise of a healthy sojourn in the country, Justyna and Mikołaj welcomed the offer. We recall

---

30. CFC, vol. 1, pp. 56–57; KFC, vol. 1, p. 67.

that thirty years earlier, during his bachelor days, Mikołaj had been employed at Szafarnia as the French tutor to Dominik's father, Juliusz, and it was through this connection that Juliusz had enrolled Domuś at the Warsaw Lyceum. Because Mikołaj's memories attached him to the area, he arranged to join Fryderyk and the Dziewanowski family at Szafarnia later in the year.

Fryderyk had first to complete his schoolwork and take the end-of-term examinations, and he burned the midnight oil to do it. The graduation ceremony took place on July 24, and the whole school assembled for this rite of passage, presided over by Bishop Kaliski. The minister of education also turned up, made a speech, and read out the roll of honor. Selected for commendation were Dominik Dziewanowski, Julian Fontana, and Wilhelm Kolberg. Two pupils were awarded special prizes: Fryderyk Chopin and Jan Matuszyński. Chopin's prize was a book titled *Outline of Statistics for the Use of Country and District Schools* by Gaspard Monge—an award that, in the droll words of Chopin's biographer Casimir Wierzyński, probably "brought more honor than pleasure."[31]

---

31. WLDC, p. 42.

EXPLORING POLAND:
HOLIDAYS IN SZAFARNIA,
1824–1825

Until now I haven't had any falls, because the horse hasn't thrown me off. But if it ever wants me to take a tumble, I may do it one day.

—*Chopin to Wilhelm Kolberg*[1]

I

The day after their graduation, Fryderyk and Dominik set out for Szafarnia in the company of Dominik's aunt Ludwika, who had come to fetch them in her carriage. The Dziewanowski family was esteemed throughout Poland, because Dominik's uncle had served as a cavalry officer in Napoléon's army and had perished during the storming of the Somosierra Pass (1808) at the head of his company of Polish lancers. His fellow officers were cut down with him, together with half his men, but the pass was taken and Napoléon occupied Madrid a week later. The story had become legend and the family basked in its reflected glory. The old manor house at Szafarnia was of baronial proportions, and displayed the family coat of arms on its walls. Fryderyk was warmly received by Dominik's parents, Juliusz and Honorata, who greeted him in person.[2] They were fond of

---

1. CFC, vol. 1, p. 13; KFC, vol. 1, p. 40.
2. Honorata was Dominik's stepmother. His father and mother (Wiktoria) had divorced in

music, adored the piano, and were well aware of his artistic gifts. Justyna
Chopin had provided Honorata with strict instructions regarding Fryderyk's
daily regimen, as recommended by Dr. Girardot. In addition to all the pills
and libations that the boy was expected to take, Girardot forbade him to
eat the rough black bread traditionally consumed by country folk, in favor
of the fine white bread eaten in the city, a sanction about which Fryderyk
complained to his parents.

II

Fryderyk's day began at 7:00 a.m. He practiced the piano to his heart's content, drew in his sketchbook whatever scenes took his fancy, and took
leisurely tours of the grounds, riding in style in the family carriage and
enjoying the fresh air. There was plenty of physical activity as well. He
and Dominik roamed across the Szafarnia estate, had close encounters
with the cows and pigs that wandered outside the house (and sometimes,
one suspects, inside as well), chatted to the local peasants, and went horse
riding. Occasionally the pair ventured farther afield, visiting a number of
nearby villages, including Sokołowo, Radomin, Rodzone, and Bocheniec.
It was the boy's first real experience of the Polish countryside, and he
reveled in it.

On August 10, Fryderyk made a brief visit to neighboring Sokołowo,
the home of his friend Jan (Jasio) Białobłocki. From there he wrote to his
parents, the first of his letters to have survived. He began by telling them
about his daily routine, making fun of his first attempts to ride a horse,
which he describes via an untranslatable pun: "I am riding on the past par-
ticiple of the French verb *connaître*" (this would be *connu*—which sounds
in Polish like *koniu*, meaning "horse"). He then returns to the all-important
question of black bread and how to remove his doctor's sanction against
eating it.

1817. The patriotism of the Dziewanowski family, incidentally, was to cost them dear. In 1833,
Juliusz was arrested by the Russians for collaborating with the Polish partisans after the
failed uprising of 1831, and was imprisoned in Warsaw. After his release he was placed under
police watch. In 1838, he transferred Szafarnia to twenty-seven-year-old Dominik and went to
live on an adjoining estate. As for Dominik, he too played an active role in the uprising, went
into exile for two years, and returned home in 1833. He was later jailed for his part in the
1848 conspiracy against Russia.

Sokołowo
Tuesday, August 10, 1824

My beloved parents,

. . . I have a keen appetite, but in order to satisfy my flat stomach, which is now starting to get bigger, I need permission to eat the country-style bread to satisfy myself. Girardot does not allow me to have any rye bread, but his prohibition applies only to the Warsaw bread, and not to countryside bread. He forbade me to eat any because it is sour, but the Szafarnia bread is not in the least acidic. The first is black, the second white. One is made from coarse flour, the other from fine flour. In the end, if he could taste it, Girardot would find it better than the other one and would certainly allow me to eat some, in accordance with the habit of doctors having their patients consume what they themselves like . . . How could Mother not grant me the permission that I desire? Haven't I indicated clearly enough that I wish to eat country bread? If Girardot were in Warsaw, I would ask Mme Dziewanowska to give me a loaf and I would send it to him at once in a little box. After the first bite he would grant me his permission. So in the hope of getting what I ask of you with so much insistence (with the consent of Mlle Ludwika and Mlle Józefa,[3] who gave me this bread on one occasion in anticipation of permission to come), I will finish my dissertation on this topic . . .

We are awaiting Father with utmost impatience; as for me, I beg him to be kind enough to purchase from Brzezina [a Warsaw music dealer] the *Variations on an Air by Moore, for piano, 4 hands* by [Ferdinand] Ries and bring it to me.[4] I would like to play it with Mme Dziewanowska. I wonder if Father could also bring me either the prescription or a bottle of pills because, according to the calculations I did today, I have enough left for only twenty-seven more days.

Now I have nothing left to write other than to ask Ludwika about Mother and Father's health. Father has, I have no doubt, fully

---

3. Dominik's aunts.
4. This newly published set of variations for four hands by Ferdinand Ries was based on one of the "Traditional National Airs" collected by the Irish composer Thomas Moore (1779–1852). The adolescent Chopin went on to compose his own set of variations for four hands on the same theme, the manuscript of which was discovered in 1965.

recovered from his kidney pains. I cordially embrace Ludka, Izabelka, Emilka, Zuzia, Mme Dekert, Mlle Leszczyńska. I am also sending greetings to the Grasshopper and to Chomentowski. I kiss my beloved parents' hands and feet.

Your son,

F. F. Chopin[5]

III

Our best information about Fryderyk's sojourn in Szafarnia comes from the satirical journal that he created and named the *Szafarnia Courier*. It was a lampoon on the leading Polish newspaper of the day, the conservative *Warsaw Courier*. Fryderyk was the editor and sole contributor, writing under the *nom de plume* of "Mr. Pichon"—an anagram of Chopin. Since the *Warsaw Courier* was subject to censorship, the *Szafarnia Courier* had to have a censor too, and this important role was assigned to Dominik's aunt Ludwika Dziewanowska. The newspaper was divided into two columns, just like the *Warsaw Courier*: "Local News," which covered Szafarnia, and "Foreign News," which covered the rest of the neighborhood. Chopin's sense of the ridiculous and his puckish humor leap from every page as he writes with mock solemnity about country life in and around Szafarnia. He describes again his failed attempts to mount a horse, the mayhem in the farmyard among the pigs and cows, his exposure to authentic Polish folk song, and the various adventures that came his way during his forays into the surrounding countryside. The *Szafarnia Courier* was dispatched at intervals to his family in Warsaw, probably in lieu of letters they had been expecting and might have preferred; but we may be sure that they smiled at the pastoral scenes he elevated to the level of news of national importance. The following extracts are drawn from the four issues of the *Szafarnia Courier* that have survived, although two more issues are known to have been written.[6]

---

5. CFC, vol. 1, pp. 6–9; KFC, vol. 1, pp. 37–38. "Grasshopper" is a nickname that has yet to be deciphered.
6. The four extant issues of the *Szafarnia Courier* are displayed in facsimile, together with their annotated texts, in CKS.

HOME NEWS
Issue of August 16, 1824

August 11. Mr. Fryderyk Chopin goes horseback riding every day, with such skill that he regularly remains stationary—on his backside. (Passed by the censor, L.D.)

August 12. A hen went lame, and a drake fighting with a goose lost a leg. A cow became so ill it is grazing in the garden . . . Consequently an edict was issued on the 14th inst. forbidding all piglets to enter the garden on pain of death. (Passed by the censor, L.D.)

There were musical evenings at Szafarnia, too. When the evening meal had been cleared away, everyone would gather around the piano for an impromptu concert. Mme Dziewanowska would play and Chopin would join her for duets. But it was as a soloist that he shone. He had recently added to his repertoire a difficult concerto by Kalkbrenner, which impressed his group of admirers. Visiting musicians also took part in these concerts, including a certain Herr Better from Berlin, a pianist of no particular merit, whom Chopin heard play and then lampooned.

August 13. Herr Better played on the piano with uncommon talent. This Berlin virtuoso plays in the same style as Herr Berger (the pianist from Skolimów). In sheer velocity he surpasses Mme Lagowska [a local pianist], and he plays with such feeling that almost every note seems to come not from his heart but from his enormous stomach. (Passed by the censor, L.D.)

Chopin was probably irritated by all the "twisting of the person" that went on at the keyboard and was alien to his own playing. In later years, after he had settled in Paris, he often parodied such players for the amusement of his friends.

15 August. Last night a cat sneaked into the dressing room and broke a bottle of juice. On the one hand he deserves the gallows, on the other he is worthy of praise, for he chose the smaller bottle. (Passed by the censor, L.D.)

FOREIGN NEWS
Issue of August 16, 1824

16 August. At Bocheniec a fox ate two helpless ganders. Whoever catches the fox is required to kindly inform the local judiciary, which will unfailingly punish the felon in conformity with its laws and regulations. The two ganders will be surrendered to whoever delivers the fox, as a reward.

HOME NEWS
Issue of August 27, 1824

The Hon. Mr. Pichon has encountered all kinds of unpleasantness from mosquitos . . . They are biting him all over, but fortunately not on the nose, or it would become even longer than it already is.

25 August. The Drake sneaked out of the Henhouse early in the morning and drowned. The reason for this suicide is not yet known, because the family is refusing to talk.

FOREIGN NEWS
Issue of August 31, 1824

29 August. As he was passing through Nieszawa [Chopin probably means Nieszkovizna] Mr. Pichon heard a village Catalani[7] singing at the top of her voice as she sat on a fence. His attention was at once caught and he listened to both song and voice, regretting however that in spite of his efforts he could not catch the words. Twice he walked past the fence, but in vain—he could not understand a word. Finally, overcome with curiosity, he fished out of his pocket three *groszy* and offered them to the singer if she would repeat her song. For a time she made a fuss, pouted, and refused; but, tempted by the three *groszy*, she made up her mind and began to sing a little

---

7. A reference to the opera singer Angelica Catalani, who had presented Fryderyk with a gold watch in 1820.

mazurka from which the present Editor, with the permission of the authorities and the censor, is allowed to quote as an example one verse:

"See, how the wolf is dancing
Beyond the hills for life;
See how he breaks his heart,
Because he hasn't got a wife."

At Radomin a cat went mad. Fortunately it did not bite anyone, but ran away and jumped into a field where it was killed. Only then did it stop its rampage. (Passed by the censor, L.D.)

HOME NEWS
Issue of September 3, 1824

September 1. As Mr. Pichon was playing the *Little Jew*, Mr. Dziewanowski called his Jewish cattle hand and asked him what he thought of the young Jewish virtuoso. Young Moshe came to the window, poked his hooked nose into the room, and listened. Then he said that if Mr. Pichon cared to play at a Jewish wedding he could make at least ten florins. Such a pronouncement encouraged Mr. Pichon to take up that kind of music as soon as possible, and who knows? he may in time devote himself entirely to this kind of profitable music making. (Passed by the censor, L.D.)

This reference to the "Little Jew" may be the first mention of an early version of Chopin's Mazurka in A minor, which he later elaborated and published as op. 17, no. 4.[8]

---

8. The long tradition of calling this mazurka the "Little Jew" goes against the grain of modern research. Scholars have questioned whether the piece we know today has anything to do with the missing sketches of a piece to which Chopin may first have attached the name. The pros and cons of the matter are summarized in CKS, p. 43.

The plangent, "ethnic" harmonies so characteristic of this particular mazurka are thought to reflect the influence of the Jewish musicians he heard in the region of Szafarnia. Its unusual opening (in the Lydian mode) also serves as its unusual ending, and the piece simply drifts away into silence on the "wrong" chord of F major. While it is not difficult to think of later compositions whose endings are abandoned (Schumann's "Entreating Child" from *Kinderszenen* and Liszt's *Nuages gris* come to mind), it is worth asking if this youthful mazurka was the first piece to do so. Fryderyk's chimerical description of himself as a "young Jewish virtuoso" must be read as an in-joke known to the family. He possessed a prominent nose and frequently disparaged it.

There was a sizable Jewish population in the region of Mazovia (the home of the Mazurka), and numerous Jews were employed on large estates such as Szafarnia. The local herdsman, milkman, and butcher were more likely than not to be Jewish. And Jewish traders turned up regularly at the manor house to bargain away their wares. Chopin found it natural to mock them, for in the Poland of his day Jews were regarded as second-class citizens. His anti-Semitic language was the *lingua franca* of the time, and it turns up in his later correspondence as well.

FOREIGN NEWS
Issue of August 27, 1824

A Jewish lease-holder in [the village of] Rodzone was letting his calf feed in the manor's cornfield every night. It wandered off safely several times, but on the night of the 24th a wolf came and ate the calf. The lord of the manor is glad that the Jew was repaid in this way for his nefarious conduct; but the Jew is angry with the wolf and offers to give the whole calf to anyone who delivers the culprit to him. (Passed by the censor, L.D.)

A few days later we find the fourteen-year-old boy describing the local Jews in a darkly comical vein.

HOME NEWS
Issue of August 31, 1824

On the 29th August a cartload of Jews was rolling along. *Die ganze Familie* consisted of *eine fat Mamele*, three big Jews, two small ones, and half a dozen little Jews. They were all huddled together like Dutch herrings. Then a stone in the road upset the cart, which overturned, and they all lay on the sand in the following order: First of all the children, each one in a different position, most of them with their legs upturned, and on top of them the *Mamele*, groaning under the load of Jewish men, whose skullcaps fell off in all the confusion. (Passed by the censor, L.D.)

The chief value of the *Szafarnia Courier* is the light it throws on the boy's personality. Its sophisticated use of satire is unusual for one so young, and springs from the same source as his talent for mimicry.

In due course Mikołaj Chopin joined Fryderyk at Szafarnia and spent a few days relaxing with the Dziewanowski family. His visit did not escape the scrutiny of the editor of the *Szafarnia Courier*, who complained to his readers that his father "eats four rolls every day, *nota bene*," a pointed reference to the constraints placed on Fryderyk's own diet, "as well as a very large dinner and a three-course supper."

Something of the color of those blissful days was captured in a letter that Chopin wrote to another school friend from the Lyceum, Wilhelm ("Wiluś") Kolberg, who was enjoying a summer holiday of his own in the Polish countryside.

Szafarnia, August 19, 1824

Dear Wiluś!

Thanks for remembering me; but I am annoyed with you, because you are such a mean and horrid *et cetera* and only write such a scrap to me. Do you begrudge the paper, pen, and ink?

Perhaps you don't have the time. That's it! He goes horseback riding enjoying himself, and no longer thinks of his friends. But whatever! Let's embrace and make peace!

I am happy that you are enjoying yourself because that is what one is supposed to do in the countryside. As for me, I also am having a good time, and you are not the only one to be riding a horse, for I can ride too. Don't ask me how I do it, but I can ride at least well enough for the horse to walk slowly wherever it feels like going, while I sit fearfully on its back, like a monkey on a bear. Until now I haven't taken any falls because the horse hasn't thrown me off; but—if it ever wants me to take a tumble, I may do it one day . . .

I won't bother you with my personal affairs, because I know that they won't interest you. The flies often alight on my lofty nose, but that's unimportant, because it's rather a custom of these annoying pests . . . Am I boring you already? If not, then write by return post, and I will continue my epistles at once.

I end this one therefore without compliments, but in friendship. Keep well, dear Wiluś, and write me soon—and not just a few words attached to another letter. We shall meet in four weeks. I embrace you heartily.

Your sincere friend,

F. F. Chopin.

My respects to your Mamma and Papa, and I embrace your brothers.[9]

After the holidays Fryderyk was able to show his friend a second mazurka that he had composed at Szafarnia, the one in A-flat major eventually revised and published as op. 7, no. 4.[10] Once again the formative experience of his stay in the Polish countryside is revealed in harmonies unexpected in an adolescent. Particularly striking is the use of the Dorian mode, with its raised submediant degree, which could hardly have been acquired from a conservatory, but rather from music

---

9. CFC, vol. 1, pp. 12–14; KFC, vol. 1, pp. 40–41.
10. The manuscript bears an inscription in the hand of Oskar Kolberg, Wilhelm's brother: "Written by Fr. Chopin in the year 1824."

he heard in the villages of Mazovia. This is musical language of close observation.

The audacious lead-back to the main theme captures our attention, situated as it is in the remote key of A major. We call it "audacious" because it seems disconnected from the rest of the mazurka, as if the youth had impulsively copied down a fragment of something heard in the distance, perhaps played by a wandering klezmer band about to move out of earshot. From here the fourteen-year-old composer pivots his way back to the home tonic of A-flat major via a single chord, seemingly plucked from nowhere. This was one of the mazurkas that some years later drew the wrath of the conservative critic Ludwig Rellstab.[11]

As the summer days grew shorter, the harvesttime approached, always the most important season in Szafarnia. The peasants took to the fields with their scythes and worked in rows, shearing the wheat in regular rhythmic movements, occasionally easing their toil with song. At noontime work would stop for food and drink, and the laborers would seek some shade from the scorching sun before resuming their work, stacking the fallen

11. "If Herr Chopin had shown this composition to a master, the latter would, it is to be hoped, have torn it up and thrown it at his feet, which we hereby do symbolically." *Iris*, Berlin, August 2, 1833.

wheat into sheaves waiting to be threshed by hand. The grain was stored near the manor house, and what was not needed for the coming winter was generally sold off. On one occasion, Fryderyk and Domuś ran into a group of Jewish merchants wanting to buy surplus grain. Chopin treated the party to an improvised *majufes*, a Jewish wedding dance, that so pleased them they formed a circle and started to sway to the music. It reached such a peak of enthusiasm that they invited the young pianist to a Jewish wedding nearby, where he was regaled with more merrymaking and music. Chopin absorbed these experiences like a sponge, and added them to a repertoire of musical memories that remained with him for life. He rarely admitted folk music into his compositions, nor did he ever go off in search of it—unlike composers of a later generation such as Bartók and Kodály in Hungary, and Vaughan Williams in England. But it nonetheless cast an invisible mantle across his long series of mazurkas and polonaises, making them ineffably "Polish" in a way that a mere quotation of a Polish folk song could not possibly have done.[12]

IV

On April 27, 1825, Tsar Alexander I arrived in Warsaw to open the third Sejm in his capacity as King of Poland. Military bands played in the public squares, gala performances were mounted in the National Theater, and glittering balls took place in the specially illuminated houses of the aristocrats. Amid all the pomp and circumstance that went along with such a solemn occasion, the Sejm was opened on May 13. Striking while the iron was hot, a local manufacturer of musical instruments named Fidelis Brunner arranged to show off a recent invention—the Aeolomelodikon—that he had constructed after a design by Professor Jakub Hoffmann, a scientist on the faculty of Warsaw University and a friend of the Chopin family. The Aeolomelodikon has been well described as a contraption that was as complicated as its name. A combination of organ and piano, its sound was amplified by a set of copper tubes with various stops and a

---

12. We have not overlooked Chopin's Grand Fantasia on Polish Airs, for Piano and Orchestra, op. 13, the only work in which Chopin "collects" Polish themes and incorporates them into a large-scale composition.

pedal board. The instrument was capable of imitating wind and brass instruments. When all the stops were out, it sounded like an orchestra of sixty players.

Hoffmann approached Mikołaj Chopin with a request to allow Fryderyk ("the foremost pianist in town") to display the instrument to the public. Whatever reservations Mikołaj may have harbored were swept away when word came from the Royal Castle that the tsar had looked with favor on a petition submitted by Brunner, and was curious to hear the instrument for himself. The Evangelical Church, with its spacious Rotunda, was chosen as the venue for this command performance (both Hoffmann and Brunner were members of the Protestant congregation there, as, incidentally, was Fryderyk's headmaster, Dr. Samuel Linde). Aside from Tsar Alexander and his entourage, Prince Radziwiłł and his family were in attendance along with other high-ranking Polish families. When Fryderyk took his bow, he was wearing the full dress uniform of a student of the Lyceum. It was the most distinguished audience before which the fifteen-year-old boy had yet played. No printed program has survived, but we know that he improvised a free fantasia that allowed him to show off the full resources of the instrument. Tsar Alexander was much taken with the boy's playing and he presented both Fryderyk and Brunner with diamond rings. The *Warsaw Courier* carried a notice of the event.[13]

It was a singular misfortune for Hoffmann and Brunner that a rival invention now took center stage, and drew attention away from theirs. The newcomer (yet another attempt to merge the piano with the organ) enjoyed the equally implausible name of the Aeolopantaleon and had been invented by a Warsaw cabinetmaker named Józef Długosz, who enjoyed the support of Józef Elsner, Chopin's future composition teacher. A charity concert was announced for May 27 in the main hall of the Conservatory, at which the Aeolopantaleon was unveiled and put through its paces by Chopin. The free fantasia that he improvised was greeted with enormous acclaim. Further accolades followed when the youth played the first movement of Moscheles's Piano Concerto in G minor. The program ended with a cantata of Elsner's, whose main theme, the anthem "God Save the King," fitted the temper of the times.[14] This concert was given by a combined orchestra and

---

13. Issue of June 7, 1825.
14. A copy of this rare program is reproduced in BFC, p. 28.

choir of more than 140 performers, and Prince Radziwiłł was once again
among the capacity audience. Such was the success of the occasion that
everyone agreed to return to the auditorium and repeat the concert on
June 10. This time Chopin played his newly published Rondo in C minor,
op. 1, which gained his first professional notice outside Poland. The article
appeared in Leipzig's *Allgemeine musikalische Zeitung* and it is generally
thought that the anonymous "Warsaw correspondent" who wrote it was
Elsner himself. Chopin's improvisation was selected for special praise,
saying that the playing was "marked by a wealth of musical ideas that
made a great impression on the audience."[15] It remains only to add that neither the Aeolomelodikon nor the Aeolopantaleon had any later success.
These hybrid instruments may well have enjoyed pride of ancestry but
they had no hope of posterity.

Tsar Alexander closed the Sejm and departed Warsaw in mid-June,
after a stay of six weeks. It was the last the Poles saw of him. Within a few
months he was dead, an event that was to have untold consequences for
the nation.

V

After the school year ended, Chopin was impatient to return to Szafarnia
for another summer holiday in the company of Domuś Dziewanowski,
and the pair arrived at the manor house in mid-July. Chopin now added
the unlikely pastimes of hunting and shooting to his pastoral activities,
joining a hunting party and coming back with a rabbit and a brace of par-
tridges tied to his waist—his "bag" for the day. Even more surprising, since
it contradicts everything we thought we knew about Chopin's delicate constitution, we learn that he tried his hand at carpentry. He first designed
some chess pieces and then went on to build some wooden benches that
were placed in the park at Szafarnia, where they remained for many years.

---

15. *AmZ*, November 16, 1825, which also contains a description of the Aeolomelodikon. Taking part in the concert was a visiting Italian singer billed simply as "Mme Bianchi." This was
not Antonia Bianchi, the mistress of Paganini—often wrongly identified as the artist—but
rather Carolina Crespi Bianchi, the divorced wife of the tenor Eliodoro Bianchi. At the time
of the concert, Antonia was eight months pregnant and living with Paganini in Palermo. Six
weeks later she gave birth to their son Achille. CPG, vol. 1, pp. 243–44.

Chopin's Poland: 1815–1830

(In 1842, after passing through the area, Ludwika Chopin told her brother, "The benches you built in Szafarnia do not exist anymore. One can only find imitations in pleasant memory of you."[16]) There were no more issues of the *Szafarnia Courier*, but a useful run of letters to his friends Jan Białobłocki and Jan Matuszyński, as well as to his family, takes up the story. Fryderyk and Domuś roamed across Mazovia more extensively than before, riding in the Dziewanowski family carriage and gaining new perspectives on rustic life in the province. One excursion took them from Szafarnia to Toruń, the birthplace of Copernicus. Fryderyk was impressed with this medieval city, featuring Gothic churches, a famous leaning tower, and a town hall "with as many windows as there are days in a year, as many

16. CFC, vol. 3, p. 116; KFC, vol. 2, p. 71.

halls as there are months, and as many rooms as there are weeks." He was indignant when he saw the derelict condition into which the old Coperni- cus house had fallen. The room in which Poland's great astronomer was said to have been born was occupied "by some German who stuffs him- self with potatoes and then allows himself to release some frequent zephyrs [i.e., farts]." "But let us put Copernicus to one side," Fryderyk told Jan Matuszyński, "and speak of Toruń's gingerbread cakes. From everything that I have seen, it is gingerbread that has made the strongest impression on me . . . Nothing surpasses the cakes!" Then, as now, Toruń was famous for its spiced pastry. Aside from the confection, Fryderyk was much taken with a German machine for moving sand, "which the Germans call a *Sandmaschine*."[17]

It was late August when the pair of travelers got back to Szafarnia and the harvest festival once again brought the holidays to a boisterous end. Fryderyk describes how he and Domuś paid a brief visit to the village of Obrowo, in the company of Mme Honorata Dziewanowska, and were just finishing their evening meal when they heard the sounds of execrable singing drifting in from the courtyard and rushed outside to find the source. A procession of old peasant women was approaching the manor house, wheezing a traditional melody through their noses. Four local girls wearing garlands of flowers and bearing the traditional gifts of freshly har- vested crops were leading the way, screeching a half-tone higher to the accompaniment of a wretched violin with a missing string. This set the scene for comedy. At the manor house two local stableboys lay in wait for the girls and threw buckets of water over them as they crossed the thresh- old. A bout of merrymaking ensued, which ended with dancing and music making in which Fryderyk also took part. It was getting dark, so candles were brought out and set up on the terrace. The violinist struck up an improvised mazurka, but the performance started to wilt. In order to keep the piece going Fryderyk seized a basetla (a kind of double bass that boasted only one string) and did his best. At one point he took hold of one of the girls and danced with her. The party finally broke up when the

---

17. CFC, vol. 1, pp. 34–35; KFC, vol. 1, p. 52. Until the 1880s, the birth house of Copernicus was erroneously identified as a run-down tenement building on the corner of Kopernika and Piekary Streets. All sightseers, including Chopin, would have paid their respects there. The astronomer was actually born at nearby 15 Kopernika Street, which is today the Nicolaus Copernicus Museum.

procession of peasants reassembled and moved on to the next village, where the harvest ritual was repeated.[18]

VI

Not long after his return from Szafarnia, the fifteen-year-old Fryderyk took on a new and unexpected role. He was appointed to play the organ during the Sunday services in the Church of the Nuns of the Visitation, situated on Warsaw's Krakowskie Przedmieście Street. This was the official church of the Lyceum, where the students and faculty members assembled for Sunday mass.[19] We speculate that this appointment came about because of his recent success in playing the Aeolomelodikon before Tsar Alexander, with all the attendant publicity it had brought in its wake. Chopin boasted to Jasio Białobłocki, "I have been appointed organist to the Lyceum. O, My Lord, what a personage I have become—the first in importance after his Reverend the Priest! I play once a week at the Visitandines' Church while the others sing."[20] Józef Sikorski, who attended those Sunday services as a boy, and later became the editor of Warsaw's leading music periodical, *Ruch Muzyczny*, retained some lively memories of those occasions.

> While the University of Warsaw was still in existence, a morning religious service was celebrated on Sundays and important holidays in the Church of the Visitation for the students. A choir composed of the pupils and ex-pupils of the Conservatory under Elsner, sang religious songs with organ, sometimes with an orchestra. Chopin was a frequent guest there, especially during the last year of his stay in Warsaw, and played the organ, be it fugues of old masters or his own improvisations. The use of the pedals, which is the difficult part of playing the organ, came to him quite easily and naturally . . .

18. Letter to his parents, August 26, 1825. KFC, vol. 1, pp. 53–55.
19. A plaque inside the building bears the inscription: "In honor of Fryderyk Chopin, who played the organ in this church as a pupil of the Warsaw Lyceum, in the years 1825–26."
20. CFC, vol. 1, pp. 44–45; KFC, vol. 1, pp. 60–61. It is often claimed, without authority, that Chopin took organ lessons from the Czech composer Wilhelm Würfel at this time. Würfel, who was a friend of the Chopin family, had taught organ at the Warsaw Conservatory since 1821. But Chopin was never his pupil.

It happened once between the parts of a Mass, which was executed by a choir and an orchestra, that Chopin sat at the organ and taking—in the manner of famous organists—a theme from that part of the Mass that had just been performed, started improvising on it. He did it with such brilliance of ideas, pouring them out in a great, continuous stream, that all those crowded around him . . . listened spellbound, forgetting all about the place and the duties for which they had congregated. They were awakened from their reverie by the irate sacristan who ran upstairs and shouted to them: "What do you think you are doing in God's name? The priest has tried already to sing *Dominus vobiscum* [the Lord be with you], the acolytes at the altar keep on ringing their hand bells, and still the organ will not stop playing." The old lady [the Mother Superior] is very cross indeed.[21]

Fryderyk's experiences in that same organ loft are recalled in the memoirs of Eugeniusz Skrodzki. The incumbent organist, one Białecki, was a player of modest achievement, whose control over the instrument left something to be desired.

Once, in the Church of the Nuns of the Visitation, Chopin had an incident with the organist, a worthy man named Białecki, who moved in his art like a horse on a treadmill. It so happened that Chopin, unable to bear the hackneyed stuff, sat himself down at the manual and extemporized without any regard, even to the priest celebrating Mass. Such volatile behavior was tolerated by the commander in chief of the organ at the Visitation. But it was worse at a students' Mass when the young musician, having heard a discord or actually a wrong note which could not be justified by any dissonance, pushed Białecki away from the manual almost by force, and sitting down, himself played instead.[22]

According to Skrodzki, Fryderyk also played "the fugues of the old masters," although he does not tell us what they were. These experiences in

---

21. "In Memory of Chopin," *Biblioteka Warszawska*, December 1849.
22. SRCY, *Bluszcz* (Ivy), no. 36, August 25 (September 6), 1882.

the organ loft were to stand Chopin in good stead. Years later he agreed to play the organ at the church of Notre-Dame-du-Mont in Marseille, during the memorial service for the tenor Adolphe Nourrit.

VII

Chopin continued to inform Jasio Białobłocki about his daily life in Warsaw during the months following his return from Szafarnia. Aside from bringing Jasio up to date with various bits of gossip about the Lyceum, and sharing news about family and friends, his letters tell us something about musical life in Warsaw as well. On October 29 the Warsaw Theater mounted a performance of Rossini's *Il barbiere di Siviglia* by a local troupe of modest talent. Chopin enjoyed the music and went home and wrote a polonaise on one of its themes. "I am thinking of having it lithographed tomorrow," he told Jasio. As far as we know, that never happened, and the manuscript is presumed lost. Chopin also wrote with humor about the production of the *Barber* and two of the amateur female singers, one of whom he described as having a cold and sneezing her way through the performance, the other clad in dressing gown and slippers, "yawning in time to the music." There is much badinage in these letters to Jasio, and for good reason. The young man was dying and Fryderyk was desperately eager to keep his spirits alive. During the recent summer holiday at Szafarnia, Fryderyk had made a detour to visit his friend on the Białobłocki family estate at Sokołowo and had found him unable to walk, crippled by tuberculosis of the bone, which had probably affected his spine.[23] He had recently undergone an unpleasant course of heat treatment at Bischofswerda without any positive results. The youth was now too ill to return to Warsaw and resume his studies, so his doctors kept him at home while doing their best to postpone his inevitable end. Fryderyk filled his letters to Jasio with every scrap of information that he thought might be of interest. There had recently arrived in Warsaw a pianist named Alexander Rembieliński, a nephew of the president of the local Education Commission. Rembieliński had studied in Paris for six years and Chopin was impressed with his

---

23. The inference that this visit had taken place may be found in Chopin's letter to Jasio, written after he had returned to Warsaw. CFC, vol. 1, p. 36; KFC, vol. 1, p. 56.

playing. "He plays the piano as I have never yet heard it played," Chopin told Jasio. "You can imagine what a joy that is for us who never hear anything of real excellence here." This was high praise coming from Chopin, who was generally critical of other pianists. What he admired about Rembieliński was his smooth and rounded playing, and the strength of his left hand, "as strong as the right," something he found unusual among pianists.[24]

As the year ended and the first winter snows began to fall, covering Warsaw in a blanket of white, Fryderyk and Ludwika received an invitation from Countess Skarbek to spend Christmas with her and her family at Żelazowa Wola. The children were delighted to return to a place so rich in memories, and after a sixty-kilometer journey by horse and sleigh with jingling bells on snow-covered roads, they arrived at Żelazowa Wola on December 24. Christmas was a magical time in Catholic Poland, and the Skarbeks celebrated it like most of the *szlachta* in their manor houses across the country. There was much eating and drinking of traditional foods and beverages, carol singing around the log fire, and the exchange of greetings and presents. Just before sitting down for his Christmas Eve dinner Fryderyk wrote to Jasio:

December 24, 1825

My dear Jaś!

You will never guess from where I am sending this letter! . . . You will certainly think it is from the second floor annex of the Casimir Palace. Wrong! So it must be from . . . from . . . Don't think about it anymore! It would be in vain: I am writing from Żelazowa Wola.

Fryderyk went on to talk about an entertaining incident that had taken place in Warsaw a couple of days earlier. He and his father had been invited to a large dinner party at the home of Józef Jawurek, a Czech musician who was professor of conducting at the Conservatory. Chopin was puzzled when Jawurek, doubtless with a strong Czech accent, explained that he would be serving *lax* (i.e., a laxative) for dinner. Was his host afflicted with colic, expecting his guests to share his condition? Chopin wondered. When the "lax" was served, however, it turned out to be a great salmon

---

24. CFC, vol. 1, p. 42; KFC, vol. 1, p. 59.

(=*Lachs* in German), which had been imported specially from Gdańsk. There was music making, too. During the evening a Czech pianist, Leopold Czapek, who had just arrived from Vienna, played to the guests; but Chopin dismissed him with the phrase "not much to say about his playing." Of greater interest was a young clarinetist from Prague, named Żak, who impressed everyone with his ability to play two notes simultaneously on the instrument. Chopin marveled that here was a clarinetist who could accompany himself. It was a desolate Christmas for Jasio, however, and Chopin's banter probably failed to raise him from his mood of despair. The letter ended with a touching declaration:

> I embrace you, my soul, and wish you nothing but good health. I hope that you will feel better every day. That is the wish of all our family, and especially of
>> Me
>> Your most sincere friend.

To which sentiment Chopin added a poignant postscript:

> Everyone, the entire household would also send you greetings if they knew that I was writing to you.[25]

Just over two years later Jasio succumbed to his cruel illness and died at his home in Sokołowo, aged twenty-two.

---

25. CFC, vol. 1, pp. 45–47; KFC, vol. 1, pp. 61–62.

THE DECEMBRIST REVOLT,
1825–1826

Tsar Nicholas—the scourge of my country.
—Prince Adam Czartoryski[1]

I

When Fryderyk and Ludwika got back to Warsaw they found an air of foreboding hovering over the city. What had happened will bear some re-telling. On December 1, 1825, Tsar Alexander I had died of typhus, in faraway Taganrog near the Crimean Peninsula, and his youngest brother Nicholas had been proclaimed his successor. Warsaw was plunged into mourning while secretly rejoicing in the demise of the monarch. For six weeks the theaters were closed, concerts were canceled, and normal life was suspended. In Saint Petersburg a group of disaffected Russian army officers, commanding about three thousand soldiers, assembled in the city's Senate Square on December 26 and refused to swear allegiance to Nicholas, proclaiming instead their loyalty to his older brother Grand Duke Constantine. But Constantine had secretly renounced his right to the throne five years earlier, his morganatic marriage to Joanna Grudzińska excluding him and his offspring from the Romanov succession. Constantine may have regretted that this formal renunciation had never been publicly

1. CM, p. 124.

promulgated and was kept from the army. Rumors had meanwhile stirred that Tsar Alexander had been murdered, that his coffin contained the remains of an unknown soldier.[2] Out of this royal confusion emerged the "Decembrist Revolt."

The newly minted Tsar Nicholas turned up in person in Saint Petersburg in order to parlay with the rebels, but his conciliator Count Mikhail Miloradovich was shot dead while making a speech. A cavalry charge was ordered by Nicholas, but the horses slipped on the icy cobblestones of the square and the charge broke up in disarray. Faced with humiliation, Nicholas ordered an artillery bombardment, which had a devastating impact on the rebels, who broke ranks and fled across the frozen surface of the Neva River. As the pursuing artillery shells broke through the ice, many of the soldiers slipped into the water and were drowned. The leaders of the revolt were arrested, taken to the Winter Palace, put on trial, and sentenced to death by hanging. The common soldiers who had supported their officers received multiple lashings and were sent to Siberia in chains.

On the morning of the public hangings of five of the Decembrists, something unusual happened. The ropes brought in to hang them broke before any of them died. It was widely assumed among the crowd of spectators that victims of botched executions would be reprieved, but Nicholas ordered new ropes and the prisoners were hanged a second time. News of this gruesome ritual reached Warsaw quickly and created revulsion, as it did across the Western world. Nicholas had shown that he intended to rule with an iron hand, and Poland had been put on notice. The patriotic resistance unleashed by this display of opposition to the tsar within Muscovy itself inspired great numbers of Poles to renew their disaffection with Russia. The cafés of Warsaw were abuzz with talk of resistance. Underground meetings were held at risk of life and limb. They functioned under cover of such umbrella organizations as the Freemasons and the Patriotic Society—perfectly legal under the Polish Constitution but which became

---

2. Among the fabrications to sweep through the ranks of the Russian intelligentsia was the tale that the pious Alexander, wracked by guilt at having done nothing to prevent the murder of his father, Tsar Paul I, had withdrawn to Siberia in order to devote himself to prayer and live the life of a monk. *Fictio cedit veritati*, as the saying goes. Yet fiction does not always yield to truth. When Alexander's coffin was opened by the Soviets, in the 1920s, it was found to be empty.

a branch of subversive activity once Nicholas became the tsar, and by extension King of Poland. There were three Masonic lodges in Warsaw, and
the one known as "Beneath the Golden Candelabra" boasted among its
members several of Mikołaj Chopin's colleagues, including Józef Elsner,
Kazimierz Brodziński, Juliusz Kolberg, and the conductor of the National
Opera, Karol Kurpiński. Mikołaj was never a Freemason, but the idea that
one is known by the company one keeps must have made him cautious.
Russia's secret police were everywhere, rooting out dissenters. Directed by
the reviled Count Nikolai Novosiltsov, they arrested hundreds of members of the Patriotic Society at dead of night and incarcerated them in the
vaults of the Carmelite Monastery. When these repositories were filled to
overflowing, Novosiltsov appropriated the cellars of the Town Hall and the
Brühl Palace, where his men continued their brutal interrogations. And
all this was going on just a stone's throw from the Chopin family's apartment in the Casimir Palace.

Passive resistance took many forms in Warsaw. One of the most effective was organized by the church. Memorial masses were held across the
city for the victims of General Alexander Suvorov's massacre of the population at Praga. That had been thirty years ago, but the event had been
burned into the national memory and was ready to be fanned into flame.
The public mood was further agitated by news of the death of the Polish
statesman Stanisław Staszic, on January 20, 1826. This eminent patrician,
who had founded the Polish National Academy of Sciences, left all his
lands to the peasants, and his funeral the following month became a ral-
lying point for a national demonstration. More than twenty thousand
mourners (almost a fifth of the population of Warsaw) lined the route followed by the coffin, which was carried by university students all the way
from the Church of the Holy Cross to the grave adjoining the Camaldo-
lese Church in the Warsaw suburb of Bielany, where Staszic had asked to
be buried—a journey of ten kilometers in the depths of winter. Fryderyk
Skarbek delivered a eulogy at the graveside.[3] By the time the coffin was

---

3. His speech was printed in full in *Zbior mow na obchodzie pogrzebowym X. Stanislawa
Sztasica* (Collection of the Speeches Delivered at the Funeral Commemoration of Stanisław
Staszic), Kraków, 1826. With fine rhetorical flourishes it refers to Staszic as "a great Statesman, a friend of the people, a savior of the nation, and someone who raised Poland from the
dead." We may be sure that Chopin read these inflammatory words and admired Skarbek for
having uttered them.

lowered into the ground the pall had been torn to shreds by mourners seeking a souvenir of this solemn event. Chopin was given a piece, which he kept as a sacred relic. Shortly afterward he composed his youthful Funeral March in C minor (op. posth.), a musical response to the death of Staszic.[4]

During these heady days Chopin, by his own account, hardly ever got home until two o'clock in the morning. The outcome might have been predicted. His delicate constitution was overwhelmed and he went down with a chronic inflammation of the throat, accompanied by headaches and swelling of the glands around the neck. A new family physician, Dr. Fry-deryk Roemer, was consulted and he applied a nightcap to Chopin's head and leeches to his throat.[5] Roemer described the young man's illness as "catarrh" in order not to alarm either Chopin or his parents. It was more serious than that, however, for the symptoms lingered and in retrospect they point to the early onset of tuberculosis. Significantly, it was the first occasion on which we find Chopin complaining to anyone about his health.

All this commotion might have had a disruptive effect on the boy's aca-demic studies, but we find him applying himself with uncommon zeal to the demanding curriculum of the Lyceum as the end-of-term examina-tions loomed. He was determined to gain his diploma, without which he

4. See Jan Ekier's authoritative *Introduction to the Polish National Edition of the Works of Fryderyk Chopin*, p. 63, Warsaw, 1974, where the later dates assigned to this march by Cho-pin's sister Ludwika (1827) and by Julian Fontana (1829) are overturned. Ekier endorses the view that the march was composed in memory of Staszic.
5. CFC, vol. 1, p. 50; KFC, vol. 1, p. 63.

would not be admitted to the High School for Music, which had recently become affiliated with the University of Warsaw. Chopin worked far into the night, applying himself diligently to the required subjects, which included Latin, history, and mathematics. He got out of bed in the small hours to improve assignments begun earlier in the day, or work surreptitiously at the piano, for he was composing as well. The other members of the household may have been disturbed by all this nocturnal activity, but Mikołaj and Justyna did not attempt to prevent it.

II

Fryderyk did not like to take part in sports, and only rarely joined the other boys in ball games. He did, however, once indulge in skating—with dire results. During the winter months the fountain on Oboźna Street near the Church of the Holy Cross used to be turned on to create an outdoor ice rink. Around the time of the New Year, 1825–26, the fifteen-year-old Fryderyk slipped while skating with his friend Eugeniusz Skrodzki and blood poured from his injured head. Eugeniusz became frightened. "He looked so pale, and could not get up. I put some snow on his cut. Fortunately, Mr. Kozłowski . . . who rarely went outside, was looking through his window and saw what had happened. He immediately called for help and a few minutes later a doctor appeared [Dr. Fryderyk Szwencki, a surgeon who lived nearby]. It turned out that there was more anxiety than pain. The next day Fryderyk went to school."[6] Because Chopin had also sprained the muscles of his leg, he hobbled around for several days on crutches. When he got better, he presented them to his lame school friend Antoni Rogoziński.[7]

With the arrival of the warm spring evenings the Lyceum students used to promenade around the botanical gardens that lay behind the Casimir Palace, or sit on benches and engage in conversation. Eugeniusz had a boyish interest in botany, and liked to explore the gardens in search of flora and fauna or to add to his collection of worms and beetles. He began to notice that Chopin was spending time in the company of a young girl

6. SRCY, *Bluszcz* (Ivy), no. 33, August 4 (16), 1882.
7. CFC, vol. 1, p. 53; KFC, vol. 1, p. 65.

with whom he was clearly infatuated. She has never been identified but may have been one of the daughters of a faculty member. Eugeniusz picked some flowers and gave them to the girl, a gesture that appeared to please Fryderyk, who gave Eugeniusz some candy that he kept in his pocket. Evidently Eugeniusz was not the only one to observe what was going on, for he continued, "One day Professor Chopin came into the gardens and asked me in his clear, positive voice: "Tell me, dear boy, did you see Fryderyk my son here?" I hesitated, judging by his expression that he might be angry with Fryderyk for being here at this moment, so I answered, "No, I did not see him." "But he does come here," insisted Professor Chopin. "Yes," I replied, "but I did not see him just now." And in order to cover my blushes because of the lie, I turned around and started to play a ball game." After a few minutes Mikołaj Chopin gave up the search, and when Eugeniusz was sure that the coast was clear, he ran over to Fryderyk, who was still conversing with the girl, and told him what had happened. "What you did was good," said Fryderyk, and he

The front façade of the Casimir Palace, 1824; a lithograph by Lassalle, after a drawing by Jan Feliks Piwarski. Chopin's apartment was on the second floor of the annex on the right.

reached into his pocket and gave Eugeniusz another candy. "I felt confused," said Eugeniusz, "for he had praised my lie."[8]

III

As the summer of 1826 approached, Chopin's symptoms had still not cleared up. More troubling was the rapid decline in Emilia's health. The thirteen-year-old girl was showing signs of tuberculosis. Dr. Wilhelm Malcz, a specialist in the disease, was brought in and all thoughts of another summer holiday in Szafarnia for Chopin were abandoned. Following Malcz's advice, Justyna took the children to the fashionable spa of Duszniki-Zdrój (Bad Reinerz) in Silesia for its famous five-week "cure." The warm mineral springs were widely considered beneficial to those with a weakened constitution and the place attracted large numbers of wealthy patrons. Accompanying the Chopins were members of the Skarbek family—Countess Ludwika Skarbek (who was herself a sufferer from tuberculosis), Count Fryderyk Skarbek and his wife, Prakseda, and their young son, Józef. The Skarbeks traveled ahead in the family's private coach in the company of Chopin's sisters Ludwika and Emilia. Chopin and his mother followed a few days later because Chopin was still awaiting the results of his final examinations at the Lyceum. On July 27 he heard that he had passed and had been accepted into the High School for Music. That same evening he celebrated by attending a performance of Rossini's opera *La gazza ladra* at the National Theater, in the company of his friend Wiluś Kolberg. As a souvenir of the event, Chopin incorporated into the Trio section of his newly composed Polonaise in B-flat minor a paraphrase of the Cavatina from Act I (*"Vieni fra queste braccia"*—"Come to these arms"), a favorite of Kolberg's. The manuscript is inscribed (probably in the hand of Kolberg's brother Oskar) with the words "Adieu! to Wilhelm Kolberg (on leaving for Reinerz) 1826."

---

8. SRCY, *Bluszcz* (Ivy), no. 33, August 4 (16), 1882.

Allegro moderato

The next day, July 28, Chopin and Justyna set out on the five-hundred-kilometer journey to Bad Reinerz. The register of the Bürgel Hof showed that mother and son arrived there on August 3.[9]

Reinerz occupied a picture-perfect location. The spa was set in beautiful parklands, crisscrossed with paths lined with flower beds, and there were low-lying mountains in the background. It was the first time that the young man had set eyes on a mountain. The family promenaded every day, took in the fresh air, and paused for occasional refreshments at the popular Bear Inn. Chopin even managed to climb one of the nearby hills. He boasted to Wiluś Kolberg that he had managed to climb the more than a hundred steps cut almost vertically out of the stone face of the Einsiedelei Hill leading to the Hermitage at the top, adjoining which was a tiny church and a vegetable garden tended by a solitary priest, "from where there is a splendid view."[10] Nonetheless, such activity exhausted him and he had to clamber down on all fours. The therapeutic regimen was strict, involving drinking two glasses of mineral water daily, the first one at 6:00 a.m., supplemented by a draft of whey. The warm water was drawn from wells situated in the *Kurhaus*, each one of which was covered with a wooden podium on which stood an attendant girl with a jug tied to a length of rope, which she would lower into the steaming water several feet below and scoop up jugfuls for the patients. Chopin's allocated well was the "Lau-Brunn" and he lined up with everybody else for his daily ration. The water tasted like ink and patients were given a ginger biscuit to mask the bitter aftertaste. Then came the mandatory promenade around the park, which took place to the accompaniment of a wretched band of wind players, whose out-of-tune playing provoked Chopin into denigrating them as "a

9. KCOL, p. 109. "Madame Chopin from Warsaw in Poland, with her son Fryderyk Chopin, [has] just arrived in order to take the cure. Resident with Herr Bürgel."
10. CFC, vol. 1, p. 62; KFC, vol. 1, p. 70.

group of nondescript caricature-figures, headed by a gaunt bassoon player with a humpy snuff-filled nose, who frightens all those ladies who happen to be afraid of horses."[11] The otherwise peaceful routine at Reinerz was disturbed by news that one of the patients had died, leaving orphaned children. Fryderyk agreed to give a benefit concert and the wealthy patrons of the spa rallied to the cause. The concert took place on August 11 in the spa's main pavilion. It was repeated on August 16. Sufficient money was raised by our young philanthropist to address the immediate plight of the children, who were taken into care by the local authorities. These recitals are noteworthy because they were the first occasions on which Chopin played beyond Poland's borders. They were briefly reported in the *Warsaw Courier*, probably at the instigation of Fryderyk Skarbek.[12]

Forty-five years after Chopin's death, in an attempt to romanticize his stay in Reinerz, the journal *Echo Muzyczne* attached some fictional details to these concerts. It published an article in its issue of August 20, 1894, containing spurious details of "Un amour de jeunesse de Chopin." We are encouraged to believe that Chopin's attendant at the Lau-Brunn was a beautiful young Czech girl named Libusza with whom he became infatuated. He visited the girl in her home in Reinerz, where he met her father, who worked in the local iron foundry. A day or two later the father was crushed to death by a heavy roller at the foundry and the children were orphaned. Through his piano playing the chivalrous Chopin raised enough money to pay for Libusza's journey to her aunt's home in Prague. This tale, an exercise in pure fantasy, is one of those touching legends with which the older Chopin biographers, and even some newer ones, have always been loath to part.

Only one thing spoiled what was an idyllic sojourn at Reinerz, and that was the lack of a good piano on which to practice. In a letter to Elsner, Chopin extolled the beauties of the town, but complained, "Imagine, there is not a single good piano and those which I have seen here give me as much pain as pleasure. Fortunately this martyrdom will not last long; the time for our farewell to Reinerz is drawing near, and on the 11th of next

---

11. CFC, vol. 1, p. 60; KFC, vol. 1, p. 69.
12. Skarbek had settled into the nearby spa of Kudowa with his family, from where he most likely dispatched his report. "This young man has often been heard on the piano in Warsaw," Skarbek wrote, describing the tragic circumstances that had brought about these concerts, "where his talent is always admired." *Warsaw Courier*, August 22, 1826.

month we intend to begin our journey."[13] One wonders how effective Chopin's concerts were, given that the piano offered him "as much pain as pleasure." Four years after the Reinerz sojourn, Ludwika Chopin published a book titled *Józio's Journey*, which adds some welcome detail to the episode. It is an autobiographical account of the journey to Reinerz, as seen through the eyes of seven-year-old Józef Skarbek, the youngest member of the party.[14] Although the book is couched in the style of a morality tale, somewhat in the manner of Klementyna Tańska, Ludwika's literary heroine, it is based on Ludwika's own observations and is therefore a primary source in the reconstruction of the Reinerz episode. Today, incidentally, the main promenade in Reinerz is called "Avenue Fryderyk Chopin."

In recent years it has been argued that the Warsaw doctors made a serious mistake in sending Chopin and Emilia to Reinerz. Hundreds of tubercular patients congregated there each summer and the risk of re-infection was real, especially from those who had entered the final stage of the disease. It was not uncommon for patients to die at the resort. If the success of the "cure" is judged by the outcome, it is worth observing that Emilia died less than a year later, in April 1827, and Ludwika Skarbek followed her to the grave just eight months after that, in December 1827. As for Chopin, his health remained uncertain, and once he was back in Warsaw his physician Dr. Malcz could do little more than compound the first error by recommending a second one: namely, another visit to the Lau-Brunn spa the following summer. The Polish medical scholar Czesław Sielużycki offered a bleak summary of the Reinerz episode when he wrote, "Reinerz continues to bask in the legend of Chopin's visit to this day, yet it was an expensive fiasco for the family."[15]

IV

Countess Skarbek, her grandson Józio, and the two Chopin sisters returned to Warsaw during the first week of September. Chopin and his mother followed them a few days later, on September 11. Both parties

---

13. CFC, vol. 1, pp. 64–65. A facsimile of this letter, the first that we have from Chopin written in French, is reproduced in KCOL, pp. 110–11.
14. *Podróż Józia* (Józio's Journey), Warsaw, 1830.
15. SHC, p. 111.

Chopin; a pencil drawing by
Princess Eliza Radziwiłł
(1826).

traveled via Wrocław (Breslau) to the village of Strzyżewo, where they
were reunited with Chopin's godmother, Anna Skarbek, and her family.
Anna was now married to Stefan Wiesiołowski, who had inherited a large
estate at Strzyżewo. She was already the mother of three small children,
with a fourth soon to be on the way. After the strict regimen at Bad Reinerz it was a pleasure for Fryderyk to relax in the warm atmosphere of
Anna's home, which was situated in the middle of a large cherry orchard
with a fruit and vegetable garden nearby.[16] The Wiesiołowskis' estate
shared a border with Antonin, the summer hunting lodge of Prince Antoni Radziwiłł, which lay just fifteen kilometers away. When the music-
loving Radziwiłł learned that Chopin was in the vicinity, he invited the

---

16. Ludwika Chopin provides a summary description of the Strzyżewo estate in *Józio's Journey*. During this stay the family took young Józio to visit the grave of his grandfather Kacper
Skarbek, who, years earlier, having fled his creditors, had returned to spend his sunset years
with his daughter Anna, until his death in 1823.

youth to pay him a brief visit. He was well aware of Fryderyk's gifts, of course, having heard him play several times in Warsaw. While the sixteen-year-old youth played the piano for Radziwiłł and his friends, the prince's daughter Eliza sat in the background and produced a pencil drawing of him that is rarely absent from modern iconographies.[17]

These visits to Strzyżewo and Antonin, brief as they were, probably did Fryderyk far more good than his entire stay in Reinerz, the much-touted health benefits of the famous spa notwithstanding, and helped to prepare him for his return to Warsaw, where he was about to become a first-year student in the High School for Music under Józef Elsner.

---

17. The Polish scholar Henryk Nowaczyk has cleared away the confusion surrounding the dates of Eliza Radziwiłł's drawings of Chopin and their connection to the composer's two known visits to Antonin, in 1826 and 1829, respectively. His detailed commentary on this matter may be read in NCGB, pp. 316–23.

AT THE WARSAW
HIGH SCHOOL FOR MUSIC,
1826–1828

With Żywny and Elsner even the greatest jackass would learn.
—Chopin[1]

I

Chopin began his formal studies in Warsaw's High School for Music toward
the end of September 1826. The details of his higher musical education
are not easy to disentangle, but the main facts are as follows. Established
in 1821, the old Warsaw Conservatory of Music was riven almost from the
start by a serious quarrel between its founding rector, Józef Elsner, and its
recently appointed principal, Carlo Soliva, an Italian singing teacher who
had been brought in to organize the practical courses. Elsner considered
Soliva incompetent, and relations between the two men declined so pre-
cipitously that Elsner withdrew from the faculty. A compromise was found
that resulted in the creation of two separate institutions, with Soliva heading a reorganized Conservatory of Music offering practical courses, and
Elsner heading a newly formed High School for Music offering theoretical
ones. The Conservatory retained its old quarters in the former Convent of
the Sisters of Saint Bernardine, while the High School became affiliated
with the University of Warsaw and occupied space in the Casimir Palace,

---

1. CFC, vol. 1, p. 112; KFC, vol. 1, p. 96.

where the Chopins lived. The quarrel between Soliva and Elsner festered for years and was still in full swing when Chopin began his higher studies. His decision to enroll in the High School rather than the Conservatory was probably influenced by his father, who wanted him to take some university courses in the humanities, not just in music. Elsner, from whom Chopin had been taking informal lessons for several months and was now to become his principal teacher, already enjoyed the rank of University Professor of Composition.

We know that Elsner treated Chopin leniently and took into account his delicate health whenever it kept him away from the classroom. From his correspondence we gather that Chopin took six hours of instruction each week from Elsner, mainly in harmony, counterpoint, and composition. He also continued to study foreign languages—German, Italian, and English—although it has to be said that the latter left few traces of a visitation in later life. For the rest, he was given a great deal of freedom by Elsner, who was well aware of the unusual gifts of his young prodigy. That Chopin had no interest in becoming a full-time university student, a path followed by several of his peers, is evident from a disclosure that he made to Jasio Białobłocki shortly after being admitted to the High School. It had to do with his unwillingness to repeat the final year of the curriculum, a requirement for anyone wishing to gain admission to the university. "It would be absurd to sit through the same lessons again when I might learn other things in the course of the year," he wrote.[2] Chopin was farsighted enough to realize that his career was already moving in a different direction from that of the other students. There was, of course, a good deal of intermingling between the Conservatory and the High School. Soliva had no hesitation in borrowing Chopin as an accompanist for his singing classes, and Chopin took part in numerous Conservatory concerts as well. For a time his musical studies overlapped with some informal university courses, which he later abandoned. He attended occasional classes in Polish literature, taught by the celebrated poet Kazimierz Brodziński, who introduced him to the epic ballads of Adam Mickiewicz. And he also enrolled in a class devoted to Polish history, taught by the distinguished historian Feliks Bentkowski. Lessons in piano playing were not pursued, because he had nothing to gain from them. The most that we can say is

---

2. CFC, vol. 1, pp. 67–68; KFC, vol. 1, p. 73.

that Chopin's studies were flexible. His main preoccupation was with composition, and it was here that his work with Elsner proved vital. Elsner
continued to live in the apartment he had always occupied in the old
Conservatory building on Mariensztat Street, next to the Royal Castle.
Because there were not so many students enrolled in the High School, he
sometimes taught Chopin and the others in his own home, rather than in
the more formal setting of the classrooms in the Casimir Palace.[3]

Elsner was a man of vastly different caliber from Chopin's earlier
teacher Żywny. Composer, performer, conductor, administrator, and
teacher, he was an all-rounder well suited to run the High School, and he
became the most important influence on the teenage Chopin's musical
development. In earlier years Elsner had traveled widely, visiting Paris,
Dresden, and Vienna, among other places, which helped him form some
important connections and develop those catholic tastes that never deserted him. Born in Grottkau near Breslau in 1769, Elsner was first drawn
to the priesthood, a vocation he abandoned in favor of medical studies,
which he pursued for a time in Vienna. It was there, in the Austrian
capital, that he found his true calling, and the study of music became his
all-consuming passion. He was an able violinist, serving as an orchestral
player in Brünn; but it was as a conductor and composer that his musical
gifts found their fullest expression. He spent his prentice years as Kapellmeister at Lemberg (Lviv), where he met his first wife, Klara Abt, who
died within a year of the marriage. In 1799, Elsner arrived at a position that
was to define him, that of chief conductor of the Warsaw Opera. Within
a few short years he had turned it into one of Poland's national institutions, freeing it from the Prussian-dominated repertoire that stifled native
enterprise. Polish opera in the Polish language became central to Elsner's
agenda. He was helped in this patriotic aspiration by his gifted young
deputy Karol Kurpiński, whom he appointed in 1810, and who eventually
succeeded him on the podium. Elsner's second wife was the Polish-born
Karolina Drozdowska, whom he married in 1802. During the years that
followed, the Elsners' home became thoroughly Polonized and he himself
became fluent in the language.

Elsner wrote a very large body of works, including twenty-seven Polish
operas (most of which were performed at the National Opera under his

---

3. MCW, p. 117.

baton); eight symphonies; six string quartets; and numerous piano pieces. A major part of his output took the form of religious and secular choral music, including no fewer than twenty-four settings of the Latin Mass and fifty-five cantatas. Many of his choral pieces show a mastery of counterpoint, which, in the happy phrase of one biographer, "seems to demonstrate that he had no ill will against the scholastic forms."[4] Elsner's music survived neither its time nor its place, but it garnered respect from his peers. As for his students, they admired him deeply, and none more so than Chopin.

Elsner brought some useful maxims about music and musicians to bear on his life as a teacher. They reveal a born mentor of wide intelligence, far removed from the petty pedagogues of the day. Elsner understood that the Latin root of the word "education" (*educere*) means "to lead forth." And he did indeed lead his students forth in their quest to discover not only the world around them, but also the world within them. Like the good teacher that he was, he had no interest in producing clones, either of himself or of others. He knew that his chief function was to make himself unnecessary, the ultimate sacrifice that any teacher must be prepared to face. His words about Chopin have secured a special place in the literature, but they tell us as much about him as they do about Chopin. After someone had criticized the young composer for not following the rules of composition, Elsner famously declared, "Let him be. He is following his own path because his gifts are unusual."

Among Elsner's maxims, scattered throughout his writings, we find the following:

1. It is a bad master who is not surpassed by his pupil.
2. To think only of playing the piano is a false idea. It should rather be regarded as a means toward a more complete understanding of music.
3. The study of composition should not be constrained by observing too many petty rules, especially by pupils whose gifts are self-evident. Allow them to discover the rules for themselves.
4. One should never expose a pupil to just one method, or just one point of view.

---

4. NFC, vol. 1, p. 37.

5. It is not enough for the pupil to equal or surpass his master: rather he should create his own individuality.

6. An artist should open himself to his surroundings. Only then, and only through such influence, can he attain his true self.

7. Each part of a composition should share the same objective: it should belong to the whole. Otherwise the beauty of a work is lost, for all beauty arises from the union of multiple parts.

This last maxim, which may be found in Elsner's "Treatise on Melody and Chant," points to his strikingly modern thinking about musical structure.[5] One can see a connection between his "union of multiple parts" and the Schoenbergian concept of the *Grundgestalt*, the basic all-embracing idea that generates the unity of contrasting themes and allows the whole structure to hang together. We do not know if Elsner openly discussed such ideas with Chopin, but Chopin's large-scale works—especially the sonatas, ballades, and scherzos—reward inspection along these lines.

We sometimes hear that Chopin was Elsner's favorite pupil, a judgment that requires some modification. The youth did not do as well as his older classmates Tomasz Nidecki and Ignacy Dobrzyński, both of whom emerged with higher marks. They applied themselves diligently to the production of church masses set to Latin texts, together with trios, fugues, and sonatas in the classical style, meant to satisfy the requirements of the syllabus, an activity in which Chopin showed so little interest that he could almost be called derelict. Elsner taught composition by taking the empty scaffolding of existing works—form, key scheme, thematic contrasts, and tempo—and having his students unfold their own music across it, bar for bar, a method that survives to this day because it helps the student to control large-scale musical forms. It was with one such composition, a "Mass for Four Voices, with Orchestral Accompaniment," that Nidecki was able to secure a grant from the Polish government for travel abroad. When Chopin applied for similar funding a year or two later, he was turned down, presumably because he was unable or unwilling to submit a composition that met the academic requirements.

---

5. Ms. 2276. Biblioteka XX Czartoryskich, Kraków.

II

Among Chopin's classmates at the High School were several who had been boarders with the Chopin family and after graduating from the Lyceum were now pursuing higher studies. Julian Fontana and Ludwik Nidecki (the younger brother of Tomasz) were in the same class as Chopin and were his own age. Ignacy Dobrzyński was in his second year and was developing into a respectable symphonist. As for Józef Stefani and Tomasz Nidecki, they were a few years older than the others and more advanced. Stefani became known for his many polonaises and his nationalistic opera *Krakovians and Gorals*, which was still playing to full houses in the 1840s, and he became the ballet master at the Warsaw National Theater. Tomasz Nidecki was the High School's star pupil and the other students looked up to him. He went first to Vienna, where he was appointed director of the Theater in der Leopoldstadt, before coming back to Warsaw in 1838, succeeding Kurpiński as director of the National Theater.

Every one of these students owed the development of his talent to Józef Elsner, without whose benevolent guidance they might have withered on the vine. Elsner often invited his musical "children" over to his apartment for impromptu get-togethers. His daughter Emilia had a good singing voice and was a frequent participant in these gatherings. Ludwik Nidecki became her regular accompanist; over time their relationship blossomed into romance and then into marriage.

The sheer number of works that Chopin wrote while he was Elsner's student continues to surprise us. Only two of the following compositions (the concertos) were finished after his graduation from the High School in July 1829. The rest were composed within a period of three years (1826–29) and all were completed before his nineteenth birthday.

1. Introduction and Variations in E major on a German National Air ("Der Schweizerbub") (1826)
2. Rondo à la Mazur, in F major, op. 5 (1826)
3. Variations on Mozart's "Là ci darem la mano," for Piano and Orchestra, op. 2 (1827)
4. Numerous pieces for solo piano, including the Nocturne in E minor, op. 72, no. 1 (op. posth.), (1827), and some juvenile

waltzes, mazurkas, and polonaises that were not published until after his death

5. Rondo in C major, for two pianos, op. 73 (op. posth.), (1828)
6. Grand Fantasia on Polish Airs, for Piano and Orchestra, in A major, op. 13 (1828)
7. Rondo à la Krakowiak, for Piano and Orchestra, op. 14 (1828)
8. Sonata no. 1, in C minor, op. 4 (op. posth.), dedicated to Elsner (1828)
9. Piano Trio in G minor, op. 8 (1828–29)
10. Concerto no. 2, in F minor, for Piano and Orchestra, op. 21 (1829–30)
11. Concerto no. 1, in E minor, for Piano and Orchestra, op. 11 (1830)
12. The earliest of the Polish Songs, including "Życzenie" (The Wish) and "Gdzie lubi" (There Where She Loves), settings of poems by Stefan Witwicki (1829)

Chopin also studied orchestration with Elsner. No fewer than five of these compositions are large-scale works for piano and orchestra. This raises a topic that has become threadbare through sheer repetition: namely, Chopin's reticence in dealing with the orchestra, which prevented him from rising much above the mundane level of adding some essential acoustical wallpaper as background for the piano. As an observation this is true enough, but as a criticism it lacks merit. Both Tausig and Klindworth thought fit to reorchestrate the two concertos, changing the balance of the sound here and there. But their editions do nothing that a sensitive conductor cannot achieve in a single rehearsal. The piano and its orchestral accompaniment are well matched, the orchestra providing a perfect foil against which the piano is able to beguile us with one virtuosic effect after another.

III

Nor should we overlook the many hours that Chopin spent at Andrzej Brzezina's music shop on Miodowa Street, browsing through the latest compositions coming out of Vienna, Paris, and Berlin. There was a piano room adjoining the premises where Chopin could play through these pieces, *prima vista*. It was an important part of his education that helped to connect him with the wider musical world beyond Poland's borders, and it was most likely at Brzezina's that the youth came across the nocturnes of John Field. He was taken by the Irish composer's treatment of *bel canto* melodies in the right hand (clearly inspired by the human voice), supported by widespread arpeggios in the left, unfolding across a variety of harmonic progressions. Chopin, open to Field's influence and perhaps recognizing something of his future self in this music, composed his early Nocturne in E minor at this time. He did not think the piece worth publishing and it remained in his portfolio until after his death. Fontana included it in his edition of the posthumous works, where it appears as op. 72, no. 1.

All the hallmarks of Chopin's mature style are present: the singing right hand, the arpeggiated rainbow chords in the left, the inventive variants added to the main melody whenever it reappears, and the whole texture washed in color by the sustaining pedal. The young composer even provides us with a vocal "duet" for his second subject (placed in the faraway key of B major), the sort of contrast we immediately recognize as signature moments in his later nocturnes—especially the ones in C-sharp minor and D-flat major, op. 27, nos. 1 and 2.

In recent times the Polish scholar Tadeusz Zieliński has argued in favor of a much later date for this nocturne, because of its great emotional range (unlikely in one so young, we are told), and because of the presence of those familiar stylistic features we have just mentioned.[6] But these same arguments are open to a different interpretation: that is, Chopin already knew how to steal from his own future, the prerogative of any genius. The piece shows that even in his teens he was moving toward his later self with the somnambulistic certainty of a sleepwalker.[7] Chopin's only encounter with Field, incidentally, which occurred in Paris in 1832 during the Irish pianist's last tour of Europe, revealed the deep ambivalence that each felt toward the other, which was not unrelated to Chopin's "poaching" of the nocturne genre from its inventor, an episode we deal with later on.

IV

Ever since Fryderyk and Emilia had returned from Reinerz the previous year, Mikołaj and Justyna had fretted over the children's health. Mikołaj was continually urging Fryderyk to drink the occasional glass of red wine, which he believed, in common with most Frenchmen growing up in the vicinity of the vineyards of Lorraine, would strengthen the constitution and "produce healthy blood." But Chopin harbored a lifelong dislike for alcohol and generally refused to drink it. The family physician Dr. Wilhelm Malcz had in any case put him on a strict regimen which he found unpleasant. "On Malcz's orders I drink emetic waters and graze on oat gruel, like a horse," he told Jasio Białobłocki. "I also have to be in bed by nine o'clock," he added ruefully, "so all soirées and dances are ruled out."[8] As for Emilia, she had been put on an equally rigorous regimen by Malcz, a diet rich in goat's milk, which the girl abhorred. Ludwika did her best to coax her young sister to drink it "for the sake of Papa," but in February 1827 the girl's health rapidly declined. She took to her bed and never left it. On April 10 the family was visited by tragedy when Emilia died from tuberculosis. She was fourteen years old. As these harrowing events were unfolding, Chopin unburdened himself to Jasio:

---

6. ZFC, pp. 812–13.
7. Julian Fontana was the first to attach the date of 1827 to this nocturne in his edition of Chopin's posthumous compositions. In an abundance of caution, the Polish National Edition, edited by Jan Ekier, suggests the time period 1828–30.
8. CFC, vol. 1, p. 68; KFC, vol. 1, p. 73.

Warsaw, [March 12, 1827]

We have illness in the house. Emilia has been in bed for the past four weeks. She started to cough and spit blood, and Mamma became frightened. Dr. Malcz ordered bloodletting. She was bled once—twice; then countless leeches, blisters, synapisms, and herbal remedies were applied. What nonsense! During the whole time she ate nothing and got so thin that she became unrecognizable; only now is she beginning to recover somewhat. You can guess what we have all been through. Imagine it for yourself, for I cannot describe it.[9]

Dr. Malcz had been brought in the previous year to replace two doctors who had treated both Emilia and Fryderyk—Drs. Girardot and Roemer. Their ineffective remedies had included the application of leeches to the swollen glands of the neck, from which both children were suffering, and in the case of Emilia constant bleedings. Dr. Malcz was vice president of the Charitable Society of Warsaw, and a leading member of the community. His high reputation made the harsh medical treatment he now proposed for Emilia difficult for her parents to resist. There is not much doubt that the girl's unexpectedly swift death was hastened by Malcz's medical care. The repeated bleedings, purges, blisterings, and fastings to which she was subjected, although delivered with the best of intentions, proved impossible for her to survive. Her treatment has been described by one medical authority as "barbarous," a term with which it is difficult to disagree.[10] It was witnessed by the seventeen-year-old Chopin, on whom the experience of watching his sister literally cough herself to death sealed the door on his youth.

Among the mourners at Emilia's funeral were Professor Józef Skrodzki

---

9. CFC, vol. 1, pp. 73–74; KFC, vol. 1, p. 76.

10. LHT, p. 5. Emilia was bled twice with a knife. The incisions were meant to "draw out the disease." A piece of cloth was placed beneath the skin, and the wound was dressed with *Daphne mezereum* to prevent the cut from healing. Leeches were also applied; hot plasters that blistered the skin were a part of the girl's treatment as well; and finally, the poisonous plant wolfsbane—containing the toxin aconite—was administered, either orally or absorbed through the skin. Aconite exerts a deadly effect if taken in overdose. Sweating, nausea, and vomiting are common side effects of this poison, which can overwhelm the respiratory system, disrupt the muscles of the heart, and result in cardiac arrest. There is no known antidote.

and his young son Eugeniusz, who gazed on Emilia's face in her open coffin and later wrote:

> A white coffin, resting on a bier bedecked with garlands of spring flowers, was placed outside the front door of the apartment. Emilcia looked radiant and appeared to be only sleeping. Her still bonny cheeks, a sweet smile, and a gentle air seemed to radiate through her emaciated and pallid face. We children could not comprehend what had happened to her. Then the hearse arrived for the coffin, and the priest, Father Rzymski, dressed in a black cape, put on his biretta, and intoned the hymn for the dead. When the procession moved off, the wailing and crying of her family drove it home to us that we would never see our Emilcia again.[11]

From the Casimir Palace the cortège wended its way toward Powązki Cemetery, where Emilia was buried. Her tombstone bears the following inscription: "Emilia Chopin passed away in the fourteenth spring of her life, like a flower blossoming with the promise of beautiful fruit—10 April, 1827."

Because the tombstone was later moved next to that of her better-known sister Ludwika, who is buried in the same cemetery, the exact location of Emilia's remains is not known. The Chopin family never fully recovered from the death of their youngest daughter, and it was said that Justyna wore black for the rest of her life. They had no regrets when later that year they had to give up their rooms in the Casimir Palace, with its sad memories of sickness and death. The university was expanding and required the space for classrooms. The Chopins were offered new quarters in the nearby Krasiński Palace, and they welcomed the move.

V

Fryderyk's first year at the High School for Music came to a close in July 1827. Despite the stress of the past few months he had applied himself diligently to his work and had held his own against the requirements

---

11. SRCY, *Bluszcz* (Ivy), no. 32, July 28 (August 9), 1882.

of the curriculum. Elsner, in his end-of-year report dated July 17, praised him in one of his famously terse entries: "Instruction in Composition and Counterpoint: 1st year Fryderyk Chopin, especially talented." In the aftermath of Emilia's funeral and the deep well of sadness into which her early death had plunged the family, the invitation that Fryderyk now received from Count Ksawery Zboiński to join him on his estate at Kowalewo, about one hundred kilometers northwest of Warsaw, was especially welcome. Zboiński had known the Chopin family for years. He was Emilia's godfather, and it was probably during the girl's funeral rites a few weeks earlier that the idea of this trip was discussed with Mikołaj Chopin. Fryderyk, it seems, was to be spared the upheavals involved in the family's move to the Krasiński Palace during this painful period of bereavement. He was to escape Warsaw, take in the bracing air of the countryside, and indulge once more in travels across Poland that had by now become a routine part of his summer holidays. The plan this time, however, was for a far more ambitious itinerary that would take him across Pomerania to the northern port city of Gdańsk.

From a letter that Chopin wrote to his parents while he was staying in Count Zboiński's residence in Kowalewo, dated July 6, 1827, we gather that he must have left the High School for Music a couple of weeks early, before the official holidays began. On the morning of his departure from Kowalewo he provided his family with details of his forthcoming trip. "It is 8 o'clock in the morning. The air is fresh, the sunshine is brilliant, the birds are chirping . . . and there is a pond on which the frogs are croaking harmoniously . . . We are first heading for Płock. Tomorrow comes Rościszewo, after that we move on to Kikół; we shall then spend a few days in Turzno, a few more in Kozłowo, and from there we shall go to Gdańsk."[12] Did Chopin ever reach Gdańsk, the gateway to the Baltic Sea? Any account of his sojourn there has to rely on speculation because not a single letter has survived in which he describes the city.[13] Chopin was too

---

12. This letter was misdated "Kowalewo, Friday [1825]" in the Sydow edition of Chopin's correspondence, an error that has worked its way through the literature. The correct date of July 6, 1827, makes clear that this planned trip to Gdańsk was separate from the one that Chopin had taken to Toruń two years earlier, a journey with which it is often confused and even conflated. The ongoing revised edition of the *Korespondencja Fryderyka Chopina*, vol. 1, p. 222, sorts out the proper sequence of events.

13. The most we can say is that the journey was planned by Chopin and no reason has ever been advanced to explain why it would have been abandoned. MSFC, p. 242.

young to have embarked on such an arduous journey alone, which involved crossing the Prussian frontier. Andrzej Bukowski has conjectured that Chopin was chaperoned by Count Zboiński and the count's two cousins who had business matters to attend to along the way.[14] A glance at the map "Chopin's Poland" (page 85) shows that the Zboiński entourage covered several hundred kilometers in the space of four weeks or so. We know that Zboiński and his cousins arrived in Gdańsk on August 9 and stayed at the Drei Mohren (Three Moors) Hotel for five days. Had the teenage Chopin been with them, he would have been registered not under his own name but by the count as *"nebst Familie"* (that is, as a family member). Gdańsk offered many memorable sights for visitors to enjoy, and it is not hard to imagine the excitement that the impressionable youth might have experienced when he first set eyes on the Baltic Sea, with its oceangoing vessels sailing in and out of the harbor. We may plausibly suggest that Chopin, like many a tourist before him, could hardly have failed to visit the imposing St. Mary's Church, with its unique astronomical clock built in the fifteenth century. He may also have gone over to the suburb of Oliwa, because its cathedral boasted something of fascination to all musicians: namely, the world's largest organ, which featured 83 stops, 5,100 pipes, and 3 manuals, complete with moving cherubs and trumpet-playing angels. The instrument required seven men to work the bellows. Pastor Johann Linde also lived in Gdańsk. He was the older brother of Dr. Samuel Linde, Chopin's former principal at the Warsaw Lyceum, and the minister of the Protestant Church of the Holy Trinity. It would have been difficult for the youth to have left Gdańsk without going to the pastor's house on Tobiasz Street to pay his respects. But all this must remain within the realm of conjecture. Chopin would in any case have left Gdańsk by August 15, because during the days following there is evidence that he stayed as a guest of the music-loving Count Antoni Sierakowski, a relative of Zboiński's, at his imposing palace in Waplewo, one hundred kilometers away. This visit to Waplewo is confirmed in a biography of Count Sierakowski, written by his grandson Adam. After reminding us that Antoni was a good violinist who composed a great deal, the author tells us that "the famous composer Chopin was his friend and

---

14. *Pomorskie wojaze Chopina* (Chopin's Travels in Pomerania), Gdańsk, 1993.

The Chopin family salon in the Krasiński Palace; a watercolor by Antoni Kolberg (1832). Sitting around the table are Mikołaj and Justyna Chopin with their daughters Ludwika and Izabella. Chopin was no longer in Warsaw.

guest at Waplewo."[15] The Waplewo Palace was described at the time as a "cultural oasis" in the heavily commercialized region around Gdańsk.

From Waplewo, Chopin traveled by stages back to Warsaw, and by early September he was ensconced in the family's new apartment on the second floor of the Krasiński Palace. He had been away from home for two months and everything had been made ready for him. Even his beloved Buchholtz grand piano had been set up in the main salon by the windows. There was an unused attic above the main room, but since it had no access they eventually built a staircase leading from one of the bedroom closets to the upper level so that Chopin could have his own study and work undisturbed on an old upright piano and a desk that Mikołaj installed for him. "It is to be my own place of refuge," Chopin wrote.[16] As for the family salon, it was to assume some importance in the musical life of

15. Andrzej Bukowski: *Waplewo. Zapomniana placówka kultury polskiej na Pomorzu Nadwiślańskim* (Waplewo. A Forgotten Institution of Polish Culture in Pomerania), p. 109.
16. CFC, vol. 1, p. 93; KFC, vol. 1, p. 86.

Warsaw because it became the venue for several concerts in which Chopin tried out new works in front of the city's artistic and intellectual elite, including his two piano concertos. The Krasiński Palace remained Chopin's home for the next three years, until his final departure from Poland, on November 2, 1830.

VI

While completing the routine exercises in harmony and counterpoint that Elsner had set him, Chopin had quietly worked at his own things, including the Rondo à la Mazur, op. 5, and the early "Schweizerbub" Variations. But it is in the variations on Mozart's "Là ci darem la mano" from *Don Giovanni* that the seventeen-year-old's mastery of the keyboard stands revealed. The work probably started out as an end-of-term assignment, set by Elsner in the early summer of 1827 to encourage his protégé to try his hand at a large-scale piece for piano and orchestra. We surmise that Chopin already had these variations in his portfolio when he set out on the long journey to Gdańsk, and he worked on them intermittently along the way. Even for the modern pianist they provide technical challenges in abundance. Since Chopin played them in public twice before his twentieth birthday, to great acclaim, we can say without hesitation that he was already a virtuoso of the front rank. Did Chopin ever see *Don Giovanni* on the stage? The opera was brought into the repertory of the Warsaw National Theater on January 5, 1823, under the direction of Kurpiński, and Chopin would have been familiar with this production—sung in Polish. The correspondent of the *Warsaw Gazette* later wrote, "Nothing has ever been sung in a Polish opera house better and more appropriately than the two finales and the duet between Don Giovanni and Zerlina, 'Là ci darem la mano.'" The same journal also makes the interesting disclosure that the duet was "often sung on the French stage here by Mlle Konstancja"—an early reference to Chopin's "distant beloved," Konstancja Gładkowska.[17]

The overall scheme of the work is simple enough, consisting of a slow Introduction, a Theme, a set of Five Variations with orchestral interludes, and a Finale in the style of a polonaise. The theme "Là ci darem la mano"

---

17. Issue of May 28, 1828.

("Give me thy hand, oh fairest / Whisper a gentle 'Yes'") is one of the most famous melodies in the realm of opera. It comes from Act One and takes the form of a seduction duet, sung by Zerlina and her enticer, Don Giovanni. Mozart sets the scene in A major, but Chopin transposes it up one semitone to B-flat major, presumably for greater physical comfort at the keyboard.

The variations that follow are typical of the "stile brillante," a genre made notable by Hummel, Clementi, Moscheles, and Weber, who were among the youthful Chopin's models for piano and orchestra. (The Beethoven concertos, with their deeper substance and weightier role for the orchestra, were slow to reach Warsaw and Chopin only became familiar with them later on.) Brilliance, facility, and the kind of bravura execution requiring what the Germans call *Fingerfertigkeit* are all features of the "stile brillante," and Chopin was not to shake off its influence until after his departure from Warsaw. The first variation is typical of the genre and is worthy of Hummel, whom Chopin would meet in Warsaw the following year.

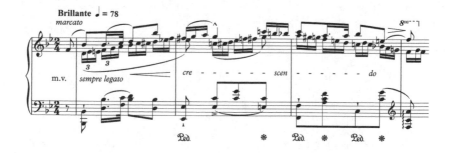

Variation IV reminds us that Chopin was known in Warsaw as "the Paganini of the piano" and was openly referred to as such in the *Warsaw Courier*. The spiccato leaps for which the Italian violinist was famous find their counterpart in this variation. Pianists remain grateful that Chopin cast the work in B-flat major, for Mozart's original key of A major would have rendered such passages yet more difficult to execute.

Variation V brings us to Friedrich Wieck's "fantastic tableau" (whose bizarre interpretation, dismissed by Chopin, was touched on in the Prologue). This is nonetheless theatrical music inspired by events on the stage, an operatic scenario filled with melodramatic asides and romantic yearning. It leads to a Finale marked "Alla Polacca" in which Mozart's famous theme is metamorphosed and clothed in the garments of Poland's national dance. This unexpected touch of patriotism was surely designed to please Elsner, although it may have been the last straw for Chopin's nemesis Ludwig Rellstab, who used it to dismiss the work as "a product of the vandalism wrought by the Slavic composer on Mozart's masterpiece."[18]

Chopin eventually handed over his "summer assignment" to Elsner, who, perceiving the exceptional qualities of the work, sent the manuscript to Tobias Haslinger in Vienna with a strong recommendation that it be published. In due course a printed copy found its way into Schumann's hands, producing one of the most famous imperatives in the annals of music criticism, "Hats off, gentlemen, a genius!"[19]

18. *Iris*, November 5, 1830.
19. *AmZ*, December 7, 1831. The original manuscript of the Variations is preserved in the Morgan Library under the call number C549.L139. On its last two pages we find several "variants" as Chopin tries out different ways of decorating Mozart's theme, and he dates them "1827." There is also a canceled variation, consisting of difficult arpeggiated chords for two hands moving in contrary motion, which was originally to have been no. IV, but was eventually set aside. Chopin's cavalier treatment of the manuscript ought not to go unremarked. With no writing paper to hand he has turned the last page into a sketch pad. It bears a drawing of a monument together with a cartoon of a military-looking figure in dress uniform, possibly a general or a sea captain, complete with epaulets, a high collar, and brushed-back hair. We speculate that since Chopin nearly always sketched from life, both the monument and the military officer may have been encountered on the recent trip to Gdańsk.

VII

One of the first concerts to take place in the new apartment in the Krasiński Palace marked Mikołaj Chopin's name day, which fell on December 6. The salon was crowded and extra chairs were brought in to seat some notable guests from the High School and Warsaw University, which on this occasion included Elsner, Fryderyk Skarbek, Professor Jakub Hoffmann, and the ever-present Skrodzki family. Wojciech Żywny, who had helped to organize everything, was highly visible in a new cravat and waistcoat proudly sported for the occasion. First came some chamber music by Mozart, Haydn, and Beethoven, followed by some pieces played by Chopin's sisters. Chopin then took his place at the keyboard. Eugeniusz Skrodzki had no recollection of what the seventeen-year-old Chopin played, but "I remember the loud and long applause given at the end of Chopin's performance. Skarbek . . . jumped from his chair, and embraced Chopin with affection, congratulating him on his fantastic playing."[20]

Three weeks after witnessing his godson's triumph, Fryderyk Skarbek found himself mourning the death of his mother, Countess Ludwika, who succumbed to tuberculosis of the throat and passed away in Warsaw on December 31. This loss affected the Chopin family as well, for Ludwika had always been a pillar of strength and had acted as a surrogate grandmother to Chopin and the other children. It was at her home in Żelazowa Wola that some of their happiest memories were enshrined. The circumstances of her death brought no comfort to the family. She passed away in the house of her doctor, Kacper Kozicki, most likely as a result of a failed surgical intervention on her throat.[21] Hardly had Chopin come to terms with her passing than Jasio Białobłocki died of tuberculosis of the bone, on March 31. Jasio's slow and painful death, while not unexpected, still came as a heavy blow. Within less than a year tuberculosis had carried off three people in Chopin's inner circle: first Emilia, then Countess Ludwika, and now Jasio, unwelcome reminders of the toll the disease could take. There is little doubt that Chopin already knew he suffered from the same illness, despite the opaque language used by his doctors.

---

20. SRCY, *Bluszcz* (Ivy), no. 33, August 4 (16), 1882.
21. MCW, p. 147.

Meanwhile, he sought refuge in work, redoubled his efforts at the High School, and composed his youthful Piano Sonata in C minor, op. 4, which he dedicated to Józef Elsner. The inscription on the title page of the manuscript, which Chopin wrote in French, reads:

> *Sonate pour le pianoforte dédiée à Mr Josef Elsner,*
> *Professeur à l'Université Royale de Varsovie, Membre*
> *de la Société Philomatique de Varsovie, Chevalier de l'ordre*
> *de St. Stanislas etc., etc. Composée par Frédéric Chopin.*

Elsner's acceptance of the dedication is written in his own hand on the same page. Obviously pleased with the work of his pupil, Elsner once again contacted Tobias Haslinger in Vienna with a recommendation that the work be published. But Haslinger set the sonata aside, fearing perhaps that a juvenile work by an unknown composer might lose money. Years later, after Chopin had become famous, the wily publisher sent some proof sheets to Chopin, who refused to correct them, because he had never been paid a penny for the manuscript. Haslinger appears to have circulated the proofs privately among musicians in Austria and Germany, because in the summer of 1839 Chopin told Julian Fontana, "My father writes that my old Sonata has been published by Haslinger and that the German critics praise it."[22] This announcement was premature, however. It was left to Karl Haslinger (Tobias's son) to publish the sonata in an unauthorized edition in 1851, after Chopin's death, without the dedication to Elsner. Fontana finally took back the rights and included the work in the posthumous edition with which we are now familiar.

In the spring of 1828, Chopin made the acquaintance of Johann Nepomuk Hummel, who came to Warsaw and gave a series of concerts during the months of April and May. The virtuoso pianist was now fifty years old and at the height of his fame. He was the leading representative of the "stile brillante," famous for his masterful fluency and the mechanical perfection of his passagework. Chopin found in his playing an ideal blend of virtuosity and classical restraint. While Hummel might not have been able to make the piano sing (a complaint made by the critic Maurycy Mochnacki in the columns of the *Warsaw Daily*, who found his playing "too German"),

---

he was able to dispatch the most difficult passages with ease while remaining immobile at the keyboard, qualities that Chopin admired and came to emulate. Hummel brought with him much more than his reputation as pianist, however. He was now the last living representative of an age that had almost vanished. As a small boy he had lodged with Mozart and had received lessons from him. Later he had studied with Haydn, from whom he had inherited the position of Kapellmeister to Prince Esterházy in Hungary. His studies with Albrechtsberger in Vienna had brought him in touch with Beethoven, with whom he had established an uneasy friendship. He was present at Beethoven's deathbed, and was a pallbearer at the composer's funeral. When Hummel walked onto the platform of the Warsaw National Theater it was as if history itself were present. Despite the wide difference in their ages, the two pianists forged a collegial relationship, and during Chopin's temporary sojourn in Vienna, following the Polish uprising, Hummel did not forget the young musician from Warsaw and was one of the first persons to greet him and take him under his wing.

On July 22, Chopin successfully completed the second-year requirements of the High School, and Elsner wrote another cryptic end-of-year report: "Instruction in Composition. Chopin Fryderyk: Special ability, second year, gone away for the improvement of his health."

VIII

In fact, Chopin had "gone away" even before the term had ended. He had accepted an invitation to spend the summer of 1828 at Sanniki, an estate in Mazovia that belonged to the wealthy parents of a fellow pupil, Konstanty Pruszak. Sanniki lay about eighty kilometers west of Warsaw, and the palace was one of the finest residences in the province, featuring its own theater where amateur plays were staged. The family traced its roots back to the fifteenth century and bore the Leliwa coat of arms. It is an indication of the wealth of Aleksander Pruszak, Konstanty's father, that when the uprising broke out just over two years later, he financed Polish troops to the tune of 20,000 złotys, which brought Russian retribution in its wake. His estates were ransacked, and much of the palace destroyed.

At Sanniki, Chopin met Konstanty's younger sister Olesia and gave her some piano lessons. He found the girl charming enough to think that she might make an excellent wife for his friend Tytus, but Tytus remained indifferent. With Konstanty and Olesia, Chopin made several forays into the nearby villages dotted around the countryside, and he renewed his contact with Polish folk music. It was at Sanniki that he probably composed the first movement of his Piano Trio in G minor, which he planned to dedicate to Prince Radziwiłł. And it was there, too, that he completed his Rondo in C major (op. 73, op. posth.), a work that he recast almost at once for two pianos, the only composition for this medium that he ever wrote. He later tried it out with his friend Maurycy Ernemann at the Buchholtz piano manufactory, "and it went pretty well." The composition was born neglected, however, which led Chopin to call it "my orphan child." It was eventually taken up by Julian Fontana, "in whom it found a stepfather."[23]

The Sanniki palace offered many comforts and Fryderyk was free to practice and compose whenever he liked. He was now eighteen years old and enjoyed strolling around Sanniki's spacious park in the company of the young governess of the family. It was an innocent-enough pastime, but the daily perambulations of the young couple caught the eye of Countess Marianna Pruszak and led to an unfortunate misunderstanding. The governess became pregnant and Chopin was wrongly suspected of being the father. After further inquiries were made the real seducer was found. It was not until everybody had returned to Warsaw three or four months later, and the Pruszak family were back in their house on Marszalkowska Street, that Chopin was able to explain his predicament in a letter to Tytus, by which time the young woman's pregnancy was visible to all. He identifies the father only by the letter "N."

Warsaw, Saturday, December 27, 1828
N. has got the governess at the house in Marszalkowska Street into trouble. The young lady is going to have a baby and her mistress the Countess refuses to have anything to do with the seducer. The worst of it is that before the whole thing came out I was suspected of being the man because I had spent more than a month at Sanniki and always used to stroll in the garden with the govern-

---

23. CFC, vol. 1, p. 93; KFC, vol. 1, p. 87.

ess. Yes stroll about but nothing more. She is anything but charming. *Like a fool I had no desire for her*—lucky for me.[24]

Chopin's parents had to be brought in before the matter was cleared up, a source of embarrassment to the young man. They acceded to Mme Pruszak's request that Chopin should take over those teaching duties that the condition of the governess did not permit her to fulfill. As if this were not enough, Chopin was asked to become the illegitimate offspring's godfather. He tells us that it was an entreaty he felt unable to refuse because it came from the girl herself![25] After the infant was baptized, the young mother was quietly dispatched to Gdańsk by the Pruszak family and her child put up for adoption.

This crisis was still working itself out when Chopin got back from Sanniki at the beginning of September and was greeted with news of a more welcome kind. He had been invited to accompany one of Mikołaj's academic colleagues, Professor Feliks Jarocki, on a short trip to Berlin, and the journey was to begin in less than one week's time.

24. CFC, vol. 1, p. 92; KFC, vol. 1, p. 86. This paragraph was written by Chopin in Italian (a language that he and Tytus had been studying), in order to protect the identity of "N" from prying eyes. The putative father was Chopin's friend and fellow student Józef Nowakowski (1800–1865), who had studied under Elsner at the High School for Music.
25. CFC, vol. 1, p. 162; KFC, vol. 1, p. 123.

FIRST TRIPS ABROAD:
BERLIN AND VIENNA,
1828–1829

Fryderyk Chopin, third-year student;
Special ability, musical genius.
　　　　　　　　　—*Józef Elsner*[1]

I

Earlier in the summer of 1828 the King of Prussia, Friedrich Wilhelm III, had issued a royal proclamation. The University of Berlin was to host a scientific congress during the two-week period September 14 through 29, to be held under the distinguished chairmanship of the explorer and scientist Alexander von Humboldt. A ripple of excitement swept across Germany's borders as invitations were sent out to the most eminent scientists in Europe. One of the recipients was Dr. Feliks Jarocki, professor of zoology at Warsaw University and a family friend of the Chopins. Jarocki was an alumnus of Berlin University who three years earlier had published an important treatise on zoology that had attracted attention. When Jarocki offered to take Fryderyk along with him, Mikołaj welcomed the idea. What the young man needed at this important stage in his life was exposure to the wider world of music, and the prospect of visiting

---

1. From Elsner's graduation report on Chopin, July 20, 1829. The document is reproduced in BC, abb. 27.

Berlin and meeting some of the scientific and artistic luminaries about to congregate there was an opportunity not to be missed. Fryderyk was also becoming a financial liability for his father. He continued to live at home and enjoyed no regular income. The prospects of a musician, however gifted, gaining a lucrative position in Warsaw were remote. Some such thoughts may have preoccupied Mikołaj as he observed the spectacular development of his son. So the decision was made. On Tuesday, September 9, Professor Jarocki and Chopin boarded the diligence and set out for the Prussian capital.

The journey took five days, and "on Sunday afternoon at about three o'clock we arrived by stagecoach in this too-huge city."[2] After the pair of travelers had checked in to the Kronprinz Inn, Jarocki took Chopin to the home of his old tutor Professor Martin Lichtenstein, rector of Berlin University and secretary of the congress. Lichtenstein in turn introduced the young man to Humboldt, an encounter about which the scholarly record remains obscure. Chopin, in fact, was singularly uninterested in the scientific conference. He managed to tour the thirteen rooms of the impressive Zoological Exhibition, and Jarocki even took him along to a fraternity dinner for the visiting scientists. But Chopin found these worthies so wrapped up in themselves and their rarefied world of intellectual discourse that he referred to them as "caricatures," and even portrayed them as such.

Of greater interest to him were visits to Schlesinger's music shop and a trip to Kisling's piano factory on Friedrichstrasse. He was disappointed to find not a single instrument on which he could practice, so for the rest of his time in Berlin he relied on the inferior piano at the Kronprinz Inn.

On his first full day he explored the city, marveling at the fine buildings, the wide thoroughfares, and the bridges across the Spree River. He found Berlin so vast and scattered in contrast to Warsaw that he told his family it could easily house twice the number of people who lived there. The order and cleanliness that were everywhere in evidence impressed him. In the company of Jarocki he visited the imposing Royal Library and was taken with the enormity of its collections. While there he observed a young man laboriously copying out, word for word, an original letter written by the Polish national hero General Kościuszko. The scribe turned out to

2. CFC, vol. 1, p. 82; KFC, vol. 1, p. 81.

be Kościuszko's twenty-seven-year-old German biographer Karl Falkenstein. When Falkenstein realized he was standing next to two Poles who could read with ease a text over which he himself was struggling, he asked Jarocki to give him a German translation, which he jotted down in his notebook verbatim.

The congress was formally opened on Thursday, September 18, in the presence of the crown prince. Jarocki got Fryderyk a ticket for the event and a seat in the assembly hall. There Fryderyk spotted Gaspare Spontini, Carl Zelter, and most notably Felix Mendelssohn, but he lacked the confidence to approach them. He begged Jarocki to excuse him from attending the private dinner that followed the ceremony, hosted by Humboldt. He felt like an outsider, he told his parents, and he did not wish "to be out of my right place."[3] Because of his diffidence, he and Mendelssohn missed meeting one another by a hairsbreadth. Mendelssohn could have opened many doors in Berlin for Chopin, but it was not to be. Chopin preferred to spend his time in the opera house. He attended performances of Spontini's *Fernando Cortez*, Cimarosa's *Il matrimonio segreto*, Onslow's *Colporteur*, and above all Weber's *Der Freischütz*, the production of which he thought inferior to the one he had attended in Warsaw two years earlier. He also visited the Singakademie and heard Handel's *Ode for Saint Cecilia's Day* directed by Carl Zelter, a work that impressed him deeply. "This is nearest to the ideal I have formed of great music," he wrote.[4]

The day before the congress closed there was a final banquet. Chopin was astonished at the copious amounts of food and drink these scientists were able to put away, and as they gradually lost their inhibitions and alcohol took hold they began to sing, with Zelter conducting. The streetwise Berliners were already making jokes about the sudden improvement in the strength of the local beer, one of which even found its way into a comedy then running at the Königstadt Theater. One beer drinker asks another, "How does the Berlin beer come to be so good just now?" The other replies, "Don't you know that we have scientists in town?"

---

3. CFC, vol. 1, p. 85; KFC, vol. 1, pp. 83–84.
4. CFC, vol. 1, p. 87; KFC, vol. 1, p. 83.

II

On September 28, Jarocki and Fryderyk began their return journey to Warsaw. Their route took them through Poznań, where they had been invited
to attend a banquet at the home of Archbishop Teofil Wolicki. But the diligence had first to pause at the small town of Züllichau for a change of
horses. When it pulled into the market square, they learned that a fresh
relay of horses was not immediately available and a delay of several hours
was expected. It was here that one of the better-known episodes in the
Chopin lexicon took place. Fryderyk noticed an unlikely old piano in an
adjoining room. It turned out to be in better condition than it looked and
it was in tune. So he sat down and began to improvise. This attracted the
attention of his fellow travelers, who entered the room one by one, and soon
a full-scale concert was under way. Chopin wove some Polish melodies
into his improvisation, and his audience was enlarged by the appearance
of the postmaster, his wife, and the couple's two pretty daughters. As Chopin's
Polish fantasia took wing, even the unpleasant German traveler who had
annoyed everyone with his inveterate tobacco smoking on board the diligence became interested and forgot to light his pipe. The spell was broken
by a stentorian voice from the other room: "Gentlemen, the horses are
ready!" The entire audience protested at this untimely interruption. First
the postmaster begged Chopin to continue, but the pianist said that they
were already late and must get to Poznań without further delay. Then the
postmaster's wife implored him to go back to the piano; finally, the two
young daughters appealed in similar vein. The postmaster even promised
extra horses if only Chopin would finish his improvisation. So Chopin ac-
quiesced and a fabric of Polish melodies was once more drawn from the
keyboard. At the conclusion of the performance a servant brought in some
wine and the postmaster proposed a toast: "To the favorite of Polyhymnia!"
A member of the audience, an elderly gentleman who had wandered into
the room when Chopin began to play, was overcome with emotion, approached Chopin, and declared, "I am old now, but am a well-trained
musician; I also play the piano. I know how to appreciate your masterly
playing. If Mozart had heard you, he would have pressed your hand and
exclaimed, 'Bravo!' An insignificant man like me dare not do that." It has
been surmised that the man who invoked the name of Mozart was Can-
tor Friedrich Kähler, who taught music at the Züllichau Pedagogium. In

response to the compliment Chopin played one of his mazurkas before resuming his journey. As the postmaster bade him farewell, he said that he would remember the name of Fryderyk Chopin for the rest of his life.[5] And what of the fantasia that Fryderyk had improvised on that indifferent piano? He remodeled it the following month and turned it into the Grand Fantasia on Polish Airs, for Piano and Orchestra, op. 13.

A few hours later Fryderyk and Jarocki were in Poznań, where they stayed for two days as guests of Archbishop Wolicki at his residence adjoining the cathedral. Aside from attending the banquet that had brought them to Poznań in the first place, Chopin took the opportunity to call on Prince Antoni Radziwiłł, the Prussian appointed governor of Poznań, who happened to be in residence with his family at the Governor's Palace a stone's throw away. Radziwiłł greeted Chopin warmly and arranged for his young guest to play that same evening in his salon, where Chopin once more found himself improvising at the piano—this time to a somewhat different circle of listeners. The scene was later interpreted by the artist Henryk Siemiradzki in his celebrated painting of 1887, *Chopin Playing in the Salon of Prince Antoni Radziwiłł*. Among those present are Prince Radziwiłł (seated); his daughters Princess Eliza (standing by his side) and Princess Wanda (behind her); and various members of the Radziwiłł family and Prussian high society. At the extreme right we also see Alexander von Humboldt, seated. Although the scene is an imaginary one, it portrays the elegance and sophistication of the evening better than many a verbal narrative that has come down to us.

Prince Radziwiłł was a gifted composer and a fine cellist, and it was for him that Chopin composed his Piano Trio in G minor, op. 8. The first movement was already finished by the time of the Poznań visit and the remaining three were slowly coming to fruition. Chopin would certainly have mentioned this work in progress to the prince and might even have rehearsed parts of it with him. By early 1829 all four movements were ready, and later that year Chopin offered Radziwiłł the dedication. Radziwiłł's warm acceptance runs:

---

5. Although modern scholars have cast doubt on this undocumented episode, we surmise that Chopin himself may have related it to his family, who in turn embroidered it before passing it along to his first biographer, Moritz Karasowski. KCLB, pp. 54–55.

Chopin Playing in the Salon of Prince Antoni Radziwiłł, an oil painting by Henryk Siemiradzki (1887).

Antonin, November 4, 1829

My dear Chopin,

I gratefully accept the dedication of your Trio which you are kind enough to offer me. I should even be glad if you would hasten its publication so that I might have the pleasure of playing it with you when you pass through Poznań on your way to Berlin. Accept, my dear Chopin, my renewed assurances of the interest which your talent arouses in me and of the high esteem in which I hold you.

Antoni, Prince Radziwiłł[6]

III

By April 1829, Chopin's studies at the High School for Music were coming to an end, and Mikołaj Chopin petitioned the government for funds to allow his son to travel abroad for further advancement in music. His request was directed to the minister of education, Stanisław Grabowski.

---

6. CFC, vol. 1, p. 139; KFC, vol. 1, p. 111.

May it please your Excellency!

Having been employed for twenty years as a teacher at the War-saw Lyceum and being convinced that I have fully performed my duties to the best of my ability, I venture to address a modest request to Your Excellency and beg for your gracious intervention with the Government, a favor which I shall regard as the best possible reward for my efforts.

I have a son whose innate gifts for music call for further development in this art. His Imperial Majesty Alexander, of blessed memory, Tsar and King of Poland, most graciously deigned to reward him with a precious ring as a token of His satisfaction when my son had the honor of being heard by the Monarch. His Imperial Highness the Grand Duke, Commander-in-Chief, has also allowed him on occasions to give proofs of his talent in His presence. Finally, many respectable persons and connoisseurs can support the view that my son might become a credit to his country in his chosen profession if he were given the opportunity to pursue his studies to their proper completion. He has finished his preliminary course of study, in witness whereof I refer to the Rector of the High School for Music and University Professor, Mr. Elsner. My son now only needs to visit foreign countries, *viz.* Germany, Italy, and France, in order to perfect himself according to the best models.

Since my modest resources, based solely on my salary as a teacher, are insufficient to cover the expense of such a journey lasting perhaps three years, I beg to submit to His Excellency the Minister a humble request that the Administration might draw from the fund which has been placed at the Viceroy's disposal some contribution toward my son's expenses.

I am, with the greatest respect, Your Excellency's humble servant,
Mikołaj Chopin
Professor at the Warsaw Lyceum
Warsaw, April 13, 1829[7]

Minister Grabowski approved the request and appended a note for the attention of Count Tadeusz Mostowski, the minister for home affairs, re-

---

7. CFC, vol. 1, pp. 95–96; KFC, vol. 1, pp. 87–88.

questing 5,000 złotys annually. Mostowski, however, turned it down and left it to one of his functionaries, General Franciszek Kossecki, to break the news to Mikołaj.

> To Mr. Mikołaj Chopin, Professor at the Warsaw Lyceum
> From the Councillor Secretary of State
>   In answer to the petition of Mr. Mikołaj Chopin, dated 13 April, for a grant of funds for his son for the purpose of foreign travel and to improve his talent for playing the piano, by order of His Excellency the President of the Administrative Council, I beg to notify him that the Council, after consulting the Minister of Home Affairs, was not inclined to accede to the request of the petitioner.
>   June 10, 1829
>   General Kossecki[8]

Scribbled in pencil in the margin of this document are the words "Give a negative answer to the petitioner." It seems strange today that Poland's greatest musician, whose name was already a household word, was denied material support by his country. But it was Count Mostowski himself who wrote bluntly, "Public funds should not be wasted [this last word was crossed out and replaced with the word 'assigned'] for the encouragement of this type of artist." If Mikołaj wanted to send his son abroad he would have to subsidize the trip himself.[9]

IV

An unusually brilliant season of musical events had meanwhile begun to unfold at the Warsaw National Theater. On May 17, Tsar Nicholas arrived in Warsaw for his coronation as "King of Poland" and brought with him the entire Imperial Family. Many aristocratic households followed in his

---

8. BC, plate nos. 23 and 24. The history of this strange matter has been traced in somewhat greater detail by the Polish scholar Stanisław Pereświet-Soltan in P-SCB, pp. 64–66.
9. It was a splendid irony, which would not have been lost on Minister Mostowski, that when he and his family were forced to flee to Paris after the failed uprising in 1831, they turned to Chopin and asked him to give piano lessons to their daughter Róża. The composer dedicated his Four Mazurkas, op. 33, to her.

wake and took up temporary residence in the capital. Prince Adam Czartoryski arrived with his retinue and so, too, did Prince Antoni Radziwiłł.
Warsaw was suddenly alive with ceremony and spectacle, and performers
of distinction converged on the city. It has been estimated that the population of Warsaw rose to 200,000 almost overnight. The sixteen-year-old
Hungarian prodigy Stephen Heller, who had made his sensational debut a
year earlier and was now in the middle of a grueling two-year tour of
Europe arranged by his father,[10] gave one of the first concerts and aroused
astonishment. The venerable Polish pianist Maria Szymanowska also
turned up and attracted a large local following. Karol Lipiński, the eminent Polish violinist, was brought in from Lemberg (Lviv) in order to lead
the enlarged National Theater Orchestra. But these artists were eclipsed
by the arrival of Niccolò Paganini, who got to Warsaw on May 21 and set
the city by its ears. The Italian violinist was at the height of his powers,
and he remained in Warsaw for nearly two months and gave twelve concerts. He made his Polish debut on May 23, and as he walked onto the
stage of the National Theater he faced a glittering assembly that may have
been exceptional even for him. The full splendor of the Russian royal court
was on display that night. Grand Duke Constantine was there with an entourage of high-ranking Russian army officers and their wives, as were
many of the aristocratic families who had congregated in Warsaw for
the coronation. Chopin, too, was present and he described Paganini's
playing as "absolute perfection."[11] Among the pieces that Chopin heard
Paganini play was the latter's popular variations on the Italian air "Carnival of Venice," which the violinist had recently published as his op. 10. It
inspired Chopin to try his hand at a similar set of roulades on this same
melody. The result is a charming piece of ninety-one measures. Resting
on a foundation of gently undulating tonic and dominant arpeggios,
Chopin unfolds an increasingly complex set of variations for the right
hand, foreshadowing a plan that he was to use many years later in his
celebrated Berceuse.

10. Unwisely, as it happens. The young man collapsed from nervous exhaustion when he got
to Augsburg, and he abandoned the life of a traveling virtuoso. BSH, pp. 7–8.
11. CPG, vol. 1, p. 342. Paganini's opening concert netted him a handsome profit of 10,953
florins. A complete list of his Warsaw concerts may be found in Xavier Rey's *Niccolò Paganini—
le romantique Italien*, Paris, 1999, pp. 327–28.

Typical of his approach is the following variation, which buries the old Italian melody beneath a cascade of notes. It reveals the nineteen-year-old to be in impressive technical form, even though the musical results quite naturally cannot rise much above the trivial nature of the theme itself. Nevertheless, this preoccupation with technical problems was necessary for Chopin. By his conquering such passages, absorbing them and making them his own, they became stepping-stones to greater things.

These double thirds spring from Paganini's own variations, which abound in them. It is as if the youthful Chopin were saying, "And I too can do this." A comparison between the two compositions, in fact, reveals the following roulades to be first cousins to the ones we find in Variation III from the Paganini set.

The "Souvenir de Paganini" remained in manuscript until 1881, when it was published as a supplement to the Warsaw periodical *Echo Muzyczne*. No one plays it nowadays, but it retains its fascination for the aficionado, and for anyone wishing to trace the evolution of Chopin's approach to the keyboard.

V

The day following Paganini's opening concert marked the occasion of Tsar Nicholas's coronation, May 24. A solemn service in St. John's Archcathedral featured a chorus of three hundred singers performing Elsner's specially commissioned Coronation Mass, directed by the composer himself. Then followed a state banquet at the Royal Castle and a command performance at which Paganini played before 130 specially invited Polish guests. As a mark of his pleasure the tsar presented the violinist with a diamond ring.

The delicate political situation surrounding the coronation led to dissent among younger Poles who were looking for a reason to assert their patriotism. Why had the foreigner Paganini been invited to play for the tsar when there was an equally great violinist in Warsaw who was Polish born and bred? This was a reference to Karol Lipiński, regarded by many as a serious rival to Paganini. The two violinists had first met more than ten years earlier, when Lipiński had traveled to Italy to seek out Paganini, and they had given two concerts in Padua. That may also have marked the beginning of their rivalry, which, it must be added, was never marred by overt hostility. Lipiński's full, rich tone, developed through his contacts with his idol Ludwig Spohr, had made him a leading representative of the "classical" school of violin playing. (Lipiński later became the teacher of Joachim and Wieniawski.) Paganini, on the other hand, who had no discernible lineage and was therefore unique, was regarded as a "romantic."

The tsar's coronation provided the unlikely venue for a musical confrontation of some importance to the Poles. Because Lipiński had been engaged to lead the National Theater Orchestra throughout the coronation festivities, he found himself in a subservient position whenever Paganini stood on the platform just a few feet away, playing his formidably difficult repertoire. The situation was made tolerable for Lipiński because his name had been placed on the roll of coronation honors, and he now enjoyed the imposing title of "First Violinist to the Tsar of Russia and King of Poland." It was the counterpart to Paganini's diamond ring, as the Italian's leading biographer puts it, but it could not placate Lipiński's supporters.[12] The controversy was taken up by the press, and Lipiński was urged

---

12. CPG, vol. 1, p. 337.

to give a concert of his own and challenge Paganini in the court of public opinion. Carlo Soliva, who had met Lipiński in Italy and truly admired him, counseled against the idea. Paganini had given concerts almost nightly since his arrival and had built up a formidable following. Better to let the matter rest.[13] Under different circumstances, the good-natured Lipiński might not have been provoked. But the rabble-rousers caught the attention of the press, and rumors were started that Lipiński was actually a pupil of Paganini's, a story that was untrue and that the Polish violinist denied. It all became too much and Lipiński announced his own concert for June 5.

It was an unfortunate decision. Warsaw witnessed a heavy thunderstorm on the day of the concert and Lipiński played to a half-empty hall, although Paganini himself was present. The reviews were good, however, and some thoughtful comparisons were made between the two violinists, not always to Paganini's advantage. One such article in the *Dziennik Powszechny* (Universal National Journal) was critical of Paganini and created a stir. It was written by Krystyn Lach-Szyrma, professor of philosophy at Warsaw University and a leading member of the "Jeunes Polonais" movement.

It is only in [Paganini's] own works that he is brilliantly effective . . . The works of others confront him with difficulties that he is unable to master, owing to the peculiar nature of his playing. Where it is a question of noble, powerful tone, of daring, passionate bowing, of a pure cantabile—in short, wherever he should bring out all the inherent beauties of the instrument, he merely displays technical dexterity . . .

To this, Lipiński presents a striking contrast. This great artist holds strictly to the canons of art. He never transgresses the standards of good taste and disdains all shimmering ornamentation. If one can call Paganini a Romantic, Lipiński justly deserves the epithet Classicist, in the finest sense of the word. His bowing is far superior to Paganini's and he is also his superior in power and fullness of tone, in soulful cantabile playing and in harmonics. He is

---

13. The Italian-born Soliva was in a delicate position and could not afford to take sides. He was acting as Paganini's host for much of the time, and his wife was looking after Paganini's three-year-old son, Achille, during the entire Warsaw visit. The violinist was inseparable from this young child, who accompanied him everywhere on the European tours.

Paganini's peer in rapid playing, but inferior to him in light staccato playing, in the less important transitions from the natural tones
to harmonics, and finally in pizzicato with the left hand.[14]

This partisan language was regarded as a libel against Paganini and stoked
the fires of a press war, with supporters of both violinists venting their conflicting views. Paganini was invited to reply but kept a monastic silence.
Lipiński, however, was drawn into the fray because he was openly taunted
by his detractors to admit not only that he was a pupil of Paganini's, but
that he had prompted Lach-Szyrma to write the article. He issued a dig-
nified denial to both charges.

> My own father taught me the rudiments of music and I am neither
> the product of a master nor of any conservatory. If I had studied
> with Paganini, I should be quite ready to admit it and should con-
> sider it a great honor . . . I made Paganini's acquaintance in Italy in
> 1818, when he was good enough to call me a "Valente Professore di
> Violine." We gave two concerts together, but that was the extent of
> our association . . .
>   Never before, at home or abroad, have false facts been used to
> humiliate me. No one has ever accused me of such things except
> the capital of my own country, which I am visiting for the second
> time. As much as I admire Paganini's great talent, I cannot, and
> never will, lay claim to a comparison with him since I have chosen
> an entirely different genre, in which I am zealously striving to per-
> fect myself so that some day I can call out to my countrymen—
> "*anch'io son pittore.*"[15]

Paganini gave his final concert on July 14, in benefit of the widows and
orphans of Polish musicians. In tribute to Elsner he played for the first
(and apparently the last) time his recently completed "Warsaw Sonata,"
which contains variations on one of Elsner's mazurkas. Two days later

---

14. Issue of June 13, 1829.
15. CPG, vol. 1, p. 340. "And I too am an artist!" This famous exclamation, often attributed to
Michelangelo, was made by Correggio when he first beheld Raphael's painting of Saint
Cecilia—the patron saint of music. Lipiński's letter appeared in the *Warsaw Gazette*, June 20,
1829.

Elsner invited the violinist to the High School for Music and introduced him to Chopin. Paganini noted in his Libro Rosso that he met "M. Chopin, *giovine pianista*" ("Chopin, the young pianist"). In an attempt to heal the partisan rift between Paganini and Lipiński, Elsner arranged to give them a farewell banquet. Unfortunately, Lipiński had to leave Warsaw before the banquet could be held, so the money that Elsner had raised to pay for it was used instead for the purchase of a gold snuffbox for Paganini. Elsner tells us that he presented it to Paganini "in the name of the artists and music-lovers of Warsaw as a souvenir of his stay, bidding him farewell among cheers and toasts drunk in foaming champagne."[16]

Paganini departed Warsaw on July 19. The following day Chopin sat for his final examinations at the High School and passed with flying colors. Elsner's concluding report ran: "Szopen, Friderik [*sic*], third year student; special ability, musical genius."

VI

The time had now come for Chopin to test himself abroad. The rejection of the petition for funds to assist in this purpose had rankled both Mikołaj and Elsner, but it could not be allowed to stand in the way of the larger goal. Chopin had continued to make plans for his first professional foray beyond Poland's borders, a journey that was to take him to Vienna and his first foreign triumphs, followed by brief sojourns in Prague and Dresden. Two days after his graduation everything was in place. Mikołaj himself advanced the money to cover the expenses of the journey—one of several similar acts of generosity toward his son. On the morning of Wednesday, July 22, Chopin and four traveling companions boarded the diligence waiting outside the Warsaw post office and began the first leg of the trip along the old postal route to Kraków—the halfway point to Vienna. Besides Chopin, the group consisted of four school friends—Ignacy Maciejowski, Marceli Celiński, Mieczysław Potocki, and Alfons Brandt. Romuald Hube, a twenty-six-year-old professor of Polish history at Warsaw University, was

---

16. The snuffbox bears an inscription in Italian: "*Al Cav Niccolò Paganini. Gli ammiratori del suo talento. Varsovia 19 Luglio 1829.*" This ceremony was reported in the *Polish Gazette*, July 22, 1829.

placed in charge of the group. The diligence traveled both day and night, with halts every forty kilometers or so to refresh the horses, and within forty-eight hours the little party was in Kraków.

Chopin was seeing Poland's ancient capital for the first time. The effect of its old buildings, which resonated with history, sincerely affected the young patriots and they lingered in the city for almost a week. On July 26, they hired a peasant and his cart to take them to nearby Ojców in order to view the ruins of the fourteenth-century castle built by Poland's former king Kazimierz III. By the time the exploration had ended it was dusk. With little chance of getting back to Kraków before nightfall, Chopin and his friends decided to put up for the night at an inn run by the Indyk family in the village of Pieskowa Skała, which lay just beyond the castle on the other side of the Prądnik River. Unfortunately the driver of the cart lost his way in the twilight and the vehicle became stuck in the swiftly flowing water. The young adventurers abandoned the cart and waded to the opposite bank. It was already 9:00 p.m. and they still had to clamber over slippery rocks and through wet grass for another kilometer or so. By the time they got to the Indyks' house their feet and legs were soaking wet. Chopin related this nocturnal adventure in a long letter to his family; but when he came to describing the Indyk house itself, he addressed his remarks especially to Izabella.

> Izabella! We stayed at the same place where Mlle Tańska stayed![17] All my friends undressed and dried themselves at the blaze kindled in the fireplace by the worthy Mme Indyk. I alone, having sat down in the corner, wet to the knees, meditated whether to undress and dry myself or not; until lo! I saw Mme Indyk leave the room in order to fetch some bedding. I had the happy inspiration to follow her and noticed a quantity of woolen Krakovian caps. These caps are of double thickness, like nightcaps. I bought one for a złoty, tore it in two, then, having taken off my shoes, I wrapped my feet in each one of the pieces. I attached them with some string,

17. This was Klementyna Tańska-Hoffman (1798–1845), who edited a periodical for young readers called *Children's Recreations*, and was famous throughout Poland for her adventure stories. Izabella, to whom Chopin addressed his remarks, was already taking a lively interest in literature and in the fate of orphans and abandoned children, themes that informed Tańska-Hoffman's work.

which certainly saved me from catching a cold. Drawing near the fireplace, I drank some wine, laughed with my good friends, and meanwhile Mme Indyk made a bed for us on the floor, where we slept soundly.[18]

He summed up the escapade with the comment, "The great beauty of Ojców was worth a soaking if nothing else." The following morning the party got back to Kraków and after two more days of sightseeing they continued their journey along the postal route and its various way stations leading to Austria. On July 31, Chopin caught his first glimpse of the imperial city.

VII

He lost no time in seeking out the publisher Tobias Haslinger and handing him a letter of recommendation from Elsner. The Haslinger music shop was located in the Graben, the most famous street in Vienna. It was a central meeting place for musicians who went there to browse among the books, try out the latest pieces on the house piano, and even use the establishment as a ticket office for their concerts. Busts of Beethoven, Haydn, Mozart, and Gluck stood like sentinels along the walls and lent dignity to the place. An ornate chandelier illuminated the main chamber. Months earlier, we recall, Elsner had sent Haslinger two of Chopin's manuscripts— the youthful Sonata in C minor and the "Là ci darem" Variations—but had received no reply, and Chopin was unsure how he might be received. Thanks to Elsner's letter of introduction Haslinger was courtesy itself. After making a fuss of the young visitor and apologizing for the absence of Frau Haslinger, who was not at home, the publisher showed him some of the latest musical novelties and then insisted that Chopin hear his young son Karl play the piano. Haslinger finally came to the point and assured Chopin that the Variations would be published within one week in his celebrated "Odeon" series. "I hardly expected that," Chopin told his parents delightedly. Haslinger then advanced another idea, one that was far less welcome. Who better than the composer himself to appear before the Viennese

---

18. CFC, vol. 1, pp. 98–99; KFC, vol. 1, p. 89.

public playing these variations? Chopin had not touched a piano for more than two weeks, and he vacillated.

Over the next few days, Chopin met a number of leading members of Viennese musical society, some of them at Haslinger's shop, who urged him to give this concert, and he gradually yielded. He was introduced in turn to the celebrated violinist and string quartet leader Ignaz Schuppanzigh, who had known Beethoven; to Count Wenzel Gallenberg, the director of the Kärntnertor Theater (and husband of Giulietta Guicciardi, often wrongly identified as Beethoven's "immortal beloved"); to the influential journalist Joseph Blahetka, whose eighteen-year-old daughter, Leopoldine, was a pupil of Czerny's and already an established pianist in Vienna; and to the two leading pianoforte manufacturers in the city, Matthäus Andreas Stein and Conrad Graf. But the most persuasive voice was that of Wilhelm Würfel, who had been on the faculty of the Warsaw Conservatory and had heard Chopin play many times. Würfel had just retired as the chief conductor of the Kärntnertor Theater, and since he knew what to do he generously offered to arrange everything for Chopin. A week after arriving in Vienna, Chopin told his parents, "I have made up my mind [to give a concert]. Blahetka says I shall be a sensation, for I am a virtuoso of the first rank, to be counted with Moscheles, Herz, and Kalkbrenner." Chopin was vastly amused when Würfel introduced him to everyone as "a young gentleman whom he has persuaded to give a concert," adding slyly, "*NB*. Without any fee!"[19] This piece of news was doubtless meant to please Count Gallenberg, who was notoriously tight with the theater's budget. All that remained was for Chopin to choose a piano. He was offered instruments by both Stein and Graf, who were willing to let him have them gratis. Everyone urged him to choose the Stein, a popular instrument in Vienna, but Chopin was more impressed with the Graf, and insisted on using it. He assured his parents that in order not to offend Stein, he would thank the piano maker personally for his kind offer, adding with mock concern, "I hope that God will be with me—don't worry!"[20]

In the event, there was plenty to worry about. The concert was announced for August 11. With just two days to go, the program had to be planned in cooperation with the incumbent conductor, Franz Lachner, and

19. CFC, vol. 1, p. 104; KFC, vol. 1, p. 91.
20. CFC, vol. 1, p. 104; KFC, vol. 1, p. 90.

Chopin decided to play not only the "Là ci darem" Variations but his *Krakowiak* Rondo as well.

Kärntnertor Theater
Tuesday, August 11, 1829

Conductor: Franz Lachner

Beethoven: "Prometheus" Overture
Chopin: *Rondo à la Krakowiak*
Rossini: Aria from *Bianca e Faliero*
          (Charlotte Veltheim, soprano)
Chopin: *Là ci darem* Variations
Vaccai: Rondo with Variations and Chorus from
          Pietro il grande (Charlotte Veltheim)

INTERVAL

A Masked Ball—Comic Ballet in two acts

The rehearsal went badly. There were so many mistakes in the hastily copied orchestral parts of the *Krakowiak* that the orchestra rebelled and Chopin almost abandoned the concert. But he was prevailed upon to do what he did best: to improvise. He dropped the *Krakowiak* and announced in its place a free fantasy on two themes: the first from Boieldieu's opera *La Dame blanche*, which he had heard for the first time the previous evening, and the second from the traditional Polish drinking song "Chmiel" (Hops).

The Kärntnertor Theater already vibrated with history when Chopin walked onto its stage. The building had been hallowed across the years by performances of the Viennese classics, from Mozart to Weber. Beethoven's "Fidelio" Overture and his Ninth Symphony had received their first performances there, as had Weber's opera *Euryanthe* and Schubert's song "Erlkönig." With a seating capacity of 1,650 the theater was not particularly large, but it wrapped both performer and listener within the mantle of its intimacy. It was an ideal location for Chopin's Viennese debut.

The theater was not full but the audience was enthusiastic. It even applauded during the *tutti* passages separating the "Là ci darem" Variations, much to Chopin's discomfiture, for at such moments the applause drowned out the orchestra. The improvisation on "Chmiel" electrified everyone, because this kind of ethnic music was unfamiliar to Viennese ears. Chopin told his parents, "My spies on the floor of the house reported that people were dancing up and down in their seats."[21] Among the "spies" were his traveling companions Marceli Celiński and Romuald Hube, who had stationed themselves at strategic points in the theater in order to eavesdrop on the audience. It was a distinguished gathering that included Count Moritz Lichnowsky, Beethoven's friend and patron; Prince Moritz Dietrichstein, the putative father of the pianist Sigismond Thalberg; and the conductor Conradin Kreutzer, equally well known as a virtuoso clarinetist and pianist. Carl Czerny was also there and he went backstage with all the others in order to compliment Chopin. Dietrichstein urged the young man to consolidate his success and stay in Vienna for the winter. Chopin, somewhat to his surprise, found that he had become an overnight celebrity.

There were naturally those whose praise was qualified. Blahetka thought that Chopin played too quietly—the sort of criticism that the pianist encountered all his life. He observed that with critics there must always be some kind of "but," and he preferred this one to the alternative of being accused of playing too loudly. A day or two later Blahetka persuaded Chopin to hear his daughter Leopoldine play, and Chopin wrote, "She is

---

21. CFC, vol. 1, p. 106; KFC, vol. 1, p. 93. The "Chmiel" drinking song that brought the audience to its feet had not yet been captured in formal music notation when Chopin improvised on its theme. Zygmunt Gloger first published it in his monumental collection of Polish folk songs (1900–1903). The aural tradition familiar to Chopin probably unfolded somewhat like this:

In a letter to Moritz Karasowski dated November 11, 1876, Oskar Kolberg recalled that Chopin had played the old folk song in 3/8 time.

The riotous words, handed down through peasant tradition, are in praise of hops that are supposed to do their work on a young couple's wedding night. KK, vol. 62, pp. 661–62.

pretty—but she bangs the piano frightfully."[22] It was also reported to Chopin that one of the ladies in the audience expressed regret that he looked somewhat unimpressive on the stage. Doubtless they were used to seeing more "activity" at the keyboard and Chopin's repose disconcerted them. Chopin again put everything into perspective. "If that is the only fault they could find with me I have nothing to worry about."[23] He also became better acquainted with Czerny, who invited him to his house to play some music for two pianofortes. "He is a good fellow, but nothing more," Chopin remarked of the renowned pedagogue. And he added the revealing comment, "There is more feeling in Czerny himself than in all his compositions."[24]

Vienna offered Chopin an opportunity to hear some unfamiliar works. He attended performances of Rossini's *La Cenerentola*, the same composer's *Mosè in Egitto*, and Meyerbeer's *Il crociato in Egitto*; and he was also present at two violin recitals by Joseph Mayseder, a pupil of Schuppanzigh's and one of Vienna's leading violinists. Chopin took tea with Countess Lichnowska, spent time with the conductor Ritter von Seyfried, and had long conversations with Conradin Kreutzer. Kapellmeister Franz Lachner also socialized with him, and their conversations would surely have turned toward Franz Schubert, who had been one of Lachner's friends and had died just a few months before Chopin arrived in Vienna. In those days Schubert and Beethoven slumbered side by side in the Währing Cemetery. No evidence has come to light that Chopin visited their graves, although it would not be surprising to learn that he had done so, since they were within easy walking distance. Everywhere he went, in fact, Chopin was welcomed with open arms by leading members of Viennese society, and the clamor grew for him to give a second concert. Flushed with the success of the first, and pressed on all sides by his new friends, he once more yielded, but it is worth noting his reasons.

I shall not give a third concert, and agreed to give a second only because they were so insistent. Besides, it occurred to me that they

22. CFC, vol. 1, p. 107; KFC, vol. 1, p. 93.
23. CFC, vol. 1, p. 106; KFC, vol. 1, p. 93.
24. CFC, vol. 1, p. 113; KFC, vol. 1, p. 96.

might say in Warsaw: "What! He gave one concert and then disappeared! Did he make a bad impression?"[25]

The second concert was announced for August 18. Once more the event took place in the Kärntnertor Theater, and once more Chopin played without a fee. This time he was determined to play the *Krakowiak* Rondo, the illegible parts of which had meanwhile been freshly copied by his old Polish schoolfriend Tomasz Nidecki, Elsner's star pupil at the High School for Music, who was now established in Vienna. Having witnessed the near-debacle of the first rehearsal, Nidecki had come to Chopin's rescue and had gone through the *Krakowiak* parts with care. By popular request Chopin also agreed to repeat the "Là ci darem" Variations, and the following program appeared on the billboards:

Kärntnertor Theater
Tuesday, August 18, 1829

Conductor: Franz Lachner

Lindpaintner: Overture to *Der Bergkönig*
Chopin: *Rondo à la Krakowiak*
Mayseder: Polonaise
        (played by Joseph Khayll, violin)
Chopin: *Là ci darem* Variations

INTERVAL

Ballet

Word had spread that Chopin was a pianist not to be missed, and a larger audience was waiting for him. As he walked onstage he was greeted by three rounds of applause, each one louder than the last, as he put it. The *Krakowiak* was a resounding success and the Czech composer Adalbert Gyrowetz (whose concerto Chopin had played as a boy in Warsaw) stood up clapping and shouting "Bravo!" Even the orchestra, now reconciled to the young genius presiding at the keyboard, gave Chopin an ova-

---

25. CFC, vol. 1, p. 110; KFC, vol. 1, p. 95.

tion. The Variations were again successful, and Chopin's reputation among the musical intelligentsia in Vienna was secured. And all this, as Chopin observed, had happened by chance. It had never been his intention to play in Vienna, but as he prepared to depart the imperial city he had the satisfaction of knowing that he had enjoyed his first international success, one that was to stand him in good stead in the months ahead.

He spent his last day taking leave of his new friends and acquaintances. Schuppanzigh urged him to return, and Chopin replied that he would like to do so in order to pursue more advanced studies. To which the violinist paid him the best possible compliment, telling him that he was already a finished artist. Chopin also went to say goodbye to the journalist Blahetka and his daughter Leopoldine, "the young and pretty pianist." In a sentimental gesture she gave him as a souvenir of his visit an autographed copy of one of her own compositions. Blahetka himself expressed surprise that the young man could have learned so much in a backwater like Warsaw. Chopin's reply has earned a permanent place in the narrative. "With Żywny and Elsner even the greatest jackass would learn."[26]

As for Tobias Haslinger, the man who had initiated all this activity, he reneged on his promise to publish the "Là ci darem" Variations within one week. The work had to wait until the following year before it appeared in print.

VIII

At nine o'clock on the evening of August 20, Chopin and his traveling companions boarded the diligence and after an all-night journey arrived in Prague around noontime the following day. They registered at the Hotel zum schwarzen Roß (Black Horse Hotel), where Chopin braved his first taste of Bohemian lager. He delivered various letters of introduction that he had brought from Vienna, beginning with one for Václav Hanka, the well-known Czech philosopher and curator of the Prague National Museum. Hanka pursued a correspondence with many Poles, especially the ones interested in supporting Czech aspiration for a separate national identity. He knew Fryderyk Skarbek and was delighted when Chopin presented himself

---

26. CFC, vol. 1, p. 112; KFC, vol. 1, p. 96.

as Skarbek's godson. He insisted that Chopin sign his visitors' book, an autograph album in which important visitors to the museum were invited to make an inscription. Chopin could not at first think of anything to say. Fortunately, his fellow traveler Ignacy Maciejowski came to the rescue with a four-line stanza for a mazurka, which Chopin quickly set to music.[27] Hanka then arranged a sightseeing tour of the city for Chopin and his companions. They explored the old Castle Hill area; visited St. Vitus Cathedral; admired various historical sites, including the ancient astronomical clock installed in the year 1410; and took in the panoramic views from the Charles Bridge across the Vltava River. Prague had been Mozart's favorite city, and Chopin was reminded of the composer's spiritual presence at every touch and turn.

The following day he went over to the National Theater, where Mozart had enjoyed some of his greatest triumphs, and presented letters of introduction from Würfel to the director Johann Stiepanek and Kapellmeister Friedrich Pixis, brother of the pianist Johann Pixis (to whom Chopin would later dedicate his Grand Fantasia on Polish Airs, op. 13). They urged Chopin to give a concert in Prague, but he wisely declined. Mindful of the fact that even Paganini had been snubbed by Prague's cognoscenti, Chopin had no desire to risk spoiling the success he had sown in Vienna by reaping a failure in Prague, "so I shall remain quiet."[28] Pixis took Chopin over to his house for a longer discussion. There in the stairwell they encountered the noted Dresden pianist August Klengel, who was passing through the city in search of possible triumphs in Italy, and had decided to call on Pixis while he was in Prague. Pixis compensated for the inconvenience that Klengel had suffered while lingering outside the apartment door by arranging an impromptu musical get-together. Chopin declined to participate, a decision he had cause to regret, for he was forced instead to listen to Klengel render his entire "Forty-eight Canons and Fugues," two in every key, a dogged continuation of Bach's 48. This mind-numbing performance took well over two hours to complete, while Chopin remained fixed to his chair, a polite smile on his face. "He plays quite nicely," Chopin conceded opaquely, "but it could be better—(hush!)." Later

---

27. The page bearing Chopin's musical setting of Maciejowski's lines, a "Mazur in G major," is reproduced in KCOL, p. 177.
28. CFC, vol. 1, p. 116; KFC, vol. 1, p. 99.

he had a long conversation with Klengel and formed an acquaintance with him "which I value far above poor old Czerny's—(hush!)."[29]

On August 25, Chopin set out for Dresden. His journey took him first to Teplitz (Teplice), noted for its thermal springs, where he stayed long enough to visit Wallenstein's castle at Dux. He saw a fragment of the great leader's skull, together with the halberd with which he was assassinated, and many other relics. Teplitz was full of Poles, and one of them, an old Warsaw acquaintance, Ludwik Łempicki, insisted on taking him that same evening to the sumptuous home of Prince and Princess Clary-Aldringen, whose vast estates encompassed the town. Well aware that he would be asked to play the piano, Chopin had changed into his evening clothes and donned the same white gloves that he had worn at his recent concert in Vienna. At 8:30 p.m. sharp he and Łempicki entered the princely residence. This was an environment in which Chopin felt completely at home. The gathering was small but select. A group of titled dandies stood in one part of the room, a military officer and an English sea captain chatted in another. There was also a Saxon general called Leiser, whose chest was covered in medals and who had a saber scar on his face. A fine Graf piano stood close by waiting to be played.

Chopin told his family:

> After tea, during which I had a long talk with the Prince himself, his mother asked me to *deign* to take my seat at the piano (a good Graf). I *deigned*, requesting for my part that they would *deign* to give me a theme for an improvisation. At once among the fair sex who sat around a large table, embroidering, knitting, or weaving, there ran a murmur: "A theme! A theme!" Three charming little princesses put their heads together; then one of them referred the matter to Mr. Fritsche (young Prince Clary's tutor, I imagine) and he with general approval proposed a theme from Rossini's *Moses*.[30]

Chopin's improvisation was well received and the princess begged him to extend his stay, but Chopin was anxious to resume his journey. "I am so

---

29. CFC, vol. 1, p. 118; KFC, vol. 1, p. 100. The indefatigable Klengel went on composing canons and fugues across the years until he had written no fewer than 120 of them, each one more impenetrable than the last.
30. CFC, vol. 1, p. 120; KFC, vol. 1, p. 101.

eager to get back to you, my dearest parents," he wrote. "What stories and goings-on I shall have to tell you! Marvelous, fabulous ones!" General Leiser, on hearing that Chopin's route back to Warsaw would take him through Dresden, dashed off a letter of recommendation to Baron von Friesen, grand chamberlain to the King of Saxony, asking him to open doors and introduce Chopin to the principal artists of Dresden. Beneath the flowery language of this diplomatic note, which was written in French, he scribbled in German: *"Herr Chopin ist selbst einer der vorzüglichsten Pianospieler, die ich bis jetzt kenne."*[31]

The next day, August 26, Chopin and his friends arrived in Dresden, where they stayed at the Hotel zur Stadt Berlin. It was Chopin's first glimpse of the "jewel on the Elbe." He wandered around the celebrated art gallery, marveled at the historic buildings, and on August 28 he went to the theater to attend a performance of Goethe's *Faust*, with Eduard Devrient in the title role. It was Goethe's eightieth birthday and the poet was being celebrated all over Germany. Chopin described the play, which lasted from six until eleven in the evening, as "a frightening but powerful fantasy."[32]

IX

When Chopin got back to Warsaw on September 12, he found an unwelcome surprise waiting for him. The Polish press had got hold of one of his best Viennese newspaper reviews and had mangled the translation. Instead of telling the reader that "Chopin placed his desire to make good music before his desire to please the public," it said that "his desire to please the public came before his desire to make good music," the exact opposite. It was an irritation that vanished only when the Viennese journals themselves reached the city and the record could be corrected. The *Allgemeine Theaterzeitung für Kunst* had, in fact, welcomed Chopin's modesty and his reluctance to exhibit his virtuosity at the expense of the music. "This is a young man who goes his own way, on which he knows how to please, although his style differs widely from other virtuosos" (September 1, 1829).

---

31. "Chopin is one of the most eminent pianists that I have yet heard." CFC, vol. 1, p. 121; KFC, vol. 1, p. 101.
32. CFC, vol. 1, p. 123; KFC, vol. 1, p. 102.

The *Wiener Zeitschrift für Kunst* drew attention to the unusual chro-maticisms of the *Krakowiak*, and added, "One is forced to admit the thoughtfulness and depth of his artistry" (August 20, 1829). Perhaps the criticism that Chopin valued most came from the *Allgemeine musika-lische Zeitung*, which referred to him as "a master of the front rank" (November 1829).

The memory of Paganini's playing earlier in the year, and the animated discussion that it had engendered in the Polish press about the place of virtuosity in performance, was still alive in Warsaw and continued to pro-vide the musical intelligentsia with food for thought. The two words "ab-solute perfection" that Chopin had used to describe Paganini are about all that we have from him. But they are all that we need in order to conclude that Paganini's impact had been profound. While there is a dearth of com-mentary from Chopin about the feast of music making that had taken place in the Polish capital during the spring and summer of 1829, we know that he was an avid consumer of the ongoing war of words in the Warsaw press concerning the pros and cons of virtuosity in performance. His Vienna reviews, translated and republished in the Polish newspapers, helped to stoke the fires of that debate and raise questions. Just how far did the overt display of virtuosity get in the way of music itself? Could the lion ever be made to lie down with the lamb? These were questions that Paga-nini's visit to Warsaw had brought to the fore, and that the nineteen-year-old Chopin was soon to resolve in spectacular fashion. For this was the moment that Chopin turned his attention to the one genre of composition whose chief function was the exhibition of virtuosity in all its forms: the study. In a letter to his friend Tytus Woyciechowski dated October 20, 1829, Chopin makes the first mention of his celebrated Studies, op. 10, telling him, with reference to the first one, in C major, "I have composed a big Technical Exercise in my own special manner; I will show it to you when we meet." And three weeks later, in a further letter to Tytus, dated November 14, 1829, he was able to write, "I have written a few exercises— if you were by my side I would play them well to you."[33] We have no means of knowing which "few exercises" they were because the sketches are lost. Some scholars maintain that these early studies included the first versions of no. 8 in F major, no. 9 in F minor, no. 10 in A-flat major, and

---

33. CFC, vol. 1, pp. 139 and 143; KFC, vol. 1, pp. 111 and 113.

no. 11 in E-flat major.[34] All we know with certainty is that the first two
"exercises" exist in manuscripts that posterity instantly recognizes as the
Studies in C major and A minor, op. 10, nos. 1 and 2. They bear the date
November 2, 1830, placed there the day that Chopin departed Warsaw for
good—suggesting that he had been putting his portfolio into some sort of
last-minute order in preparation for a much longer journey abroad.[35]

X

From the moment that he had returned to Warsaw the idea of a more
ambitious tour beyond Poland's borders had preoccupied Chopin's thoughts.
An extended trip lasting perhaps three years, taking in Germany, France, and
Italy, was being considered—the sort of itinerary that Mikołaj had in
mind when he petitioned the government for funds earlier in the year. Warsaw had nothing more to offer Chopin, and it was becoming clear that if
he was to acquire a European reputation he must seek his fortune abroad
under the direction of the best masters. He had continued to study foreign languages; he was bilingual in French, and his German and Italian
were improving. Mikołaj was ready to put up the money for such a journey. So why were Chopin's plans marked by endless procrastination and
irresolution? A glance through his correspondence shows that he changed
the date of his departure time and again, in a continuous state of uncertainty, and often on the basis of no more than a passing whim. The young
man was in love. Or, as Józef Elsner was later to put it, he had fallen under
the influence of "a pair of beautiful eyes."[36]

---

34. They are listed in Maurice Brown's catalogue, entry no. 42.
35. These manuscripts are fair copies, probably in the hand of Ludwika Chopin, from which
we infer that they rest on versions going back to the time of Chopin's correspondence with
Tytus a year earlier. They are held in the Chopin Museum, Warsaw, under the call numbers
M/190–91.
36. CFC, vol. 2, p. 81; KFC, vol. 1, p. 221.

KONSTANCJA GŁADKOWSKA: THE DISTANT BELOVED, 1829–1830

. . . I have already found my ideal, whom I have served faithfully for six months, though without saying a word to her.

—Chopin[1]

I

We cannot be sure when Chopin first met the young singer Konstancja Gładkowska, but it was probably during the early spring of 1829. That is when Carlo Soliva put on a series of vocal concerts featuring his best pupils at the Conservatory, and Chopin was in attendance. Contrary to the literature, Konstancja was not the daughter of the Burgrave of the Royal Castle, but rather of the manager of a tenement building in Old Warsaw.[2] She possessed a fine mezzo-soprano voice and had ambitions to succeed on the operatic stage. Her concert took place on April 21, and Chopin fell under the spell of her voice and then of her feminine charm. He was too unsure of himself to declare his feelings openly and for months he worshipped Konstancja from afar. She was one of six girls who studied with Soliva and boarded in the hostel attached to the Conservatory. The Italian conductor was heavily criticized by his nemesis Elsner for allowing

---

1. CFC, vol. 1, p. 132; KFC, vol. 1, p. 107.
2. MSFC, p. 257.

these attractive young ladies to sing duets with Russian officers from the local garrison, even permitting them (Elsner said "encouraging them") access to the hostel. Soliva himself had married one of the girls, Maria Kralewska, in 1825, while she was still his student, and had raised a few local eyebrows, including those of Elsner. Konstancja herself had no difficulty in attracting male admirers, by whom she was frequently surrounded. Chopin lacked the experience to compete with his rivals, bottled up his emotions, and suffered in silence. When her father passed away, Konstancja's musical studies were paid for through a state bursary. Her mother, Mme Salomea Gładkowska, who lived in Radom, thereafter harbored but one thought: to find a wealthy husband for her daughter and bring about her rescue from the operatic stage, a place of dubious repute for unmarried girls. Salomea often visited Warsaw, spent time with her daughter, and, we imagine, scrutinized many a young man through her lorgnette, with a view to weighing his credentials as a prospective suitor.

Warsaw was a small city and it would have been hard for the young couple not to notice each other at the soirées and social events that were a fixture during the season. Chopin was by now a celebrity and Konstancja was well aware of his standing in the world of music. But in the absence of any correspondence between the pair we cannot be sure if she was alert to his feelings, let alone returned them. And those feelings were intense, for Chopin was in the middle of his first sexual awakening. One Sunday morning while sitting in church, where attendance was mandatory for all the music students, he was struck by a single unexpected glance from Konstancja, and he left the building in such a daze that he stumbled on the pavement. In his trancelike state he bumped into Dr. Parys (a family physician) and the best pretense that he could think of to explain his confusion was that a dog had run between his legs and he had lost his balance. "It is terrible to think what a lunatic I sometimes seem to be," he remarked.[3] On another occasion he was playing the Spohr Piano Quintet at a soirée and his gaze was captured by a young lady who reminded him so forcefully of Konstancja that he could hardly remove his eyes from her. By the end of the evening he felt that his heart had been enslaved forever.[4] The clearest indication we have of Chopin's infatuation with Konstancja comes in a

---

3. CFC, vol. 1, p. 199; KFC, vol. 1, p. 142.
4. CFC, vol. 1, p. 193; KFC, vol. 1, p. 139.

written confession that he made to his friend and confidant Tytus Woyciechowski, on October 3, 1829. His words have often been quoted, for
they have become an essential part of the story.

> It is perhaps my misfortune that I have already found my ideal,
> whom I have served faithfully for six months, though without say-
> ing a word to her about my feelings; whom I dream of, who inspired
> the Adagio of my Concerto, and also this morning the little waltz
> that I am sending you. No one but you will know what it means.
> Notice the passage marked "X." How I should enjoy playing it to you,
> dearest Tytus! In the Trio the melody in the bass must stand out as
> far as the upper E-flat in the treble in the 5th bar. But what need is
> there for me to tell you this, when you feel it?[5]

Whatever it was that Tytus was supposed to know and feel the world
has never been quite able to fathom. This passage from the middle section of the Waltz in D-flat major (op. posth. 70, no. 3) must have conveyed
the memory of an intimate nature, because Chopin later expressed regret at having sent it and feared that he might have incurred his best
friend's anger. "I swear I only wanted to give you pleasure—for I love
you very much."[6]

II

Tytus had been a pupil of Mikołaj Chopin's since the autumn of 1824,
the year he enrolled as a student at the Warsaw Lyceum, where Chopin

5. CFC, vol. 1, p. 132; KFC, vol. 1, pp. 107–108.
6. CFC, vol. 1, p. 135; KFC, vol. 1, p. 109.

had got to know and admire him. Two years older than Chopin, Tytus was physically strong and self-assured. In brief, he possessed the very qualities that Chopin lacked, and the composer looked up to him as the older brother he never had. That Chopin was emotionally dependent on Tytus and craved his approval is evident from their correspondence. "A single glance from you after each of my concerts would mean more to me than all this praise from . . . people like Elsner, Kurpiński, Soliva, and so on,"[7] he wrote in extravagant vein. Tytus was a good amateur pianist, and although music was not his special field he may have taken some casual lessons at the Conservatory. In 1826 he gained a qualifying diploma from the Lyceum, which admitted him to the university, where he studied law and administration. By then he had become Chopin's *alter ego*, his bosom friend, and the recipient of his innermost thoughts. In 1828, following the death of his father, Tytus abandoned his studies to help his mother run their large estate at Poturzyn, which lay three hundred kilometers southeast of Warsaw, a property that he would eventually inherit. That simple fact explains the existence of an important run of letters from Chopin to Tytus, which began after Tytus left the Polish capital and coincides with the period of the young composer's growing infatuation with Konstancja.

With Tytus no longer at his side, Chopin lapsed into a state of psychological confusion, and he began to divert some of his innermost thoughts of love and even of sexual desire away from his "distant beloved" and transfer them onto his best friend. This opens the door to a large topic through which more than one Chopin biographer has wandered only to return with no satisfactory explanation as to what was found on the other side. It is clear that Chopin had no idea how to handle the emotions surging within him, or to whom he should confess them. In the event, he turned not to Konstancja, perhaps fearing rejection, but to Tytus. This mental twist has given rise to a number of conjectures, including the notion that Chopin was experiencing some latent homosexual feelings brought to the surface as his unrequited love for Konstancja intensified. His letters to Tytus bear witness to this strange fact, as the following extracts show.

You don't like to be kissed. Allow me to do so today.[8]

---

7. CFC, vol. 1, p. 145; KFC, vol. 1, p. 114.
8. CFC, vol. 1, p. 94; KFC, vol. 1, p. 87.

I don't want to write any more news. I just want to caress you and be with you.[9]

Give me your lips, dearest lover. I'm convinced you still love me, and I am as scared of you as ever, like some sort of tyrant, I don't know why but I am scared.[10]

I keep your letters like a lover's ribbon. I have the ribbon, so write to me and in a week's time we shall pamper one another again.[11]

I know my love for you is hopeless, and I only scribble this non-sense to make you love me more . . . My feelings for you have to seek out some superhuman means of forcing your heart to respond to them.[12]

These are sentiments that should more properly have been addressed to Konstancja, but were instead directed toward Tytus. It has been pointed out that the Polish language lends itself to extravagant forms of address between two men that the rest of the world might regard as uncomfortably sensual. This was particularly true in a bygone age when chivalrous, high-flown salutations were the norm. We should, of course, make allowances for these differences in the difficult business of translation. It might even be permissible to paraphrase such language in a way that would render the modern English equivalent of "give me your lips, beloved" as "let me em-brace you, dearest friend," but a certain amount of poetry might be lost along the way, and still more truth. Yet what are we to make of the fol-lowing, where no such linguistic considerations obtain?

Now I am going to wash myself. Please do not embrace me as I have not washed yet. And you? Even were I to anoint myself with fra-grant oils from Byzantium, you would not embrace me—not unless forced to by magnetism. But there are forces in Nature! Today you

---

9. CFC, vol. 1, p. 144; KFC, vol. 1, 114.
10. CFC, vol. 1, p. 206; KFC, vol. 1, p. 146.
11. CFC, vol. 1, p. 184; KFC, vol. 1, pp. 134–35.
12. CFC, vol. 1, p. 194; KFC, vol. 1, p. 140.

will dream that you are embracing me! You have to pay for the night-mare you caused me last night![13]

This language is frankly erotic and it is fair to ask, as several biographers have done, whether there might have been a passing homosexual affair be-tween Tytus and Chopin. We are much inclined to doubt it but cannot know for sure because not a single letter from Tytus to Chopin has sur-vived. Tytus was, in any case, a reluctant recipient of overt declarations of love, as Chopin's side of the correspondence confirms. It seems far more likely that Chopin wrote these and similar passages in an exalted frame of mind when, in the seclusion of his sanctuary in the Krasiński Palace, he put pen to paper and gave free rein to his adolescent fantasies. After the Warsaw Uprising, incidentally, and Tytus had been discharged from the Polish army, he went on to enjoy married life with Countess Aloy-sia Poletyło (of the Trzywdar coat of arms), who bore him four children. They named their second son Fryderyk after Chopin.[14]

If Chopin's "confession" to Tytus in October 1829 is to be taken at face value, the image of Konstancja could rarely have been absent from his thoughts during his six-week tour of Vienna, Prague, and Dresden made earlier in the year. By the time he had returned to Warsaw, in Septem-ber 1829, with such accolades as "pianist of the front rank" bestowed on him by the Viennese press, his position had been transformed. Yet his new-found confidence did not extend to his private life and he could not sum-mon up the courage to declare himself to Konstancja.

---

13. CFC, vol. 1, p. 189; KFC, vol. 1, p. 137. In his biography of Chopin, Arthur Hedley warned his English-language readers not to attach literal meanings to these and similar passages (HC, p. 17), but he then went on to exclude most of them from his "Selected Correspon-dence" of Chopin's letters and drained the ones that remained of their erotic overtones. "It must be remembered that the highly coloured language used by the Slavonic peoples a hun-dred years ago did not correspond to realities which would in many cases scandalize and embarrass western Europeans," he wrote. Pierre Azoury makes a very good point when he asks in reply why Chopin did not express himself as effusively to his other close friends, such as Jan Białobłocki and Jan Matuszyński, as he did to Tytus. "The only convincing answer," Azoury points out, "is that Chopin's feelings for Tytus were different and exclusive to him." ACC, p. 190.
14. CFC, vol. 2, p. 351; KFC, vol. 1, p. 355.

III

In the autumn of 1829, Chopin accepted another invitation to stay with Prince Antoni Radziwiłł and his family at Antonin, the hunting lodge that the prince had constructed on his estates near the Duchy of Poznań's border, and named for himself. Three years had elapsed since Chopin's last visit there, in 1826. He traveled first to nearby Strzyżewo in order to pay his respects to his godmother, Anna Wiesiołowska, and then took up residence at Antonin. The prince, whose talents as a composer and an accomplished cellist were widely admired, delighted in the company of musicians. He had his own in-house string quartet in which he himself sometimes participated, performing the quartets of Haydn, Mozart, and Beethoven. Radziwiłł was an enthusiastic hunter, but his residence at Poznań was never large enough to house the many guests he wanted to join him during the summer months. So in 1821 he commissioned the noted Berlin architect Karl Schinkel to draw up some plans and within five years Antonin was brought into being. According to a contemporary description, wild boar, red deer, roe, and wolves roamed freely among the surrounding forests, and "called for the clamor of the hunt."

> On a site completely surrounded by forests of fir and pine there stood as if conjured up by magic a stately building . . . Its exterior, shape, and construction were suited to the hushed wildness of the woods; it was not of stone, nor of brick, but constructed entirely of wood, bearing the hues of the forest itself.[15]

The many rooms of Antonin were lavishly furnished. The Radziwiłł family occupied the ones on the ground floor, while the guest chambers were on the floors above. For eight days the young composer relaxed in the company of the Radziwiłłs, and especially the prince's attractive daughters, Eliza and Wanda, whom he had got to know on his earlier visit in 1826. He happily agreed to give piano lessons to the younger of the two ladies, Princess Wanda, because her youthful charm took his mind off Konstancja. "She is young, seventeen [in fact she was twenty-one], and

---

15. *Przyjacyel Ludu czyli Tygodnik Potrzebnych i Pożytecznych Wiadomości* (The People's Friend, or The Weekly Vital and Useful News), vol. 3, no. 1, July 2, 1836.

Antonin, Prince Radziwiłł's hunting lodge.

pretty," he wrote. "God knows how pleasant it was to place her little fingers on the keys," he confessed to Tytus.[16] During one of the lessons he played her his recently composed Polonaise in F minor (op. posth. 71, no. 3). Wanda became so fond of it that she made him play it to her every day, and when she insisted on learning it for herself he had to ask Tytus (to whom he had sent the only manuscript copy) to return it to him posthaste, because he did not want to write it out from memory and risk making mistakes. In the meantime, he composed for Wanda an *Alla polacca* for piano and cello in order to give her something challenging to practice with her cello-playing father. The cello part contains a number of special effects that Chopin disparaged as "tinsel," including double-stops and runs with turns, about which Prince Antoni himself would have been con-

16. CFC, vol. 1, p. 141; KFC, vol. 1, p. 112.

sulted. (It was later published as the Introduction and Polonaise brillante, op. 3, and dedicated to the eminent Viennese cellist Josef Merk.) While the three of them rehearsed, the twenty-five-year-old Princess Eliza sat in the background and made a second pencil drawing of Chopin to go along with the one she had made of him three years earlier, which she dated November 4, 1829.[17] It was at this time, too, that Chopin handed over his newly completed Piano Trio, op. 8, with its dedication to Prince Radziwiłł, and received Radziwiłł's gracious letter of acceptance. The prince in turn took pleasure in showing Chopin the score of his recently completed opera *Faust*, a work that contained some novel effects (including an off-stage orchestra and an overture that ran straight into the first act without the usual break) and that was well-enough regarded to be performed in Berlin and Poznań. Radziwiłł had in earlier years enjoyed the advantage of meeting Goethe and talking to the great poet about his literary master-piece. What particularly captured Chopin's imagination was the way in which the seduction aria, sung by Mephistopheles beneath Marguerite's window, was combined with the solemn chanting of a choir from a nearby church—a simultaneous mixture of the sacred and the profane. "I would never have expected [such things] from a Governor-General," he remarked.[18] Chopin's stay at Antonin was made still more pleasant for him by the unassuming presence of Radziwiłł's wife, Princess Ludwika. "She knows that it is not birth that makes a person," he remarked, "and her manner is so attractive that it is impossible not to love her."[19]

Chopin would have preferred to linger "until they had kicked me out of that Paradise," but he was obliged to depart because of what he de-scribed as "my private affairs"—a veiled reference to the fact that the im-age of Konstancja was beckoning him back to Warsaw, to say nothing of the Finale of his F minor Piano Concerto, which was still unfinished. As he took leave of his "two Eves," as he called the princesses, there was no hint of the shadow of misfortune that was shortly to cast its pall across this highly cultured family. Within a year of Chopin's visit, Prince An-toni had been removed as governor-general of Poznań for showing too much sympathy toward the Poles, and died in 1833. Princess Eliza followed him

17. The earlier drawing of 1826 is reproduced on page 102.
18. CFC, vol. 1, p. 140; KFC, vol. 1, p. 112.
19. Ibid.

to the grave a year later, when she was just thirty-one years old. Within two short years her mother, Princess Ludwika, had also slipped into the arms of death. Only Princess Wanda was left, but shortly after marrying into the Czartoryski family she, too, went to meet her maker, when she was thirty-seven years old. The joy, laughter, and sheer delight in the arts that were part of daily life at Antonin disappeared, and as the family members returned one by one to be entombed in the chapel's burial vault, the place took on the trappings of a morgue and only the ghosts remained.

IV

Posterity remains grateful to Konstancja for being the inspiration behind the Larghetto of the F minor Piano Concerto. The movement contains one of the composer's most ravishing melodies. It reaches such expressive heights that the roulades and grace notes with which it is adorned become virtually indistinguishable from the melody those ornaments were meant to decorate. If music of this caliber is the result of unrequited love, we can only stand back and marvel that Chopin, for all his youth, was able to sublimate his feelings and pour them into a composition of such depth of emotion. It marks a defining break from the more superficial "stile brillante" with which he had been associated until now. More than that, this music is nothing less than a tribute to the human voice itself.

In the weeks following his return from Antonin, Chopin managed to put the finishing touches to the Concerto. The work was given a semi-private run-through in the family's drawing room in the Krasiński Palace on March 3, 1830, with Kurpiński conducting a small ensemble before a specially invited group of friends. We learn that "Elsner beamed with joy" and "Żywny was moved to tears." The *Warsaw Courier* declared, "Young

Chopin surpasses all the pianists that we have heard here. He is 'the Paganini of the Piano.'"[20] The next step was to introduce the Concerto to the Warsaw public, and within two weeks everything was arranged. On March 17, Chopin played the work in the National Theater before an audience of eight hundred people. The second half of the concert included the premiere performance of his Grand Fantasia on Polish Airs, op. 13. He was not happy with his playing, however, partly because his own soft-toned piano (specially transported into the theater for the concert) could hardly be heard beyond the front rows of the stalls. Elsner called the bass end of the keyboard "woolly." It was decided there and then to give a second concert, and on March 22, Chopin was back in the theater, this time playing on a Viennese grand with a more aggressive sound, an instrument loaned to him for the occasion by a music-loving Russian general, Piotr Diakow. He again played the Concerto but replaced the Fantasia with the *Krakowiak* Rondo, op. 14, ending with an improvisation on the popular folk song "In the Town They Have Queer Customs." The concert was a triumph for Chopin, producing a standing ovation and shouts of "Let's have one more concert!" The *Ladies Journal* extolled him with a sonnet, while the *General Daily News* declared that there was no one but Mozart with whom to compare him. This was all that was required for the *Official Journal* to caution against the use of such extravagant language and weigh in with a rebuttal, which in turn started a small press war with the *Warsaw Gazette* and reignited an old argument about the respective merits of Kurpiński and Elsner, and the differing traditions they represented. Chopin, his spirits dampened by such partisan warfare, complained about it in an emotional letter to Tytus (dated "the anniversary of Emilia's death"), in which he drew comfort from the couplet

> "Unborn is he for whom mankind
> Nought but words of praise can find."

One review might have consoled him, however. It appeared in the *Polish Courier* and likened his playing to "a beautiful declamation, which happens to be the natural condition of his music."[21] It was written by a then-

---

20. Issue of March 4, 1830.
21. Issue of March 26, 1830. And Grzymała added perceptively that the land that gave

unknown writer named Wojciech Grzymała, who had just been released from a three-year jail sentence imposed on him by Tsar Nicholas for his part in the "Decembrist revolt." Grzymała was to become one of Chopin's closest friends and staunchest supporters in Paris in the years ahead.

V

Chopin's first group of "Polish Songs" dates from this time. They have always been a neglected part of his output, but they assume significance once we place them within the story of his life. When Chopin set the following texts by two of Poland's greatest poets, it is not hard to imagine that he was thinking of Konstancja.

"Życzenie" (The Wish)
(Stefan Witwicki) (1829)
"If I were the sun in the sky I would not shine except for you . . .
If I were a bird in the thicket I would sing in no other land . . .
but forever at your window, and for you alone."

"Czary" (Enchantment)
(Stefan Witwicki) (1830)
"In every place, at any time . . . I see her always there
　　　before me . . .
by day my thoughts are with her, by night shadows take
　　　her shape,
she is with me in dreams and reveries. I am certain that this
　　　is enchantment."

"Precz z moich oczu!" (Out of My Sight!)
(Adam Mickiewicz) (1830)
"In every place and at every corner,
where we wept and played together,
everywhere and forever I shall be there with you."

Chopin birth had left its mark on his music; that the "echoes of its fields and forests, as well as the songs of its villages," could be heard in his compositions.

Konstancja Gładkowska; an
anonymous pencil drawing
made about ten years after
Chopin had left Warsaw.

These songs languished in manuscript until after Chopin's death, although
some of them were copied and privately circulated. In this regard they were
not unlike his suppressed feelings for Konstancja, destined to remain mute
as far as the wider world was concerned.

The first evidence of personal encounters between Chopin and Konstancja comes in a letter dated April 10, 1830, addressed to Tytus. Chopin writes that he had attended a grand soirée in the home of Colonel
Friedrich Philippeus, an aide-de-camp to Grand Duke Constantine, during
which he accompanied a comic duet from Rossini's *Il turco in Italia*
sung by Carlo Soliva and Gresser, a Russian officer. He told Tytus, "Mme
Gładkowska inquired after you." We infer that if Konstancja's mother
was present at this concert, Konstancja was probably there as well.
But it is from a letter dated June 5, 1830, that it becomes clear that
Chopin was already well-enough acquainted with her to attempt to promote
her career.

How this came about is not without interest. The celebrated soprano

Henrietta Sontag had recently arrived in Warsaw and gave eleven concerts, chiefly for the tsar and members of the aristocracy who had returned to the Polish capital for the opening of the Polish Sejm. The twenty-four-year-old singer was already famous across Europe. Seven years earlier Weber had composed the title role of his opera *Euryanthe* for her. A year later, in 1824, Beethoven had agreed to have the eighteen-year-old girl sing in the premiere performances of his Ninth Symphony and his Missa Solemnis, a gesture that assured her immortality. Chopin attended her Warsaw concerts and raved about her singing, praising the sound that Sontag could produce within this register:

Her diminuendos, he wrote, were *non plus ultra*, her *portamenti* wonderful, and her scales, particularly the chromatic ones, unsurpassable. Sontag's admirers described her as an "envoy from heaven," a phrase that Chopin endorsed. It was Prince Radziwiłł who brought them together, and Chopin helped her rearrange a Ukrainian folk song that Radziwiłł wanted her to sing at a concert in his Warsaw salon. Such encounters were not easy to arrange, for Sontag always had a crowd of admirers at her door— "chamberlains, senators, district governors, generals, and adjutants," all hanging around, as Chopin put it, gazing into her pretty eyes and talking about the weather. Yet Chopin penetrated the security cordon and made it into the inner sanctum. "You can't imagine how delighted I was to make her closer acquaintance," he wrote. "I mean in her room, sitting beside her on the sofa." From this privileged position, he added somewhat archly, he found her a million times prettier and more attractive in casual morning dress than in full evening attire.

Chopin would have been well aware of the whiff of scandal hovering over Sontag, involving her clandestine marriage to Count Carlo Rossi in 1827 (she was of low birth), her secret pregnancy and confinement, and the recent decision by the King of Prussia, who was ravished by her singing, to raise her to the ranks of the aristocracy so that she could live openly with Count Rossi in The Hague. In exchange for this privilege Sontag had given up the stage, as befitted a countess, and limited herself to "command performances" for the aristocracy, which is what she was now doing in

Warsaw. When Tsar Nicholas heard her, he called her a *"Rossi-*gnol*"*—a nightingale—a play on words that could hardly have originated with him, who was much more at home with generals than with poets.

Seduced by Sontag's charm, and comfortable in her presence, Chopin turned to her for advice about Konstancja's prospects for a wider career. We conjecture that it was Chopin who arranged (through Soliva) to have Sontag audition Konstancja. Chopin tells us that this happened in early June and he attended the session. When he got to Sontag's hotel room, he found not only Sontag, but also Carlo Soliva with both Konstancja and Anna Wołków (another of the maestro's star pupils) in attendance. They sang one of Soliva's duets, "but Mlle Sontag told them that their voices were strained." She said that "although their training was good they must produce the voice in a different way if they don't want to lose it altogether within two years. In my presence she told Wołków that she had great facility and many pretty effects but had 'too shrill a voice,' and she invited them to come to her frequently so that she could show them her own method as far as possible."[22] Sontag was evidently willing to help prepare these two girls for their public debut in the National Theater, now only a month or so away.

Tsar Nicholas's presence in Warsaw attracted other artists to the Polish capital. The King of Prussia's court pianist, sixteen-year-old Sigismund Wörlitzer, arrived and so did Czerny's talented pupil Anna de Belleville. "She plays the piano charmingly," wrote Chopin, "with an extraordinarily light touch, and very elegantly." Toward the teenage Wörlitzer he extended but faint praise. "The young fellow plays quite nicely, but he is far from justifying the Court title which he bears."[23] Wörlitzer's party piece was Moscheles's famous Variations on the "Alexander March," which aroused universal admiration. It was a politically correct gesture, the work having been composed in honor of Tsar Alexander I at the time of the Vienna Congress, and it was now being laid at the feet of his youngest brother, Tsar Nicholas. In June, these three artists—Sontag, Wörlitzer, and Belleville—gave a command performance for Nicholas and his court at the Royal Castle, from which Chopin was excluded. "People were

---

22. CFC, vol. 1, p. 171; KFC, vol. 1, p. 128.
23. CFC, vol. 1, p. 164; KFC, vol. 1, p. 124.

surprised at my absence, but I was not" was his laconic response.[24] Chopin's patriotic sentiments were becoming well known, and he may have been observed mixing with young radicals in the Warsaw coffeehouses—Dziurka (Little Hole), Suchy Las (Dry Forest), and Kopciuszek (Cinderella)—places which in these politically charged times had become hives of subversion. In any case, the rebuff was quickly forgotten. On June 28, the tsar closed down the Sejm and left Warsaw together with his entourage. No sooner were the royals out of town than Chopin was invited to play his newly published "Là ci darem" Variations in the National Theater at a benefit concert for the singer Barbara Majerowa, on July 8. The unexpected arrival of copies of the printed score in Brzezina's music shop (after Schlesinger had sat on the work for more than a year) had created a buzz of interest in the piece and brought the season to a fitting end.

VI

Just two days after the concert, on July 10, Chopin set out on a three-hundred-kilometer journey to Poturzyn and spent nearly a fortnight with Tytus Woyciechowski at his country seat. The two young men had not seen each other for more than a year and there was much catching up to be done. They rode around the estate on horseback and raced across fields now turning gold with the approaching harvest, and Chopin absorbed once again the songs of the Polish peasants. Every morning he was awakened by the sound of a rustling birch tree outside his bedroom window, which he later recalled nostalgically in a letter to Tytus. There were even lessons on how to handle a crossbow, but Chopin lacked the strength to manipulate it. It was most likely at this time that Chopin presented Tytus with a copy of the "Là ci darem" Variations, which bears a dedication to Tytus, and they would have gone through the work on the piano. It was a handsome tribute that put a crowning touch on their friendship. In the pastoral surroundings of Poturzyn they would also have talked of Konstancja, and perhaps of an unnamed girl with whom Tytus appeared to have fallen in love, a subject that aroused Chopin's curiosity. Hovering over

---

24. CFC, vol. 1, p. 172; KFC, vol. 1, p. 128.

everything else was the question of Chopin's departure from Poland   a topic on which he had vacillated for months, testing Tytus's patience. Procrastination, the thief of time, was part of the very weft and weave of Chopin's character, a burden that could paralyze his ability to make decisions, sometimes for weeks on end.

When Chopin learned that Konstancja was to make her stage debut at the National Theater on July 24, singing the title role in Paër's opera *Agnese*, he cut short his stay at Poturzyn and hurried back to Warsaw. "Gładkowska leaves little to be desired," he told Tytus. "She is better on the stage than in the concert hall." Soliva had composed a special aria for her in order to show off her particular talents, and it was inserted into the second act of the opera. "It is most effective," wrote Chopin. "I knew that it would be, but I hardly expected the effect to be quite so great."[25] The *Polish Courier*, by contrast, published a harsh review, accusing her of having shouted her voice away. "Just because one can produce a sound, even if it be accurate, it may not be worthy to be called singing . . . Perhaps Mlle Gładkowska once had a voice, but today, alas, she no longer possesses one." The review ruffled many feathers, but the journal came back undaunted in a second article and said that neither Konstancja nor Anna Wołków (who had meanwhile made her own debut in Rossini's *Il turco in Italia*) were destined for the operatic stage because "their voices are devoid of charm, which is the soul of singing."[26] These stinging words, published anonymously, were written by Maurycy Mochnacki, a lawyer and journalist, whose trenchant pen earned for him the title of "the Robespierre of polemics." It has been suggested that his article was motivated by local politics, that he wanted to destroy the singing school established by Soliva at the Conservatory, and that he did not mind sacrificing the careers of these two young ladies in order to do it. Whatever the case, the cordial relationship that he enjoyed with Chopin was terminated and Mochnacki was removed from the composer's circle of friends. He and Chopin had often socialized with other artists in Warsaw's popular cafés, but once Mochnacki had poured public scorn on Konstancja, Chopin finished with him.

---

25. CFC, vol. 1, p. 175; KFC, vol. 1, p. 130.
26. Issues of July 31 and September 1, 1830.

VII

It was now mid-August and Chopin was still in a state of indecision about when to leave Poland. Since his family had gone to Żelazowa Wola for a short holiday, he decided to join them there, the last occasion on which he is known to have visited his birthplace. In these relaxed surroundings Chopin was presented with an ideal opportunity to unburden himself about Konstancja, but he failed to do so. There is truth to the idea that his highly developed sense of *amour-propre* got in the way—that self-regard which is nourished by the admiration that flows from others, and which Rousseau reminds us we hardly know we have until faced with its loss. (Years later George Sand noticed the same thing. "He is afraid of what people might say."[27]) Mikołaj and Justyna were loving parents, but Mikołaj was an authority figure whose approval Chopin would not lightly squander. In any case, Mikołaj would hardly have wanted to hear of a secret love affair just as his son was about to leave the country. So Chopin did what he and his sisters had always been raised to do and simply "kept up appearances." In a revealing letter, written after he had left Warsaw, his sister Izabella confessed to Chopin, "As long as you kept quiet about it, then I did too. But I knew about it."[28] We may be sure that she spoke for the entire family as well.

Of growing concern was the civil unrest that was creeping across Europe and might get in the way of Fryderyk's travels. The July Revolution had broken out in Paris, and after three days of hand-to-hand fighting at the barricades (the "Three Glorious Days"), King Charles X was swept from the throne and replaced by Louis-Philippe, the former Duke of Orléans, who had no real claim to the succession. He was a citizen king, a creation of the middle classes. Tsar Nicholas disparaged him as "the king of the grocers." As the unrest spread through Germany, Austro-Hungary, and then Italy, there was fear that it might reach Warsaw. The cafés and underground meeting places started to buzz with student plots to cast off the Russian yoke. Since the official newspapers were censored, underground printing presses worked overtime and subversive pamphlets began to circulate through Warsaw, keeping the population informed about what was

---

27. CFC, vol. 2, p. 252; KFC, vol. 1, p. 324.
28. CFC, vol. 2, p. 102; KFC, vol. 1, p. 231.

happening in the outside world. Novosiltsev's spies were hard at work and arrests were widespread. When graffiti was plastered on the walls of the military barracks ("Soldiers, prepare to defend your homeland!"), panic set in at the Belvedere Palace and Grand Duke Constantine drilled his soldiers for twenty-four hours a day. One enterprising group of revolutionaries managed to place a sign at the entrance to Belvedere, "Apartment for rent in the New Year." At dusk it was not uncommon to hear rifle shots from Praga, in the area of the Vistula River, as the ringleaders were rounded up and summarily executed.

While he was on holiday in Żelazowa Wola, with talk of insurrection in the air, Chopin visited the music-loving General Piotr Szembek, who was encamped with his Polish regiment at nearby Sochaczew. When the general heard that Chopin was visiting his birthplace, he sent Adjutant Alfons Czaykowski to fetch him to the camp in his carriage. "Szembek is very musical," wrote Chopin, "and he is an excellent violinist, having studied earlier with Rode, and he is a confirmed admirer of Paganini." General Szembek ordered his band to perform for Chopin, "and I heard some amazing things," Chopin observed. He was particularly impressed with the virtuosity of a bugle player who could play chromatic scales at incredible speed, and with subtle dynamic shadings. The general had a piano in the camp and he kept Chopin playing so long that the young man was late getting back to Warsaw and he missed much of Rossini's *Il turco in Italia*, which was being performed in the theater that night. "It was the Adagio of the F minor Concerto that impressed the general most," wrote Chopin.[29]

September came and went, and Chopin still lingered. He wrote to Tytus, "I am still here; I do not have the strength to fix a date." But then he did just that and announced that he would leave Warsaw on October 16, a few days after giving a "farewell" concert. He purchased a traveling trunk, packed it with a set of new clothes, acquired some monogrammed and hemmed handkerchiefs, and corrected and bound his manuscript scores, including his unpublished studies and concertos. And still he procrastinated. The departure date gave way in turn to October 20, which also came and went. It was not until the end of the month that he purchased a ticket to leave Warsaw on November 2.

---

29. CFC, vol. 1, pp. 181–82; KFC, vol. 1, p. 133.

VIII

All of Chopin's energies had meanwhile been concentrated on his "farewell" concert, scheduled to take place in the National Theater on October 11. He invited Gładkowska and Wołków to participate, and Soliva to conduct. The Italian was more than willing to help but he obliged Chopin to seek permission from the minister of education before allowing his two soloists and a supporting female choir to appear in the theater. Such permission was necessary because these students were being educated at the expense of the state. "You would not believe the trouble I had getting permission for those young ladies to sing,"[30] Chopin complained. His own contribution to the concert was to be the premiere performance of his newly completed Concerto in E minor, op. 11 (now called number one, because it was published before its predecessor in F minor), and the Grand Fantasia on Polish Airs, op. 13. On September 25 he held a private rehearsal at home with a small orchestral ensemble, before a specially invited audience that included Elsner, Kurpiński, Żywny, Soliva, Czapek, Kaczyński, Kessler, and other representatives of Warsaw's musical elite. He secretly relished the prospect of seeing this diverse gathering marshaled under one roof. Kurpiński and Soliva disliked each other, and there was no love lost between Elsner and Soliva either. "History offers no precedent for all these gentlemen being brought face to face," Chopin remarked. "Our house will witness the event."[31]

On the morning of the rehearsal Chopin went over to the Conservatory to borrow some music stands and pick up some mutes for the strings. "Without them my Adagio [the Larghetto] would be a failure." Everyone agreed that the Concerto was an impressive work, but it was the Rondo finale that gained the most approval. Soliva told him that it did him the greatest credit. Kurpiński praised its originality. Elsner was taken by its rhythm. All that was now required was the approval of the Warsaw public.

---

30. CFC, vol. 1, p. 202; KFC, vol. 1, p. 144.
31. CFC, vol. 1, p. 197; KFC, vol. 1, p. 141.

Warsaw National Theater
October 11, 1830
Karol Görner: Symphony
Chopin: Allegro from the E minor Piano Concerto, op. 11
    (played by the composer)
Soliva: Aria with chorus
    (sung by Anna Wołków)
Chopin: Larghetto and Rondo from the E minor Piano Concerto, op. 11
    (played by the composer)

Intermission

Rossini: Overture to "William Tell"
Rossini: "O quante lagrime per te versai" from *La donna del lago*
    (sung by Konstancja Gładkowska)
Chopin: Grand Fantasia on Polish Airs, op. 13
    (played by the composer)
Conductor: Carlo Soliva
Streicher piano

The day after the concert Chopin waxed lyrical about the evening to Tytus. His "farewell" appearance had exceeded all expectations, he said. It was a full house, the applause was tremendous, Anna Wołków was "dressed like an angel in blue," and she sang charmingly. Konstancja was dressed in white with roses in her hair, "her attire divinely arranged to suit her complexion." Soliva had transposed Konstancja's aria from Rossini's *La donna del lago* down a tone, the better to suit her voice. At the words *"tutto detesto"* she descended to the low B-natural in such a way that "Zieliński declared that one note to be worth a thousand ducats."[32] We conjecture that it was this concert, and the rehearsals preceding it, that led Konstancja and Chopin to share their first intimate thoughts. The words of the aria "O quante lagrime per te versai" mean "Oh, how many tears have I shed for you." Its inclusion in the concert may have been fortuitous but

---

32. CFC, vol. 1, p. 208; KFC, vol. 1, p. 147. Faustyn Zieliński, a teacher of singing at the Conservatory, had rehearsed the chorus for this concert.

we cannot help wondering about the symbolism. Somewhat to his surprise Chopin was not nervous while he played, and he told Tytus that he performed with confidence, "just like I do when I am alone." The Concerto "went like clockwork" on the Streicher piano. Since the applause would not stop, he took four curtain calls. As for Soliva, his conducting made a great impression "and he showed me so much kindness that it is hard to repay him."[33] Soliva, in fact, had found Chopin's orchestral parts to be so full of mistakes that he had taken them home and spent hours correcting them.

Does another musical symbol lie beneath the surface details of this "farewell" concert? We ask the question because Chopin called the Larghetto movement of his concerto a "Romance," the only time he is known to have used the term. And since it is the only piece of music about which he ever attempted to provide a literary program, his commentary is not easily set aside. Once again Tytus becomes the recipient of some private thoughts.

> The Adagio of the new concerto is in E major. It is not meant to create a powerful effect; it is rather a Romance, calm and melancholy, giving the impression of someone looking gently toward a spot which calls to mind a thousand happy memories. It is a kind of reverie in the moonlight on a beautiful spring evening. Hence the accompaniment is muted: that is, the violins are muffled by a sort of comb [Chopin's description of the violin mute] which fits over the strings and gives them a nasal and silvery tone . . . In spite of myself some idea comes into my head and I take plea-. sure in indulging it, perhaps quite wrongly. I am sure you will understand me.[34]

33. CFC, vol. 1, p. 208; KFC, vol. 1, p. 147.
34. CFC, vol. 1, p. 166; KFC, vol. 1, p. 125.

ROMANCE

Larghetto ♩ = 80

When Chopin talks of a "reverie in the moonlight" and "a spot which calls to mind a thousand happy memories," he comes close to suggesting that the movement enshrines an imagined love scene. His description is notable, coming as it does from a composer who generally chose to say nothing about his music in order not to let the daylight spoil the magic. Is it possible that thoughts of Konstancja lay behind this music too? The Romance is obviously the sibling of its predecessor, the Larghetto from the F minor Concerto, whose shared features are everywhere in evidence—in the operatic aria, in the vocally inspired roulades that decorate it, and in the dreamlike nocturne style that pervades it. The strings are muted throughout, an idea that Chopin may have derived from the slow movement of Mozart's Piano Concerto in C major, K. 467 (nicknamed "Elvira Madigan" by a later, less sophisticated generation), and their veiled sonority provides a perfect backdrop to the cascade of notes with which the piano adorns the main theme on its return.

Historians are fond of placing Chopin's concertos in a direct line of descent from the ones by Hummel and Moscheles, but Chopin's slow movements make such an idea difficult to sustain. Nothing prepares us for the kaleidoscopic range of color that emerges from the keyboard as the Romance unfolds, for which it is impossible to find a precedent in a work for piano and orchestra. Rather it proffers a glimpse of the later concertos of Schumann and Grieg, whose slow movements are also veiled with muted strings.

Few moments in the whole of Chopin are more compelling than the bars leading up to the recapitulation of the opening theme, which hover over Chopin's "reverie in the moonlight" like a benediction. In terms of sheer keyboard radiance these matchless measures appear to have been stolen from the pages of Debussy's Studies or from Ravel's *Miroirs*, turning the young Chopin into a time traveler.

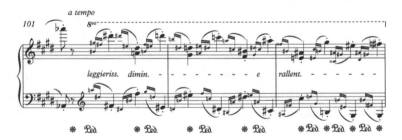

In the afterglow of this concert Konstancja and Chopin exchanged rings, although there is no evidence that this symbolized a betrothal. Still, Chopin arranged to correspond with Konstancja through his friend Jan Matuszyński, who was studying medicine at the university and agreed to act as a go-between. There was secrecy involved, but the mere fact that these arrangements were put in place indicates that the relationship had been taken to a new level, one in which it was not impossible for the couple to contemplate a future together after Chopin had returned from his foreign travels. The idea is borne out by some affectionate lines that Konstancja wrote in Chopin's album on October 25, just two weeks after the "farewell" concert, most likely in the Chopin family apartment in the Krasiński Palace.

> Sorry twists of fate you weave
> Yet yield we must to fortune.
> Remember well, as now you leave
> In Poland they do love you. K.G.

Two or three pages further on Konstancja added more lines, conveying the patriotic sentiment that "in foreign lands they may appreciate and reward you better, but they cannot love you more." She never saw the words that Chopin was to add in pencil after he had left Poland and she herself had married: "Oh yes they can!"

What of the rest of Konstancja's story? On January 31, 1832, she married Józef Grabowski, whose wealthy family owned the imposing Tepper Palace in Warsaw. Józef was attached to the Polish legation in Saint Petersburg and returned to Warsaw shortly after the uprising broke out. Konstancja's mother saw in him a good match for her daughter and with Chopin safely out of the way she had no difficulty in arranging a betrothal. Almost two years after the wedding, Izabella, in an attempt to console her brother for the loss of his "distant beloved," remarked, "I am as surprised as you that she could have been so insensitive. The palace was clearly more alluring to her."[35] After the wedding Józef purchased an estate near the village of Raducz, in the region of Piotrków, where he and his young bride settled down to country life. Konstancja was content to retire from the stage and devote herself to hearth and home, eventually producing five children. In later life the macular degeneration from which she had suffered as a student grew worse, and despite consultations with leading ophthalmologists in Poznań and Paris, she became blind. She bore her affliction with exemplary patience. When as an elderly woman Karasowski's biography of Chopin was read to her, she expressed surprise at how much she had meant to the young composer, but harbored no regrets. "I doubt whether Chopin would have been such a good husband as my

---

35. CFC, vol. 2, p. 102; KFC, vol. 1, p. 231.

honest Józef," she said. "He was temperamental, full of fantasies, and unreliable."[36] Just before she died, in December 1889, she burned all her letters and other souvenirs of Chopin, taking many secrets to the grave.

IX

As Chopin prepared to leave Warsaw, several farewell parties were arranged for him. One of them took place in the home of his schoolmate Józef Reinschmidt on Dzielna Street, who later left a reminiscence of the evening. Mikołaj Chopin was there, as was Dr. Ludwik Köller, a family friend of the Chopins who had recently returned from his medical studies in Paris. A group of Chopin's fellow students was also present, including Domuś Magnuszewski (who helped Józef to host the party), Tytus Woyciechowski, Wiktor Chelmicki, Konstanty Gaszyński, and Julian Fontana. After dinner there was a round of speeches led by Dr. Köller, who wished Chopin much success and fame abroad, and urged him "never to erase from his memory his native land and the friends he was leaving." Fontana seated himself at the piano and played some Polish folk music, which moved everyone to sing and dance. Chopin was finally persuaded to go to the keyboard. "Then from his fingers flowed so many wonderful national melodies that at times we listened with trembling hearts and tears in our eyes."[37] That same night he also composed his drinking song "Hulanka" (Merrymaking), to words by Stefan Witwicki.

On the eve of his departure, Chopin went over to Katarzyna Brzezińska's coffeehouse on Kozia Street to say farewell to some of his friends, before spending the rest of the evening at the theater.[38] The following day, November 2, he set out for Vienna. He waited for the diligence at the old post house by the city boundary in the district of Wola, where a surprise had been arranged for him. Elsner was there with a small male-voice choir from the Conservatory, gathered to sing a farewell cantata with guitar accom-

36. HFCZ, vol. 2, p. 68.
37. "Chopin's Farewell Party," recollections of Józef Reinschmidt in the periodical *Pion* (The Plummet), no. 24, June 16, 1934.
38. Rossini's *Il barbiere di Siviglia* was performed at the National Theater that night. See Kazimierz Wladyslaw Wojcicki's *Kawa literacka w Warszawie (1829–1830)*, Warsaw, 1873, p. 23.

paniment, composed for Chopin by Elsner himself. Each verse ended with the patriotic stanza

> Although you leave our native land
> Still will your heart remain with us,
> And the memory of the genius within you.
> And so, from the bottom of our hearts we say:
> "Good luck wherever you go!"[39]

It was a beautiful gesture, made all the more poignant by the tide of events that was shortly to drown Poland in blood. Tears may well have been shed at the moment of parting. But it was made bearable for Chopin by news that Tytus had at the last moment agreed to accompany him as far as Vienna, and they arranged to meet at Kalisz, near the Silesian border. Chopin boarded the diligence, the postilion blew his horn, and the old tollgate disappeared from view. He had made similar journeys in the past, but this one turned out to be different. Although he did not know it, he was leaving his homeland forever.

---

39. The words were by Ludwik Dmuszewski, the editor of the *Warsaw Courier*. A thoughtful posterity has placed on the post house at Wola a plaque that reminds us, "In this place on November 2, 1830, Chopin's friends said goodbye forever as he left his native home and Poland."

THE WARSAW UPRISING,
1830–1831

Every Pole should all his life be prepared for oppression or exile.
—Prince Adam Czartoryski[1]

I

The Warsaw Uprising began on the evening of November 29, 1830, when a group of disaffected Polish army cadets stormed the Belvedere Palace and attempted to assassinate Grand Duke Constantine. From the start everything went wrong. The fire at the old brewery near the Vistula that lit up the night sky was meant to mark the commencement of hostilities, but it was started thirty minutes early and the Russian garrison was alerted. When the conspirators reached the Belvedere Palace, they ran through the building but found the grand duke's bedroom empty. Warned by his guards, he had fled to the chambers of his wife, Joanna, via a secret passageway, clad in his nightwear. One of his functionaries, Major Mateusz Lubowidzki, a high-ranking official in the secret police, intercepted the cadets as they tried to break down the bedroom door, but he was pierced by bayonets. Meanwhile, in the grounds outside, a Russian major general, Alexander Gendre, fled the palace by the back door and ran into an ambush of Polish insurgents, who shot him to death. In all the confusion

---

1. CM, vol. 2, p. 331.

he was mistaken for Constantine, and the cry went up, "The grand duke is dead!" This false alarm probably saved Constantine from capture and death, for it gave him time to gather what was left of his wits, withdraw from Belvedere, and save himself from a conflagration with which he was singularly unprepared to deal. He eventually encamped outside the city with his bodyguards and a detachment of his troops, there to await instructions from his brother, Tsar Nicholas.[2]

Thus began an epic struggle to cast off the Russian yoke that would last for ten months. Some heroic battles were fought along the way, but through sheer force of numbers the Poles were driven onto the defensive and Warsaw fell once more under Moscow's control.

II

Chopin, we recall, had left Warsaw in the company of Tytus on November 2, more than three weeks before the uprising began. Their route had taken them through Wrocław, Dresden, and Prague. They spent four days in Wrocław, where, at the insistence of the local Kapellmeister Joseph Schnabel (an old friend of Elsner's), Chopin gave a concert in the "Ressource" Hall on November 8, and played the Romance and Rondo from his E minor Concerto. This happened by chance, for Chopin had no plans to give concerts. Schnabel had issued a friendly invitation to Chopin to attend a morning rehearsal he was conducting with an amateur pianist who was preparing to play the Moscheles E-flat piano concerto that evening. During a break in the rehearsal Schnabel turned to Chopin and asked him if he would like to try out the piano. Chopin had not practiced for a couple of weeks, but not wishing to seem discourteous he sat down at the instrument and dashed off a couple of his "Là ci darem" Variations. That was sufficient incentive for the official soloist to take fright, leaving Schnabel with no alternative but to invite Chopin to take his place. The German orchestral players were struck by Chopin's unusual technique. "*Was für ein leichtes Spiel hat er!*" ("What a light touch he has!"). As for

---

2. There are conflicting accounts of the events that took place during the first few hours of the uprising. We have mainly followed the one in DGP, vol. 1, pp. 318–19. Constantine never lived to see the final outcome of the conflict. He succumbed to cholera on June 15, 1831, before the fall of Warsaw.

the audience, they were especially pleased with his encore, an improvisation on themes from Auber's *La Muette de Portici*. Otherwise, this concert is today almost forgotten and produced no income for the pianist.

By November 12, Chopin and Tytus had arrived in Dresden, where many people remembered him from his visit the previous year, and he spent a week in the Saxon capital pursuing his contacts and being pursued by them in turn—"like a dog," as he put it. Every evening found him in the opera house, where he attended performances of Auber's *Fra Diavolo* and Rossini's *La donna del lago*. During his stay in the city he met Countess Honorata Komar and her three daughters—Delfina, Ludmila, and Natalia. Twenty-three-year-old Delfina, famous for her radiant beauty, was already estranged from her husband, Count Mieczysław Potocki, and later on, after the Komar family had moved to Paris, she took some occasional piano lessons from Chopin. The alleged romance between Chopin and Delfina proposed by an earlier generation of biographers, and the run of salacious letters that their torrid affair is supposed to have engendered, is a topic to which we propose to return in the Epilogue. In Prague, the last leg of their journey, the pair of travelers stayed just long enough to consume a hearty meal, wait for fresh horses, and board the diligence that took them across the Austrian border en route to the imperial capital. They arrived in Vienna on November 23 and checked in to the fashionable Stadt London Hotel, which proved to be so expensive that they moved almost at once to the Golden Lamb Hotel in the district of Leopoldstadt, in order to gain time to find more permanent quarters.

Barely five days later, news of the Warsaw Uprising reached them. After a couple of sleepless nights and some anguished discussions with Chopin, Tytus hurried back to Warsaw in order to join the fight. (He became a second lieutenant in the Polish army and after seeing combat was decorated with the Gold Cross for Valor.) Chopin was eager to accompany him, but was deterred by a letter from his family urging him not to risk coming home. Even so, within a few hours he impulsively packed his bags and caught the next diligence in pursuit of Tytus, only to abandon the idea when the futility of what he was doing had sunk in. He later wrote, "I curse the moment of my departure [from Warsaw]."[3] His sisters, he observed,

---

3. CFC, vol. 1, p. 237; KFC, vol. 1, p. 162.

could at least help by rolling strips of lint into bandages for the wounded, but if he returned he would simply be a burden on his father.

Chopin and Tytus had found a beautiful three-room apartment on the third floor of a house on the Kohlmarkt in the center of the old city, but with the departure of Tytus, Chopin found that he could not afford the rent of 70 florins a month. Yet he was loath to leave his new abode, because the location was ideal. The music shops of Arteria, Haslinger, and Mechetti were just around the corner, as was the Kärntnertor Theater. Quite by chance, some friends of the previous tenant (an English admiral) wanted to view one of his rooms and were so pleased with what they saw that they offered to rent the entire apartment for 80 florins on the spot. Chopin's landlady, Baroness Lachmanowicz, who had Polish connections and was well disposed toward Chopin, showed him a spacious room on the fourth floor for 10 florins, which he accepted, well pleased with the exchange. "I am now housed as well for 10 florins as I was for 70," he told his parents.[4] Conrad Graf also came to his rescue and hoisted one of his finest pianos up all four floors, free of charge.

Chopin's own description of his living quarters and daily routine can hardly be bettered. His room was large and neat and had three windows overlooking the Kohlmarkt. Whenever he looked down at the street beneath him, he tells us, the people appeared like pygmies. The mirrors placed on the walls between the windows created light and a sense of space. His bed was positioned next to the wall opposite the windows. On one side was his Graf piano, on the other a sofa. A large mahogany table occupied the center of the room. The resident servant woke him every morning and served coffee. Still in his dressing gown he would play the piano and let his coffee go cold. Meanwhile, his German-language teacher turned up around 9:00 a.m. and gave Chopin a lesson. Whenever the weather permitted, he would walk around the ramparts of the old city and take lunch at a popular restaurant called Zur Boemischen Koechin, where all the university students liked to eat. In the afternoons he called on friends and colleagues, returned home at dusk, changed into evening attire, and then ventured to some party or other, not getting back until 10:00 p.m. or later. "I come home, play the piano, have a good cry, look at

---

4. CFC, vol. 1, p. 233; KFC, vol. 1, p. 160.

things, have a laugh, get into bed, blow out my candle, and always dream about all of you."[5]

His dreams included Konstancja, as his letters to Jan Matuszyński (who was still the official go-between) readily show. "Am I still loved?" he asks plaintively. He was worried that his messages to her might be intercepted and her reputation compromised. In his next letter to Jan we find him eulogizing Konstancja as "my angel of peace." He instructed Jan to tell her that "my ashes shall be laid at her feet." Konstancja did not respond to such an extravagant notion, which led Chopin to ask his intermediary, "Did you hand over my note? Today I regret having written it. Perhaps she is fooling me and treating it as a joke." The Russian officers who spent time in her company aroused his jealousy and he disparaged them as "the epaulets." His feelings sometimes came boiling to the surface. "How I tear my hair when the thought comes that she may forget me! Those fellows! Gresser! Bezobrazow! Pisarzewski! It's too much for me. Today I feel like Othello!"[6] The image was extreme, but it was not plucked out of the air at random. Chopin had just heard a performance of Rossini's *Otello* in the Kärntnertor Theater, with Sabine Heinefetter singing the role of Desdemona, wife of Othello, and it had left its mark. The scene to which he alludes is known to all Shakespeareans. Othello, roused to a pitch of fury by rumors of Desdemona's infidelity with the young lieutenant Cassio, murders her. Othello then kills himself after discovering that Desdemona was innocent after all, her virtue intact. If the twenty-year-old Chopin really did see himself as Othello, with Konstancja as Desdemona and one of the Russian "epaulets" as Cassio, then he gives the lie to the idea that once he had left Warsaw, Konstancja was of little concern to him. In fact, she haunted his imagination for months to come.

III

One of Chopin's earliest visitors was his former traveling companion Romuald Hube, who had unexpectedly returned from a trip to Italy, had been unable to cross the frontier back to Poland, and was now stranded in

5. CFC, vol. 1, pp. 246–47; KFC, vol. 1, p. 166.
6. CFC, vol. 1, p. 245; KFC, vol. 1, p. 166.

Vienna. He lodged with Chopin for a time and looked after him when Chopin went down with a bad cold. Hube later recalled that "Chopin was always practicing on the piano, usually reworking phrases, and sometimes improvising."[7] Another visitor was Hummel, who sought him out within days of his arrival, a gesture that Chopin regarded as a great compliment. Hummel had not forgotten his encounter with the young pianist from Warsaw more than two years earlier. He was accompanied by his son, Eugen, whose aptitude for drawing was well exhibited in a portrait he drew of Chopin, as well as a picture of Chopin's room for the composer's album. Another visitor, who climbed the four flights of stairs on a daily basis, was his Polish friend Tomasz Nidecki, who arrived every morning to practice on Chopin's piano, determined to master the E minor Concerto, which he hoped to play with Chopin in a version for two pianos.

Wilhelm Würfel, who had been so helpful to Chopin in the past, was now terminally ill and could not manage the stairs (within two years he died of tuberculosis), so Chopin went over to Würfel's house to pay his respects in person. It was there that he met the Bohemian violinist Josef Slavík, whose playing aroused his admiration. Four years older than Chopin, Slavík was the leader of the imperial court orchestra and a great virtuoso. Chopin described him as a second Paganini who made the listener speechless. "He can play ninety-six notes staccato with one stroke of the bow," Chopin marveled.[8] They rehearsed together and for a time Chopin thought of writing a set of variations on a theme by Beethoven that they might play in Vienna, but the idea came to nothing. Slavík took Chopin to the home of Mme Konstancja Bayer, whose marriage to a Pole from Dresden did nothing to hide her strong infatuation for the attractive young violinist. The two musicians played for the Bayers' friends and even danced a mazurka at one of Mme Bayer's parties, an event that stimulated Chopin's puckish pen into activity. At one moment, he tells us, Slavík lay on the floor like a sheep—a posture that was doubtless meant to remind everyone of the pastoral origin of the dance. At another, an old German countess with a long nose and a pockmarked face attempted to hold up her skirt gracefully with the tips of her fingers "like they did in olden times," while performing some waltz steps (to a mazurka!) with her long, thin legs.

---

7. HRP, p. xxv.
8. CFC, vol. 1, p. 235; KFC, vol. 1, p. 161.

She kept her head at such a stiff angle in relation to her partner that her neck bones stuck out, to the dismay of her aristocratic friends, a scene that Chopin relished describing to his parents. Chopin felt at home at Konstancja Bayer's parties, but her first name brought on bouts of nostalgia. "I like to visit her because it evokes memories of . . . . ," he told Jan Matuszyński, unable to write the name of his distant beloved. "All her music, handkerchiefs, and table napkins are marked with her name."

Chopin also encountered Sigismond Thalberg and attended one of his concerts, but was not impressed.

> Thalberg plays famously but he is not my man. He is younger than I, popular with the ladies, writes pot-pourris on themes from [Auber's] *Masaniello*, produces *piano* with the pedal instead of with the hand, takes tenths as easily as I take octaves, and wears diamond shirt-studs. Moscheles does not impress him, so it is hardly surprising that Thalberg likes only the *tuttis* in my concerto. He also writes concertos.[9]

Thalberg's piano playing was like his diamond shirt-studs: there for effect. It was a deft response to the Austrian pianist's criticism of Chopin's concertos, which implied that they could be endured only when the piano itself remained silent. Chopin could wield irony with the best of them, of course. When he heard Aloys Schmidt, a pianist-composer from Frankfurt who had recently been savaged by the Viennese press, he observed, "He is already over forty years old and composes eighty-year-old music."[10]

As Christmas approached, and with no news from his family, Chopin succumbed to homesickness. On Christmas Eve he wandered near midnight into St. Stephen's Cathedral. The congregation had not yet arrived for the traditional nativity service and he found himself standing in a dark corner by a gothic pillar. Overwhelmed by the splendor of the cathedral, and by its vast silence, he fell into a kind of trance. Only the sound of the sacristan's footsteps, as this worthy went around lighting tapers in the depths of the shrine, aroused Chopin from his somber thoughts. "A grave lies behind me, another lies beneath me; the only thing missing is a grave above my head," he wrote. "A gloomy harmony arose within me—

---

9. CFC, vol. 1, p. 243; KFC, vol. 1, p. 165.
10. CFC, vol. 1, p. 254; KFC, vol. 1, p. 172.

I felt my isolation more than ever."[11] People and lights began to appear on the scene, and the service was about to begin, so Chopin pulled up the collar of his greatcoat to shield himself against the cold and joined a crowd of revelers walking toward the Imperial Chapel, where he listened to Christmas mass. He got home at 1:00 a.m. and sank into his bed, and once more dreamed of his friends and family in Warsaw.

Chopin soon found that the Vienna of 1831 was not the Vienna that he had visited less than two years earlier. The November Uprising had changed the public mood and Poles were regarded with suspicion. Austria had been the recipient of a large portion of Polish territory when the country was dismembered at the time of the last partition. If the Poles continued to make trouble, Austria would side with her two neighboring powers, Prussia and Russia. As he was eating his Christmas dinner at an Italian restaurant, he was infuriated by the conversation that drifted toward him from a nearby table. "God made a mistake when he created the Poles!" declared one diner. "Yes," responded another. "Nothing good comes out of Poland"—an echo of Metternich's rhyming aphorism "*In Polen ist nichts zu holen.*"[12] Chopin fumed at the smugness of his fellow diners. "The b——s are really enjoying themselves just now," he declared, allowing himself an expletive. Of the bloodbath that was to follow during the months ahead, no one had the slightest conception.

IV

From the depths of this despond emerged the first sketches of the Scherzo in B minor. Scholars are divided on when, exactly, Chopin began work on this composition and they sometimes assign to it the later date of 1835, the year it was published. But there is a persuasive argument to be made for placing its origins in the emotional desolation of Christmas 1830. Niecks likened the opening chords to "a shriek of despair," and what followed to the bewildered efforts of a soul shut in by a wall of circumstance "through which it strives in vain to break."[13]

---

11. CFC, vol. 1, p. 240; KFC, vol. 1, p. 163.
12. CFC, vol. 1, pp. 242–43; KFC, vol. 1, p. 165.
13. NFC, vol. 2, p. 257.

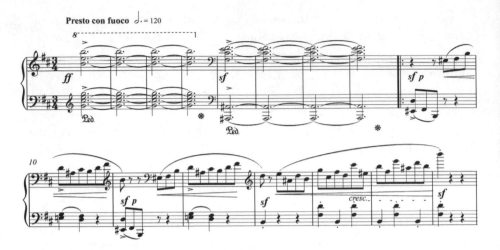

The word "scherzo," of course, is the Italian noun for "joke." But there is not much humor in the four Scherzos of Chopin, and particularly not here. This contrast between title and content drew from Schumann a penetrating observation when he reviewed the work. "If *jest* wears such dark veils, how is *gravity* to clothe itself?"[14] And this Scherzo is gravity personified, for it plumbs the depths. The music is not only agitated, it is angry. It pours out of the piano in a torrent of fury made placid only with the arrival of the Trio (not so-called by Chopin), where the connection to Poland becomes clear. Chopin paraphrases the well-known Polish Christmas carol "Lulajże Jezuniu" ("Sleep, Little Jesus"), familiar to every schoolchild in Poland. The words of the lullaby evoke the Nativity.

> Sleep, little Jesus, my little pearl,
> Sleep, my favorite little delight.
>
> Sleep, little Jesus, sleep, sleep,
> But you, lovely Mother, solace him in tears

This was the first Christmas that Chopin had spent beyond Poland's borders, and the carol summoned memories of hearth and home. Nostalgia for Christmas past pervades his setting. Of the several variants of the melody that have come down to us, the Paderewski edition of Chopin's works gives the following:

---

14. *NZfM*, May 12, 1835, p. 156.

Chopin's paraphrase of this tune (it is not a mere quotation) is magical and elevates it to an altogether higher level. The harmonic progressions are beautified here and there, while the right hand rocks back and forth in the manner of a cradle. The repeated upper F-sharp (a pedal point that runs throughout much of the episode) has been likened by one biographer to the star that shimmered over the Nativity—an image that does no harm to the passage and might even enliven an otherwise opaque interpretation of it.

The last time that Chopin heard this carol sung in Poland may well have been one year earlier, when he visited the Bernardines' Church in Warsaw for the Christmas Day service. The church, known as Saint Anne's, was located next to the music conservatory and was the official place of worship for the female singing students, including Konstancja. Something of the nostalgia evoked by these memories comes out in an inscription that he wrote at the top of a letter addressed to Jan Matuszyński on Christmas morning: "Vienna. Christmas Day [1830], Sunday Morning. Last year at this time I was at the Bernardines' Church. Today I am sitting all alone in my dressing gown, gnawing at my ring and writing."[15] We do not know if this ring was the one given him by Konstancja. But the music that follows seems to suggest that it was, because it offers a striking confirmation that she was still much on his mind. As the Christmas carol reaches its final cadence, a new melody takes over, with connections of a different kind.

15. CFC, vol. 1, p. 236; KFC, vol. 1, p. 161.

This is a direct quotation from the song "Życzenie" (The Wish) composed by Chopin the previous year and inspired by Konstancja. ("If I were the sun in the sky, I would not shine except for you.") Three times the phrase is repeated, each entry appearing at a higher level than the one before, in an upward-moving spiral that fails to reach its objective and simply falls back on itself, as if the wish remained unfulfilled. The carol then returns to cast a benediction over this memory and round off the Trio.

The spell of the lullaby is shattered by the abrupt return of the two hammer blows with which the Scherzo began—the "shriek of despair." By telescoping the return of the Introduction into the tail end of the carol, Chopin obliterates the carol. The first blow does not kill the reverie, but the second one does. It is a sovereign moment in the drama of the piece. When the Polish novelist Stanisław Przybyszewski first heard these measures, he likened them to "a primal scream of a soul" in torment.[16]

The frenzy then resumes, and the first part of the Scherzo is recapitulated in its entirety. But what are we to make of the final chords toward the end of the Scherzo? We begin to see what Chopin meant when he disclosed to Jan Matuszyński that on the outside he pretended to be calm, "but on returning home I vent my rage on the piano."[17] That rage becomes palpable on the final page of this violent piece. The dissonant chords,

16. PPS, p. 102.
17. CFC, vol. 1, p. 236; KFC, vol. 1, p. 162.

hammered out *fff*, stretch bone and sinew to the limit, as if not only the piano but the pianist too must be made to experience Chopin's pent-up violence.

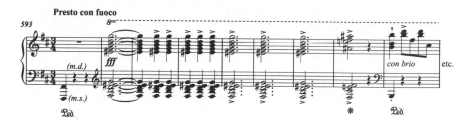

V

The ink had barely time to dry on this manuscript when news of a crucial turning point in Poland's struggle for independence came, on January 25. After several weeks of fruitless negotiations with Russia, the Sejm in Warsaw voted for the dethronement of Tsar Nicholas I as King of Poland. This was the only excuse that Nicholas required to declare war on the Poles. After making certain that his brother Grand Duke Constantine was safely out of Warsaw, the tsar mustered an army of 120,000 soldiers under the command of General Hans von Diebitsch, which crossed the Polish border on February 4 and advanced toward the capital. The Poles blocked his advance in a series of brilliant rearguard actions with an army of only 30,000 men. The opening shots of what was now the Russo-Polish War of 1831 were fired on February 14 at Stoczek, when a small detachment of the Polish army under General Józef Dwernicki routed the Russians and stopped their advance in its tracks. This had a tremendous effect on Polish morale and led to the conviction that here was a war that might actually be won. More victories followed. At the Battle of Grochów on February 25 the Russians suffered almost ten thousand casualties, but it was a costly victory for the Poles, who suffered seven thousand casualties of their own. At the Battle of Dębe Wielke, on March 31, the Poles crossed the Vistula by night, caught the Russians by surprise, annihilated an entire Russian corps, and captured a further ten thousand prisoners, including two generals. The battle raged for two days, resulting in a further Polish victory and the capture of guns and Russian flags. Another Russian corps was scattered at Iganie on April 10.

After these early successes on the battlefield, why did the Poles languish and enable General Diebitsch to regroup? In Warsaw there were those who favored a negotiated settlement with Moscow, and the Sejm was riven by dissent. Chief among the negotiators was Prince Adam Czartoryski, who, even while these early battles were being fought, had sent his emissaries to Paris, Vienna, and London in hopes of gaining political support for a peace settlement. But it all came to naught because of the obduracy of Tsar Nicholas, who refused to negotiate with anyone. When Prince Xavier Lubecki-Drucki turned up in Saint Petersburg earlier in the year with a set of formal peace proposals from Warsaw, Nicholas not only refused to meet with him, but demanded as a precondition to any negotiations the unconditional surrender of the Congress Kingdom—which rendered conversation pointless. One further setback for Czartoryski occurred when General Diebitsch, who had shown himself disposed to compromise, died of cholera, which was already reaping a harvest of death among the ranks of the Russian army. Tsar Nicholas replaced him with General Ivan Paskevich as his commander in chief, a military hero who had covered himself in glory in a number of battles in Russia's endless war against its southern neighbor Turkey. The mandate given to Paskevich was clear: crush Poland by whatever means necessary. It was to be a war to the finish.

VI

Despite the turbulent news coming out of Poland, Chopin continued to compose. The Four Mazurkas, op. 6, date from the Vienna period, as do the Five Mazurkas, op. 7. With these compositions the mazurka emerges for the first time as a sophisticated art form, a genre worthy of a place on the concert platform. Chopin himself wrote of them that "they are not for dancing,"[18] an important clue as to their true nature. They are really "mazurkas about mazurkas," recollections of the homeland, whose spirit would be sullied were they to function as music to which peasants danced. There is something else worth noting, too. These mazurkas marked the beginning of what was to become a very long succession of pieces in the genre—about sixty of them altogether.

---

18. CFC, vol. 1, p. 236; KFC, vol. 1, p. 161.

Every stage of Chopin's creative development is reflected in his mazurkas. That cannot be said of the other genres that he made famous—the polonaise, nocturne, ballade, and scherzo. Years might elapse between the composition of one such piece and another. But not with the mazurkas, the creation of which was a lifelong preoccupation.

Four Mazurkas, op. 6	Five Mazurkas, op. 7
No. 1, in F-sharp minor	No. 1, in B-flat major
No. 2, in C-sharp minor	No. 2, in A minor (a reworking of the 1824 version)
No. 3, in E major	No. 3, in F minor
No. 4, in E-flat minor	No. 4, in A-flat major (a reworking of the 1824 version)
	No. 5, in C major

Removed from their peasant origins, while remaining irrevocably linked to them, the nostalgia Chopin felt for his native country is evident on every page of these pieces. We detect in these mazurkas the first traces of that emotional world which Chopin himself described with the Polish word *Żal*. The term can mean "longing," "regret," "nostalgia," "melancholy," "grief," and even a combination of these things. Chopin's music is shot through with this inexpressible quality, familiar to all who hear it, elusive to all who attempt to analyze it. It makes its presence felt in the very opening measures of the Mazurka no. 1, in F-sharp minor, composed shortly after his arrival in Vienna and the first realization that he was cut off from his homeland.

Liszt writes about *Żal* in his book on Chopin. One evening when they were together in Paris, he tells us, Chopin was asked by one of the aristocratic ladies present, overcome by the music he had just played, to identify the source of its melancholy. He could find no appropriate expression except in his own language: the Polish word *Żal!* "Seeming to relish the sound," Liszt observed, "he repeated it frequently, as if dwelling on its meaning . . . its ability to convey intense regret."[19]

The Five Mazurkas, op. 7, were completed about the same time. Chopin's Graf piano was once again the recipient of these "songs of the soul." The first of them, the Mazurka in B-flat major, made its way around the world very quickly, and within a year or two of its publication in 1832 it had become known by the sobriquet "The Favorite," especially in Warsaw. Later on it was picked up by Kalkbrenner and used as the basis of his "Variations brillantes pour le PF, sur une Mazurka de Chopin," op. 120.

The very popularity of this mazurka has deafened us to its originality. The contrasting middle episode is an uncommon example of "emotion recollected in tranquillity." Wordsworth was talking about poetry but his epithet applies with peculiar force to music such as this. Memories are stirred of sounds heard in happier times. Recollections of childhood summers spent in the countryside of Mazovia are never far away. The "bagpipe drones" in the left hand, combined with the haunting modal melody in the right, are drawn directly from the treasury of memories that Chopin brought with him from the homeland.

---

19. LC, pp. 79–80.

The passage brings us closer to Chopin's frame of mind than many of the sentiments that he was sharing in his letters to family and friends. Words may obfuscate, but the mingled chimes of music require no translation.

The *Lento con gran espressione*, composed about the same time, bears out that thought. It emerged from the feelings of isolation and homesickness that Chopin experienced in the wake of the November Uprising. In Poland the work is sometimes called the "Reminiscence Nocturne," and for good reason. It is unique in Chopin's output because of the number of self-quotations it contains. Chopin sent a copy of the work in a letter to his family bearing the inscription "For my sister Ludwika to play before she starts to practice my second concerto" [i.e., the one in F minor]. In her own list of Chopin's compositions, Ludwika described the piece as a "Lento, with the character of a nocturne." And she appended a note with the words "Sent to me from Vienna." The manuscript was discovered in 1875 by Chopin's first Polish biographer, Marceli Antoni Szulc, who persuaded the Leitgeber publishing house in Poznań to issue it under the generic title "Adagio." Modern editions have reverted to Ludwika's description, and today the piece is classed among the nocturnes. The *Lento con gran espressione* is musical autobiography made manifest. No other work of Chopin's is constructed in quite this manner. Composed in simple reprise form, the four-bar introduction and the subsequent nocturne-like melody set the scene for reminiscences about to be stirred.

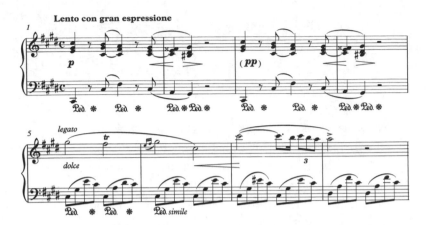

A montage of no fewer than four self-quotations follows in short order: one from the song "Życzenie" (The Wish), which Chopin had used in the B minor Scherzo, and three from the outer movements of the F minor Piano Concerto. Chopin draws this material together with such consummate ease that the twenty-five bars across which they unfold (21 to 46) sound as if they were born on the page, rather than smuggled in from other works. The first quotation, which comes from the opening of the Rondo finale of the F minor Concerto, assumes this form:

Of uncommon interest is the way in which the passage was originally notated in the autograph. The melody remained in 3/4 time, just as it was in the Concerto, while the accompaniment remained in 4/4, the time signature of the nocturne itself. The result is a pioneering example of bi-metrical notation, rare in 1830, and a harbinger of the important role that cross-rhythms were to play in Chopin's later works.

Chopin modified this passage when in 1836 he asked Ludwika to make a copy of the work for inclusion in a portfolio of his pieces for his fiancée Maria Wodzińska, and he "regularized" the notation to make the piece easier to play.[20] To this melody are attached two measures stolen from bars 41–42 of the first movement's second subject.

They lead straight into a reminiscence of the song "Życzenie" (The Wish).

From the song we are ushered seamlessly into the "village dance" section of the finale of the Concerto (bars 145ff, marked *scherzando*), an unmistakable reminder of the homeland. In the orchestral version of this passage, the rustic nature of the material is enhanced by Chopin's direction to play *col legno*—striking the strings with the stick of the bow rather than with the hair.

We do well to remember that Chopin's "reminiscences" all came from compositions as yet unpublished, which turned the *Lento con gran espressione* into an essentially private matter, intended first for Ludwika and then for those within Chopin's inner circle, the only people who might be expected to recognize the quotations. The first public performance was given by Mily Balakirev on October 17, 1894, the forty-fifth anniversary of

20. The autograph, showing Chopin's original bimetrical notation, is reproduced in KCOL, p. 264.

Chopin's death, during the celebrations surrounding the unveiling of the obelisk erected outside Chopin's birthplace in Żelazowa Wola. It was a fitting choice. By then the memories of times past enshrined within the piece were more widely shared, and the celebrations of which the *Lento* was a part can now be seen as an event that marked a turning point in Chopin's wider recognition in his native land.

VII

In Vienna, Chopin developed a warm friendship with Dr. Johann Malfatti, Beethoven's physician during the composer's final illness. Malfatti enjoyed the patronage of the royal court, some of whose members were his patients, and his marriage to the Polish countess Helena Ostrowska gave him a special insight into the plight of the Poles. He took Chopin under his wing, dined with him frequently, and prescribed various medications for him. Malfatti was a consoling presence and Chopin was able to unburden himself to "the incomparable Malfatti," as he called him. During the bouts of sadness and uncertainty to which Chopin fell prey, Malfatti reminded him of who he was and what he might accomplish. It was Malfatti's view (developed, perhaps, through his friendship with Beethoven) that an artist belonged to the world and not to any particular country, and he urged Chopin to detach himself from the anguish of Poland and develop a cosmopolitan outlook, advice that Chopin was unable to accept. Malfatti owned a spacious villa in Hietzing, on the outskirts of Vienna, and in early May Chopin journeyed there in the company of Hummel to spend the day with the doctor and his family.

Chopin also visited the Imperial Library, whose impressive collection of music manuscripts captured his attention. As he surveyed the bound volumes on the shelves, he noticed one bearing the name CHOPIN. He took it down and was surprised to see that it was his manuscript of the "Là ci darem" Variations, which Haslinger had given to the library without his knowledge. The discovery gave him pause. He was happy to be represented in one of Europe's important repositories, but his pleasure was diluted by the fact that Haslinger had never paid him for this work. Such underhand dealing bothered him, and helped to form his later ambivalence toward publishers in general and Haslinger in particular.

Chopin was meanwhile living off money that his father had transferred to him in the form of Russian rubles, converted to Austrian florins at usurious exchange rates. By June he had almost run out of funds and Mikołaj was obliged to help out again. "I notice that you have already drawn on the money intended for the remainder of your travels," Mikołaj wrote, "so I am sending a little extra allowance—we should like to send more, but it is all that we can afford . . . I rely on your prudence . . . Be as economical as you can. My heart bleeds that I cannot give you more."[21] Chopin assured his parents that although he lived thriftily, "I shall have to draw a little more money than Father has provided for me, otherwise I shall have to start my journey [from Vienna] with a very light purse."[22] This exchange between father and son is revealing. Despite Chopin's oft-repeated wish not to be a burden on his father, he often emptied the latter's purse whenever the need arose. He never did master the art of managing money, and after he had settled in Paris, Mikołaj had to chide him for his financial carelessness. Among his few personal assets was the diamond ring given him by Tsar Alexander, so Chopin instructed Mikołaj to sell it and add the proceeds to whatever money might be transferred from Warsaw.

He often went over to the Prater and wandered around the great amusement park, enjoyed the scent of the spring flowers, visited art galleries and the opera house, and suffered intermittent bouts of melancholy. During these moments of gloom he liked to go over to the home of one Mme Szaszek, a Polish émigré who put on parties for her Polish friends, and in whose company his spirits were revived. He amused everybody with what he called his "latest parlor trick"—a parody of Viennese generals, whose tight uniforms with chests full of medals and a lot of puffed-up pomposity he imitated so marvelously that those who saw his charade split their sides with laughter. He also discovered the Vienna beer halls, where he heard Johann Strauss (senior) and Joseph Lanner

---

21. CFC, vol. 1, p. 286; KFC, vol. 1, p. 179.
22. CFC, vol. 1, p. 275; KFC, vol. 1, p. 182.

play waltzes during supper. Strauss had formed his orchestra in 1825 and it had become enormously popular. Hundreds of people sat at tables, drinking beer and chatting to one another while Strauss regaled them with one waltz after another. Strauss brought the Viennese waltz indoors, transforming it from a simple Austrian pastoral dance into the sophisticated ballroom music we know today. Out of these visits arose one of Chopin's own best waltzes, in E-flat major, op. 18. It was not the first waltz he had composed, but it was the first that he allowed to be published, in 1834.

The influence of Strauss is not hard to detect, particularly in the way the episodes are deployed, providing not only thematic but key contrast as well. The first episode, presented in the subdominant key of A-flat major, requires the fingers of a virtuoso, to say nothing of a piano with an excellent repetition action, a quality we assume Chopin's Graf piano did not lack.

As the waltz unfolds, the ear is constantly refreshed by such contrasts. One of the later episodes, in the remote key of B-flat minor, mimics the "sleigh bell" effect that is found in numerous Strauss waltzes. When placed on the piano keyboard, the device acquires a special charm as the stream of acciaccaturas jostle against the main notes of the melody, almost dislodging them, and creating a frisson of dissonance in the process.

VIII

Chopin had long since lost hope of putting on concerts of his own and re-plenishing his slender resources. It was as if Vienna had become a closed city, for all memory of his earlier successes there seemed to have vanished. The new, hard-nosed manager of the Kärntnertor Theater was the ballet master Louis Duport, determined to stanch the flow of red ink created by his predecessor Count Gallenberg, who had been so well disposed toward Chopin in 1829. Duport was happy enough to open the theater to Chopin, provided that the young man assumed the costs and allowed the ad-ministration to keep the receipts. In an unusually frank letter to Józef Elsner, Chopin confessed,

> I meet with obstacles on all sides. Not only does the continuous round of mediocre pianoforte concerts ruin this genre of music, but it frightens away the public. The events in Warsaw have also af-fected my position in Vienna for the worse, just as they might have improved my chances in Paris. Nonetheless, I hope that everything will turn out for the best and that before the Carnival is over [a pop-ular Viennese holiday] I shall produce my first concerto, which is Würfel's favorite.[23]

On April 4, Chopin was offered a cameo appearance at a benefit con-cert in the Redoutensaal for the singer Mme García-Vestris, featuring ten other performers of local repute. He was billed simply as a "pianoforte player." It was a humiliating description and he was not paid. In order to avoid a looming defeat, Chopin resolved to mount a concert of his own in the Kärntnertor Theater on June 11, playing his E minor Concerto under

---

23. CFC, vol. 1, p. 251; KFC, vol. 1, pp. 170–71.

the baton of a local conductor, D. Mattis. The summer was approaching, the season was effectively over, most of the aristocratic families had left the city for their vacation homes, and there was no trace of a newspaper critic to be found. Cholera was also stalking the land, and it affected the attendance. (Rather than close the building against the disease and rob the orchestra of work, the ever-resourceful Duport had thrown caution to the wind and let Chopin mount his excursion into the unknown.) Inevitably the expenses were greater than the receipts and Chopin lost money.[24] It was a further worry for Mikołaj, who saw his bank transfers evaporating into thin air. Out of pocket, and out of sorts with everything in Vienna, Chopin knew that he would have to get out of what was rapidly turning into a financial wasteland.

His preferred destination had always been Italy. But riots had broken out and civil unrest was sweeping the country. Bologna, Modena, Ancona, Parma, and then Rome had succumbed to violence; the Carbonari had set up revolutionary cells across the country, making travel risky. Paris was a safer alternative, but the Russian embassy was reluctant to issue Chopin with travel documents to France, a country that had barely emerged from its own revolution, was unfriendly toward Russia, and was already filling up with Polish refugees bent on making trouble for Moscow. Why add Chopin to their number? So Chopin requested permission to travel to London instead, which was a beacon of stability in these troubled times. The Russians at first "mislaid" his passport, causing further delays. Meanwhile, he had to secure a *Gesundheitspass* (health certificate) declaring him to be free of cholera, without which he would not be permitted to move across the Austrian frontier. It was mid-July before he received a visa from the Russians, but it allowed him to travel only as far as Munich. "Never mind," he observed, "I'll have Monsieur Maison, the French ambassador, sign it."[25] That is how he came to have his passport endorsed "To London via Paris." He often quoted this phrase—*Passeport en passant par Paris à Londres*—in order to garner amusement after he had settled permanently in Paris: "I am here only in passing."

On July 20, Chopin set out for Munich in the company of Alfons

24. There is a brief mention of this little-known concert in the *Allgemeine Theaterzeitung*, June 18, 1831.
25. CFC, vol. 1, p. 272; KFC, vol. 1, p. 181.

Kumelski, a Polish biologist who had just finished his studies and was now returning to Warsaw. Their route took them through Linz and Salzburg, where they visited the birthplace of Mozart. In a letter to his family, Kumelski observed that just as they alighted from the diligence the ancient clock above the residence of the archbishop was striking six o'clock. Chopin was puzzled by what he heard. The clock was chiming a well-known duet from a recent opera by Auber, *Le Maçon*. How was it possible that this old clock, with its antique mechanism, had anticipated Auber by a century or more? Had Auber copied the melody from the clock? Inquiries were made, and Chopin was amused to discover that the clock keeper, who was a keen opera lover, had mastered the mechanism of this timepiece and liked to change it to reflect his latest enthusiasms.

Chopin was obliged to linger in Munich because the additional funds that his father had promised to send him had not yet caught up with him. In order to save money he and Kumelski lodged with the court cellist Carl Schönche, whose apartment on Briennerstrasse lay in the center of the city. Chopin had brought several letters of introduction from Vienna, and during the enforced delay they helped him form some useful contacts in the Bavarian capital. When he decided to arrange a concert, the local musicians rallied to his side. Assisted by four singers from the opera house and a clarinetist, this midday concert took place in Munich's Odeon Theater on August 28, under the aegis of the Philharmonic Society. Chopin played his Concerto in E minor and the Grand Fantasia on Polish Airs in the chamber versions of these pieces. The Concerto was divided into two parts, with the tenor Herr Bayer singing a Cavatina with clarinet and piano accompaniment (the one by Schubert?) placed between the first and second movements. It secured for Chopin a favorable review in Munich's *Flora* journal, which noted his "charming delicacy of execution" in the Concerto—a bouquet thrown perhaps in the direction of the pianist and away from the composition. The Polish Fantasia fared better ("these Slavonic folk songs seldom fail to arouse the listener") and both composer and composition "gained unanimous applause."[26]

Chopin's money arrived at last and he left Munich at the beginning of September, en route for Stuttgart, where he booked into a local hotel. Kumelski stayed behind in Munich and Chopin found himself a stranger

---

26. Issue of August 30, 1831.

in a strange city. The news from Poland was bad and daily growing worse. The Poles had suffered grievous losses on the battlefield and were digging in around Warsaw for a last-ditch defense of the city in anticipation of a final Russian assault. It was only after Chopin arrived in Stuttgart that he learned of the true scale of the battle and the bloodbath that had taken place.

IX

General Ivan Paskevich had assumed command of the Russian army in mid-June 1831. He had at his disposal seventy-four infantry battalions, more than a hundred squadrons of cavalry, fifty companies of Cossacks, and 318 heavy guns—approximately 200,000 men all told. The Poles for their part had mustered an army of 150,000 men, but many of them were required to garrison other parts of the country considered at risk.

For the defense of Warsaw the Poles had put in place an army of 40,000 men and 95 horse-drawn cannon. The civilian population was recruited to help excavate a series of redoubts, or earthworks, which were thrown up in the shape of a wide horseshoe around the city, behind which the troops dug in and waited. The Russians deployed 80,000 men and 390 cannon, and they encircled the city. The final assault was launched on September 6, at 4:00 a.m. The Russians directed their main attack against a key position, the heavily defended Redoubt no. 54 at the Catholic churchyard in the district of Wola. General Józef Sowiński, "the soldier with the wooden leg," was charged with defending this key position and given command of a single regiment of soldiers comprising about thirteen hundred men. The Russians threw eleven battalions at him and overwhelmed his troops; Sowiński himself was killed in the battle. At the climax of the hand-to-hand fighting, a Polish soldier in a suicidal attempt to turn the tide of battle put a match to the powder store, and the resulting explosion blew up the entire redoubt, resulting in carnage that decimated both defenders and attackers alike. The bodies of the newly dead were now strewn across the graves of those long dead. Hours after the conflict had swept into the center of the city, Sowiński's corpse was still pinned against a gun carriage in the Wola churchyard, pierced by bayonets and "standing eerily erect on its wooden leg."[27] Warsaw capitulated at midnight on September 7 and 8, with the suburbs in flames and convoys of refugees attempting to flee the city.

Russian retribution was swift and harsh. Paskevich was under orders to punish the Poles, and he went to work with a will. Ten thousand Polish officers were cashiered and condemned to penal servitude in Russia. About eighty thousand rankers in the Polish army were forcibly drafted into the Russian army and sent to the Caucasus to fight in the tsar's ongoing war against the Shamils in Dagestan, near the Turkish border. For the civil population the reprisals were especially ruthless. Eight hundred "orphaned" children, whose fathers had been killed in battle, were forcibly removed from their mothers at bayonet point and handed over to Russian infantry regiments to be "reeducated." Beyond Warsaw itself, the punishment may have been still more severe. More than five thousand families in Podolia were dispossessed, stripped of their lands and personal possessions, and transported to the Caucasus, joining the millions of serfs already under Muscovy's dominion. Their elegant manors and surrounding estates, which had belonged to these families in some cases for generations, were treated as spoils of war and handed over to Russian generals and their friends.

Most remnants of the Congress Kingdom were abolished—the army, the courts, the universities, the ministries. Only the church escaped.[28] Poland was effectively wiped from the map, absorbed into the Russian empire, and ruled by military decree. Paskevich was given a new title, "Prince of Warsaw," but the Poles preferred to call him "the Hound of Mogilev" in light of the wholesale public hangings carried out in that province by his subordinate Governor-General Mikhail Muravyov. At the personal insistence of Tsar Nicholas, Prince Roman Sanguszko, of royal blood, was sentenced to hard labor for life, chained to a gang of convicts, and forced to walk to Siberia, a terrible journey of 3,300 kilometers, which took ten months to accomplish. (Joseph Conrad immortalized

---

27. DGP, vol. 2, p. 238.
28. The papal encyclical of Pope Gregory XVI *cum primum* (June 9, 1832), which was addressed to "all the archbishops and bishops residing in Poland," may explain why. It implicitly criticized the uprising by abjuring violence. "We shed abundant tears at the feet of God," lamented Gregory from the safety of Rome, "grieving over the harsh evil with which some of our flock was afflicted. Afterward We humbly prayed that God would enable your provinces, agitated by so many and so serious dissensions, to be restored to peace and to the rule of legitimate authority." By "legitimate authority," of course, Gregory meant the authority of Moscow.

The Abduction of Polish Children by Russian Soldiers, September 1831, a lithograph
by Nicolaus Maurin, after a painting by M. Twarowski (c. 1832).

the trial of Sanguszko in his short story "Prince Roman.") The remaining population was subjected to punitive taxation and forced to pay for
the huge army of occupation that took over the country. Since the minis-
try of finance had been abolished, the coin of the realm—the złoty—no
longer existed and was replaced with the Russian ruble. This caused severe
economic problems for Polish families—including for a time the Chopin
family—who suddenly found their savings worthless. Ten thousand Poles
left the country and formed the core of what became known as "The
Great Emigration." They sought sanctuary in Western Europe, and even in
America. Liberal opinion in Paris, London, and New York, firmly opposed
to the suffering that Poland was made to endure, fueled an anti-Russian
sentiment that smoldered for the rest of the century.[29]

     And what of the leaders of the insurrection? Prince Adam Czartoryski
and nine of his peers were condemned to death by decapitation. Three

---

29. DGP, vol. 2, pp. 232–45.

hundred and fifty others were sentenced to be hanged. Most of them escaped capture, including Czartoryski, who with the help of the army made his escape through Galicia and finally settled in Paris. By his refusal to negotiate, Tsar Nicholas transformed Czartoryski, who was always prepared to seek accommodation with Moscow, from a passive conservative into an active rebel. In his memoirs, Czartoryski excoriates Nicholas and calls him "the scourge of my country."[30]

X

These catastrophic events had just started to unfold as Chopin's journey to Stuttgart took place. His "Stuttgart Diary" tells of his growing anguish. This album had been given to him a year or so earlier in Warsaw, but aside from containing some random lines from Gładkowska and Żywny, Chopin himself had hardly touched it. Suddenly this small notebook became the recipient of his most turbulent thoughts, and the outpouring of feelings he confided to its pages transformed it into a document of capital importance. As he contemplated the bed in the room he was renting in the Stuttgart hotel, his morbid thoughts often got the better of him.

---

30. CM, p. 124. A few further words about Czartoryski are in order. After narrowly evading capture by the Russian army at Kraków, Czartoryski secured a passport from Metternich, issued to him under the name of "George Hoffman." Because of the uncertain political situation in Paris, Czartoryski headed first for Britain, where he hoped to gain the ear of Parliament. He arrived incognito in London on December 22, 1831, with little more than the clothes he stood up in. It took more than a week before Czartoryski was granted an interview with the foreign secretary, Lord Palmerston. He found Palmerston somewhat aloof, a cautious politician who was in no hurry to enter into a confrontation with Russia. There were two crucial debates in the House of Commons during Czartoryski's protracted stay in London. At the first of them, on June 28, the condemnation of Russia's actions was unanimous. Tsar Nicholas was described as a "miscreant," and when Palmerston expressed regret at such unparliamentary language, there were verbal exchanges in the House during which the tsar was degraded still further to the level of "a monster in human form." (CM, vol. 2, p. 336.) The British newspapers were highly sympathetic toward the Poles ("The cause is glorious— and the sentiment of Polish freedom beats in every British heart," wrote The Times at the height of the conflict, in its issue of August 11, 1831). Czartoryski's wife and three children joined him briefly in London, where he at first wanted to settle, but he finally took up permanent residence in Paris because, as he himself said, his wife, Princess Anna, could not adapt to the British climate.

How strange! This bed on which I shall lie has been slept on by more than one dying man, but today it does not repel me! No doubt more than one corpse has lain on it, and who knows for how long? And am I any better than a corpse? Like a corpse I am without news of my father, mother, sisters, or Tytus. Like a corpse I have no lover. It cannot speak in its own language to those around it. Like a corpse I too am pale and cold and indifferent to everything. A corpse has ceased to live, and I too have had enough of life.[31]

When Chopin wrote these words, he did not know that Warsaw had already fallen. The news that the Russians had taken the city on September 8 only reached him ten days later, together with graphic accounts of the massacre that followed.[32] The words that come to mind when we think of Chopin generally include "fastidious," "aristocratic," "remote," and "refined." But the language that he went on to confide to his diary seems to flow from a different pen.

Stuttgart. I wrote the above lines not knowing that the enemy has reached my home! The suburbs are stormed—burned down! Jaś [Matuszyński], where are you? Wiluś [Kolberg] has surely perished on the ramparts. I see Marcel [Celiński] in chains. Sowiński, that good patriot, is a prisoner in the hands of those scoundrels. Oh God! Do you exist? You exist but you do not avenge us. Have the Muscovites not yet committed crimes enough for you, or are you yourself a Muscovite?

Chopin's thoughts now turn to his family.

My poor kind father! Perhaps he is starving. Maybe he has nothing to buy bread for my mother? Perhaps my sisters have fallen victims to the fury of the Muscovite soldiers! Paskevich, that dog from Mogilev, seizes the residence of the first Monarchs of Europe!

31. SAC, p. 41.
32. News of the collapse of Warsaw could not have reached Chopin before September 18, which is when the Berlin and Munich newspapers first published their descriptions of the entry of Paskevich's army into the city. See the persuasive argument advanced in favor of this date by Zofia Helman and Hanna Wróblewska-Straus in HW-S.

Moscow rules the world? O Father, is this the consolation of your old age? Mother, poor suffering Mother, is it for this that you out-lived your daughter? O churchyard of Powązki! [Where Emilia was buried.] Did they respect her grave, or has it too been trampled underfoot, a thousand other corpses piled above it? They have burned down the city! O why could I not kill a single Muscovite! O Tytus, Tytus!

As for Konstancja,

What has happened to her? Where is she? Poor girl. Perhaps she is in some Muscovite's hands. Maybe some Muscovite is beating her, strangling her, murdering, killing her. Ah, my darling! Here I am, alone. Come to me. I'll wipe away your tears. I'll heal your wounds by reminding you of the past—of the days when there were no Muscovites, of the days when a few Muscovites strove to win your favor, but you scorned them because of me—me—not because of Grabowski![33] Do you have a mother? Yes, you have a mother, such a cruel one. Mine is so kind, but perhaps I have no mother now. Perhaps some Muscovite has killed her—murdered her. My sisters, raving, resist. My father, in despair, is helpless. There is no one to help my mother. And I am here doing nothing, empty-handed, groaning and suffering, only able to pour out my grief at the piano. But what more can I do? O God, make the earth tremble so that it may swallow up this generation. May the most frightful torments seize the French for not coming to our aid.[34]

Chopin utters three curses in this heartfelt cry—against Russia, against France, and against God. According to legend his fury overflowed into his "Revolutionary" Study, op. 10, no. 12, although Chopin himself is silent on the matter and the title is not his. In Stuttgart the mask of genteel

---

33. Józef Grabowski, Konstancja's future husband. The reference indicates that Chopin had learned about their forthcoming nuptials during his recent stay in Vienna.

34. SAC, pp. 43–44. This source gives a history of the album and reproduces two of the original pages of the "Stuttgart Diary." The album was destroyed during World War II, but a photocopy of the document, including the pages of the "Stuttgart Diary," is preserved in the Chopin Museum, Warsaw, under the call number M.67-1953.

A fragment from Chopin's "Stuttgart Diary," September 1831. "The enemy has reached my home."

civility that Chopin always presented to the outside world was removed and for one unique moment we catch a glimpse of unbridled aggression striking out in all directions. The "Stuttgart Diary" reveals a crucible of emotions impossible to contain. There was hatred against those who had sacked his country; venom for all things Russian; a need for vengeance; overwhelming fear for the safety of his family; genuine remorse at his own helplessness; and feelings of deep inferiority mixed with a peculiar brand of self-loathing, born of the knowledge that he was too impotent to take up arms in defense of his homeland. Such naked revelations were never to be repeated, for within days the mask was back in place, and the world was not given a second chance to witness the emotions that lay behind it. His peroration tells it all. "My heart died in me for a while . . . No words can describe my misery." When the text of the diary was first published (in 1871, by Count Stanisław Tarnowski, a professor of Polish literature at the University of Kraków), its authenticity was doubted. It seemed impossible that the fastidious Chopin, who was always so careful to groom himself in word and deed when presenting himself to others, could have penned such violent lines. But graphological evidence provided by the document proves that the handwriting is his. Of greater psychological interest is the turning point that Stuttgart represented for Chopin. One line commands attention. "I am . . . only able to pour out my grief at the piano." Whether he was conscious of some deeper purpose guiding him at that moment, we cannot know. But those words were rich in prophecy.

Chopin remained in Stuttgart for at least a week before gathering himself for the final leg of his journey and boarding the mail coach that would convey him via Strasbourg to Paris. It was a bone-breaking trip of 650 kilometers, which with various rests along the way took about ten days to complete.

AN EXILE IN PARIS, 1831–1833

I am forced to think of making my way in the world as a pianist . . .
Nothing can extinguish my perhaps too audacious but noble wish
and intention to create for myself a new world.

—Chopin[1]

I

During the early evening of October 5 the diligence conveying Chopin and his fellow travelers from Strasbourg came to a halt outside the terminal building on the rue des Messageries, Paris.[2] It was already getting dark and no one was there to greet him. The other passengers soon dispersed and went their several ways, swallowed up in the labyrinth of narrow streets and medieval alleyways that constituted the Poissonnière district of the old city, adjoining Montmartre. With a heavy traveling trunk and a thick portfolio of manuscripts to manage, Chopin had to set about finding somewhere to stay. Travelers in transit were often recommended to lodge at a small inn on the nearby rue de la Cité Bergère, and that is where Chopin rented accommodation until he had found his bearings. He remained there for six weeks.

---

1. CFC, vol. 2, pp. 52–53; KFC, vol. 1, p. 205.
2. Until recently the date of Chopin's arrival in Paris was unknown. The city's police records confirm that it was October 5. HW-S, pp. 100–101.

Chopin had no fixed plans to stay in Paris. His travel documents, obtained through the Russian embassy in Vienna, merely gave him permission to pass through the French capital en route to London. Yet in the end Paris became his home. By mid-November he had found a small apartment on the fifth floor of 27 Boulevard Poissonnière, with a small balcony that offered magnificent views across Paris to the distant Panthéon. Shortly after taking possession of his new abode Chopin set down some first impressions in a letter to his traveling companion Alfons Kumelski, the biologist in whose company he had journeyed from Vienna as far as Munich, and who had now moved on to Berlin. Paris, a teeming metropolis of about one million inhabitants and ten times larger than Warsaw, was a complete contrast to anything Chopin had so far experienced.

November 18, 1831

You find here the greatest splendor, the greatest squalor, the greatest virtue, and the greatest vice; at every step you see posters advertising cures for ven[ereal] disease—nothing but cries, noise, din, and mud, past anything you can imagine. One is able to disappear in this paradise and in one respect it is very convenient: no one inquires how anyone else manages to live. You can walk about in winter dressed like a tramp and yet frequent the best society. One day you may eat the most copious dinner for thirty-two *sous* in a restaurant full of mirrors and gilded moldings and lit by gas—and the next day you may go for lunch to a place where they will give you just about enough to feed a bird, making you pay three times as much . . . And so many sisters of mercy [i.e., prostitutes]! They pursue the men, and there are plenty of strong, tough fellows about. I regret that the souvenir of Teresa (despite the ministrations of Bénédict, who considers my misfortune to be insignificant) has not allowed me to taste the forbidden fruit. I have already got to know a few lady vocalists—and the ladies here are even more eager for "duets" than those from the Tyrol.[3]

The passing reference to "Teresa" points to an encounter with a prostitute somewhere en route from Vienna to Munich, an incident that evidently

---

3. CFC, vol. 2, pp. 15–16; KFC, vol. 1, pp. 186–87.

took place while he and Kumelski were passing through the Austrian Tyrol. Teresa's "souvenir," an unwelcome case of a sexually transmitted infection, was treated by one Bénédict, which temporarily inhibited further sexual activity—the "forbidden fruit," to use Chopin's euphemistic phrase. This disclosure by Chopin is unusual, for nowhere else in his correspondence does he come close to confessing to such liaisons. We are left to conclude that this may have been his first sexual encounter, a traveler's tale worth recounting. His entertaining description of the "lady vocalists" who frequented his neighborhood and who were desirous of performing "duets" suggests that he was not displeased at being propositioned by them.

From his lofty perch on the fifth-floor balcony Chopin observed far more than the normal hustle and bustle of life on the streets. Paris was riven by political dissent. The reign of King Louis-Philippe was barely six months old, but the poverty-stricken lower classes whom he professed to represent, calling them "my comrades," were already in rebellion against their "citizen king." Riots broke out just below Chopin's balcony as the various political factions confronted one another.

> There are medical students, the so-called Young France group, who wear beards and have a special way of tying their cravats—I must mention that each political party wears them differently (I'm speaking of the extremists): the Carlists have green waistcoats; the Republicans and Bonapartists, i.e., "Young France," have red ones; the Saint-Simonists or "New Christians" (who are devising an original religion of their own and have already a huge number of converts—they, too, preach equality) have blue ones, and so on.[4]

When the crowds got out of hand, the gendarmes moved in, blowing their whistles, attempting to restore order. There was a further surge of excitement when General Girolamo Ramorino moved into an apartment opposite Chopin's and large numbers of expatriate Poles and their sympathizers converged on the area to greet him. This general, an Italian military adventurer who had served under Napoléon and had fought with the Poles during the Warsaw Uprising, was regarded as a national hero.

---

4. CFC, vol. 2, p. 57; KFC, vol. 1, p. 208.

"A thousand anti-government agitators made their way across town with a tricolor banner to salute Ramorino," wrote Chopin.[5] Despite the cheers that went up from the crowd ("*Vive les Polonais!*"), Ramorino failed to appear, perhaps not wishing to provoke the government of Louis-Philippe. He sent instead to subdue the throng his Polish aide-de-camp Tytus Dzialyński, who assured them, "General Ramorino will appear another day." It is doubtful that the famous swashbuckler did, but the damage was already done. Chopin tells us that a massive demonstration took place in front of the Panthéon, which was within his distant view. It grew like an avalanche, he said, as the crowds gathered force then rushed the left bank of the Seine and reached the Pont Neuf, intent on moving toward General Ramorino's residence. The cavalry was brought in to stop them, many demonstrators were wounded, and arrests were made. A separate crowd had meanwhile assembled beneath Chopin's windows, waiting to be joined by the mob approaching from the other side of town. A detachment of infantry was brought in, and when that proved ineffective they were joined by mounted hussars and gendarmes who cleared the sidewalks and arrested the ringleaders. ("And all this in a free nation!" Chopin observed in wonderment.) The shops were closed, the streets were patrolled, and the orderlies were hissed as they passed through. Unknown to the demonstrators, General Ramorino had secretly vacated his apartment, having concluded that discretion was the better part of valor. After twelve hours it was all over, and ended with the crowd singing the "Marseillaise." "You cannot imagine what impression the menacing voice of the people made on me," Chopin wrote from his ringside seat on Boulevard Poissonnière.[6] He generally disliked crowds and hated yet more the mentality of the mob, but he was clearly buoyed by the revolutionary turmoil going on around him.

---

5. Ibid.
6. Ibid. To Ramorino is owed a distinction rare in the annals of military history. After being found guilty of incompetence and insubordination at the Battle of Novara (1849), he requested and was granted the privilege of commanding the firing squad himself.

II

The "Great Emigration" was by now well under way and thousands of displaced Poles were settling in France. Most of the Polish intelligentsia spoke French, and memories of Napoléon and the former Duchy of Warsaw were still fresh in the minds of the older generation. It has been estimated that between six thousand and seven thousand Polish exiles settled in Paris after 1831. They consisted of poets, journalists, painters, musicians, aristocrats, statesmen, and generals. Among the poets were Adam Mickiewicz, Juliusz Słowacki, Zygmunt Krasiński, and Cyprien Norwid; the painters included Teofil Kwiatkowski and Piotr Michałowski, whose famous portrait of Napoléon mounted on a white charger has become iconic; among the generals were Karol Kniaziewicz, Henryk Dembiński, and Józef Bem, whose skills as an artillery officer were later recruited by the Hungarians in their own fight for independence against Austria during the Transylvanian campaign of 1848. The aristocrats and statesmen included Count Ludwik Plater, Count Władysław Ostrowski, and Prince Casimir Lubomirski. As for musicians, several of Chopin's boyhood friends drifted into Paris shortly after he himself arrived there, including Antoni Orłowski and Julian Fontana, who became Chopin's trusted amanuensis, his chief music copyist, and the editor of his posthumous works. Fontana played a vital part in Chopin's affairs, shared an apartment with him on the rue de la Chaussée d'Antin for a couple of years (1836–38), and eventually took on the unrewarding role of general factotum.

No one among the members of the Polish diaspora was more closely attached to Chopin than Wojciech (Albert) Grzymała. By the time Grzymała first got to know Chopin, toward the end of 1832, this flamboyant personality had experienced the kind of adventures that could well have been drawn from the pages of a novel. He was a polyglot who spoke five languages—Polish, Russian, German, French, and Italian, with a smattering of English for good measure—a legacy that reflected a career that had taken him to every one of those countries. Grzymała has been described by his modern biographer as "Chopin's most trusted confidant," an assessment with which it is difficult to disagree.[7] Chopin wrote more than seventy letters to Grzymała, more than to any other known corre-

---

7. ACC, pp. 109–26.

spondent. As for Grzymała, his devotion to Chopin was complete. He adored the music and he loved the man.

Grzymała had been a participant in the Decembrist movement to overthrow Tsar Nicholas I, which earned him a three-month stretch in jail. After delivering a fiery speech at the memorial service for Stanisław Staszic, Grzymała found his sentence increased to three years by a vengeful Nicholas, who had him incarcerated in the dungeons of the Peter and Paul Fortress in Saint Petersburg. After his return to Warsaw, the thirty-six-year-old Grzymała was recruited by the Polish government to serve as a director of the Bank of Poland, in which capacity he was sent to Britain to negotiate loans and the purchase of weapons to aid the Polish insurgency. Thanks to his knowledge of the Bourse, he made a small fortune trading on the stock exchange and became independently wealthy. When the Warsaw Uprising broke out he was in England, where he aligned himself with the rebel government. Condemned to death in absentia by the Russians, he moved in 1831 to Paris, joining the stream of expatriates already flooding into the city. There he became chairman of the Polish Bank and president of L'Avenir Maritime Insurance Company. His wealth gave him entrée into the highest circles, and he mixed as easily with the military as with politicians, aristocrats, and the literati. Always a ladies' man, the strikingly handsome Grzymała had entered into matrimony in Warsaw with a much younger girl, Michalina Krüger, a union that had produced a son (Wincenty, born out of wedlock in 1820), but about which hardly anything else is known. His matrimonial bond did not prevent him from forming close ties with other women, including George Sand, whom he got to know as early as December 1831. Sand refers to him at that time as "her friend and table companion."[8] He played an important role in bringing Chopin and Sand together in 1836, acting as confidant and counselor to both of them. Grzymała was a co-founder of the Polish Literary Society (a political organization in everything but name), under cover of which he formed a vibrant network of subversive contacts, which later got him into difficulties with the French authorities, forcing him into hiding after the 1848 revolution had driven King Louis-Philippe into exile.

---

8. CGS, vol. II, p. 195.

III

History might well have marginalized these disparate individuals as the flotsam of an insurrection washed up on the shores of a democratic France. And that would have remained their fate had it not been for the arrival in Paris of Prince Adam Czartoryski, in the summer of 1832, who gave the Polish diaspora a political face by forming a *de facto* Polish government in exile. They rallied around his inspired leadership and within a year Paris had become the new capital of Poland, with Czartoryski referred to as its uncrowned king.

Chopin's biographers have been generally reluctant to tackle the question of just how vigorously he attached himself to the Polish cause. His correspondence contains hardly a word about it, so the question always remained moot. Yet the evidence that he enjoyed a high profile within the Polish diaspora lies everywhere to hand. He was proud to join the Polish Literary Society when he was offered membership in 1833. He often played at the Czartoryskis' sumptuous home on the Faubourg-du-Roule. Later on, after Czartoryski had acquired the Hôtel Lambert, a splendid property at the far end of the Île Saint-Louis on the Seine, and turned it into the official address of the Polish government in exile, Chopin performed there, too, playing the piano in support of Polish causes. One of his best pupils was Princess Marcelina Czartoryska (*née* Radziwiłł), the niece of Czartoryski—a connection that gave him a privileged position within Czartoryski's family circle. Years later, during Chopin's celebrated visit to Britain, in 1848, he was greeted by two of Czartoryski's agents (Major Karol Szulczewski and Leonard Niedźwiedzki), who helped him smooth over some of his travel and living arrangements. Such connections are not easily glossed over and speak to a stronger bond with Polish exiles than is generally conceded. Meanwhile, the Russian embassy in Paris was a veritable nest of spies, reporting back to Moscow from its headquarters in the Place Vendôme, and Chopin was watched along with everybody else.

Among the non-Polish musicians whose acquaintance Chopin made during these first few months in Paris—Liszt, Berlioz, Hiller, and Mendelssohn among them—none was closer to him than the cellist Auguste Franchomme, for whom he would eventually write his Cello Sonata, op. 65. Franchomme was one of the few individuals in whose company Chopin felt completely at ease. Quiet, reserved, and tactful in conversation, Franchomme had much in common with Chopin, who recognized in him a kindred spirit. In Franchomme's presence Chopin was able to drop the mask of polite formality that he generally wore for the benefit of others, and be himself. They dined often together, enjoyed occasional outings to the theater or the opera, and once made a joint excursion to Enghien-les-Bains to take the waters. Above all, they played chamber music together. Franchomme admired Chopin's nuanced piano playing and found in him a perfect partner, responsive to the inflections in his own performance. They often held impromptu rehearsals at each other's apartment, where they might sometimes play before a select audience of friends. After Franchomme's marriage to Amélie Paillot in 1837, Chopin continued to be a welcome visitor in the cellist's home, where he adored the couple's three children, Cécile, René, and Louise, and was adored by them in turn. Franchomme was the only non-Polish friend, other than his pupil Adolf Gutmann, whom Chopin addressed with the intimate *tu* in his correspondence. And in the dark days toward the end of Chopin's life, Franchomme provided him with emotional and material support. He was one of the pallbearers at Chopin's funeral.

IV

Chopin had brought with him two letters of introduction to Paris, one from Dr. Malfatti addressed to Ferdinando Paër, the director of the Italian Opera; and another from Elsner to the venerable opera and oratorio composer Jean-François Le Sueur, who taught composition at the Conservatoire and whose distinguished roster of pupils included Berlioz, Ambroise Thomas, and Charles Gounod. The letter to Paër proved especially useful, because it was in his home that Chopin met Rossini, Henri Herz, and Friedrich Kalkbrenner, a pianist of European renown and a leading member of the musical establishment, whose early support was to prove vital to Chopin. Kalkbrenner introduced him in turn to his business partner Camille Pleyel, the piano manufacturer with whose instruments the name of Chopin was soon to become permanently linked.

Chopin's first encounter with Kalkbrenner was one of those meetings at which one wishes a camera had been present, to say nothing of a microphone. Kalkbrenner was renowned for the clarity and precision of his piano playing. The rapidity of his scales and passagework aroused universal admiration. Each individual note shone like a jewel, whatever its velocity. Arpeggios would cascade up and down the keyboard with no apparent effort on the part of the pianist himself, who sat immobile before the instrument that obeyed his every whim. Paër described Kalkbrenner's playing as "polished as a billiard ball," and he provided a fine military analogy when he observed that Kalkbrenner "directed his fingers like a well-drilled company of soldiers," somewhat like a general surveying the conflict from his headquarters situated some distance behind the battle lines. Not for him the mud and gore of trench warfare, with its hand-to-hand combat. Whatever the demands of the keyboard, Kalkbrenner played with an aristocratic disdain for the difficulties confronting him, observing the battle with Zen-like detachment from afar.

Chopin had always wanted to hear Kalkbrenner play in order to test the legend against reality. He was sincerely impressed by the perfection of the virtuoso's playing and his response is worth noting because it reveals the qualities that Chopin valued in piano playing: "Herz, Liszt, Hiller, and the rest are nobodies compared with Kalkbrenner . . . It is impossible to describe his *calm*, his enchanting touch, his incomparable evenness and mastery, which he reveals in every note. He is a giant who tramples underfoot the Herzes, Czernys, and of course me!"[9] This was a judgment that Chopin might later have wished to retract, but it was true for him at the time. Kalkbrenner invited Chopin to play something, and the young man obliged with a performance of his E minor Concerto. Kalkbrenner then inquired whether he had ever been a pupil of Field's, observing that he played in the style of Cramer but had the touch of Field. "I was terribly pleased to hear that," Chopin wrote, "but even more pleased when Kalkbrenner took his seat at the piano in order to show off to me but got lost and had to stop." This was a passing slip from which Kalkbrenner quickly recovered, for Chopin added, "You should have heard how he took the repeat—I never imagined anything like it." Thereafter the two musicians met almost daily and their friendship blossomed. Kalkbrenner then made his storied proposition that Chopin should become his pupil for a period of

9. CFC, vol. 2, p. 41; KFC, vol. 1, pp. 199–200.

three years, during which time he would acquire a "solid foundation," ought not to appear in public, but would emerge as a "finished artist."

It was a breathtaking proposal, given everything that we know about Chopin's accomplishments up to that moment. But it was typical of Kalkbrenner's inbred sense of superiority. Chopin was at first unsure what to do and wrote to his family for advice. Mikołaj Chopin was baffled and could not imagine why it would be necessary for his son to spend three years as Kalkbrenner's apprentice, acquiring a "solid foundation." He consulted Elsner, who was strongly opposed to the idea. "They've recognized genius in Fryderyk," he wrote, "and are already scared that he will outstrip them, so they want to keep their hands on him for three years in order to hold back something which Nature herself might push forward."[10] Ludwika went even further when, after cautioning Chopin to have nothing to do with the proposal, told him that she had picked up some gossip that the celebrated Polish pianist Maria Szymanowska had called Kalkbrenner "a scoundrel," that his real aim was to cramp Chopin's genius. In the event, Chopin did not need any of this well-meant advice; he decided to heed his inner voice and follow his own path. There is no evidence that this decision affected his relationship with Kalkbrenner; they remained on friendly terms and even gave concerts together. Their early connection was strengthened when Chopin dedicated his E minor Piano Concerto to Kalkbrenner, the highest tribute he could have made at that time.

V

Kalkbrenner traditionally disappears from Chopin's biography at this point, but it is worth dwelling on his personality for a moment, if only to reveal the sort of influence that Chopin had managed to avoid. Kalkbrenner had

---

10. CFC, vol. 2, p. 25; KFC, vol. 1, p. 192. Stephen Heller has some interesting things to tell us about Kalkbrenner that throw further light on Chopin's decision to go his own way. When Heller arrived in Paris, in 1838, he called on Kalkbrenner, played to him, received one or two consultation lessons from him, but then decided to break the connection. Aside from imposing a usurious "apprentice fee" of 500 francs a year, which the impoverished Heller could ill afford, he required that Heller remain his pupil for five years, pass a monthly examination for which he would be prepared by one of Kalkbrenner's own assistants, and agree to publish no music without Kalkbrenner's consent, lest it compromise the reputation of the master! BSH, p. 14.

The Salle Pleyel, at 9 rue Cadet, Paris; a contemporary engraving.

moved to England in 1814, where he remained for ten years and amassed a fortune through his many publications, his famous Piano Method, and above all through the promotion of his "guide-rail," which ran the entire length of the keyboard and on which the luckless pupil was supposed to rest his wrists in order to discourage all vertical movement of the arms.[11] When Kalkbrenner returned to Paris with his English money, he bought shares in the firm of Pleyel and Co., became a director of the company, and helped to promote its pianos. Henceforth, whenever Kalkbrenner played in Pleyel's showrooms it ranked as activity on the stock exchange.

Kalkbrenner's absolute belief in himself and his accomplishments formed, in the dry words of Niecks, "the centre of gravity" upon which all the other qualities of his character balanced themselves.[12] He liked to instruct even his oldest friends how they might conduct themselves in society and how they might refine their table manners. Fresh from informing a student how to hold his hands at the keyboard, Kalkbrenner would happily go on to demonstrate to a dinner companion how one must

11. *Méthode pour apprendre le piano-forte à l'aide du guide-mains,* op. 108.
12. NFC, vol. 1, pp. 235–36.

hold a knife and fork. His constant boasting about the many honors bestowed on him by the king, and about his contacts with the aristocracy in general, amounted to an obsession. Every success to come his way he regarded as his birthright; conversely, no success to come the way of others could even be acknowledged, unless it was seen to have been influenced in some measure by Kalkbrenner's own precepts. Delicacy, refinement, and a love of order amounting to fetish were hallmarks of his personality—just as they were hallmarks of his playing. The pianist was an extension of the man.

Kalkbrenner was known for his vanity and was sometimes ridiculed for it. He was often observed walking along the Paris boulevards, a man of fashion decked out in full sartorial splendor, with dress coat, top hat, and walking cane in perfect alignment. Hiller's memories of Kalkbrenner are not without interest here. One day, Hiller tells us, Mendelssohn, Chopin, Liszt, and Hiller himself were sitting outside a café on Boulevard des Italiens chatting noisily. Suddenly they observed the picture-perfect figure of Kalkbrenner approaching. Knowing how easily he lost his poise, the young band of bohemians surrounded him in the street and taunted him with their noisy banter, driving him to despair and his tormentors to laughter. *"Jugend hat keine Tugend,"* quipped Hiller, by way of justifying this boisterous behavior.[13] The memoirs of Louis Moreau Gottschalk help to round out the picture. Although they refer to encounters that took place ten years after Chopin arrived in Paris, they confirm that Kalkbrenner ended up becoming a caricature of himself.

> The perfect elegance of his manners, his cultivated intelligence, and his talent gave him great success in society; but his extreme vanity, which had become proverbial, had in time rendered him insupportable. He thought of himself as infallible in everything, and had said forcibly, like a celebrated dancer of the last century, Vetris, I think, "there are in Europe three great men—Voltaire, Frederick [the Great], and myself."[14]

---

13. "Boys will be boys." HMBE, pp. 22–23.
14. GNP, pp. 220–21. Kalkbrenner had a young son, Arthur, whom he hoped to make the inheritor of his glory. Having boasted to the French court about the eight-year-old boy's ability to improvise, Kalkbrenner was delighted when the king expressed a desire to witness this musical miracle for himself. Seated at the piano, the child began to play. All went well at first,

Then there was Kalkbrenner's smile, a permanent fixture on a face that seemed to express constant self-satisfaction with everything that he had accomplished. After attending a concert that Kalkbrenner gave in 1843, Heine pilloried him: "On his lips there still gleamed that embalmed smile which we recently noticed on those of an Egyptian pharaoh when his mummy was unwrapped at the museum here."[15] Clara Schumann noticed the same thing. She once went to a concert at which a Kalkbrenner sextet was being played, and observed the composer sitting in the front row, "smiling sweetly and highly satisfied with himself and his creation. He always looks as if he were saying: 'Oh, God, I and all mankind must thank Thee that Thou hast created a mind like mine.'"[16]

VI

These first few weeks were difficult and Chopin's funds were low. The money that his father had sent him in Vienna and Munich had been spent. At this moment the outlook for Chopin was bleak. It was rapidly becoming his winter of discontent. A turning point came when Chopin made his first public appearance in Paris at a concert in the Salle Pleyel, thanks to the influence of Kalkbrenner. Under the imposing title "A Grand Concert of Vocal and Instrumental Music, given by M. Frédéric Chopin from Warsaw," the event was announced for January 15. The programs had already been printed when Kalkbrenner fell ill, so the concert had to be postponed until February 26. Chopin played his Concerto in E minor in the first half and his "Là ci darem" Variations in the second. Several artists assisted— including Ferdinand Hiller, George Osborne, Wojciech Sowiński, Camille Stamaty (a last-minute replacement for Mendelssohn), and Kalkbrenner himself. These pianists combined forces for a performance of a monstrous new work for six pianos, specially composed by Kalkbrenner in honor

---

but suddenly the music ceased. The boy turned to his father and remarked innocently: "Papa, I have forgotten . . ."! To rehearse and then forget one's "improvisations" was an embarrassment not easily overcome. It was Arthur's charming display of reticence that prompted Heine to throw another squib in the direction of Kalkbrenner, "whose hopeful son already surpasses his father—in modesty." HMB, p. 276.

15. HMB, p. 276.
16. A characterization uttered by the music dealer Heinrich Probst, which Clara quotes in her diary with obvious relish. LCS, vol. 1, p. 303.

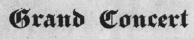

Grand Concert

VOCAL ET INSTRUMENTAL

DONNÉ

Par M. Frédéric Chopin, de Varsovie,

Dimanche 15 Janvier 1832, à huit heures précises du soir,

DANS LES SALONS DE MM. PLEYEL ET Cⁱⁱᵉ.,

Rue Cadet, N°: 9.

PROGRAMME.

Première Partie.

1°. **Quintetto** composé par Beethoven, exécuté par M^{rs}. BAILLOT, VIDAL, URHAN, TILMANT et NORBLIN.

2°. **Duo** chanté par Mlles. TOMÉONI et ISAMBERT.

3°. **Concerto** pour le Piano, composé et exécuté par M. F. CHOPIN.

4°. **Air** chanté par Mlle. TOMÉONI.

Deuxième Partie.

1°. **Grande Polonaise**, précédée d'une Introduction et d'une Marche, composée pour six Pianos, par M. Kalkbrenner, et exécutée par Messieurs KALKBRENNER, MENDELSOHN-BARTHOLDY, HILLER, OSBORNE, SOWINSKI et CHOPIN.

2°. **Air** chanté par Mlle. ISAMBERT.

3°. **Solo** de Hautbois, par M. BROD.

4°. **Grandes Variations** brillantes sur un thème de Mozart, composées et exécutées par M. F. CHOPIN.

On trouve des Billets aux Magasins de Musique de M^{rs}. SCHLESINGER, rue de Richelieu, n°. 97; l6. PLEYEL et C., boulevart Montmartre ; PACINI, boulevart des Italiens ; LEMOINE, rue de l'Échelle.

PRIX DU BILLET 10 FR.

VINCHON, Fils et Su^{ccesr} de Mme V^e. BALLARD, Imprimeur, rue J.-J. Rousseau, n°. 8.

Chopin's first concert in Paris, February 26, 1832 (postponed from January 15).

of Chopin and aptly titled "Grande Polonaise preceded by an Introduction and March."

The concert was poorly attended and Chopin lost money. The critic
François-Joseph Fétis was in the audience, however, and Chopin's playing
elicited from him an important and farsighted review.

> . . . Here is a young man who, abandoning himself to his natural
> impressions and taking no model, has found, if not a complete
> renewal of pianoforte music, at least a part of that which we
> have long sought in vain—namely an abundance of original
> ideas of a kind to be found nowhere else. We do not mean by
> this that M. Chopin is endowed with a powerful organization
> like that of a Beethoven, nor that there arise in his music such
> powerful conceptions as one remarks in that of this great man.
> Beethoven has composed pianoforte music, but I speak here of
> pianists' music, and it is by comparison with the latter that I find
> in M. Chopin's inspirations an indication of a renewal of forms
> which may exercise in time much influence over this depart-
> ment of the art.[17]

These were perceptive comments. Fétis had grasped the fact that Chopin
was creating a new kind of music—music that emerged from the piano,
as opposed to music that was merely played on it—and his observation that
it would come to have influence on what followed was prophetic. There
was one other person of note in the audience that evening on whom the
concert left a lasting impression: the twenty-two-year-old Franz Liszt. Years
later Liszt recalled the occasion in his biography of Chopin. "We remember his first appearance in the rooms of Pleyel, where we were so delighted
that the most vociferous applause seemed insufficient for the talent that
was opening a new phase of poetic sentiment and presenting happy innovations in the substance of his art."[18]

This is perhaps the place to dispel the popular notion, never supported
by much evidence, that there were strong ties of friendship between Liszt
and Chopin. Whatever camaraderie existed between them in the early

---

17. *La Revue musicale*, March 3, 1832.
18. LC, p. 147.

years was of brief duration and ended in discord. The connections were confined to a few externals, and we must not make too much of them. Nor were the musical links between the pair particularly profound. It is true that Liszt admired Chopin's music, and in later years he welcomed it into his influential masterclasses in Weimar and elsewhere; he also included it in his recitals and he gave memorable lessons on some of these compositions. But his admiration was not reciprocated. Chopin came to disparage what he considered to be the empty virtuosity of Liszt's music and its superficial brilliance. And he was critical of Liszt in the role of *grand seigneur*, especially in the 1840s, when the Hungarian pianist enjoyed an unparalleled success as a touring virtuoso, bringing the crowds to their feet while dispensing largesse along the way. The "triumph of spectacle" dismayed Chopin and dampened their friendship.

VII

Artistic success was one thing, financial success another. Mikołaj Chopin, deeply worried at the obstacles that his son was facing, issued one injunction after another not to tire himself out in the fruitless quest to arrange concerts guaranteed to lose money. "It entails expenses that must end by causing you embarrassment," he wrote anxiously.[19] The family was in reasonable health, he added, and they were able to put bread on the table, a veiled reminder of the hardships imposed on them by the Russian occupation. It was probably this letter that prompted Chopin to take the uncharacteristic step of writing to the concert committee of the Paris Conservatoire, asking for a place in one of their prestigious concerts, which might at least produce a fee.

Paris, March 13, 1832

Gentlemen of the Concert Committee,

I would very much like the favor of being permitted to appear at one of your admirable concerts and beg to submit an application to you. Having confidence in your kindness toward artists and having

---

19. CFC, vol. 2, p. 64; KFC, vol. 1, p. 212.

no other title to put forward in order to obtain this favor from you, I do hope that you will accept my request.

I have the honor to be, Gentlemen, Your very humble and obedient servant.

F. Chopin[20]

The application was turned down. The letter bears a marginal note, probably from the secretary, "Request arrived too late—Answered." It was yet another setback on the path to wider recognition.

VIII

In April 1832, six months after Chopin arrived in the French capital, there was an outbreak of cholera and a large exodus from the city. At its height more than a thousand people died every day from the disease, including King Louis-Philippe's prime minister, Casimir Périer. When the tally of the dead approached 18,000, the city ran out of coffins, so the corpses were placed in makeshift sacks and left at the curbsides to be picked up by wooden carts wending their way through the cobbled streets to local cemeteries. More than 120,000 passports were issued by the authorities at the Hôtel de Ville, but many of the recipients never managed to get out of the city because of the traffic jam of corpses that brought the boulevards to a standstill. Heine left a graphic account of one such scene in his *Berichte aus Paris*. Wishing one day to visit a friend, he arrived just as they were putting his corpse onto a cart. He caught a cab and followed the body to Père Lachaise Cemetery. There he found himself trapped by hundreds of vehicles bearing the dead. One coachman tried to get ahead of the others, a disturbance broke out, and the gendarmes moved in with bared sabers. Some of the carts were overturned, and their grim cargo toppled to the ground. Heine wrote, "I seemed to see that most horrible of all *émeutes*—a riot of the dead."[21]

Chopin had meanwhile relinquished his apartment on Boulevard Poissonnière and moved into a more spacious one close by, located on the

---

20. CFC, vol. 2, pp. 66–67; KFC, vol. 1, p. 213.
21. HMB, vol. 4, p. 121.

second floor of 4 Cité Bergère. Its great advantage was that there were fewer stairs to climb, although Chopin wondered if he would be able to afford the rent. The critic Ernest Legouvé visited him not long after he had settled in and left an interesting pen sketch of the occasion.

> We climbed to the second floor of a small furnished apartment and there I found myself in front of an elegant, pale, sad young man, with a light foreign accent, brown eyes of an incomparable pure and gentle expression, and with chestnut hair almost as long as Berlioz's and falling on his forehead in the same way . . . Chopin can best be described as a *trinité charmante*. His personality, his playing, and his compositions were in such harmony that they could no more be separated than can the features of one face.[22]

Another visitor at this difficult time was Chopin's fellow émigré the twenty-year-old violinist Antoni Orłowski, a former student at the Warsaw Conservatory, who found Chopin so melancholy that the two friends barely exchanged a word. "He is homesick," Orłowski wrote to his kinsfolk in Warsaw, "but please don't mention it to his parents: it would worry them. Things are bad here. There is great poverty among artists. The cholera is causing rich people to flee to the provinces."[23] The only public appearance that Chopin made during the spring of 1832 was to take part in a charity concert on May 20, arranged by the princesse de la Moskowa in aid of the cholera victims, for which he received no fee. Chopin had by then become so worried about his financial position that he thought of leaving France. This is evident from a letter that Mikołaj wrote to his son on June 28. "Let me advise you to save what you can, so as not to find yourself without a penny, especially as you intend visiting other countries."[24]

There is an unproven story that a chance meeting with Prince Walenty

---

22. LSS, vol. 2, pp. 158–59.
23. CFC, vol. 2, p. 70.
24. Ibid., p. 71. Five months later we find Mikołaj returning to this theme, expressing the hope that the publication of his son's music would generate enough money "to enable you to realize your project of going to England next spring . . ." (CFC, vol. 2, p. 76; KFC, vol. 1, p. 218.) And in April the following year Mikołaj warns him, "You mention going to England. What with? In a country like that, where everything is so dear!" (CFC, vol. 2, p. 88; KFC, vol. 1, p. 225.) There is no evidence that Chopin planned to go to America, a notion to which several of his modern biographers remain attached.

Fryderyk Chopin; a
lithograph by Gottfried
Engelmann, after a portrait
by Pierre-Roch Vigneron
(1833).

Radziwiłł, the younger brother of Prince Antoni, changed the course of
Chopin's destiny. When Walenty learned of Chopin's plans to leave France,
so the story goes, he decided to thwart them. We are told that he took
Chopin along to a soirée in the home of Baron James de Rothschild, head
of the most powerful banking family in Europe. The baroness asked
Chopin to play. His command of the keyboard, his refined style of playing,
and the unusual music he conjured from the instrument made an immediate impression. So did the elegance of his manners, honed to perfection in Poland, where he had so often played at similar gatherings. Some
of the ladies present immediately asked him for lessons, and recommended him as a teacher for the sons and daughters of their friends. True
or false, we know that a link with the Rothschild family had been established by the beginning of the winter season of 1832 and Chopin's prospects had been transformed.[25] It was these aristocrats who fixed his fee at

25. The story is descended from Karasowski's biography of Chopin (1877), which acquired it
from Chopin's Paris-based Polish colleague Wojciech Sowiński.

20 francs a lesson—a very large sum for private tuition in those days. By the end of the year he had as many pupils as he could manage and was financially independent. He had a carriage and a manservant, and mixed in the highest circles. In an unusually immodest letter to his old school friend Domuś Dziewanowski, Chopin boasted about the unexpected change in his fortunes.

> I have found my way into the very best society, among ambassadors, princes, ministers—I don't know by what miracle, because I have not pushed myself forward. But it is necessary, because they say that good taste depends on it. You have a bigger talent if you have been heard at the English or the Austrian embassies. You play better if Princess Vaudemont, the last of the old Montmorency family, was your protector . . . After having lived here only one year I already enjoy the friendship and respect of artists. One proof is that even those artists with great reputations dedicate their compositions to me before I do so to them.
>
> Fryderyk[26]

IX

On Christmas Day, 1832, John Field, the creator of the nocturne, made his Paris debut and offered a smorgasbord of his own compositions to a packed audience in the concert hall of the Paris Conservatoire. Chopin was curious to hear the Irish pianist with whom he had so often been compared. Field had not been heard in the West for many years. He had lived in Russia since 1802, where his successes in Saint Petersburg and Moscow had turned him into a celebrity and where he had made a fortune as a fashionable teacher, enabling him to pursue a notoriously lavish lifestyle. Glinka, his most famous pupil, used to say, "It seemed that he did not strike the keys. But his very fingers poured on them, like large drops of rain, and were scattered like pearls on velvet." This phrase, "pearls on velvet," attached itself to Field's playing and it was what the great public came to hear. His arrival in the French capital had been anticipated for weeks,

---

26. CFC, vol. 2, pp. 82–83; KFC, vol. 1, pp. 222–23.

following some successful concerts for the Philharmonic Society in London. He was billed as "Clementi's most distinguished pupil," a representative of "a school of playing that nowadays exists only in our memories,"[27] an oblique reference to the noisy piano playing to which the Parisians were being subjected on a daily basis. The program included a performance of Field's recently composed Concerto no. 7 in C minor, a work that bristles with difficulties and that the pianist played from manuscript. The newspaper reviews were excellent (Fétis wrote of a "veritable delirium" among the audience and dutifully referred to the "marvelous mechanism of Field's fingers"[28]). Two more concerts followed in the salon of the piano maker Jean-Henri Pape, on January 20 and February 3, 1833, which were somewhat less successful. There were complaints about the large and drafty hall at 19 rue des Bons-Enfants, in which waves of cold air swept through the auditorium as the doors opened to receive each new batch of listeners, "who then had to sit in the unbearable vicinity of the canes and umbrella vestibule."[29] M. Pape had no reason to expect any compliments on his music rooms, intoned the *Gazette musicale*. Field had formed a special bond with Pape, however, and used his pianos exclusively for the Paris concerts, finding them responsive to his touch. Chopin had tried the Pape pianos and found them wanting.

Pape was in fact a mechanical genius who took out more than three hundred patents on piano design. His instruments appeared in all shapes and sizes. Square pianos, hexagonal pianos, oval pianos, and pianos with an expanded eight-octave keyboard all sprang from his fertile mind, enjoyed a brief celebrity, and disappeared from view. He was particularly brilliant when it came to improving the interior mechanism of the instrument, with its complicated system of checks and balances, and he experimented constantly with the position of the hammer in relation to the soundboard, frequently changing the covering of the hammerhead with materials ranging from felt to leather in his search for a purer sound. His greatest innovation was the introduction of cross-stringing, which permitted him

27. *La Revue musicale*, November 24, 1832. As a youth Field had entered into a seven-year apprenticeship under Muzio Clementi in London, where, in exchange for lessons from the Italian master, he worked in Clementi's piano warehouse as a salesman and promoted his pianos.
28. Ibid., December 29, 1832.
29. Ibid., February 4, 1833.

to reduce the size of the instrument without sacrificing its tonal qualities and to build instruments that saved a lot of space; his "pianino" stood just over one meter high. But his most remarkable invention was surely the "oven-piano," which allowed the player to cook a meal via a hidden heating unit while practicing—a boon to those aspiring pianists whose metaphorical desire to set fire to the keyboard now stood every chance of becoming a reality. Pape had mounted an exhibition of his pianos in London a few months earlier, attended by Thalberg, Moscheles, and others, and that is where Field may have come across his latest models, which gained for Pape the title of "the Broadwood of Paris."

Chopin attended all three of Field's concerts but was disappointed with what he heard, finding the Irish pianist's playing dry and colorless. Field may well have been past his prime at this time. His addiction to alcohol and tobacco, part and parcel of his indulgent lifestyle in Russia, had begun to take its toll. In Saint Petersburg he was referred to unkindly as "drunken John" and was known to fall asleep during his lessons. He had lost the slender contours of his youth and stood on the brink of a fatal illness (rectal cancer), which overwhelmed him when his European tours took him to Naples the following year and condemned him to a nine-month stay in the hospital and an operation for fistula. The powerful drugs that had been prescribed for him by his Russian doctors to suppress his symptoms merely added to his burdens. Antoine Marmontel, who was then a young piano student, recalls visiting Field during the latter's sojourn in Paris. He was sitting in an armchair, smoking an enormous pipe, surrounded by mugs and empty bottles, his features reddened, and was obviously inebriated. He reminded Marmontel of Falstaff. Despite Field's physical condition, Marmontel claimed that he "could obtain sonorities of exquisite color from the keyboard, and his lightness in rapid passages was incomparable."[30] Field was notoriously lacking in *savoir-faire*, however, which was particularly noticeable whenever he entered the best society. Once invited to play at a soirée in the house of Duchess Descazes, he arrived with his dress in disarray and shoes that were too tight for his swollen feet. The evening grew hot, so Field, oblivious to his surroundings, simply loosened his clothes and removed his shoes. And it was in this state of undress that the duchess led

---

30. MPC, pp. 98–99.

him to the piano, past a group of simpering women, where he charmed
the cream of Paris society with his piano playing.

Field lingered in Paris until May (possibly to consult the famous French
surgeon Baron Guillaume Dupuytren), but he made no attempt to meet
Chopin, whom he notoriously dismissed as "a sickroom talent."[31] He was
displeased at the similarity between Chopin's recently published Nocturne
in E-flat major, op. 9, no. 2, and his own Nocturne no. 1 in the same key,
composed years earlier and titled "Romance."

Field (1814)
"Romance" in E-flat major

Chopin (1833)
Nocturne in E-flat major, op. 9, no. 2

Chopin had got to know Field's "Romance" while he was still a student
in Warsaw, together with a number of other piano pieces by Field that he
admired. One can readily understand Field's annoyance when Chopin's
Three Nocturnes, op. 9 (the first pieces that Chopin had ever composed
in a genre that had hitherto belonged exclusively to Field), were published
in Paris by Schlesinger at the very time that Field's presence in the city

31. *"Un talent de chambre de malade."* GFF, p. 16.

was being celebrated. What made this particular pill so much harder for Field to swallow was that Schlesinger had placed Chopin's nocturnes in a collection called *Album de Pianistes: morceaux inédits* side by side with Field's eleventh nocturne, in E-flat major—inviting a direct comparison between the two composers. Today it has become fashionable to downplay Field's influence on Chopin, but what one of Field's modern biographers has called "the close concordances" between the two composers cannot be ignored. Nothing can take away from Field his crowning contribution to the history of piano music, the nocturne. After all, it was Field who discovered that inner world of dreamy melancholy that became the mark of the nocturne style. Marmontel's description of these pieces as "miniature meditations" comes to mind. By the same token, nothing can take away from Chopin the fact that he infused Field's invention with his own genius, transforming the nocturne into one of the major genres of the Romantic era.

X

A week or so after these encounters with Field, Chopin received an accolade more precious to him than anything he had boasted about earlier in his letter to Domuś Dziewanowski: namely, confirmation that he had been elected to the membership of the Polish Literary Society in Paris. Despite its euphemistic name, this politically motivated organization contained radical members with a price on their heads. Chopin's patriotic reply runs:

> To the President of the Polish Literary Society in Paris
> Paris. January 16, 1833
>
> I received yesterday, the 15th, the notification of election to associate membership, with which the Literary Society has been pleased to honor me.
>
> I would ask you, Mr. President, to convey my expression of gratitude to my compatriots who have given me such a convincing proof of their encouragement and indulgence. The honor of belonging to their circle will be for me a spur to fresh endeavors in keeping with the aims of the Society, at whose disposal I readily place my entire service and strength.

I remain, with deep respect,
Your obedient servant,
F. F. Chopin.
Born 1 March 1810 at the village of Żelazowa Wola in the Province
of Mazovia.[32]

In just over fourteen months Chopin had become a highly visible
member of the Polish diaspora, and his career had taken wing. This first
season of concertizing was crowned for him when he appeared in the
prestigious "Athénée musical" series at the Hôtel de Ville, on April 25,
1833, playing the Larghetto and Rondo from his E minor Piano Concerto
under the baton of Narcisse Girard. Mikołaj Chopin, as prudent and
levelheaded as ever, was not impressed with his son's successes and upbraided him for his indifference to money. "I am very glad, my dear boy,
that you have got over your concert," he wrote, "but I see all the same that
you cannot fall back on such enterprises if you are in need of money, since
the expenses swallow up the takings. However, if you are satisfied, we
are. But I must go on repeating that as long as you have not put a couple
of thousand francs on one side, I shall regard you as one to be pitied, notwithstanding your talent and the flattering compliments you receive.
Compliments are so much smoke which won't keep you alive in times of
need."[33]

His father's accusatory words evidently fell on deaf ears, for in June 1833
Chopin moved into a yet more expensive apartment, at 5 rue de la Chaussée
d'Antin, taking with him his childhood friend Dr. Aleksander Hoffman,
who had lodged with him at the Cité Bérgère since the previous Decem-

---

32. CFC, vol. 2, p. 86; KFC, vol. 1, p. 224.
33. CFC, vol. 2, p. 88; KFC, vol. 1, p. 225. Chopin had given three concerts in Paris during
the weeks preceding the arrival of his father's letter, which is dated Warsaw, April 13, 1833.
Perhaps the event to which Mikołaj alludes was the widely reported concert in the Théâtre
des Italiens on April 2 arranged in benefit of the actress Harriet Smithson, who, just one
month earlier, had fallen while alighting from a carriage and had fractured her right leg in two
places just above the ankle. She was totally immobilized. Hector Berlioz, who was shortly to
marry Harriet, was beside himself with worry and enlisted a galaxy of actors and singers in
support of the cause—including Rubini, Tamburini, Giulia Grisi, Liszt, and Chopin. Chopin
evidently joined Liszt in a performance of George Onslow's Sonata, op. 22, for four hands. It
was doubtless to show support for Hector as much as for Harriet that Chopin agreed to take
part in the concert. The event raised 6,500 francs for Harriet. Mikołaj, from his vantage point
in faraway Warsaw, simply saw money flowing in the wrong direction and expressed himself
accordingly.

ber and would remain under his roof for two years. Hoffman, who had studied at the Lyceum under Mikołaj Chopin and had graduated from the department of medicine at the University of Warsaw, was now a physician with his own practice in Paris. During the uprising he had served in the Polish army as a medical officer, reaching the rank of major, but after the defeat of the insurrection he joined the Great Emigration and sought refuge in France. It was a useful arrangement for Chopin, because it helped to cover his ongoing expenses and Hoffman also became his "in-house doctor." Hoffman's presence in Chopin's apartment had a calming effect on Mikołaj, for toward the end of the year we find him writing to Chopin, "A thousand beautiful greetings to Mr. Hoffman. How delighted I am that you are together!"[34]

XI

Chopin had already come to a resolution with regard to the direction his career must take: namely, to produce something new in the world of piano music. Since the life of a touring virtuoso was anathema to him, teaching would have to become his salvation and enable him to buy the time necessary to produce that body of music on which his fame rests today. Once the first steps were taken he never looked back. As early as December 1831 there had been an exchange of letters on this topic between Chopin and Józef Elsner. Elsner was convinced that the best way for Chopin to attract international attention was to compose an opera on some Polish national theme, and have it performed in one of the major European opera houses. But that is not how the newly independent Chopin saw his situation. His reply to Elsner was respectful but firm as he pointed out to his old mentor the manifold difficulties of getting an opera produced in Paris. "Nearly a score of gifted young men, pupils at the Paris Conservatoire, are sitting waiting with folded hands for someone to produce their operas, symphonies, or cantatas, which no one but Cherubini and Le Sueur has seen in manuscript." He then came to the nub of the matter.

---

34. CFC, vol. 2, p. 99.

Although in 1830 [the year that Chopin had left Warsaw] I realized how much I still had to learn and how far I was from being able to follow successfully any of the examples which you offered me . . . nevertheless I dared to think to myself: "I *will* approach his achievement, in however small a measure, and if I cannot produce an opera like his *Lokietek*, perhaps some sort of *Laskonogi* will come from my brain."[35] But I have lost all hope for anything in that direction. I am therefore forced to think of making my way in the world as a pianist, postponing only to a later period the loftier artistic aims which you rightly put before me in your letter . . . Nothing can extinguish my perhaps too audacious but noble wish and desire to create for myself a new world.[36]

"To create for myself a new world." These were the prophetic words that the twenty-one-year-old Chopin had been bold enough to address to his teacher. They marked the direction that his career would follow, one from which he never wavered. In the two years that had elapsed since Chopin had first given voice to this idea, he had taken great strides toward his objective. His growing portfolio of unpublished compositions contained the Two Nocturnes, op. 15; the Twelve Studies, op. 10; the Scherzo in B minor, op. 20; the Ballade in G minor, op. 23; and a medley of mazurkas and waltzes, among other things. It was an extraordinary body of work to slumber so silently for so long, but it was entirely in keeping with Chopin's desire not to release anything with which he was not satisfied. These compositions prove conclusively that Chopin had moved away from the "stile brillante" of his earlier years, which had yoked him to models handed down by Hummel and Moscheles, and had already begun to create for himself that new world of which he had spoken. The promise that Chopin had made and shared with Elsner was now on the way to fulfillment, and it is to that world we must turn.

---

35. Chopin refers here to two famous Polish kings by their popular nicknames "The Dwarf King" and "Longshanks"—otherwise King Stanislas IV (1260–1333) and Stanislas III (1168–1231)—the first of whom had been the subject of one of Elsner's own operas. Elsner himself left a rich legacy in this field of Polish patriotism. As recently as January 1831, just six weeks after the Warsaw Uprising had broken out, he had produced an opera, *Powstanie narodu* (The Insurrection of a Nation), whose intention was to rally the population and summon its will to fight.
36. CFC, vol. 2, pp. 51–53; KFC, vol. 1, p. 205.

CHOPIN AND THE KEYBOARD:
THE RAPHAEL OF THE PIANO

The mechanism of playing took you little time. Your mind was busier than your fingers. If others spent whole days struggling with the keyboard, you rarely spent an hour at it.
        —*Mikołaj Chopin to his son (1831)*[1]

I

Chopin had barely been in Paris for two years and he was already being compared with the leading pianists of his time. He was only twenty-three years old, was virtually self-taught, and was composing a body of work that has meanwhile found a permanent place in the repertory. We can do no better than to pause at this juncture and take stock of what he himself described as "the new world" that he was creating for himself.

When Chopin arrived in the French capital, it was full of composer-pianists, each one vying with the others for a place of supremacy at the keyboard. Alkan, Dreyschock, Herz, Hünten, Kalkbrenner, Liszt, Pixis, Osborne, Sowiński, Stamaty, Thalberg, and Zimmerman—the list is endless—either lived or made important appearances there. They were obsessed with technique and are sometimes affectionately referred to within the profession as "the flying trapeze school." There was Kalkbrenner with

---

1. CFC, vol. 2, p. 23; KFC, vol. 1, p. 189.

his pearled passagework, Dreyschock with his powerful octaves, and Thalberg with his trick of making two hands sound like three. What the *Revue et Gazette musicale* described as "a theater of stunts" was in full swing.[2] It did not take Chopin long to assess the situation in which he found himself, and he delivered an opinion from which he never wavered: "I really don't know whether any place contains more pianists than Paris, or whether you can find anywhere more asses and virtuosos. Is there a difference?"[3]

Heinrich Heine likened the Paris virtuosos to "a plague of locusts swarming to pick Paris clean." As he cast his baleful gaze across what he regarded as a musical circus, he was moved to pick up his pen and puncture the vanity of these keyboard technicians in a series of essays known as *Musikalische Berichte aus Paris*. Satire was his rapier, sarcasm his cudgel. Of Dreyschock's noisy piano playing he declared, "He makes an infernal racket. One seems to hear not one pianist, Dreyschock, but *drei Schock* [i.e., three times three score] of pianists." And lest his readers failed to understand his German pun he made the point yet clearer by delivering the *coup de grâce*. "Since the wind on the evening of the concert lay in a southwesterly direction, you could have heard him in Augsburg. Go hang yourself, Franz Liszt." Kalkbrenner was dispatched in a couple of sentences. "He is like a bonbon fallen in the mud. There is nothing wrong with it, but everybody leaves it where it lies." When Pixis played the piano, Heine declared, his pretty melodies were so simple that they were eagerly sought after by dealers in singing canaries who could teach their caged feathered friends to whistle them back after a single hearing, to the delight of their customers. As for Henri Herz, he was grouped among the musical mummies, like Kalkbrenner and Pixis. "He has long been dead, but was recently married," a mischievous allusion to the pianist's recent and possibly bigamous union with Thérèse Lachmann, a French courtesan whose profligate spending was to ruin him financially even as she was reenergizing him physically. Liszt and Thalberg were also cut down to size when their fabled ivory duel in the Paris salon of Princess Belgiojoso was reduced by Heine to "a melancholy misunderstanding." Not only pianists, but composers and

---

2. Issue of November 24, 1832.
3. CFC, vol. 2, p. 39; KFC, vol. 1, p. 199.

literary figures had cause to fear Heine's banter. When he heard of Meyerbeer's phobia about cats, he remarked, "That is because in a previous incarnation he was a mouse!" Alfred de Musset (a former lover of George Sand's) was dismissed as "a young man with a great future behind him."[4] Not even his bitterest enemies would have wished on Heine the Calvary of suffering he was called upon to endure during his final years. As the syphilis he had contracted in earlier times gained dominion over his body, he became paralyzed and confined to his "mattress grave," as he described it. But even there he continued to hurl invective at the world. *"Vergiftet sind meine Lieder"* ("My songs are poisoned") was a line he had once written in one of his best-known poems. It was the poison that the world in general remembered after the brilliant wordsmith had departed this vale of tears. Still, Heine remains by far the most colorful chronicler of these times and without his pungent prose our descriptions of Paris in the 1830s would be the poorer.

There was one shining exception to the roll call of pianistic and artistic personalities whom Heine placed in the public pillory. Chopin was and remained his favorite pianist. It was Chopin's exquisitely nuanced performances that the German poet admired, together with the endless variety of tone color he could draw from the keyboard. It led Heine to eulogize him as the "Raphael of the piano."

> When he plays I forget all other masters of the instrument, or mere skill, and sink into the sweet abyss of his music, into the melancholy rapture of his exquisite and profound creations. Chopin is the great and genial poet of sweet sound, who should only be named with Mozart, or Beethoven, or Rossini.[5]

What distinguished Chopin from the acrobats was his lack of interest in technique as an end in itself—a saving grace that he might never have possessed if he, too, had endured a formal piano education. He belonged to no school, he subscribed to no dogma. Everything he knew about piano playing he had discovered for himself. While his contemporaries—the

---

4. Heine's scabrous comments on the music and musicians of his time may be found in HMB, vol. 9, pp. 275–86.
5. HMB, vol. 9, p. 279.

gladiators of the keyboard—were fighting it out in the open arena of the concert hall, Chopin quietly lay siege to the instrument, creating a series of compositions that broke fresh ground, that are absolutely typical of the piano, and that have dominated the repertory ever since.

II

Chopin's approach to the keyboard is well documented. He advocated the unrestricted use of the thumb on the black keys, and often used it to strike two adjacent keys simultaneously, much to the dismay of the conservative pedagogues; he would sometimes pass the longer fingers over the shorter ones without the intervention of the thumb if that would secure a better legato; he recommended a flat finger for a singing touch; he employed the organist's favorite device of finger substitution to sustain melodic lines; and he favored a low piano stool, finding it more comfortable than the high one adopted by the hard-hitting virtuosos who liked to descend on everything from a great height. Above all, there was his "flutter pedaling," that continuous *vibrating* of the sustaining pedal that cast a warm glow over everything he played, yet gave it at the same time its unusual clarity. Such originality could never have come from someone drilled in the restrictive methods then in vogue in the conservatories of Europe. He reacted strongly against the "finger equalization" school made famous by Czerny and his followers, maintaining that each finger has individual characteristics that are there to be enhanced, not equalized away. "The third finger," he would tell his pupils, "is a great singer," and he would then go on to unfold entire phrases with this finger taking a major share of the work. He accepted that the third and fourth fingers were "the Siamese Twins of the hand," joined from birth by a ligament, but unlike many of the pedagogues of the day he made no special attempt to separate them. His "Sketches Toward a Piano Method" remained unfinished at his death, but the pages that survive illustrate that he had no interest in pedantry for pedantry's sake.[6]

---

6. The manuscript is held in the Morgan Library, New York, and is somewhat more extensive than we are generally led to suppose. It was published complete by Jean-Jacques Eigeldinger

It was Chopin's misfortune that, unlike Liszt, he had no great pupils to carry on his tradition. His most gifted student may well have been the young Hungarian prodigy Károly Filtsch. But Filtsch died when he was only fifteen years old, his promise unfulfilled. Another pupil was Karol Mikuli, who later produced his own edition of Chopin's music and left some useful personal observations about Chopin's playing. Nor should we overlook Adolf Gutmann, to whom the composer dedicated his C-sharp minor Scherzo, and who was present at Chopin's bedside when Chopin died. The pupil whose playing most resembled that of Chopin himself, so we are told, was Princess Marcelina Czartoryska, but her elevated position in society precluded any possibility of a public career. These names were the exceptions. For the most part Chopin was reduced to teaching the sons and daughters of the French aristocracy, where wealth usually stood in inverse ratio to talent. The outcome might have been foreseen: Chopin's tradition died with him. Liszt fared better. Of the four hundred or so pupils who are known to have passed through his hands, a number of them became eminent—von Bülow, Tausig, Rosenthal, Friedheim, Lamond, and von Sauer among them. And because some of them lived well into the twentieth century and made notable gramophone records, they created a special posterity for Liszt, which gave him an enviable advantage over his contemporaries.[7]

III

Any meaningful discussion of Chopin and the keyboard will founder unless it acknowledges one influence that held him daily in its thrall: the human voice. His adoration of opera, and Italian opera especially, was unconditional. Having heard and admired countless operas sung by many of the leading singers of his time—Sontag, Catalani, Schröder-Devrient, Malibran, Viardot, Nourrit, and Lablache among them—it is hardly surprising that Chopin attempted to enshrine the memory of their singing in his

---

(ECE, pp. 190–97). Chopin bequeathed the document to the composer Charles-Valentin Alkan, his friend and neighbor in the Square d'Orléans, for whom he had both affection and admiration, and with whom he discussed many of the ideas it contains.
7. There are reasonably complete roll calls of the pupils of Liszt and Chopin in LL and ECE, respectively.

melodies. This love affair with the human voice comes out especially in his nocturnes, whose inner spirit comes from the world of opera and that style of singing we call *bel canto*. Consider the "portamento" effects in bars 18 and 20 of his Nocturne in F-sharp major, op. 15, no. 2. They have their origin not in the keyboard and the five fingers of the pianist, but in the throat and larynx of the singer.

The piano is incapable of a true portamento—that imperceptible gliding from one tone to another through all the intermediate pitches. Chopin, imprisoned as he is within the twelve notes of the chromatic scale divided equally across the keyboard, nonetheless comes close to imitating one of the great expressive devices of the singer. And given some nuanced playing on the part of the pianist, the illusion can be made complete. One of the best ways to prepare this passage for performance is first to sing it. Hans von Bülow's aphorism comes to mind: "Whoever cannot sing (whether the voice be beautiful or unbeautiful) should not play the piano."[8]

If it is axiomatic that all good music making begins with the voice, then all instruments should aspire to sing. That is especially hard in the case of the piano because it is a percussion instrument whose sounds begin to decay from the moment they are born. Ways must therefore be found to create the illusion that the piano sings. And this is where a deeper study of Chopin's keyboard textures begins to pay a dividend. Fingering, pedaling, phrasing, nuance, agogic accents, light and shade (not just between the individual notes of a melody but within the individual notes that make up chords as well) all play a role in the grand deception. Meanwhile, it

---

8. BAS, part 2, p. 275.

remains the case that inside every successful Chopin interpreter is a singer trying to get out.

Among the myriad ways in which Chopin connected himself to the great singers of his time, one of the more striking occurs in his B major Nocturne, op. 62, no. 1. Here he finds an unusual use for the trill. This ornament had of course been employed from time immemorial to decorate individual notes. But had it ever been used to decorate an entire melody—except, perhaps, by the coloratura singers in the opera house? When Chopin recapitulates the Nocturne's opening theme, he recalls it in the form of a series of shimmering trills coiled around the notes of the melody.

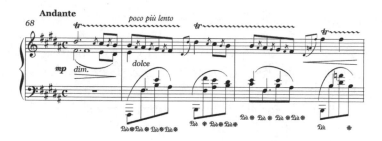

Both Jenny Lind and Henrietta Sontag were famous for delivering phrases in this manner. For the rest, one can draw a straight line from this passage to the slow movement of Ravel's Piano Concerto in G major, written eighty-five years later, where a similar technique is used—the French master doffing his hat to his Polish predecessor, so to say. Note also the use of "flutter pedaling," the rapid changes of pedal (seven times within one bar) designed to keep clean a texture that the trills might otherwise make cloudy.

The final bars of the Nocturne in B major, op. 32, deserve an entry in the lexicon of musical notation. They, too, spring directly from the world of opera. Some prescient "drum taps" herald a dramatic "recitative," sung by baritone and soprano, punctuated with orchestral chords. All bar lines have been removed—save at the end. This is music that could have been plucked straight out of one of the tragic operas of Bellini or Donizetti—the final bars of Act II (say) before the curtain falls and we await the denouement in Act III. Let us note, too, the care that Chopin exercises in the disposition of the rests among the inner parts, creating the illusion that here is a piano reduction of a full operatic score.

Is this nocturne the only composition in Chopin's output that begins in the tonic major and ends in the tonic minor? There are few similar examples in the history of classical music. Schubert's Impromptu in E-flat major, op. 90, no. 2, springs to mind, ending as it does in E-flat minor. Brahms's Rhapsody in E-flat major, op. 119, no. 4, is also a contender, for it, too, ends in E-flat minor. But finding similar examples can exhaust one in the chase.

In the vocally inspired Barcarolle we encounter an unusual word, *sfogato*. It, too, comes from the world of the coloratura singer. This Italian term means much more than "light and easy," as one music dictionary has it. Rather it conveys the notion of being "let loose" or "freed up." In bar 78 Chopin tells the player, *dolce sfogato*.

The direction is so unique that André Gide was led to ask: Has any other composer than Chopin ever used this word to describe his piano music? The answer is yes, but we know of only one example. It occurs in Liszt's

Fourteenth Hungarian Rhapsody, composed a few years later, where the *friska* "lets loose" toward the climax of the piece. Still, Chopin should receive whatever bouquet is offered for being there first.

It is easy to detect the operatic duet as the inspiration behind the opening pages of the Nocturne in C-sharp minor, op. 27, no. 1. At bar 20 the soprano voice is joined by a contralto, which adds an independent part in counterpoint to the main theme.

Richard Wagner disparaged Chopin as "a composer for the right hand." It is one of those remarks that he might well have wished to withdraw had he thought it through. For it was Chopin's right hand that transformed the world of piano playing beyond imagining, especially when it took on the trappings of a human voice, or in this case two voices. Since both melodies have to be contained within one hand, the challenge becomes how best to distribute their notes among the five fingers in such a way that the phrasing of each voice is preserved. Chopin's fingering is exemplary in this regard, because while it is not easy for a small hand, it shows how much trouble he took to avoid having to rely on the right foot to see his melodies through. The pedal was there to add color, not to paper over whatever cracks might appear in the player's legato line.

There is more counterpoint in Chopin than one might suppose. Many inner voices lie buried within Chopin's textures, longing to be discovered and brought out. The great players know where they are, and bring them out accordingly. Not to be outdone, there are other players who discover melodies that do not even exist, but insist on bringing them out anyway. (Both the Andante Spianato and the Study in A-flat major—the "Aeolian Harp," op. 25, no. 1—are among the pieces that have provided pianists across the generations with an endless supply of phantom melodies.) Charles Rosen went so far as to say that Chopin was the greatest contrapuntist since

Mozart.[9] The point is not easily dismissed, although Mendelssohn surely has an important claim to the title since he had mastered the fugue, a form into which Chopin hardly ventured beyond some elementary exercises. Chopin, however, had few peers in his ability to weave textures from two or more melodies of equal interest. Mention of Mozart reminds us that it was his classical restraint and coolness under fire that Chopin admired. Despite the romantic passion and emotion that sometimes burns at white heat in Chopin's music, there is an aristocratic detachment that prevails over everything that he wrote.

IV

It is when we turn to the sketches of Chopin's unfinished "Piano Method" that some of his fundamental ideas on piano playing come to the fore. The ideal playing position, Chopin maintained, is when the five fingers are placed over the notes E, F#, G#, A#, and B. This conforms to the natural shape of the hand and is therefore the most comfortable position for the player.

Heinrich Neuhaus (the teacher of Richter, Gilels, and others) observed that this first step was nothing short of inspired. In winged words, and in specific relation to Chopin, he waxes lyrical about this hand position.

> You cannot find anything more natural on the keyboard than this position . . . Thanks to this simple exercise the beginner immediately makes friends with the instrument, and feels that the piano and the keyboard are not an alien, dangerous, and even hostile machine but a familiar, friendly being ready to meet you if you treat it lovingly and freely, and yearning for the closeness of the human

9. RRG, p. 285.

hand as the flower yearns for the approach of the bee, ready to yield all its pollen.[10]

"Yearning for the closeness of the human hand." Behind the poetry lies something profound. For the first time in the history of piano pedagogy, precedence was being given to the physical comfort of the hand, rather than to the ungainly scale of C major—the scale normally handed out to beginners for no other reason than that there are no sharps or flats in its key signature. By considering the natural placement of the hand on the keyboard, Chopin emancipates himself from the tyranny of C major and all its discomforts—which was never anything more than a legacy of the widespread solfège system, which used to dominate the training of singers and instrumentalists alike.[11] It helps to explain the large number of pieces by Chopin whose key signatures are loaded with sharps and flats. The comfortable "lie" of the hand was always a vital consideration with him, although of course it was never the only one.[12]

It followed that in their scale-playing Chopin required his pupils to begin with B major, because it is the simplest scale physically, and proffers the hand all five black keys.

Naturally this scale also fits the left hand to perfection when the notes are played in descending order. The two scales, like the hands themselves, are mirror images of each other. And what is good for scales is also good for arpeggios. In a series of basic exercises that Chopin sent from Paris to his niece, Ludka, in Warsaw, he recommends the following:

10. NAP, pp. 84–85.
11. An argument that is persuasively elaborated by Jean-Jacques Eigeldinger in ECE, p. 100.
12. NAP, pp. 84–86. Neuhaus expressed bewilderment that so many studies and exercises continued to be written in C major long after Chopin's death. And he adds, somewhat artfully, "except for an excessive love of ivory and a contempt for ebony, it would be difficult to find an explanation for this one-sided approach."

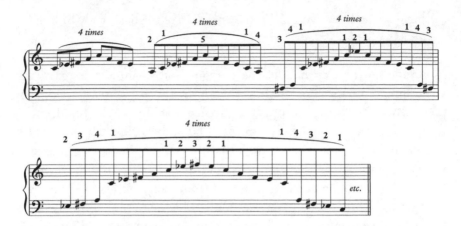

It is the arpeggio on the diminished seventh that must first be cultivated, he says, because it fits the shape of the hand and the topography of
the keyboard better than other configurations. And if one starts from the
top and reverses the direction of the arpeggio, a mirror image is created
for the left hand, too. Chopin developed this point in his "Sketch Toward a
Piano Method."

> One cannot overpraise the genius who presided over the construc-
> tion of the keyboard, so well adapted to the shape of the hand. Is
> there anything more ingenious than the elevated keys (i.e. the black
> ones)—destined for the longer fingers—so admirably serving as
> pivot-points? Many times, without thinking, minds who know noth-
> ing about piano playing, have seriously proposed that the keyboard
> be levelled: this would eliminate all the security that the pivot-points
> give to the hand, and would consequently make the passage of the
> thumb in those scales involving sharps and flats extremely difficult.[13]

He went on to argue that those who wanted to see the keyboard leveled to a
single horizontal plane should logically be prepared to remove a joint from
each finger, otherwise thirds and sixths and all legato playing would become
extremely difficult, if not impossible.[14] It is notable that the only teacher
Chopin censures in his Method is Kalkbrenner—the pianist he once thought

13. ECE, p. 192.
14. Ibid., p. 195.

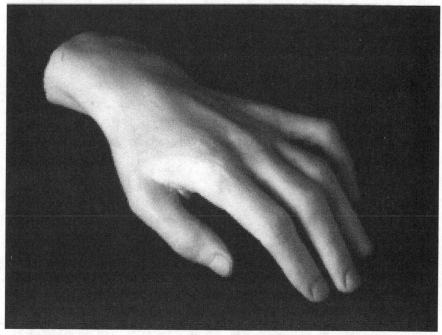

Chopin's left hand; a marble cast by Auguste Clésinger (1849).

of as perfection itself. His objection to Kalkbrenner's axiom that everything be played from the wrist is nothing less than a criticism of the latter's "hand-rail," which was designed to force the player to do just that. Similar considerations must have led Chopin toward one of his deeper insights.

> For a long time players have been acting against nature by training our fingers to be all equally powerful. As each finger is differently formed, it is better not to attempt to destroy the particular charm of each one's touch, but on the contrary develop it. Each finger's power is determined by its shape: the thumb having the most power, being the broadest, shortest and freest; the fifth finger, at the other extremity of the hand; the third as the middle and the pivot; then the second, and then the fourth, the weakest one, the Siamese twin of the third, bound to it by a common ligament, and which people insist on trying to separate from the third—which is impossible, and fortunately, unnecessary. There are as many different sounds as there are fingers.[15]

---

15. Ibid., pp. 32–33.

Attributing individual "personalities" to the fingers had never before been introduced into piano pedagogy. The touch of each finger, Chopin implies, has its own peculiar charm. At first sight the idea seems naïve, for it is tantamount to turning the player into a painter, the fingers into brushes. But for Chopin the ten fingers represented nothing less than a palette of differing hues, enabling him to color his interpretations in a variety of shades. The poet Théophile Gautier said that when Chopin's fingers touched the keys "they seemed brushed by angels' wings"—an observation that is worth pursuing.

V

A Niagara of ink has been spilled over the question of just what happened "when Chopin's fingers touched the keys." Dozens of earwitness accounts have come down to us, and if we sift through them with care they allow us to reconstruct with some certainty what it was about his playing that so attracted his contemporaries. The testimony comes not only from prominent musicians such as Schumann, Berlioz, Liszt, and Charles Hallé, but also from seasoned critics such as Fétis, Legouvé, and Henry Chorley. Some of Chopin's pupils, too, left firsthand reminiscences. These observers may have disagreed about many things, but when it came to Chopin's playing they were united. It was color, nuance, and phrasing that set him apart and made his playing unique—the opposite of the *Sturm und Drang* approach, which was rapidly overtaking the world of piano playing and turning the pianists themselves into machines. It was the still, small voice that they detected and admired in Chopin, a voice that stood out from the clamor of the crowd because it had something important to say. While many of his contemporaries manipulated a keyboard producing nothing more than senseless sound, Chopin coaxed the keys into sounding sense. This division between senseless sound and sounding sense still cuts across the world of piano playing today. Chopin was merciless in his criticism of the "piano pounders" and we have already encountered more than one example of the contempt in which he held them. According to his pupil Karol Mikuli he compared the thumping noise they made to a dog's barking. Since their playing lacked nuance, they deprived themselves of speech—for nuance, after all, is where meaningful speech resides. With-

out it, the language of music is ineluctably returned to its postnatal beginnings, where the only sounds to be heard are the inarticulate cries of
an infant.

Chopin was surely thinking along such lines when he wrote in his
Piano Method, "We use sounds to make music, just as we use words
to make language." With singers constantly in his mind's ear, it was perfectly natural for him to produce "breathing points" in his playing, akin to
those places where the singers themselves would inhale before beginning the next phrase. Frustrated by the mindless phrasing he heard all
around him, and which had become anathema to him, Chopin once told
Mikuli,

> It is as if someone were reciting in a language not understood by
> the speaker, a speech carefully learned by rote, in the course of
> which the speaker not only neglected the natural quantity of the
> syllables, but even stopped in the middle of words. The pseudo-
> musician shows in a similar way, by his wrong phrasing, that
> music is not his mother tongue, but something foreign and in-
> comprehensible to him, and so must, like the aforesaid speaker,
> quite renounce the idea of making any effect upon his hearers by
> his delivery.[16]

When Chopin arrived on the scene, piano playing was dominated
by the "finger equalization" school, whose aim was to make all ten fingers equally strong. To this end a host of technical exercises flooded the
market, together with a promise that they would create a "democracy of
the hand." Czerny was the acknowledged leader of this school, and his
bone-breaking exercises are still a blight on the happiness of piano students
everywhere. His most famous pupil, Franz Liszt, was living proof that
Czerny's method might contain the keys to the kingdom. Many others pursued similar aims and produced their own exercises, including Cramer,
Clementi, Stamaty, and Stephen Heller. The chief problem facing these
pedagogues was one that would not go away: how to separate the fourth
finger from the third, how to separate what Chopin called the "Siamese
twins" of the hand. It is a fact, well established, that many a promising

---

16. MCPW, p. iii.

career fell by the wayside in pursuit of this endeavor. Its most famous victim was Robert Schumann, who in 1829, not long before Chopin first met him, had invented a "finger tormentor," a kind of lever on which the fourth finger was secured and independently worked, while the remaining fingers were constrained. The result for Schumann was a partially paralyzed right hand, and a performing career that had to be abandoned.

Chopin's ideas on how to deal with the matter were refreshingly different. Rather than try to separate the Siamese twins, why not let them remain conjoined? In brief, he chose to work with nature rather than against it. He was, in any case, interested in a different, though related, question. What caused the wealth of color and nuance that the master pianist was able to coax from the instrument? Chopin's answer was to attribute color and character to each of the fingers themselves. This was long before the next generation of pedagogues—Matthay, Leschetizky, and Breithaupt among them—had started to grapple with the question of tone color and come up with answers of their own. But not one of them would have disagreed with Chopin's central proposition that the fingers themselves were accountable for the quality of sounds produced. While the volume of sound that Chopin created may have been relatively small, the kaleidoscopic range of tone color that he drew from the instrument was immense, and remained unmatched by other pianists. This, after all, was what had led Heine to dub Chopin the "Raphael of the piano" in the first place.

A distinctive feature of Chopin's playing was smoothness and ease of execution, qualities he cultivated in his pupils as well. He often recommended massaging and flexing the hands and fingers away from the instrument in order to reduce stiffness and prepare the player for that first vital contact with the keyboard, where comfort and ease had to prevail. Suppleness above all was his watchword. Adolf Gutmann made the interesting observation that Chopin's fingering was always calculated to achieve this end. Fingering, in fact, was the mainspring that propelled everything else. Niecks was not wrong to call Chopin's fingerings "revolutionary." They represent the Royal Road along which all students of Chopin's music must travel in their quest for a deeper understanding of his unique connection to the keyboard.

VI

Chopin's inventive use of finger substitution to sustain melodic lines drew from Alfred Hipkins the comment "He changed fingers as often as an organ player."[17] In the Prelude in G major, Chopin calls for substitutions in which the first and fourth fingers are relieved of their duty by the second and fifth.[18]

Such examples remind us that in his younger years Chopin played the organ. He learned much from the instrument, above all the difficult business of sustaining legato lines through ingenious fingerings. Organists do not keep melodies alive by throwing their hands and arms into the air, after the fashion of the piano virtuoso who relies on the right foot and the sustaining pedal to retain the sound and save the day. At the organ the fingers alone must do it. When an organist loses contact with the keyboard, he loses the sound as well, a lesson not lost on Chopin the pianist. We know from contemporary accounts that when Chopin played the piano his fingers remained in contact with the keyboard, giving his arms few opportunities to demonstrate "virtuosity." The Prelude in B minor offers instances of finger substitution in the left hand. We understand the logic behind these exchanges. With each substitution, additional fingers are made available to take on the notes of the incoming melodic line— guaranteeing smoothness and evenness of expression. An organist would do such things without thinking about it.

---

17. HHCP, p. 5.

18. Chopin's fingerings are drawn from a variety of sources, including the scores used by his pupils Karol Mikuli, Jane Stirling, Camille Dubois-O'Meara, and Friederike Müller-Streicher, which Chopin frequently annotated during their lessons. Above all, there are the scores of his sister Ludwika Jędrzejewicz, which are believed to have belonged to Chopin himself and were acquired by her after his death.

The Royal Road offers other vistas, too. When Chopin told his pupils that "the third finger is a great singer," he also provided them with abundant examples of what he had in mind. The unorthodox use of a repeated third finger in the Nocturne in G minor, op. 37, no. 1, can best be understood as an attempt to change the timbre of those notes, in much the same way as singers might choose to darken the hue of their voice in order to characterize certain vowels of a phrase.

The third finger is also called upon to bear the burden of the opening cantilena in the Nocturne in C minor, op. 48, no. 1. And while the inner meaning of one of Chopin's favorite directions, *mezza voce* (half voice), might not be immediately understood by a pianist, there is hardly a singer who would not know at once what to do, both in terms of timbre and volume.

In the Nocturne in E-flat major, op. 9, no. 2, it is the fifth finger that is charged with the task of bringing out much of the melodic line. This fingering, highly idiosyncratic at first glance, would not readily occur to the player, so we are entitled to ask why it occurred to Chopin. The only plausible answer is that he was seeking a timbre that he thought the fifth finger was best fitted to provide.

Much of the teaching in vogue in Chopin's time revealed an ambivalent attitude toward the thumb. Its use on black keys was generally frowned upon, especially when the fingers themselves could do such work. Chopin did not hesitate to emancipate the thumb. His best-known act of audacity in this respect was to provide the pianist with a work that *obliges* all five digits of the right hand to play exclusively on black keys, an activity in which the thumb is promoted to full partnership with the fingers. The "Black Keys" Study remains a landmark in the history of the literature, because it shuts the door so firmly against the older, more conservative approach to the keyboard.

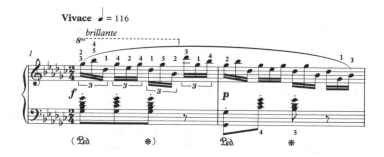

Chopin liberated the thumb in other ways as well. He frequently used it to depress a series of successive notes, as for example in the F minor Study from the Trois Nouvelles Études.

Its employment in this example from the Barcarolle is particularly bold.

Since the thumb, according to Chopin, is the most powerful digit of the hand, it is well suited for the creation of strong melodic lines. In the central episode of the Study in E minor, op. 25, no. 5, we come across an example in which every note of the melody (save one) is played by alternating thumbs, producing a "three-handed" effect, the sort of texture made famous by Thalberg, one in which he may well have been preceded by Chopin.

The two hands alternate in sharing this melody, which emerges from the middle of the keyboard and evokes Busoni's remark about "the enthroned golden sound." Whichever hand is not engaged in the task of playing the melody provides an accompaniment to the one that is, creating the illusion of a third hand. Note also the deft "finger substitution" in bars 81 and 83, in which the fifth finger of the left hand must swiftly take over from the thumb in order to enable the latter to continue the melody. Chopin was meticulous in matters that continue to confound the modern pianist.

VII

"Finger sliding" was a common practice with Chopin. Because the keyboard consists of two planes, the upper plane providing the black keys and the lower one providing the white ones, it is not difficult for a single finger to slide from the upper to the lower level, although the purists of the day objected. Chopin left many examples that show his disdain for orthodoxy. In the Waltz in A minor, op. 34, no. 2, the thumb slides quite easily from D-sharp to E-natural.

Another "finger slide" occurs in the Trio of the Funeral March of the B-flat minor Sonata, op. 35, where both the third and fourth fingers are slipped discreetly from black to white keys.

Chopin occasionally requires the player to depress two adjacent keys with one digit. In the C minor Nocturne, op. 48, no. 1, the right thumb does duty for two fingers, and depresses the notes C and D simultaneously.

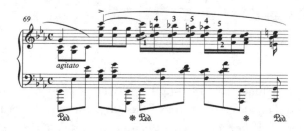

Sometimes, too, Chopin will pass one finger over another, the better to secure legato playing, as in the following passage from the Berceuse where the fourth finger of the right hand is passed over the fifth.

His pupil Mme Elise Peruzzi, who was among the first for whom Chopin played the Berceuse, recalled that "his pianissimo was extraordinary. Every little note was like a bell, so clear. His fingers seemed to be without any bones; but he would bring out certain effects by great elasticity."[19] And it is elasticity above all that is required to play the next example, which also comes from the Berceuse. The third finger and the thumb are simultaneously passed over and across the fourth and fifth fingers. At first sight Chopin's fingering appears quixotic; but it turns out to be quite logical and not as difficult as it looks. Those pianists with sufficient digital flexibility to follow the path marked out by Chopin's fingers will have no difficulty in preserving the independence of the two intertwined melodies. Those without it will have to come up with a different solution.

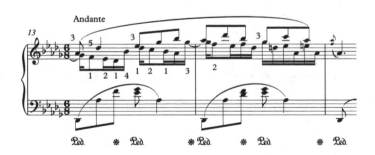

Chopin's insistence that his pupils cultivate a proper legato often produced a pointed rejoinder when they failed to achieve it. According to Friederike Müller-Streicher, his severest criticism was "You do not even know

19. NFC, vol. 2, p. 339.

how to join two notes together,"[20] a remark that might have come straight out of old Carlo Soliva's singing studio.

Chopin's music is notable for requiring unusual rhythmic independence between the hands. It is common to find all manner of uneven groupings, including sevens against threes, nines against fours, and, as in the case of the B-flat minor Nocturne, op. 9, no. 1, elevens against sixes.

Such piano writing readily betrays its origins. It could only have emerged from improvisation at the keyboard, followed by the much more laborious process of capturing everything on paper—that is, of "composing" it. A more complex example of rhythmic independence, this time within the hands as well as between them, occurs in the F minor Ballade, op. 52. Here we find nines (RH) against sixes (LH), with an upper melody formed out of every fourth note from a long sequence of triplets—resulting in a theme that unfolds in 5/8 time across a metrical background of 6/8.

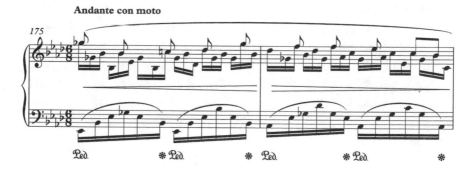

Mikuli observed that such was the flexibility of Chopin's wrists, it was relatively easy for him to pass the little finger over the thumb as, for

20. Ibid., p. 341.

example, in the Impromptu in A-flat major, op. 29, which calls for an abrupt inward-turning of the wrist, as the fifth finger "leapfrogs" over the thumb, with no break in the line.

VIII

There is a commonly held view among pianists that one of the most difficult pieces Chopin ever wrote was the Study in C major, op. 10, no. 1. We recall that this was one of the early "exercises" that he composed a year or so before he left Warsaw, when he was nineteen years old. Chopin himself did not consider this study particularly challenging, and he rejected the idea that it required a large hand, notwithstanding the widespread arpeggios covering a span of a tenth. At one of their lessons he assured Friederike Müller-Streicher that only a flexible hand was required to play the piece well. He advised her to practice it in the mornings when the hand was relaxed, and to play it very slowly at first. "If you study this piece as I intend it to be played, it opens up the hand and offers a range of broken chords like a bow sweeping across the strings," he told her. "But unhappily," he cautioned not without irony, "instead of teaching you how to do it, it can often teach you how to undo it."[21]

21. NFC, vol. 2, p. 341.

Chopin's hands may have been small but they were very supple. Heine was astonished to observe their deceptive span—"like the jaws of a snake suddenly opening to swallow its prey." Mikuli once again throws some welcome light on such passages. "A genuine piano hand, extremely flexible though not large, enabled him to play arpeggios of most widely dispersed harmonies and passages in wide stretches, which he brought into vogue as something never attempted before; and everything without the slightest apparent exertion, a pleasing freedom and lightness being a distinguishing characteristic of his style."[22] Chopin was spared having to contend with the heavier action of the modern concert grand, which adds a measurable burden to the pianist's work. And because he took the decision to place this arpeggiated study cheek by jowl with the "chromatic" one in A minor, op. 10, no. 2, the problems they pose as individuals are compounded by the far greater problems they pose once they are yoked. The first study may stretch the hand to the limit, but the second one immediately contracts it, testing the endurance of all but the hardiest of virtuosos.

This "chromatic" study confronts the player with a difficulty justly celebrated among pianists. The thumb and second finger of the right

22. MCPW.

Study in A minor, op. 10, no. 2. Chopin's corrected proof sheet.

hand are simultaneously engaged in providing an accompaniment to the chromatic scales, which have to be played mainly with the fourth and fifth fingers—the weakest digits of the hand. If ever a piece was designed to remind one of nature's gift to the pianist, the "Siamese twins," we find it here. For Isidore Philipp this study was "the most difficult in the entire repertory of Etudes" bar none, an interesting judgment with which we think Chopin himself might not have agreed.[23] Even so, it is worth adding that it was the only one that Chopin fingered in minute detail, an indication of his concern for the player, as an inspection of his corrected proof sheet shows.

Chopin's injunction to relax and remain supple leads inevitably to a consideration of his own bearing at the keyboard. It was quiet, almost immobile. He avoided those overt displays of body language, so beloved of other pianists, that involved torsos swaying back and forth, with hands and arms thrown aimlessly into the air. Chopin called such actions "catching pigeons." His default position was simplicity itself. With his elbows level with the keyboard, and hands pointing slightly outward (their natural position), his arms could reach the full compass of the piano without inclining him either to the left or the right. He leaned back slightly, hardly ever forward, the only visible movement being the hands and their lateral

23. "Les Études de Chopin," *Musica* 134, Paris, November 1913, p. 216.

Chopin seated at
the piano; a pencil
drawing by Jakob
Goetzenberger
(October 1838).

movements across the keyboard. His right foot rested on the sustaining
pedal, even when not depressing it.

IX

We mentioned Chopin's pedaling. It captured the attention of Antoine
Marmontel, the doyen of piano teachers at the Paris Conservatoire, who
heard Chopin play many times and wrote,

> No pianist before him employed the pedals alternately or simulta-
> neously with so much tact and skill. With most modern virtuosos,
> excessive, continuous use of the pedal is a capital defect, producing
> sonorities eventually tiring and irritating to the delicate ear.
> Chopin, on the contrary, while making constant use of the pedal,

obtained ravishing harmonies, melodic whispers that charmed and astonished.[24]

Marmontel's observation that Chopin occasionally used both pedals simultaneously makes us regret that the composer never once indicated that fact in his scores. Still, there is no shortage of those "ravishing harmonies" and "melodic whispers" resulting from pedaling that continued to live in Marmontel's memory long after Chopin was dead. The dissonant E-flat toward the end of the F major Prelude, totally unexpected, leaves the work floating in the air, a magical effect that would be impossible without the sustaining pedal—which remains depressed even after the work has ended.

It is well known that whenever Chopin played four-hand music, he insisted on taking the *secondo* part, which traditionally gave him control over the pedals. Whether his partner was Liszt, Kalkbrenner, Moscheles, Czerny, or any other pianist with whom he is known to have played, the outcome was always the same. They had to take the *primo* part, leaving him in charge of what Anton Rubinstein called "the soul of the piano."

Quite difficult for the player is the problem of how to manage the ending of the D-flat major Nocturne, op. 27, no. 2.

---

24. MPC, pp. 10–11.

Few pianists have the courage to hold down the sustaining pedal through-out the last three bars, as Chopin indicates (in fact, he never indicates that the pedal is to be lifted), fearing the harmonic chaos that might ensue. On a Pleyel of Chopin's time, however, the effect would have been utterly charming. It is as if he wanted the Nocturne to disappear into the night, trailing a mist of mingled harmonies in its wake. This dreamlike effect can be transferred to the modern keyboard through half-damping—a slight easing away of the dampers from the strings—and it is worth any pianist's while to attempt.

A similar challenge lies in wait for the performer in the slow movement of the Sonata in B minor, where Chopin requires the sustaining pedal to be held down for almost four bars.

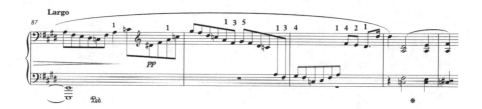

This is an inordinately long time. But the "halo" that is cast over this music when the pedal is fully depressed, and not released until after the chord of the second beat of bar 90 has been struck, is an essential part of the character of the music. Half-damping would hardly be the best way to handle this passage, unless we wish to rob it of luster.

X

Any discussion of Chopin and the keyboard must take into account what he does not do. We search almost in vain for the tremolando, that stock-in-trade device used by so many of Chopin's contemporaries and generally cheapened by them. The tremolando is an orchestral effect that sounds ungainly on the piano keyboard because it does not spring naturally from it. Liszt uses it to splendid purpose in his operatic paraphrases and sym-phony transcriptions, of course; but even Liszt warned his pupils to treat the device with care, to avoid surplus movements of the hand and arm, and "not to make omelets." Chopin needed no such counsel because he had already divested himself of what he must have considered a branch of vulgarity.[25]

Likewise, we find no trace in Chopin of those quick-fire single-note reiterations that Liszt turned into a signature effect. Once Sébastien Érard had introduced the repetition action into his pianos (the "double-escapement," in 1823), the way was open for the virtuoso pianist to create the illusion that the instrument could sustain its sound into infinity, a sound that would never decay. Few better examples exist in the whole of the piano's repertory than the radiant middle section of the Tarantella in Liszt's "Venezia e Napoli" Suite, where the device is used to feed a stream of sound into the melodic line, one of the "Neapolitan Songs" of Guillaume Cottrau that Liszt had heard in Italy.

Chopin eschews this kind of piano writing. He had already found other ways to make the piano sing. Nor must we neglect to mention those alternating octaves which Liszt made so much his own that they bear his name: "Liszt octaves." With thumbs interlocked, the hands move rapidly across the keyboard, producing octaves that alternate with each other. Our ears are deceived into thinking that double octaves are being played, but twice as fast and twice as powerful. It was the kind of torrential sound that brought Liszt's audiences to their feet. His "Paganini" Study no. 2 provides a typical example.

---

25. Three small exceptions spring to mind that prove the point. There is a modest "drum roll" in the juvenile Funeral March (1826), an obvious attempt to reproduce the sound of side drums in the military parades of the time. And there is an equally solitary and unobtrusive left-hand tremolando in bar 97 of the Polonaise in E-flat minor, op. 26, no. 2. As for the neglected Largo in E-flat major, a sketch of 16 bars that was never published in Chopin's lifetime, its furtive tremolando in bar 13 comes close to showing indifference for the device.

Chopin will have nothing to do with it. As for the glissando, there is not a single example to be found in the whole of his music, while the device abounds in Liszt.

XI

Chopin was fortunate to encounter the Pleyel piano at the very moment that his genius was achieving its fullest expression. When he first touched its keyboard, toward the end of 1831, he knew that he had found an ideal instrument. "Pleyel's pianos are the last word in perfection," he wrote in December of that year.[26] Today what Chopin valued in the instrument is much better understood.

> Pleyel sought a sound with a basically dark hue, capable of as much nuance in color as in dynamic range. In order to pick up the least vibration produced by his soft-surfaced hammers, he employed thin soundboards with light, low bridges. Every whisper of sound thus became audible. The powerful action compensated for the relative inefficiency of the soft hammers in exciting the strings—power used not for loudness, but to permit the veiled clarity of tone so characteristic of Pleyel's pianos. In playing with more force, the sound of the instrument became brighter, due to the firmer inner layers of the hammers being brought into play . . . The cushioning of every part of the action gave to the player a feeling of comfort and control over the tiniest nuance. Finally, the

---

26. CFC, vol. 2, p. 48; KFC, vol. 1, p. 203.

una corda provided further tone colors at the quiet end of the spectrum.[27]

It nonetheless remains extraordinary that Chopin's music was composed mostly for an instrument with a keyboard compass of a mere six and a half octaves. What a universe he unfolds within the confines of those 78 notes! The seven-octave keyboard was available to him, but he rarely used it.[28] The modern concert grand has 88 notes at its disposal, some models offering more. But Chopin's music ignores such bounty. "Stone walls do not a prison make / Nor iron bars a cage."[29] Some such philosophy always governed Chopin's relationship to the keyboard. Throughout his entire output he rarely went beyond a keyboard with 78 notes, and we admire his inventiveness within such constraint. Still, there are times when a certain discomfort becomes evident.

In the Scherzo in C-sharp minor, for example, Chopin obviously requires a low B-flat in the left hand, bar 197, which was not available to him but which every modern pianist is happy to provide.

A more serious situation arises in the Fantaisie in F minor in bars 110–12, where Chopin is obliged to provide octave E-flats (tonic degree) in the left hand at bar 112, instead of octave B-flats (dominant degree), which he would obviously have preferred—

27. CSP, pp. 234–35.

28. Chopin's last piano, which was loaned to him by Pleyel during the final months of his life, has a compass of 82 notes (serial number 14810). After Chopin's death it was purchased by his Scottish pupil Jane Stirling and sent to Warsaw, where it is today displayed in the Chopin Museum. Chopin composed nothing on it that made use of its wider compass.

29. Richard Lovelace was not thinking of music when he penned those perceptive lines. But their continuation—"Minds innocent and quiet take / That for an hermitage"—apply with peculiar force to Chopin. The "hermitage" of the Pleyel keyboard became for him a place in which he was perfectly at home. The Pleyel upright that he used during his stay in Majorca is confined to 78 notes.

—the model for this preference being found in the recapitulated (and transposed) version in bars 277–79. The modern pianist who is not confined to Chopin's reduced keyboard generally rejoices in making the adjustment.

There are a number of similar examples worth considering, and they are well known to the player. In the Trio section of the Scherzo in B-flat minor it is the right hand that runs out of notes. Consider the first appearance of the upward-sweeping arpeggio with which Chopin adorns this melody, in bars 281–84.

When this theme is recapitulated in its transposed version, at bars 307–309, Chopin runs out of keyboard, and has to subject the decoration to an unexpected contraction.

Held hostage to the limitations of Pleyel's keyboard, Chopin here produces a rather beautiful contradiction of our expectations. We would not readily forgo it by sacrificing it on the altar of the modern concert grand, whose generous keyboard would do no more than offer the possibility of repeating what has already been heard.

XII

Chopin's widely acclaimed harmonic innovations, which made a genuine contribution to the history of harmony, arose, like so much else, from his daily contact with the keyboard, where his fingers easily led his ears into uncharted territory. This passage, from the Mazurka in C-sharp minor, op. 30, no. 4,

comprises chains of "chords of the seventh" resolving only onto themselves, and they never find a proper tonal resolution until the pattern is abandoned. It is at such moments that Józef Brzowski's description of Chopin as "the Copernicus of the piano" comes to mind.[30] It was not an idle image. Copernicus, the celebrated Polish astronomer, had three hundred years earlier opened up the heavens for his successors, just as Chopin was now opening up new worlds of sound for those who came after

---

30. BJT, p. 92.

him. It is sufficient commentary on the modernity of this passage that René Lenormand included it in his "Étude sur l'harmonie moderne," a treatise that was published almost seventy years after Chopin had composed this unusual sequence of chords.

The mazurkas, in fact, contain a gold mine of advanced harmonic procedures that have been prospected to the point of exhaustion by theorists. Among them we find such passages as the emotional climax to the Mazurka in C-sharp minor, op. 50, no. 3 (bars 164–73), with its forward-looking glimpse of the Prelude to *Tristan*, a work that would not make its appearance for another generation.

Liszt, in his later years, was said to have been puzzled by certain passages in the mazurkas that seemed not to belong there, as if inserted at random. That, at any rate, was the burden of a conversation that Niecks reported having had with him when he interviewed Liszt while doing research for his Chopin biography. Liszt remarked that one encountered in the mazurkas "bars which might just as well be in another place." But he added, as if to soften the criticism, that where Chopin puts them, "perhaps nobody else could."[31] Reaping a random harvest of harmony was ever Chopin's good fortune; but the many chance discoveries that came his way had to earn their place in his finished compositions,

31. NFC, vol. 2, p. 231.

or be jettisoned. It has been well said that "Chopin the composer was ruthless in dealing with Chopin the improviser."[32] Ideas that sprang spontaneously to life on the keyboard were not allowed to remain there until subjected to scrutiny, refined, modified, and when found wanting banished—the ultimate chastisement that Chopin was able to bring against himself.

The closing, dissonant bars of the Ballade in G minor must have sounded chaotic to their first listeners, because they are still capable of sending a shock through the ears of audiences today, who have heard them many times.

These grinding discords, which begin with an augmented fourth (*diabolus in musica*), pick up all manner of "forbidden" intervals along the way, including sevenths and ninths, as the two hands sweep across the keyboard with broken octaves in contrary motion. All the conventional distinctions between consonance and dissonance are swept aside.

XIII

Two important techniques of composition may be considered here because they, too, sprang out of Chopin's daily contact with the keyboard, and are symptomatic of the kind of discoveries that probably came to light during moments of improvisation. The first may be called "the apotheosis of themes," the recasting of simple melodies brought back "clothed in grandeur." First introduced by Beethoven in such works as the finale of the "Choral" Symphony, with its great outburst in the "Ode to Joy," it became a quintessentially Romantic device. Chopin provides some telling exam-

---

32. Jon Newsom's perceptive observation, quoted in SCP, p. 180.

ples in his ballades, especially. Consider the second subject of the G minor Ballade, op. 23, which is first heard in its simpler, straightforward form.

When Chopin comes to recapitulate it, he "apotheosizes" it, elevating it into one of the grand climaxes of the Ballade.

The other technique is known as "developing variation." The term was first introduced by Arnold Schoenberg, but the process it describes was already more than two hundred years old when he coined these words. They describe to perfection a creative process that Chopin made very much his own: namely, the practice of loading his melodies with an ever-increasing abundance of ornamentation—an effect whose true home may once more be found in the opera house. At its typical best, the model is pushed ever further into the background as each repetition is called upon to bear the weight of yet greater layers of variation. Chopin's music teems with examples, but these excerpts from the early Nocturne in B major, op. 9, no. 3, can stand for the others. The opening melody is first presented in its basic form, its outline unadorned.

At its second appearance, the melody has acquired all the trappings of the *fioratura* singer, with the basic shape of the original theme still audible behind the decorations.

The process is carried still further as the old is continually made new. At its third appearance, Chopin pushes his melody yet deeper into the background, decking it out with more variants, while never losing touch with the model that first gave them life.

There are historical precedents for "developing variation," and we find them at every touch and turn in Chopin's beloved Mozart, whose music, both instrumental and operatic, provides textbook examples of the process in action.[33]

XIV

By 1849 the Paris Virtuoso School had run its course and had begun to fade from memory. Its leading personalities had all dispersed. After their famous "ivory duel," Liszt and Thalberg had gone their separate ways— Liszt to conquer the rest of Europe with his transcendental piano playing, and Thalberg to embark on those marathon tours of North and South America that made him a multimillionaire and allowed him the luxury of ending his days in comfortable retirement, cultivating grapes at his impressive villa near Posillipo, Italy. Kalkbrenner perished in the cholera

---

33. We need look no further than Mozart's Rondo in A minor, K. 511, a sovereign composition whose "developing variations" gain dominion over the rondo theme with each passing appearance. It could well have served as a model for Chopin, for it was well known to him.

epidemic of 1849, while his most famous pupil, Stamaty, was obliged to stop playing in public because of persistent muscular problems (described as "rheumatism") and withdraw behind the protective walls of the Conservatoire, where he became a respected teacher numbering Saint-Saëns and Louis Gottschalk among his pupils. Hiller returned to his native Frankfurt and became music director of the Lower Rhenish Music Festival, while Pixis abandoned his concert career, retreated to Baden-Baden, and opened a private teaching studio. Henri Herz suffered a particularly mournful fate. His spendthrift wife, the courtesan Thérèse Lachmann, having acquired access to his purse strings, had brought him and his piano factory to the brink of financial ruin and he had to flee to America in an attempt to rebuild his fortune.[34] Alkan was meanwhile about to enter that long period of self-imposed seclusion from the world during which even his friends and colleagues found it notoriously difficult to gain access to him. "Alkan, who was Alkan?" inquired Le Ménestrel when it published his obituary notice in 1888. As for Heinrich Heine, who had so brilliantly captured the activities of these pianists, his pen was now paralyzed along with much of the rest of his body as he lay on his "mattress grave" and enjoyed the dubious privilege of seeing his baleful forecast come true. The plague of locusts that had descended on the French capital in the early 1830s had indeed "picked Paris clean" and departed, leaving it bereft of anything that could be identified as a school. What a burial service Heine could have conducted as the Paris Virtuoso School was laid to rest!

Paradoxically it is Chopin whose legacy from those times is the one that posterity has come to treasure—the same Chopin "who belonged to no school and subscribed to no dogma." There is hardly a work that Chopin wrote during the thirties and forties that is not today in the standard repertoire. And there is hardly a work written by the others that is. As we

---

34. Shortly after his arrival in the New World, in 1848, Herz went in for what he called some musical *extravaganzas*, the best way to liquidate his debts. He once mounted a gala concert involving eight pianos and sixteen players. Having come up short of one player, he asked a lady in the audience, who was innocent of all knowledge of piano playing, simply to mimic the movements of the others without her fingers actually touching the keys. The deception was revealed when she continued her uncertain choreography during a long silence in the music, reducing the audience to laughter. (HMVA, pp. 300–306.) On another occasion Herz advertised that the hall was to be illuminated by a thousand candles. A man in the audience counted the candles, and finding that there were only 992, he reported the discrepancy to Herz. Nothing daunted, the pianist bought eight candles and sent them to his disgruntled detractor. HMVA, pp. 123–25.

turn the pages of Chopin's music, it opens up new vistas on the world of the piano, on the physical attributes of the keyboard, and on the connection of the keyboard to the human hand. The wealth of opportunities it proffers to the virtuoso is widely recognized. But if that were all, Chopin's music would not rise much beyond that of his contemporaries. Over and above everything else is its timeless power to move its hearers to a better place. It constantly brings to mind Alfred Cortot's beautiful aphorism: "Music forces Mankind to confront its nobility."

MARIA WODZIŃSKA: "MY MISFORTUNE," 1834–1837

"Ave Maria!"
—*Juliusz Słowacki*[1]

I

Among the students who had lived in the boarding school of Mikołaj Chopin were three brothers—Antoni, Kazimierz, and Feliks Wodziński—the sons of a wealthy landowner, Wincenty Wodziński, who owned a large estate at Służewo in the region of Toruń. It was through Chopin's early friendships with these boys that he first met their sister Maria, who was nine years younger than he, and he gave the girl some occasional piano lessons whenever she was in Warsaw. At the end of 1831 the Wodziński family departed Poland in order to escape the upheavals of the failed insurrection. They settled temporarily in Geneva, while Maria's uncle Maciej Wodziński—the patriarchal head of the family—went to live in Dresden. As early as 1834 the Wodzińskis issued an invitation for Chopin to visit them in Switzerland, but he was unable to accept. He did, however, send Maria a copy of his newly published Waltz in E-flat major, op. 18, inscribed with the words: *"Hommage à Mlle M. W. de la part de son ancien*

---

1. From Słowacki's poem *W. Szwajcarii* (In Switzerland).

professeur F. F. Chopin. 18 jui. 1834."[2] Maria had meanwhile sent Chopin a set of variations of her own, evidence not only of her growing ability as a musician, but also of the regard in which she held her former teacher, who was now famous in the wider world of music.

An invitation from Ferdinand Hiller to attend the Lower Rhine Music Festival at Aachen, in mid-May 1834, was one that Chopin felt unable to refuse, and the two friends traveled to the Rhineland together from Paris. Arrived at Aachen, the first thing they did was to go over to the theater where Handel's oratorio *Deborah* was being rehearsed in an edition prepared by Hiller. They followed the score from their seats in the circle. As they were coming downstairs, they bumped into Felix Mendelssohn, whom Chopin had last seen in Paris two years earlier. "[Hiller] tumbled into my arms, ready to squeeze me to death for joy," wrote Mendelssohn. "Chopin had cut his lessons to come with him, and so we met once more."

> The next morning, [he continued,] we were all at the piano, and that was a great delight to me. They have both improved in execution, and as a pianoforte player Chopin is now one of the very finest; quite a second Paganini, doing all sorts of wonderful things that one never thought could be done.[3]

For three days the friends reveled in one another's company, and Mendelssohn rented a private box in the theater so that they could hear the oratorio in style. After the festival the trio traveled by steamer along the Rhine from Düsseldorf to Cologne, where Mendelssohn took leave of his friends and went back to Leipzig, while Chopin and Hiller continued on to Coblenz. On board the steamer Hiller wrote a letter to his mother, Régine, to which Chopin added a whimsical postscript, indicative of the buoyant mood in which the trip along the Rhine had left him.

> Gracious Lady! Today I am like the steam from our boat which vanishes into thin air. I feel as if one part of me were floating away to

---

2. "To Mlle M[aria] W[odzińska] with respects from her former teacher F. F. Chopin, 18 July 1834." From the evidence of Chopin's covering letter to Maria's brother Feliks, we gather that the abbreviation *18 jui* referred not to June (*juin*) but to July (*juillet*).
3. HMBE, p. 31.

my homeland, while the other comes to greet you respectfully in Paris, finds you in your boudoir, and presents its compliments . . .
Your servant,
Ch.[4]

Chopin's public appearances were widely reported in the press and the Wodziński family followed them from afar. On December 14 we find him at the Paris Conservatoire playing the Larghetto from his E minor Piano Concerto under the conductor Narcisse Girard. This was an otherwise all-Berlioz concert, featuring such big works as *Harold en Italie* and the *Francs-juges* overture, and Chopin's intimate music might well have been pushed into the shade by the noontide glare of the massive orchestra. Nonetheless the *Gazette musicale* thought the contrast beautiful and hailed Chopin as a "spiritual composer and an inimitable pianist."[5] Things went still better on Christmas Day, when he participated in a gala concert in the salon of François Stoepel (located in the Hôtel de Gèvres), featuring a galaxy of singers and instrumentalists, including Liszt, who joined Chopin in a performance of the Moscheles Sonata for four hands. We read that their rendering "electrified" the audience, so the two pianists increased the voltage by playing a (newly composed) set of variations by Liszt on a theme of Mendelssohn, which drew enthusiastic reviews in the *Gazette musicale* and *Le Temps*. Never far from Chopin's thoughts was the plight of Polish refugees, and on April 4, 1835, he took part in a benefit concert for his compatriots in the Théâtre-Italien, playing once more the slow movement from his E minor Piano Concerto.

II

The Wodziński family had meanwhile moved from Geneva and joined Uncle Maciej in Dresden, where large numbers of Polish expatriates had taken up residence. From this coign of vantage they renewed their invitation to Chopin to join them for a holiday and he agreed to meet them there in the late summer of 1835. Quite by chance Chopin's parents, Mikołaj and

---

4. CFC, vol. 2, p. 114; KFC, vol. 1, p. 239.
5. December 28, 1834.

Justyna, were making their first excursion abroad—to the nearby watering spa of Carlsbad (Karlovy Vary) in Bohemia—and Chopin hurried to join them, en route to Dresden. Before setting out from Paris, he acquired French travel documents in order to thwart any Russian attempt to delay his journey, and a French passport was issued on August 1, 1835.[6] Free to travel across Europe's borders, he set out on the ten-day journey to Carlsbad and was reunited with his parents on August 15. Because he had forgotten to tell them at which one of the more than thirty hotels he would be staying, they had no idea where to find him. Mikołaj embarked on a search, tracked him down in the early hours of the morning, woke him from his slumbers, and brought him back to the Golden Rose Hotel, where he and Justyna were staying. ("You always were absentminded" was Mikołaj's laconic comment.) The family had not been together for nearly five years and they basked in one another's company. Mikołaj and Justyna had brought with them their two-year-old grandchild, Henryk, the son of Ludwika, who had given birth to her second child just two or three weeks earlier and was convalescing.[7] Chopin spent an entire month in his parents' company, reliving the past, adoring his young nephew, catching up with all the unsettling news from Warsaw (both the University and the Conservatory had been shut down), and acquainting them in turn with everything that he was doing in Paris. Mikołaj would have lost no time in giving his son some firsthand details about the tragedy that had unfolded a few months earlier at Żelazowa Wola and had profoundly shaken them. Michał Skarbek, the new owner of the estate and a younger brother of Chopin's godfather, Fryderyk, had committed suicide by hanging himself on a rope in one of the rooms of the manor house. In his will, written two days before he killed himself, he had left everything to the unknown Franciszek Kwiatowski, and died owing Mikołaj Chopin the considerable sum of 22,726 złotys, which Mikołaj had loaned Michał without any of the usual securities. The Chopins endured much anxiety as they attempted to recover the money from the new owner of Żelazowa

---

6. SCP, p. 69.
7. Ludwika had married the lawyer Kalasanty Jędrzejewicz on November 22, 1832, in the church at Brochów where Chopin himself had been baptized. The wedding reception was held at nearby Żelazowa Wola because, as Mikołaj Chopin put it, he could hardly serve the many guests who had traveled all the way from Warsaw "just a glass of water." Fryderyk for his part had sent the newlyweds a polonaise and a mazurka "so that you may dance and your souls may rejoice." These works have never been identified and are presumed lost. They are mentioned in CFC, vol. 2, p. 75; KFC, vol. 1, p. 217.

Wola, who finally assumed the debt and took out a mortgage to raise the capital. It was probably this "windfall" that allowed Mikołaj to indulge in the luxury of an expensive, monthlong sojourn in Carlsbad.[8]

The day after their reunion father and son wrote a joint letter to Chopin's two sisters in Warsaw, which captures the pleasure they experienced at being together again.

Carlsbad, August 16, 1835

My dear children,

This is the first letter written by Papa and me that you have ever received. Our joy is indescribable! We never stop embracing each other—what more can we do? What a pity that we can't all be together here! The little one [Henryk] is adorable. How good God is to us. I can't write sensibly—it's better not to try to think of anything today—only enjoy the happiness that life offers us. What it brings me today is unique. Our parents look exactly the same, only a trifle older. We go for walks arm in arm with darling Mamma; we talk about you all, we imitate the tantrums of my little nephew, and we tell how much we have been thinking about each other. We all eat and drink together; we exchange tender caresses and then shout at each other. I am *at the summit of my happiness*. I see again those little mannerisms and habits which I grew up with, and that hand which it is so long since I kissed.[9]

The first thing they had to do was register with the local police and pay the mandatory "resort tax." The police records reveal that Mikołaj described himself as a "Professor, born in Nancy, France" [instead of Marainville]; while Chopin registered as a "Professor from Paris." This attempt to cover up their Polish background suggests that the Chopins were under surveillance. Carlsbad was known as a gathering place for disaffected Poles. Metternich's spies were everywhere, and we will shortly come to some circumstantial evidence that Fryderyk was being watched.[10] After three idyllic weeks in Carlsbad, Chopin traveled with his parents to

---

8. The matter has been given detailed attention by Mariola Wojtkiewicz in WZW, pp. 90–95, "The History of a Debt."
9. CFC, vol. 2, pp. 147–48; KFC, vol. 1, pp. 260–61.
10. This supposition is pursued in *Fryderyk Chopin v Karlovych-Varech*, by Jaroslav Prochazka, Carlsbad, 1951.

Maria Wodzińska; a self-portrait, undated.

Tetschen (Děčín), close to the Polish border, where they had been invited to spend a few days during the second week of September in the château of the rich and cultivated Count Franciszek Thun-Hohenstein. Three of the count's five children—Anna, Josefina, and Bedřich—had taken lessons from Chopin the previous autumn and were delighted at the prospect of seeing their famous teacher once again. Josefina especially became attached to him, and she left a touching account of the visit in her diary. Chopin entertained everyone at the piano, and sometimes reduced his audience to shrieks of laughter when he mimicked to perfection an Englishman speaking pidgin French, a character he had probably come across at the Carlsbad spa. On September 14 the idyll came to an end and Mikołaj and Justyna returned to Poland. It was the last time that Chopin saw his parents. Justyna could not contain her tears at the time of parting, and Chopin hardly ventured from his room for the rest of the day. He lingered at Tetschen for a few more days, and on September 15 he copied out his Waltz in A-flat major, op. 34, no. 1, and dedicated it to Countess Josefina. On September 19 he set out on the final leg of his journey to Dresden in the company of one of Josefina's brothers, booking rooms at the Stadt Gotha Hotel.

III

Chopin lost no time in searching out the Wodzińskis. His first sight of Maria enchanted him. The girl that he remembered had meanwhile developed into a young woman who was starting to turn heads. The poet Juliusz Słowacki had fallen in love with her in Geneva, but his passion had gone unrequited and was left to burn itself out when the family moved to Dresden.[11] Chopin and Maria spent some pleasant hours together, making music (she was by now an accomplished pianist[12]), conversing, and going for long walks, activities that were carefully chaperoned by Maria's mother, Teresa. Dresden formed the perfect backdrop for a growing romance. The "Florence on the Elbe" was famous for its culture, and Maria happily played the role of tourist guide. During the day the couple took strolls along the banks of the river and visited various art galleries and museums, the famous opera house, and the historic Frauenkirche with its chiming clock. The evenings they spent with the rest of the family in the house of Uncle Maciej Wodziński, which was situated on the fashionable Rampische Strasse within sound of the Frauenkirche bells. This patriarch had lost all his lands in Poland, and preferred to live out the rest of his days as an exile under the protection of the King of

---

11. Słowacki was inspired to write one of his most romantic love poems for Maria, titled *In Switzerland*. Written in 1835, immediately after the young girl had been torn from the twenty-six-year-old Słowacki's side, the impassioned opening lines run: "*Since the day she vanished like a golden dream, I wither from grief and am faint with longing, nor do I know why from these ashes my soul does not fly after her to the angels, why it does not fly beyond the heavenly lists to her who is redeemed and my love.*" Did Maria ever read these romantic lines? And perhaps more to the point, did Chopin? *In Switzerland* was not published until 1839, but it is entirely possible that he came across it through his network of Polish connections in Paris. At one point in the long poem, Słowacki turns Maria into a virtual goddess, ending two of the later stanzas with the invocation "*Ave Maria!*"

12. Maria never abandoned her piano playing. There was a report in the Warsaw press that she gave a concert in March 1843, playing a Chopin ballade "in a really masterly fashion and with great talent."

Saxony, rather than negotiate a return to his homeland and place himself under Russian rule. A lover of the arts, he possessed a wonderful collection of prints and books in whose company he spent much time. He was described as being a stickler for etiquette. He could hardly have failed to recognize Chopin's talent, but he clearly wanted more for his niece than a musician as a husband, someone who might become a drain on the family's dwindling resources and who had no estate to offer in return. In the end it would be Uncle Maciej and the men of the family who dashed Chopin's hopes. But that was more than a year away. Before long Maria had captured Chopin's heart and he began to entertain notions of a permanent relationship. Lacking the courage to declare his feelings outright, he tried at first to show his affection through music. On September 22 he copied out for her the first bars of his Nocturne in E-flat major, op. 9, no. 2, beneath which he wrote *"Soyez heureuse"* (Be happy).[13] Two days later he composed (or more likely copied out) for her his famous Waltz in A-flat major, op. 69, no. 1, bearing the inscription *"pour Mlle Marie."* The manuscript bears the dateline "Dresden, Sept. 1835." The Waltz remained unpublished until Julian Fontana included it in his posthumous collection of Chopin's works in 1855. Posterity has come to know it by the sentimental nickname that Maria herself wrote on her copy, "L'Adieu," a designation that Chopin himself would not have recognized.[14]

---

13. Chopin appears to have forgotten that his most famous nocturne was notated in 12/8 time. He absentmindedly misplaced one of the bar lines, unfolding part of the melody in 6/8! The holograph is reproduced in BFC, p. 104.

14. The facsimile of the Waltz first appeared in a biographical novel titled *Les Trois Romans de Frédéric Chopin* (1886), written by Maria's nephew Antoni Wodziński. Despite his family connection to Maria, Antoni's book is largely a work of fiction, a poisoned chalice from which a number of later biographers drank too deeply. Still, it is to Antoni that we owe a possible explanation of the twelve accented D-flats that occur somewhat incongruously in the right hand between bars 65 and 95, which Chopin marks *tenuto*—held. The notion that they represent the chiming of the great bell of the Frauenkirche tolling midnight, before the rolling wheels of Chopin's carriage take him away from Maria in bars 81–88, is the product of a fertile imagination. And it is somewhat spoiled by the discovery that after the count of twelve, six more random chimes put in an appearance. But stranger images have been attached to Chopin's music, and this one was obviously part of family lore. At one point the author has Chopin and Maria walking hand in hand around the park at the family mansion in Służewo, a place that Chopin never visited. And years after their parting, he sends Maria off to Paris for a sentimental reunion with Chopin. Maria was a child when Chopin first met her, and the possibility of an early romantic connection between the pair did not exist. After 1836 they never saw each other again, least of all for a reunion in Paris. Maria lived to see the publication of Antoni's novel, but her reaction to it remains unknown.

Chopin gave no public concerts in Dresden, but he was persuaded by the Wodziński family to take part in a soirée at their home, to which a number of distinguished guests from the Polish diaspora were also invited. It suited Teresa to cultivate these illustrious families and take on the role of a regal hostess. On this occasion she went down to defeat. A curious incident occurred that gives credence to the idea that Chopin was under political surveillance. From the diary of Józef Krasiński, an emissary who represented Poland's interests in the Saxon capital, we learn that after playing a number of his own pieces Chopin began to improvise at length on the old patriotic song "Poland Has Not Yet Perished." Known as the Dąbrowski Mazurka, this melody stirred memories among Poles that went back to Napoléon and the Polish regiments that served under him after the catastrophe of the Third Partition. The text contains the lines "What the aliens have taken from us / We shall retrieve with a saber"—which was nothing less than a call to arms.[15] Sitting in the audience were two diplomats from the Russian embassy whom Krasiński identifies as "Schröder the Envoy, a courteous but cold man, and his despicable secretary Richter." The Russians were outraged and next morning Krasiński was summoned to the Russian embassy and interrogated. How could he permit Chopin to play such inflammatory music? they asked. Krasiński came back with the perfectly reasonable reply that he had no idea what Chopin had intended to play, and he could hardly be expected to order a musician as to how and on what he was supposed to improvise in somebody else's house. "I will never forget Richter's response," Krasiński continued. "If you wish to be a faithful subject of the Monarch and not appear to be sojourning in a foreign land like a rebel, then you should have thrown out of the house a demagogue like Choppin [sic] or at least have compelled him to silence and left that house."[16]

Krasiński tells us that when his passport came up for renewal, the Russians punished him by declining to process it. For the Wodziński family it was even worse. Although their passports had not expired, they were told it might be in their best interests to leave Dresden. If Krasiński's account of this diplomatic incident is true, it would go far to explain the growing

---

15. The melody was officially adopted as the national anthem of the Republic of Poland in 1926.
16. GJK, Appendix I.

unease of Wincenty Wodziński as he contemplated a possible marriage of his daughter to someone the Russians considered a "demagogue," even as he was negotiating with them for the return of his properties in Poland.

IV

Chopin departed Dresden on September 26, with a promise to join the Wodziński family the following year in Marienbad, where they already planned to take the waters. Shortly after he left, Maria put pen to paper and wrote him a very long letter in which it is evident that the young girl not only missed him, but had begun to fall in love with him. When Chopin read these lines, he could be forgiven for supposing that not only Maria but the entire Wodziński family now regarded him as a worthy suitor. He is referred to as a "fourth son"; the chair on which he sat in "Fryderyk's corner" is to be left undisturbed; his writing pencil, which he forgot to take with him, is now a relic; and his vacant place at the dinner table symbolizes the void created by his absence. Here is how the sixteen-year-old expressed herself.

[Dresden, September 1835]
. . . On Saturday, after you had left us, we all walked sadly about the drawing room, where you had been with us a few minutes earlier. Our eyes were filled with tears. My father soon came home and was upset at not having been able to say goodbye. My mother kept on reminding us mournfully of some little characteristic of "her fourth son, Fryderyk," as she calls you. Felix looked quite dejected; Casimir tried to make his usual jokes but they didn't come off, for he was acting the comedian, half laughing and half crying. Papa made fun of us and laughed too, but it was only to prevent himself from crying. At eleven the singing master came; the lesson went very badly for we couldn't sing. You were the sole topic of conversation. Felix repeatedly asked me to play that Waltz (the last thing you played and gave to us). They enjoyed listening as I enjoyed playing, for it brought back the brother who had just left.
I took the Waltz [i.e., "L'Adieu"] to be bound. The German bookbinder stared when he was shown just one sheet. (He didn't know,

this German, who had written it!) No one could touch anything at dinner; we kept on looking at your usual place at table and then at "Fryderyk's corner"—the little chair is still in its place and will probably stay there as long as we are in this house . . .

She then goes on to ask Chopin to look after her brother Antoni, who was en route to Paris, intent on fighting in Spain's civil war, and hoped to lodge with Chopin for a time. "Please don't be indifferent to him," pleaded Maria. "He will be glad to find a friendly heart to understand him." And she concluded:

> We never cease to regret that you are not called Chopiński, or at least that there isn't some other indication that you are Polish. If there were, the French could not question our pride in being your compatriots. But I am boring you. Your time is so valuable that it is really a crime to make you waste it in reading my scribblings. Anyhow I'm sure you won't trouble to read it all. Little Maria's letter will be thrown aside when you've read a few lines—so I need not blame myself for wasting your time . . .[17]

One sentence from Maria's final paragraph calls for comment: her expression of regret that Chopin was not called Chopiński, a sentiment that was shaped by the Wodziński family. Behind her bland words lay something profound. Many Poles whose families bore foreign names had changed them to indicate their immersion into Polish society. This was especially true of German names. Schmidt became Szmit; Schroeder became Szreder; Schulz became Szulc. Mikołaj had integrated as fully as anyone, but he always refused to change the spelling of his family name and hide his French roots. Fryderyk himself was often referred to in the Polish press as Choppen, Szoppen, or Szopen, a practice that was a source of amusement to him. As for Chopiński, Maria must have known that he was immovable on the topic.

There were more immediate problems confronting Chopin's relations with the Wodzińskis than the lack of a Polish name. Looming over everything else was the uncertain state of his health. That Teresa Wodzińska at first supported her daughter's growing attachment to Chopin is evident from the correspondence. But she also knew that Maria would require the blessing of the male family members, including Uncle Maciej, and that might be more difficult to obtain. It was obvious to everyone that Chopin had a delicate constitution, and Teresa may already have guessed that he was consumptive—to judge from her repeated urgings that he take better care of himself and pursue the various remedies she prescribed for him.

V

Chopin returned to Paris by way of Leipzig, where he spent two days in the company of Mendelssohn. They had promised themselves this meeting ever since their encounter in Aachen a year earlier. They made music together, Mendelssohn playing parts of his new oratorio *St. Paul*, and Chopin inserting a few of his own Studies from op. 25 between the sections of the oratorio. While this was going on, Mendelssohn tells us, groups of inquisitive Leipzigers tiptoed in and out of the music room so that they could say they had seen Chopin. Mendelssohn was so taken with Chopin's performance of what he described as "a pretty new Nocturne" (probably the still-unpublished one in D-flat major, op. 27, no. 2) that within a couple of hours he had committed most of it to memory so that he could play it to his brother Paul. He later told his sister Fanny Hensel, "There is something so profoundly original and at the same time so very masterly in his piano playing that he may be called an absolutely perfect virtuoso."[18] The next day Mendelssohn took Chopin over to meet Friedrich Wieck at the latter's house on Grimmstrasse. It was there that Chopin had a surprise encounter with Robert Schumann, whom he had not yet met. Schumann, whose colorful review of his "Là ci darem" Variations four years earlier had so bemused Chopin, was now the editor and proprietor of the influential *Neue Zeitschrift für Musik* and he had continued to lavish attention on Chopin's music. Behind the civilized veneer of these meetings with two of his great contemporaries lay something that cannot be overlooked. Mendelssohn and Schumann were full of praise for

---

18. CFC, vol. 2, p. 154; KFC, vol. 1, p. 264.

Chopin's music; Chopin was almost completely indifferent to theirs. It is true that Schumann and Chopin were shortly to dedicate two of their greatest works to each other—Chopin inscribing his Ballade in F major, op. 38, to Schumann, and Schumann his *Kreisleriana* to Chopin. But while Schumann extolled the Ballade, all that Chopin could find worthy of note in *Kreisleriana* was the nice design of its front cover. Wieck introduced Chopin to his sixteen-year-old prodigy daughter, Clara (one day to become Schumann's wife), who played several works of her own and then launched into a performance of Schumann's F-sharp minor Piano Sonata, which was dedicated to her. She redeemed what might have been a tedious experience for Chopin by playing two of his Studies from op. 10 in such a polished manner that he was sincerely impressed. He later declared that she was the only woman in Germany who knew how to play his works.

Despite his best efforts to please Mme Wodzińska, Chopin had the misfortune to fall ill in Heidelberg on his journey back to Paris and went down with what he called "influenza." He had gone there to visit the parents of his young pupil Adolf Gutmann, but became so ill that he had to take to his bed and remained in Heidelberg for nearly a week. Not wishing to alarm the Wodzińskis, he kept quiet about his setback. This turned out to be a mistake. Rumors of his death began to circulate in Germany and it became necessary to deny them. Chopin's parents suffered needless anguish for several weeks, which turned into inexpressible relief when they read the following announcement in the *Warsaw Courier* in its issue of January 8, 1836: "We wish to inform the many friends and admirers of the eminent talent of the virtuoso Fryderyk Chopin that the report of his death which has been circulating during the last few days is without foundation."

The torment of uncertainty and the fear that Fryderyk might still be in danger ended only when Chopin himself informed them that all was well. His letter has not survived, but we surmise that it arrived in Warsaw on January 9, the very day that Mikołaj replied to it, for the latter's response begins with an outburst of emotion, expressing unmitigated relief that his son was alive. "Never was a letter more longed for or more impatiently awaited than the one we have just received," he wrote. "The dreadful news [of Fryderyk's death] came to us just before Christmas, and you cannot imagine what a state we were in, nor our mortal anxiety."[19] Mikołaj was

---

19. CFC, vol. 2, pp. 164–65; KFC, vol. 1, p. 270.

justified in chiding his son for his silence. The family, Mikołaj wrote, had to learn the true state of affairs from others. Good friends had tried to assure them that all was well. Mme Fontana, he went on, had called on them personally to tell them that her son Julian had written to her as recently as December 12 and had mentioned Fryderyk in his letter, with no indication that anything was amiss. Faustyn Zieliński had then rushed over to Ludwika's house, having read in the *Journal des débats* that Chopin was going to improvise at a soirée in the rue de la Chaussée d'Antin. Mikołaj was with Ludwika at that moment, and together they ran over to Lourse's café, where Mikołaj was able to read the article for himself. There is one other piece of information in Mikołaj's letter to which we must attach importance, because it explains what happened during the months that followed. Maria's father, Wincenty, had called on the Chopin family during the Christmas holidays, curious about the rumors concerning Fryderyk's demise. In the absence of solid information Mikołaj had been unable to provide him with any satisfactory answers. From this moment can be traced the first signs of division among the Wodzińskis: the men of the family were solidly against a marriage between Chopin and Maria. Only Teresa continued to support her daughter's aspirations, but that support eventually slipped away.

Chopin got back to Paris during the third week of October 1835, and picked up the threads of his earlier routine: teaching (still a vital source of income), composing, and socializing at all hours in the homes of the aristocracy, where he improvised on the piano, sometimes not getting back to his apartment until one or two o'clock in the morning. It was not an itinerary calculated to please Mme Wodzińska, whose contacts kept her fully informed. Chopin's social calendar during the winter of 1835–36 reads like a combination of pages from *Burke's Peerage* and *Who's Who*. He dined with Kalkbrenner. He attended a soirée in the Petit-Luxembourg Palace hosted by Duke Élie Decazes, who had earlier been the prime minister of France, and for whose guests he played one of his waltzes (probably the one in E-flat major, op. 18). He joined a select party in the home of General Karol Kniaziewicz (a veteran of Napoléon's campaign against Russia), where he found himself sitting next to the exiled national poet Adam Mickiewicz and statesman Julian Niemcewicz. He was present at Polish functions in the home of Prince Adam Czartoryski. And a place at the table of the influential banker Auguste Léo was regularly open to him. Our attention is particularly captured by a party hosted by Liszt, where

Chopin dined with the writer and philosopher Pierre-Simon Ballanche, the composer Giacomo Meyerbeer, and the painter Eugène Delacroix, who was to become a close friend. Liszt was on a passing visit from Switzerland and he gave two notable recitals in the Salle Érard, at one of which (May 18) he introduced Beethoven's "Hammerklavier" Sonata to the Parisians. No one had yet dared to play this impenetrable work in France. Berlioz was present, score in hand, and he extolled Liszt as "a new Oedipus, who has solved the riddle of the Sphinx."[20] If Chopin was present his reaction to this concert remains unknown. It featured parts of Liszt's piano arrangement of Berlioz's *Harold en Italie*—the kind of music to which he was averse.

VI

For much of the time, Chopin was preoccupied with his plans to join the Wodzińskis in Marienbad, and on July 19, 1836, he set out on the long journey, which took him through Strasbourg, Nuremberg, and Bayreuth, arriving in Marienbad on July 28. He moved into the fashionable White Swan Hotel, where the Wodzińskis were also staying, this time describing himself in the official register as "a property owner from Paris"—which we may plausibly assume to be yet another attempt to avoid surveillance by the Russians. The three weeks that he spent at Marienbad with Maria and her family were for him a blissful time. It was plain to everyone that he and Maria were in love, and Chopin had every reason to suppose that the family would look favorably on the idea of a marriage. When the Wodzińskis returned to Dresden toward the end of August, Chopin traveled with them. Nonetheless, he was slow to declare himself and waited until the eve of his departure before finding the courage to do so. On September 9, 1836, at "the twilight hour,"[21] Chopin finally proposed to Maria and was accepted. Teresa lent her blessing to the engagement, asking only that it remain secret until she had brought her husband around to her way of thinking. It was a difficult condition, but Chopin went along

---

20. *Gazette musicale*, June 12, 1836.
21. The poetic Polish expression "the twilight (or gray) hour" (*o szarej godzinie*) describes the close of day when reason is at its weakest and emotion at its strongest.

with it. Meanwhile, he was to be placed on probation, his health carefully monitored.

Chopin's return journey to Paris took him once again through Leipzig, where he paid a second visit to Schumann, on September 12. "Who should walk in but Chopin!" declared Schumann. "What joy it brought us. We spent a beautiful day together, which we celebrated again yesterday."[22] This second celebration was a reference to Clara Wieck's seventeenth birthday, which fell on September 13. Chopin played for Schumann his newly published Ballade in G minor, op. 23, "dearer to me than anything," Schumann remarked, "followed by a host of studies, mazurkas, and nocturnes, everything unparalleled." Schumann left a description of the visit in an issue of the *Neue Zeitschrift*, in which he picks out for special mention Chopin's performance of the Study in A-flat major, op. 25, no. 1.

> Imagine an Aeolian harp that had all the scales, and that these were jumbled together by the hand of an artist into all sorts of fantastic ornaments, but in such a manner that a deeper fundamental tone and a softly singing higher part were always audible, and you have an approximate idea of his playing. No wonder that we have become fondest of those pieces that we heard him play himself, and therefore we shall mention first of all the one in A-flat, which is rather a poem than a Study. It would be a mistake, however, to think that he brought out every one of the little notes distinctly; it was more like a billowing of the A-flat major chord, swelling from time to time by means of the pedal. But in the midst of the harmony were heard the sustained tones of a wondrous tenor voice, which came into greater prominence to join the principal *cantilena*.[23]

Clara Wieck was present and played in turn some of her own newest pieces, including her Soirées musicales, op. 6, and her Piano Concerto, op. 7. Schumann could not resist making a comparison and privately observed, "Clara is a greater virtuoso, and invests [Chopin's] compositions with still more meaning than he does himself." But he added, "The very sight of him

22. SBNF, pp. 77–78.
23. *NZfM*, December 22, 1837.

at the piano is moving."[24] Through Schumann, Chopin also made the acquaintance of Henriette Voigt, the wife of a local merchant. Henriette, who was a good amateur pianist, liked to receive distinguished artists in her Leipzig salon. She took Chopin across to her home and he played for her, which led her to record this vignette in her diary:

> Chopin was here yesterday and played on my piano for half an hour. He improvised and played his new Etudes. He is an interesting person, whose playing captures the listener with a sensitive ear, and I indeed listened with bated breath. The lightness with which those velvet fingers glide, or rather flit, across the keyboard is astonishing. He captivated me, I cannot deny it, in a way that I have never known before. What enchanted me most was the freedom of both his bearing and his playing.[25]

Henriette had not heard a note of Chopin before that memorable afternoon, but she immediately rushed out to purchase every one of his compositions she could lay hands on. Before resuming his journey to Paris, Chopin laid a wreath at the monument of Prince Józef Poniatowski, the Polish field marshal who had been killed fighting on the side of Napoléon at the Battle of Leipzig. The memory of Poniatowski, the brother of the last King of Poland, was woven deeply into the fabric of Polish nationalism, and Chopin's floral tribute is generally lost in the fog of history. From Leipzig, Chopin went on to Cassel, where he called on Ludwig Spohr, whose Piano Quintet he used to play in Warsaw. He also sought out Hiller and Mendelssohn in Frankfurt. Mendelssohn had recently enjoyed a triumph conducting the first performance of his *St. Paul* oratorio at the Lower Rhine Festival, held this year in Düsseldorf, and he was presently on an extended visit to Frankfurt, where he had just become engaged to his future wife, Cécile Jeanrenaud.

---

24. SBNF, p. 79. At the time of Chopin's visit, Schumann was putting the finishing touches to his unpublished *Carnaval* (1837), one of whose numbers he called "Chopin." This tribute has the distinction of being the first attempt by anyone to imitate Chopin's musical style. Chopin's response to a piece bearing not only his name but his unmistakable musical "fingerprints" as well remains unknown.

25. Selections from Voigt's diary were published by Wolfgang Boetticher in his "Weitere Forschungen," BWF, pp. 53–55.

VII

By late September, Chopin was back in his Paris apartment on the rue de la Chaussée d'Antin, dogged by illness. Eighteen days and nights traveling across Germany by diligence and back again to France had taken their toll. He remained in bed, coughed up blood-flecked sputum, and developed a high fever. His old friend Jan Matuszyński, who was now a physician, was there to look after him, having arrived from Warsaw the previous year, and had moved in with him just as their mutual friend Dr. Aleksander Hoffman had moved out. So Chopin once more had his own "in-house physician." No one was better qualified to treat Chopin's illness than Matuszyński, for like Chopin he had arrived from Poland with similar symptoms. Tuberculosis claimed him just over six years later, at the early age of thirty-four. During the uprising, Matuszyński had served in the Polish Rifles Regiment and had been awarded the country's highest military honor, the Cross of Virtuti Militari. After settling in Paris, where he continued to pursue his medical practice in the local hospitals, Matuszyński provided his brother-in-law in Poland with a brief description of his daily life with Chopin.

> Chopin is now the leading pianist in Paris. He gives many lessons, never for less than twenty francs. He has composed a good deal and his works are much sought after. I am living with him at 5, rue de la Chaussée d'Antin. It is rather far from the Medical School and the hospitals, but I have very good reasons for staying with him— he's the only friend that I have. We spend our evenings at the theatres or pay visits or we stay in and enjoy ourselves quietly at home.[26]

Despite Chopin's wretched health, or perhaps because of it, he and Matuszyński moved during October 1836 from no. 5 to no. 38 rue de la Chaussée d'Antin—the same street, but with a different entrance. It was a more spacious apartment, offered more sunlight, and might have provided Matuszyński himself with greater freedom had he stayed. In the event, he moved out a few weeks later in order to marry Thérèse Boquet,

---

26. HSCC, p. 123.

the widow of a French cavalry officer. Chopin was a witness at their wedding, which took place on December 21, 1836, at the Polish church of St. Roch on the rue Saint-Honoré. Julian Fontana, who had meanwhile returned to Paris after a longish stay in England and was attempting to establish his career in the French capital, took over the rooms vacated by Matuszyński and lived with Chopin for the next two years, acting as his secretary and amanuensis.

VIII

No sooner had Chopin said goodbye to the Wodzińskis than Teresa began to regret that she had not discussed his engagement to Maria more fully. On the day of his departure, she explained, she had been ravaged with toothache and had undergone an extraction. "I was so unwell that I could not give enough attention to 'the twilight hour' and we did not discuss it sufficiently. Had you stayed, we could have gone into it more fully the next day . . ."[27] Teresa had already begun to fear that this secret engagement might end in grief. She began to chide Chopin for not taking better care of himself, urging him to go to bed by eleven o'clock and drink gum water (an aromatic syrup drink, laced with opium). Just before she and Maria returned home to Poland, Teresa sent him a firm directive. "I will write to you from Warsaw: and now I must repeat: Take care of your health and all will be well." And later in the same letter she returned to the old refrain: "Remember, this is a testing time."[28] She fussed about a pair of specially made slippers she had sent Chopin and some woolen stockings that Maria had knitted for him, pressing him to wear them in order to safeguard his health. Teresa had exacted a solemn promise from Chopin that he would wear these trappings, and because he had remained silent on the matter she assumed that her orders were being ignored, and accused him of lying about them: "I gather from your letter that you were not telling the truth when you solemnly promised to obey my orders, for you do not say a word about wearing woolen stockings with your slippers and going

---

27. CFC, vol. 2, p. 198; KFC, vol. 1, p. 286.
28. CFC, vol. 2, p. 199; KFC, vol. 1, pp. 286–87.

to bed before eleven."[29] To this Chopin responded with quiet dignity, "As I respect you I assure you that I am not lying: I *do* remember my slippers, and when I play I think of 'the twilight hour.'"[30] These injunctions about wearing a pair of slippers and woolen stockings may perplex the modern reader. But in accordance with the folklore of the time, "colds" were presumed to enter the body through the feet—and a first line of defense was to keep them warm.[31]

During the whole of Chopin's stay with the Wodziński family, an air of expectancy hovered over everything that they did and marginalized their daughter's secret betrothal to the composer. For some time now the Wodzińskis had been making preparations for their return to Poland and the repossession of their estates, after a five-year exile. Maria's father, Wincenty, had already gone back to Warsaw ahead of the family to oversee the arrangements. Behind these plans lay an important assumption. If Chopin's engagement to Maria ever became official, it was taken for granted that he would return to Poland as well, and the correspondence contains tantalizing glimpses of such a scenario. Maria herself had written shortly before her departure for Poland that she hoped to hear Chopin playing on the new piano at Służewo that they had asked him to send them. And she had concluded her final letter from Dresden (October 2) with the sentence "Goodbye until May or June."[32] Despite her optimism, it was not to be.

Maria was a passive daughter, easily dominated by her parents. Teresa Wodzińska has been memorably described as a "harridan."[33] That was a harsh judgment, but we must not forget that it was Teresa who played a major role in breaking off Chopin's engagement to her daughter after first approving it, under circumstances that were unnecessarily cruel to him. From the moment that the Wodzińskis arrived back in Poland a marked change of mood overtook their dealings with Chopin. Distance was now to be allowed to exert its inevitable influence. The language of the letters

---

29. CFC, vol. 2, p. 203; KFC, vol. 1, p. 290.

30. CFC, vol. 2, p. 207; KFC, vol. 1, p. 292.

31. The contemporary French journal *Almanach populaire* was a fountain of knowledge on such matters. It kept its readers rigorously informed about such wide-ranging topics as astrology, financial investments, temperance societies, and of course home remedies for whatever ailed one.

32. CFC, vol. 2, p. 205; KFC, vol. 1, p. 291.

33. HSLC, p. 323.

becomes more polite and formal, and Maria's messages to Chopin take the form of brief postscripts to her mother's letters. Meanwhile, instead of informing Chopin of her change of mind, Teresa kept his hopes alive and manipulated him for her own trivial ends. Examples of her duplicity abound, and it is easy to list them. Her comment to Chopin that when she got back to Warsaw and met his parents she would remain silent about his "secret" engagement to Maria was contemptible. Did she really think that Chopin's family was so out of touch with their son that he would have kept such news from them? In fact they learned of it almost at once, and were pleased at the prospect of happiness that this engagement might bring him. As for Chopin himself, his naïveté was such that he was slow to realize he was being "taken for a ride," as one popular biographer expressed it.

When the Wodziński family repossessed their manor in Służewo, they found it neglected. The old house piano was so broken down that it was unplayable, so that was the cue for Teresa to ask Chopin to send a replacement from Pleyel and ship it to Poland, while making no clear provision for its payment. Chopin was happy to oblige and the piano was shipped to Gdańsk, from where it was supposed to be conveyed by wagon for the remaining 140 kilometers to Służewo. Not long afterward Teresa asked Chopin to provide autographs of prominent people in Paris for her growing collection, as if he had nothing better to do than go around knocking on doors and picking up signatures from his friends. Once more he obliged. He not only acquired the autographs but also got Ludwika to copy out seven of his Polish Songs, together with his *Lento con gran espressione* (1830), for Maria. After proofing everything, Chopin placed these manuscripts in an elegant red leather-bound volume with Maria's name inscribed on the cover in gold letters and sent the collection to Służewo. For these acts of kindness he received no thanks, but rather a reproof. Teresa's irritable letter to Chopin, dated January 25, 1837, marks a turning point, and must have indicated to him that his hopes of matrimony were fading. The letter is long, and we quote only the essential parts of it.

Służewo, January 25, 1837

My good Frycek,

It is a long, long time since we received your letter, followed shortly afterward by the parcel of music about which I shall rather scold you than *thank* you for sending. And that "keepsake" [the handsomely bound album], what folly! Moreover, when you wrote about the piano you did not state what sum was to be sent, for we must know in advance in order to get the money together. Please let me know also to what address in Gdańsk the piano is being sent. We have calculated that if Adolphe were informed of its arrival there, a cart could be sent to fetch it—it is only twenty-five leagues away [140 kilometers]—and we could have the piano before the spring. Life here is rather sad. Since our return from Warsaw we have not set foot outside the house and have entertained no guests . . . (T.W.)

To this litany of complaints Maria herself provided a postscript.

Mamma has scolded you so I will thank you very nicely, and when we meet I shall thank you still more nicely. You can see that I am lazy about writing, for the fact that I am postponing my thanks until we meet frees me from the obligation to write at length for now. Mamma has described our mode of life so I have nothing left to report except that a thaw has set in—an important piece of news, is it not?—especially important for you to know. The quiet life we lead here suits me and that is why I like it—for the time being, of course: I would not wish it to be like that always. One has to make the best of things when one has no other choice. I try to find things to do to pass the time. At the moment I am reading Heine's *Deutschland*, which is awfully interesting. But I must stop now and give you my blessing. I hope that I do not need to reassure you of the sentiments of
		Your faithful Secretary,
		Maria[34]

There is not a syllable of real affection from Maria, whose lines consist in the main of dull platitudes. As for Teresa, she merely initialed her part of the missive "T.W." Ferdynand Hoesick describes this letter as thoroughly

---

34. CFC, vol. 2, pp. 210–12; KFC, vol. 1, pp. 294–95.

unpleasant, dry, and devoid of affection, and in parts simply rude.[35] Chopin was at this point a musician of European stature. Teresa, adds Hoesick, appears to have had no idea to whom she was actually writing.

IX

With prospects of his marriage to Maria Wodzińska fast disappearing, Chopin sank into despair. In February 1837 he also fell victim to the influenza epidemic that was raging across Europe and confined him to his room for several weeks. He was forced to cancel a number of engagements, including his participation in a concert with Liszt on April 9 in the Érard salon. High fever and frequent hemorrhaging were among the symptoms and this time he may even have contracted pneumonia. He swallowed crushed ice to calm the inflammation of his throat, but was left with a chronic cough and a hoarse voice.[36] In the midst of these travails he received a letter from his mother (marking his twenty-seventh birthday, on March 1) informing him that Teresa Wodzińska had been in touch with her to complain that he had broken his promise to keep early hours and was neglecting his health. This busybody alarmed Justyna, and Chopin must have been furious. Through her network of informants Teresa had been keeping herself supplied with tittle-tattle about Chopin's lifestyle in Paris, had learned of his illness, and had used it to place further distance between the Chopins and the Wodzińskis.

From this same letter we learn that Chopin had consulted a clairvoyant, doubtless believing that she might prove to be a more reliable source of information about his future than Mme Wodzińska herself. This fortune-teller was the celebrated Mlle Marie Lenormand, who lived in the rue de Tournon, then one of the seamiest quarters in Paris. She sat in an old leather armchair in a darkened room with a black cat circling around her feet and a pack of cards of her own design spread on the table before her. Many eminent clients had consulted her across the years, including Tsar Alexander I of Russia and the Duke of Wellington, who wanted to discover who had tried to assassinate him. Known as the "Sibyl of the Faubourg

---

35. HFCZ, vol. 2, p. 204.
36. SHC, p. 118, and BJT, p. 108.

Saint-Germain," Mlle Lenormand's best days were now behind her. She foretold not merely a happy future for Chopin but a singularly bright one. To anyone familiar with his biography the prophecy fell wide of the mark. A year or two earlier, Marie d'Agoult had also consulted her before eloping with Liszt, and had received similar words of hope and encouragement, with a rose-tinted future as far as the eye could see. D'Agoult herself was soon to discover that Lenormand's compass was not merely out of order but was capable of pointing in two directions simultaneously. Justyna disapproved of fortune-telling and she admonished her son, "Promise me, dear Fryderyk, that you won't see her again."[37] Whether he took this advice to heart and wasted no more money in vain attempts to pierce the veil of the future we do not know. In any case, that future seemed bleak, and for the first time he was confronted with the reality of an encroaching disease that seemed to defy treatment.

Ever since Chopin had arrived in Paris one of his most fervent admirers had been the Marquis Astolphe de Custine, author and travel writer, who emerges from the literature as a devoted friend with a genuine concern for the composer's well-being. Custine was dismayed to observe Chopin's rapid decline and he lavished a series of urgent invitations on the composer to join him at his villa in Saint-Gratien by Lake d'Enghien, not far from Paris, telling him, "I think that such an excursion would be salutary for your health . . . You are ill. What is worse, your illness might become serious. You have reached the limit of physical and spiritual suffering." Custine must have been well informed about Chopin's problems, however hard the composer tried to conceal them, for he added these perspicacious comments:

> To preserve your *past*—which holds such a promising future—there is only one way open to you: to let yourself be treated as a sick child. You must be persuaded that one single thing is of consequence: your health. The rest will take care of itself. I am sufficiently your friend for you to allow me to go to the heart of the matter. Is it money that is keeping you in Paris? If so, I can lend you some; you can pay me later, but you must take three months' rest! If it is love that has failed

you, let us see what friendship can do. Live for yourself, for us. There
will be plenty of time later on to get rich.[38]

Chopin declined to pursue Custine's generous offer of a three-month holiday in Germany, nor as far as we know did he accept the money offered
him, but he did spend one weekend in May at Custine's villa in Saint-
Gratien, where he found a Pleyel piano waiting for him and a ready audience of distinguished guests eager to hear him play. After a splendid banquet hosted by Custine at a nearby restaurant, washed down with copious
quantities of champagne and burgundy, the guests returned to the villa,
where Chopin performed two of his Studies from op. 25 and the first part
of the still-unfinished Ballade in F major, op. 38. This visit was captured in detail by Chopin's old school friend the composer Józef Brzowski,
who was on an extended visit to Paris and went along with him to Saint-
Gratien.[39] "I need hardly talk about the impression he made on his listeners," Brzowski wrote.

> He played his new Etude in A-flat major, the beginning of his sec-
> ond Ballade, and the F minor Etude. The delighted audience wanted
> to hear a Mazurka as well. Chopin immediately offered them one
> of his patriotic poems, and then, inspired like a nationalistic poet,
> started to improvise a war song. Its melody was marvelous and the
> fiery hue with which he performed it electrified the legitimist souls,
> who were transported by the nostalgic emotions that the Mazurka
> aroused in them. When he finished, and stood up from the piano,
> everybody also stood up and surrounded the triumphant virtuoso;
> and because they all had a genuine legitimist background, they
> asked him what was the war song that he had played. Nobody knew
> that he was actually improvising, so he told them that it was an old
> song of the Ulany Regiment [the famous light cavalry of Polish
> Lancers, based in Poznań]. The ladies that surrounded him insisted
> that he arrange it for choir, and said that they would like to sing it.
> Chopin promised that he would do so, but turning to me he said in
> Polish: "Tomorrow they will have forgotten about it." This revealed

---

38. CFC, vol. 2, pp. 220–21; KFC, vol. 1, p. 302.
39. CJFC, pp. 223–27. See also BJT, p. 121.

to me that Chopin knew a lot about the sort of people who frequented the salons of Paris.[40]

The fact that Chopin attended Custine's villa at all is not without interest. Everyone knew that the marquis was engulfed in a homosexual
scandal that had led to his banishment from the "best" Parisian society,
though not from its artistic circles in which he much preferred to mingle.
His admiring messages to Chopin convey overt expressions of love mingled
with insinuations that the composer simply ignored. Chopin would certainly have met Custine's in-house lover, Édouard de Sainte-Barbe, and
also the young Polish count Ignacy Gurowski, with whom Custine was
wont to share his ample bed. Another personality of equally licentious
repute whom Chopin met at Saint-Gratien was the Englishman Edward
Hughes Ball, who had as a young man inherited a vast fortune from an
English aunt, which had earned for him the dubious nickname "Golden
Ball." His reckless gambling and the purchase of three castles from the
King of England had collapsed his bank balance to the point that he had
been forced to flee his creditors and seek refuge in France. There he modeled himself on his hero Beau Brummel, and created a niche for himself
in the annals of sartorial splendor by inventing the black necktie. He is
known to have sired at least six children via numerous mistresses while at
the same time mingling with Custine and his circle of intimates. As for
Count Ignacy Gurowski, he had lived in France as an exile since 1831
and had become Custine's lover in 1835. His profligate and unstable nature introduced much agitation into Custine's private life. Gurowski was
later banished from France for eloping with and secretly marrying the
nineteen-year-old Princess Isabella de Bourbon, niece of King Ferdinand
VII of Spain. This was no mean feat, since the princess was at that time
living in a monastery and chaperoned by the monks who were educating
her. The hasty marriage ceremony appears to have been conducted in the
getaway coach hired by Gurowski to take the couple to England. The
union produced three children and generated much scandal. If there is
any truth to the notion that one is known by the company one keeps, we
can only wonder what the Wodziński family made of it all. Brzowski
returned to Poland two weeks later with a rich treasury of memories to

40. BJT, p. 121.

divulge to his Polish acquaintances. Before setting out, he accompanied Chopin to Enghien's thermal baths in an attempt to improve the composer's breathing and get rid of the incessant cough that had plagued Chopin for weeks, especially during the morning hours.

One other invitation arrived in the spring of 1837, which Chopin firmly rejected. Tsar Nicholas made it known that he wanted to bestow on Chopin the title of "Pianist to the Imperial Russian Court." This unexpected offer, which carried with it a lifetime pension, was conveyed through the office of Count Carlo Pozzo di Borgo, the Russian ambassador to Paris, who explained that since Chopin had played no part in the Warsaw Uprising he was not considered a political fugitive. According to Chopin's nephew Antoni Jędrzejewicz, Chopin turned down the invitation with some blunt words to Pozzo di Borgo. "Even if I did not take part in the Revolution of 1830, my sympathies were with those who did. Therefore I consider myself an exile: it is the only honor to which I am entitled."[41] It is at this point that Robert Schumann's celebrated words likening Chopin's music to "cannons buried in flowers" take on their true meaning, for they are often misconstrued. If Chopin's works were akin to weapons of war, as Schumann implied, the military-minded Tsar Nicholas would be well advised to bring them to Saint Petersburg and place them in the service of the Romanovs.[42] By declining the tsar's invitation Chopin made it clear that he and his music were on the side of Polish resistance.

X

The Wodziński family had meanwhile sealed themselves off at Służewo and Maria no longer wrote to him. Neither she nor her parents could summon the good grace to thank Chopin for his proposal of marriage, nor give him the reasons for declining it. Teresa continued to tantalize him with the occasional letter, which rarely contained a word about her

---

41. HFCZ, vol. 2, p. 150.
42. Schumann's description of Chopin's music is generally detached from its context. It was meant as a political reference, not a poetical one. His original words were: "If the autocratic, all-powerful monarch of the North knew what a dangerous foe was threatening him with these utterly simple mazurka melodies, he would doubtless ban this music. The works of Chopin are cannons buried in flowers." NZfM, April 22, 1836.

daughter. Her chief concern was her eldest son, Antoni, and here she took particular advantage of Chopin. Antoni had long been a source of worry to Teresa. He had fought in the uprising, had escaped from Poland, and had then drifted from one place to another, arriving in Paris and even moving in with Chopin for a time. Mikołaj Chopin cautioned his son not to loan Antoni money, having fallen victim to the young man's spendthrift ways himself, and having failed to recover a substantial sum he had advanced to the wayfarer. The warning went unheeded and Chopin, too, eventually joined the ranks of Antoni's creditors. The young man enlisted in a regiment of Polish lancers, was sent to fight in the civil war in Spain, and was wounded during the Battle of Huesca (May 24, 1837). Teresa became frantic for news of him and shamelessly turned to Chopin for help. She may not have wanted Chopin for a son-in-law but was not above appealing to him when he could be useful in other matters. On June 18 he gave her what information he could about the gravity of Antoni's wounds, and provided some details of the military catastrophe, which he gleaned from his Polish contacts in Paris. The regiment of Polish lancers to which Antoni had been attached, he told her, had been completely wiped out, but Antoni was safe.[43]

By August 1837, Chopin knew that his ill-fated engagement to Maria was over, since meaningful contact with the Wodziński family had all but ceased. It was probably at this time that he bundled all her letters together and placed them in a large envelope, which he tied with ribbon and marked *Moja bieda* (My misfortune). The package was discovered after his death in his Paris apartment. Chopin later referred to the Wodziński family as "thoughtless, unscrupulous, and heartless."[44]

In retrospect we are bound to conclude that Chopin was fortunate to have escaped this marriage. Maria was an ordinary girl, lacking in sophistication. Had Chopin married into the Wodziński family he would have lost his independence, his creative output would have been stifled, and the world might have been deprived of a treasury of music that was still to seek its full expression. He might also have been expected to return to Poland. After the refined life he was leading in Paris, that would have sounded the creative death knell. It would also have robbed him of

---

43. CFC, vol. 2, p. 222; KFC, vol. 1, pp. 303–304.
44. CFC, vol. 2, p. 309; KFC, vol. 1, p. 340.

"My misfortune." Chopin's correspondence with Maria Wodzińska.

his pupils, his major source of income. If you add to this the fact that the Wodziński family no longer held him in particularly high esteem, you have a burden too great for Chopin to have borne. It was always vital for him to have the unconditional support of family, friends, and colleagues who admired his genius, for without it he could not flourish.

XI

The story of Maria Wodzińska is not quite finished. In 1840 she became engaged to Józef Skarbek—the son of Fryderyk Skarbek—and on July 24, 1841, she married him. This wedding of Chopin's former fiancée to someone the Chopin family not only knew very well but who had belonged to their inner circle since childhood was looked upon with some bitterness by Chopin's sister Ludwika, who regarded it as a betrayal. "May God forgive them," she wrote.[45] Evidently God had other plans for the couple,

---

45. CFC, vol. 3, pp. 40–41; KFC, vol. 3, p. 16. Ludwika's sense of betrayal is better appreciated when we recall that Józef Skarbek was the young hero of her literary endeavor *Józio's*

because their Roman Catholic marriage was eventually annulled on grounds of *nullum in radice*—code words for nonconsummation of the union. After waiting for the obligatory two years, Maria married again, this time to Władysław Orpiszewski. There was one son of the marriage, named Tadeusz, who died when he was only four years old. The Orpiszewskis eventually migrated to Florence, where their home on the Piazza d'Azeglio became a gathering place for Polish artists and writers. Once a slender beauty, Maria became stout and matronly in later life.[46] After the death of her second husband in 1881 from tuberculosis (an irony that could hardly have failed to impress itself on her), she returned to Poland and lived with her niece Maria Orpiszewska. She died in 1896, aged seventy-seven, almost half a century after Chopin himself, to whom she owes her only claim to the attention of posterity.

Journey, mentioned on pages 36 and 101. When Ludwika enshrined the character of this seven-year-old boy in her book during his stay with the Chopin family at Bad Reinerz in 1826, she would have been mortified to know that he would one day grow up to marry the woman to whom her own brother was for a time engaged, before being jilted.

46. A photograph of her taken in her sunset years bears out this observation. It is reproduced in ECIB, p. 211.

AN ENGLISH INTERLUDE, JULY 1837

What enormous things they have here! The urinals are huge, but there is nowhere to have a proper pee.

—Chopin to Fontana[1]

I

Numerous invitations came Chopin's way that were meant to lift him from the slough of despond into which he had descended as a result of the Wodzińska affair. But he refused to stir, preferring to nurse his bruised feelings in Paris. Even the three days in June that he spent at the thermal baths at Enghien in the company of Józef Brzowski, following their joint trip to the Marquis de Custine's villa at Saint-Gratien, had failed to raise his spirits and he was not sorry to get back to his apartment on the rue de la Chaussée d'Antin, which he now shared with Julian Fontana. It was Camille Pleyel who came to his rescue by suggesting that Chopin accompany him on a trip to London. Pleyel himself stood in need of diversion, for he had recently cast off his young wife, the pianist Marie Pleyel, for her serial infidelities, and the process of separation had been painful for him. Marie had given birth to an illegitimate daughter in 1836 (fathered

1. CFC, vol. 2, p. 225.

most likely by her latest lover, the Hamburg merchant George Parish), which added to his marital burdens.[2]

Marie Moke (as she then was) had married Camille Pleyel in 1831 after her stormy engagement to Berlioz had been broken off. The marriage was problematic from the start. There was a twenty-three-year difference in their ages and Marie was persistently unfaithful to her older husband, who, as is so often the case, was the last to hear the news. For additional illumination we need look no further than the correspondence of Meyerbeer, who picked up a dramatic piece of scandal and passed it along to his wife, Minna, who had earlier been a pupil of Marie Pleyel's. "Your former piano teacher Camille [Marie] Moke, the present Madame Pleyel, has been given a terrible beating in her own house, by one of her lovers whose jealousy she aroused. He dragged her by the hair into the street. Her husband, who until then had supposed the contemptuous creature to be the most virtuous of wives, has had his eyes rudely opened. All Paris is talking about her infamy."[3] This scene evidently took place in May 1835, about the time that Marie became pregnant. Later that year Marie and Camille Pleyel were formally separated and Pleyel cut her out of his will.

A complete change of scenery was obviously in order for Pleyel, too, tired as he was of being rolled through the public mire. Since London had always been Chopin's destination of choice, he was happy to fall in with Pleyel's wishes, but made one stipulation: he must remain incognito. His professional friends must not know where he was going, and neither must the Wodziński family. Only if he were protected from prying eyes by a cloak of anonymity, he felt, would he be able to enjoy the simple pleasures of a sightseer and tourist, and be allowed to forget his dismal relations with the Wodziński family. Chopin acquired a French passport (dated July 7, 1837), and he and Pleyel set out from Paris on July 9. They boarded the ferry at Boulogne and crossed the English Channel to Dover, the first time that Chopin had ever been on the open sea. "I will tell you later what charming thoughts and disagreeable sensations the sea gave me," he told Fontana,[4] and after a journey of eighteen hours they arrived in London the following day.

---

2. Marie's daughter was legitimized on October 9, 1858, after Pleyel's death. Her name was also Marie, and she became a singer. See FLSL, p. 984.
3. GMB, vol. 2, p. 459.
4. CFC, vol. 2, p. 225; KFC, vol. 1, p. 306.

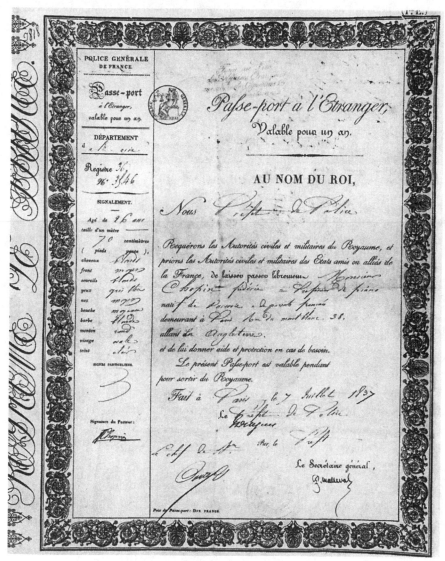

Chopin's French passport, dated July 7, 1837.

The details on Chopin's passport give one of the best descriptions of his physical characteristics to have come down to us:

Age: 26 years	Nose: Normal
Height: 1.70 meters	Mouth: Normal
Hair: Blond	Beard: Blond
Forehead: Normal	Chin: Round
Eyebrows: Blond	Face: Oval
Eyes: Gray-blue	Complexion: Clear

The pair of travelers stayed at the fashionable Sablonnière Hotel, situated at the corner of Cranbourne Street and Leicester Square. Julian Fontana had already contacted one of his old Warsaw friends, the poet Stanisław Egbert Koźmian, who now lived in the British capital, and alerted him to the composer's impending arrival. "He will be staying in London for a week or ten days at the most," wrote Fontana, "and he wishes to see no one . . . I ask you to keep [this visit] entirely to yourself."[5] So determined was Chopin to remain incognito that he used the name "Mr. Fritz" to mask his identity, and few people knew that he was there.[6]

Koźmian took the tourists under his wing and arranged to show them the sights. Fontana had rashly promised Chopin "an Italian sky" during this brief summer sojourn. In reality Chopin found the air of London sooty, and the gray columns of smoke rising above the city from hundreds of chimneys irritated his lungs. But he nonetheless eulogized London, finding the English women, horses, buildings, squares, palaces, and trees impressive. He was especially taken with the enormous English urinals, marble palaces "with nowhere to have a proper pee."[7] It is to Koźmian that we owe the best account of this underreported trip to England. Writing home to his brother in Poland, Koźmian observed:

> July 25, 1837
> Chopin has been here for two weeks incognito. He knows no one and does not wish to know anyone, except me. I spend the whole

---

5. Fontana's letter is dated July 3, 1837. OFCL, p. 44.
6. The pseudonym is hardly impenetrable. "Fritz," the German nickname for Frederick, has a similar-sounding Polish equivalent, "Frycek," by which Chopin's family and his intimate friends knew him.
7. CFC, vol. 2, p. 225; KFC, vol. 1, p. 306.

day with him and sometimes even the whole night, as yesterday. He is here with Pleyel, famous for his pianos and for his wife's adventures. They've come "pour se régaler de Londres" [i.e., "to do London"]. They are staying at one of the best hotels, they have a carriage, and in a word, they are simply looking for an opportunity of spending money. So one day we went to Windsor, another to Blackwall, and tomorrow we are going to Richmond. This is why I must postpone till later the rest of my story, because of the pleasure I get from the company, the playing and the conversation of my "seraph."[8]

II

In their quest "to spend money" the trio traveled in their hired carriage not only to Richmond, Hampton Court, Blackwall (famous for its "fish dinners"), and Windsor, but even farther afield to Chichester and Arundel, where they met Lord Dudley Stuart, a leading champion of the Polish cause in Britain, who was at that moment standing for a seat in the parliamentary elections, which he lost. It was there that Chopin witnessed the hurly-burly of an English rural election (of the kind described to perfection by Dickens at "Eatanswill" in The Pickwick Papers), perched on top of the carriage that had brought them there. Almost every evening found them at the opera or the theater. Giuditta Pasta was at that moment singing to packed audiences at the King's Theatre, and Chopin admired her in the leading roles of Cherubini's Medea and Bellini's I Capuleti e i Montecchi. He also heard Schröder-Devrient in Beethoven's Fidelio, a work that appears to have left little impression on him. A concert in aid of the Beethoven Memorial Fund, at which Moscheles played the "Emperor" Concerto under the direction of Sir George Smart at the Drury Lane Theatre, likewise failed to move him and he made no attempt to go backstage and meet the famous pianist, whose playing he found "frightfully baroque."[9] Had

---

8. HFCZ, vol. 2, p. 145.
9. This was a reference to a concert on July 20 in which Sir George Smart also conducted a performance of the Ninth Symphony for the Philharmonic Society. It was "given to empty benches," according to Moscheles, who complained bitterly about the jingoistic sentiments that one British newspaper had published against the proposed Beethoven monument: "The Germans never contributed anything to the monuments of illustrious Englishmen." MAML, vol. 2, pp. 23–24.

Moscheles had the slightest inkling that Chopin was in London, let alone in the audience, he would almost certainly have sought him out, because he had long wished to make his acquaintance. But Chopin was reluctant to come out of his shell. That was soon to change, however. Pleyel was invited to a soirée in the home of his English counterpart, the piano manufacturer James Shudi Broadwood, who lived in Bryanston Square, and he took Chopin along with him, introducing him to the other guests as "Mr. Fritz from Paris." And he might have got away with the deception were it not for the fact that after dinner the guests moved into the music room and one or two of them began to play on Broadwood's latest piano. Chopin could not resist the urge to follow suit. After a few measures the audience was spellbound and Chopin was unmasked. "Nobody else played like that." This marked the beginning of a fruitful relationship between Chopin and the house of Broadwood, which was to stand him in good stead when he returned to Britain in 1848. The Broadwood piano became his instrument of choice for all his major concerts that year.

Pleyel's presence in England raises a topic of a rather different kind. His failed marriage to Marie Moke, and the birth of her illegitimate daughter, had continued to make him vulnerable to gossip. Even Koźmian, in the letter quoted earlier, referred to him somewhat unkindly as "Pleyel, famous for his pianos and for his wife's adventures." Divorce was not a possibility under French law, but other options were. It may have been at this time that Pleyel met a twenty-one-year-old Englishwoman named Emma Osborn, and arranged to take her back to Paris as his common-law wife. We know that within eighteen months of this trip to London, Emma was already ensconced in the Pleyel household, for Chopin makes an oblique reference to her, inquiring after her health in a letter to Pleyel, dated January 22, 1839. At Pleyel's request Emma changed her name to Emma Osborn Pleyel. She became a Chopin enthusiast and, after Pleyel's death, in 1855, she came into possession of an important cache of Chopiniana—consisting of manuscripts and a number of personal items, which eventually found their way back to England. Emma died in 1906, at the venerable age of ninety, leaving behind some reminiscences that stretch credulity.[10]

---

10. They may be found in Victor Gille's *Souvenirs romantiques: Madame Emma Pleyel*, Paris 1954. A formal photograph of Emma Osborn, taken in the Paris studio of Clément Lagriffe in the 1860s (included in CCPLS, p. 8), reveals her to have been a strikingly handsome woman. She is buried in Père Lachaise Cemetery in a plot located opposite the tomb of the Pleyel

III

Moscheles, who had lived in London for several years, makes a plaintive reference to Chopin's visit in his diary. "Chopin, who passed a few days in London, was the only one of the foreign artists who visited nobody and also did not wish to be visited, as every conversation aggravates his chest complaint. He went to some concerts and disappeared."[11] Mendelssohn arrived three weeks after Chopin had left. When he learned that he had just missed seeing Chopin, he wrote to their mutual friend Ferdinand Hiller. "It seems that Chopin came over here quite suddenly a fortnight ago, paid no visits and saw nobody. He played one evening most beautifully at Broadwood's, and then hurried away again. They say that he is still very ill and miserable."[12]

Ill and miserable he may have been, but the impression he made when he played at Broadwood's lingered. The following year *The Musical World* carried some retrospective remarks about his playing in its issue of February 23, 1838.

> During his short visit to the metropolis last season, but few had the high gratification of hearing his extemporaneous performance. Those who experienced this will not readily lose its remembrance. He is, perhaps, *par éminence*, the most delightful of pianists in the drawing-room. The animation of his style is so subdued, its tenderness so refined, its melancholy so gentle, its niceties so studied and systematic, the *tout ensemble* so perfect, and evidently the result of an accurate judgement and most finished taste, that when exhibited in the large concert-room, or the thronged salon, it fails to impress itself on the mass.

IV

That is about all the official record has to tell us about Chopin's first visit to England. We know, however, that during this fleeting trip he contacted

---

family itself. On her tombstone, prepared half a century after the death of Camille, she is described as "Pleyel's widow."
11. MAML, vol. 2, p. 20.
12. HMBE, p. 90.

his English publisher, Christian Wessel, whose offices in Frith Street lay less than a kilometer from Chopin's hotel in Leicester Square, and on July 20 he signed various contracts. Wessel's impressive catalogue of Chopin's music, which now included dozens of his compositions, represented an important stake in the composer's affairs. It is true that Chopin could hardly speak a word of English, and that might have increased his sense of isolation; but Pleyel stood ready to act as an intermediary on any business matters with Wessel, and he actually countersigned the contracts.[13] There is moreover abundant evidence that Chopin did not cross the English Channel empty-handed, but brought various manuscripts with him in his travel trunk. By October 1837, just two months after Chopin had departed London, Wessel brought out the Impromptu in A-flat major, op. 29. A month later he expanded his catalogue to include Chopin's Four Mazurkas, op. 30, the Scherzo in B-flat minor, op. 31, and the Two Nocturnes, op. 32. All these pieces (save the Impromptu) appeared in England before Wessel's rival publishers in Leipzig (Breitkopf) and Paris (Schlesinger) were able to issue them. The jewel in the crown was the second volume of Twelve Studies, op. 25, which Wessel published in October, about the same time as Schlesinger and Breitkopf. Wessel was particularly inventive in attaching descriptive titles to Chopin's music for the delectation of English pianists. But when he provided the Scherzo in B-flat minor with the pendant "La Méditation," one wonders if he had even heard the work. The two nocturnes carried the appellations "Il lamento" and "La consolazione," respectively. Wessel knew that an army of English lady pianists was waiting in the wings, ready to have their lamentations aroused by the first Nocturne in G minor and consoled by the second one in A-flat major. Later would come such gems as "La Gracieuse" for the F major Ballade, op. 38, and "Les Soupirs" (Sighs) for the Two Nocturnes, op. 37. Despite Chopin's protests Wessel could not be deterred, fearing that he might lose money if he published these compositions under their generic titles.[14]

---

13. WCB, p. 29.
14. Chopin's exasperation with Wessel over these fatuous nicknames comes out in his correspondence and particularly in his letter to Julian Fontana dated October 9, 1841. "Now, as regards Wessel, he is a fool and a swindler . . . Tell him that if he has lost money over my compositions, it is certainly on account of the ridiculous titles he has given them, in spite of my prohibition and my repeated rows with Mr. Stapleton [Wessel's business partner]. You can tell him also that if I listened to the voice of my conscience I wouldn't send him another thing after those titles." (CFC, vol. 3, p. 86; KFC, vol. 2, p. 42.) We are left to wonder how this

After a mere three weeks Chopin's English interlude came to a close. We are told that the loyal Koźmian accompanied him as far as Brighton,[15] where they visited the recently completed royal folly, Brighton Pavilion, after which Chopin embarked on the cross-channel ferry from Dover, and got back to Paris toward the end of July. His brief sojourn in London had done him a world of good, even though it was there that he received a letter from Teresa Wodzińska (now lost) informing him that his engagement to Maria was terminated. He had long awaited this news with trepidation, but its arrival finally released him from the misery that had bound him to the Wodzińskis. Pleyel remained behind in London, making arrangements for the improvement of his domestic life in Paris, of which Emma Osborn would soon become a part.

---

problematic relationship between Chopin and Wessel was formed in the first place, doomed as it was to one rough passage after another. Edwin Ashdown, the proprietor of the company that eventually bought out Wessel, provides a possible answer. After pointing out that scarcely anybody played Chopin's music in England during the composer's lifetime, he went on: "Frederick Stapleton, Wessel's partner, was not particularly musical, but he heard Chopin play in Paris, and the performance had an extraordinary effect upon him. He felt sure that there was a fortune in publishing such music, and he persuaded Wessel to buy everything that he could of Chopin's. Few people could play it at the time, and the firm had rather a long experience of the unpopularity of Chopin. They decided to take no more of his music. Cramer published the next composition." *The Musical Herald*, April 1, 1903, pp. 99–101.

15. HFCZ, vol. 2, p. 148. This puzzling piece of information, which has been ensconced in the Chopin literature for more than a hundred years, carries the imprimatur of Ferdynand Hoesick. If Koźmian and Chopin visited Brighton on their way back to Dover, it would have represented a very wide detour, complicating Chopin's return journey. Dover was the only port of exit to France at that time. Neither Newhaven nor Folkestone (both closer to Brighton) had yet opened its cross-channel ferry services, although Chopin was able to use the latter port when he returned to London in 1848.

BUFFETS AND REWARDS,
1833–1838

*He is indefatigable . . . in his search for ear-splitting discords, forced
transitions, harsh modulations, ugly distortions of melody and
rhythm . . .*

—Ludwig Rellstab[1]

*The marvellous charm, the poetry and originality, the perfect free-
dom and absolute lucidity of Chopin's playing at that time cannot
be described. It was perfection in every sense.*

—Charles Hallé[2]

I

Despite the turbulence in Chopin's private life, it remains the case that by
the time that he and Maria Wodzińska parted company his position in the
world of music had been transformed. A cornucopia of his music had been
published, revealing a composer increasingly sure of himself, someone who
had carved out a new path and had made it uniquely his own. He had
moreover developed solid connections with three of Europe's leading
publishers—Schlesinger in Paris, Breitkopf and Härtel in Leipzig, and
Wessel in London. And since in the absence of proper copyright laws he

1. *Iris im Gebiete der Tonkunst*, July 5, 1833.
2. HLL, pp. 31–32.

was able to sell his compositions to all three publishers simultaneously, and generally did so, his income from composing can properly be described as handsome.

Yet it is worth recalling that Chopin was hardly known to the wider world as a composer before 1833. Until then the only composition to have enjoyed broad circulation was the "Là ci darem" Variations, op. 2. It is true that the Rondo in C minor, op. 1, and the Rondo à la Mazur, op. 5, had been published earlier in Warsaw, but these teenage pieces had not yet crossed Poland's frontiers. At his debut concert in Paris, on February 26, 1832, Chopin was known simply as "a pianist from Warsaw." Not until the publication of the Four Mazurkas, op. 6, and the Five Mazurkas, op. 7, in December 1832, which Chopin had brought to Paris with him, were the floodgates opened with a stream of compositions following in swift succession. Among them were the Three Nocturnes, op. 9; the Three Nocturnes, op. 15; and the Concerto in E minor, op. 11, all of which had been published by June 1833. In the two or three years following, Chopin found himself in the enviable position of having his publishers vie with one another for such pieces as the Concerto in F minor, op. 21; the Scherzos in B minor and B-flat minor, opp. 20 and 31; the two volumes of Studies, opp. 10 and 25; the Two Nocturnes, op. 27; the Two Polonaises, op. 26; and the Ballade in G minor, op. 23.

It was a considerable body of work, which elevated Chopin's reputation. That fact was acknowledged by the musicologist F.-J. Fétis, who in 1836 decided to include an entry on Chopin in his ongoing *Biographical Dictionary of Musicians*, and sent the twenty-six-year-old composer a questionnaire requesting some firsthand information about his life and work. Chopin returned the form on March 27, 1836. Next to "Date of Birth" he wrote, "1 March, 1810," offering further proof that the date on his baptismal certificate in the Church of St. Roch, Brochów, reflected an aberration on the part of the officiating cleric.

II

Pride of place among the works completed at this time must be given to Chopin's Twenty-four Studies, opp. 10 and 25, which occupy a unique place in the literature. They are the first such pieces to have made the hazardous journey from the practice studio to the concert hall, where they have always remained secure. Countless pieces called "studies" by Czerny, Clementi, Cramer, Döhler, Hummel, Moscheles, and others failed to find a place in the pantheon because they lacked the superior musical substance required to put them there. By contrast, it is the sheer beauty and polish of Chopin's studies, each one in reality a miniature tone poem, that beguiles the ear, their obvious technical demands notwithstanding. It is not uncommon to find them described as "comprehensive," embracing the entire range of piano technique. That is not entirely true, for we search in vain for tremolandos, trills, far-flung leaps, rapid single-note repetitions, and alternating hands (the "vamping effect"), which typify other studies with specific pedagogical goals in mind. And by disdaining to inscribe them with an overarching title (such as we find in Czerny's "School of Velocity" or Clementi's "Gradus ad Parnassum"), Chopin avoids grounding his work in the field of keyboard gymnastics, the graveyard of so many similar efforts in the genre, leaving pedagogy with no foothold.

TWELVE STUDIES, op. 10	TWELVE STUDIES, op. 25
Dedicated to Franz Liszt	Dedicated to Countess Marie d'Agoult
(June 1833)	(October 1837)
1. C major	1. A-flat major ("Aeolian Harp")
2. A minor	2. F minor
3. E major	3. F major
4. C-sharp minor	4. A minor
5. G-flat major ("Black Keys")	5. E minor
6. E-flat minor	6. G-sharp minor ("Thirds")
7. C major	7. C-sharp minor
8. F major	8. D-flat major ("Sixths")
9. F minor	9. G-flat major ("Butterfly")
10. A-flat major	10. B minor ("Octaves")
11. E-flat major ("Arpeggio")	11. A minor ("Winter Wind")
12. C minor ("Revolutionary")	12. C minor ("Ocean")

The Twenty-four Studies may be played as complete cycles (rare in Chopin's time, but not in ours) or they may be presented in smaller groups resting on nothing more than the whim of the player. It is even possible to create families of studies drawn from both books, so homogeneous are these pieces in their totality. There is some evidence, based on the key scheme pursued by the first six studies from op. 10, that Chopin may have had a predetermined sequence of paired keys in mind for that set (C major / A minor; E major / C-sharp minor; G-flat major / E-flat minor), with each alternating study appearing in the relative minor key of the one that preceded it—a pattern that was broken with the abrupt arrival of the seventh study, in C major, a latecomer to the scene. These twelve pieces were in any case composed over a scattered period of three years (1829–32), and were only assembled for publication during the first half of 1833. Nor were they composed in the order in which they were published. While the first two Studies were indeed written first, in November 1829, the most famous one of the set (no. 3 in E major) was probably the last to be composed, in August 1832. And Chopin is known to have shuffled the others around before determining their official running order.

This first book of Studies was published in Paris by Schlesinger on June 8, 1833, with a dedication to Franz Liszt. Within two weeks they were already in Liszt's repertoire. On June 20 we find Chopin writing some famous lines in a letter to Ferdinand Hiller: "I am writing without knowing what my pen is scribbling because at this moment Liszt is playing my studies and putting honest thoughts out of my head. I should like to steal from him the way to play my own studies."[3] Liszt took them on tour with him, playing individual numbers in various European cities, and when he returned to Paris after a prolonged absence, he featured two of them (nos. 11 and 12) in a recital he gave in the Érard salon on February 4, 1837. Just over two months later (April 9) he was back at the same venue playing from manuscript the still-unpublished Studies nos. 1 and 2, from op. 25. It seems unlikely that Chopin was present at either concert, because he was unwell for much of the early part of 1837. "Chopin continues to cough with infinite grace" was Countess Marie d'Agoult's delicate way of putting it.[4]

The dedication of the second book of Studies to Marie d'Agoult, Liszt's mistress, may be regarded as unfortunate in light of the hostility that later developed between her and George Sand (and by extension to Chopin, who was soon to become Sand's lover). When Liszt wrote to Sand from Italy asking her to pass along his thanks to Chopin for the recent dedication of these pieces to d'Agoult, one wonders what mingled thoughts passed

3. CFC, vol. 2, p. 93; KFC, vol. 1, p. 227.
4. CFC, vol. 2, p. 216.

through his mind. For we now know that it had been Chopin's intention to dedicate the second set of studies to Liszt as well as the first, but he had a change of heart and placed Marie d'Agoult's name on the title page instead.[5]

It is hardly possible to do more than touch on a few of the highlights of these pieces here. Some of them have already drawn comment in an earlier chapter ("Chopin and the Keyboard"), where the hand-stretching and hand-contracting properties of no. 1 in C major and no. 2 in A minor were remarked. The Study no. 3, in E major, commands attention because it has made its way around the world. Can any other "exercise" make a similar claim? According to Adolf Gutmann, Chopin once admitted that he had never written a melody to compare with this one. Ever suspicious

---

5. The story emerges from a run of letters in the Breitkopf archives held in the Hochschulbibliothek in Darmstadt, published for the first time in 1997. (SDNL, pp. 167–80.) When Breitkopf invited Liszt to join the editorial team for the firm's Collected Edition of Chopin's works (1878–80), they assigned him the Preludes. Liszt told Breitkopf that his preference was to edit the Studies "because the first volume was dedicated to me," to which he added the revealing comment, "and the second one, too, for that matter (at that time)." (LLB, vol. 2, p. 258.) Breitkopf was placed in the uncomfortable position of having to tell Liszt that the Studies had already been assigned to Ernst Rudorff, the head of the piano faculty at the Berlin Hochschule für Musik, and Liszt's nemesis. Liszt graciously yielded and agreed to fall back on the Preludes. But what had prompted Chopin's change of mind regarding the dedication of the op. 25 Studies? We conjecture that it was connected to Liszt's indiscreet tryst with Marie Pleyel two or three years earlier, while she was still the wife of Chopin's friend and colleague Camille Pleyel, and to Liszt's unauthorized use of Chopin's rooms for this purpose while Chopin was out of town. Niecks found the incident sufficiently intriguing to interview one of Chopin's pupils, Mme Vera Rubio, about it. What he discovered produced the memorable line, "The circumstances are of too delicate a nature to be set forth in detail." He felt constrained to add some detail anyway. "The discovery of traces of the use to which his rooms had been put justly enraged Chopin." (NFC, vol. 2, p. 171.) Chivalry prevented Niecks from identifying Marie Pleyel as the woman in question. But he had no need to do so, because it was tacitly confirmed by Liszt himself. When, in 1839, Liszt encountered La Pleyel in Vienna, and told Marie d'Agoult about this chance meeting, he added, "She asked me if I remembered Chopin's room . . . Of course, Madame, how to forget?" (ACLA, vol. 2, p. 379.) Chopin was not one to forget either. He felt compromised and his friendship with Liszt never regained the camaraderie of former times. Had Liszt been content to take into Chopin's apartment any one of the numerous lady admirers fluttering around him at that time, it is unlikely that anything much would have been made of the matter. What colored everything in Chopin's eyes, however, was that Marie was the wife of his friend and piano manufacturer. Pleyel had been cuckolded under Chopin's roof not by any old piano strummer eager to enjoy the favors of his beautiful wife, but by Franz Liszt, who was moreover the leading promoter of the Érard piano, Pleyel's chief business rival. It was as if the competition between the two contending houses had been transferred from the concert hall to the boudoir. We may never know what took place in that room on the rue de la Chaussée d'Antin, of course. In such matters perception generally trumps reality. Chopin himself provided a finely nuanced description of the abrupt change in his relationship with Liszt when he observed, "We are friends; we were comrades," a remark transmitted to Niecks by Chopin's pupil Wilhelm von Lenz. NFC, vol. 2, p. 171.

of its wide popularity, the purists always placed distance between themselves and this piece, dismissing it as hackneyed. Yet even the tasteless
lyric ("Tristesse") that Hollywood attached to the melody failed to destroy
it, and may even have prompted thousands of listeners to return to the
original and partake of the magic at its source.

Chopin originally marked the theme "Vivace" (lively), as if he had at
first failed to identify its true character. It is impossible for us today to
imagine the tempo as anything other than "Lento" (slow), one of the more
welcome afterthoughts in the history of piano music. Chopin indicated a
metronome mark for this opening theme of ♪ = 100, which is fast, but
suggests that the excess of sentiment with which the melody is nowadays
infused is something that he anticipated and wished to avoid. Still, this
somewhat swifter tempo is what the middle section requires. The diminished seventh chord had already become a timeworn component of romantic harmony, but no one before Chopin had employed it in the service
of such sonic marvels as we find at the climax of this study.

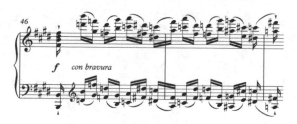

We mentioned Chopin's metronome marks. He supplied them for every
one of these studies. They are important and with one or two controversial exceptions they should be observed. Maelzel had invented the machine
that bears his name in 1816. After Beethoven was persuaded in 1817 to
issue metronome marks for his first seven symphonies, the practice was
taken up by leading musicians across Europe. Chopin probably acquired

one of these early models in Warsaw, for we find metronome marks on a number of his compositions written before he left Poland. During his Paris years he used it consistently until 1836, when he abandoned it after completing the Twelve Studies, op. 25, and the Two Nocturnes, op. 27. Any metronome marks that appear after that are not by him but have been provided by his editors. That having been said, Chopin always had a metronome standing on his piano and he was not above switching it on if his students were not keeping strict time. He probably stopped indicating its use in his compositions in order to allow some flexibility on the part of his interpreters. By then it was not difficult to deduce what tempi he had in mind when he used such terms as Lento, Andante, Allegro, and Presto, because he had already established firm links between these expressions and the metronome marks in his earlier works.

One of the "controversial exceptions" occurs in the Study in C-sharp minor, no. 4. The tempo mark of ♩=88 is generally considered too fast, even for a Presto, and it has had an unfortunate effect on several generations of Young Turks who have been provoked into playing it yet faster, to the detriment of the music. Like other fast-moving studies in the collection, the tempo of this one would have been easier to manage on Chopin's Pleyel, with its lighter action, than on the heavier keyboards of a Steinway or a Bechstein confronting the player today. Chopin emphasized the link between the third and fourth studies, by writing at the end of the manuscript of no. 3 the words *"attacca il presto con fuoco"*—meaning no. 4.[6]

6. In light of the controversy surrounding some of these metronome marks, it is worth asking the question: Was Chopin's metronome accurate? It was examined by Arthur Hedley, who confirmed in a letter to me, dated May 17, 1965, "In August 1936 (in Warsaw) I saw and checked Chopin's metronome; it was quite accurate." (AWC, box 4, f.8.) The instrument perished during the destruction of Warsaw in World War II. One possible explanation for the fast tempi of some of these studies is that they were optimal speeds recommended for practice purposes, not necessarily to be adopted for a finished performance in the concert hall.

The E-flat minor Study (no. 6) would not be out of place among the Nocturnes. It is one long lamentation that plumbs the depths. More than one commentator has pointed to its chromatic harmonies, which foreshadow Wagner's *Tristan*. This grief-laden music has a sibling in the second book, which could likewise be mistaken for a nocturne: namely, the great Study in C-sharp minor, op. 25, no. 7, whose tragic grandeur conveys a sorrow that runs too deep for tears. It would cause no surprise if we were to learn that these two pieces had been composed simultaneously, even though they ended up in different books. Chopin places each of these two studies between ones exhibiting bright virtuosity, which has the effect of casting yet deeper shadows across their somber surface.

Hans von Bülow offered the highest accolade to the Study in A-flat major, no. 10, when he wrote, "He who can play this Study in a really finished manner may congratulate himself on having climbed to the highest point of the pianist's Parnassus."[7] The piece is undoubtedly the most deceptive in the collection. From the listener's point of view everything sounds straightforward enough. We hear an engaging melody for the right hand, with an arpeggiated accompaniment for the left. From the player's point of view, however, nothing is straightforward. Chopin has placed him inside a veritable hornets' nest of cross-rhythms and syncopations. The melody first emerges from a background of triplets, then of duplets. Accents are changed without warning, shifting the balance of the phrase sideways, so to speak, together with the place of each note within it. Material played legatissimo is then repeated staccato. Having unfolded all this in A-flat major, Chopin, seeming to trifle with the player, repeats much of it in A major, which involves an entirely different set of hand positions on the keyboard. And what are we to make of those random notes in the left hand (the E-flats) that must be held down, the demands on the other fingers notwithstanding? To borrow a phrase from Dr. Samuel Johnson (who was admittedly holding forth on a somewhat different topic), the wonder is not that it is done well, but that it is done at all.

---

7. From Bülow's commentary to his edition of the studies, BCS.

The "broken chords" Study (no. 11) breaks new ground with regard to the manner in which widespread chords may be unrolled across the keyboard. One may search the repertoire in vain for any previous study quite like this one. It demands difficult extensions of an eleventh and even an occasional thirteenth as these upward-rolling chords strive to maintain the melody articulated by the top notes.

This study reminds us that to Chopin we owe a profound discovery about the pianist's hand. In spanning large distances across the keyboard, the central pivot finger of the hand is not always the third, as Chopin generally advocated, but the index finger. In these arpeggiated chords it is the index finger that temporarily becomes the hand's "center of gravity." And by concentrating on where that finger is to be placed, the other notes are made immeasurably easier to play.

The first book of Studies is brought to a dramatic conclusion by the "Revolutionary" Study, no. 12 in C minor, which was composed against the turbulent political background of the Warsaw Uprising and its collapse, discussed earlier. Whether or not it was Chopin's direct response to the fall of Warsaw in September 1831, that legend is now so deeply woven into the fabric of the piece that it cannot be separated from it. No such association existed in the minds of its first hearers, however, deprived as they were of a nickname that was not attached to the Study until after Chopin's death. It is hard to improve on Kullak's description of the piece as "a bravura study of the highest order for the left hand"—an observation whose deeper point will be lost if it fails to remind us that everywhere else in the collection the emphasis is on the right, a peculiarity of the op. 10 Studies that generally goes unremarked.

Karasowski evokes the image of Zeus hurling thunderbolts at mankind.[8] It is a telling idea, but for younger pianists with nothing more than thunderbolts to hurl it is a dangerous one, for in callow hands the work itself is turned into the battlefield, instead of depicting one. Even the normally verbose Cortot was given pause before writing about this "exalted outcry of revolt," and seemed to balk at the task of setting down his usual mundane preparatory exercises and fingerings for a composition in which "the emotions of a whole race of people are alive and throbbing."[9] After the tumult of the middle section (featuring enharmonic changes considered so bold by Hans von Bülow that he simplified the notation in his edition of the work), Chopin brings back the opening impassioned theme (bar 50), whose muffled eruptions finally come to rest in C major. The closing measures (bars 77ff) reveal a curious resemblance to the coda of

8. KCLB, p. 201.
9. From the Commentary of Cortot's edition of the Studies, vol. 1, p. 78.

the first movement of Beethoven's Sonata in C minor, op. 111 (bars 134ff),
a work that is cast in the same key and expresses a similar mood of
defiance. We do not know if Chopin got to know this sonata during his
extended stay in Vienna, but we may be sure that he would not have been
flattered by the comparison.

III

Although the second book of Twelve Studies, op. 25, was not published
until October 1837, they must be considered as a logical continuation of the
earlier set. A few of them had even been written before the first book was
released, but were held back for inclusion in the second. These early com-
ers were probably among the ones numbered 4 through 10, although the
order in which they were composed is far from clear. When Chopin played
the first of them for Robert Schumann in Leipzig, in September 1836,
the piece was still in manuscript. Schumann, we recall, had invited his
readers to imagine "an Aeolian harp" whose harmonies "billowed" in the
wind, providing posterity with an image that continues to define this music.

His recollection that Chopin brought out a tenor voice "in the midst of
the harmony" is a fine testament to his memory of what the manuscript
clearly shows; but it has encouraged many a modern editor to go off in
search of additional melodies lurking in the undergrowth of these Aeolian
harmonies, melodies that Chopin may not have suspected were there, and
stem the notes accordingly. For the rest, it is a sound editorial principle
not to make visible what is already audible.

Hugo Leichtentritt has drawn attention to the ingenious construction
of the third Study, in F major. He points out that the middle section is in
the unusual key of B major and asks: Why B major for a piece in F? Since

the octave F–F″ is divided at the halfway point by the augmented fourth F–B, any sequence of modulations that leads from F to B will, if repeated from that point, lead back again from B to F. So Chopin adopts the plan F–B–F, in which the last part of the study is an exact harmonic reflection of the first.[10]

Three of the studies that follow are known by didactic titles ("Thirds," "Sixths," and "Octaves") behind which lies music of profound expressiveness. They offer textbook examples of Chopin's gift for turning treadmill figures into art of a high order. When we hear the study in thirds (no. 6, in G-sharp minor), it is the gossamer lightness of the piece that lingers. James Huneker put the matter succinctly when he wrote that this study is first music, and only then does it become a technical problem, an interesting reversal of concepts that could apply to the entire set. True, Chopin shows a cavalier disregard for the trifling matter of the "Siamese Twins"— those conjoined third and fourth fingers that he mentions in his Piano Method. But he does make a secret concession to the pianist by deploying the piece in G-sharp minor. It would become yet more difficult in any other key. An aphorism of Saint-Saëns has a bearing on such matters: "In art, a difficulty overcome is a thing of beauty."

The Study no. 8, in D-flat major, the "Sixths," remains one of the most forbidding in the set. Bülow thought it "indispensable" for the development of an advanced technique, while admitting that this term had lost its currency through overuse. But he added helpfully, "As a remedy for stiff fingers before performing in public, playing it through six times is recommended even to the most expert pianist."[11]

10. LACK, vol. 2, pp. 165–67.
11. BCS, p. 34.

Bülow's advice may not be as tyrannical as it sounds. The Study is only thirty-six measures in length, is the shortest in the book, and lasts just over one minute in performance. Still, to use this musical jewel as a "warm-up" exercise for other things is perhaps an extravagance too far.[12] As for the powerful "Octaves" Study in B minor (no. 10), it offers an object lesson in the contrasting ways in which octaves may express themselves. In the thunderous first part we have double octaves (rare in Chopin) played with full force from the shoulders, while the quiet middle section presents single octaves for the right hand as weavers of romantic melody, before the thunder returns. Niecks waxed biblical over this piece when he described it as "a real pandemonium; for a while holier sounds intervene, but finally hell prevails."[13]

Chopin originally began the "Winter Wind" Study (no. 11) with a spectacular plunge into the abyss. The slow introduction was added

---

12. When one of Bülow's students, Emma Grosskurth, joined Liszt's masterclass in Weimar, she amused Liszt and the other students by playing this study backward, note for note. Carl Lachmund, from whom this anecdote comes and who was in the class at the time, described the effect as "a modern pleasantry." We have always assumed that Fräulein Grosskurth picked up this droll idea from Bülow himself. LL, p. 309.

13. NFC, vol. 2, p. 254.

later, so we are told, at the suggestion of Dr. Aleksander Hoffman, the physician who lodged with Chopin during the years 1833–34 in his apartment on the rue de la Chaussée d'Antin, where he heard the composer play the piano every day. This story comes to us from Hoffman's young widow, Emilia Borzęcka. Hoffman, who played the piano well (he had been a student at the Warsaw Conservatory before taking his medical degree), was steeped in the same cultural ambience that had nurtured Chopin himself. Emilia tells us, "Chopin, who did not like re-working something once it had been written down, was resolved to leave this Study as it was, if only for the reason that no better opening came to his mind." But the idea of a "lead-in" evidently lingered. "It preyed so long on his mind," Emilia reported, "that one night he had the idea of a four-bar melancholic preface to the Study—and on rising from his bed he immediately added it. The next day he played it to my husband, who wholeheartedly approved of it. And that is how the first four bars of the A minor Study, the penultimate in the set, came into being."[14] They have the desired effect of throwing the following Allegro con brio into startling relief.

14. Emilia Borzęcka's recollections took the form of an extended interview that she gave Ferdynand Hoesick in 1900, which he incorporated in his article "Z rozmów o Chopinie" (Conversations About Chopin) in *Kraj* 32, pp. 437–39, and no. 33, pp. 449–51. See also HFCZ, vol. 2, pp. 56–57.

Cast in the bleak key of A minor, the "Winter Wind" Study ranks among the most physically demanding of the collection. It has given rise to a small but legitimate criticism about the way in which the second book of Studies has been put together. What could possibly follow such a tempest? This turbulent piece closes with an upward-rushing scale covering four octaves, marked *fff*. It is a veritable whiplash that shuts down the storm. The fact is, the "Winter Wind" overshadows the final Study, no. 12 in C minor, despite the obvious nobility of the latter work. Commonly referred to as the "Ocean," the closing Study derives its name from the tidal waves of sound that arise from the continuous flow of arpeggios sweeping up and down the keyboard.

In lesser hands, these configurations would remain at the mundane level of those "treadmill figures" we mentioned earlier, old-fashioned endurance exercises that lurk within the covers of many a faded pedagogical publication of bygone years. But Chopin redeems them, thanks to the rich series of harmonic progressions through which he propels them. And with a further touch of magic he draws from these same majestic columns of sound a theme that has more than a passing resemblance to plainchant, and is sometimes mistakenly referred to as such.

The study comes to a close with an extended *tierce de Picardie*, marked *fff*. Sir Donald Tovey extolled the piece as "the greatest Étude of the greatest of Étude-writers,"[15] and many would agree with him. But a dissent would not be out of place. Regal as the waves of the "Ocean" Study are, they cannot dispel the memory of its impassioned predecessor, to say nothing of one

---

15. TCM, p. 163.

or two of the earlier numbers, which never cease to jostle for attention, once we allow them to vie for the title of "the greatest."

With the publication of his Twenty-four Studies, Chopin had attained a position of unassailable superiority in the realm of piano music, a position that he has on rare occasions been asked to share, but from which he has never been dislodged. These matchless compositions are best understood as a gateway to Chopin's own music. There are few technical hurdles in his entire output that are not foreshadowed here, and the solutions come tumbling from the page. The Studies also remind us that to Chopin belongs the honor of setting clear boundary lines between the piano and the orchestra. While other composers frequently cross them, Chopin never does. Beethoven, Schumann, Mendelssohn, and Brahms all wrote music that, with minor adjustments, fits either medium. But Chopin's music resists such efforts. Born and bred on the keyboard, the piano remains its homeland. When perforce it is transferred to the orchestra, the results generally range from the ungainly to the absurd.

IV

While Chopin's music was well received in most parts of Europe, it was subject to regular abuse at the hands of the Berlin-based critic Ludwig Rellstab, the editor and owner of the journal *Iris im Gebiete der Tonkunst* (Iris in the Realm of Music). Rellstab, who had in earlier years been an officer in the Prussian army, was an amateur pianist and poet who found a niche for himself in the burgeoning profession of music criticism. His trenchant opinions were widely feared, and in 1827 they earned him a stretch in Spandau prison for defaming the reputation of Henriette Sontag. He was jailed for a second time in 1836 for maligning Spontini, the director of the Berlin Opera and a personal favorite of King Friedrich Wilhelm III. When a copy of the first book of Studies, op. 10, reached Rellstab's desk, he published a review that has entered the annals of musical invective: "Those who have deformed fingers may put them right by practicing these studies; but those who have not, should not play them, at least not without having Messrs. von Gräfe or Dieffenbach [two well-known orthopedic surgeons] standing by."[16] The time would come when

16. *Iris*, January 31, 1834.

Rellstab would regret writing these words. But this was a bell that could not be unrung. His dislike of Chopin's music was in any case already well established. He had declared war on the composer months earlier with his vitriolic condemnation of the Five Mazurkas, op. 7, for their "ear-splitting discords" and "their harsh modulations."[17] But worse was to follow. Everyone acknowledged that John Field was the inventor of the nocturne, so when Chopin published his first set of Nocturnes, op. 9, the opportunity to compare him unfavorably with Field was too tempting for Rellstab to resist.

> Where Field smiles, Chopin makes a snickering grimace; where Field sighs, Chopin groans; Field shrugs his shoulders, Chopin arches his back like a cat; where Field adds seasoning to his food, Chopin throws in a handful of Cayenne pepper . . . If one holds Field's charming romances before a distorting mirror, so that every finer expression becomes exaggerated, one gets Chopin's work.[18]

This abuse from Rellstab went on for years, and Chopin's friends wondered how he could possibly remain aloof. So, for that matter, did Rellstab. In an act of journalistic infamy he published a spurious letter containing threats purporting to come from Chopin, but which is now considered to have been written by Rellstab himself, in order to provoke his quarry into a reply.

> You are really a very bad man, and not worthy that God's earth either knows or bears you. The King of Prussia should have imprisoned you in a fortress; in that case he would have removed from the world a rebel, a disturber of the peace, and an infamous enemy of humanity, who probably will yet be choked in his own blood. I have noticed a great number of enemies, not only in Berlin, but in all the towns which I visited last year on my artistic tour, especially very many here in Leipzig, where I inform you of this, in order that you may in future change your disposition, and not act so uncharitably towards others. Another bad, bad trick and you are done for! Do

---

17. *Iris*, July 5, 1833.
18. Ibid., August 2, 1833.

you understand me, you little man, you loveless and partial dog of a critic, you musical snarler, you Berlin wit-cracker, etc.

Your most obedient servant,

CHOPIN[19]

In a move calculated to throw his readers off the scent, Rellstab wrote at the foot of the text: "Whether Mr. Chopin has written this letter himself, I do not know, and will not assert it, but print the document that he may recognize or repudiate it." Chopin did neither. A moment's reflection is enough to prove that it could not have issued from his pen. Chopin never visited Leipzig in 1833–34, the letter's place of origin, and he did not undertake an "artistic tour" of Germany in 1833. The missive was moreover written in German, a language in which Chopin was not fluent; and the menacing tone of its content is unlike anything else that he wrote. As each new work of Chopin appeared, Rellstab took a malignant delight in tearing it to shreds. At last he began to see that he was making himself look foolish, because practically every other leading critic in Europe was falling in line behind Robert Schumann's imperative "Hats off, gentlemen, a genius!" Rellstab may have been reluctant to remove his hat, but remove it he did. By 1839 he had started to reverse himself and was saying of the Nocturne, op. 9, no. 2 (which he had earlier mocked), "It is gracefully ornamented and replete with subtle harmonic effects . . . and may rightly add to the fame of the celebrated composer." He confessed that either the times had changed or he had changed; whatever the reason, he blustered, Chopin's music now sounded quite beautiful to him. Rellstab finally fell on his sword when he visited Paris in 1843. By now Chopin enjoyed a European celebrity and Rellstab was uncertain how he might be received. He thought it expedient to bring with him a diplomatically worded letter of introduction from Liszt, which he presented in person to Chopin in an attempt to repair the relationship.[20] Neither Chopin nor Rellstab left an

---

19. Ibid., January 31, 1834. When Chopin's family in Warsaw became aware of this unpleasant situation, Mikołaj Chopin advised his son, "Just keep getting under the skin of this progeny of Zoilus, and you will prove to them that it is impossible to set limits to art." (CFC, vol. 2, p. 110.) This arcane reference to "Zoilus and his progeny" would not have displeased Chopin. Zoilus, the Greek grammarian and nit-picking scourge of Homer, was said to have been crucified for his criticisms of the king.

20. CFC, vol. 3, pp. 128–29. Liszt's letter is a masterpiece of diplomacy. "There is no need for a go-between where you and Rellstab are concerned," it began. And it ended with the saccha-

account of the meeting. But we may fall back on some words of Confucius to summarize their difference: "When a wise man points to the stars, only a fool looks at his finger."

V

Among Chopin's growing circle of admirers few were more important than Charles Hallé, who left some valuable recollections of the composer. Hallé had arrived in Paris in the autumn of 1836 from Germany, intent on taking piano lessons from Kalkbrenner. He auditioned for the great technician, but was disappointed when Kalkbrenner made some disparaging remarks about his playing and recommended that he take instruction from one of his pupils instead. A few days after this setback he received a dinner invitation from the banker Louis-Jules Mallet, and found himself sitting next to Chopin.

Autumn 1836

The same evening I heard him play, and was fascinated beyond expression. It seemed to me as if I had got into another world, and all thought of Kalkbrenner was driven out of my mind. I sat entranced, filled with wonderment, and if the room had suddenly been peopled with fairies, I should not have been astonished. The marvellous charm, the poetry and originality, the perfect freedom and absolute lucidity of Chopin's playing at that time cannot be described. It was perfection in every sense. He seemed to be pleased with the evident impression he had produced, for I could only stammer a few broken words of admiration, and he played again and again, each time revealing new beauties, until I could have dropped on my knees to worship him.[21]

Thereafter the two men saw much of one another and became friends. Hallé lived in Paris until the Revolution of 1848 drove him to England,

---

rine sentence "My affection and respect for you will remain unchanged and, as your friend, I am always at your service." Liszt and Chopin had not met for several years. Rellstab did not know that whatever intimacy had existed between the two composers in earlier days had long since evaporated, a situation that rather reduced the letter's value.
21. HLL, pp. 31–32.

and during the twelve years that intervened he heard Chopin play his newest works many times. In his memoirs (1896) he made the interesting point that although Chopin's compositions had in the meantime become the property of every schoolgirl, "nobody has ever been able to reproduce them as they sounded beneath his magical fingers." In listening to him, Hallé wrote, one lost all power of analysis and gave oneself up, as it were, to the improvisation of a poem, under whose charm one remained as long as it lasted. The rhythmic freedom of Chopin's playing Hallé found remarkable. He never forgot the occasion when Chopin was playing a group of his mazurkas, which, though written in 3/4 time, sounded under Chopin's hands as if they were in 4/4. When Hallé drew attention to the contradiction, Chopin denied it strenuously. So Hallé made him play one of them again, while audibly counting four beats to a bar. Chopin laughed, and pointed out that a short delay on the first beat of the bar was part of the national character of the dance. "The more remarkable fact," said Hallé, "was that you received the impression of three-four rhythm whilst listening to common time."[22] Hallé was right to conclude that Chopin must have been very well disposed toward him to tolerate such a discussion. When Meyerbeer a few years later made a similar observation about the way Chopin played his own mazurkas, it led to a "scene" between them, as we shall discover.

VI

Polish expatriates were not the only refugees flooding into France. Italy had also begun its own struggle for national independence, from Austria, forcing large numbers of exiles to seek sanctuary in the French capital. By the mid-1830s, Paris was teeming with the disaffected, the dispossessed, and the disenfranchised from both countries. The Italians, unlike the Poles, had no government in exile in Paris, but they rallied around those patrician families who were willing to open their salons and put on various charitable events to ease their burdens. One of the most prominent was the colorful Princess Cristina Belgiojoso-Trivulzio. Often called the "revolutionary princess," she was a friend of both Garibaldi and Mazzini, and supported them in their struggle for a unified Italy. Charged with high

---

22. Ibid., p. 34.

treason by a criminal tribunal in Milan, Cristina fled to Paris, bought a palatial home on the rue d'Anjou, and surrounded herself with a brilliant circle of composers and writers, which included Liszt, Bellini, Meyerbeer, Dumas, Musset, and Heine. She also got to know Chopin, who became an occasional visitor. Cristina was a keen lover of opera. Bellini had given her piano lessons and she had earlier been a singing pupil of Pasta's. She was often observed in her box at the Italian opera, weeping during the arias of Donizetti and Bellini, emotional reminders of a homeland to which she could not return.

On March 31, 1837, La Belgiojoso opened her Parisian home for a lavish three-day charity bazaar in an attempt to raise money for the rising tide of Italian refugees. A number of artists took part, but the event to which everyone looked forward was the "ivory duel" between Liszt and Sigismond Thalberg. The two pianists had recently appeared in separate venues—Thalberg in the Paris Conservatoire and Liszt at the Paris Opera—arousing their respective followers to such a pitch of enthusiasm that the question now on everyone's lips was "Who is the greatest pianist?" By attempting to find out, La Belgiojoso scored the social coup of the season. On March 26 the *Gazette musicale* carried the following advertisement: "The greatest interest . . . will be without question the simultaneous appearance of two talents whose rivalry at this time agitates the musical world, and is like the indecisive balance between Rome and Carthage. Messrs. Listz [*sic*] and Thalberg will take turns at the piano."

So great was the demand to see the two rivals "take turns" that the princess was able to charge 40 francs a ticket. The profligate entertainment included contributions from the instrumentalists Lambert Massart, Chrétien Urhan, Pierret, and Matthieux; and from the opera singers Taccani and Puget. But these worthies might as well have stayed at home. All eyes were on "Rome" and "Carthage." Thalberg appeared first and played his old warhorse, the *Moses* Fantasy. Liszt then went to the keyboard and played his *Niobe* Fantasy. The critic Jules Janin was there and preserved an account of the evening in the *Journal des débats*:

> It was an admirable joust. The most profound silence fell over that noble arena. And finally Liszt and Thalberg were both proclaimed victors by the glittering and intelligent assembly. It is clear that such a contest could take place only in an Areopagus. Thus two victors

and no vanquished: it is fitting to say with the poet ET AD HUC SUB JUDICE LIS EST.[23]

Two victors and no vanquished. La Belgiojoso was not satisfied with this verdict. When asked to give her own opinion, she came out with a diplomatic aphorism that has found a permanent niche in the literature: "Thalberg is the first pianist in the world—but Liszt is unique."[24] Liszt, in brief, was incomparable.

Chopin did not turn up to witness the ivory duel, a spectacle he would doubtless have found demeaning; but he forms an essential element in what followed. Some weeks prior to her charity bazaar, La Belgiojoso commissioned a group of composer-pianists to write a variation each on the stirring march "Sound the Trumpet for Liberty" from Bellini's *I puritani*—a patriotic call to arms—deliberately crafted to give the Austrian authorities occupying her part of Italy a severe case of heartburn.

She sent the theme to six pianists—Liszt, Thalberg, Pixis, Herz, Czerny (who was just then visiting Paris), and Chopin—and called the work *Hexaméron* (=six). The idea was to have the work published and make yet more money through the sale of its copies. Liszt was charged with holding the team together and took on the task of composing the Introduction, the Interludes, and a virtuosic Finale. La Belgiojoso clearly hoped to have all six pianists physically present in her salon, each one playing his own variation. The title page bears the proud inscription:

---

23. Issue of April 3. The "poet" in question is Horace: "Critics contend and the question is still undetermined." This attempt on the part of Jules Janin to unburden himself of an excess of classical learning was doubtless designed to flatter La Belgiojoso. Given her democratic political leanings, she would not have been displeased to see her luxurious home described as an "Areopagus," an arena in ancient Greece where a council of elders used to meet in order to pass judgment on conflicting issues.
24. LLF, p. 45.

HEXAMÉRON
Grandes
Variations de Bravoure
pour piano
sur la
Marche des Puritains de Bellini
composées
pour le concert de Mme la Princesse Belgiojoso
au Bénéfice des Pauvres

Perhaps it was this inscription, together with an earlier announcement in the March 21, 1837, issue of the *Journal des débats* and a confusing report in the *Neue Zeitschrift für Musik*, that led later writers to assume all six composers had turned up. Alas, no such gathering took place, and neither did the performance of *Hexaméron*, because it was not finished in time. Chopin failed to meet the deadline, and without his contribution Liszt could not complete his Interludes. The princess expressed her ongoing frustration in a letter to Liszt written on June 4, 1837, more than two months after her charity event had taken place: "No news from M. Chopin, and since I am proud enough to fear making a nuisance of myself, I do not dare ask him. You do not run the same risk with him as I, which prompts me to ask if you would find out what is happening to his Adagio, which is not moving quickly at all. It will be one more kindness on your part, for which I shall be as grateful as for the others."[25] Her whimsical allusion to an Adagio "which is not moving quickly at all" is the first reference we have to Chopin's "Largo," which turned out to be the jewel of the entire composition.

---

25. OAAL, pp. 135–36.

Unlike some of the other variations, which are brash and assertive, Chopin's piece treats "liberty" as a dreamlike vision, a yearning for some distant homeland. This was a feeling that he alone among the other composers had actually experienced, for he was the only one among them to know what it meant to live in exile. Chopin casts his variation in E major—the faraway, twilight key of the flattened submediant. The tonal contrast is profound, for all the other variations are rooted in the key of Bellini's theme, A-flat major. One wonders by what happy chance this contrast came about. It could hardly have come from Liszt, whose job it was to provide some necessary continuity among the variations, but we have no way of knowing.

VII

The question has often been asked: How much was Chopin influenced by Bellini, whose March from *I puritani* was the inspiration for *Hexaméron*? Chopin did not hear a note of Bellini in Warsaw, where the operas were never performed, and by the time he arrived in Paris his creative personality was already formed. The first Bellini operas he heard were *Il pirata* and *La sonnambula* at the Paris Opera, in 1832, and in them he would have recognized his second self. The similarities between the two composers stem from their mutual admiration for the operas of Mozart and Rossini, whose cantilenas provided the models for Chopin's singing piano and Bellini's decorated arias. Hiller has described the powerful effect that Bellini's music had on Chopin. During a performance of *Norma* that they attended together Chopin had tears in his eyes as he listened to Giovanni Rubini singing the great extended cantilenas toward the end of Act II.

Bellini and Chopin met each other at the beginning of 1834, first in the salon of Princess Belgiojoso and later in the home of Mme Lina Freppa, an Italian singing teacher whom Bellini had known in Naples. At her soirées Chopin played the piano and Bellini held forth on his operas, illustrating his ideas at the keyboard. Bellini spoke execrable French (Heine likened it to "breaking words on the wheel like an executioner") and even his Italian, so we are told, was delivered in a mangled Sicilian accent; but the two composers found common ground in music. They were not dissimilar in temperament either, for both composers obsessed over the details of their works in progress. And Bellini, like Chopin, was drawn to fashionable society. Heine (who once again provides us with a memorable image) spotted Bellini at a society event and described him as "a sigh in dancing pumps and silk stockings." Bellini was thirty-three years old when he died in September 1835, following an attack of amoebic dysentery, the symptoms of which he had endured since 1831.[26] He was buried in Père Lachaise Cemetery, following an impressive requiem mass held in Les Invalides, sung by a chorus of 350 singers and soloists from the Paris Opera. Members of the royal family were present, an indication of the wide esteem that he enjoyed. Gioacchino Rossini, Ferdinando Paër, Michele Carafa, and the septuagenarian Luigi Cherubini formed the distinguished quartet of Italian pallbearers. The funeral cortège wound its way through driving rain past large crowds of mourners lining the boulevards until it reached the cemetery, where Rossini, soaked to the skin, delivered a graveside oration. Chopin was in Dresden visiting the Wodziński family when these mournful events unfolded, so he was spared the ordeal of participating in the obsequies. While Chopin may or may not have requested that a Bellini aria be sung at his bedside as he lay dying, there is no truth to the story that he requested to be buried next to Bellini. Everyone knew that Bellini's grave in Père Lachaise was to be a makeshift affair. His soaring posthumous reputation only strengthened the demand from his Italian compatriots that his remains should come home. But that was not possible until the political upheavals in his native land had been quietened. In 1876, Bellini's body was finally exhumed and returned to his birthplace in Catania, Sicily, with full national honors.

VIII

Chopin's appearances in the salons and stately homes of the aristocratic families in Paris during this period continued without respite. He played

---

26. The autopsy report prepared by Dr. Adolphe Dalmas, professor of medicine at the University of Paris, may be read in WVB, pp. 415–16. Despite the clarity of its findings, it failed to silence the rumors that swirled around Bellini's death and lingered for years: namely, that he had been poisoned. Dalmas found a malignant tumor growing on the liver, the ultimate cause of death.

for the Duke of Orléans, the eldest son of King Louis-Philippe; for Baron Adolphe d'Eichthal, a member of the French banking dynasty; and for Countess Thérèse d'Apponyi, wife of the Austrian ambassador to France. The wealthy Mallet brothers (Louis-Jules and Adolphe-Jacques, "bankers to the nation") and Auguste Léo—Chopin's own banker and occasional representative—were also happy to present the "pianist from Warsaw" at their postprandial gatherings. Chopin's connections with these families improved his standing in society, and he acknowledged it in the obvious way, by flattering their vanity and dedicating to them some of his best music. A glance at the list of his dedicatees reveals a generous scattering of princes, dukes, and counts, together with their consorts, siblings, and offspring, names that might have disappeared into the mists of time save for the fact that they were placed on the title pages of Chopin's compositions. It is to one of them, Countess Pauline Plater, the dedicatee of the Four Mazurkas, op. 6, and the daughter of Count Ludwik, that we owe a well-worn anecdote, indicative perhaps of nothing more than the vapid conversation pursued by the chattering classes during breaks between the musical items at their soirées. When asked to compare the merits of three pianists who had appeared in her salon—Hiller, Liszt, and Chopin—Pauline replied that she would choose Hiller as a friend, Liszt as a lover, and Chopin as a husband.[27]

It is unfortunate that there exists no reliable record of what Chopin played at these functions. We know only that he featured his own works exclusively. He also improvised music that was kept aloft for hours on the wings of inspiration. These were experiences to treasure, for by their very nature they could not be repeated. Something of the delight and sense of anticipation that was aroused whenever word spread that Chopin was about to play the piano is caught in a hastily scribbled message that George Sand sent to Delacroix in May 1838: "Chopin will be playing to an intimate circle. Please come at midnight."[28] It led Berlioz to complain, "Chopin always keeps himself aloof . . . Unless you are a prince, a minister, or an ambassador, you might as well give up hope of hearing him."[29]

---

27. RLKM, vol. 1, p. 229.
28. CGS, vol. V, pp. 407–408.
29. *Journal des débats*, April 13, 1842.

IX

Berlioz's rueful comment notwithstanding, Chopin did take part in several high-profile concerts in the early part of 1838 that brought him wide publicity and good reviews, but again no money. On February 16 he played before the royal family and their guests in the Tuileries. After performing a number of his own compositions, he improvised on a theme handed to him by the king's sister Princess Adélaïde, which, in the diplomatic language of the *Journal des débats*, "obtained the greatest success and repeated felicitations from the Queen and the princesses."[30] It also gained for him a silver tea service decorated in gold and inscribed with the words *Louis-Philippe, Roi des Français à Frédéric Chopin*. Just over two weeks later, on March 3, Chopin took part in a benefit concert for his friend Charles-Valentin Alkan that, despite being held in Jean-Henri Pape's famously windswept piano rooms, succeeded in attracting a large audience. Alkan, who was only twenty-four years old, was already showing those prodigious gifts as a pianist and composer that set him apart from his contemporaries, and several artists happily donated their services in support of "the young beneficiary," as the *Revue et Gazette musicale* called him. They included the violinist Heinrich Ernst; the cellist Alexandre Batta; the singers Maria Alizard and Mlle d'Hennin; and Pierre Levassor, the leading tenor at the Palais-Royal Theater, who specialized in performing witty "chansonnettes," which generally sent waves of laughter across the audience and were there to lighten the load of the rest of the program. The main item was the premiere performance of Alkan's unpublished Third Piano Concerto *da camera*, played by the composer with his gifted twelve-year-old brother, Napoléon, accompanying him on a second piano. Alkan then returned to the platform and played "several remarkable pieces of his own composition,"[31] including two studies for solo piano. The *pièce de résistance* came toward the end of the program when Chopin (who had been waiting in the wings) joined Zimmerman, Gutmann, and Alkan in a performance of the Allegretto and Finale of Beethoven's Symphony no. 7, arranged for two pianos and eight hands by Alkan himself. When we consider Chopin's thinly veiled aversion to Beethoven's music, and his lack of enthusi-

---

30. Issue of February 19, 1838.
31. *Le Ménestrel*, March 11, 1838.

asm for Henri Pape's pianos (to say nothing of his drafty showrooms), this public appearance is best described as a sacrifice placed on the altar of his affection for Alkan.

But it was Chopin's participation in a benefit concert in support of his old Warsaw school friend the violinist Antoni Orłowski, held in the city of Rouen on March 12, that garnered the most attention. Orłowski had moved from Paris to Rouen in 1835 to become leader of the Rouen Philharmonic Orchestra. He enjoyed an uneasy relationship with the management and by the time of this concert he stood in need of a boost, both moral and financial. Anxious to make his mark, he announced a gargantuan concert to include his own arrangements for large orchestra of a Schubert symphony and an overture by Ferdinand Ries, together with a special appearance by Chopin playing his Concerto in E minor, op. 11, and the Grande Polonaise, op. 22. Fifteen rehearsals were held in order to bring everything together. Orłowski hired the main salon of Rouen's Hôtel de Ville and sold tickets to a capacity audience of five hundred people. On the day of the concert he found himself with a depleted band, most of whose players had been diverted to the Théâtre des Arts by an unfriendly management and ordered to take part in a performance of Halévy's opera *La Juive*. It was a Machiavellian situation that ruffled feathers and led to a protest in the columns of the local *Journal de Rouen*. "In spite of all previous assurances [the Théâtre management] yesterday staged a major opera, and thus deprived M. Orłowski of the presence of his orchestral musicians."[32] Denied an orchestra, Chopin performed his E minor Concerto in the version for piano and string quintet and the Grande Polonaise in the version for solo piano. Determined to help Orłowski, who faced a full hall and a vastly curtailed program, Chopin played much else besides, including his recently published Impromptu in A-flat major, op. 29.

The Impromptu had drawn a vituperative review in *La France musicale* just five weeks earlier, on February 4, 1838. "The best thing that can be said about this Impromptu," it jeered, "is that M. Chopin has composed some very lovely Mazurkas." It then went on to accuse Chopin of searching for an idea, pursuing it through all the major and minor keys, and on failing to capture it simply doing without it, bringing matters to a close with a few trite chords: "Voilà! An impromptu." The review was published anonymously but it was generally believed to have been the work of Henri Herz, who had a financial interest in this journal. His motives are not difficult to ascertain, for he was well aware of the *bon mot* going the rounds of the Paris salons. "Thalberg is a king, Liszt is a prophet, Chopin is a poet, and Herz is a solicitor."

The Rouen concert was a triumph for Chopin. Several critics had followed him from Paris, intent on hearing him play, which had the unfortunate effect of marginalizing poor Orłowski, who was simply referred to in the press as "a Polish professor." That the spotlight had been switched from him to Chopin was largely the work of Chopin's wily publisher Maurice Schlesinger, who had earlier brought out the aforementioned Impromptu as a supplement to the *Gazette musicale*,[33] and now dispatched the critic Ernest Legouvé to cover the concert for the same journal. Legouvé gave Chopin one of the finest reviews of his career. "Here was an event that was not without importance in the world of music," it began. Legouvé then surveyed the subtle refinements that characterized Chopin's playing and made it unique. He ended with a glancing reference to the clamor that had surrounded the Liszt-Thalberg contest the previous year, urging Chopin, "Put an end to the great debate that divides the artists; and when it shall be asked who is the first pianist of Europe, Liszt or Thalberg? let all the world reply, like those who have heard you—'it is Chopin.'"[34]

Chopin had no interest in settling the question of who was the first pianist of Europe. Notwithstanding the success he enjoyed at Rouen, he

---

33. Issue of October 29, 1837. The hostility that prevailed between *La France musicale* and Schlesinger's *Gazette musicale* had festered for years and reached a climax of sorts when Schlesinger fought a duel with one of Herz's pupils. The matter was brought to court and the trial was heard on April 29, 1834. Chopin was called as a witness for Schlesinger, an experience that caused him acute embarrassment.
34. Issue of March 25, 1838.

did not appear as a pianist in any public forum again for three years. The unexpected direction that his life was about to take would in any case have banished all thoughts of concertizing, for it was to remove him from Paris as well—at least for a time. In order to understand what had happened, and how the events that were about to overtake him were already falling into place, we must go back a couple of years.

ENTER GEORGE SAND,
1836–1838

Until now, I have always been faithful to those I have loved.
—*George Sand*[1]

[George Sand] used words for garments and she hid in their folds.
—*Jarosław Iwaszkiewicz*[2]

I

In mid-October 1836, Paris was enlivened by news of the return of Liszt and Countess Marie d'Agoult, seeking to rehabilitate themselves after the scandal of their elopement to Switzerland eighteen months earlier, and the birth of their illegitimate daughter, Blandine. The affair had been followed avidly by Liszt's wide circle of admirers, to say nothing of the gossip-mongers, and Liszt himself had not been slow to provide a surfeit of detail about the couple's sojourn in Geneva and their forays into the Swiss country-side in the first of his "Bachelor of Music" essays, published for the whole world to read in Schlesinger's *Revue et Gazette musicale*. Earlier in the summer they had been joined by George Sand and her retinue, and she had added her own dispatches back home in the form of her "Lettres d'un voyageur," one of which described their visits to the Chamonix valley

---

1. CGS, vol. IV, p. 435.
2. IC, p. 344.

GEORGE SAND'S FAMILY TREE

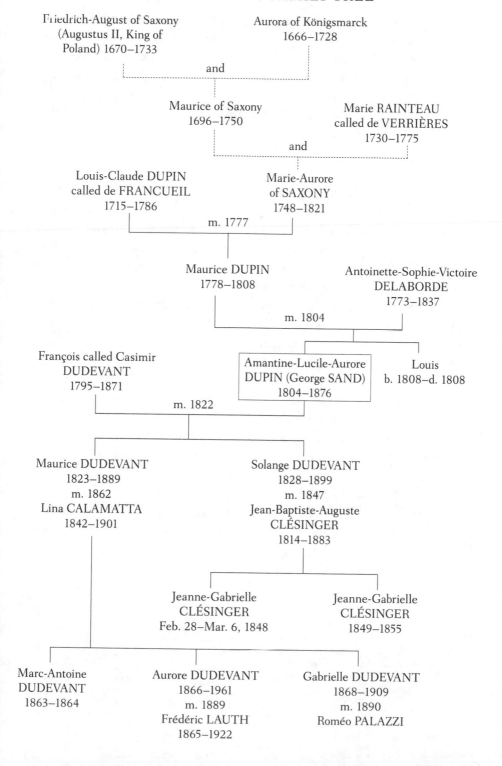

Friedrich-August of Saxony (Augustus II, King of Poland) 1670–1733 **and** Aurora of Königsmarck 1666–1728

Maurice of Saxony 1696–1750 **and** Marie RAINTEAU called de VERRIÈRES 1730–1775

Louis-Claude DUPIN called de FRANCUEIL 1715–1786 — Marie-Aurore of SAXONY 1748–1821 — **m. 1777**

Maurice DUPIN 1778–1808 — **m. 1804** — Antoinette-Sophie-Victoire DELABORDE 1773–1837

François called Casimir DUDEVANT 1795–1871 — **m. 1822** — Amantine-Lucile-Aurore DUPIN (George SAND) 1804–1876 — Louis b. 1808–d. 1808

Maurice DUDEVANT 1823–1889 m. 1862 Lina CALAMATTA 1842–1901

Solange DUDEVANT 1828–1899 m. 1847 Jean-Baptiste-Auguste CLÉSINGER 1814–1883

Jeanne-Gabrielle CLÉSINGER Feb. 28–Mar. 6, 1848

Jeanne-Gabrielle CLÉSINGER 1849–1855

Marc-Antoine DUDEVANT 1863–1864

Aurore DUDEVANT 1866–1961 m. 1889 Frédéric LAUTH 1865–1922

Gabrielle DUDEVANT 1868–1909 m. 1890 Roméo PALAZZI

and to Fribourg, where Liszt had played on the newly installed Mooser organ and had famously improvised an extended fantasy on the Dies Irae from Mozart's *Requiem*, an event captured in prose by Sand and published in the *Revue des deux mondes*.[3] These bulletins by Liszt and Sand are widely consulted by scholars today and form mandatory reading for anyone with an interest in piecing together the minutiae of a scandal that had set the French capital on its ears.

The lovers of Geneva installed themselves in the fashionable Hôtel de France, 23 rue Laffitte, wondering how they might be received. They did not have to wait for long. They were inundated by a stream of well-wishers—including Rossini, Meyerbeer, Berlioz, and Chopin himself—come to welcome them back to Paris. Marie arranged several soirées attended by such literati as Sainte-Beuve, Balzac, Heine, and Victor Hugo; soon the Hôtel de France was abuzz with intellectual and artistic activity. She wrote enthusiastically to George Sand, who had meanwhile returned to her country home at Nohant, inviting her to rejoin them. By the end of the month Sand was in Paris and had rented a suite of rooms adjacent to the ones occupied by Liszt and Marie. They even shared a common sitting room where they could entertain their mutual friends. "Those of mine you don't like," wrote Sand, "will be received on the landing."[4] It was in the Hôtel de France, possibly toward the end of October, that Chopin and Sand had one or two chance encounters. But it was not until the evening of November 19, 1836, that she heard him play the piano at one of Marie d'Agoult's soirées, and was enthralled. The feeling was not reciprocated. Chopin was offended by her cigars, her male attire, and her flamboyant manners. "What an antipathetic woman that Sand is!" he exclaimed to Ferdinand Hiller as they walked home after the party. "Is it really a woman? I am ready to doubt it."[5] And to his family in Warsaw he expressed himself even more strongly, telling them that there was "something about her that repels me."[6]

Sand was aware that the evening had not gone well and looked for a chance to repair the damage. After some behind-the-scenes prodding from Liszt and Countess d'Agoult, Chopin held a soirée of his own at his place

---

3. SLV, p. 309. This was the tenth of Sand's "Lettres d'un voyageur," which covered the Swiss sojourn with Liszt and Marie d'Agoult.
4. CGS, vol. III, p. 528.
5. CFC, vol. 2, p. 208.
6. Ibid.

on the rue de la Chaussée d'Antin, on December 13. Among the distinguished company were Heine, Eugène Delacroix, Marquis Astolphe de Custine, and the novelist Eugène Sue. The musicians included Meyerbeer, Ferdinand Hiller, Johann Pixis, and the tenor Adolphe Nourrit, who was at that moment having some notable triumphs at the Paris Opera. A number of Polish expatriates were present, including Adam Mickiewicz ("the Dante of the North," as Liszt liked to call him), Albert Grzymała, Jan Matuszyński, Count Bernard Potocki, and the frail and elderly Count Julian Niemcewicz, one of the revered sponsors of the Polish Constitution of 1791. Józef Brzowski, Chopin's chronicler in chief at this time, left a detailed description of the evening in his diary.[7] Liszt and Marie d'Agoult turned up and brought Sand along with them. Eager to make a better impression this time, Sand made her entrance sporting a pair of white pantaloons and a scarlet sash—the colors of the Polish flag. This secured a diplomatic victory for her, especially among the expatriates. She then sat quietly on a chaise longue by the fireside, smoking one of her "poetic" cigars (which was almost certainly laced with opium) while Nourrit sang some Schubert songs, including "Erlkönig," accompanied by Liszt.

Liszt was not wrong when he observed that there was always a certain misanthropic resistance on the part of Chopin to opening his apartment, even to those within his inner circle, but when he did so the result was never less than memorable, as it was on this occasion. Many years later Liszt reminisced about this evening in his book about Chopin. He attached no date to his memory, but it can be inferred from the details he provides in his text.[8] In lyrical language, he described how the room appeared extended into the shadows beyond, from whose semidarkness the sounds of an unseen Pleyel piano emerged as if from a disembodied source, while the audience sat in the flickering candlelight, captivated. The spell was broken only when Chopin got up from the keyboard and Marie d'Agoult passed tea and ices around. Then came the highlight of the evening, a performance by Chopin and Liszt of Moscheles's Sonata in E-flat major for four hands, with Chopin playing the *secondo* part and Liszt the *primo*. Pixis turned the pages, casting approving glances at the audience to register his pleasure at what was being offered. From these unlikely seeds there would

7. BJT, pp. 98–101.
8. LC, pp. 90–93.

soon blossom one of the famous love affairs of the nineteenth century. The *grande passion* between Chopin and Sand, so slow to emerge with him, so swift with her, perplexed even their closest friends, so mismatched a pair did they seem to be. Despite some learned commentary to the contrary, the Chopin-Sand affair was from its uncertain beginning aided and abetted by Marie d'Agoult, who was doubtless more than happy to switch the spotlight from herself and give Paris a different scandal to gossip about.

We called the pair mismatched. He was reserved, aloof, somewhat effeminate in his bearing, always immaculate in his attire, and looked the perfect dandy. She was brash, flamboyant, outspoken in the dissemination of her radical political ideas, and decidedly masculine in appearance, donning men's clothing as an outward symbol of equality with the opposite sex. Already she had written plays and novels that had attracted attention for their advanced social ideas, especially on the emancipation of women, and she had been involved with a string of lovers—the writer Jules Sandeau, the journalist Henri de Latouche, the poet Alfred de Musset, the doctor Pietro Pagello, and the lawyer Michel de Bourges among them. Her novel *Lélia*, published in 1833, had brought her notoriety through its portrayal of "free love" and was assumed by everyone who read it to be a portrait of Sand herself. Six years older than Chopin, she would eventually take the initiative in their affair. But that was more than a year away. Chopin was still secretly engaged to Maria Wodzińska, uncertain of the outcome, while Sand had not yet disentangled herself from her latest lover, the dramatist Félicien Mallefille, who was presently the tutor of her son, Maurice.

II

It may be useful to pause at this point in order to consider the complex personality of the woman with whom Chopin was to spend nine years of his life. Some biographers have seen in George Sand a wholly negative influence. But she gave Chopin exactly the right domestic environment in which to compose. During their long liaison he was to create some of his greatest works, and when the break came the fountain of music started to die within him. Nor must we forget that Sand became his chief caregiver as his illness made fatal inroads into his health, and she saw him through more than one life-threatening crisis. Sand's life was to touch on Chopin's at a hundred different points, and it would be dere-lict to gloss over it as if it had no bearing on the events that were about to follow.

Our best source of information about George Sand comes from Sand herself. The torrent of words that constitutes her autobiography, *Histoire de ma vie* (1850–54), required no fewer than four volumes before the flow was exhausted. Sand was adept at bending life into literature, so we do well to treat her prose with caution. Her vast correspondence, consisting of thousands of letters to and from hundreds of correspondents, provides us with a better picture of her complex character. But it, too, is not always above blending fact and fiction, and it contains pitfalls for the unwary. It has been well said that Sand "used words for garments and she hid in their folds."[9]

III

Sand's earliest memories were of Nohant, the château in the Berry re-gion of France that she had inherited from her grandmother, the wid-owed Mme Marie-Aurore Dupin de Francueil, and which was now her home. Her father, Maurice Dupin, could trace his ancestry from a blood-line going back to Friedrich-August of Saxony, who became King Augus-tus II of Poland. Born into privilege, young Maurice Dupin longed for somewhat more adventure than his sheltered lifestyle and his doting mother allowed, and at twenty-two he became a lieutenant in Napoléon's army and was posted to Italy as an aide-de-camp attached to the high command. Here his eye fell on an attractive woman of dubious repute, Sophie-Victoire Delaborde—Sand's future mother—under circumstances that Sand may have embroidered in the telling in order to make her story more compelling.

Sand described her mother as "one of the world's gypsies." Sophie-Victoire was the impoverished daughter of an innkeeper and professional bird fancier who had fallen on hard times and had been reduced to selling

---

9. IC, p. 344.

canaries on the Paris quays. She was a sexually attractive young woman, became a dancer in the Paris theater, gave birth to an illegitimate daughter by one of her several lovers, and went to Italy in the wake of the French army as the mistress of a general. It was there that she met the general's aide-de-camp, Lieutenant Maurice Dupin, who succumbed to her charms and detached her from the general—an act that did not prevent him a year or two later from being promoted to the rank of captain and then of major. His mother, Mme Dupin de Francueil, was beside herself with anxiety when she saw how besotted her son was with someone she regarded as little better than a harlot, and when Maurice tried to bring Sophie-Victoire back to Nohant would not have her in the house. So Maurice installed his lover at nearby La Châtre and chose to ride out the family storm. This was not long in coming. Sophie-Victoire became pregnant shortly before Maurice was posted to a military camp in Boulogne, and on June 6, 1804, she married him in a secret civil ceremony in Paris, just in time to legitimize the child. Less than one month later, on July 1, their daughter, Amantine-Lucile-Aurore—the future George Sand—put in her appearance. When news was brought to Mme Dupin, she tried to have the marriage annulled on the grounds that it lacked benefit of clergy. It was the start of a long period of discontent between Sophie-Victoire and her mother-in-law, who remained implacably opposed to having the daughter of an impecunious bird fancier in the family.

When Aurore (the name by which Sand preferred to be known) was only four years old, her mother gave birth to a son, Louis. The family was in Spain, having been taken there by Maurice, whose regiment was now involved in the Napoléonic campaigns on the Iberian Peninsula. Aurore was convinced that this child, who had fallen ill, was deliberately blinded by Spanish doctors out of hatred for the French. Given leave to return to France, Maurice took his family back to Nohant, but during the return journey the child contracted smallpox and died. The parents buried the infant in the garden at Nohant near one of the pear trees. Within one week of this tragedy, the family had to bear a far greater one. Maurice was riding back to Nohant from La Châtre through heavy rain at night, when the horse reared and threw him to the ground, breaking his neck. Aurore was haunted by the anguished cries of her mother as they carried his body into the house. Fifty years later she was still able vividly to recall that childhood trauma.

I can still see which part of the room we were in. It is the same room I now inhabit and where I am now writing of these terrible events. My mother fell into a chair behind the bed. I see her ashen face, her long black hair spread across her chest, her bare arms that I cover with kisses. I hear her piercing cries. She was deaf to my own and did not register my caresses. Deschartes [the abbé, Aurore's tutor, who had brought the sad news] said to her: "Look to this child and live for her."[10]

During the funeral, the four-year-old Aurore failed to understand why everyone was dressed in black, and was told it was because of the death of her father. She then said something that caused her mother the greatest pain. "Is my papa still dead?" She understood death, she tells us, but did not think that it lasted forever. And she half believed the servants who had witnessed the ghost that walked in her father's full dress uniform through the rooms of Nohant at the very moment she was trying to comfort her mother. He, too, was laid to rest not far from Louis. Ravaged by grief and with no one to offer her the consolation she craved in this house of strangers, Sophie-Victoire went back to Paris to be with her family and her natural daughter, Caroline. To make sure that she stayed there, Grandmother Dupin paid her an annual pension of 1,500 francs in exchange for signing a piece of paper granting her legal control over Aurore, who spent her early childhood living either at Nohant or in Mme Dupin's luxurious Paris apartment.

Not long after the death of her father, Aurore learned she had an illegitimate half brother, Hippolyte Chatiron, the result of an affair that Maurice Dupin had conducted with one of her grandmother's servant girls, the daughter of a local carpenter, five years before Aurore herself was born. Hippolyte, who was brought up in the neighborhood around Berry, became a frequent visitor to Nohant, and despite their different personalities a bond of affection sprang up between him and Aurore, strengthened by the knowledge that they shared a father who had been taken from them as children.

---

10. SHV, vol. 1, p. 597.

IV

Aurore's mother and grandmother quarreled constantly over her upbringing. The legal agreement that was supposed to have prevented such things produced nothing but a perpetual tug-of-war between the two women. Aurore called herself "the apple of their discord." When she was thirteen, her grandmother placed her in a convent, insisting on the advantages of a religious education. Despite its forbidding name and its somewhat grim history, the Convent of the "Dames Augustines Anglaises" (which had been used as a prison following the French Revolution) was one of the best boarding schools in Paris. It was run by English nuns whose order had fled to France after Cromwell began his persecution of Catholics. Aurore remained there for three years. She learned English, donned the same regulation habit of purple cloth worn by the nuns, studied *The Lives of the Saints*, and had the rough edges of her country upbringing smoothed away by the brides of Christ in their cloistered environment, one in which she soon felt at home. Even at this tender age Aurore had a sharp mind and a quick pen. She looked around and divided the girls into three groups: those who were stupid, those who were compliant, and those who were devils. She placed herself in the last category, and as a "devil among the nuns" she sometimes created such mayhem that the Mothers dubbed her "madcap." This made her very popular with the other girls, who nicknamed her "Some Bread," the English translation of "du pain"—a wretched pun on her name, Dupin. The only men she saw were her two chaplains, Abbé de Villèle and Abbé de Prémord, the latter of whom heard her confession and drew up the moral code by which she was expected to conduct her daily life. A high premium was placed on chastity, and any attempt to undo it "by anyone, no matter how honorable," must be reported. Whenever a girl was heard to utter "an evil word," the nuns forced the miscreant to get down on bended knees and kiss the floor. The rooms of the junior girls were unheated and the food was basic. Letters home were censored. When one of Aurore's letters to her grandmother was opened by the Mother Superior and found to contain a litany of complaints about everybody connected with the establishment, including the Mother Superior herself, only the intervention of Mme Dupin (who sided with her granddaughter on this issue) averted punishment. Small wonder that Aurore later became a rebel, turned her back on the Church, transformed herself into Lélia, became an enemy of censorship, and drew on her rich supply of teenage memories whenever she wanted to pull aside the veil of hypocrisy behind which human beings generally like to practice their indiscretions.[11]

Released from the confines of her English convent, Aurore went back to her grandmother at Nohant. The thing she feared most was an arranged marriage, the usual fate for a girl with prospects. But Mme Dupin had been laid low with a stroke, and matchmaking was not on her mind. Their intimate conversations during her grandmother's illness drew them closer, and the old lady made Aurore her heiress. Mme Dupin died at Nohant on December 26, 1821, after a second stroke, which had left her immobilized. Her last words to Aurore, who was at her bedside as she expired, were "You are losing your best friend." At her grandmother's death Aurore inherited Nohant, and found herself independently wealthy. She was only seventeen years old. Sophie-Victoire, who was fobbed off with a small pension, tried to contest the will, but legal counsel ruled against her. It was an aggravation that drove a permanent wedge between mother and daughter.

V

Suitors soon came calling at Nohant and were sent packing by Aurore, and once or twice by Sophie-Victoire as well, who started to exercise an unwelcome control over her daughter's personal affairs. Over the objections of her mother, and perhaps to get away from her influence, Aurore married twenty-seven-year-old Casimir Dudevant on September 17, 1822.[12] She brought with her a dowry of 100,000 francs as well as the Nohant château, which is where they began their married life. Aurore tells us that

---

11. SHV, vol. 1, pp. 961ff.

12. We sometimes read that Aurore was elevated to the aristocracy at the moment of her marriage. Casimir was the illegitimate son of Baron Jean-François Dudevant and his mistress Augustine Soulé, but had no claim to the title. In Aurore's words, her husband bore a rank no higher than a second lieutenant in the French infantry (SHV, vol. 1, p. 13), and she scolded those who addressed her as a "marchioness." Many years later, after Casimir's death in 1871, their son, Maurice Sand, petitioned to have his grandfather's title restored to his branch of the family. It was probably Maurice who had the word "Baronne" inscribed on his mother's tombstone at Nohant. We are left to wonder what the republican-minded Aurore might have made of it all, averse as she was to hereditary titles of any kind.

she was "completely innocent," never having shared her bed with a man, an experience she found pleasurable, even blissful. Within a month she was pregnant. During the months that followed, Casimir spent his days in the fields and woods around Nohant, indulging in his favorite pastimes of hunting and shooting, while Aurore took up dressmaking and sewing baby garments. Needlework, in fact, became a lifelong preoccupation, an activity to which she liked to return in moments of stress.

When her time was due, the couple left for Paris and moved into the Hôtel de Florence, where Aurore gave birth to a son, Maurice, on June 30, 1823, one day before her nineteenth birthday. She now learned the full meaning of what it meant to marry in haste and repent at leisure. It is not difficult to chart the erratic course of the marriage as it slowly wended its way downhill. At Nohant she found that she had exchanged one prison for another. Casimir was an assertive husband who liked to be master of the house—even though the house was not his. At first the days were tranquil enough, but when Aurore installed a piano with the intention of returning to her early love of music, Casimir objected. "I saw that you did not like music and I ceased to play," she wrote. It has been claimed by some biographers that Aurore was indifferent to music, but the opposite was the case. Grandmother Dupin had given the girl lessons on the piano and had also taught her the rudiments of harmony. In later life she was able to notate some folk songs she heard sung in the province of Berry, "including a bourrée of which Chopin had been fond." And in her autobiography she confessed that "the beauty of music affects and transports me more than that of any other art."[13] By stifling her enjoyment of music, Casimir knew that he was introducing some unhappiness into her life. And more was to follow.

Casimir was a skirt chaser who, when the day was done, liked nothing better than to climb the stairs to the servants' quarters and enjoy the favors of two of the girls, Claire and Pepita. Claire became pregnant and Aurore was never sure whether her husband or her half brother, Hippolyte, was the father because Claire had smiled on both men. In any case, Aurore had her own way of dealing with a crowded marriage, and that was to make it more crowded still, a matter we shall come to presently. There were in

---

13. SHV, vol. 1, pp. 625–26. Sand's novel *Consuelo* could only have been written by someone who brought an insider's knowledge of music to bear on the plot.

the meantime some growing confrontations with Casimir concerning his incompetent handling of the estate and his wasteful expenditure of her money. It drove her to draw up a legal document that was meant to protect their respective interests, and, if matters should go that far, might even serve as the basis for an amicable annulment. The terms of this agreement gave Casimir no peace, for the document proffered him a glimpse of a future without hearth and home. Frequent flare-ups took place over the dinner table, often in the presence of guests, during which Casimir, having drunk one glass of wine too many, became verbally abusive. A real tempest blew up on one occasion when his wife refused to give ground and he ordered her to leave the room. "I am in my own house," she reminded him in front of their guests, and refused to budge.[14] An apoplectic Casimir reached for his hunting rifle, which was hanging on a nearby wall, but before he had a chance to fire it in anger it was forced from his grasp by Alexis Duteil, one of his drinking companions.

VI

Hovering over everything else at Nohant were the uncertain circumstances surrounding the birth of Aurore's daughter, Solange. There are good reasons to suppose that Solange was not fathered by Casimir, but was the illegitimate daughter of Stéphane Ajasson de Grandsagne, from whom a few years earlier, in André Maurois's delicate phrase, "Sand had learned the elements of sentimental anatomy in her room in Nohant."[15] When Aurore first met him, Stéphane was a young medical student who had been engaged by her tutor, the elderly Abbé François Deschartres, to give her some lessons in anatomy and even the opportunity to assist at surgery. In this capacity Aurore witnessed amputations and autopsies. Her nursing experience made her used to dealing with medical crises and thereafter she never shrank from the sight of blood.[16] She also acquired some knowledge

---

14. ML, p. 212.

15. Ibid., p. 92.

16. In her autobiography, Sand offers some explicit details about her work with Stéphane, "who brought over the heads, arms, and legs which Deschartres needed in order to show me where to begin." (SHV, vol. 1, p, 1076.) She also acquired the skeleton of a young girl, which she suspended in her room at Nohant, the better to become familiar with human anatomy.

of pharmacy and was able to advise the residents of La Châtre about the best way to deal with whatever ailed them. Stéphane fell in love with Aurore at that time but she was too young to entertain thoughts of marriage, nor would her grandmother have allowed her to sacrifice herself on the altar of poverty, for Stéphane came from an impoverished family of ten children.

A turning point came in the autumn of 1827 when Stéphane visited Nohant while Casimir was in Paris. The pair were inseparable during Stéphane's sojourn in Berry, and they made no attempt to hide their obvious attachment to each other from the local population. When Stéphane returned to Paris, Aurore resolved to continue the relationship. No sooner had Casimir got back to Nohant than his wife departed for the capital in pursuit of Stéphane. She arrived there on December 5, and moved into the Hôtel de Florence, where three years earlier she had given birth to Maurice. She prolonged her stay in Paris for more than two weeks, offering Casimir the explanation that she was consulting a variety of doctors about her health. She was indeed far from well, and thanks to Stéphane's medical connections she was examined by some of the foremost doctors of the day, including Professor Landré-Beauvais, head of the Faculty of Medicine at Salpêtrière Hospital, who found nothing seriously wrong with her. Aurore's problems were more of mind than of body, for she was wracked by conscience, and with good reason. We now know that some intimate love letters were being exchanged with Stéphane at this time.[17] They lead to one conclusion: she had come to Paris for the express purpose of continuing an extramarital affair. When she finally got back to Nohant, around December 20, she was pregnant.

Solange was born on September 13, 1828. The pros and cons of her paternity were carefully balanced by André Maurois. He concludes that conception took place in Paris on December 13, 1827, nine months to the day before Solange was born. On that day, in fact, Aurore wrote Casimir an unusually frank letter telling him that Stéphane was now at her place, and would remain there for several days.[18] She was back in Nohant by the end of the year, where she evidently resumed sexual relations with her

---

This early medical experience stood her in good stead in later life, and is worth bearing in mind when we consider that Sand was shortly to become Chopin's chief caregiver.
17. They remained for many years in the possession of Stéphane's son, Paul-Émile. See *Le Moniteur général*, January 6, 1900.
18. ML, pp. 467–69: "A Note on the Birth of Solange Dudevant-Sand."

husband. But how to explain the early arrival of Solange, just eight months later? She liked to maintain that Solange was born prematurely because of a fright she had received when Hippolyte's young daughter Léontine Chatiron had fallen down the stairs at Nohant. That remained her official position for years. But in her *Histoire de ma vie* she drops a powerful hint about the true state of affairs when she reports an interesting scene that took place at the beginning of September, two weeks before the birth of Solange. An old admirer, Aurélien de Sèze, had turned up unexpectedly at Nohant and had caught her unawares at an early hour, laying out baby clothes in the drawing room. "What on earth are you doing?" he asked. "Surely it must be obvious," she replied. "I am working against time in preparation for somebody who looks like arriving earlier than I thought."[19]

Whether Solange arrived late or early was by now a matter of indifference to Casimir. The situation between him and Aurore had reached such a low point that even while she was in labor she overheard an intimate conversation between him and the Spanish servant Pepita going on next door, which left no doubt that they were in the middle of an affair. As if that were not enough, Aurore tells us that Hippolyte then staggered into her bedroom after a bout of drinking, and fell to the floor intoxicated. These were the circumstances in which Solange made her entrance into the world.

If more evidence of Solange's paternity is required, it lies readily to hand. Aurore often referred to Solange by the affectionate nickname "Mademoiselle Stéphane." As for Stéphane himself, he seemed more than ready to acknowledge paternity. Whenever his friends inquired why he was visiting Nohant, he liked to tell them, "Why shouldn't I go? I am going to see my daughter."[20] It is worth dwelling on Solange and her origins because it provides a clue to her dysfunctional relationship with her mother and especially with her brother, Maurice, in later years. Just what the young girl herself knew, and when she knew it, remains obscure. But she would surely have picked up the usual tittle-tattle that always swirled around Sand and her paramours at Nohant. And whenever Stéphane Ajasson de Grandsagne turned up, and the tongues started wagging again, Solange must have realized that she was the special object of his curiosity. For

19. SHV, vol. 2, p. 90.
20. VGS, p. 122.

the rest, Solange's increasingly rebellious behavior as a teenager, and her malicious tongue, especially with regard to her brother, would eventually bring down on her head the full wrath of her mother, who expelled her from the family circle, a dramatic event that helped to bring about the final rupture with Chopin as well.

Casimir's acceptance of his mournful situation is not hard to explain. He had recently lost 25,000 francs of the fortune he shared with his wife in a series of reckless business ventures and was humiliated by his own incompetence. Sand, who had yielded to his wishes in money matters, gave vent to her anger and accused him of stupidity. "When one has made a blunder, one does not repair it by swearing and groaning, and indulging in orgies of self-reproach until you make yourself and everybody else ill. Be a man!"[21] Casimir feared a separation, but where was he supposed to go? His ancestral home at Guillery belonged not to him but to his putative mother, Baroness Gabrielle Dudevant, who had never reconciled herself to having her husband's illegitimate son brought up at Guillery and passed off as if he were her own flesh and blood, so she disinherited him. Casimir sought consolation in the traditional activities for a man in his position: drinking and womanizing. At the end of a busy day, filled with remorse for having wasted so much of his wife's capital, the penitent would collapse in an armchair and snore the evening away. A sort of truce descended on the marriage. Casimir clung to Nohant, to his son, and even to his wife, for he needed the material security such things offered. As for Aurore, she turned the situation to her own advantage. After the birth of Solange, she abandoned the marital bed and moved into a room on the ground floor of Nohant, next to the children and their nurse, where Casimir had no access to her. Here she spent the nights at her writing table, and when the first rays of daylight penetrated her room, she went to sleep on a small cot that she had installed in what was now a haven from her husband and her collapsing marriage.

She still had to summon the resolve to make a final break. Casimir obliged her in a scene that could have come straight out of one of her novels. One day, after he had left Nohant on one of his hunting trips, she opened his desk in search of some promissory notes, because she feared the true extent of their joint debts. Among his papers she found an envelope addressed to her, but marked: "Not to be opened until after my death!" It was

---

21. CGS, vol. I, p. 584.

Casimir's will, but since her name was on the cover she opened it, she tells us, without any fear of indiscretion. What she read devastated her. "What a will!" she wrote. "Nothing but curses!" Casimir had poured into this document all his pent-up anger against his wife, and all his scorn for her character. She thought that she was dreaming, for she had no idea how much she was despised. "This finally aroused me from my slumbers," she wrote.[22]

There was a tense confrontation during which Aurore remained inflexible and reduced him to tears. She herself laid down the terms of their separation, on which she refused to waver. She informed Casimir that she was leaving him, and intended to spend several months of each year in Paris. She demanded a monthly allowance from the revenues of the Nohant estate, which had in any case been guaranteed her in their prenuptial agreement. A resident tutor must be engaged to look after the education of the children, for whose salary Casimir would be responsible. The final settlement would come later, once the lawyers had sorted everything out, but Casimir knew that he was now on notice to leave Nohant. Aurore packed her bags, embraced her children, and caught the stagecoach to Paris. She arrived there on January 6, 1831.

Waiting for her was a young friend whom she had met earlier in La Châtre, the handsome blond-haired Jules Sandeau, who like Aurore herself harbored ambitions to become a writer. Within a few weeks they had started an affair and had moved into a small apartment on Quai Saint-Michel. They embarked on a joint novel, *Rose et Blanche* (1831), which eventually ran to five volumes but earned little money. In the middle of this work Aurore was obliged to return briefly to Nohant, in part to take control over her impending legal fight against Casimir, which was about to turn ugly, and in part to pick up some furniture for transfer to the Paris apartment. Casimir, Hippolyte, and her mother, Sophie-Victoire, were waiting for her and pressed her to remain at Nohant and give up her newly acquired liberty. This provoked her to put pen to paper and explain her views in a celebrated letter to her mother.

> May 31, 1831,
> My husband does exactly as he likes. Whether he has mistresses,
> or does not have mistresses, rests entirely with him. He can drink
> wine or water just as the fancy takes him, and is free to save or

---

22. Ibid., p. 737.

spend. He can build, plant, sell, buy, run the house and the estate, as he thinks fit . . . But it is only fair that he shall grant me the same liberty that he enjoys. If he does not, then I shall think him odious and contemptible—and he would hate that to happen. Consequently, I am completely independent. I go to bed when he gets up, I visit La Châtre or Rome as I please. I come home at midnight or at six a.m. All that is my business and no one else's.[23]

Lélia had found her independence. Toward the end of 1832 she not only broke off the affair with Sandeau, but took with her an important souvenir: the first syllable of his name. "George Sand" was the famous *nom de plume* by which she came to be recognized. And it was as George Sand, freighted with all the emotional baggage that had constituted her life so far, that in the autumn of 1836 she first got to know Chopin, and attempted to draw him into her inner circle.

VII

The soirée that Chopin had given in his apartment on December 13 of that year had lingered in Sand's memory. She made several attempts to entice him down to Nohant (using Marie d'Agoult as her intermediary) but he always found a reason not to go. Sand even instructed Marie, "Tell Chopin that I idolize him."[24] From February 1837, d'Agoult stayed as Sand's guest at Nohant for the better part of six months, and was joined by Liszt whenever his concert engagements allowed. Other guests floated in and out of the old house, including the tenor Adolphe Nourrit, and there were glorious evenings of lieder recitals, with Liszt accompanying the singer at the Érard piano that Sand had installed especially for the pianist. "When Franz plays the piano, the burden is lifted from my heart," she declared.[25] But despite Sand's urgings Chopin never appeared. In May he used the excuse that he was leaving for Germany to meet his old friend Tytus, a trip that never materialized. In June his pretext was that

23. CGS, vol. I, p. 888.
24. CGS, vol. III, p. 765.
25. SJI, pp. 45–46.

he was enjoying the thermal baths at Enghien in the company of Józef Brzowski. And in July, Camille Pleyel took him to London as his traveling companion. It must have seemed to Sand as if her quarry—it is difficult to find a better word—might elude her grasp. But in April 1838 all that changed when she visited Paris. She heard Chopin play in the home of her friend Charlotte Marliani (April 25) and fell once more under the spell of his music. She sent him a scrap of paper on which she scrawled the words "I adore you." (Her friend Marie Dorval the actress, who was with her, added, "And me, too!") It was Sand's first declaration of love for Chopin, found among his papers after his death. Sand heard him again at a soirée in the home of Astolphe de Custine (May 8) at which Jules Janin and Victor Hugo were present, by which time she knew that she must take the initiative.

Chopin seems to have held himself in reserve for an unconscionably long time, at least by Sand's standards. She unburdened herself about this problem to their mutual friend Albert Grzymała in a letter that went on for more than six thousand words across thirty-two pages, an epistle on love, fidelity, morals, and the temptations of the flesh. When Sand wrote it, she was under the illusion that Chopin was still involved with Maria Wodzińska, and did not know that the engagement had already been broken off, for the simple reason that Chopin had not told her. The letter is too long to present in full, but we can profitably consider those fragments from it that shed light on her growing attachment to Chopin. She begins her missive by registering her amazement at the effect that Chopin's presence continues to have on her, and goes on to weigh the pros and cons of an affair with him.

May, 1838.

Until now, I have always been faithful to those I have loved, perfectly faithful . . . I am not of an inconstant nature. On the contrary. I am so used to giving my exclusive affection to one who loves me truly, so slow to take fire, so accustomed to living with men without reflecting that I am a woman, that I was rather disturbed at the effect Chopin had on me. I still have not got over my amazement, and if I were very proud I should feel humiliated at allowing my heart to fall straight into infidelity just when my life seemed calm and settled forever . . . But if Heaven would have us remain faithful to earthly affections, why does it sometimes allow angels to lose their way among us and meet us in our path?[26]

After blaming Heaven for placing an angel in her path and bringing confusion into her life, Sand comes to the nub of the matter: whether to capitulate, body and soul, or whether to abstain.

> And so the great question of love arises once more within me. I once said: "There is no love without fidelity," and this is the point I was coming to—to discuss with you the question of possession. For certain minds, the whole question of fidelity is inseparable from it. It is, I believe, a wrong idea; one may be more or less unfaithful, but when one has allowed one's soul to be invaded and when one has granted the simplest caress, urged to it by feelings of love, the infidelity has already been committed and what follows is less serious, for he who has lost the heart has lost everything. Better to lose the body, and keep the soul intact. And so, when two persons wish to live together, they should not violate nature and truth by retreating from a complete union, but should they be compelled to live apart, the wisest thing for them—and hence a duty and a true virtue—is to abstain. I had not yet seriously thought about all that, and if he had asked for it in Paris I should have yielded, obedient to that innate uprightness which makes me hate caution, restrictions, false distinctions, and subtleties of any kind whatsoever.

Throughout her screed Sand also seeks to remove herself from the moral consequences of her betrayal of her current lover, Félicien Mallefille. She warms to her theme and comes to Chopin himself, the real reason for all this angst.

> As I am being absolutely frank with you I must admit that one thing does not quite please me in Chopin: and that is, his reasons for abstaining are bad ones. Up to this point I have thought it fine of him to abstain out of respect for me, from shyness, and fidelity to his old flame. All that involved sacrifice, and in consequence meant strength and real chastity.

---

26. The letter is reproduced in full in CGS, vol. IV, pp. 428–39.

. . . I do not remember exactly the words he used. I think he said that *certain facts* might spoil our memories. Wasn't that a stupid thing to say, and do you think he really believed it? What wretched woman left him with such impressions of physical love? Has he had a mistress who was unworthy of him? Poor angel! I should like to see all women hanged who have soiled in men's eyes the thing in life most worthy of respect, the most sacred fact in all creation, the divine mystery the most serious of all human actions and the most sublime in the whole universal range of life. The magnet attracts iron inexorably; the animals seek each other out, in obedience to the law of sex. Even vegetable life knows this law of attraction, and man, who alone in the whole terrestrial world has received from God the gift of feeling divinely what the animal, vegetable, and mineral world only feel materially, man in whom the electrical attraction is transformed to a consciousness in his intelligence, felt and understood, man alone, I say, takes upon himself to regard this miracle which is simultaneously accomplished in his body and soul as a miserable necessity, speaking of it with scorn, iron, and shame! It is very strange. And this way of separating spirit and flesh has simply resulted in the establishment of monasteries and brothels.

It was an astonishing outburst. Sand had made the first move toward intimacy and Chopin had rebuffed her, a situation that probably made him all the more desirable in her eyes. The letter allowed her to clarify her thoughts, of course, but there remained the problem of poor Mallefille, at this moment blissfully unaware that he was about to be thrown aside. Sand had always claimed that she could handle Mallefille, that he was simply a piece of "yielding wax on which I have set the imprint of my seal, and when I want to change the superscription, I shall, if I go carefully and have patience, succeed."[27] To give herself a bit more time to "change the superscription," she sent her piece of "yielding wax" on a two-week trip down the Seine in the company of Maurice, where they lingered in Rouen and Le Havre while she decided how best to deny Mallefille access to her bedroom once he got back. She resolved to treat him to one of her homilies on the advantages of friendship over physical love, and hoped that he

27. Ibid., p. 409.

might see reason as she removed him from the lowly rank of lover and promoted him to that rarest and most elevated level of chaste friend and companion. It should have come as no surprise to Sand that when the dramatist's eyes were finally opened to what was going on, he became unhinged. What made his humiliation complete was that a week or two earlier, and innocent of all knowledge that Chopin was the cause of his misfortune, Mallefille had written an effusive essay in honor of the composer that had been published in the *Gazette musicale* and warmly inscribed "To M. Frédéric Chopin, as a proof of my affection for you and my sympathy for your heroic country."[28] Overnight Mallefille was turned into a laughingstock and became dangerous. He prowled around Chopin's apartment on the rue de la Chaussée d'Antin for nights on end, brandishing a dagger, and when he caught Sand leaving Chopin's address he pursued her down the street, forcing her to flee in a passing cabriolet in fear of her life. From melodrama the situation descended into farce. Mallefille pounded on Chopin's door intent on committing physical injury, from which the composer was saved only through the intervention of the burly Grzymała, who stood well over six feet tall and was more than a match for whatever Mallefille could throw at him. Mallefille challenged Chopin to a duel, but was talked out of such an absurd idea by Sand's friends. When Alexandre Rey, another of Maurice's tutors, had the temerity to point out how ridiculous he was becoming, the enraged Mallefille challenged Rey himself to a duel, and sufficient blood was drawn for some sort of satisfaction to be obtained. Eventually Mallefille did what countless abandoned lovers have done before him. He withdrew from the world, took to his bed for a couple of weeks, and drowned in self-pity. In her gleeful summary of the affair, Marie d'Agoult, who had brought Sand and Chopin together in the first place, wrote to a friend, "Confess, now, that is a far better story than any novelist could invent."[29]

---

28. Issue of September 9, 1838.
29. BRRS, p. 152. Georges Lubin makes a passing reference to the duel between Mallefille and Rey in CGS, vol. IV, p. 487. Curtis Cate enlarges on the matter in CS, pp. 457–58.

VIII

By July 1838, Chopin and Sand had become lovers. They still did not live together. In an unusual act of discretion, almost certainly made out of consideration for Chopin, Sand rented a small room in a nearby hotel on the rue Laffitte, using her maiden name, Mme Dupin, and on those nights she did not spend with Chopin she followed her usual routine and worked at her writing desk until breakfast the following morning. In August she persuaded Delacroix to paint them in what has meanwhile become one of the most celebrated portraits in the Chopin iconography. They posed for him in his atelier on the rue des Marais, Saint-Germain. Sand is doing her embroidery while listening to Chopin playing a small upright piano. This context is generally lost because after Delacroix's death the canvas was cut in two and sold at auction. Chopin's half of what was originally a joint portrait came into the possession of the pianist Antoine Marmontel, who later bequeathed it to the Louvre.

George Sand; an oil painting by Delacroix (1838).

Chopin; an oil
painting by Delacroix
(1838).

Although Sand told Delacroix before he left for the country in September, "I am still in the same state of bliss before you left me, and not the smallest cloud darkens our clear sky,"[30] it was an uncertain arrangement. Chopin was nervous of public notoriety and Sand of further menaces from Mallefille. Her life had long been in need of tranquility and the means of acquiring it now seemed more elusive than ever. Many factors continued to roil her. Her judicial separation from Casimir Dudevant, conducted through the district court at La Châtre, had dragged on for months and had drained her resources. The case had been a seamy one, involving charges of assault, lesbianism, the division of property, and good old-fashioned adultery. Sand's subsequent dealings with Casimir in the aftermath of such a public display of their mutual contempt for each other had fretted her nerves and rendered her search for serenity difficult. Still, she had secured Nohant from Casimir's grasp and the courts had granted her custody of the children, which were major victories. Just how much of this mayhem was known to Chopin remains an open question, but the more squalid details were almost certainly kept from him. Sand's friend Charlotte Marliani, the wife of the Spanish consul, proved to be a tower of strength at this difficult time, and in the evenings Sand often went for dinner to Charlotte's place, where she unburdened herself of her load of care.

As the autumn of 1838 approached, what to do and where to go were questions that loomed large. Sand was concerned about Chopin's health and the cough that never left him. She was also worried about Maurice, who was suffering from a form of rheumatism and would, like Chopin, benefit from a milder climate. When Charlotte suggested the Spanish island of Majorca as a solution to these problems, with its warm Mediterranean sunshine, Sand took to the idea. She knew nothing about the island—few people in "civilized" Europe then did—but its mystery was all part of its appeal and once the idea was fixed in her mind she rationalized away every objection.

This trip was to be a honeymoon in everything but name. Majorca was far enough away from Paris to rob gossip of its oxygen, and news of the true nature of the liaison between her and Chopin could be kept from his religious-minded family in Warsaw—at least for a time. Maps were produced and a route was plotted that would take them via Lyon and Nîmes down to Perpignan and Port-Vendres, from where they could board ship to Barcelona and thence to Majorca. Emmanuel Marliani, in his capacity as a Spanish diplomat, provided some letters of introduction that were to prove useful along the way. By mid-October the die was cast. Sand withdrew Solange from her boarding school, picked up Maurice from Delacroix's atelier, where the sixteen-year-old boy had started to take painting lessons from the master, and on October 18 she and the children left Paris on the first stage of their adventure. Chopin stayed behind because he needed a few more days to put his affairs in order. He asked Julian Fontana to take care of the apartment they shared, and he arranged with Pleyel to have a piano shipped out to Majorca; the banker Auguste Léo was also approached for a loan to help cover the expenses of his trip. Only when these matters were settled was Chopin able to follow Sand and the children down to Perpignan.

A WINTER IN MAJORCA,
1838–1839

Another month in Spain and we should have perished there,
Chopin of melancholy and disgust; I of fury and indignation.
                                                    —*George Sand*[1]

I

Chopin left Paris on October 27, and traveling by diligence he caught up with Sand and her children at Perpignan, on November 1. "Chopin arrived looking fresh as a rose and rosy as a turnip," she told Charlotte Marliani, "having borne heroically four nights in the mail coach."[2] At Port-Vendres the small party boarded a steamer that took them down the Catalonian coast to Barcelona, where they put up at the Four Nations hotel while Sand busied herself arranging a passage to Majorca, a delay for which she had not bargained. Spain was in the grip of civil war. Sand knew full well that this conflict, which had already claimed tens of thousands of casualties across the Iberian Peninsula, was in full swing when she planned the route to Majorca. But with typical indifference to the facts, she thought nothing of putting Chopin and her children in harm's way in order to pursue her bliss. On one of their forays into the surrounding countryside, which

1. CGS, vol. IV, p. 577.
2. Ibid., p. 512.

they made on donkeys, they saw detachments of Spanish troops, supporters of Queen Cristina, on their way to Barcelona.[3] These soldiers had
been engaged in battle, and Sand observed that they were haggard, hun-
gry, and exhausted. It was a dangerous situation. Barcelona itself was
heavily fortified with ramparts and gun emplacements, and freedom of
movement was greatly curtailed. At night the sound of gunshots echoed
across the distance, as sentries returned the sporadic fire of the guerril-
las who now roamed the countryside unchecked and were probing the city's
perimeter. For five days the travelers waited in Barcelona, unsure when
they might leave. Meanwhile, they formed connections with the French
consul and even dined aboard a French brig at anchor in the harbor, contacts that were to prove lifesaving when, three months later, the return
journey to the mainland became hazardous.

II

Just after dusk on the evening of November 7, Sand and her entourage
boarded *El Mallorquin*, a small Spanish paddle steamer that plied twice
a week between Barcelona and Palma.[4] After a warm and calm night
crossing, they sailed into Palma Harbor late the following morning under
blue skies and a blazing sun.

While Sand went off in search of lodgings, Chopin and the two
children stood aimlessly on the quayside, arousing the curiosity of the local

---

3. They were almost certainly the defeated remnants of the Battle of Maella (October 1,
1838), in which the royalist army had lost more than three thousand dead and the stragglers
were now heading back to Barcelona. This first "Carlist War" had lasted for nearly six years,
and would not end until 1839, with a roll call of the combined dead and wounded running to
more than 150,000 soldiers.
4. *El Mallorquin*'s modest celebrity as the vessel that transported Chopin and Sand from the
Spanish mainland to Majorca and back invites us to enlarge on its identity. It was built in
Aberdeen by the firm of Duffus & Co. It had a wooden hull lined with copper, weighed 400
metric tons, and was approximately 45 meters long and 9 meters wide. The engine was pow-
ered by two boilers producing 120 horsepower; it was also fitted out with a schooner's sailing
rig. The vessel was delivered to Palma on September 7, 1837, and after various trials it undertook its maiden voyage from Palma to Barcelona on October 6, 1837, carrying twenty-two
passengers, some animals, and local farming produce. Depending on weather conditions, and
the prevailing swell in the Mediterranean Sea, the 220-kilometer journey could take upwards
of twelve hours to complete. The names of Chopin, George Sand, her two children, and her
kitchen maid Amélie are to be found in the ship's passenger list for November 8, 1838.

El Mallorquin, the paddle steamer on which Chopin and George Sand sailed to Majorca; a watercolor by Ramón Sampol Isern.

bystanders. She got back several hours later, having been unable to find suitable quarters. What rented rooms might normally have been available had been taken over by refugees trying to get away from the conflict on the mainland. It was a major setback, and her mood was not helped by the philosophy that prevailed among the islanders, and was proffered to her whichever way she turned, *mucha calma.* The best that she had been able to do was to rent a couple of semifurnished rooms in a disreputable quarter of the town—the Calle de la Marina—the main street leading to the port. It was noisy and dirty, and after a week they left because the rooms were situated over a cooper's workshop and the sound of hammering made it impossible for Sand to work.[5] As for Chopin, he could not work anyway, because the Pleyel piano shipped out for him before he left Paris had not arrived, and without a piano, composing was impossible for him.

Sand was desperate to find fresh accommodation. Although she possessed letters of introduction to the Marquess of Majorca, to the wealthy Canut banking family, and to various other prominent people on the is-

5. SHM, p. 33.

land, nobody seemed willing to help. In her memoirs Madame Hélène Choussat de Canut tells us why.[6] The Majorcans did not know what to make of Sand and her fellow travelers. She was unattached, wrote books, wore trousers, and smoked cigars; and horrors! this woman signed herself with the name of a man—George Sand! She was, moreover, accompanied by two long-haired boys and a young girl who, like her, was dressed in male attire; nor did the group go to church, which meant that their activities were probably immoral. In frustration Sand appealed to the French consul in Palma, Pierre-Hippolyte Flury,[7] who put her in touch with one Señor Gómez, the owner of a picturesque villa at Establiments, just outside Palma, called So'n Vent—a Catalan phrase meaning "House of Winds." The villa was sparsely furnished and like similar dwellings in Majorca it had unglazed open windows, the better to let the balmy air circulate freely through its rooms. It lacked a proper fireplace, but there was a brazier in each room should it become necessary to light a fire. Both Sand and Chopin were pleased with their new dwelling and on November 15 they moved in. That same day Chopin wrote ecstatically to Fontana,

> Here I am at Palma, surrounded by palms, cedars, cactuses, olives, oranges, lemons, aloes, figs, pomegranates, etc., everything that the Jardin des Plantes has in its hothouses. The sky is like turquoise, the sea like lapis lazuli, the mountains like emeralds, the air as in heaven. During the daytime it is sunny and hot, and everyone walks about in summer clothes; at night you hear guitars and singing for hours on end. There are huge balconies overhung with vines; the ramparts date back to the Arabs. Everything, including the town, has an African look. In a word, life is marvelous![8]

Sand settled down to her writing while Chopin went for long walks into the surrounding countryside with Maurice. The exercise did him good, and his health improved to such an extent that Sand eulogized the island, declaring, "It is a Promised Land . . . surpassing all my dreams."[9] Her optimism was premature, however. Paradise quickly turned into purgatory.

---

6. GVM, pp. 54–55; also CHS, pp. 110–12.
7. Often misnamed "Fleury" in the literature.
8. CFC, vol. 2, pp. 265–66; KFC, vol. 1, pp. 327–28.
9. CGS, vol. IV, p. 522.

As Chopin was returning from one of his walks, it started to rain and he went down with bronchitis. The villa became cold and the unglazed windows were now a liability. So were the braziers, which produced a lot of smoke and little heat. The fumes created havoc with Chopin's breathing, and Sand had to bring in a workman to build a Lhomond stove, which could heat the place without the noxious effect. Soon the winter rain was coming down in torrents and the walls began to swell with moisture. Chopin became seriously ill, coughing uncontrollably and spitting blood. Sand called in a doctor to examine him, who unexpectedly turned up with two of his colleagues. Chopin left a droll description of his encounter with this trio of experts.

> I have been as sick as a dog these past two weeks. I caught a cold, despite the eighteen degrees of heat, the roses, oranges, palms, and figs. Three doctors—the most celebrated on the island—have examined me. One sniffed at what I spat, the second tapped where I spat from, and the third sounded me and listened as I spat. The first said that I was going to die, the second that I was about to die, and the third that I was dead already. However, I feel the same as always . . . It was all I could do to stop them from bleeding me or applying blisters and setons . . .[10]

Sand was infuriated when the doctors diagnosed tuberculosis and reported the presence of the disease to the authorities. This disclosure was a requirement under Spanish law, but it had unfortunate consequences. Señor Gómez insisted that his tenants get out, that all the bedding be burned, that the walls be whitewashed and the furniture destroyed. He then presented Sand with the bill. As word spread through Palma of Chopin's condition, they were treated like lepers. Shopkeepers refused to serve Sand with essential provisions and her children were stoned in the streets. It was at this point that she decided they must leave.

A week or two earlier, on one of her first expeditions into the island's interior, Sand had come across a deserted Carthusian monastery in the village of Valldemosa. This fourteenth-century charterhouse, which had recently been secularized, had been taken over by the local authorities and

---

10. CFC, vol. 2, p. 274; KFC, vol. 1, p. 330.

the cells rented out to whoever wished to stay there. Sand took an option on one of them (containing three adjoining modules) for the absurdly low rent of 35 francs annually, with no other thought in mind than that she might escape there from time to time and get on with her writing. Valldemosa now became her best hope. Chopin and Sand piled their personal effects onto a handcart and with the help of a carter began the seventeen-kilometer journey to the monastery. It was December 15. They would remain at Valldemosa for fifty-nine days.

III

Perched halfway up a hillside, about a thousand feet above sea level, the monastery at Valldemosa was difficult to access because roads were non-existent. "Roads are made by torrents and repaired by landslides" was Chopin's wry description. "You can't drive through this way today because it has been plowed up, tomorrow only mules can pass—and you should see the local vehicles!!"[11] Still, once they had taken possession of their unusual abode Chopin and Sand were overcome by the majestic view of the surrounding countryside. Sand declared that it was one of those views that overwhelm one, "because they leave nothing to be desired, nothing to the imagination. Whatever poet and painter might dream, Nature has here created."[12] Their cell, consisting of three adjoining rooms, was simply furnished with camp beds, old tables, wicker chairs, and rush matting strewn across the clay floors. Sand engaged a local village woman, María Antonia, to help with the chores of cleaning and cooking. There was also a young girl, Catalina, who acted as a chambermaid. María Antonia occupied her own cell next to theirs, which acted as a kitchen for the entire family. Sand described her as "light-fingered" and complained that she helped herself to Sand's old clothes as well as to the best things in her larder. María Antonia had a more serious strike against her, however. She had friends in the village and opened up her cell to them whenever there

---

11. CFC, vol. 2, p. 283; KFC, vol. 1, p. 333. The Spanish travel writer José de Vargas Ponce used more dramatic language when describing Majorca's roads: "What they call a road is a string of impassable precipices, and the unfortunate traveler journeying from Palma to the hills of Galatzo is confronted with death at every step . . ." PDM, p. 38.
12. SHM, p. 99.

was something to celebrate. Once she hosted a noisy wedding party for a local farmer, Rafael Torres, and his young bride, during which the guests drank and danced the local *jota* and *fandango* throughout the night, to the accompaniment of an "orchestra" consisting of castanets, a violin, and an out-of-tune mandolin. Sand complained that they had a prostrate invalid next door who required rest, but all they could do was endure the disturbance with *mucha calma*, because the local police would have offered no protection and might well have joined in the merrymaking. There were other disruptions, too. On one occasion a macabre torchlight procession, meant to mark the feast day of Saint Antoni, made its way through the dark cloisters toward María Antonia's cell.[13] Disturbed by the noise of the singing and the clattering castanets, Sand opened the door of her adjoining cell ("a double door of solid oak that protected us"), raised her lantern for greater illumination, and beheld a fearful Lucifer dressed in black and sporting devil's horns, his face painted blood red. He was surrounded by his cohorts—imps wearing birds' heads and horses' tails, with virgin shepherdesses dressed in white and pink. Sand described this bizarre scene as "an ugly masquerade," an uncivilized way to observe a religious festival. She was relieved when "King Beelzebub" addressed her in Spanish, revealing himself to be nothing more than a lawyer with the prosaic name of Jaime Prohens.[14]

Chopin likened his cell to a tall, upright coffin with enormous vaulting. It was a prophetic image. The rains that winter went on for days without end. At night, huddled around the stove, the little party attempted to cheer themselves up by relating the events of the day—a sodden excursion through the surrounding countryside, an encounter with a local villager, the discovery of unusual flora and fauna, and perhaps as a special treat a glance through the portfolio of pictures that Maurice had sketched that day.[15] And all this with the wind howling down the nearby ravine,

13. Sand was confused in calling it a "Shrove Tuesday" celebration, misled no doubt by the colorful costumes worn by the villagers. Saint Antoni's Day, which falls on January 17, is one of the most joyful religious celebrations in Majorca. On that day Chopin received a visit from his Polish compatriot Karol Dembowski, who was on an extended tour of Spain and Portugal, writing a book about the Spanish war that contains a brief description of his meeting with Chopin and Sand. (DDEP, p. 300.) Georges Lubin enlarged on this visit in CGS, vol. IV, p. 559.
14. SHM, p. 110.
15. Some of these drawings have assumed documentary significance, and occupy a prominent place in the Chopin iconography.

The monastery at Valldemosa; a watercolor by Maurice Sand (1839).

and the rain beating mercilessly against the windowpanes. When the downpour eased, a thick mist sometimes rolled down the mountainside, enveloping the monastery in a wintry shroud. Under its cover the eagles and vultures that circled overhead would swoop down and snatch the sparrows perched on the branches of the pomegranate tree just outside Sand's window.

It was a primitive and potentially deadly environment for Chopin, and by mid-December his health had declined to the point that Sand was forced to bring in a doctor from Palma. It was then that the full impact of what she had done by bringing Chopin to Majorca in the first place struck her with force, and the responsibility "weighed like lead on my heart."[16] When the doctor diagnosed tuberculosis, she accused him of making a mistake. She herself claimed, without the benefit of any superior knowledge, that the patient was merely suffering from laryngeal phthisis. She rashly asserted that Chopin "was no more consumptive than I am." It is

16. SHM, p. 149.

indicative of Sand's stubbornness in such matters that even after Chopin's widely reported death from consumption, in 1849, she did not erase these words from her text when it was published in a revised version in 1855, six years after he had expired.[17] She insisted to the end that Chopin's malady was an infection of the larynx. Chopin at first shrank from the regimen that this particular physician recommended: bleeding, starvation, and a milk diet. Sand was warned that unless Chopin was bled he would die. She tells us that an inner voice in turn warned her that only *if* he was bled would he die, so she refused to permit it.

Starvation was tried for a time, but it did not suit Chopin and he abandoned it. He did, however, attempt to follow the prescription of a milk diet, which led to some amusing consequences. There were no cows in the mountains, so Sand procured with difficulty a supply of goat's milk, brought to them in a jug, which she claimed was sampled along the way by the children who delivered it. The miracle was that the jug always seemed to be fuller on arrival at the monastery than on its departure from the village. Sand decided to resolve these "religious phenomena," as she put it, by purchasing a goat, which María Antonia milked daily. To this source of nourishment was added the milk of a long-haired sheep, which kept the goat company. When these liquid supplies in turn began to dry up, the finger of suspicion fell once more on María Antonia, and the animals were placed under lock and key.

Chopin was still without a piano and could not compose. He told Pleyel, "I dream of music but I can't write any because there are no pianos to be had here . . . In that respect it is a primitive country."[18] Even before leaving Palma he had complained to Fontana,

> The only news I have received about my piano is that on December 1 it was loaded onto a merchant vessel at Marseille. I suppose it will spend the winter in port or at anchor, and I shall receive it only when I am ready to leave. That will be delightful, as I shall have the pleasure not only of paying 500 francs duty but of pack-

17. Sand's blunt account of Chopin's deteriorating condition, found in *Un hiver à Majorque*, runs: "We could almost see Death hovering over our heads, waiting to seize the sufferer, whom we were single-handedly battling to keep alive." SHM, pp. 148–49.
18. CFC, vol. 2, p. 271.

ing it up again. Meanwhile, my manuscripts sleep, while I get no
sleep at all. I can only cough, and, covered in poultices, await the
spring or something else.
Palma, 14 December 1838.[19]

At the end of December, Chopin received news that the Pleyel upright had not only been shipped out of Marseille, but had been sitting
in the Palma customs house for more than a week, awaiting clearance
until the import tax ("a huge sum for the damned thing"[20]) had been paid.
The instrument was finally released, hauled up the mountainside to Valldemosa, and installed in Chopin's cell. The presence of a decent keyboard had a transforming effect on him. Until then he had made do with an
inferior local piano, which, in Sand's words, brought him more vexation
than consolation, and had been abandoned in Palma. He quickly put the
finishing touches to his Preludes, and by January 22 had sent the manuscript to Fontana with instructions to make a fair copy for Pleyel, who had
agreed to pay Chopin the large sum of 2,000 francs for the entire set. That
agreement soon started to unravel, as we shall presently discover.

IV

The Preludes are wonderful miniatures, the shortest lasting no more than
forty seconds, the longest lasting five minutes or so. Some of them come
across with the force of an aphorism. They are best described as outcries
and asides, mood pictures ranging from joy to sadness, containing both
sunshine and shadow. Although they can be played separately, and often
are, they sound best when presented as a set. This is clearly what Chopin
intended, because the Preludes unfold all twenty-four major and minor
keys in a rising circle of fifths—with every alternating Prelude in the relative minor key of its predecessor—a feature that is lost whenever we adopt
a smorgasbord approach to these precious cameos, picking and choosing
along the way.

---

19. CFC, vol. 2, p. 278; KFC, vol. 1, p. 332.
20. CFC, vol. 2, p. 285; KFC, vol. 1, p. 333.

1. C major	7. A major	13. F-sharp major	19. E-flat major
2. A minor	8. F-sharp minor	14. E-flat minor	20. C minor
3. G major	9. E major	15. D-flat major	21. B-flat major
4. E minor	10. C-sharp minor	16. B-flat minor	22. G minor
5. D major	11. B major	17. A-flat major	23. F major
6. B minor	12. G-sharp minor	18. F minor	24. D minor

Some of the Preludes had already been composed in Paris, and were brought to Majorca in a portfolio containing his works in progress. Others were still in an embryonic state, mere sketches requiring something more than a final polish before Chopin was satisfied with them. The remainder (at least four of the Preludes) were composed on the island itself.[21] Pleyel, to whom the Preludes were to be dedicated, had already advanced Chopin 500 francs against their completion, and Chopin's chief priority was to fulfill the commission without delay.

When Sand began to rearrange her memories and offer the world her own account of their stay in Valldemosa, she described Chopin as "a detestable patient."[22] Nor could the novelist in her refrain from offering her readers some lurid descriptions of the gloom into which Chopin sometimes sank, and the anxieties from which he suffered. She and the children loved to explore the deserted monastery at night, walking through the dark and silent cloisters, which were illuminated only by moonlight or a couple of candles they brought along with them. For them it was an adventure. For Chopin those same cloisters were filled with phantoms and terrors, she reports. Very often she and the children returned from their nocturnal ramblings at ten in the evening, only to find Chopin in a state of near terror, sitting at the keyboard, "his eyes struck with dread, and his hair standing on end."[23] Then, when he had recognized them, he would play whatever

---

21. Scholarship is in disarray when it comes to a more precise understanding of the chronology of the Preludes. We know with certainty that the one in A major had been composed as early as 1836, because Chopin had already copied it into an album belonging to Delfina Potocka. Likewise, the A-flat major Prelude dates from no later than 1837, the year he asked Fontana to make a copy of the piece so that he could pass it along to Count Léon de Perthuis, an aide to King Louis-Philippe. Maurice Brown's "Index" identifies four Preludes composed in their entirety on Majorca: no. 2 in A minor, no. 4 in E minor, no. 10 in C-sharp minor, and no. 21 in B-flat major respectively. See Index nos. 107 and 123.
22. SHV, vol. 2, pp. 419–20.
23. Ibid., p. 419.

he had just composed—"the terrible and heart-rending obsessions which had stolen over him in that hour of loneliness, sorrow, and fright." When reading such passages, we do well to recall that they were penned more than fifteen years after the events they purport to describe, after Chopin had died and was no longer able to dispute them. Sand goes even further when she attempts to describe the genesis of the Preludes, and she writes of one incident that has gained wide currency in the literature. She tells us that she and Maurice went to Palma to purchase some provisions. The rains came down in torrents that day and turned the rocky paths into overflowing rivers. Abandoned by their cart driver, they arrived back at the monastery after nightfall, shoeless and soaked to the skin. There they found Chopin in a state of despair, convinced that they were dead. Tormented by imaginary ghosts, he sat at the piano and saw himself drowned in a lake—"heavy, icy drops, falling rhythmically on his chest." Thus was the famous "Raindrop" Prelude born, according to Sand. "His composition that evening was full of raindrops resonating on the tiles of the monastery," she wrote.[24]

The repeated A-flats (heard by Sand as raindrops) become enharmonically changed into G-sharps in the middle section of this Prelude, and take on a brooding, ominous character.

24. Ibid., p. 420.

When Sand pointed out to Chopin that in his distress he had uncon-
sciously incorporated into his music the sounds of water dripping onto the
roof—she called it "imitative harmony"—he protested against the naïveté
of such an idea, of thinking that his notes copied the sounds of nature.[25]
Nonetheless it is Sand's account of the birth of this piece that is retailed
whenever it is played, rather than Chopin's denial of it.

Liszt always maintained that it was the F-sharp minor Prelude to
which the appellation "Raindrop" should be applied. His choice remains
enigmatic and has never had much support from Chopin scholars.
Rather it is Sand's vivid description of the eagles and vultures circling
on the thermal currents around Valldemosa's mountaintops, the better
to swoop on their prey, that has once again captured posterity's imagination. Chopin, as usual, is silent on such matters and lets the music
speak for itself.

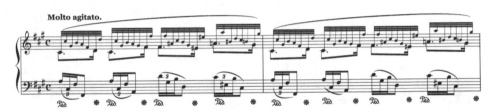

No mention of the Preludes, however cursory, can overlook the
second one, in A minor, one of Chopin's most desolate creations. This
brief utterance of twenty-three measures begins in the "wrong" key of E
minor, then slowly wends its way through G major and D major before
finally coming to its fateful rest in the cold key of A minor. And all the
while it features a left-hand accompaniment containing some of the most
grinding dissonances in the whole of Chopin. If there is anything to the
idea that music is a direct expression of the life of the mind, then this
Prelude reflects to perfection the dark moods into which Chopin sometimes descended while living in his "coffin cell" at the Valldemosa
monastery.

---

25. SHV, vol. 2, p. 421. Sand's translator the poet Robert Graves, who lived in Majorca for
more than half a century, issued a dissenting footnote on the matter. "This proves to have
been impossible," he wrote. The architecture of the charterhouse would have prevented her
from hearing anything more than "rain dripping from the roof into the garden." SHM, p. 171.

If we wish to gain a healthier impression of Chopin's state of mind at this time, one that is more firmly grounded in reality than that provided by Sand, we have only to turn to his correspondence. It contains not a word about "phantoms and terrors," or water drops for that matter. Chopin was preoccupied with problems more secular than satanic. The financial agreement that he had reached with Pleyel regarding the sale of the Preludes had started to founder, causing him some vexation. Lurking beneath the surface was the fact that Chopin was having difficulty in paying his share of the Majorcan expenses. The day before he left Paris he had secured an advance of 1,000 francs from the banker Auguste Léo in order to help defray the costs of the trip, but Léo was now pressing Chopin (through Fontana) to repay the loan. The only way that Chopin could settle the debt was by diverting to Léo money owed him by Pleyel for the Preludes, but Pleyel was reluctant to increase the advance he had already forwarded to Chopin, because the bill for the piano was still unpaid. Chopin now developed what can only be described as a Machiavellian plan to turn matters to his personal advantage, and the long-suffering Fontana was charged with the unpleasant task of carrying everything out. Chopin instructed Fontana to bypass Pleyel if the latter continued to procrastinate, and offer the Preludes to other publishers, including Heinrich Probst (the Paris-based agent for Breitkopf and Härtel in Germany), Maurice Schlesinger in France, and Christian Wessel in England. In order to make the offer more attractive to Schlesinger he dangled the prospect of further manuscripts to come, including the second Ballade and the Two Polonaises, op. 40. Chopin, in fact, was infuriated by this money mix-up, involving Pleyel, Léo, and Schlesinger, which drew from him some blistering anti-Semitic comments. "Léo is a Jew! . . . I'll send [him] a short open letter with my thanks which he can swallow right down to his heels (or wherever you like). Scoundrel!" And later on, with particular reference to Schlesinger and Probst, "All these lice bite me less where I am now."[26] Two months later he was still venting his frustration. "If we have to deal with Jews let it at least be with the orthodox ones."[27] And the tirade continued in a separate letter to Grzymała: "Jews will be Jews and Huns will be Huns—that's the truth but what can one do? I am forced to deal with them."[28] This picture of Chopin as an anti-Semite, railing against his Jewish publishers for wanting their pound of flesh, stands in contrast to the received image of him as a rarefied dandy, disdaining to sully his hands with the grime of filthy lucre.[29]

V

It has often been remarked, without much reason, that the Majorca episode was one of the most unproductive periods in Chopin's life. Yet he not only finished the Preludes there but one or two other important works besides, including the Ballade in F major, op. 38, to which he attached a new ending, and the Polonaise in C minor, op. 40, no. 2.[30]

---

26. CFC, vol. 2, p. 284; KFC, vol. 1, p. 333.

27. CFC, vol. 2, p. 307; KFC, vol. 1, p. 339.

28. CFC, vol. 2, p. 309; KFC, vol. 1, p. 341.

29. It is not easy to disentangle the complications surrounding the publication of the Preludes, but the final outcome was this: they eventually appeared in three separate editions, much to Chopin's financial advantage: in Germany (Breitkopf and Härtel, 1839); in France (Adolphe Catelin, 1839); and in England (Wessel, 1840). Pleyel evidently withdrew from the whole thing, selling his rights in these pieces to Catelin, although both the French and the English editions are dedicated to him. These contracts netted Chopin a combined sum of 2,500 francs, after the cost of the Pleyel piano had been deducted. For the second Ballade he demanded a further 1,000 francs, and for the Two Polonaises, op. 40, the sum of 1,500 francs. These and other details may be gleaned from two letters that Chopin wrote on the same day, January 22, to Pleyel and Fontana. (CFC, vol. 2, pp. 287–88.) The German edition was dedicated to Joseph Kessler, the pianist and composer whom Chopin had known and admired in Warsaw. It is worth recalling that Kessler had dedicated his own set of Twenty-four Preludes, op. 31, to Chopin, when the Italian edition came out in Milan, in 1835. Kessler's pieces are generally understood to have provided the antecedents for Chopin's own set of Preludes, for they, too, are composed in all the major and minor keys, albeit in random order, and also take the form of fleeting aphorisms. An even closer link with Kessler may be found in the latter's Twenty-four Etudes, op. 20 (composed in 1825), which move through all the major and their relative minor keys in a *descending* circle of fifths—that is, in the opposite direction from Chopin's Preludes. Chopin is known to have attended the musical soirées that Kessler put on in his home in Warsaw after the latter had settled there in 1829, and it is likely that Chopin heard him play these études at that time.

30. The Polonaises in A major and C minor, op. 40, nos. 1 and 2, were dedicated to Julian Fontana. The one in A major had already been completed in Paris and was originally intended for Tytus Woyciechowski; but in the end Chopin placed Fontana's name on both works. When Fontana received the manuscripts for copying in readiness for publication, he

One composition of unquestioned genius to emerge from the Majorca trip was the Scherzo no. 3, in C-sharp minor, op. 39, to which Chopin put the finishing touches after he got back to the mainland. It is dedicated to Chopin's pupil Adolf Gutmann, perhaps because of its powerful octave passages on the opening page—the sort of keyboard technique in which Gutmann was said to excel. For the rest, the Scherzo is full of musical wonders. The opening is keyless—one is tempted to describe it as atonal—as it searches for the home key of the piece.

And when that home key arrives, it does so, in the words of the composer Alan Rawsthorne, with the abruptness of someone switching on the light.[31]

was bold enough to ask Chopin to change the middle section of the one in C minor. It is one of the rare occasions on which the mature Chopin accepted the criticism and agreed to make revisions. "I will go on altering the second half of the Polonaise for you until I die," wrote Chopin, in a burst of gratitude for all the mundane chores that his friend was presently carrying out for him in Paris. "Perhaps you won't like yesterday's version of it either—although I racked my brains on it for about 80 seconds." CFC, vol. 2, p. 371; KFC, vol. 1, p. 365.

31. WFC, p. 69.

The chorale-like melody in the middle section seems to conjure up the image of a procession of monks, chanting as they move through the deserted cloisters of a monastery. Enthroned in the middle register of the keyboard, each phrase ending of this chorale is adorned with showers of notes that come cascading from above—diamond dust settling on holy robes. The effect is memorable and is vintage Chopin.

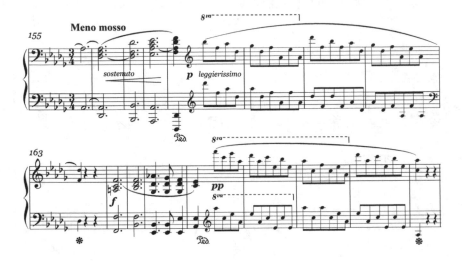

From time to time fragments of plainchant come drifting through those same cloisters, as if a distant door had been opened to reveal monks at prayer.

The scherzos that we find in the sonatas of Chopin are clearly modeled on the old minuet and trio movements contained in the sonatas and symphonies of Haydn, Mozart, and Beethoven. But his four independent scherzos are better understood as modifications of sonata form itself. The internal structural divisions separating "minuet" from "trio" are swept aside, and we are proffered instead exposition and development sections akin to those in a full-fledged sonata form. The Coda of the present Scherzo is 110 measures long, by far the longest section of the work, and amounts to a climactic summing-up of what has gone before. Its paramount feature is a return of the earlier chorale, transformed through apotheosis, during which Chopin "lets the glory in."

It is a stimulating exercise for one's sense of form to hear this example (twelve bars, 542–54) unfolding across its model (twelve bars, 155–67) with metrical exactitude. The idea that Chopin was a simple miniaturist who could not control large-scale structure has no dominion.

VI

By the first week of February 1839 it had become clear that Chopin was so gravely ill he would be unable to tolerate another month of rain and cold, so Sand made plans for their return to the mainland. Her earlier dream of staying on the island for an extended period and finding a peaceful environment in which her writing might flourish had come to nought. On February 12 the party set out on a nightmare descent through the mud and rubble that was now the only way down the mountainside to Palma. Because no one from the village would rent them a carriage for fear of infection, Chopin had to make the hazardous journey in an open two-wheeled cart, known locally as a *birlocho*, drawn by a donkey, a debilitating experience that caused him to hemorrhage violently. The following day, the bedraggled party boarded the steamer *El Mallorquin* at anchor in Palma and made the twelve-hour sea crossing back to Barcelona.[32] As they went

32. CGS, vol. IV, p. 475. The subsequent fate of the Pleyel piano on which Chopin had brought to life his recent music is worth relating, because the facts surrounding its history are

on board, they met with an unpleasant surprise. No one had told them that
the vessel regularly transported a cargo of a hundred or more hogs to the

---

almost stranger than fiction. Within fifty years of his visit to the Valldemosa monastery, the
inevitable process of romancing the entire dreadful episode had begun. The cell where Sand
and Chopin lived had become a shrine for the faithful and was attracting pilgrims from
across the world. In 1917, Bartolomeu Ferrà opened a Chopin Museum in cell no. 2, which he
rented at that time and later owned, and which he claimed had been occupied by the composer, the centerpiece of which was an upright piano declared to have been the one used by
Chopin. No one could deny it, because by now all the key players in the story were dead.
Across the years millions of tourists visited this museum, and paid good money for the privilege of entering "Chopin's cell" containing "Chopin's piano." Some came in silent homage;
some came to place flowers on the keyboard; others—including some of the leading concert
pianists of the day—came to play on this instrument in order to attach themselves to a golden
thread that would connect them to Chopin. We now know that they were not only worshipping
at the wrong shrine but worshipping a graven image as well. In 2011 both the piano and the cell
in which it was exhibited were declared by a judge of the mercantile court in Palma to have no
connection to Chopin, and all claims to the contrary were deemed to be "fraudulent." Among
the findings was one that sent ripples of disbelief across the world of music. The piano in cell
no. 2 was not even built, by the Spanish firm of Oliver y Suau, until the 1850s, years after
Chopin's death. But who had brought the lawsuit, and why?
    Just hours before they left Palma, Sand had managed to sell the Pleyel piano to the
banker Bazile Canut for the handsome sum of 1,200 francs, and the debt to Camille Pleyel
was discharged. The instrument eventually passed into the possession of Gabriel Quetglas
Amengual, an industrialist who owned cell no. 4 of the Valldemosa monastery. A cloud of uncertainty naturally hovered over the provenance of the piano, and for good reason. Three
generations had passed and the paper trail was obscure. Édouard Ganche traveled to Valldemosa in an effort to identify Chopin's cell and establish the provenance of its piano. After a
careful examination he concluded that the piano owned by the Quetglas family was without
doubt the one that Pleyel had sent to Chopin (the instrument bears the serial number 6668,
which also appears in the Pleyel factory's registry book). Ganche published his findings in the
journal *La Pologne*, June–July 1932. That same year Gabriel Quetglas Amengual set up his
own Chopin Museum in competition with that of the Ferrà family. For many years the two
families continued to feud over the matter, but it was the instrument owned by the Ferrà
family, perhaps because of superior marketing skill and the impressive collection of manuscripts that adorned their museum, that tourists continued to flock to see. By 2010, the Chopin
bicentennial year, the Quetglas family had had enough and went to court. The official assigned
to the case, Judge Catalina Munar of the Second Mercantile Court in Palma, went to the
monastery to examine the place for herself. She studied a number of documents, including
letters to and from George Sand about the rental of the cell and its furniture, and also some
drawings by Maurice Sand, which could only have been done from Chopin's cell because of
the view they revealed beyond its windows. Judge Munar concluded that cell no. 4, owned by
the Quetglas family, was Chopin's cell. She also condemned the piano exhibited in cell no 2,
hitherto admired by the world as the recipient of the Preludes and the Third Scherzo, describing it as "a poor Majorcan piano of inferior make" never having been played by the composer.
(The full text of the judgment is preserved in Palma's mercantile court records under the sentence number 00023/January 31, 2011. The Ferrà family tried to have this verdict overturned,
but it was upheld by a panel of three appellate judges in Palma, sentence number 00332/Octo-
ber 19, 2011.) If there is a moral to the tale it is this: the rush to purchase proximity to genius
can so easily lead one astray that it is often better to keep one's money in one's pocket.

mainland, and because the animals required fresh air they were given the run of the open deck. Hogs were Majorca's chief export, and on its return journey to Barcelona *El Mallorquin* gave hogs priority over passengers. The ship's captain, Gabriel Medina, obliged Sand and Chopin to stay in their cabins below deck, where the atmosphere was stifling. The foul stench became unbearable and Chopin could not sleep. He began, in Sand's graphic words, "spitting bowlfuls of blood," and she became thoroughly alarmed at his condition. Around midnight she reported that they were awakened by the cracking of whips being used by the crew against the animals, in order to keep them moving. This was supposed to prevent the hogs from succumbing to *mal de mer* and making the fetid conditions on deck still worse.[33] Even after the ship cast anchor in the shallow waters off Barcelona, the passengers remained confined to their cabins until the last of the hogs had been herded off the rolling vessel and onto the small boats waiting to transfer them to shore. Only after these "gentlemen" had left the ship (to use Sand's mordant description) were the human beings allowed to set foot on dry land. There was an altercation with the captain, who insisted that the bed on which Chopin had slept should be burned, and he charged Sand double its true cost. While they were bargaining, Sand tossed a coin and a note to a passing fisherman, begging him to row over to a French brig-of-war, the *Méléagre*, that she had spotted at anchor in the bay. In an act of chivalry appreciated by Sand, the captain himself came over in response to her plea and transferred the party to his own vessel, where Chopin was at once treated by the ship's surgeon, who managed to stop the hemorrhaging and in Sand's words "reanimated him."[34]

Back on the Spanish mainland, they spent the next few days exploring the countryside around Barcelona, and even went on an excursion to the fishing village of Arenys de Mar, a trip that slowly brought about an improvement in Chopin's health. Finally, on February 21, they were able to board a splendid French steamer, *Le Phénicien*, bound for Marseille. As they stepped on deck, Sand and her children shouted, "*Vive la France!*"

---

33. SHM, p. 26. Robert Graves once more disputes this part of Sand's account and claims that what she heard was the whacking noise of the waves against the sides of the ship once the southern headland had been cleared.
34. The name of the surgeon who "reanimated" Chopin was Jacques-Hubert Costa. The names of the three doctors who treated Chopin on Majorca remain unknown.

From Barcelona they sailed across the Gulf of Lion, a voyage of thirty-six hours, during which the vessel pitched and rolled alarmingly. They finally docked at Marseille on February 25, and Sand lost no time in bringing in the physician Dr. François Cauvière, a friend of the Marlianis, who examined Chopin and extended some excellent care. Cauvière diagnosed Chopin's condition as extremely serious and had him stay in his home, 71 rue de Rome, for a couple of days. With the onset of warmer weather, and the regimen of the milk-rich diet that Cauvière prescribed, Chopin's health improved to such an extent that Sand could write to Charlotte Marliani, "He is much, much better . . . He has stopped spitting blood, sleeps well, coughs but little, and, above all, he is in France! He can sleep in a bed that will not be burned because he has used it. No one draws back when he proffers his hand."[35]

VII

The distressing experiences that Sand and Chopin endured in Majorca continued to fester in her imagination. She purged them in the only way that she knew, by writing about them and inviting the whole world to share her pain. Although she had brought many of these misfortunes on herself, someone else had to be held accountable. Her book *Un hiver à Majorque* makes plain on every page that it was the fault of the Majorcans themselves, and no one else's. Looking back on the ten-week sojourn on their island, she wrote: "Another month in Spain and we should have perished there, Chopin of melancholy and disgust; I of fury and indignation. They wounded me in the most sensitive spot in my heart, under my very eyes they pierced a suffering person with pinpricks. I shall never forgive them, and if I ever write about them it shall be with venom."[36] And it was venom into which she dipped her pen and settled her account with this "stupid, thieving, and bigoted race." The first version of the text was written at Nohant in the months that followed. In it she describes the 160,000 islanders as cowards, hypocrites, and pickpockets, and even likens them to Indian monkeys and Polynesian savages. She also implies that the

---

35. CGS, vol. IV, p. 578.
36. Ibid.

monks of Valldemosa had in earlier years fathered most of the villagers by impregnating the local women. "Can it be only twenty years since the monks ceased to interfere with the privacy of the home?" she asked archly after observing the uniform physiognomy of the younger generation of the islanders, confident that she knew the answer. Whether she showed her jeremiad to Chopin while it was still a work in progress is not known. In any case, when the installments began to appear in the *Revue des deux mondes*, in January 1841, he must have read them and been relieved to know that he was nowhere mentioned by name, even though his inner circle of friends understood very well where he had been, and with whom.[37] There was at the moment no question of continuing on to Nohant—their eventual destination. Chopin was too weak to face such a journey, and Sand herself was by no means certain how to resolve the issue of their *ménage à deux*. Their friends in Paris were abuzz with questions about how the lovers of Majorca would present themselves to the world now that they were back in France. So she temporarily moved her entire "family" into the Hôtel de Beauvau, in Marseille, while considering what to do, and proceeded to cover up to twenty pages a day with prose, working through the night. There she revised her novels *Lélia* and *Spiridion*, which she had brought back with her from Majorca, despite the constant interruptions from her children and from casual sightseers—"the time-

---

37. Nor does Chopin's name appear in the various editions of the book itself, the first of which was published in 1842 by the firm of Hippolyte Souverain, Paris. The nearest Sand comes to identifying Chopin is in such oblique phrases as "a member of our family, who had a delicate constitution and suffered from a serious inflammation of the larynx." (SHM, p. 46.) That Sand took care to wrap Chopin in a mantle of anonymity was a decision not hard to fathom. We recall that they went to Majorca in part to hide their intimate relationship from society, but also to spare Chopin's family in Warsaw, who might now be embarrassed to read details of a "honeymoon" gone so badly awry. Sand's purpose in writing *Un hiver à Majorque* was not to claim Chopin as her latest lover, but to settle her grievances with the Majorcans. And on this last point she may have bitten off more than she could chew. Not generally known is the "Refutation of George Sand," a vigorous rebuttal of her impressions of Majorca, written by the longtime Majorca resident and intellectual Don José Quodrado, who published a detailed response to Sand's text in *La Palma: A Weekly Journal of History and Literature*, on May 5, 1841. The article is worth anyone's time to read because it represents a balanced reply to Sand's more hostile descriptions of the island and its people. M. Quodrado allowed himself to end his reproaches with words he later appeared to regret because, as he put it, he feared he might have debased himself by using similar language to Sand herself: "George Sand is the most immoral of writers, and Madame Dudevant the most obscene of women." Whether Sand ever read the obscure magazine is not known. At any rate, she never responded to it in later editions of her book.

wasters, the curious, the literary hangers-on," as she described them—who besieged her door while she continued to nurse the patient. Chopin himself was reasonably content because he daily felt much better, and on the piano they installed in the hotel for him "he kept boredom at bay, and brought poetry into our lodgings," in Sand's eloquent words.[38]

Did Chopin make a will before setting out for Majorca? There is a strong hint that he may have done so in a letter that he addressed to Fontana while resting at the Hôtel de Beauvau. After instructing Fontana to carry out a variety of chores for him, including disposing of his furniture should he decide not to return to Paris, Chopin continues, "I told you that in my desk, in the first drawer next to the door, there is a letter which you, Grzymała, or Jan [Matuszyński] might unseal. I now ask you, please, to take it out and burn it *without reading it*. I adjure you, in the name of our friendship, to do this—the document serves no purpose now."[39] We do not know what the document contained, nor do we know its date, and since no trace of it has ever been found we are left to conclude that Fontana burned it. But whatever was expressed in that letter Chopin's return from Majorca had made null and void. It is one more loss that his biographers have cause to lament.

VIII

During the second week of March 1839, while he was still recuperating in Marseille, Chopin received news that the celebrated tenor Adolphe Nourrit had committed suicide by flinging himself from a third-floor window of the Hotel Barbaie in Naples. He was only thirty-seven years old and left a grieving widow with six young children and a seventh still in the womb. For years Nourrit had been the leading tenor at the Paris Opera, and he was among Chopin's favorite singers. He had quarreled with the administration after they brought in another tenor, Gilbert-Louis Duprez, with whom he refused to share top billing. In 1837, Nourrit had moved to the San Carlo opera house in Naples, in an attempt to shore up his career, but he fell into depression when his voice started to show signs of

---

38. CGS, vol. IV, p. 625.
39. CFC, vol. 2, p. 305; KFC, vol. 1, p. 337.

wear. His memory also began to fail—a possible consequence of his growing dependence on alcohol. During the early hours of March 8, after taking part in a benefit concert the previous evening that he feared had not gone well, Nourrit had jumped to his death. His body was brought back to Marseille, en route to Paris for its final burial, and on April 24 a requiem mass was held in the small church of Notre-Dame-du-Mont. Madame Nourrit asked Chopin to play the organ during the service. In a letter to Fontana, dated April 25, Chopin wrote: "Yesterday I played the organ for Nourrit, so it shows that I am better . . . His body was brought here on its way to Paris; there was a requiem mass for him, and the family asked me to play, so I played during the Elevation."[40]

Sand had some caustic things to say about the way the service was conducted. The bishop was ill-disposed to take part, perhaps because of the circumstances of Nourrit's death, and she wondered if the choir had been deliberately instructed to sing out of tune. The poor organ she described as "a false, screaming instrument—its wind had no other purpose except to blow it out of tune." Chopin, she claimed, sacrificed himself on this instrument by playing Schubert's *Die Gestirne* (The Stars), a favorite with Nourrit in earlier years, but the organ would not allow him to perform the song in the glorious and exalted manner of Nourrit, as she expressed it. So he used the less discordant stops of the instrument and played the piece "with a plaintive sound as soft as an echo from another world."[41] Sand was incensed that many members of the large congregation, who had been relieved of a 50-centime admission charge at the door, had come expressly to hear Chopin and were disappointed with the small sound of the instrument, expecting him to raise the rafters. She further complained that neither she nor Chopin could be seen, because they were hidden out of sight in the organ loft—as if the congregation had come to see them and regarded Nourrit's corpse as an irrelevance.

Throughout March and April, Chopin continued to be plagued by money problems, and the sale of his Majorcan manuscripts had come to dominate his correspondence with both Fontana and Grzymała. It is clear that Sand was still paying most of the bills, a situation that Chopin wanted to remedy. His financial position was complicated by the fact that the

40. CFC, vol. 2, pp. 328–29; KFC, vol. 2, p. 347.
41. CGS, vol. IV, p. 645.

money he had earlier loaned Antoni Wodziński had not been repaid. In a letter written from Marseille on March 2 he mentioned the matter to Fontana, choosing not to mince words. "If Antek goes without paying back my money, it will be quite a Polish trick—I mean the trick of a *stupid* Pole—but don't tell him I said so."[42] He may also have written to the Wodziński family in Warsaw about the matter, a fact we deduce from a further letter to Fontana written about ten days later. "Antek's parents must be terribly forgetful to let such a thing come to pass between him and me [a reference to his broken engagement to Maria, which Antoni may have used as a reason to dishonor the debt]. Between ourselves he has gone off without paying the money he owed me. What worthless people. They have no scruples and they lack heart!"[43]

IX

Thanks to the warm spring sunshine bathing Marseille, together with the devoted care of Dr. Cauvière, Chopin started to regain his strength. By early May he was well enough for Sand to arrange a short trip with her "family" to Genoa. Chopin at first declined to join them, fearing that he could not withstand another Majorca fiasco. But as the warmer weather approached he changed his mind and looked forward to seeing Italy for the first time, a country to which he had once thought of moving during the unsettled days following the Warsaw Uprising. As for Sand, she harbored some nostalgic memories of an earlier visit to Genoa in the company of her old flame Alfred de Musset, in the autumn of 1833 at the height of their romance. On May 3, Sand, her two children, and Chopin boarded the paddle steamer *Pharomond* for the sea crossing to the picturesque Italian port. For ten days Sand and the children explored the city, admiring the architecture of its palaces, visiting its galleries, contemplating its paintings and sculptures, and enjoying some magnificent views of the surrounding coastline. It is doubtful that Chopin kept pace with such physical activity, but this short stay in Italy lifted his spirits.

All that changed during the sea crossing back to Marseille on May 16

---

42. CFC, vol. 2, p. 305; KFC, vol. 1, p. 337.
43. CFC, vol. 2, pp. 308–309; KFC, vol. 1, p. 340.

when they ran into a storm. The boat was tossed back and forth, making little headway against the heavy waves, and everyone in the party was seasick. After almost two days at sea, the boat finally docked in port on May 18. Chopin was obliged to rest once more in the home of the ever-attentive Dr. Cauvière, leaving Sand to observe somewhat ruefully, "I do not like journeys anymore; or rather, I am not in a condition to enjoy them."[44] The lovers of Majorca finally left Marseille during the last week of May 1839 and made their way to Nohant in slow stages. They traveled by ferryboat along the Rhône River as far as Arles, where they transferred to a diligence, "sleeping at inns along the way like a good middle-class couple."[45] The honeymoon was over.

44. CGS, vol. IV, p. 655.
45. Ibid.

AT NOHANT, 1839

It seems to me that I am living in a Garden of Eden here.
—*George Sand*[1]

I

Chopin and Sand arrived at Nohant on June 1. She was euphoric to be back and within hours had explored every nook and cranny of the old house, as if to reassure herself that everything was as she had left it, seven months earlier. Nohant enshrined her most precious memories and reverberated with recollections of times past. The rooms containing her grandmother's old furniture, the courtyard, the gardens, the copse of chestnut trees and the wider landscape beyond, all carried their sentimental associations, which she would later weave into the fabric of her autobiography with compelling effect.

Some memories were too deep for tears. Her grandmother slumbered in the local churchyard a stone's throw away, side by side with her father, Maurice Dupin. The body of her infant brother still lay where her parents had buried it in the garden, marked by a pear tree now grown to full stature. Nohant was more than bricks and mortar. For Sand it was a living repository of her past and it gave her strength to go forward. No wonder

---

1. CGS, vol. IV, p. 664.

that within three days of her return she was likening Nohant to a Garden of Eden.

Sand settled into her usual routine, writing through the night until daybreak, and then snatching a few hours' sleep on the small cot near her writing desk. Shortly before noon she would get up and help supervise lunch before joining the others. During the day there might be excursions into La Châtre, a simple picnic on the patio facing the garden, or a ramble down to the banks of the Indre River, which flowed past the Nohant estate less than two kilometers away. Sand also set aside time to educate her two children. While in Majorca she had tried to organize a course of daily lessons for them, but Chopin's illness had got in the way, and the trunkfuls of books she had taken to the island were left largely untouched. In the more peaceful surroundings of Nohant she brought new energy to the task. She refreshed her memory of Greek and Roman history in order to prepare herself for each day's lesson. She also introduced the children to philosophy and art. Maurice, already sixteen years old, absorbed his mother's teaching quickly, and revealed himself to be an apt student. Solange was, in the words of Sand, "a different story." The eleven-year-old girl was an unruly pupil, harboring seeds of rebellion against her mother, which increased with the passing years. Chopin had a softening influence on the girl and started to give her piano lessons. Soon she was able to accompany him in simple four-handed arrangements on the instrument that Sand had installed in the drawing room for Franz Liszt, when he and Marie d'Agoult had stayed at Nohant two years earlier. Chopin did not like this instrument, and it was eventually replaced by a new one from Pleyel.

Chopin at first enjoyed life at Nohant, unfettered as it was by conventional constraints. He was free to organize his time as he wished. He generally retired to bed early and slept while Sand worked. His room was on the upper floor, next to Sand's, and overlooked the garden. He had a commanding view of the surrounding lawns and flower beds, and would have been able to see the two cedar trees that she had planted years earlier, and named Maurice and Solange. Today they tower over the house. His breakfast, consisting of a cup of hot chocolate, was brought to his room, and after he had dressed and attended to his toilette, he would spend the rest of the morning working on his compositions. He rarely joined Sand and the children for their afternoon forays into the neighboring countryside, because he tired easily. His leisurely "walks" around the Nohant

The Nohant château; a photograph taken from the garden side. Chopin's room was on the upper floor, third window from the left.

estate generally took place on a donkey's back, the animal being led by Sand or one of the children. Otherwise he would settle beneath a tree, or pick a few flowers, but such things soon palled and he would return to the house and shut himself away in order to resume work on whatever music he had set aside earlier in the day. One of the first things that Sand did was to bring in Dr. Gustave Papet, a twenty-seven-year-old physician who lived in the neighborhood, to give Chopin a thorough examination. Papet's verdict was reassuring. There was nothing wrong with Chopin, "save for a minor chronic inflammation of the larynx, which he could not promise to cure, but need not cause alarm."[2] One has to wonder whether Papet was telling Sand what she wished to hear or what he thought to be true. Chopin was so weak that he was unable to walk any distance without losing his breath.

Dinner was served at five o'clock, and after the meal was finished the evening hours might be given over to entertainment. Sand often received

2. SHV, vol. 2, p. 425.

visitors, and when the postprandial atmosphere was particularly relaxed it was not difficult to persuade Chopin to play the piano and even amuse the audience with his celebrated mimicries. After enthralling them with his piano playing, he would willfully break the spell he had just created. Glancing in the mirror, he would rearrange his cravat, ruffle his hair, comport his features, and reduce his audience to laughter with imitations, in the words of Sand, "of a phlegmatic Englishman, an impertinent oldster, a sentimental English lady, or a mercenary Jew. They were pathetic types, however comic, but so perfectly rendered that one never tired of wondering at his gift."[3] It was Chopin who began the tradition of putting on pantomimes and plays at Nohant, which were improvised and contained roles for anyone who wanted to take part. These entertainments eventually inspired Maurice Sand to create Nohant's puppet theater, with a cast of characters drawn from the old *commedia dell'arte*—Arlecchino, Pantalone, Il Dottore, and Zanni among them.

II

The unexpected situation in which George Sand now found herself calls for comment. There can be no doubt that when she first conceived the idea of a romantic getaway to Majorca, she believed that this was the beginning of a great adventure of the heart, and she was setting the scene for a very long and passionate love affair with Chopin. Every word that she had uttered and every action that she had undertaken supports this notion. She had always maintained that Chopin's illness, given the right treatment, would go away. But it had not gone away. Within four short months she had been obliged to face a new reality: her role as a lover, such as it now was, had been replaced with that of a caregiver; her self-image as an object of sexual desire had been replaced with that of a sister of mercy. Sand could not have got out of the relationship easily, even if she had wanted to, without appearing heartless and calculating, and she was neither.

Most scholars of the topic are agreed that it was during these first few weeks at Nohant, in the summer of 1839, that Chopin and Sand ceased having sexual relations. The date of June 19 that Sand scratched on the

---

3. Ibid., p. 442.

left-hand panel of the embrasure of her bedroom window (less than three weeks after her return to Nohant) is believed to have been her way of marking her newfound chastity, the day on which she became the "mistress of her own bedroom," so to say. Sand herself declared that from this time she lived like a virgin, "both with him *and with the others*."[4] Many years later she left an account of the sort of life that she faced.

> A kind of terror seized me in the presence of a new duty which I was to take upon me. I was not under the illusion of passion. I had for the artist a kind of maternal adoration which was very warm, very real, but which could not for a moment contend with maternal love, the only chaste feeling which may be passionate.
>
> I was still young enough to have perhaps to contend with love, with passion properly so called. This contingency of my age, of my situation, and of the destiny of artistic women, especially when they have a horror of passing diversions, alarmed me much, and, resolved as I was never to submit to any influence which might divert me from my children, I saw a less, but still possible danger in the tender friendship with which Chopin inspired me.
>
> Well, after reflection, this danger disappeared and even assumed an opposite character—that of a preservative against emotions which I no longer wished to know. One duty more in my life, already so full of and so overburdened with work, appeared to me one chance more to attain the austerity toward which I felt myself attracted with a kind of religious enthusiasm.[5]

Sand here presents herself as a paragon of self-sacrifice, someone who had to struggle to wall herself off from the lusty temptations of the flesh in order to devote herself exclusively to the interests of her children and the genius whom fate had entrusted to her care. Everything we know about Sand suggests that it was not difficult for her to cast off the shackles of hymeneal bondage. This had been her destiny in every affair she had pursued so far, and she was well practiced in the role. Sand's modern biographer Curtis Cate goes so far as to suggest that she found the physical act

---

4. Sand's italics. CGS, vol. VII, pp. 700–701.
5. SHV, vol. 2, p. 433.

of lovemaking with Chopin considerably less exalting than his music, given the uncontrollable bouts of coughing brought on by the slightest exertion of his cadaverous physique.[6] At this point in his life he was so thin that he weighed less than ninety-five pounds. Nobody will ever know what discussions passed between the pair concerning the nature of their new-found platonic relationship, but it would be doing Sand a grave injustice to suppose that there was no discussion at all. We know only the following with certainty: by the summer of 1839 passion had given way to compassion. The sexual chastity that Sand imposed on their relationship was never to be lifted, and there were times when it was a difficult burden for Chopin to bear. At Nohant they occupied separate bedrooms and pursued different itineraries—she writing for most of the night while he slept, he composing for much of the day while she slept. This was the symbiotic relationship that they managed to retrieve, to their vast credit, from the emotional debris of the Majorca disaster. For the next eight years Chopin received from Sand all the maternal care she was so supremely able to offer him. That was a very great deal, and the devotion she brought to the task cannot be dismissed without acknowledgment.

The list of works that Chopin composed while living with Sand is impressive, for it includes some of his greatest creations, among them:

Twelve Mazurkas, opp. 50, 56, 59, 63	Ballade in F minor, op. 52
Six Nocturnes, opp. 48, 55, 62	Polonaise in F-sharp minor, op. 44
Four Waltzes, opp. 42, 64	Polonaise in A-flat major, op. 53
Sonata in B-flat minor, op. 35	Scherzo in E major, op. 54
Sonata in B minor, op. 58	Berceuse, op. 57
Fantaisie in F minor, op. 49	Barcarolle, op. 60
Ballade in A-flat major, op. 47	Polonaise-Fantaisie, op. 61

Many of these pieces were composed either in full or in part at Nohant, and the list is not complete. Sand, in turn, did much of her own best work during the seven summers that she and Chopin lived at Nohant, writing twelve novels, six short stories, and one play—all of which were published during

---

6. CS, pp. 485–86.

the period 1839–46. No other conclusion is possible than that the relation-ship was mutually supportive, of which their work provides eloquent proof.

III

To Sand we owe some of the best insights into Chopin's complex personal-ity. She shrewdly observed of him that "he was a creature of habit, and the slightest change was a terrible thing in his life." He would get upset for days over the least provocation, over the smallest adjustment to his daily routine; but when confronted by something really serious he appeared indifferent to all its consequences, walling himself off. She summed it up in a poetic phrase: "The heave of emotion was out of scale with its spring."[7] There was a darker side, too. Woe betide the person charged with the task of tearing him away from the piano, "more often his torment than his joy," as some-times had to happen when mealtimes arrived or unexpected visitors dis-rupted the general flow of events. On such occasions he could reveal flashes of ill humor best avoided. "Chopin was terrifying when angry, and when, as with me, he contained himself, he looked ready to suffocate and die."[8]

Sand's pen sketch of Chopin's composing process has entered the lexicon.

> His composing was spontaneous, miraculous. He found ideas with-out looking for them, without foreseeing them. They came to his piano, sudden, complete, sublime—or sang in his head while he was taking a walk, and he had to hurry and throw himself at the instru-ment to make himself hear them. But then began a labor more heartbreaking than I have ever seen. This was a series of efforts, of irresolution and impatience to grasp again certain details of the themes he had heard: what he had conceived as a whole he over-analyzed in putting on paper, and his retreat in not recapturing it whole (according to him) threw him into a kind of despair. He shut himself up in his room for whole days, weeping, walking about, breaking his pens, repeating or altering a measure a hun-

---

7. SHV, vol. 2, p. 422.
8. Ibid., p. 447.

dred times, writing it down and erasing it as often, and starting over the next day with a scrupulous and desperate perseverance. He would spend six weeks on one page, only to return to it and write it just as he had on the first draft.[9]

IV

Despite the maternal care that Sand lavished on him, Chopin was often frustrated with daily life at Nohant. "His thirst for rusticity was soon assuaged" was her way of putting it. Whenever he was at Nohant, she said, he yearned for Paris; but once he was in Paris he yearned to be back at Nohant.[10] Some of Sand's rural friends, who had a habit of dropping in unannounced, he could hardly bear. Sand's half brother, Hippolyte Chatiron, who was addicted to the bottle, he found rough and uncouth. Hippolyte's wife, Émilie, who was as subdued as Hippolyte was brash, was a mouselike personality who did even less to elevate Chopin's mood. Sand enshrined her character in a backhanded compliment when she said that Émilie was not bad company—"when she was sleeping."[11] It was not uncommon for Hippolyte to turn up with three or four of the locals in tow. After drawing generously on Sand's hospitality, he and his cohorts would repair to another part of the house, smoking and drinking, and round off the evening with a noisy game of billiards, activities in which Chopin was singularly unfit to participate. He preferred to withdraw into his own world and do what he did best. For part of the summer of 1839 he became absorbed in correcting the Paris edition of Bach's 48. He corrected "not only the engraver's mistakes, but those which are backed by the authority of people who are supposed to understand Bach. Not that I have any pretensions to a deeper understanding, but I do think that I sometimes hit on the right solution. There now—I have gone and boasted!"[12] He made these revisions from memory because he did not have any other edition to hand—one more indication of how thoroughly he knew the 48.

After five weeks at Nohant, Chopin had had enough and on July 8 he

---

9. Ibid., p. 446.
10. Ibid., p. 441.
11. CGS, vol. I, p. 715.
12. CFC, vol. 2, p. 349; KFC, vol. 1, pp. 353–54.

wrote to Grzymała, begging him to drop whatever he was doing in Paris and join them in Nohant. "Take the mail coach as far as Châteauroux. You will get there by noon the next day. From there you will have two and a half hours' ride in the stagecoach that goes to La Châtre . . . Dinner will be ready for you after we have greeted each other warmly." To this Sand added a postscript:

> So there! You fickle husband, we await you in vain. You trifle with our impatience and deceive us with false hopes. You really must come, my dear friend, because we need you. The little one's health is only so-so. As for me, I feel that he needs a little less quiet, solitude, and regularity than life at Nohant offers. Who knows? Perhaps a little trip to Paris. I am prepared to make any sacrifice rather than see him waste away in melancholy.[13]

For some time now Sand and Grzymała had taken to addressing each other in jocular fashion as "Your dear Wife" or "Your dear Husband," with references to Chopin as their "little one," for whose welfare they felt responsible. From this time, too, Sand started to refer to "my three children" and call Chopin her *invalide ordinaire*—her everyday patient—a telling indication of the light in which she now regarded him. It was nothing less than an attempt to rearrange the family circle, to put a new face on it, one that she could present to the outside world once she got back to Paris. Since the relationship had been drained of passion, the right words had to be found to describe what was left. Chopin seemed ready enough to accept his new role, for he reciprocated by coming up with some oblique vocabulary of his own, referring to Sand in his correspondence as "the mistress of the house" or even as "my hostess." This was the sanitized script that they began to rehearse at Nohant during the summer of 1839 so that it was ready to be put into full production, so to speak, once they got back to Paris.

Grzymała arrived at Nohant toward the end of August and stayed for two weeks. It was probably the first time in almost ten months that Chopin had conversed in his mother tongue, and he and Grzymała enjoyed some intimate exchanges in Polish. The children were immensely amused

---

13. CFC, vol. 2, pp. 345–46; KFC, vol. 1, pp. 351–52.

Solange and Maurice Sand;
a drawing by Nancy
Mérienne (1836).

at hearing this Slavic language in full flow. They came and sat by the two friends and tried to imitate certain Polish words, with their rolled "rrr"s and granulated "szczyn"s, breaking into fits of laughter at their failed attempts. During his stay in Nohant, Grzymała would have been fully apprised by Sand of the new situation that she and Chopin now faced. It was Grzymała, in fact, who was charged with the task of finding separate accommodations in the city, in an attempt to help them ease their way back into Parisian society.

Sand was almost as eager as Chopin to return to Paris. Financial considerations loomed large. Nohant was an expensive estate to run, costing her about 1,500 francs a month. Revenue from the land did not begin to meet this figure. She was moreover legally bound to pay Casimir 10,000 francs as part of the final separation settlement, which had guaranteed that Nohant would remain her property. She was also in debt to her half brother, Hippolyte, who had lent her 14,000 francs to help get her out of this financial hole. Her main source of income was from writing—she called it "laying eggs." Ever since her return to Nohant she had worked mainly on her play *Cosima: or Hatred Within Love*, a work that may have been inspired by her declining relationship with Marie d'Agoult, and is named after the second daughter that the runaway countess had borne Franz Liszt eighteen months earlier. Sand now pinned all her hopes on this drama, knowing that were it to succeed she would be able to pay off her debts and balance the books. Her old publisher François Buloz, who had just been appointed manager of the Comédie-Française, was cajoled into traveling down to Nohant to discuss the project. The play, Buloz told her, could go into rehearsal in the New Year, and the premier performance take place in April 1840. These were compelling reasons for Sand to return to Paris without delay. She wanted to meet the actors and supervise the rehearsals.

That Chopin and Sand had already decided not to live together once they got back to Paris is confirmed in a letter that Chopin wrote to Grzymała on September 20, in which he urges his friend to find two separate apartments for them. Hers was to be close enough to his for them to enjoy some intimacy, while at the same time it must enable them to lead separate lives.

> My Dear!
> Rent the small apartment for me, but if we are too late for that then take the large one—it doesn't matter which so long as I have one of the two. As for her apartment, she thinks it is too expensive and she cannot be persuaded that it is better to pay more rather than have a lot of other tenants in the house.[14]

To this Sand added a long postscript, containing a whole series of injunctions. Chopin's rooms had to face south, attracting some essential sunshine. He must also have a separate room for his manservant. As for her apartment, the dining room need not be large, she wrote, because she never entertained more than a dozen people at a time. The children's rooms must have fireplaces but should be located well away from her bedroom. Finally, the whole place should be clean and fresh so that when they arrived they would have nothing more to do than to buy some furniture and move in.

Chopin's biographers have tended to gloss over this arrangement, finding nothing particularly unusual about it. But when placed against the background of the Majorca fiasco and the physical and psychological chaos

---

14. CFC, vol. 2, p. 352; KFC, vol. 1, p. 355.

it had introduced into their lives, we see that it represented a turning point in the relationship. Many factors were at play here, but the obvious (and always unspoken) advantage for Chopin was that his family in Warsaw would continue to be protected against the gossip that would ensue had he decided to openly engage in a *ménage à deux* with Sand.

Five days after dispatching his letter to Grzymała, Chopin wrote another one, to Fontana, enlisting his help in choosing wallpaper (dove gray with dark green borders), buying some new furniture, and getting the old furniture (especially his writing desk and bed) out of storage. Fontana was also charged with engaging the services of a manservant, preferably a Pole, for no more than 80 francs a month, out of which this worthy must buy his own food. The cost of all this was to be paid for with money borrowed from Grzymała. But how to repay him? Chopin had thought of that, too. Fontana must write at once to Wessel in London, saying that Chopin had six new manuscripts for sale at 300 francs each. The long-suffering Fontana carried out his duties manfully, as usual, and by October everything had fallen into place. Chopin would move into 5 rue Tronchet behind the Madeleine Church, while George Sand and her children would rent accommodation nearby, located behind 16 rue Pigalle, which she described as two adjoining pavilions at the far end of a garden.

V

Despite his periodic complaints against the rustic lifestyle imposed on him at Nohant, Chopin brought several works to completion at this time, including the Four Mazurkas, op. 41, the Nocturne in G major, op. 37, no. 2, the Impromptu in F-sharp major, op. 36, and most notably the Sonata in B-flat minor, op. 35. To judge from a letter that Chopin wrote to Fontana, the Sonata was well on the way to completion by early August 1839: "I am writing here a Sonata in B-flat minor that will contain the March that you already know. The Sonata consists of an Allegro, a Scherzo in E-flat minor, the March, and a short Finale—which takes up about three pages of my handwriting. The left and right hands gossip in unison after the March."[15]

---

15. CFC, vol. 2, p. 348; KFC, vol. 1, p. 353. Chopin uses the made-up Polish word *ogadują* in his last sentence ("*Lewa ręka* unisono *z prawą ogadują po marszu*"), which may carry a multiplicity of meanings, including "to gossip with malice" and "to crab, or pull apart." Jeffrey Kallberg has provided a discerning commentary on these distinctions, in KCM, p. 4.

Chopin's passing mention of "the March that you already know" refers to the celebrated Funeral March, which had been in his portfolio for two years, and was now elevated to the role of the Sonata's slow movement. When Robert Schumann reviewed the work, shortly after its publication in 1840, he was bothered by the seeming lack of unity among the movements, and went so far as to call Chopin's use of the word "sonata" to describe the work as "capricious, if not downright presumptuous." And in a phrase that has become famous in the annals of music criticism he told his readers, "Chopin has here tied together four of his most unruly children," accusing him of smuggling four separate pieces "into places that they could otherwise never have reached."[16]

Chopin provides no tempo marks for either the opening four-bar introduction ("Grave") or for the first-movement sonata form that follows it. He tells us only that the latter should be played "Doppio movimento," or double the speed of the former, indicating that there is a precise relationship between them. This has led some observers to proclaim a mystery where none actually exists.[17] If we read Chopin's letter to Fontana, we know that he conceived the exposition as an Allegro, which determines the speed of the introduction.

The first subject, marked *agitato*, establishes the turbulence that underlies most of this movement and provides much of the material on which

16. *NZfM*, February 1, 1841.
17. WFC, pp. 158–59.

the development is to be based. It modulates without the assistance of any definable transition section straight into the second subject, which is cast in the key of the relative major and presents two quite distinct themes, (a) and (b).

(a)

The first of these themes was about the only thing in the Sonata that Schumann thought praiseworthy, finding that its continuation "could almost have been written by Bellini." A subsidiary theme returns to the general agitation that informs this movement.

(b)

In recent years some learned discussion has hovered over the question of what to do about the repeat of the exposition. Does the pianist go back to the beginning of the Sonata and play the four-bar "Grave" introduction again, or go back just to the "Doppio movimento," thereby excluding it? Convention has always come down firmly on the side of the latter decision, and so have most of the published editions, with one or two notable exceptions. The only surviving manuscript (a copy in the hand of Adolf Gutmann) raises doubts and could be said to support either side of the argument. Brahms was the editor of the sonatas for the celebrated Breitkopf and Härtel Complete Edition (1878–80), and it was Brahms who, invariably scrupulous in such matters and working from this manuscript, decided

Manuscript page of the Sonata in B-flat minor, op. 35, showing the opening measures. A copy in the hand of Adolf Gutmann.

that the double bar at the beginning of the "Doppio movimento" section was not a repeat sign because it lacked the necessary dots. The controversy gained ground in recent years when the authoritative Polish National Edition went beyond Brahms and eliminated the double bar entirely, and with it all traces of the problem. This conundrum, which is of no more than marginal interest to the biographer, is naturally of great importance to the player. After all, several generations of pianists have never included the introduction as part of the exposition's repeat, as their recordings show; and it is no small thing to change a major feature of one of the pianistic masterworks of the nineteenth century. We reproduce the only extant copy of the manuscript so that the reader may ponder for himself what Chopin's editors thought he may have had in mind.[18]

At the climax of the development section, Chopin combines the opening motif of the introduction with the first subject, weaving them together

---

18. The manuscript originally belonged to Breitkopf and Härtel but is today in the possession of the Polish National Library, under the call number MUS. 22. Adolf Gutmann made this copy from Chopin's autograph, which is now lost. Three editions of the Sonata were published more or less simultaneously, in 1840. Gutmann's copy was used for the Leipzig (Breitkopf) edition, while the autograph was used for the Paris (Troupenas) and London (Wessel) editions. Of these three early publications, only the Breitkopf edition carried a repeat sign at the "Doppio movimento," which for the next century was followed by most other editions, with the notable exception of Breitkopf's own Collected Edition (1878–80), when it was removed by Brahms, who, following his interpretation of Gutmann's calligraphy, replaced it with double bar lines. For a fuller account of the problem facing the player, see the argument put forward by Charles Rosen in support of the repeated "Grave" introduction, in RRG, pp. 279–82, and a vigorous rebuttal of that argument by Anatole Leikin, in LRC, pp. 568–82. Leikin reminds us that publishers in the eighteenth and nineteenth centuries habitually failed to print repeat signs after the introduction in fast sonata movements, taking them for granted.

with a triplet figure derived from the subsidiary theme of the second subject (b). This simultaneous unfolding of three separate strands of musical thought (shown here on three staves) results in an acoustical fabric of compelling intensity.

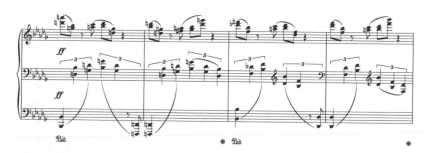

With the arrival of the lead-back over a dominant pedal point (bars 162–70) we expect Chopin to usher in a full-blown recapitulation, beginning with a return of the first subject, after the time-honored fashion of the First Viennese School. But at this juncture Chopin reveals his independence. Having worked his first subject to the point of exhaustion in the development section (one writer puts it somewhat differently, charging him with "worrying it to death"[19]), its reappearance in the recapitulation would have amounted to a tautology. Chopin's preference for concision and economy comes to his rescue at this point, and to the rescue of the piece. The development rolls right over the expected point of return, omitting the first subject entirely, and forces the incoming second subject to bear the brunt of the recapitulation (bar 170). While the exposition was 104 bars long, the truncated recapitulation is reduced to a mere 60 bars (excluding the coda); yet these two sections remain in perfect equilibrium and prove yet again that metrical balance is not the same thing as musical balance. As far as we know, such structural foreshortening through the loss of a sonata movement's first subject had never before been attempted, and it has turned this recapitulation into a *locus classicus* for music analysts.

---

19. ACMS, p. 59.

Chopin was to repeat the procedure in the first movement of his Sonata in B minor, op. 58 (and later still in the first movement of his widely undiscussed Cello Sonata in G minor, op. 65), a sure sign that he saw the idea not only as one with merit but also as one that might make an important contribution to the history of sonata form. More than thirty years elapsed before it happened again—in the first movement of Tchaikovsky's Symphony no. 4, in F minor, whose first subject likewise fails to return, and whose development section moves straight into the recapitulated second subject. If there is anything to be learned from Chopin's pioneering example it is surely this: when content trumps form, it may offer a glimpse of the future; when form trumps content, we are generally offered only a glimpse of the past.

While Chopin's four scherzos helped to emancipate the genre and elevate it to the level of an independent movement displaying some highly individual structures, the scherzos in his sonatas by contrast cleave to tradition. They stem directly from the scherzo inherited from Beethoven, which was itself an outgrowth of the old minuet and trio in the sonatas of Mozart and Haydn. Such movements were generally undemanding from a technical point of view. The present Scherzo, by contrast, bristles with difficulties and remains the most physically challenging movement in the Sonata. Only the heroes of the keyboard are able to dispatch it with ease.

As the Scherzo hurtles along at breakneck speed, the right hand is called upon to negotiate some formidable scales in double fourths, the left hand in double thirds. There are also flying leaps in contrary motion to extreme ends of the keyboard, where disaster lies in wait for the unwary player.

Although this movement unfolds across a metrical background of 3/4 time, Chopin achieves some stimulating contrasts when he occasionally "displaces" his bar lines and breaks into 2/4, as the accents in bars 73–77 show—following the fashion of Beethoven in his scherzos.

Time has turned the Funeral March into a musical icon. It has been used on countless occasions to mark the passing of crowned heads, military heroes, and celebrities in the arts and sciences. A symbol of universal mourning, the March transcends time and place. From the moment we hear the solemn tread of its opening chords, we become part of a great processional that conveys us to a world of pomp and circumstance, a place where the spirits of the great and glorious are enshrined.

Yet the March was never played at any burial service during Chopin's lifetime. There is some irony in the fact that the first occasion it was enlisted in the service of the dead was at Chopin's own funeral, in the Madeleine Church, on October 30, 1849, in an orchestral arrangement by Henri Reber. When Chopin put the finishing touches to the Funeral March, in 1837, and set the manuscript aside for a time before finding a permanent home for it, he had no idea that he had just penned music that would be used to mark his own passing from this vale of tears. An inspection of the only remaining autograph fragment of the Trio reveals that Chopin placed the date November 28, 1837, beneath the closing bars, and then signed it.[20] It was the eve of the anniversary of the November Uprising, the date on which the Polish diaspora in Paris marked this national catastrophe. We join with the Polish scholar Mieczysław Tomaszewski in saying that the Funeral March was originally a lament for Chopin's homeland, a connection that was lost after the movement was incorporated into the wider context of the Sonata. The movement has meanwhile become as famous in its way as the Funeral March from Beethoven's "Eroica" Symphony. It is difficult to understand why Schumann described it as "largely repulsive," and then went on to say that an incomparably better effect would have been achieved had Chopin composed an Adagio, "perhaps in the key of D-flat major,"[21] a remark that reveals Schumann to have been an occasional prisoner of the past. He is referring, of course, to the fact that all four movements are in a minor key, an unusual occurrence in classical sonatas, and one that Chopin never adopts elsewhere. Yet the Funeral March is the central pillar of the Sonata, one that defines the composition. All the other movements lead up to or away from it. Nor is it simply the sepulchral mood of the March that casts its shadow across the rest of the composition. There are thematic connections at work as well, which not only link this movement to the others but may even have helped to generate them.[22] Far from being "unruly children," we have come to understand that they were always members of a united family.

The Finale, marked *Presto*, ranks among the most extraordinary movements that Chopin composed. Consisting of a mere seventy-five bars of music, it generally lasts no longer than the same number of seconds in performance. The continuous whirl of unison octaves, which follow so hard on the heels of the Funeral March's closing chords, reminded Anton Rubinstein of "night winds sweeping across churchyard graves," an image that has become firmly attached to this music. Schumann did not regard the Finale as music at all, dismissing it as a "mockery," while Mendelssohn is said to have abhorred it.[23] The dichotomy between sight and sound,

---

20. A photograph of this fragment was published in KCM, p. 5. The manuscript may at one time have been in the possession of Arthur Hedley but is now presumed lost.
21. *NZfM*, February 1, 1841.
22. Some of them are traced in an earlier essay of mine, "Chopin and Musical Structure." WFC, pp. 245–47.
23. NFC, vol. 2, p. 227.

between what we hear and what we see on the printed page, makes it almost impossible to form any impression of how this music might sound until we hear it performed. It is athematic and virtually atonal—played *sotto voce* throughout—until the final cadence brings everything to a close with a fortissimo chord in the home key of B-flat minor. Analysts have not been slow to observe that the contours of this idea were already present in the opening intervals of the Grave introduction to the first movement.

It is here that Chopin's creative use of the word *ogadują* (*obgadują* = crab), quoted in his letter to Fontana, comes into play, because the hands, locked in unison, do indeed move across the keyboard sideways, in the manner of a crab. Chopin left no pedal markings, and his injunction *sotto voce* is generally interpreted to mean that the music should be drained of feeling. But in his perceptive comments about this movement, Heinrich Neuhaus tells us that the howl of the wind in the graveyard absolutely requires the pedal. He points out that there are many marvelous harmonies concealed behind these voices that "chatter in unison," which the pedal helps to reveal. "Try to set down the harmonic skeleton of this wonderful Finale," he writes, "and you will immediately see what it is all about."[24]

It took the Sonata a long time to outlive its critics. The keyless music of its final pages, especially, won few supporters until modern times, when the avant-garde rushed to embrace them. Meanwhile, the fine balance that Chopin achieved between his respect for tradition and his urge to inno-

24. NAP, pp. 166–67.

vate was neither immediately recognized nor then immediately forgiven by our forefathers. Along the way the work had to endure some dry academic scrutiny from which it was slow to escape. As late as 1960 we were informed that the Sonata was "something less than first-rate Chopin."[25] Behind all such criticism was Chopin's perceived lack of control over large-scale musical structure. The model set down by Beethoven and the First Viennese School was the one against which all subsequent sonatas must be judged. "He was great in small things, and small in great ones." This oft-quoted judgment, memorable only for its wordplay, was uttered by the English cleric Reginald Haweis,[26] and it haunted Chopin's reputation for years, helping to confine him to the ranks of the salon composer. It now haunts the shade of its instigator. The power and majesty of Chopin's ideas have prevailed over all such commentary, and today the work stands before us as a monument of Romantic piano music, one that is likely to last as long as the piano itself survives.

VI

Sand always maintained that the journey from Paris to Nohant was simple. In fact, it took thirty hours and called for some stamina. The Messagerie Royale, the horse-drawn coach that carried the mail, some merchandise, and some passengers, set out at 7:00 in the evening and traveled through the night. By 6:00 the next morning it had reached Orléans, where the passengers would alight for breakfast. By 3:00 p.m. they were in Vierzon taking a late lunch and waiting for fresh horses and a different coach to take them to Châteauroux. From there, anyone wishing to go to Nohant had to switch to a smaller horse-drawn carriage for the final leg of the journey, and that took another four hours. The return journey from Nohant to Paris was yet more demanding because the coach left at 5:00 a.m., arriving in the capital during the early evening of the following day, so travelers from Nohant generally lost sleep. This grueling trip was undertaken by Chopin many times. In the summer and autumn of 1844, for instance, when his sister Ludwika and her husband visited him, he

---

25. ACMS, p. 59.
26. *Music and Morals* (1872), p. 262.

made the return journey between Nohant and Paris no fewer than five times. Pets were allowed to travel with their owners, adding to the general discomfort, and one could never be certain what combination of fur and feather might take up the remaining space when the coach halted at the next station. Sand herself used to travel with her dogs, Pistol and Mops, while Delacroix (who soon became a regular at Nohant) was accompanied by his cat, Cupid.

Just before sunrise on the morning of October 10, Chopin and Sand left Nohant with the two children, and after breaking their journey in Orléans that night they arrived in Paris the following evening. For the first few days Maurice moved in with Chopin at the latter's new apartment on the rue Tronchet while Sand and Solange stayed with the Marlianis until her apartment on the rue Pigalle was ready. By mid-October, Sand and Chopin had taken up residence in their separate quarters in an attempt to convince the outside world they were living independent lives. These domestic arrangements, so carefully supervised by Grzymała and Fontana, quickly foundered. The winter was approaching, Chopin's apartments became humid and cold, and his cough became worse. He often arrived at Sand's place looking pale and drawn. Sand also found the distance between their two abodes involved too much to-ing and fro-ing to offer him proper care. Chopin eventually gave up his apartment, renting the smaller of the two pavilions that comprised Sand's quarters, so that he could join the family for dinner in the evenings and participate in whatever social gatherings she cared to organize, while at the same time retaining his independence. As she deftly put it, once this new reality had been accepted, "We are not living under the same roof, but we share a common wall."[27]

---

27. CGS, vol. V, p. 551.

GROWING FAME, 1839–1843

Chopin is a pianist apart, who cannot be compared with anyone.
                                                              —Léon Escudier[1]

I

Installed in her pavilion on the rue Pigalle, Sand worked ceaselessly to bring her play *Cosima* to the stage. From the start there were problems. The unruly troupe of actors who worked at the Comédie-Française did not like the play, considering it the work of an amateur, and they wanted some changes to the text. The role of Cosima, Sand insisted, must be played by her old friend the actress Marie Dorval. But Dorval was not a member of this state-subsidized theater and there were delays while the new manager, François Buloz, sought permission from the minister of the interior, Count Charles Duchâtel, to override this inconvenient house rule. A further setback occurred when Joseph Lockroy, one of the leading actors at the theater, withdrew from the play, leaving everything once more in jeopardy. By January 1840, Sand was at her wits' end. Buloz had first thought that he could bring out the play "within fifteen days," but that was a boast he came to regret. The opening night was delayed until April 29. Meanwhile, the press got wind of Sand's problems and her ene-

1. *La France musicale*, May 2, 1841.

mies gathered to witness her defeat. They were already contemptuous of the banality of the plot, which concerned a virtuous husband's attempts to save his beautiful wife from the consequences of a fatal infatuation with a cold-hearted lover. The play, in brief, was about the preservation of marriage—and this from the pen of a woman who, in word and deed, had shocked society with her promotion of "free love" and mocked the institution of matrimony. *Cosima* smacked of hypocrisy, and Sand's conversations with Sainte-Beuve and Balzac, both of whom read the script and warned her of an impending fiasco, prepared her for the worst.

While the play was in rehearsal an opening salvo was fired by Charles Lassailly, a minor poet and dandy, who for a time had been a secretary to Balzac. Lassailly was a religious fanatic who attacked the play and excoriated Sand herself, calling her "a woman of double sex," a hermaphrodite, whose son dressed like a girl and whose daughter dressed like a boy. (Within weeks of writing his "preview," Lassailly was admitted into the nursing home of the psychiatrist Dr. Esprit Blanche, where he was treated for a mental disorder. He died insane two years later.) On the opening night the theater was packed with Sand's adversaries. There were some supporters, of course, including Liszt, Marie d'Agoult, Balzac, and Chopin himself, but their presence only made Sand's humiliation complete. Within minutes of the curtain going up there was booing and whistling. The actors were put off their stride and missed their cues. The audience became restless and even Mme Dorval, who had seen her share of theatrical mishaps, was unable to contain her poise. Sand wanted the play taken off at once. Buloz allowed it to run for seven nights, after which it expired of shame. Far from resolving Sand's financial difficulties, the play had cost her ten months' labor and 10,000 francs to stage, and she was now worse off financially than if she had never bothered to write it in the first place. That is one reason she and Chopin did not return to Nohant in the summer of 1840. It was cheaper for her to stay in Paris.[2]

---

2. Sand recouped some of her losses by selling the hardcover rights of *Cosima* for 5,000 francs.

II

As for Chopin, his financial situation had been transformed. He had sold his B-flat minor Sonata to Breitkopf and Härtel, together with the Third Scherzo, op. 39, Four Mazurkas, op. 41, Two Nocturnes, op. 37, and the Impromptu in F-sharp major, op. 36, for 500 francs per opus number, which had netted him 2,500 francs by the early spring of 1840.[3] The publication of such an important body of work also raised his profile, and his reappearance in Paris after an absence of almost a year attracted pupils. Four or five of them visited him daily in his small apartment on the rue Tronchet, and played their pieces to him on his newly installed Pleyel grand piano at 20 francs a lesson. Many pupils were nonentities of whom the world has little recollection, but they could afford his fee, which was paid in cash and left discreetly on the mantelpiece. He either sat next to them, listening patiently, or he would demonstrate on a small cottage piano that stood nearby. Although the winter had taken a toll on his health, he was unfailingly good-natured toward his students. During his lessons it was not unusual to see him dab his forehead with eau de cologne or sip gum water laced with opium to ease the chronic inflammation of his throat.

Not all his pupils came from the ranks of the ungifted, and it is worth opening a short parenthesis to consider the exceptions. Shortly after Chopin's return from Nohant the twenty-three-year-old Friederike Müller arrived from Vienna and approached him for lessons. She had studied with Czerny, was technically advanced, and had drawn attention to herself when a few weeks earlier she had received an ovation at a matinée concert in the home of Countess Thérèse d'Apponyi, who enjoyed the sobriquet "the divine Thérèse" and was the dedicatee of Chopin's Two Nocturnes, op. 27. After handing over various letters of introduction, Friederike told Chopin that she had come to Paris for the express purpose of studying Chopin's works with the composer himself. "It would be sad if people were not in a position to play them well without my instruction," Chopin replied somewhat sardonically. When Friederike modestly responded that she was not one of their number and still had much to learn, Chopin warmed to her discretion and said, "Well, play me something," and they moved over to the

---

3. Chopin had threatened to break off relations with Breitkopf unless they met his conditions, "beneath which I am not prepared to go." CFC, vol. 2, p. 376.

piano. "In a moment his reserve had vanished," wrote Friederike. "Kindly and indulgently he helped me overcome my timidity, inquired if I were comfortably seated, let me play until I had become calm, then gently found fault with my stiff wrist, praised my correct comprehension, and accepted me as a pupil. He arranged for two lessons a week."

Friederike studied with Chopin for the next eighteen months. She became one of his best interpreters, and her memoir of the time she spent with him throws valuable light on his teaching.[4] Chopin gave her his Studies and Preludes to learn, an indication of her technical prowess. After their lessons had come to an end, in the spring of 1841, he dedicated to her his challenging Allegro de Concert, op. 46—which after its publication a few months later led Liszt to dub her "Mademoiselle opus quarante-six." To Friederike we owe some of our best descriptions of Chopin as a teacher.

> Mikuli used to say that "A holy artistic zeal burnt in him then, every word from his lips was incentive and inspiring. Single lessons often lasted literally for hours at a stretch, until exhaustion overcame master and pupil." There were for me also such blessed lessons. Many a Sunday I began at one o'clock to play at Chopin's, and only at four or five in the afternoon did he dismiss us. Then he also played, and how splendidly; but not only his own compositions, also those of other masters, in order to teach the pupil how they should be performed. One morning he played from memory fourteen Preludes and Fugues of Bach's, and when I expressed my joyful admiration at this unparalleled performance, he replied: "Cela ne s'oublie jamais."[5]

On December 20, 1840, just a few weeks after the lessons had begun, Chopin made Friederike play his newly published Sonata in B-flat minor "before a large assemblage," as she put it. The event took place in Sand's apartment, which was more spacious than his own. On the morning of the concert Friederike went to see Chopin in order to run through the

---

4. This memoir takes the form of extracts from a diary, made available to Niecks, who published them in NFC, vol. 2, pp. 340–43.
5. "One never forgets that sort of thing."

Sonata one last time, but was nervous. "Why do you play less well today?" inquired Chopin. She replied that she was afraid. "Why? *I* consider that you play it well," Chopin assured her. "These words restored my composure. The thought that I played to his satisfaction possessed me also in the evening; I had the happiness of gaining Chopin's approval and the applause of the audience." Emboldened by Chopin's words, Friederike went on to play the Larghetto from his Piano Concerto in F minor, "which he accompanied magnificently on a second piano." At her last lesson, which probably took place in April 1841, Chopin showed his appreciation of Friederike's talent by giving her the autograph pages of two of his Studies, op. 10, nos. 3 and 4. In 1849, Friederike married the Viennese piano maker Johann Baptiste Streicher and, following the conventions of the day, gave up her career as a performer.

There were not many other pupils to elevate Chopin's teaching day. Adolf Gutmann was an exception, of course, and although he had been with Chopin for the past several years he continued to take lessons from him. Nor must we forget the fourteen-year-old prodigy Georges Mathias, who became his pupil during this very year of 1840 and later enjoyed a teaching career at the Paris Conservatoire spanning more than three decades. This select circle of students was enlarged three or four years later by Thomas Dyke Tellefsen, who came from Norway especially to study with Chopin, and by Karol Mikuli, whose devotion to his master's memory was symbolized by his monumental edition of Chopin's works, a labor of love that took him many years to complete. Special mention must be made of an eighteen-year-old opera singer, Pauline García, who was introduced to Chopin by George Sand during the winter of 1839–40. The daughter of the celebrated singing teacher Manuel García, and younger sister of the equally celebrated soprano Maria Malibran, Pauline longed to become a concert pianist and had studied for two years with Franz Liszt, who predicted a virtuoso career for her. But after the early death of her famous sister, Pauline's mother, the soprano Joaquína Sitchez, insisted she abandon this calling and follow in the family's footsteps, pursuing a career in the opera house. When Chopin first met Pauline, she stood on the brink of international glory, having just created a sensation in London in the role of Desdemona in Rossini's *Otello*. Their common love of opera and her devotion to the piano did the rest. Pauline fell under the spell of Chopin's music and became not only his pupil, taking informal lessons from him

for several years, but also a loyal friend. They frequently played duets to-
gether and he allowed her to arrange some of his mazurkas as vocal display
pieces, which she took on tour with her.[6] In April 1840, Pauline married
Louis Viardot, twenty-one years her senior and the director of the Théâtre-
Italien, a career he abandoned in order to manage that of his young wife.
Thereafter she preferred to be known simply as Pauline Viardot.[7]

What did Chopin have his students practice? For technique he prescribed the studies of Cramer, Moscheles, and Clementi (especially the
latter's *Gradus ad Parnassum,* by which he set great store). For repertoire
he recommended above all Bach's 48 together with the sonatas of
Mozart. He also included music by Field, Hummel, Hiller, Schubert, and
Weber, depending on the competence of the individual student. One or
two of the sonatas of Beethoven would sometimes appear on the music
desk—including the "Moonlight" and the "Funeral March" sonatas—but
he was out of sympathy with most of the others. He ignored the compositions of his contemporaries Liszt and Schumann, and most of Mendelssohn as well. Of course, Chopin's own music occupied a central place in
his teaching, especially when the students themselves requested it, and
their annotated scores containing his fingerings, pedal markings, and
tempo indications offer a portal through which the modern pianist may
enter his pianistic world.

We referred earlier to the exemplary patience that Chopin extended
toward his pupils, and the pains he took to make sure that they got everything
right. The lessons were not always tranquil, however. Georges Mathias recalled that Chopin could occasionally be pushed over the edge by a particularly obtuse pupil. On one occasion he lost his temper, lifted a chair by
its back, and threw it on the floor.[8] The daily burden of his chronic illness
sometimes drove him to extremes, breaking through the mask of polite
reserve behind which it could no longer be contained.

---

6. For a brief discussion of these brilliant arrangements, see page 564, footnote 17, in the
"Twilight in Britain" chapter of this volume.
7. Sand played a pivotal role in brokering this marriage. When she learned that Pauline was
being pursued by one of Sand's former lovers, Alfred de Musset, who had fallen madly in love
with the young singer and proposed to her, she sensed a disaster in the making and brought
Louis Viardot into Pauline's orbit.
8. GC, pp. 241–42.

III

Chopin's growing reputation was burnished through an important brush with French royalty. Not long after his return from Nohant, in the autumn of 1839, he was invited to appear before Queen Marie-Amélie and her entourage at the royal residence, Saint-Cloud. It was brought about as a result of Chopin's burgeoning friendship with Ignaz Moscheles, who was now back in France after an extended visit to England and was presently staying with his wife, Charlotte, in the luxurious home of her uncle, the banker Auguste Léo. Léo, we recall, had loaned Chopin money for the trip to Majorca and Chopin was now his occasional dinner guest.

Moscheles had long expressed a wish to meet Chopin, so it was natural that the two composers had their first encounter at one of Léo's soirées, about which Moscheles left an account in his diary. He asked Chopin to play something and was delighted with what he heard. "He played me some of his Studies and his latest work, 'Preludes.' I played in return several things of my own." A week later they met in Chopin's apartment, where Moscheles heard Chopin play his Prelude in A-flat major, "the one in 6/8 time, with the perpetually recurring A-flat resembling the pedal bass of an organ." Chopin's pupil Gutmann was there, and played from manuscript the newly completed Scherzo in C-sharp minor. Chopin then treated the company to a performance of his Sonata in B-flat minor, a work that was also still in manuscript. What struck Moscheles most about Chopin's playing was that those "hard inartistic modulations," which he could never accept when he himself was playing them, ceased to shock him when he heard Chopin, "for he glides over them almost imperceptibly with his elfish fingers. His soft playing being a mere breath, he requires no powerful forte to produce the desired contrast."[9] It was the start of a respectful friendship. One of their listeners was Count Léon de Perthuis, adjutant to King Louis-Philippe, who mentioned it to members of the royal family. Within days an invitation had been issued for Chopin and Moscheles to give a command performance at Saint-Cloud, on October 29. Count de Perthuis himself picked them up at 9:00 p.m. and drove them to the palace. It was pouring rain and the party got drenched. Moscheles takes up the story.

---

9. MAML, vol. 2, pp. 39–40.

The Queen asked if the instrument—a Pleyel—was placed as we liked it; was the lighting what we wanted? If the chairs were the right height, etc.; and was as anxious for our comfort as a Citizen Queen might well be. First of all Chopin played a mélange of Nocturnes and Etudes, and was extolled and admired as an old court favorite. I followed with some old and new Studies, and was honored with similar applause. We then sat down together at the instrument, he again playing the bass, a thing he always insists on. The small audience now listened intently to my E-flat major Sonata, which was interrupted by such exclamations as "divin! délicieux!" After the Andante the Queen whispered to one of her suite: "Ne serait-il pas indiscret de le leur redemander?" which was tantamount to a command; so we played it again with increased abandon, and in the Finale gave ourselves up to a musical delirium.[10]

Moscheles adds that he and Chopin reveled like brothers in the triumphs that each of their individual talents received that evening. "There was no tinge of jealousy on either side," he remarked. It was 11:30 p.m. when they left the palace and the rain had stopped. They went home "this time only under a shower of compliments."

There is an unsubstantiated coda to this story that shortly after the concert the palace contacted Moscheles, inquiring if he would accept a nomination for the Legion of Honor. The pianist is supposed to have replied that he would prefer something "less common." The king then sent him a beautiful leather traveling case that Chopin slyly observed was a royal hint for the pianist to leave town. Chopin's own gift from the king was a magnificent Sèvres porcelain vase on a tooled bronze mounting.

IV

These were the circumstances that led Moscheles to invite Chopin to make a contribution to his *Méthode des Méthodes*, an elaborate three-part work that he was in the middle of publishing, with a detailed commentary and

---

10. Ibid., p. 44. A review of the concert appeared in the *Revue et Gazette musicale* on October 31, 1839.

introduction by the music critic F.-J. Fétis. Part Three consisted of twenty advanced studies ("Études de perfectionnement") for the finished artist, whose composers included Benedict, Döhler, Henselt, Liszt, Mendelssohn, Méreaux, Rosenheim, Taubert, Thalberg, Édouard Wolff, and of course Moscheles himself. There is hardly a technical device, however extreme, that fails to find a refuge in this collection. One or two of these pieces still bring gymnasts to their feet. Chopin's studies, known as the Trois Nouvelles Études, stand out from the rest. It is not simply that they are the only ones that have entered the standard repertory (although Liszt's "Ab irato"—"In anger"—has recently emerged from obscurity). What strikes the listener is the antivirtuosic character of these pieces, situated as they are within a context where virtuosity is about the only thing being celebrated. Chopin concentrates not on fast fingers and powerful chords but on rhythmic and textural subtleties, both between and within the hands. Study no. 1, in F minor, for example, presents threes against fours,

while Study no. 2, in A-flat major, presents threes against twos. It also happens to be the most frequently played of the set, its singing melodic line having an instant appeal not only to the player but to a broader audience.

Study no. 3, in D-flat major (the most deceptively difficult of the set), is an exercise in contrasting textures, presenting legato and staccato lines simultaneously within the same hand, a difficult proposition. While the first two studies require hands that are rhythmically independent of each other, this third study calls for a hand that is divided against itself, so to speak, the lower half dealing with the staccato notes, the upper half dealing with the legato ones. As if to draw attention to the problem, from which there is no escape, the pianist is enjoined to play "*la melodia sempre legato.*"

Moscheles's earlier description of Chopin's "elfish fingers" here takes on an unexpected meaning, because the five digits of the right hand are not only called upon to work independently, but occasionally in opposition to one another. We have it on the authority of Ignaz Friedman that Moriz Rosenthal used to play the inner notes with the thumb alone, leaving a wider choice of fingers for the melody. Sir Donald Tovey placed a high premium on this study and elevated it "to an altogether higher plane than several of the lighter ornaments in the two great sets," opp. 10 and 25. And referring to the unique technical problem it posed for the pianist's right hand, he pointed out that "Chopin was the only important writer who systematized it in this extreme form."[11] Anyone wishing to understand what differentiates Chopin's approach to the keyboard from that of his contemporaries can point to few better examples than the Trois Nouvelles Études. They immediately unmask the player possessed with more brawn than brain. They disclose a world in which subtlety abounds, in which the steel-fingered, chromium-plated virtuoso can find no sanctuary. And they lend a new and unexpected meaning to the title "Études de perfectionnement," where perfection resides in the ability to reveal the still, small voice lying at the center of it all.

While Moscheles admired Chopin the pianist, his opinion of Chopin

---

11. TCM, p. 160.

the composer was qualified. His scattered comments on the topic reveal a conservative musician unable to rise above the constraints of time and place. "In his compositions Chopin shows that his best ideas are but isolated; he leaves them fragmentary, and fails to produce a work of complete unity . . . I often find passages that sound to me like someone preluding on the piano, the player knocking at the door of every key and clef to find if any melodious sounds are at home."[12] It is true that these remarks, written in 1847, were directed mainly toward the Cello Sonata, which had just been published. But they apply equally to Moscheles's opinion of Chopin in general. Not long after Chopin died, Moscheles offered but faint praise when he wrote that Chopin possessed many fine and original qualities, but "he was not a classic."[13]

V

Still smarting from her defeat over *Cosima*, Sand worked more furiously than ever on her new novel, *Horace* (1841). She was still in debt and this was the only way that she could keep her creditors at bay. *Horace* is a roman à clef that Sand used to settle an old score. Sitting among the "supporters" who had witnessed her humiliation on the opening night of *Cosima* was a false friend, Marie d'Agoult, the mother of a real-life Cosima fathered by Liszt. For months Marie had harbored a secret resentment against Sand and gloated over her downfall. Just three years earlier, while staying as Sand's guest in Nohant, Marie had no hesitation in describing her as "a great woman in whom God has kindled a sacred flame."[14] Now she mocked Sand openly in letters to their mutual friends—Balzac, Sainte-Beuve, and Charlotte Marliani—in terms so derogatory that Marliani advised Sand to break off relations with her. That Marie was envious of the apparent success of the Sand-Chopin *ménage* while what was left of hers with Liszt was about to go into free fall, leaving her abandoned and the mother of three illegitimate children, cannot be doubted, and she let her pen run away with her. "I don't think that it will be long before the Chopin

---

12. MAML, vol. 2, p. 171.
13. Ibid., p. 207.
14. AM, p. 75.

household breaks up," she told Liszt, just before *Cosima* made its disastrous debut. "Some of our friends consider him morbidly jealous, a man who is being killed by his passion, who is tormented by it and torments others. [Sand] is exasperated by it and only fears that he would die if she were to leave him!"[15]

Whether d'Agoult knew that Sand had imposed conditions of celibacy on Chopin after the pair had returned from Majorca is uncertain, but in light of the intimate thoughts they were used to sharing in the early days of their friendship we think it likely. It is in any case difficult to put any other construction on her words "killed by his passion." Among the salacious observations that Marie distributed among their friends was that Sand had put on weight, and she wondered idly if Sand were pregnant, in which case who might the father be? The implication was that since Chopin was denied access to Sand's bedroom he was hardly in a position to assume the honors of paternity.[16] Whether this choice morsel reached the ears of Chopin we do not know; but his relationship with d'Agoult cooled noticeably. One thing is beyond question. Sand was well aware that the celibate nature of her liaison with Chopin was difficult for him to bear. Whenever he perceived Sand's numerous male admirers fluttering around her, both in Paris and in Nohant, paying her compliments and receiving compliments in return, he became frustrated and suspicious. Sand's biographers have contemplated that one or two of these admirers may have been admitted to her bedroom, a fact that she tried to keep from Chopin, although it does not appear to have escaped the attention of Marie d'Agoult, who used it as ammunition in her campaign against her erstwhile friend.

Sand did not follow Marliani's advice and break with Mme d'Agoult at once, because she knew that revenge was a dish best served cold. She bided her time while suggesting to Balzac that the story of Marie and Liszt's

---

15. ACLA, vol. 1, pp. 412–13.
16. The unpublished journal of the Swiss writer Charles Didier is a mine of information on this matter. Rejected by Sand as a prospective lover before Chopin came on the scene, he wrote in January 1840, "G.S. is said to be pregnant: by whom?" Didier passed this piece of gossip along to Marie d'Agoult, certain that she would pass it along to others. If we continue to turn the pages of Didier's journal we come across another entry that is not without interest in the present context. Didier hints that Marie submitted to him on the night of January 30, 1842, after an evening at the opera. (VCA, vol. 2, p. 122, n. 179; and SCD, p. 113.) Had this well-kept secret reached Sand's ears, we may be certain that it would have resulted in a second edition of *Horace*.

elopement might make a rattling good tale if only he cared to tell it, and she even supplied him with a title, "The Galley Slaves of Love." Balzac obliged her by producing his novel *Beatrix*, part of his famous cycle titled *La Comédie humaine*, in which Sand is metamorphosed into the saintly heroine Félicité des Touches, while Marie d'Agoult is cast as Beatrix, the Marquise de Rochegude, a vainglorious socialite whose empty thoughts vanish within the folds of her flowing gowns or are obscured by the elegance of her coiffure. Marie never forgave Sand for this betrayal, but Sand was not finished. Having seen what Balzac could do with the story, she came through with an elaboration of her own and placed Marie in the center of *Horace*, depicting her as the Vicomtesse de Chailly—a would-be patroness of the arts, filled with pretension. She was flat chested, skinny, and had obvious dental problems. Even her golden tresses, widely regarded as her crowning glory, were the work of her maid, who spent hours grooming her mistress for exposure to society. In the salons she pretended to know a bit about everything, Sand wrote, but her conversation was shallow, generally consisting of information she had gleaned earlier in the day or had overheard the previous evening. It was a cruel portrait and drove a stake through the heart of their friendship.

Nothing deflected Sand from the routine to which she was long accustomed—working through the night by candlelight, and emerging at the crack of dawn "like a bat coming out of its cave blinking in the sunlight," as Balzac described her. He was among Sand's regulars at the rue Pigalle, and gave us the best description of her residence there.

> George Sand lives at 16 rue Pigalle, at the end of a garden above the coach house and stables of a mansion that faces the street. She has a dining room whose furniture is of carved oak. Her small drawing room is decorated in a café-au-lait color, and the reception room has superb Chinese vases, full of flowers. There is always a flower pot in bloom. The upholstery is green. There is a side table full of bric-à-brac, and there are paintings by Delacroix as well as a portrait of herself by Calamatta . . . The piano is a magnificent square upright, of rosewood. Chopin is always there. She smokes only cigarettes, nothing else. She doesn't get up until four o'clock. At that hour Chopin has finished giving his lessons. One goes up to her flat by a narrow, steep staircase. Her bedroom is brown. She

slccps on two mattresses laid on the floor, Turkish style. *Ecco, contessa!*[17]

Chopin dined nearly every evening with Sand and her children. After the last of his pupils had departed the rue Tronchet, he would travel the short distance to the rue Pigalle by fiacre and enjoy what was now his family life. Whenever Sand put on parties for her large circle of friends, Chopin found himself mingling with a cross-section of the Parisian intelligentsia. Louis Blanc, Pierre-Simon Ballanche, Sainte-Beuve, Balzac, Eugène Delacroix, Marie Dorval, and Heine all graced her salon. The Polish contingent was well represented by such figures as Grzymała, the poets Stefan Witwicki and Adam Mickiewicz, his fellow musician Julian Fontana, and the elder statesman Julian Niemcewicz. On these occasions Sand's apartment became more Polish than Poland. When the conversation began to flag, Chopin might be persuaded to take his seat at the piano. He would then play for hours, to the point of exhaustion, beguiling his audicnce with one improvisation after another, after which Sand would say good night to her guests, mount her steep staircase, and scribble the night away. Chopin would call for his fiacre and return to his apartment on the rue Tronchet, or later on, after he had moved under Sand's roof, walk across the linking garden to his own wing of the same house.

VI

On December 15, 1840, Paris was brought to a standstill by the state funeral of Emperor Napoléon I, whose remains had been exhumed and transferred from the island of Saint Helena, where he had been confined as a prisoner of the British after his defeat at Waterloo. Nearly twenty years had elapsed since the emperor's death, but the French had never abandoned the idea of bringing his body back home. After years of wrangling, King Louis-Philippe and his advisors managed to get a bill passed by the legislature in the spring of 1840, to which was attached the sum of two million francs to cover the cost of the expedition. In July a frigate named

---

17. BLH, vol. I, p. 527.

La Belle Poule, escorted by two other vessels, set out from Toulon under the command of the king's third son, the Prince de Joinville (who was a career naval officer), and after a voyage lasting ninety-three days the flotilla cast anchor off the remote British island, there to await the transfer of the emperor's remains. It carried on its steerage deck a specially designed candlelit chapel, draped in black velvet bearing Napoléon's insignia, with a catafalque in the middle guarded by four gilded wooden eagles. The exhumation took place at midnight, October 14, carried out by torchlight. Two of Napoléon's old generals, Henri-Gratien Bertrand and Gaspard Gourgaud, sailed aboard the frigate from France to witness the exhumation, together with some of the emperor's former servants, including Count Louis Marchand, his chief *valet de chambre*, who had lived with him in exile on Saint Helena. Three heavy stone slabs covering the tomb were moved to one side by a contingent of British soldiers, and the coffin beneath was then raised to the surface. When this coffin, made of mahogany, was opened, it revealed a second one within it made of lead, which had been sealed. As the screws of this interior coffin were removed and the lid raised, a wave of emotion swept through the group of onlookers as they saw Napoléon's perfectly preserved body within. General Gourgaud, Count Marchand, and one or two others who had known him well in life began to weep. The emperor's head was resting on a cushion, his face was serene, the lips slightly parted, making one or two incisors distinctly visible. He had been dressed in the uniform of a colonel of the Chasseurs de la Garde Impériale, decorated with the Legion of Honor, his hat placed across his thighs. The buttons on his uniform had begun to tarnish, and the seams of his boots had started to split, but no other signs of decay were visible. After the ship's doctor, Rémy Guillard, had examined the body, General Gourgaud ordered the lead coffin closed and placed within the imposing ebony casket brought from France, designed in the style of the old Roman emperors, bearing the words in gilded bronze, *Napoléon Empereur mort à Sainte-Hélène le 05 Mai 1821.*

The details of Napoléon's exhumation and the return of his body to France transfixed the nation. It was the only topic of conversation on the boulevards and in the salons, and it dominated the press. The Polish diaspora, especially, had good cause to revere Napoléon's memory, for many of them had fought and died beneath his banner; and his creation of the Duchy of Warsaw, into which Chopin himself had been born, was still a vibrant part of their past. The frigate bearing the emperor's body docked at Cherbourg on November 30, and the coffin was transferred by land to a smaller vessel, which made its way slowly from Le Havre down the Seine to Paris. More than a million people lined the banks to get a glimpse of the ship as it passed by. The route would not have displeased Napoléon. In a codicil to his will, he had expressed the wish to be buried on the banks of the Seine in the midst of the French people. The government, however, had already decided that his reburial would take place in Les Invalides, the nation's military museum, and the body would rest in the Chapel of Saint Jérôme. Victor Hugo's description of the funeral cortège as it made its way down the Champs-Élysées remains unsurpassed. The boulevards were thronged with people come to pay their final homage. Many of them stood on the rooftops of houses, he tells us, in order to keep their appointment with history. As the procession came into view, accompanied by the rumble of cannon fire, echoed every fifteen minutes by the guns at Les Invalides, Hugo found the effect overwhelming. "The gilded catafalque was enormous," he wrote. It was ten meters high and five meters wide, and resembled "a golden mountain drawn by four teams of four horses . . . It was an enormous mass whose stages rose in a pyramid atop the four huge gilded wheels that bear it. The sixteen horses were covered from head to foot in gold cloth, only their eyes visible, giving them the air of phantom beasts." Detachments of the National Guard marched alongside, and eighty-six officers of Napoléon's legions carried the banners of his eighty-six *départements*. "The procession drew after it the acclaim of the whole city, just as a torch is followed by its smoke."[18]

Meanwhile, at Les Invalides, one hundred and fifty of the best singers and players from the Conservatoire and the Paris Opera had been brought together for a performance of Mozart's *Requiem* under the direction of François Habeneck. When George Sand learned that Pauline Viardot was to be one of the four soloists, she requested tickets from her young friend so that she and Chopin could attend one of the final rehearsals. "For two days, Chopin has been busy making sure that we are able to listen to you," she told Viardot, "but we do not know when or where this rehearsal will be. Please think of me so that I can be there when the greatest lady of

18. HCV, "Funérailles de l'Empereur," pp. 98–112.

the present sings the music of the greatest man of the past."[19] Sand eventually discovered that the dress rehearsal was to be held at the Conservatoire (December 12), and both she and Chopin occupied the box that had been set aside for them. Sand also secured tickets admitting them to Napoléon's interment in Les Invalides on December 15 and another performance of the *Requiem*. The temperature that day plunged to minus 14 degrees Celsius, so we are not sure that Chopin himself was present. Sand produced a spare ticket that she offered to Delacroix. Was it the experience of hearing Mozart's *Requiem* that moved Chopin to express his well-known wish to have the work performed at his own funeral? We can only speculate. We know that when his wish was granted, Pauline Viardot was again brought in as a soloist. There is one other thing that lends itself to speculation. On an earlier page we learned that on December 20, just five days after Napoléon's interment, Chopin had arranged a soirée for a number of guests and had persuaded Friederike Müller to perform his "Funeral March" Sonata. The choice could hardly have been fortuitous, and for many in the audience the Finale's "night winds sweeping across churchyard graves" brought the year to a somber close.

VII

With the arrival of the New Year, 1841, Paris began to offer a welcome smorgasbord of diversions. In January, Sand and Chopin began attending a series of lectures by Adam Mickiewicz at the Collège de France on the history of Slavonic language and culture. Mickiewicz had recently been appointed to the Chair of Slavonic Literature at the Collège, having given up his academic appointment in Lausanne, and was now a resident of the French capital. The Poles turned out in force to support their national bard. At two o'clock on the afternoon of December 22, 1840, the famous author of Poland's epic poem *Pan Tadeusz* walked onto the platform and delivered his inaugural address before a packed audience, whose ranks included Prince Adam Czartoryski, the eighty-three-year-old Julian Niemcewicz (now just a few months away from the grave), and members of the French Institute and the Chamber of Deputies. By the time that Mickiewicz had

---

19. CGS, vol. V, p. 182.

The lecture auditorium at the Collège de France (1844).

completed his soaring oration, many members of the audience were overcome with emotion. Poland had found its voice.

Caught up in the general excitement, Chopin and Sand attended the lectures on January 5 and 19. They found themselves sitting next to Grzymała, Witwicki, and Seweryn Goszczyński, the romantic novelist who was under sentence of death imposed by a Warsaw court for his subversive activities in Kraków. Eustachy Januszkiewicz, a journalist and one of the co-conspirators of the November Uprising, was present and wrote, "Mickiewicz is attracting increasingly large audiences. He is becoming bold and shows us a succession of different landscapes on the vast canvas of Slavic culture. Yesterday he talked of the Slavic language . . . We listened to him in inexpressible rapture. Mme George Sand sat next to him, and by her stood Chopin."[20] The historian Ault-Dumesnil reported, "[Mickiewicz] reveals to us a world completely unknown . . . I attend with Mme Sand . . . She comes with the famous pianist Chopin and leaves in his carriage."[21]

20. HFCZ, vol. 2, p. 358.
21. MZM, vol. 3, p. 130, n. 54.

There were other diversions, too. On February 7, Pauline Viardot gave a concert in the Conservatoire, where Chopin heard her sing several arias by Handel, a composer he admired even though the Parisians thought him old-fashioned. The Viardots were getting ready to leave for London, where Pauline had been offered a lucrative contract to appear at Her Majesty's Theatre. Just before their departure Sand managed to extract a firm promise from them to visit Nohant that summer. In March, Chopin attended a recital by a twelve-year-old piano prodigy named Anton Rubinstein, but history makes no mention of his reaction to the boy's playing. One wonders what he might have made of the fact that within a generation Rubinstein would become a leading exponent of his music.

VIII

On April 26, 1841, after much procrastination, Chopin was persuaded to give a recital in the Salle Pleyel. Sand has some entertaining things to say about the nervous state into which Chopin worked himself as the day of the concert approached. "An astounding piece of news is that little Chip-Chip is going to give a *Grrrrand* Concert. His friends plagued him so much that he has given way." No sooner had he agreed to play than he regretted it, and would have canceled; but before any formal announcement had been made three quarters of the tickets were sold. "There is no more amusing sight than our meticulous and irresolute Chip-Chip compelled to keep his promise," wrote Sand. "He will have nothing to do with posters or programs and does not want a large audience. He wants to have the affair kept quiet. So many things alarm him that I suggest that he should play without candles or audience and on a dumb keyboard."[22]

Chopin prepared for the concert by practicing Bach's 48 Preludes and Fugues, his preferred way of "warming up" for a public concert, because these pieces loosened his fingers. He was assisted by the opera singer Laura Cinti-Damoreau (for whom Rossini had composed leading roles in the Italian opera) and the violinist Heinrich Ernst. But the distinguished audience that crowded into the auditorium that evening

---

22. CGS, vol. V, p. 282.

was there to hear Chopin. He placed several of his latest works on the program, including the F major Ballade, op. 38; the C-sharp minor Scherzo, op. 39; a group of Preludes; the Four Mazurkas, op. 41; and the A major Polonaise, op. 40, no. 1. The concert was made memorable because it was reviewed in the *Revue et Gazette musicale* by Franz Liszt, who had temporarily suspended his European tours and happened to be in Paris. Ernest Legouvé, the regular critic for the *Gazette*, would normally have reviewed the concert, but Liszt approached the journal's publisher, Schlesinger, and requested the honor of writing about his old friend himself. When Legouvé mentioned that he was handing over his duties to Liszt, Chopin expressed some misgivings. "I should have preferred it to have been you." "You must not think that, my dear friend," replied Legouvé. "An article by Liszt would be a piece of good fortune, both for the public and for you. Believe in his admiration for your talent. I promise you that he will create a beautiful kingdom for you." "Yes," replied Chopin without smiling, "in his empire."[23]

Liszt is at his poetic best in this article. But because he treated the concert as a social event rather than a musical one he aroused Chopin's displeasure. The article is long and we quote only a truncated version of it here.

> Last Monday, at 8:00 o'clock in the evening, the salons of M. Pleyel were magnificently lighted; to the foot of a staircase, which was carpeted and perfumed with flowers, a stream of carriages brought the most elegant women, the most fashionable young men, the most famous artists, the richest financiers, the most illustrious noblemen, the whole elite of society, an entire aristocracy of birth, fortune, talent, and beauty.
>
> A grand piano stood open on the platform; everyone sought the nearest seats and settled down to listen. They told themselves in advance that they must not miss a chord, a note, a suggestion, a thought that might fall from him who was to play. They were right to be so eager, attentive to the point of worship, for they awaited not merely a skilled virtuoso, nor even an artist of renown: he was someone far beyond all this—they awaited Chopin!

---

23. LSS, vol. 2, p. 161.

Coming to France some ten years ago, Chopin did not struggle for the first or second place among the crowd of pianists that surged around us at that time. He stood aloof from this hurly-burly that for many years tossed performers everywhere into a chaotic battle for survival . . . This refined and delicate artist has remained undisturbed by any attack. Criticism is silent, as though posterity had already delivered its judgment . . . From the striking of the first chords a bond of closest sympathy was established between the artist and his audience. He had no need to startle or grip his listeners; he was playing in an atmosphere of quiet understanding. Every note seemed to be utterly spontaneous and inspired. Two Studies and a Ballade had to be encored. Had it not been for the fear of adding to the fatigue already visible on his pale face, the audience would have encored every item.

Chopin's Preludes are unique compositions. They are not simply, as their title would suggest, pieces intended as an introduction to something further; they are poetic preludes similar to those of a great contemporary poet that gently ease the soul into a golden world of dreams and then carry it aloft to the highest realms of the ideal. Admirable in their diversity, they require scrupulous examination of the workmanship and thought that have gone into them before they can be properly appreciated. Even then, they still retain the appearance of spontaneous improvisations produced without the slightest effort. They possess that freedom and charm which characterize works of genius.

What can one say about the Mazurkas, those miniature masterpieces so capricious yet so polished? "A perfect sonnet is worth more than a long poem," said an authority on the finest century of French literature. We are tempted to say the same of these Mazurkas if not more. For us, some of them are worth more than certain *very long* operas . . .

Franz Liszt[24]

---

24. Issue of May 2, 1841. It used to be thought that Marie d'Agoult had written this review for Liszt, and the older generation of Liszt biographers was not slow to say so. More recent scholarship does not support them. WFL, vol. 2, pp. 368–96.

And in a final flourish of praise for Chopin the man he remarked, "Is not the noblest and most justifiable satisfaction that an artist can experience that sense of being above and beyond his fame, superior even to his success, greater still than his glory?"

There is nothing here that Chopin could reasonably have found offensive. Yet the article vexed him. Liszt had dipped his pen in purple ink and Chopin felt patronized. This seal of approval was an "honor" he did not want, especially when offered in so public a forum as France's leading music journal. And he probably found the reference to his frail health superfluous. Comments such as "the fatigue already visible on his pale face" that prevented him from giving more encores could be read as an effort to attract the sympathy of the crowd. All the talk of elegant women, famous artists, and rich financiers arriving in a stream of carriages seemed to rob the concert of *gravitas* and reduce it to the level of a fashion statement. It confirmed Chopin's growing belief that Liszt, who was now in the middle of his greatest European triumphs, had become a tuft hunter, too easily diverted by the jewels and tiaras in the audience.[25] Liszt, in fact, had

---

25. This is perhaps the place to shed more light on the deeper reasons for Chopin's discomfiture with Liszt's review. Liszt had been on the road for the past two years, bringing Europe to its feet. He was now the brightest star in the pianistic firmament and was providing daily fodder for the popular press. The hysteria surrounding his concerts, the idolatry of his audiences, and the souvenir hunters especially, seemed to many to bring the profession of music into disrepute. "Lisztomania" (that wonderful term first coined by Heine) was sweeping Europe and the reception accorded the pianist can best be described as unhinged. Admirers swarmed all over him, fighting for possession of his silk handkerchiefs and his velvet gloves, which they then tore to pieces as relics. Insane female "fans" sought clippings of his hair, and there are well-documented tales of them acquiring Liszt's cigar butts, which they then placed in their cleavage. The sexual undertones were unmistakable. Sober-minded musicians such as Mendelssohn, Schumann, and Hiller were privately appalled at such vulgar displays of hero worship and they came to despise Liszt because of it, as an inspection of their correspondence readily confirms. Liszt's career had reached its apogee just a few months earlier when, after giving some hugely successful concerts in benefit of his native Hungary, he was presented with his famous "Sword of Honor" by six of Hungary's leading magnates, with Count Leó Festetics at their head. The ceremony took place on the stage of the Hungarian National Theater, following his performance of the *Rákóczy* March (music that was banned under the Austrian rules of censorship then governing Hungary). The resulting furor was, in the words of one observer, "almost enough to have awakened the dead." A crowd of five thousand people gathered outside the theater, forcing the pianist to dismount from his carriage and join a torchlight procession that led him all the way back to his hotel. The Paris newspapers had a field day and Liszt was openly mocked. Cartoons appeared of him dressed as a "piano hussar," mounted on a horse and decked out in full Magyar regalia, with his sword of honor absent-mindedly buckled to his right side—that is, the wrong side for fighting. Even the professional journals joined in the chase, and pilloried Liszt. One need look no further than *La Revue des*

come to represent everything in the sphere of music making that Chopin scorned—shallow virtuosity, the roar of the crowd, and the pursuit of newspaper glory. As the Hungarian made his triumphal progress through Europe, acknowledging the cheering masses that always seemed to line his route, Chopin disparaged him with lines that continue to echo in the literature. "One of these days he will be a member of parliament, or perhaps even King of Abyssinia or the Congo—but as regards the themes from his compositions, well, they will remain buried with the newspapers . . ."[26]

When Chopin communicated his irritation with Liszt's article to his family in Warsaw, Mikołaj Chopin responded, "I am curious about one thing: did you see Liszt after his article, and are you on as friendly a footing as you used to be?"[27] Chopin's reply must have been negative, because Mikołaj returned to the topic later in the year. "So you met Liszt at a dinner. I know how tactful you are. You are quite right not to break with him completely, in spite of all his boasting. You used once to

---

deux mondes, which ridiculed both him and the saber, an article that provoked an agitated response from the pianist (issue of October 1840). The editor of the journal then stooped to a personal attack in which he observed that Liszt's Hungarian nationality was clear to everybody from the style of his French prose (issue of November 1840). These unpleasant exchanges were published just six months before Chopin's concert.

And now Liszt was here, "resting" in Paris. What would happen? The locals were soon to find out. During his monthlong stay in the city Liszt gave several concerts, the most noteworthy being in the Salle Érard, on March 27, in which he played his newly composed "Reminiscences" on Meyerbeer's *Robert le Diable*, an arrangement filled with keyboard pyrotechnics, worthy of the Devil himself. It brought the house down. Such was the success of this virtuoso work that it led to a famous incident on April 25 (one day before Chopin's own concert) at a fund-raising concert for the Beethoven memorial, given at the Conservatoire. This all-Beethoven program featured the "Emperor" concerto, with Liszt as soloist and Berlioz conducting. "Lisztomania" immediately took over. The crowd would not allow the concert to proceed and noisily clamored for a repetition of *Robert le Diable*, leaving Liszt no alternative but to oblige, while Berlioz and the orchestra stood idly by, Beethoven's memory temporarily pushed into the sidelines. Richard Wagner, who was at that moment trying to scrape a living in Paris, reviewed the concert for the Dresden *Abend-Zeitung* and describes the furor that Liszt's playing created. He was affronted by the unexpected insertion of this flashy work into an all-Beethoven concert, and wrote sarcastically: "Someday Liszt in heaven will be summoned to play his Fantaisie on *The Devil* before the assembled company of angels" (issue of May 5, 1841). The important point to note is that Chopin witnessed this hubbub for himself. And it took place just twenty-four hours before his own appearance in the Salle Pleyel and his last-minute discovery that Liszt was to write the review.

26. CFC, vol. 3, p. 73; KFC, vol. 2, p. 34.
27. CFC, vol. 3, p. 97; KFC, vol. 2, p. 50.

be friends, and it is a fine thing to be his rival in tact."[28] Far more pleasing to Chopin was the review in *La France musicale*, which correctly defined him as the creator both of a new school of piano playing and of composition.

> Chopin is a pianist from conviction. He composes for himself and performs for himself . . . One may say that Chopin is the creator of a school of pianism and of a school of composition . . . In truth nothing equals the lightness, the sweetness with which this artist preludes on the piano; moreover, nothing can be placed beside his works, which are full of originality, distinction, and grace. Chopin is a pianist apart, who cannot be compared with anyone.
> Léon Escudier[29]

By any measure Chopin's concert was a resounding success, his earlier misgivings notwithstanding. It not only confirmed his reputation in Paris but brought in an astonishing sum. Sand could not get over the fact that "by giving a two-hour concert and batting out a few chords he has put six thousand and a few more hundred francs in his pocket amid the bravos, the shouts of 'encore,' and the flutterings of the loveliest women in Paris. The scoundrel!"[30] She lamented that she had to chain herself to her desk for three months in order to make a similar amount.

IX

From Paris, Chopin and Sand proceeded to Nohant, where they arrived in mid-June. Two years had elapsed since they had lived there, and Sand was overjoyed to be back once more in her "Garden of Eden." Chopin, too, looked forward to a relaxing time in the countryside and the leisure to compose. The summer got off to a disturbing start, however. On the night of

---

28. CFC, vol. 3, p. 115; KFC, vol. 2, pp. 69–70.
29. Issue of May 2, 1841.
30. CGS, vol. V, pp. 290–301. The poet Stefan Witwicki added his voice to the chorus of disbelief. "Just try to recite verse for three quarters of an hour," he exclaimed, "and try to get six thousand francs for that!"

July 5 the Berry region experienced a major seismic tremor, which was also felt in Paris. The floors and walls of the old house were rocked by an invisible hand, pictures fell off their hangings, and crockery was smashed against the kitchen floor. The moonlit sky was darkened as if by a veil and the village women were convinced that "the Devil had a hand in it." Sand's dog Pistol started to howl and a herd of cows in Hippolyte's nearby field began to bellow in fear. Sand later told Delacroix that Chopin was thoroughly alarmed because he had never experienced an earthquake before. Violent thunderstorms followed and the rest of July remained damp and gloomy. Since the in-house piano was in poor shape, Chopin could not work. Sand observed his frustration with the instrument. "When his palfrey fails to obey his commands, he deals him a mighty blow with his fist, *which the poor piano does not even notice!*"[31] Pleyel sent down a replacement on August 9, and Chopin was at last able to put some finishing touches to his latest compositions—the Allegro de Concert, op. 46; the Ballade in A-flat major, op. 47; the Two Nocturnes, op. 48; and the Fantaisie in F minor, op. 49. He sent off the manuscripts to Fontana for copying, with instructions to offer them to Breitkopf for a nonnegotiable fee of 2,000 francs for all four works. Fontana fulfilled his commission with his usual doglike devotion, but not before receiving several follow-up messages from Chopin laced with the usual sprinkling of pejoratives—"Swindlers," "Jews," "Haslinger is a fool," etc.—which were apt to put in an appearance whenever he was dealing with publishers.[32] Meanwhile, Chopin's old lost longing for some sophisticated company at Nohant was satisfied when Louis and Pauline Viardot fulfilled their earlier promise and turned up flushed with the success of Pauline's London triumphs. They stayed for two weeks, bringing with them not only some firsthand accounts of musical life in Britain but also a disclosure of a more intimate nature. Pauline, who

---

31. CGS, vol. V, p. 391. Chopin sent an urgent message to the ever-obliging Fontana: "Tell [Pleyel] to send me a better piano because mine is no good." CGS, vol. V, p. 335, *n*. We are left to ponder whether this was the Érard piano that Sand had installed for Liszt two years earlier.
32. The long run of letters that Chopin sent to Fontana during the summer of 1841, and in particular the ones written in September and October of that year, reveal his mounting agitation with publishers. It is an indication of the restlessness that Chopin experienced when dealing with matters he was obliged to leave in Fontana's hands that the letter dated September 13 was written at "3 in the morning" and bears the notation "Stars." CFC, vol. 3, pp. 72–91; KFC, vol. 2, pp. 34–48.

had just celebrated her twentieth birthday, was pregnant with their first child, Louise, whose birth was expected in mid-December.

The life of unruffled calm that Sand and Chopin had hoped to enjoy at Nohant during this long summer of 1841, and could not seem to find, experienced a further setback far removed from earthquakes and skirmishes with publishers. Not long after their arrival a personal crisis arose that gave Sand an unexpected glimpse into the interior character of the man with whom she now shared her life. A year earlier Chopin had recommended his thirty-five-year-old pupil Marie de Rozières to Sand, suggesting that she would make an excellent piano teacher for Solange. Sand was happy to take her on, and de Rozières became a regular member of the household, both in Paris and at Nohant; more important, she was admitted to Sand's inner circle and became a confidante. No one could have foreseen what happened next, least of all Chopin himself. In the summer of 1841, de Rozières embarked on a passionate love affair with Antoni Wodziński, the ne'er-do-well brother of Chopin's former fiancée, Maria Wodzińska, who had left his regiment of Polish lancers in Spain and was now wending his way back to Poland via Paris. Chopin, who was informed about what was going on by Julian Fontana, became agitated about the tittle-tattle that Antoni might pass along to de Rozières concerning his difficult relationship with the Wodziński family and the intimate details of his broken engagement to Maria Wodzińska, wanting at all costs to prevent such gossip from reaching the ears of Sand. In a fit of petulance he described de Rozières to Fontana as "a tart" and even as "a slut," hoping no doubt that by destroying the messenger he might also destroy the message.

To judge from the correspondence that the worldly-wise Sand exchanged with de Rozières about the topic, she attached little importance to what she dismissed as idle chatter, assuring her, "You have never been anything but perfect for all of us, and we have long known how to value you." For Chopin it was different, and the thought that Sand might consider inviting de Rozières and Antoni to join them in Nohant drove him to a rare confrontation with her. "I thought he would go crazy," Sand wrote. "He wanted to leave the house, saying I was making him look like a ridiculous, jealous lunatic . . . that my gossiping with you was the cause of it all." And she added, "Two days ago he spent the whole day without uttering a word to a single soul." Chopin was, in fact, seething with anger at the thought that his earlier love life had become the object of gossip. ("I am regarded by the Wodziński family as something quite other than a pianist."[33]) Fortunately, the crisis had blown over by the end of the summer, for the simple reason that de Rozières's hopes of matrimony were shattered after Antoni seduced and then abandoned her before returning to Poland. Seeing de Rozières jilted by a man he had long since ceased to admire, who was moreover the brother of the woman who had earlier jilted Chopin himself, it was not difficult for Chopin to soften his attitude toward her and patch up their friendship. The episode serves to remind us of how jealously Chopin guarded his private life, and how agitated he could become if he feared that it had been breached. As for Sand, she sealed away the memory of their confrontation until the time came for her to draw on it some four years later, when she appropriated it for one of the scenes in her novel *Lucrezia Floriani*, the fictional account she was to offer the world of their lives together.

Chopin's overriding concern was to get his latest crop of manuscripts published. Fontana had done his work well, and by the time that Sand and Chopin got back to Paris, during the first week of November, all that Chopin had to do was to look over Fontana's copies and give final approval to the deal with Breitkopf.

November 12

Gentlemen,
I am sending you my four manuscripts:
    Allegro de Concert, op. 46
    Ballade, op. 47
    Two Nocturnes, op. 48
    Fantaisie, op. 49
Please let me know as soon as you receive them.
Yours most sincerely,
    F. Chopin
    16 rue Pigalle[34]

---

33. CFC, vol. 3, p. 67. Sand's letters to de Rozières may be found in CFC, vol. 3, pp. 52–55, 70–72, and 77–78.
34. Ibid., p. 92.

Within three weeks he had received a bank draft from the publisher ("I beg you to accept my thanks for your punctuality") and was once more flush with money and temporarily freed from financial worries.

X

On December 1, 1841, Chopin took part in a command performance at the newly restored Pavillon de Marsan, located on the north side of the Tuileries Palace. It was the residence of Prince Ferdinand-Philippe, Duke of Orléans, the oldest son of King Louis-Philippe, and was reputed to be the most opulent stately home in France, exceeding by far the luxury of Saint-Cloud, the palatial home of the royal family itself. Five hundred guests had been invited for the concert, including diplomats from the Prussian, Swedish, and Saxon embassies. Louis-Philippe's former prime minister, Adolphe Thiers, added luster to their ranks, and he was flanked by a galaxy of artists, including Delacroix, Delaroche, and Ary Scheffer. Louis-Philippe and Queen Marie-Amélie arrived early with three of their young children, and were accompanied by Queen Maria Cristina of Spain, who had sought sanctuary in France after her forced abdication. It was by far the most glittering assembly before which Chopin had ever appeared. An orchestra had been assembled under the direction of Jacques Halévy to accompany the singers Giulia Grisi, Luigi Lablache, and Fanny Persiani in a medley of Italian operatic arias by Donizetti, Mercadante, and Rossini. Chopin was the only instrumentalist, and he captured the attention of the press with a performance of his Ballade in A-flat major, op. 47, followed by an extended improvisation at which, in the hushed language of La France musicale, "the royal audience marveled." The same journal observed that while pianists who played in public had a habit of playing on new pianos, "Chopin did not hesitate to play on the Pleyel grand piano sold to the court five or six years ago, and drew from it sounds of admirable purity—which testify to the durability of M. Pleyel's pianos."[35] After he had finished playing, Queen Marie-Amélie came over to the piano to congratulate him in person, an unusual gesture that was widely reported. From a letter that his sister Ludwika

---

35. Issue of December 5, 1841.

wrote to him shortly afterward, we gather that Chopin's fee that evening was an expensive set of Sèvres porcelain dishes, while the other artists merely received cash. This distinction charmed Ludwika ("they would not dare offer you money . . . for fear that you might not accept it"), but Chopin was not amused.[36] A couple of days later, Sand wrote to her brother, Hippolyte, "Chip-Chip played at court in a white tie the day before yesterday, but isn't very happy about it."[37] Chopin might have preferred to pocket Luigi Lablache's fee and have the singer walk away with the porcelain dinner service.

Chopin's teaching mill continued to occupy most of his time and provide most of his income. Sand became indignant when "a few fine ladies protested that the rue Pigalle was too far from their elegant districts." These worthies must have been surprised when they received his response: "Ladies, I give much better lessons in my own room and on my own piano for twenty francs than I do for thirty at my pupils' homes, and besides, you have to send your carriages to fetch me, so take your choice." Chopin would never have thought of this strategy by himself. "It was I who suggested it," confessed Sand, "and I had a lot of trouble making him agree."[38]

XI

Despite the routine bouts of ill health that Chopin endured during the winter of 1841–42, he roused himself sufficiently to give another concert in the Pleyel salon on February 21, assisted by Pauline Viardot and August Franchomme. This time the receipts totaled 5,000 francs. Sand, having spent all her superlatives raving about the profits of the concert Chopin had given a year earlier, was reduced to calling it "a unique achievement in Paris." Chopin played among other things three Mazurkas; three Studies from op. 25; four Nocturnes (including the newly published one in F-sharp minor, op. 48, no. 2); the Ballade in A-flat major, op. 47; and the

36. CFC, vol. 3, p. 95; KFC, vol. 2, p. 52.
37. CGS, vol. V, p. 522. Chopin wrote to his father about the concert the same day, December 4. Although the letter is lost, its existence may be inferred from Mikołaj's reply on December 30: "You told us that you attended the *soirée* but were not in a good mood." CFC, vol. 3, p. 96; KFC, vol. 2, p. 50.
38. CGS, vol. V, pp. 522–23.

still-unpublished Impromptu in G-flat major, op. 51. "If music really is architecture in sound," wrote the *Revue et Gazette musicale*, "then Chopin . . . is a most elegant architect."[39] The laudatory review in *La France musicale* painted an extravagant picture of the "social" aspect of the concert, and talked of "the perfumed heads and snowy white shoulders of the most charming women for whom the princely *salons* contend." We are told that George Sand made her entrance in the company of two young girls (Solange and Augustine Brault) and became the observed among the observers. "Others would have been disturbed by all those eyes turned on her like so many stars; but George Sand contented herself with lowering her head and smiling."[40] By now one could no longer talk of a mere audience. Chopin had created a congregation that, in a happy phrase of Liszt, assembled to worship at "the Church of Chopin."

As if to rob him of whatever satisfaction the concert had brought, Chopin learned that his old teacher Adalbert Żywny had passed away that same evening at the ripe age of eighty-six, and the shroud of sadness that settled over him increased his physical woes. Sand once more had a semi-invalid on her hands, and she had to minister to him daily. Her burden was soon to be doubled, as was Chopin's, because his old friend Dr. Jan Matuszyński, who for years had suffered from tuberculosis, had entered the final stages of the disease and was brought over to the rue Pigalle so that he could be cared for properly. And it was there that Chopin and Sand watched him die an agonizing death on April 20. It was a horrifying experience for Chopin, as he witnessed his old friend overcome by violent hemorrhages and terrible convulsions. "He died in our arms," Sand told Pauline Viardot, "after a slow and cruel agony, which caused Chopin as much suffering as if it had been his own . . . When it was all over he broke down."[41] Matuszyński's funeral and burial, which took place in Montmartre Cemetery, filled him with gloom, as did the sight of his friend's grieving widow, Thérèse Boquet, standing at the graveside. Sand knew that she had to get Chopin away from the rue Pigalle, away from the pall of death that hung over their two pavilions. Within a fortnight she had wound up her affairs and was ready to set out with Chopin for an extended

39. Issue of February 27, 1842.
40. Ibid.
41. CGS, vol. V, pp. 647–48.

stay in the country. They departed for Nohant on May 5, arriving the following day. With one brief interruption they remained there until the
end of September.

That summer saw a steady stream of visitors follow them to Nohant,
including Eugène Delacroix (who was giving regular painting lessons to
Maurice), the lawyer Michel de Bourges, the actor Pierre Bocage, the
poet Stefan Witwicki, Louis and Pauline Viardot, and Marie de Rozières,
who was now back in the family fold after her unfortunate brush with
Antoni Wodziński. Dr. Papet also turned up, examined Chopin, and found
his lungs to be in good order. This cheerful news must have surprised his
patient, who could hardly get through the morning before coughing up
copious quantities of phlegm, which made him feel as if he were choking.
Only when the new grand piano that Pleyel had loaned him for the summer
was finally unpacked and installed, on July 19, did his mood brighten. It
was on this instrument that he brought to completion three of his masterpieces: the Ballade in F minor, op. 52; the Polonaise in A-flat major,
op. 53; and the Scherzo in E major, op. 54. Composing, when it went well,
was his redemption.

XII

In the A-flat major Polonaise, Chopin turns his pen into a sword. Of all his
works, this is the one in which the flame of patriotism burns most brightly.
A later generation bestowed on it the subtitle "The Heroic," for pageantry
and heraldry are imprinted on every page. Before we dismiss such views as
mere hyperbole, it is instructive to recall that as early as March 1842, not
long before this Polonaise appeared, the Polish magazine *Tygodnik Liter-
acki* (Literary Weekly) had drawn a startling parallel between Poland's national bard Adam Mickiewicz and Chopin himself. Hitherto, the article
said, it had been Mickiewicz who had spoken for Poland. But "since he has
smashed his fiddle and has become instead a deep thinker, Chopin has
inherited his power, and it is he who feeds the holy flame of nationhood in
our hearts."[42] This open criticism of Mickiewicz by the Poles themselves,
laced as it was with barely concealed sarcasm, and Chopin's elevation to

---

42. Issue of March 7, 1842.

that of national bard in his place, was nothing short of astonishing. What had happened to bring about this shift of opinion?

On December 14, 1841, Mickiewicz had embarked on a second round of lectures on Slavonic literature at the Collège de France, following the ones that Chopin and Sand had attended at the beginning of the year, and they were being critically received. The soaring rhetoric that he had placed in the service of the Slavs and their tormented history was now joined to a different cause. Mickiewicz's conversion to Messianism, and his belief that only divine intervention could save Poland from her enemies, surprised many of his followers who preferred to live by the old adage "God helps those who help themselves." On March 7 the *Literary Weekly* broke with him and declared, "The stance of Chopin in our present situation is more commendable than that of probably anyone."[43] Since Mickiewicz had "smashed his fiddle" he was no longer the Rhapsode of the Poles. It was Chopin's piano that would give voice to Poland's aspirations.

That poetic phrase, "the holy flame of nationhood," could well have been coined to describe what the A-flat major Polonaise has come to symbolize. Its rousing introduction has been likened to a call to arms, punctuated by the rumble of drum rolls in bars 3–4 and 7–8, which come as close to onomatopoeia as anything that Chopin wrote.

---

43. The *Literary Weekly* was published in Poznań, a focal point of resistance to Prussian domination of western Poland and the site of some serious military conflicts during the 1848 uprising.

Not the least interesting feature of this introduction is that it emerges from the "wrong" key of E-flat major, which the ear at first accepts as the tonal center of the piece, but which in retrospect turns out to have been a sustained dominant pedal, heralding the entry of the main theme in the tonic key of A-flat major. Excalibur has been drawn from the stone.

Chopin did not like this polonaise to go fast, and his heading "Maestoso" is not always heeded. Charles Hallé recalled an occasion when Chopin "laid his hand upon my shoulder, saying how unhappy he felt, because he had heard his Grande Polonaise in A-flat *jouée vite!* thereby destroying all the grandeur, the majesty, of this noble inspiration."[44]

Liszt sometimes introduced the Polonaise into his Weimar masterclass, together with commentary drawn from old memories. His Scottish pupil Frederic Lamond was present on one such occasion and recalled "a pianist who was performing Chopin's Polonaise in A-flat major, and playing it with great gusto. When he came to the celebrated octave passage in the left hand, Liszt interrupted him by saying: 'I don't want to listen to how fast you can play octaves. What I wish to hear is the canter of the horses of the Polish cavalry before they gather force and destroy the enemy.'"[45] The image of a cavalry charge is compelling and the fanfare-like motifs in the right hand complete the picture. Lamond's anecdote dates from 1885, but Liszt was simply repeating what had become commonplace in the more than forty years since the Polonaise was composed. Six rolled chords introduce this storied episode, which is set in the unexpected and brilliantly contrasted key of E major.

---

44. HLL, p. 34.
45. LM, p. 68.

These left-hand octaves have given rise to some idle speculation about a possible connection between this work and Liszt's "Funérailles," which bears the inscription "October 1849"—the month of Chopin's death. We are led to believe that "Funérailles" was a posthumous tribute from Liszt, cemented by the striking similarity between Chopin's octaves and those of Liszt in "Funérailles." But the inscription "October 1849" does not refer to Chopin. It memorializes the executions by hanging of thirteen Hungarian generals who had fought in the country's War of Independence against Austria (1848–49) and of the execution of Prime Minister Lajos Batthyány by firing squad that same day, October 6, the anniversary of the Hungarian uprising. Any lingering doubts about this issue are dispelled by a glance at the manuscript, whose title page contains the word "Magyar" (i.e., "Hungarian").

In bars 96–97 there occurs one of the most visually stunning moments in keyboard topography. Because of the layout of the keyboard, the rotating left-hand octaves in E major force the hand to move in a counterclockwise direction. Chopin then abruptly sideslips into D-sharp major, forcing the hand to reverse direction and move clockwise. The choreography is striking, and continues to provide many a heyday for concert pianists. Several editions, including that of Ignaz Friedman, transpose the D-sharp major passage into its enharmonic equivalent key of E-flat major (a change of notation without a change of pitch) to make it easier to read. But Chopin's notation carries with it a different psychological feeling, reflecting as it does the extreme end of the tonal universe he wishes to occupy. An inspection of the manuscript[46] shows that Chopin took pains to write

46. Held in the Morgan Library under the call number Heinemann MS 42.

one double sharp after another as he captured this passage on paper, as if to imprint the struggle on the eye as well as the ear.

Liszt once told his Weimar masterclass that in the lead-back to the main theme one should hear the rumble of distant cannon fire, "as if the passing cavalry a few moments earlier had conjured up recollections of a distant battle"—a prolongation of his earlier image. He then sat down at the piano and achieved the effect of muffled guns by not only emphasizing but slightly delaying the *sf* bass notes and holding them with the pedal. "The unique effect he produced with the accented basses, coming as they do first at longer intervals, then at every measure, came to us as a revelation," wrote his American pupil Carl Lachmund. Liszt added that he had heard Chopin play the passage that way, although there is no record of when that might have happened.[47] Whether onomatopoeia falls within the province of the performer as well as the composer remains an open question, but the possibility cannot be discounted.

Several times in the course of the Polonaise the main theme is recapitulated in apotheosis, bringing with it some additional trills on the second beat—a touch of the side drum and all the panoply associated with it.

The A-flat major Polonaise fulfills one of the basic requirements by which a masterpiece may be defined: it cannot be consumed through use. Each time it is played it invites a further repetition. Here, if anywhere, it is possible to say *Vox populi, vox Dei*. Not surprisingly the work became part of the national solemnities surrounding the return of Chopin's heart to Warsaw in October 1945. Completed during the summer of 1842 at Nohant, the Polonaise was published the following year with a dedication to Chopin's banker, Auguste Léo.

And what of Chopin's response to his widely perceived "displacement" of Mickiewicz as Poland's national bard? It remains unknown. But he and Sand, together with many members of the Polish diaspora, looked on with dismay as Mickiewicz, at the very time this Polonaise was being composed, fell under the spell of the charismatic Polish philosopher Andrzej Towiański, whose strange ideas were leading Mickiewicz from Messianism to Spiritualism and were having a negative influence on his lectures at the Collège de France. Whether "the Bard of Poland" actually believed that Towiański had received a visitation from the Virgin Mary with instructions to divert the course of history and call for the intervention of supernatural forces in the liberation of Poland may never be known. But he certainly knew that Towiański had anointed himself leader of a sect known as "The Circle of God's Cause," which had attached itself to this half-baked agenda. Many thought Mickiewicz had become delusional and belonged in a mental institution. Not surprisingly, the poet lost credibility through his connection to Towiański, and his lectures expired after one more term. "My name is Million," Mickiewicz had written in one of his best-known poems.[48] After 1842, the appellation could easily have been attached to Chopin and the A-flat Polonaise. As for Sand, the glowing

---

48. From the poetic drama *Forefathers' Eve*, Part III, Scene I. Chopin, too, was troubled by Mickiewicz's conversion to Messianism and wrote to Stefan Witwicki about it. "Can

essay on Mickiewicz that she had written not long after her return from Majorca, in which she had hailed him as a prophet of an indomitable Poland, had been rendered pathetic by this turn of events. Thereafter the name of Mickiewicz is notably absent from the list of those who were invited to join her and Chopin at Nohant.

XIII

As in many of the country houses of Europe, Sand's guests at Nohant were at liberty to follow their own pursuits and were never forced on one another's company. Her idea of a house party was not unlike a Greek symposium where the brightest and best could exchange ideas or just get on quietly with their work. Chopin never got used to the more boisterous of Sand's friends, especially those who smoked and drank to excess, so he avoided them by keeping to his room. Sand herself had recently given up smoking cigars in favor of cigarettes out of consideration for Chopin's cough.

Delacroix was making his first visit to Nohant that summer, a place he came to regard as a second home. He had been so ill in Paris, suffering from a stubborn infection of the larynx (he would one day succumb to tuberculosis), that on the orders of his physician he had abandoned work on the murals of the library of the Luxembourg Palace and sought to convalesce in the countryside. Sand had come to his rescue by inviting him to Nohant, and it was here that his friendship with Chopin took wing. They now had the chance to build on their earlier acquaintance and engage in some intimate conversations about painting and music, in which they sought to find a rapport "between the tones of painting and the sounds of music." Delacroix found Chopin surprisingly receptive to such ideas. He already loved Chopin's music and began to love the man. He was transported by Chopin's improvisations, which wafted daily through the rooms of the château and reached the atelier where he painted. Sand, for her part, wanted to attract Delacroix to Nohant on a regular basis, and the pair started talking about converting one of the buildings adjoining the manor

---

you conceive of greater madness?" he asked. CFC, vol. 3, pp. 191–92; KFC, vol. 2, pp. 130–31.

house into a permanent studio where he and Maurice might work. Here
is how Delacroix described life at Nohant in the summer of 1842.

> When you are not assembled for dinner or lunch or billiards or for
> walks, you can go and read in your room or sprawl on your sofa.
> Every now and then there wafts through your window, opening on
> to the garden, a breath of the music of Chopin, who is at work in
> his room, and it mingles with the song of the nightingales and the
> scent of the roses . . . I have endless conversations with Chopin, of
> whom I am really very fond and who is a man of rare distinction.
> He is the truest artist I have ever met, one of the very few whom
> one can admire and value.[49]

There were times when it must have seemed to Sand that she was
running a hotel, rather than a symposium, with an endless procession of
guests coming and going. She was as gregarious as ever, which meant that
money flowed out as soon as it flowed in. One way to keep it flowing in,
of course, was to finish her novel *Consuelo*, which had occupied her for
the past several months and was about to be serialized in *La Revue indépendante*, a monthly magazine that she herself had founded with Pierre
Leroux a short time earlier. Sand modeled the heroine of the novel, a Spanish opera singer named Consuelo, on the personality of Pauline Viardot,
whose fictional counterpart lived a life of "moral purity over the manifold
temptations of the flesh." Central to the plot is the figure of Consuelo's
old maestro Nicola Antonio Porpora, who decries flashy virtuosity in favor
of pure musicality—an idea that Sand probably derived from Chopin. The
novel became a best seller, but whatever it did for Sand's bank balance it
proved that she could never have set up shop as a clairvoyant. Within a few
short years Pauline Viardot, Consuelo's real-life model, had succumbed to
"the manifold temptations of the flesh" by having an affair with Sand's
son, Maurice, under the nose of her husband, Louis, creating panic at
Nohant—a topic to which we will return. Pauline then went on to fan the
flames of a passion she had aroused in the heart of the young Russian novelist Ivan Turgenev, who fell madly in love with her during her concerts in
Saint Petersburg, followed her back to France, and installed himself under

---

49. LED, pp. 161 and 164.

the Viardots' roof as a "novelist in residence"—or, as some would have it, her lover in residence and the possible father of one of her four children.

XIV

For much of the summer Sand fretted about where she and Chopin might live when they returned to Paris. She knew that to go back to the rue Pigalle was impossible, filled as it was with memories of the illness and death of Jan Matuszyński. The best medicine would be a complete change of scenery, unencumbered by the old associations. Charlotte Marliani once again came to the rescue and alerted Sand to the advantage of moving into apartments in the newly fashionable Square d'Orléans, located in the ninth arrondissement, not far from Montmartre. Charlotte had recently moved there and she acted as Sand's go-between. The Square d'Orléans was modeled on the neoclassical design of the Regent's Park residences in London and was the work of the English architect Edward Cresy. A private portico led to a tree-lined courtyard within, where the white stone apartments were adorned with pillars in the classical style. The central fountain was a later addition, dating from the 1850s. Named after King Louis-Philippe, who was then Duke d'Orléans, the square was finished in 1829 and became known as "the new Athens." One of the first residents was Alexandre Dumas *père*, and other distinguished tenants followed. They included the composers Charles-Valentin Alkan and Charles Gounod; the Conservatoire piano professor Pierre-Joseph Zimmerman; the sculptor Jean-Pierre Dantan; the writer Louis Énault (who later published a popular biography of Chopin); the actress Mme Mars; and the ballerina Marie-Sophie Taglioni. Friedrich Kalkbrenner had also lived there for a time. The place was a veritable *Who's Who* in the arts.

Sand and Chopin came up from Nohant to view the Square d'Orléans at the end of July 1842, and immediately fell in love with the place. They signed two separate leases on August 5, and the rent was not cheap. Sand acquired the more spacious apartment (no. 5), which cost her 3,000 francs a year; Chopin's smaller dwelling (no. 9) cost him 600 francs a year, but he knew that he could raise this sum in a few weeks by giving piano lessons. Charlotte Marliani lived between them (no. 7). The enclosed courtyard offered plenty of room for the carriages in which Chopin's wealthier pupils generally arrived. The square was also reasonably close to the theater and the opera house, an unexpected bonus for Chopin. He could see Sand's apartment from his study windows, and was able to walk across the courtyard to her place for meals after he had finished teaching, or join her or Mme Marliani and their guests whenever one or the other of them wanted to act as hostess. It was a perfect solution to the continuing problem of their *ménage à deux* and how to present it to the outside world. At the Square d'Orléans Sand and Chopin were able to enjoy an intimate family life, yet at the same time live as independent people. Sand described the arrangement in her autobiography.

> We left our apartment in rue Pigalle, which [Chopin] came to find unpleasant, and had established ourselves on the Square d'Orléans, where the enterprising Marliani had arranged a family life for all of us. She occupied a lovely apartment between our two [at no. 7]. In order to visit one another—sometimes at her apartment, sometimes at mine, sometimes at Chopin's, when he felt inclined to play for us—we had only to cross a large, clean sandy courtyard decorated with plants. We would all eat together at Marliani's and share expenses. It was a good economical arrangement and it allowed me to see all manner of people at Mme Marliani's, to visit more intimately with friends in my own apartment, and to resume my work whenever I felt like retiring. Chopin, too, was delighted to have a beautiful, isolated drawing room where he could go to compose or dream. But he loved people, and rarely took advantage of his sanctuary, except to give lessons.[50]

A week after signing their respective leases, Sand and Chopin rejoined their houseguests at Nohant. It was not until September 27 that they traveled back to Paris in the company of the Viardots, and moved the following day into their separate quarters. The Square d'Orléans remained Chopin's residence for the next seven years, until just a few weeks before his death.

---

50. SHV, vol. 2, pp. 435–36.

XV

Among Chopin's first visitors was the Russian diplomat Wilhelm von Lenz, who left a memoir of the occasion and became Chopin's pupil. "He was a young man," von Lenz recalled, "not very tall—slim and haggard, with a sad, but most expressive face, and an elegant Parisian bearing. I have seldom met with an apparition so entirely engaging." After telling Chopin that he had studied some of the Mazurkas with Liszt, von Lenz must have been surprised when Chopin inquired, "Then why do you need me?" The meeting looked as if it might end before it had properly begun, but the diplomat in von Lenz rose to the occasion. "I want to have the privilege of studying them with you. I regard your Mazurkas as Literature." With that the atmosphere warmed noticeably. Chopin pulled an elegant little watch from his waistcoat pocket with the remark, "I still have a few minutes—I was going out—I had forbidden the door to anyone—you must pardon me." Not wishing to waste a moment more on pleasantries, von Lenz went over to the piano.

It was a Pleyel; I had been told that Chopin never used any other instrument. The Pleyel has an easier action than that of any other Parisian manufacturer. I struck a chord before seating myself, to get the depth of touch ("le gué," I called it). This, and my manner, seemed to please Chopin. He smiled and leaned wearily against the piano, and his keen eyes looked me directly in the face: I dared only one glance toward him, then, taking my courage in both hands, I started the B-flat major Mazurka—the typical one, to which Liszt had given me the variants.[51] I played it well. The "volata" through the two octaves went better than ever before, and the instrument was easier to the touch than my Érard. Chopin whispered engagingly: "That little bit is not your own, is it? *He* showed you that! *He* must have his hand in everything! Well, he may dare. He plays to thousands, I seldom to one! Very well, I will give you lessons. But only twice a week—that is the most I ever give. It will be difficult to find three quarters of an hour . . . But you must be very

51. This was the well-known Mazurka in B-flat major, op. 7, no. 1, the "volata" mentioned by von Lenz being a Lisztian flourish that has not come down to us.

punctual. With me everything goes by the clock—my house is like a dovecote."[52]

Von Lenz always turned up early and waited in the antechamber. One lady after another would come out of Chopin's music room, "each one more beautiful than the last." Among them was Mlle Laure Duperré (the daughter of Admiral Victor Duperré), to whom Chopin had the previous year dedicated his two Nocturnes, op. 48. "She was a most lovely woman, tall and straight, like a palm tree," von Lenz remarked, and she was at that time one of Chopin's favorite pupils. When the lesson was over, Chopin liked to play the cavalier, accompanying Laure to the stairs and taking his leave of her in the vestibule, a courtesy he rarely extended to others. The thirteen-year-old Hungarian prodigy Károly (Carl) Filtsch was also observed coming and going. Friederike Müller had introduced this gifted youth to Chopin a year or so earlier, having attended some of his sensational concerts in Vienna. Von Lenz became mildly jealous when Chopin allowed young Filtsch to play the B-flat minor Scherzo after refusing to let von Lenz himself learn it, because "it was too difficult for me." Chopin did encourage von Lenz to sit in on one or two lessons, however, so that he "often heard this wonderful work at its very best." Filtsch was at that time studying Chopin's E minor Concerto with the composer, who claimed that the boy played it better than he did. We shall have more to say about Filtsch, because he was the only pupil of unquestionable genius that Chopin ever taught.

To von Lenz we owe the preservation of a celebrated encounter between Chopin and Meyerbeer and their heated argument about "tempo rubato." It would be derelict not to report it here because it reveals the distance that sometimes separated Chopin from his contemporaries, even the most distinguished, on matters of musical interpretation. Von Lenz was having a lesson on the Mazurka in C major, op. 33, no. 2, when Meyerbeer unexpectedly walked in. Chopin invited the great composer to sit down and indicated to von Lenz that he should continue playing.

"That is two-four time," said Meyerbeer. In reply, Chopin told me to repeat it, and kept time by tapping loudly upon the instrument with his pencil. His eyes glowed. "Two-four," repeated Meyerbeer quietly.

---

52. LPZ, p. 35.

I only once, in all the time I knew him, saw Chopin angry. A delicate flush covered his pale cheeks—he looked very handsome. "It is three-four," he said loudly—he who always spoke so softly! "Let me use it," said Meyerbeer, "as a ballet for my opera. Then I will show you." (He was writing *L'Africaine*, then kept secret.) "It is three-four," Chopin almost screamed, and he played it himself. He played it several times, counting loudly, and stamping the time with his foot in rage! It was no use. Meyerbeer insisted it was two-four. They parted not on the best terms! It was anything but agreeable to me to have been present at this little scene. Chopin disappeared into his room, without saying a word, leaving me alone with Meyerbeer.[53]

Von Lenz has the reputation of being a chatterbox, and there are aspects to his story that make us yearn for greater clarity. Still, at its heart it contains a ring of truth. When he reflected on this unfortunate scene, he remarked, "All the same, Chopin was right. Though the third beat in the Mazurka is slurred over, it certainly exists—but I took care not to press this point with the composer of *Les Huguenots*!"

It does not do to dwell on how Meyerbeer could have heard this passage in 2/4 time. Nor is the mystery resolved when we read in the memoirs of Berlioz that Chopin could never play strictly in time[54]—Chopin, who had a metronome always standing on the piano and whose pupils were reprimanded if they played too freely. Liszt is particularly informative here. He heard Chopin play many times and came forward with an image that bears contemplation: "Look at these trees. The wind plays in the leaves, develops life in them. But the tree remains the same. That is *Chopin's Rubato*!"[55] To

53. LPZ, pp. 45–46.
54. "Chopin chafed under the restraints of time . . . [He] simply could not play in strict time." BM, p. 436.
55. LPZ, p. 47. Liszt developed this image in his biography of Chopin. Chopin's rubato "is like

which it only remains to add that when not only the leaves begin to sway but also the boughs, then the piece itself is about to be blown away.

Toward the end of the year, December 1842, Chopin received a letter from the pianist Anna de Belleville, whose nuanced playing of the classics he had admired when he heard her play as a teenager in Warsaw. She was now married to Antonio Oury, a violinist in Her Majesty's Theatre Orchestra, London, and wondered if Chopin had anything new in his portfolio that she might introduce to the London public. All his recent compositions, he replied, were destined for his English publisher, Wessel. By way of reparation he offered her what he called a little Waltz "which I have had the pleasure of writing for you, but please keep it for yourself. I should not like it to be made public."[56] This was the Waltz in F minor, op. 70, no. 2, which Anna probably thought had been composed especially for her. In fact, it was one of those pieces that Chopin copied out several times and circulated among his friends, "especially for them"—an economical way of flattering their vanity. There were at least eight manuscript copies of this Waltz in circulation during Chopin's lifetime, most of them dedicated to women, including one that he placed in Delfina Potocka's album two years later. Fontana published an edited version of the Waltz in his posthumous edition of Chopin's piano music, in 1855.

XVI

We mentioned Carl Filtsch. A few more words about this musical prodigy are in order because of his unique position in the roll call of Chopin's

---

the flickering of a flame in the drifting air, like the swaying of a field of corn responding to a gentle breeze, like the treetops which the involuntary movement of the wind bends back and forth." (RGS, vol. 1, p. 82.) It is worth recalling that Chopin was the first composer in history to write the words "tempo rubato" into his scores.
56. CFC, vol. 3, p. 125; KFC, vol. 2, pp. 75–76.

pupils. The eleven-year-old boy had turned up on Chopin's doorstep toward the end of November 1841, in the company of his older brother and traveling companion Josef, the pair having journeyed all the way from their native Transylvania, then part of Hungary. Sons of a Protestant pastor in the town of Szászebes, both brothers were musically gifted, but eleven-year-old Carl was considered by all who heard him to be a genius. Josef, older than Carl by seventeen years, acted as a surrogate father, looked after the boy's interests, and sent informative letters back home to the parents, from which some of our present information is gleaned. Thanks to the generosity of Hungarian aristocrats, Filtsch was rescued from obscurity and brought first to Vienna, where he had some lessons from Friedrich Wieck before being sent to Paris to study with Chopin.

Chopin read the letters of introduction handed to him by Josef, and then asked Carl to play something. The boy went over to the piano and plunged into Thalberg's *Don Giovanni* Fantaisie, op. 14, which he had studied with Wieck and with Thalberg's old teacher August Mittag. After the opening cascades had landed him on the main theme, Chopin stopped him with the remark, *"Brave, mon enfant.* You have had very good masters." He then left the room for a moment and returned with George Sand, who also wanted him to play something. When he had finished, she "kissed Carl warmly," wrote Josef, "and we left with the happy certainty that we had the hour from 10 to 11 every other day."[57] Sand took to the boy and often invited him over to her place in the rue Pigalle, and later to her new address in the Square d'Orléans. The Filtsch brothers were living at that time in the home of the Duke de la Rochefoucauld, head of one of the most distinguished families in France, and Carl liked nothing better than to bring his young friend, ten-year-old Arthur de la Rochefoucauld, with him so that they could indulge in a game of billiards after Carl's lessons were finished. George Sand's billiards table, which she had installed the moment she moved into the Square d'Orléans, provided hours of diversion for her guests.

Filtsch remained with Chopin for eighteen months (1841–43), and Chopin invested much time in fostering his talent. He gave Filtsch three lessons a week, more than he generally allowed his other pupils, and the boy made rapid strides. Among the works Filtsch studied with Chopin (aside from the E minor Piano Concerto and the Scherzo in B-flat minor, already

---

57. GNCF, p. 172.

Carl Filtsch; a
lithograph by
Franz Eybl (1841).

mentioned) were the recently composed Ballade in A-flat major, op. 47,
the Two Nocturnes, op. 48, and the still-unpublished Impromptu in G-flat
major, op. 51. Works by Bach and Beethoven, as well as Thalberg, Moscheles,
and Weber, also found a place in Carl's repertoire. Chopin was delighted
with the boy's playing and came to regard him as the best interpreter of
his works, calling him affectionately "my little *gamin.*" "My God!" Chopin
once exclaimed, after hearing him play. "What a child! Nobody has ever
understood me as this child has . . . It is not imitation, it is the same sentiment, an instinct that makes him play without thinking that it could go
any other way. He plays almost all my compositions without having heard
me [play them], without being shown the smallest thing . . ."[58] Some worried that the youth was modeling himself so closely on Chopin, whom he
obviously idolized, that he ran the risk of losing his artistic identity. But
Filtsch replied that he was incapable of playing with someone else's feelings.

58. Reported by Ferdinand Denis in Vienna's *Der Humorist,* February 1843.

"Even Chopin was stupefied by this bold and original reply, which pleased him greatly," Josef informed his parents.[59] By all accounts Carl had a fabulous musical memory. He was able to copy out Chopin's Impromptu in G-flat major, op. 51, after hearing Chopin himself play it at his lessons.[60] But this feat was soon put into the shade by another one. While Carl was preparing for a public performance of the E minor Concerto in London, a few months later, it was impossible to get hold of the orchestral parts in time, so Carl copied them out from memory—a feat reported by J. W. Davison, the music critic of the London *Times*.[61]

Chopin and Sand often invited guests to the Square d'Orléans to hear Carl play. One such appearance included a performance of the great C minor Nocturne, op. 48, no. 1, given before a group of aristocratic ladies. Chopin turned to them, placed his hand on Carl's shoulder, and said, "That, ladies, is called *talent*." During the summer of 1842, after Chopin and Sand had departed on their annual sojourn to Nohant, Filtsch took a few lessons from Liszt, who had just got back to Paris fresh from his triumphs in Saint Petersburg. When Liszt heard Filtsch, he recognized in the Hungarian prodigy his second self. "When that young man sets out on his travels, I shall shut up shop," he declared.[62] Liszt then did his patriotic duty, took the boy under his wing, and gave him lessons *gratis*. In a charming letter written after Liszt had resumed his tours and left for Cologne, he addressed Filtsch as "Dearly Beloved Conjuror."[63]

Filtsch was the only pupil to whom Chopin gave composition lessons. From a brochure that remains strangely neglected, we learn that Chopin instructed the boy to compose an Impromptu of his own, based on the one in G-flat major by Chopin that he knew so well. The sketches for this work bear corrections in Chopin's hand and were preserved in a dossier of manuscripts and letters assembled by Josef Filtsch as a memorial tribute to his brother after the latter's early death.[64]

---

59. HSCC, p. 217.
60. Carl's manuscript copy of Chopin's Impromptu is mentioned in Maurice Brown's Index of Chopin's Works (no. 149), and also in Krystyna Kobylańska's Manuscripts of Chopin's Works (no. 724).
61. NFC, vol. 2, p. 175.
62. LPZ, p. 36.
63. LLB, vol. 1, p. 47.
64. The dossier was described in a little-known thirty-page brochure titled "About One Whom Chopin Loved," written by Josef Filtsch's daughter, Irene Andrews, and privately pub-

During the eighteen months that Filtsch was with Chopin he made some high-profile appearances at which Chopin was either his collaborative artist or a visible member of the audience. To no other pupil did Chopin extend similar endorsements. They shared the same platform at least five times, and on three occasions they played Chopin's E minor Concerto with Chopin accompanying at a second piano, a work that became the boy's signature piece. Count Emmanuel de Las Cases, the venerable president of the Phrenological Society, attended one of these performances and after examining Carl's cranium proclaimed him to be "a child with a great intellect and an indomitable will." In mid-January 1843, Baron James de Rothschild opened his palatial home on the rue Lafitte and arranged a *grande soirée musicale* so that young Filtsch could display his talents to a larger audience. His wife, Baroness Betty, had heard the boy at George Sand's a few weeks earlier and was determined to draw him into the Rothschilds' circle. Never had their famous residence glittered with such a display of gold and silver candelabra, crystalware, luxurious tapestries, priceless paintings and sculptures, with liveried servants standing vigil at tables filled to overflowing with flowers and ices. Five hundred guests were present, including members of the royal family, and numerous distinguished artists took part, including the singers Pauline Viardot, Giulia Grisi, and Luigi Lablache. But all eyes were on Filtsch, who once again played the E minor Concerto with Chopin at the second piano. When the success of this performance reached the ears of the conductor François Habeneck, he

---

lished in New York, in 1923. It contained striking proof of Carl's gift for composition, for enclosed with the sketches of the Impromptu there was also a *Konzertstück* for piano and orchestra, which was published in 2005 in an edition by Ferdinand Gajewski. These documents were dealt with by Gajewski in his article "New Chopiniana from the Papers of Carl Filtsch." (*Studi musicali* XI [1982], pp. 171–77.) The dossier also contained a run of letters from Carl and Josef to their parents, from which we have quoted some random excerpts. When Arthur Hedley first brought out these letters in his *Selected Correspondence of Fryderyk Chopin*, doubt was cast on their authenticity, which still lingers. Hedley claimed to have copied the texts directly from the dossier, which had meanwhile found its way to England and was made available to him by a descendant of Josef Filtsch, Sir Francis Gwynne-Evans (better known as Francis Loring, the singer). It is not known if Hedley worked from autographs or from typed copies, because the dossier itself is no longer in the public domain. While we cannot rule out the possibility that the texts were "edited" by family members, the many references to Chopin that they contain, together with the composer's special relationship to Carl that they reveal, can in the main be verified from other sources. In this regard, the biographical sketch of Carl Filtsch by Marie Klein, *Chopin Magyar tanítványa Filtsch Károly* (Chopin's Hungarian Disciple Károly Filtsch), should not be overlooked.

arranged for the boy to repeat the Concerto with the Paris Conservatoire Orchestra.

But it was the concert that took place in the Érard salon on April 24, 1843, which created the greatest sensation and obliged Filtsch to give encores. The boy had been ill, having exhausted himself through overwork and the stress of appearing so often in public. As he seated himself at the piano and observed the familiar faces of Chopin, Sand, and his brother Josef in the audience, he rallied and summoned all his resources. Although the documentary record is incomplete, it appears that he played Liszt's *Lucia di Lammermoor* paraphrase and Thalberg's *Don Giovanni* Fantaisie, performances that brought the house down. "This is how we imagine Mozart must have played," wrote the critic of *Le Monde musical*, "thus we remember Liszt twenty years ago."[65] But the greatest applause was reserved for a group of Chopin's studies and the Nocturne in C minor, op. 48, which once again revealed Carl's singing touch and his control over the thundering octaves in the middle section of the latter piece. The boy had to return to the platform several times before the audience let him go and he was able to rush up to Chopin, who embraced him, uttering once more the simple words, "*Brave, mon enfant.*"[66]

Filtsch left Chopin's orbit as abruptly as he had entered it, not yet thirteen years old. When Chopin set out for Nohant, on May 22, 1843, he had every expectation that Filtsch would be waiting for him when he got back to Paris in the fall. But the young genius was already garnering fresh laurels in England, and Chopin never saw his "little *gamin*" again. Two years later Filtsch was taken ill in Vienna just as he was about to walk onto the concert platform to play his *Konzertstück*. He was brought to Venice by his Hungarian patrons, where he died, his shining promise unfulfilled.

---

65. Ibid., p. 28.
66. Ibid. The concert was reviewed for the *Revue et Gazette musicale* by Henri Blanchard in its issue of April 30, 1843. He wrote, "In him one could recognize those qualities so rarely present in seasoned pianists who think of themselves as being front-rank performers."

THE DEATH OF
MIKOŁAJ CHOPIN, 1844

The medals one possesses are worthless, if one is not a good human being.

—*Mikołaj Chopin*[1]

I

On May 3, 1844, after a long illness, Mikołaj Chopin died in the home of his daughter Izabella Barcińska. He was seventy-three years old. The funeral took place on May 6, and Mikołaj was interred in the Powązki Cemetery, where years earlier Chopin's sister Emilia had been buried. A graveside oration was delivered by Bishop Jan Dekert, Mikołaj's former pupil and a lifelong family friend.[2] A mass for the dead was celebrated the next day in the Church of the Capuchins on Miodowa Street. Many of the scientific and artistic elite of Warsaw were among the mourners. "He was a great father and husband, and a noble friend," wrote the *Warsaw Courier* in its obituary notice on May 5. "He left two daughters and one son of whom the whole nation is proud." And on May 12 the same journal published a panegyric to Mikołaj, which took the form of a poem extolling his virtues, which now lived on in his famous son.

---

1. SRCY, no. 32, p. 249.
2. The manuscript of this oration, which contains valuable information about Mikołaj's early years in Poland, is preserved in the Chopin National Institute, Warsaw, under the call number F. 4528.

The noble Chopin has died, but he left us
His son, to whom talent gave fame.
With his great qualities
He brings glory to our country,
In him as in all his family
The paternal virtues will continue to shine forth.

Three weeks elapsed before Fryderyk received news of his father's death, which devastated him. He shut himself away in his apartment in the Square d'Orléans and refused to see anyone. "He declined visibly," George Sand wrote, "and I did not know what remedies to use to combat the increasing irritation of his nerves." She asked Auguste Franchomme to come over and spend time with him, "for you are one of the two or three people who can do him good. I myself suffer too much from his grief: I have not the strength to console him."[3] Such was the depth of Chopin's despair that he was unable to summon the energy to write to his mother. It was left to Sand herself to compile a tactful, and somewhat flowery, letter of condolence to Justyna and describe the despair that Chopin was suffering at the loss of his father. After assuring Justyna that her son was not ill, and that he was showing both courage and resignation in the face of such grave news, she told her that they would shortly be leaving for the country, "where he will rest after this terrible crisis." She then continued,

[Paris, May 29, 1844]
He thinks only of you, his sisters, and all his family, whom he so warmly cherishes, and whose sorrow distresses and occupies his mind as much as does his own grief. For your part at least, please do not worry about the outward circumstances of his life. I cannot

---

3. CFC, vol. 3, p. 150. Sand's letter is dated May 26, 1844. The context makes it clear that Chopin did not learn of his father's death until May 25, when Sand herself broke the news to him after they had visited the theater to see a performance of Sophocles's *Antigone*. The very next day, May 26, she told Franchomme: "Our poor Chopin has just received news of the death of his father." On May 29 she conveyed the same information to Pierre Bocage, informing him of Chopin's profound sadness, and then wrote a letter of consolation to Justyna Chopin. See Georges Lubin's interesting commentary on this inexplicable delay, in CGS, vol. VI, p. 556. The distinguished editor of Sand's correspondence is not alone in finding it "astonishing" that news of Mikołaj's death should have taken so long to reach Paris.

hope to remove his deep, lasting, and well-justified sorrow, but I can at least care for his health and surround him with as much affection and watchfulness as you yourself could show. This loving duty is one which I have been happy to take upon myself, and I promise that I shall never fail in it, and I hope that you, Madame, have confidence in my devotion to him.

I will not say that your bereavement affects me as much as it would have done had I known the admirable man whom you mourn. My sympathy, sincere as it is, cannot lessen that terrible blow; but I know that by telling you that I will consecrate my days to his son, whom I regard as one of my own, I shall in some measure offer you tranquility of mind. It is for this reason that I have taken the liberty of writing to express my profound attachment to you as the adored mother of my dearest friend.

George Sand[4]

Several things strike us about this letter. For five years Sand and Chopin had enjoyed a widely publicized *ménage à deux*, yet there is no suggestion here of any romantic attachment between them. Sand refers to Chopin as "my dearest friend" and implies that she regards Chopin as one of her own children. Justyna replied in similar vein, tactfully using the same sort of veiled language and entrusting her son to Sand's "maternal care," as she put it. She implored Sand to be Chopin's guardian angel "as you have been an angel of consolation to me, and accept our respectful gratitude, which you may be sure equals your invaluable devotion and care."[5] It should not surprise us that this correspondence was initiated by Sand, and not by Chopin. Chopin's helplessness in the face of adversity was well known, and his penchant for placing a protective wall of silence between himself and the cruel world beyond was never more in evidence. But it does seem extraordinary that he was unable to write to his mother and be the first to console her in her hour of grief.

---

4. CFC, vol. 3, pp. 150–51.
5. Ibid., p. 152.

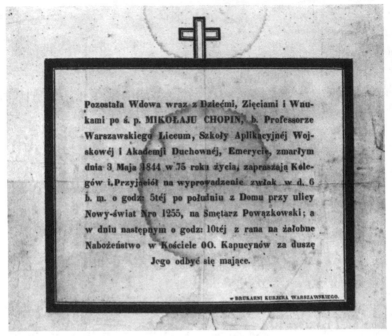

Pozostała Wdowa wraz z Dziećmi, Zięciami i Wnu-
kami po ś. p. MIKOŁAJU CHOPIN, b. Professorze
Warszawskiego Liceum, Szkoły Aplikacyjnéj Woj-
skowéj i Akademji Duchownéj, Emerycie, zmarłym
dnia 3 Maja 1844 w 75 roku życia, zapraszają Kóle-
gów i Przyjaciół na wyprowadzenie zwłok w d. 6
b. m. o godz: 5téj po południu z Domu przy uliey
Nowy-świat Nro 1255, na Smętarz Powązkowski; a
w dniu następnym o godz: 10téj z rana na żałobne
Nabożeństwo w Kościele OO. Kapucynów za duszę
Jego odbyć się mające.

▾ DRUKARNI KURJERA WARSZAWSKIEGO.

Mikołaj Chopin's funeral announcement, Warsaw, May 5, 1844.

II

Chopin contacted his brother-in-law Antoni Barciński, and asked him for a full account of what had happened during the weeks leading up to his father's death and funeral. From Antoni's long and highly informative reply we learn that Mikołaj and Justyna had given up their own home and had moved in with the Barcińskis, who had acquired more generous accommodation to make this possible. The family was now living at 1255 Nowy Świat (New World) Street, one of the most fashionable thoroughfares in Warsaw, with buildings of neoclassical proportions. There Mikołaj had access to a garden, where he spent his declining years cultivating grapes and producing his own wine—a return to the occupation of his forefathers in Lorraine. He gradually lost his strength as the tuberculosis from which he had long suffered took its toll. Izabella helped to nurse her father during the final weeks, and Ludwika and her husband, Kalasanty, came every other day. Throughout the final ordeal Mikołaj remained calm, and observed, "I thank Almighty God for having given me such good, loving, and virtuous children!" He was not afraid of death, and bore his illness with fortitude. During his last night on earth Izabella and Antoni sat by his bedside. Toward morning, as he felt his end approaching, Mikołaj called out, "Antoni, dear Antoni, do not leave me today." So Antoni stayed. Mikołaj's gaze often wandered across the room to Chopin's portrait and bust, from which he drew comfort. And then, in Antoni's words, "he went to sleep, in every sense of the word, and I wish that everyone may live as he lived and die as he died."[6]

By far the most significant revelation in this letter is Mikołaj's request that his body be opened after his death, in order to avoid the fate of awakening in the tomb. He was greatly influenced in this decision by Professor Józef Bełza, a Polish scientist and close family friend who had lived for a time with the Barciński family. Here is how Antoni described the situation.

A very learned man of honest heart [Bełza] has been trying for years to organize in Warsaw an establishment where the departed would be kept for a few days before their burial. He knows all about such things and used to tell our father when the latter still enjoyed full health about certain random cases of apparent death. Our dear father encouraged him to realize his project. This is why—his very vivid memory having reminded him of such circumstances in the last days of his life—*our father asked us to have his body opened after his death, so as to spare him the terrible fate of those who awake in the tomb. There is nothing surprising about that.* [My italics]

There is not much doubt that the famous scrap of paper that Chopin was supposed to have written on his deathbed, requesting that he may not be buried alive, was in fact written by Mikołaj himself.[7] The matter

---

6. Barciński's letter is dated "Warsaw, June 1844." CFC, vol. 3, pp. 152–58; KFC, vol. 2, pp. 93–98.

7. See the image of this document on page 474. *"Comme cette toux m'étouffera, je vous conjure de faire ouvrir mon corps pour [que] je [ne] sois pas enterré vif"* ("As this cough will suffocate me, I implore you to have my body opened lest I be buried alive"). Mikołaj supported Józef Bełza in the latter's attempts to organize an establishment in Warsaw whose function would be to observe the dead for several days in order to avoid interring someone alive. (CFC, vol. 3, p. 156; KFC, vol. 2, pp. 96–97.) The document was preserved by Ludwika among other family relics

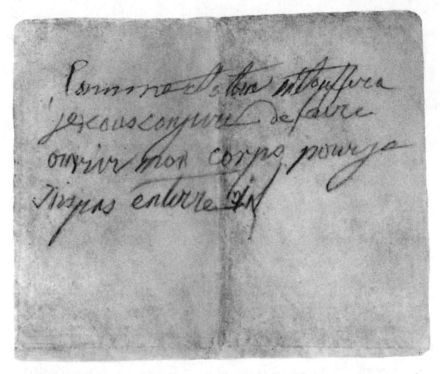

Mikołaj Chopin's last words: "As this cough will suffocate me, I implore you to have my body opened lest I be buried alive."

has been forcefully debated across the years, but Antoni Barciński's letter provides compelling evidence that such a request came from Mikołaj, shortly before his demise. And these written instructions would have served a practical purpose: they would have protected Bełza himself had he been subjected to unwelcome scrutiny by those members of the religious, medical, and legal communities who happened not to support his radical ideas about the setting up of a warehouse for the "undead" in Warsaw.

---

in her possession, and was eventually passed to her daughter, Madame Ludwika Ciechomska. There is no evidence that this scrap of paper came from France. In fact, there is not a single mention of it in the recollections of those who were present at Chopin's bedside during his final days. Had it not been for the fact that the document was reproduced by Mieczysław Karłowicz in his book *Souvenirs inédits de Frédéric Chopin*, first published in Warsaw and Paris in 1904, we might never have learned of it. This deathbed note perished in Poland during World War II.

Anxious to assure Chopin that his father's decision had not been taken without reflection, and that Mikołaj had been of sound mind, Barciński provided some additional details.

You know that Father had a far-sighted spirit and an extremely active brain. When I pointed out to him that his illness was not dangerous and that—thank God—we were still playing, like we always did, with that wooden stake in the garden, he smiled and said: "My dear Antoni, I am requesting this to cover all eventualities. If I get better, my caution will not be necessary this time." Do not think, my dear Frycek, that he made this request because of physical suffering (which might lead him to believe that his end was near). It was his general way of seeing things. He had already mentioned it to me several years ago. Do not imagine anything terrible about this, and do not attribute this request to physical suffering or to a torment greater than what your father actually had to endure, for you would do him wrong. A fair man, full of justice, of righteousness; breathing only for the happiness of others and who sacrificed his whole life for them, such a man is not afraid of death. Our father felt no agony. He died with serenity, and with the sweet certainty that he would survive through his children, whose hearts he had formed according to his. He was absolutely calm and penetrated by the pleasant assurance that unity of feeling, fraternal love, mutual tenderness of all the members of a family, small in number but fundamentally honest, gave him the formal guarantee of our felicity on earth; and just as this admirable father in the twilight of life was breathing only through our happiness and through our successes, he therefore did not have the slightest reason to torment or sadden himself. Every day, he repeated to us that it would be difficult to find a happier father than he. God will bless you, he used to say, if you keep loving and respecting one another; look after your health, be full of solicitude for your mother. Thus believe, my dear Frycek, in what I have just written to you about our father, who is so deserving of admiration. No one possessed his trust more than myself, no one had freer access to the secrets of his heart; it is for these reasons that I have been able to reveal to you the pure truth with the certainty that you will find in my assertions some slight source of consolation.

III

This was the emotional background against which Ludwika and her husband, Kalasanty, decided to travel to France and visit Chopin. Nine years had elapsed since Chopin had seen any members of his family, and fourteen since he had said farewell to his sister, and he was overjoyed at the prospect of seeing her again. Kalasanty he had not yet met. Sand, too, was delighted at this visit and she invited the couple to make use of her apartment in the Square d'Orléans for a few days and then travel as her houseguests to Nohant, where she and Chopin were spending the summer. Chopin could not wait to see his sister, so he traveled back to Paris by himself and on July 16 he and Ludwika were reunited.

Chopin told Mlle de Rozières (who had been instructed to prepare Sand's apartment for Ludwika and Kalasanty) that he was experiencing "happiness enough to send one crazy and to make me wonder whether you will understand my French today."[8] He had been conversing with Ludwika and Kalasanty in Polish without pause, eager to receive from their own lips an account of his father's last days and a description of the funeral. For the next ten days Chopin became a tourist guide, showing his special visitors the sights of the city. He introduced them to his Polish friends and even put on a reception for them in his own apartment in the Square d'Orléans. The homes of Auguste Léo, the Franchommes, and the Marlianis were also opened to them, and they attended the opera. Kalasanty was a technology enthusiast and he happily went off to various exhibitions in search of the latest mechanical novelties, while Chopin and his sister drove around Paris in a carriage so that she could admire the city's architectural landmarks in comfort. In the midst of all this activity the trio did not forget to go to Montmartre Cemetery and lay some flowers on the grave of Jan Matuszyński.

After ten days of nonstop to-ing and fro-ing, Chopin was completely worn out, and on July 25 he returned to Nohant ahead of his relatives in order to get everything ready for their three-week stay as guests of Sand. He wanted to escape the city and avoid the noisy celebrations about to

---

8. CFC, vol. 3, p. 166.

mark the anniversary of the "Three Glorious Days," the revolution of July 1830, which had swept the Bourbons from power and brought the people's monarch, Louis-Philippe, to the throne. Ludwika and Kalasanty did not want to miss the excitement of the carnival atmosphere and stayed on. As a special treat for them, Chopin asked Grzymała to use his influence at court and procure a pair of window seats at the Tuileries so that Ludwika and Kalasanty might enjoy a ringside view of the fireworks display due to commence a day or two later. Grzymała was unable to join them, having a few days earlier fallen down the stairs of his apartment and cracked his tailbone, making it difficult for him to walk. He was now seeking relief by immersing himself daily in the mineral baths at Enghien.

Ludwika and Kalasanty arrived at Nohant on August 9, where they were greeted by Sand and Chopin, who acted as "master of the house" and assumed the role of host. Ludwika often joined her brother in the mornings for his usual breakfast of hot chocolate, and sat on his bedroom sofa, chatting and reliving the memories of their childhood in Warsaw. Sand had given up her own room next to that of Chopin so that Ludwika could be nearer to her brother. Kalasanty frequently went out with Maurice to explore the surrounding countryside, but he was badly bitten by harvester bugs. This became the basis of a family joke because the following year, when these insects failed to return in large numbers, Kalasanty was credited with their demise. "They gorged themselves so much on Kalasanty they have died as a result," Chopin observed drily of his brother-in-law's difficult personality.[9] There was also a lot of music making. Ludwika expressed interest in the local folk songs of Berry, so Chopin jotted down some of these regional tunes for her, and later dispatched the manuscript to Poland. (Two of these airs were used by George Sand as incidental music for her play *François le Champi* and have become known as Chopin's Bourrées in G major and A major.) One evening he and sixteen-year-old Solange played music for four hands to the family, after which Chopin persuaded the girl to return to the piano and play a Beethoven sonata that she had been studying with him. We can only speculate whether Chopin played parts of his latest masterpiece-in-progress to Ludwika, the Sonata in B minor, on which he had been working for much of the summer; but

---

9. CFC, vol. 3, p. 210; KFC, vol. 2, p. 144.

knowing Ludwika's intense interest in everything that her brother did, it seems likely. In any case, she would have heard the strains of this sovereign composition drifting through the house as it gradually took shape beneath his fingers.

IV

Our attention is first drawn to the choice of key. There is not a single piano sonata by Mozart or Beethoven in B minor, and Chopin would have known it. What he may not have known is that the key of B minor occurs nowhere in the piano sonatas of Schubert either, to say nothing of Dussek, Hummel, and Weber, and that both Mendelssohn and Schumann were busily avoiding it—a fact that throws Chopin's sonata into sharp relief. There is always a danger in musicology of making too much out of too little. But the question still arises: Why should Chopin be among the first to pioneer the key of B minor in a large-scale, multi-movement piano work? The answer surely lies in the way he viewed the topography of the keyboard. While the key of B minor does not "yearn for the human hand," to fall back on a phrase of Heinrich Neuhaus, it opens up a direct route to those keys that do—to the "flat finger" keys of D major, B major, E major, and F-sharp major, in which much of the rest of the Sonata unfolds.

The first movement contains an abundance of themes sufficient to provide material for two more sonatas. From its six contrasting ideas, the two that head the main groups in the exposition are quoted here: the first subject with its bold, march-like theme, which establishes the tonic key of B minor,

and a highly contrasted second subject in the relative major key of D major, which has been well described as "an aria without words."

Fresh as this theme sounds, it does not come from nowhere. We find it searching for its identity as early as the transition section in bars 23–24, where Chopin introduces it in embryonic form and treats it as a canon at the octave between soprano and contralto voices. It is a sophisticated touch that lends integrity to the theme it heralds. Oddly enough, it was for the integrity of its thematic connections that this Sonata always had to contend. Almost from the moment of its publication, in fact, the Sonata attracted criticism for its lack of unity, which, in the words of Niecks, "is as little discernable in this sonata as in its predecessor."[10] This lamentation echoed the censorious voice of Moritz Karasowski (Chopin's cello-playing biographer), who wrote that "the composer seemed to have found it difficult to keep the profusion of thought within due proportion."[11] And in his wholesale dismissal of Chopin's ability to handle sonata form, Hanslick, while more poetic, provided what amounted to a kiss of death by saying that Chopin "was never able to unite the fragrant flowers that he scattered by handfuls into beautiful wreaths."[12] No one who is interested in what modern musicology has come to call "reception history" will want to neglect such commentary, for it allows us to marvel afresh at the slings and arrows directed against the Sonata by its early critics, whose views became so deeply entrenched that we still encounter them today. It was left to Hugo Leichtentritt to demonstrate for more modern ears that the first and second subjects hang together so closely they can be performed simultaneously, with slight textural adjustments. His analytical demonstration is reproduced here.[13]

10. NFC, vol. 2, p. 228.
11. KCLB, p. 362.
12. HAC, p. 167.
13. LACK, vol. 2, p. 249.

When music's two solitudes, Analysis and Performance, work in harness like this, the results can be revelatory.

In the first half of the development section Chopin gives his first subject a rigorous workout, and clothes it in passages of advanced chromatic harmonies. Niecks described these pages as "a comfortless waste," a devastating description of a significant passage whose function he evidently failed to grasp. Like the Sonata in B-flat minor, the first subject is developed so exhaustively that its reappearance in the recapitulation would have amounted to a tautology; so Chopin abandons it. In brief, the first thirty-one measures of the Sonata are omitted entirely, leaving the second subject to bear the brunt of the return. The seamless manner in which Chopin accomplishes this shows his understanding not only of the history of sonata form but also of the way in which it might have a future. Simply put, he has found a new function for the closing measures of the exposition's transition section (bars 31–41) by placing them at the tail end of the development section (bars 142–51) and transforming them into a lead-back. In this new role, this passage moves ineluctably over a dominant pedal (F-sharp) into the second subject and the home tonic of B major, bypassing the first subject altogether. This is the kind of structural compression that led Debussy to exclaim, "Why must one repeat, at any price, the same thing twice? What use is it to say, 'Get this into your head'?" Debussy's question was a rhetorical one. But when we hear how convincingly Chopin suppresses the first subject, and brings in the second subject via the lead-back, we come to understand why he made it.

Lead-back, formerly the Transition   Second Subject

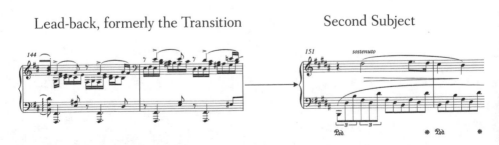

The loss of thirty-one measures results in a recapitulation reduced to just over half the size of the exposition; yet this drastic truncation causes no "lack of symmetry," a pejorative phrase that has sometimes been attached to this movement. Parallels between architecture and music, between the spatial and the temporal, are all very well, but when pushed too far they are liable to break down.

The word "Mendelssohnian" has been used to describe the character of the fleet-fingered Scherzo that follows, but there is little in this movement that resembles anything that Mendelssohn might have composed. Rather it brings to mind something Schumann once said: "Chopin could publish everything anonymously; everyone would recognize him anyway."[14] Chopin's personality is woven into the very fabric of this Scherzo. Like its predecessor in the B-flat minor Sonata, it unfolds across a form that was already a century old when Chopin acquired it, and had its origins in the minuet and trio.

Form is what all pieces of the same genre have in common, while their structure is what makes them unique. For confirmation of this observation one need look no further than the way in which Chopin links the Scherzo to the Trio (not so called by Chopin). After shutting down the Scherzo with emphatic octaves on the tonic degree of E-flat, Chopin quits them as D-sharps and pivots enharmonically into B major, the contrasting key of the Trio.

14. *NZfM*, November 2, 1841.

The "pivot motif" (*x*) reappears twice in the middle of the Trio, binding the Scherzo to it, a reminder that both Scherzo and Trio are two halves of an inseparable whole.

The distribution of the movements in Chopin is rather different than in a Beethoven sonata, where the slow movement generally comes second. In all five Chopin sonatas (we include the Cello Sonata and the Piano Trio) the slow movement comes third. Marked "Largo," the slow movement of the present work bears the trappings of a nocturne, and could easily be mistaken for one, a point made by its first reviewer in the *Allgemeine musikalische Zeitung*.[15]

It is worth extending this observation, for the Largo really consists of two "nocturnes," the second one (consisting of a contrasting middle episode in the subdominant key of E major) serving as a languid foil to the first. We choose the word "languid" with care. The more musical the pianist, the more he will fear this episode, which Kullak was not wrong to describe as "self-absorbed." The impression conveyed is of music suspended in some vast, timeless space. The challenge for the player is not to lapse into self-absorption himself, but to make the timeless tem-

---

15. *AmZ*, February 4, 1846. The review went on to inform its readers that the Sonata was better suited for small salons than for large concert halls—an observation that the subsequent history of the work has never supported.

poral. So much *gravitas* is trailed in the wake of this Largo that care must be taken not to shift the balance of the Sonata away from the first movement, where it belongs, and place it on the third, where it does not; but that will happen only if the player allows it. In musical interpretation there are few local events that do not exert an effect on the whole.

Anyone interested in the subtleties of keyboard notation cannot fail to notice the care with which Chopin has stemmed these notes. Blake's phrase "the holiness of minute particulars" comes to mind. What compels attention is Chopin's demand that each note in the right hand, with one or two exceptions, be sustained past the arrival of the note that follows it. The result is a delicate series of overlaps, a *legatissimo*, or a wash of color, produced by the fingers alone rather than by the sustaining pedal. It is the sort of exquisite detail that belongs to a world of piano playing now vanished almost beyond recall.

The Rondo Finale, marked *Agitato*, is a movement of great brilliance and its unflagging energy must be maintained to the end, or the work is lost. That it requires a virtuoso technique goes without saying. Many a pianist has gone down to defeat who heedlessly ignored Chopin's warning "*Presto, non tanto*"—"Very fast, but not too much." The coruscating brightness of the incoming passagework must not be obscured by the meaningless fog of sound that would otherwise envelop it. Thinking fingers are always a necessary thing in Chopin, but never more so than here.

By comparison with the first movement's wealth of thematic contrasts, the Finale is positively starved of them. If the Sonata's first movement had almost too many melodies for the form to contain, the last movement has almost too few. But those few are enough. Confined to two clearly contrasted ideas, Chopin succeeds magnificently in creating a full-fledged sonata-rondo out of them. The time-worn phrase "less is more" is often used to describe Chopin's celebrated ability to compress his musical thinking. Moreover, the Finale is one of the few sonata-rondos in musical history whose main idea returns outside the tonic key, yet another reminder of Chopin's ability to do new things with old forms. The rondo is ushered in with an eight-bar introduction over a dominant pedal leading to a dramatic pause, and then begins,

Chopin stemmed this theme differently for each one of its three appearances. Its contour emerges gradually, in stages, so to speak. At its first appearance (bar 9) the theme jostles for recognition among the surrounding notes of the right hand, accompanied by triplets. The second time we hear it (in the unexpected key of E minor, bar 100), the notes are stemmed to reveal the theme emerging from its new context, this time accompanied by quadruplets.

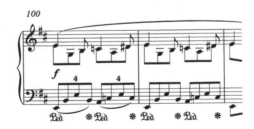

It is as if Chopin wanted to make the audible visible. At its third appearance, in fact, the theme breaks free of its neighboring notes, and is accompanied this time by sextuplets. This accumulation of notes in the left hand—triplets leading to quadruplets, leading in turn to sextuplets—imparts a gathering sense of urgency to each succeeding statement of the theme, a constant reminder that Chopin had, after all, marked the movement *Agitato*.

Between each appearance of the rondo theme, Chopin has placed a sharply contrasted second subject, whose initial bars (52–54) offer a rich supply of material for future development.

Rarely could the Pleyel piano on which Chopin composed this sonata in his room at Nohant have been called upon to respond to the sort of diamond brilliance we find in the coda. It has become part of the folklore surrounding the movement that when Professor Hans Schmidt, head of the piano faculty at the Vienna Conservatory, made his first acquaintance with it, he placed it at the forefront of all Chopin's compositions for technical difficulty.

The B minor Sonata has never enjoyed the massive following accorded to its companion in B-flat minor, although many musicians today regard it as the greater work—a change of attitude that came about slowly. Captivated by the siren song of the Viennese classics, most of its first critics found the work wanting. Then there were the players. The Sonata requires a grasp of strategy rather than tactics and this, combined with its deep emotional content, places it beyond the reach of all but the sovereign pianist. Tactics, alas, are what Chopin interpreters are generally admired for—a ravishing rubato here, an unusual pedal effect there, a torrential climax somewhere else. But more is required of those who wish to play this Sonata well. Of all Chopin's works, this is the one whose qualities are most likely to remain mired within the limitations of the player.

Published in the summer of 1845, the Sonata in B minor was inscribed with a dedication to the Countess Émilie de Perthuis, whom Chopin, in an artful pun on her husband's name, describes as the "amiable wife" of Count Léon-Amable de Perthuis, adjutant to King Louis-Philippe. The work was never played in public during Chopin's lifetime. It had to wait until January 1866 for its first performance, when it was rescued from obscurity by the Polish pianist and composer Aleksander Zarzycki, who gave the world premiere in Warsaw.[16]

V

Even while Chopin was putting the finishing touches to the Sonata, Sand was toiling every night on her latest novel, *Le Meunier d'Angibault* (*The Miller of Angibault*), and was happy to read aloud the latest passages to Ludwika the following day, in whom she found the perfect listener. Sand had come to admire Ludwika, who impressed her with her well-stocked mind, her socially advanced ideas, and her elegant French. Sand later confessed that it was one of the happiest summers she ever spent at Nohant. She observed the calming effect that the sister had on her brother's uncertain moods, and after Ludwika's departure for Warsaw she wrote, "I can tell you that you are the best doctor he has ever had, for one only needs to speak of you to restore his will to live."[17]

On August 28, Chopin accompanied Ludwika and Kalasanty back to Paris. Sand insisted that they use her comfortable carriage to take them

---

16. Zarzycki's recital, reported in Warsaw's *Musical and Theatrical Gazette* (January 1866, no. 17), included a Liszt rhapsody, a Schumann novelette, and a study by Henselt. The *Gazette* described the Sonata as "the crowning work of the concert."
17. CFC, vol. 3, p. 171.

as far as Orléans, where they took the train to the capital, because the newly opened railway line reduced the journey by several hours. Installed once more at the Square d'Orléans, Chopin, in his own words, spent the days "continually on the go, running around with my sister," while in the evenings they all went to the opera, where they saw Meyerbeer's *Les Huguenots* and Balfe's *Les Quatre Fils Aymon*, which had opened earlier in the season. With time running out they managed to squeeze in one last visit to the Comédie-Française, where they saw the celebrated actress Mlle Rachel, whom Chopin had always admired, in one of her classical roles. The final evening, September 2, was spent in Chopin's apartment listening to him play the piano. On this farewell occasion he was joined by Franchomme and the select audience was treated to a medley of chamber music. That night the group stayed up very late. It was already 2:30 a.m. when Chopin wrote in Ludwika's album a copy of his song "Wiosna" (Spring). A few hours later, in the early morning of September 3, Ludwika and Kalasanty began their long journey back to Warsaw.

VI

After six weeks of constant activity Chopin was exhausted and needed rest. Ensconced once more in Nohant, he wrote to Ludwika that he planned to stay there for several weeks. During the Indian summer that prevailed over Berry that year, with its long sunset evenings, Sand was able to get on with some necessary renovations to the old house and make further improvements to the garden. She was in her element and in no hurry to get back to Paris. Chopin, seeing time slip by, became restless, as he generally did at Nohant. His pupils were waiting for him and he had some business transactions to conclude with his publishers. Schlesinger had promised to pay 600 francs for the Two Nocturnes, op. 55, and the Three Mazurkas, op. 56, but he was dithering. Chopin instructed Franchomme to collect the money in person, keep 500 for himself (evidently the repayment of a loan the cellist had made to Chopin during the recent and somewhat expensive visit of Chopin's sister to Paris), and set aside the remaining 100 francs for Chopin himself. "Be civil!" Chopin cautioned his friend, speaking from long experience in such matters.[18] On November 13 he wrote to Marie de

---

18. Ibid., p. 172.

Rozières telling her to expect him within the next few days. "Be so kind as to have a fire lit in my rooms," he told her. He always feared the cold.

When Chopin got back to Paris, probably on November 29, he was greeted by the first of the winter blizzards sweeping the city. He looked out over the courtyard of the Square d'Orléans and described to Sand how everything was covered in deep snow. He urged her to postpone her return until the latest possible date, "so that it may be less cold . . . everyone says that the winter is coming too suddenly." He even put on three layers of flannels under his trousers to stay warm. It took Jan the manservant several days to clean out the apartment, which had been empty for the past six months, so for the first week or so Chopin dined with the Franchommes and Mlle de Rozières. Sand meanwhile wrote to him from Nohant and got him to run various errands for her, including making purchases for her winter wardrobe. "The dress you ordered is of black *levantine* of the finest quality," he told her. "I chose the material from a selection of ten . . . The dressmaker has thought of everything and she is resolved to please you." These were frivolous requests that perhaps robbed Chopin of time better spent looking after his own affairs. He had not yet installed a piano and many of his pupils had no idea that he had returned to Paris, so he was losing income. "It was only today that I had my first inquiries from prospective pupils," he told Sand. "They will all come back gradually, so I am not worried."[19] Of greater concern was to get the chimney sweeps to Sand's apartment, in readiness for her own arrival, "for I dared not light big fires before they came."[20] In the end, the bitter winter that had been forecast caught up with him and he went down with a severe cold and bouts of uncontrollable coughing. When Sand got to Paris in the middle of December, she once more found herself acting as caregiver.

The inclement weather, which was reluctant to loosen its grip, made Chopin feel "as old as a Mummy."[21] He complained that the Parisians did not know how to celebrate Christmas and New Year, and he compared their casual observance of these feast days with the fervent way in which they were celebrated in deeply Catholic Poland. In his weakened state he often had to be carried by his servant Jan across the Square d'Orléans to Sand's apartment; for longer trips it was impossible for him to get in and

---

19. CFC, vol. 3, p. 183.
20. Ibid., p. 181.
21. Ibid., p. 183.

out of his carriage without help. He was cheered by the visits of friends, however, including Franchomme, Delacroix, and above all Grzymała, who had made such a splendid recovery from his recent injury that he was now "dancing like a twenty-year-old."[22] The return of his pupils gave Chopin a sense of purpose and allowed him to structure his day. They had been formally alerted to his presence in the city by a brief news item in the *Gazette musicale*, in its issue of January 5, 1845. "Chopin has returned to Paris. He brings with him a big new sonata and some variantes [*sic*]. Soon these important new works will be published."

VII

The "big new sonata," of course, was the recently finished Sonata in B minor; but what were the "variantes"? This was Chopin's informal description of his Berceuse, op. 57, a term that is justified by the manuscript sketches, which are filled with numerous metamorphoses of a single idea. Having sketched out these embryonic "variantes," Chopin puts them in order by numbering them 1 through 14, a sequence that governs the direction the composition is going to take, although "variantes" is a word that does scant justice to the cascade of notes with which this matchless lullaby is adorned. Chopin has composed a cradle song to end all cradle songs.

There is no trace in Chopin's correspondence of the identity of the infant who might have inspired the Berceuse. Yet it is possible to speculate that he did have a particular child in mind when he wrote it. In the summer of 1843, Pauline Viardot's infant daughter, Louise, had been cared for by George Sand in Paris and Nohant, while the singer herself had gone off to Vienna to appear in the role of Rosina in Rossini's *Il barbiere di Siviglia*. Sand wrote several letters to Pauline during this period of separation, but it is the one dated June 8, 1843, that draws attention: "Whether you like it or not, Louise calls me 'Maman' and her way of saying 'petit Chopin' disarms all the Chopins on earth." And she added, "Chopin adores her and spends his time kissing her hands."[23] Pauline brought Louise to Nohant with her in June 1845, just one month before

---

22. Ibid., p. 192; KFC, vol. 2, p. 131.
23. CGS, vol. VI, p. 163.

the Berceuse was published. We should add that a sketch of the cradle
song later found its way into Pauline's possession, presumably given to
her by Chopin. Chopin brings all further speculation to an end, alas, by
dedicating the Berceuse to his pupil Mlle Élise Gavard; but such in-
scriptions from Chopin are notoriously misleading. This one simply
reads: "*À Mlle Élise Gavard, son vieux professeur et ami, F. F. Chopin.*"

The entire composition of seventy bars unfolds across a sustained pedal
point on D-flat, part of a left-hand figure that rocks gently back and forth
between tonic and dominant harmonies, and remains virtually unchanged
until the last two bars of the piece.

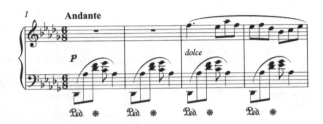

It has been likened to the imitation of the backward and forward motion
of a cradle. Hypnos, the god of sleep, is being summoned. While the left
hand "rocks the cradle," the right hand introduces a simple four-bar melody that is called upon to bear the burden of an extraordinary number of
"variantes"—roulades, arabesques, grace notes, and *fioriture* passages of
myriad kinds. Chopin uses seventeen of the twenty-four "variantes" found
in his sketches—an indication that when he worked on the material in its
earlier stages, the Berceuse was to have been somewhat longer than the
version he actually published. Typical of the unstoppable flow of decorations are the two "variantes" below—(a) and (b):

(a)

(b)

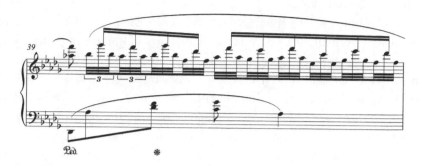

Tovey liked to draw attention to the aesthetic problem peculiar to variation form: namely, how to stop the momentum that arises when one variation follows another with the predictability of a planet in orbit. With each revolution there is the inevitable expectation that another is to follow. In brief, having started the process, how do you stop it and bring the work to a satisfactory close? There were two traditional solutions, both of them employed by Beethoven and both well known to Chopin. One was to write an extended coda, the other was to attach a fugue to the final variation. Such methods served to provide a cushion against what would otherwise be a crude and abrupt finish to the composition, and with it the feeling that the piece had simply stopped for want of ideas. Chopin's solution has become yet another *locus classicus* worthy of inclusion in textbooks on variation form. In a stroke of pure magic he unexpectedly introduces a C-flat in bar 55, presaging a change of key. This single note, which arrives unbidden, is sustained for four measures and is at first reluctant to resolve; but ultimately it sinks into the subdued key of G-flat major, producing a prolonged "dying fall."

Whether or not this moment was intended to suggest a child gradually falling asleep, that is the image most readily conveyed as the music comes to rest in a land of dreams and a final unadorned statement of the opening theme in the tonic key.

Chopin himself gave the first performance of the Berceuse for some of his Polish friends in his apartment at the Square d'Orléans on February 2, 1844—Stefan Witwicki, Józef Zaleski, and Klementyna Hoffmann-Tańska among them. At that time it was still a work in progress and was one of the things he perfected at Nohant later in the year. The Berceuse is a jewel of a work whose very enchantment places it beyond the realm of analysis. We are left to fall back on the story of the Chinese emperor of legend who, in a vain attempt to discover the secret of the nightingale's song, opened its throat only to find nothing there. As so often with Chopin, there is a ghost in the machine of which the machine knows nothing.

VIII

Chopin continued to give four or five lessons daily, but by the end of February 1845 he had to suspend them because of attacks of "asthma," and Dr. Jean Molin was called in to treat him. The Easter holidays brought some relief and a couple of special pleasures. On Good Friday (March 21), Chopin and Sand went to hear Mozart's *Requiem* performed at the Conservatoire. Two days later (Easter Sunday) they heard Haydn's *Creation* at the same venue and took Delacroix along with them. These two choral masterpieces mark the Christian calendar in a special way, and this particular juxtaposition—death followed by life—was symbolic of the Christian creed. If Chopin noticed it, he is not known to have attached any importance to it. By now his agnosticism, years in the making, was virtually complete.

Throughout much of the winter of 1844–45, Sand herself had not been well and was sleeping badly. "The apartment is dark," she complained, "with neither sky nor light," and she resented "trudging around in fine ankle boots in the black mud of the streets" after developing rheumatism and catching a sore throat in the salons. How much better to be at Nohant wearing clogs in the real mud of the countryside![24] Even as late as

---

24. DCSN, p. 140.

March we find her railing against the severe frosts that lingered in Paris and kept her indoors. Her health had not been much better at Nohant, where she had suffered from migraines and poor vision, symptoms that had appeared when she had written eleven chapters of *Consuelo* in ten days, sustained only by coffee and cigarettes. When she emerged from the semidarkness of her study, having toiled the night away by candlelight, she found that she could not stand the bright morning sunshine and had to wear thick blue glasses to shield her eyes against the light. These disfigured her face to the amusement of the locals, but Sand was worried about her eyesight. She also had difficulties in getting her latest novel, *Le Meunier d'Angibault*, published in a hardcover edition, and had to settle for it appearing by installments in the liberal newspaper *Réforme*, an imperfect solution that hardly covered her expenses and the investment of her time. Further gloom descended on the Square d'Orléans when Chopin learned of the death of his young pupil Carl Filtsch, and his sadness affected Sand as well.

There were highlights along the way, of course, including a memorable encounter with the Shakespearean actor William Macready, who had crossed the Channel to take part in the English-language productions of *Macbeth* and *Hamlet* before a capacity audience of twelve hundred people in the Salle Ventadour, now run by the Théâtre-Italien. Sand was pleased and flattered when Macready responded to her flowery letter of invitation and turned up at the Square d'Orléans in the company of the noted American traveler George Sumner and launched into an animated discussion with Sand about the theater, Shakespeare, and England—a vigorous exchange of opinions to which the generally taciturn Chopin made an occasional contribution. She and Chopin also attended one or two Polish balls at the Hôtel Lambert, hosted by the Czartoryskis, including what Chopin called "a great Easter banquet" on March 24, 1845, and an equally sumptuous event on May 26, at which he played. The Paris season came to a colorful end on May 29 when Sand took Chopin and the children to the theater to see *Les Indiens Ioways*, a presentation featuring a troupe of native Indians brought over from the American Midwest. Sand's reaction to her first encounter with North American "savages" is enshrined in her essay "Relation d'un voyage chez les sauvages de Paris." It contains echoes of James Fenimore Cooper's book *The Last of the Mohicans*, which had been published in 1826 and told the story of the virtual annihilation of an old and once-proud Native American culture overcome by encroaching "civilization." These passing diversions did nothing to assuage Sand's overriding frustration with Paris, however, and by the end of May she had had enough. "I no longer have anything to do here, and I am bored."[25] She would happily have returned to Nohant had it not been for an epidemic of typhus that broke out in the Berry region. She was also short of cash, a situation she remedied in the usual way by burning more midnight oil and turning out at breakneck speed a novelette titled *Teverino*—an unlikely story of a horse-taming minstrel who brought merriment into the lives of a dull Italian couple set in their ways. It helped Sand pay some pressing bills, and by mid-June she and Chopin were able to close their apartments at the Square d'Orléans and depart for Nohant. They were glad to turn their backs on Paris after one of the longest and most depressing winters within memory.

A week or two earlier Chopin had made a special purchase. "Le Maestro a acheté une voiture!" proclaimed Sand in disbelief. And it was in Chopin's brand-new carriage that they set out for Berry on June 12. The vehicle could seat four people but on this occasion it had to contend with five: Sand, Maurice, Solange, Chopin, and Pauline Viardot, who had once more been invited to Nohant for a few days, and stayed for three weeks.

---

25. CGS, vol. VI, p. 881.

A HARVEST OF SORROWS,
1845–1847

Chopin is [Sand's] evil genius, her moral vampire.
—Adam Mickiewicz[1]

If he had not had the bad luck to know George Sand, who poisoned his whole life, he might have lived to be as old as Cherubini.
—Wojciech Grzymała[2]

I

During the summer and autumn of 1845 the first fissures in Chopin's relationship with Sand began to appear and he became increasingly discontented with daily life at Nohant. Several things had started to vex him. He had been forced to dismiss his Polish manservant Jan, who had begun to quarrel with Sand's maidservant Suzanne. She taunted him constantly over his thick Polish accent, while he in turn abused her in execrable French. "He tosses off such lively epithets as 'ugly as a pig' and 'a face like a backside,' and even prettier phrases," wrote Chopin.[3] Sand called the fellow "stupid and humorless." One of her complaints was that he rang

1. KGS, vol. 3, p. 189.
2. CFC, vol. 3, p. 442; KFC, vol. 2, p. 324.
3. CFC, vol. 3, p. 207; KFC, vol. 2, p. 141.

the dinner bell loudly, sometimes for a full quarter hour, and she finally threatened to throw a pail of water over the poor man's head if he did not stop. Even the children disliked him. In the face of such united opposition, Chopin knew that he would have to let Jan go. He regretted parting with him because Jan was the only person in the household with whom he could speak Polish. Another source of frustration was that Chopin's piano, which had stood idle during his six months' absence in Paris, was in need of some urgent attention that was slow in coming. He could not enjoy playing the instrument until it had been tuned and voiced, and he could not compose either. And hovering over everything else was the appalling weather.

When Chopin and Sand set out for Nohant, they had expected to be greeted by the usual summer warmth. They were met instead by chilly winds and leaden skies, which finally opened up to deliver rainstorms of biblical proportions that deluged the entire region; and when the Indre overflowed its banks it put fields, roads, and homesteads underwater. Many families were made homeless. Hippolyte Chatiron's house and adjoining garden were flooded, although Nohant itself was spared. "No one can ever remember seeing anything quite like it in our peaceful countryside," Sand wrote, as she surveyed the surrounding meadows that had been turned into lakes.[4] To which Chopin added a typical understatement, "I am not cut out for life in the country."[5] When Louis Viardot tried to collect his wife, Pauline, and bring her back to Paris, he was forced to turn back, finding the swollen river impassable, vital bridges swept away. In July, when the summer finally arrived, nature made up for its earlier neglect by providing so much heat that everyone suffered from the sweltering humidity. As the waters receded, the crops that had been underwater began to rot in the fields, and the smell of decaying vegetation pervaded the entire area.

Marooned at Nohant, and unable to return to Paris because of the washed-out roads, Pauline Viardot remained as Sand's guest for three weeks. Chopin was delighted at the prospect of making music with the famous diva, who had been bringing audiences to their feet in the opera houses of Vienna, Berlin, and more recently Saint Petersburg. He wrote to Auguste Léo on July 8 that his mind was always on beautiful music "now that we

4. CGS, vol. VI, p. 906.
5. CFC, vol. 3, p. 200; KFC, vol. 2, p. 136.

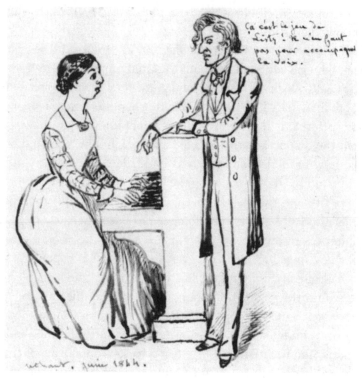

"That's the Listz [*sic*] way of playing. You must not play like that
when accompanying the voice." An ink drawing by Maurice Sand
(June 1844).

have Mme Viardot with us."[6] Pauline, an advanced pianist whose earlier
studies with Liszt had given her a virtuoso technique, was now Chopin's
occasional pupil, and he was curious to know what Liszt had taught her.
Their conversations at Nohant must have been overheard by Maurice Sand,
who had earlier captured one such exchange in a droll cartoon, "Chopin
reprimands Pauline Viardot."

It was at Nohant that Pauline most likely busied herself with arranging a number of Chopin's mazurkas for voice and piano, showpieces designed to feature her both as soloist and accompanist. Chopin encouraged
her efforts and did not object when she took these arrangements on tour.
He even invited her to appear with him in concert at Lord Falmouth's

6. CFC, vol. 3, p. 197.

house in London, in 1848, where she performed a group of these mazurka arrangements in his presence.[7]

Mindful as ever of Chopin's health, Sand brought in her physician
Dr. Papet, who gave him a thorough examination and declared him to be
"perfectly healthy in every respect, though inclined toward hypochondria."[8]
To attribute imaginary illnesses to Chopin, when there were real ones from
which he suffered, makes one wonder if Papet knew what he was talking
about; but the diagnosis satisfied Sand. As for Chopin, he could not overcome the state of inertia into which he had fallen. There were unfinished
manuscripts on his desk (including the Three Mazurkas, op. 59; the Barcarolle, op. 60; and the Polonaise-Fantaisie, op. 61), and since he knew
that it was impossible for him to compose in Paris, because of his teaching mill, he was thrown into a panic. He retired to his room daily, where
he tormented himself trying to get everything down on paper, crossing out
what he had already written and starting all over again. Unable to compose, he would throw down his pen and idle away his time on triviali-
ties, pottering around the house in search of things to do. He occasionally
wandered into Ludwika's old room, where she and Kalasanty had stayed
the previous August, in an attempt to revive old memories of that visit.
Solange, who had recently returned from boarding school, often caused
random interruptions—to bring him a cup of hot chocolate, to play duets
with him, or to ask him to go with her for a walk in the garden and witness
one of the trees being chopped down. Chopin generally complied, even
though in the mornings he was plagued by a hacking cough for which he
continued to sip opium-laced gum water.

II

Solange was approaching her seventeenth birthday and had developed into
an attractive, golden-haired young woman, mature beyond her years; and
she had begun to turn heads. She was adept at playing the coquette and
liked to exchange harmless banter with Chopin, who knew exactly how to

---

7. Viardot's arrangements are considered in more detail later; see page 564, footnote 17, in the
"Twilight in Britain" chapter of this volume.
8. CGS, vol. VII, p. 159.

respond to her whenever she turned on her feminine charms; he had, after all, grown up in a household filled with women. Sand saw things differently and knew that her daughter was treading a delicate line when she indulged in the pastime of flirting with Chopin before her guests. It has been suggested that Chopin may even have been half in love with Solange, that the sexual chastity Sand had imposed on him for the past five years made him vulnerable to the girl's attractions. Willful and headstrong, Solange sought one confrontation after another with her mother, who began to find her behavior unmanageable. The gentle kitten of earlier years had become an aggressive cat with sharp claws, which she did not mind using when family members and the servants got in her way. The source of her hostility is not hard to find. The girl had endured an unsettled past, to say the least. Three years earlier she had been sent to a private boarding school in Paris, directed by Ferdinand Bascans, after having been taken out of the one run by Mme Michelle Héreau, who evidently did not know what to do with her. And before that there had been a private Swiss tutor, Mlle Caroline Suez, who had also failed to make any headway with the young girl. In the hope of taming her rebellious daughter, Sand had handed her over to Bascans, at whose institution she spent three resentful years, seeing relatively little of her mother and feeling shut out of the family.[9] Discipline was particularly rigorous at this establishment, where Bascans tried with might and main to bring about a resurgence in the field of thought in the minds of his young charges, but with little success in the case of Solange. His difficulties were compounded by the fact that Sand took an active part in arranging the curriculum she wanted her daughter to pursue. In a revealing letter she told Bascans, "Solange is far more skeptical than I would like," and she instructed him to suppress the mass from her daughter's daily worship "because it is a waste of time, for she employs it above all to mock the devotions of others."[10] In earlier years Sand's nickname for Solange had been "Mignonne"—or "little darling." Now that the girl was beginning to show her claws, Sand called her a vixen, and even the "Queen of Sloths,"[11] an indication of the precipitous decline into which their relationship had fallen. There seems little doubt

---

9. RGSF, p. 51.

10. CGS, vol. V, pp. 617–19.

11. CGS, vol. VII, p. 631.

Solange Sand; a drawing
by Auguste Clésinger
(spring 1847).

that Solange had become aware through local gossip that she had been
sired outside the marriage bed. And because she had been parted from
Sand during her formative years (unlike Maurice, who had remained at
his mother's side) her resentment festered and she felt like an outsider. In
the summer of 1845, a round of bickering broke out between mother and
daughter in which Maurice was involved because he inevitably came to
his mother's defense. Chopin was wise enough to stay clear of these arguments. He was, in any case, cocooned in his study for much of the time
and required tranquility for his work. But everyone knew that Solange
could take her bruised feelings to him for solace and comfort; and she often
did, much to Sand's chagrin.

It would be difficult to imagine a greater contrast to Solange than her
brother, Maurice, who was withdrawn by nature and never enjoyed the
intimate relationship with Chopin that Solange experienced. He was now
twenty-two years old and was being groomed by Sand to become the "master of Nohant." Already showing talent as an artist, Maurice liked nothing

better than to don his *biande* (a loose-fitting blouse from the Berry region) and work at his canvases, sometimes setting up his easel out of doors when the weather permitted. He loved Nohant and rarely wanted to leave. The high life of Paris, which attracted Solange like a moth to a flame, held little interest for him. Rarely a week went by during the social season without Solange attending some dinner party or other, or perhaps a concert, a ballet, or an art exhibition. Sand, the famous author, received many complimentary tickets from her peers wanting to attract her attention, tickets she was happy to make available to her society-minded daughter because she knew that Maurice, chafing to get back to Nohant, would not use them. Whenever Solange and Maurice were together, they were like the proverbial mixture of oil and water, and if you stirred them too vigorously the result could be unpleasant. The household was often roiled for days by arguments that broke out without warning and drove Sand to distraction.

More serious complications arose when Sand brought nineteen-year-old Augustine Brault to live at Nohant, during this fateful summer of 1845. Augustine had been born into an impoverished family in Paris, distantly related to Sand through relatives of her mother. She was the daughter of a penurious tailor, Joseph Brault, and experienced a rough childhood at the hands of her domineering mother, Adèle. Sand took an exceptional interest in Augustine, a pretty young brunette, and across the years helped the family with periodic gifts of money. She even secured a place for Augustine in the Paris Conservatoire, where the girl studied piano and voice, the latter under the guidance of Manuel García, the brother of Pauline Viardot. When it became apparent that Augustine lacked the talent for a career in music, Adèle thought to put her daughter on the stage. For this profession Augustine had even less aptitude. Sand intervened, knowing full well that in the absence of even minor roles this could lead to a life of prostitution for young women. She offered to adopt Augustine in exchange for some modest compensation, an idea to which Adèle, after some initial misgivings, finally agreed. So Maurice was dispatched to Paris to bring the girl down to Nohant. And that is how "Cousin Augustine," as she became known, joined the family circle. Sand waxed eloquent about her new daughter. "She has everything in her favor, beauty, goodness, youth, honesty, refinement, and simplicity of heart."[12] Sand even entertained

---

12. CGS, vol. VII, p. 149.

the idea that Augustine might make an excellent wife for Maurice. The road to hell is paved with good intentions, and no one doubted that Sand had acted from the best of motives. But she had reckoned without Solange, who, from the moment that Augustine crossed the threshold, had perceived her as a rival jostling for a position within the family circle, and she resolved to oppose her, with devastating consequences that we shall come to presently.

Sand now had an extra mouth to feed. As well as looking after Augustine's board and lodging, she had committed herself to paying the girl's parents 50 francs a month for the privilege of doing so. In the summer of 1845 she buckled down to the task of making ends meet by writing a novella, *La Mare au diable* (*The Devil's Pool*), which she claimed to have thrown off in four days. It is generally regarded as one of her more beautiful stories, a pastoral fairy tale set in the heart of the rustic countryside around Berry. We gather from one of her letters to Delacroix that she had intended to dedicate the book to Chopin, but for reasons unknown she changed her mind.[13] It is an interesting fact that has drawn scant attention, that neither Chopin nor Sand dedicated a single work to each other.

Among the dark secrets buried at Nohant that summer was one that no one could have foreseen. Maurice had fallen passionately in love with Pauline Viardot, a volatile situation that had to be hidden at all costs, especially from her manager-husband, Louis. Pauline was twenty-four and the mother of an infant daughter. Maurice, two years her junior, had succumbed to her charms the previous year and was now bewitched by her. No great harm might have come of this situation save for one thing: astonishingly, Pauline reciprocated his feelings. Thanks to the sleuthing of Georges Lubin we now have what amounts to a confession from Pauline in the form of a letter to Sand, in which she wrote on September 20, 1844, after an assignation with the lovesick swain in her country home, "How is Maurice after his little trip? We promised each other to be brave . . . I can't say more about it at the moment . . . I love him very seriously . . . Write to me soon—a *double-entente* if it's possible."[14] The reference to a

13. *Corr. générale d'Eugène Delacroix* (vol. 1, p. 278), ed. André Joubin. Paris, 2 vols., 1936–38. Sand contented herself with sending an autographed copy to Chopin's sister Ludwika in Warsaw.
14. CGS, vol. VI, p. 632.

"*double-entente*" was a request for Sand to use coded language in her reply, lest it arouse the suspicions of Louis Viardot. Curtis Cate calls the situation "more astounding than fiction."[15] We are now better able to understand why Sand thought a marriage between Maurice and Augustine Brault desirable, and why she did so little to discourage the girl's deflowering by him. (Solange would later accuse Maurice of making Augustine pregnant.[16]) Such a marriage, had it occurred, would have put paid to a sexual liaison between her son and the wife of one of her best friends. Augustine would hardly have tolerated it. It was an impossible situation for Maurice, of course, and he finally gave up the chase. Faced with the inevitable loss of his ideal, he sublimated his feelings in the time-honored way: his oil painting of the famous diva now on display at the Musée Renan-Scheffer in Paris shows him at his artistic best, a worthy pupil of his teacher Delacroix.

Chopin had already divined what was going on. When he accompanied his relatives back to Paris, in the summer of 1844, Maurice had insisted on coming with them, ostensibly to act as Chopin's traveling companion on the way back. Instead, the besotted young man took himself off to Pauline's château at Courtavenel near Brie, where he dallied with the singer for more than a week, while Chopin traveled back to Nohant alone. "You will remember that I predicted when we left here that I should be returning by myself in the stagecoach," Chopin told Ludwika, "and that the whole of our journey was simply designed to conform to certain conventions."[17]

III

Altogether the summer of 1845 was a bleak one for Chopin. The only works that he managed to complete during his five-month stay in Nohant were the Three Mazurkas, op. 59.

---

15. CS, p. 531.

16. So, too, would Augustine's father, Joseph Brault, who, having failed to part Sand from more of her money, defamed her in his pamphlet "The Biography and Intrigues of George Sand," in which he not only accused her of luring his virgin daughter into Maurice's bedchamber, but implied that Sand herself was a lesbian.

17. CFC, vol. 3, p. 170; KFC, vol. 2, p. 109.

No. 1 in A minor
No. 2 in A-flat major
No. 3 in F-sharp minor

All three pieces are highly inventive in their use of simple rondo form. Well aware of the tyranny of the formula, Chopin refreshes the form in ways that are both bold and charming—the charm often masking the boldness. He may bring back the main theme in the "wrong" key (no. 1); he may recapitulate it in a different register of the keyboard (nos. 1 and 2); and he may even recast it altogether and have it return in the form of a canon (no. 3). Memories of the homeland are never far away. While Chopin may have composed them at Nohant, he might just as well have been living in Mazovia. There is nostalgia here aplenty, but there are also veins of native wit gleaming in the background that, once they have caught our attention, become part of the complex pleasures we derive from these pieces. We have no trouble in spotting the humor that lurks behind the surface gravity of the Mazurka no. 1, in A minor, even though the opening theme gives no indication of what the listener is about to experience.

The modulations that Chopin introduces at the tail end of this melody have been described as "self-willed," but they allow him to sidestep adroitly from one key to another before returning to the main idea. Huneker attached much value to this Mazurka and in a fit of verbal extravagance he told his readers that "a subtle turn takes us off the familiar road to some strange glade wherein the flowers are rare in scent and odour."[18] Whatever one thinks of such language, it probably has the merit of bringing the listener closer to the music's content than might a chord-by-chord analysis of its harmonic structure.

---

18. HCM, p. 367.

At the third appearance of the theme Chopin breaks the rules of classical rondo form by bringing back this melody in the remote key of G-sharp minor, instead of the home key of A minor. In terms of pitch it is only one semitone away, but all musicians understand that this places it at the other end of the tonal universe. If one does not possess absolute pitch, one might miss the deception.

Chopin "corrects" himself through an adroit recasting of the material he introduced at bar 13 (Huneker's "strange glade"), which brings him back to the tonic key of A minor and a final statement of the theme, this time in the lower register for the left hand. The Mazurka is a perfect example of Chopin the improviser placed under the firm control of Chopin the composer.

The Mazurka no. 2, in A-flat major, is the best-known piece in the set. In response to an earlier request from Mendelssohn, Chopin made a copy for the composer's wife, Cécile ("her favorite works are those you have written"), and sent it to Berlin for inclusion in her album.[19]

---

19. The copy is inscribed *"hommage à Madame F. Mendelssohn-Bartholdy de la part de F. Chopin. Paris. 8 Oct. 1845."* Cécile's album is preserved in the Bodleian Library, Oxford, under the call number "MSS. M. Deneke Mendelssohn b.2, item 42." Mendelssohn had clearly hoped to give Cécile something from Chopin's pen in time for Christmas 1844, but Chopin had procrastinated for almost a year. "Just try hard to imagine, my dear friend, that I am writing by return post," he wrote, tongue in cheek. CFC, vol. 3, p. 218.

It is a quixotic thought, but even as the residents of Nohant were quar-
reling within earshot over material matters, both past and present,
Chopin had removed himself to a different world, one more timeless
than temporal. There is one passage in the A-flat major Mazurka that
repays study, because Chopin here offers a glimpse into the future of
harmony.

One wonders what the conservative Mendelssohn thought when he
looked at the copy Chopin had made for Cécile. This is not simple sequen-
tial writing, as an examination of the separate voices shows, and it contains pitfalls for the unwary. It presents the kind of modulations over which
Moscheles's fingers used to stumble when he tried to make sense of what
was going on. Even Liszt was puzzled by the unexpected appearances of
such passages, which seemed to him to convey the impression of *non se-
quiturs*, until he heard Chopin himself play them. As for the F-sharp minor Mazurka, the last in the set, it comes as a surprise to learn that it was
first composed in the key of G minor, an upward transposition that some-

what changes the character of the piece as we have come to know it. Is this the only composition in Chopin's output that he is known to have written in two different keys? Far from being a "sketch," the designation frequently assigned to it in the main catalogues, an inspection of the unpublished manuscript of the G minor version of the Mazurka shows it to be complete in that key.[20]

The final choice of F-sharp minor as the key of the piece appears to have been put off until shortly before the publication of the Three Mazurkas as a set, in November 1845. We cannot say why Chopin changed his mind. Perhaps it had to do with the sheer physical comfort of the piece. When played in F-sharp minor, the Mazurka lies more conveniently beneath the hand, especially the central episode in F-sharp major, and that might have been a consideration with him. For the rest, the two versions of the Mazurka when placed side by side provide an object lesson not only in how well musical ideas may fit into the keyboard's topography, but how they are sometimes determined by it.

Chopin's final recapitulation of this rondo theme interferes with tradition by coming to us as a canon at the octave, a charming contradiction of our

---

20. Held at the Morgan Library, under the call number 114343.

expectations, and a reminder that at Nohant he had a copy of Cherubini's *Treatise on Counterpoint* within arm's reach.

A similar example may be found in the Mazurka in C-sharp minor, op. 63, no. 3 (composed the following year), in which Chopin recapitulates his main theme in strict canon at the octave, the trailing voice following the leading voice one beat later.[21]

21.

The mazurkas had always taken pride of place in Chopin's output when it came to innovation. But with the appearance of these later examples it is clear that the potential of the genre was not yet exhausted.

IV

Chopin set out for Paris on November 28, 1845, where his teaching mill awaited him. Shortly before his departure Sand was sufficiently concerned about his health to bring in Dr. Papet once again, who subjected the composer to a thorough examination, this time using his newfangled stethoscope to check Chopin's pulse, and palpating (or sounding) various organs of the body for signs of disease. After declaring that all the organs were fit, Papet stuck to his earlier diagnosis, claiming that Chopin was subject to hypochondria. By now even Sand had her doubts. Under different circumstances she might have delayed Chopin's departure, but she had arranged to leave Nohant the following day, together with her two children and Hippolyte Chatiron, in order to visit her cousins the Villeneuves, at the Château de Chenonceau, near Tours. When she finally reached Paris, on December 9, it was clear that Chopin was very ill and had gone down once more with influenza, which was sweeping across the city. He had a hoarse voice and could hardly speak. He had to cancel several lessons, including one with Baroness Betty de Rothschild, who generally paid him the handsome sum of 50 francs a lesson—more than double his normal fee. Sand once more found herself in the unenviable position of caregiver, going back and forth across the Square d'Orléans through the increasingly bitter cold to make sure that his needs were met. Soon she herself was ill and had lost her voice. Mme Marliani was also laid low, unable to help. On December 13, Sand wrote to her cousin Apolline de Villeneuve, cursing the city. "Paris is blacker, sadder, gloomier than ever."[22] By Christmas Eve the entire family was coughing and sneezing, and Sand was confined to her room, rendered almost speechless, a condition she bore with difficulty. Chopin summed up their plight.

> I ask you, how can one keep one's head on one's shoulders here just before the New Year? The doorbell never stops ringing. Today they are all down with colds—I have my miserable cough—nothing surprising in that—but the Mistress has such a cold and her throat is so sore that she can't leave her room, and that exasperates her terribly. The better one's health usually is, the less patience one has in

---

22. CGS, vol. VII, p. 208.

illness. There is no cure for it and one can't reason about it. The whole of Paris is coughing this week. Last night there was a terrific storm with thunder and lightning, hail and snow. The Seine is enormous.[23]

Sand became so poorly that Chopin, in an unusual reversal of roles, summoned his homeopathic physician, Dr. Molin, to her bedside. Despite these interruptions to his daily routine, Chopin managed to see his Three Mazurkas, op. 59, through the press. They were brought out by the Berlin publishing house of Stern for 600 francs, and the composer also managed to extract an additional 300 francs from Schlesinger for the French edition.

By Christmas, Chopin's spirits were at such a low ebb that he tried to persuade his mother to join him for a brief visit to Paris. He told her that she could make the journey in the company of the Obreskoff family, who happened to be passing through Warsaw on their way back from Athens after visiting their daughter. Justyna's reply was a model of motherly solicitude mixed with her usual common sense. Her rheumatism made it impossible for her to travel even short distances, she explained, for it was as much as she could do to cross Warsaw and visit his sister Ludwika.

> I should have to stay with you the whole winter, and you, my poor boy, what would you do with me? I should only be a source of worry to you, and knowing your good nature I also know full well that you would always be uneasy about me, that you would feel I was bored, not comfortable and a thousand other things. No, my dear child, I won't do it, especially as you have people with you who take the greatest care of you, to whom I am infinitely grateful.[24]

One visitor who did come to see Chopin was Franz Liszt, who was in the middle of a concert tour of the French provinces and unexpectedly turned up at the Square d'Orléans in mid-December to pay his respects. Liszt's triumphs in Bonn the previous August surely hovered over the conversation. He had rescued from almost certain collapse the inaugural

---

23. CFC, vol. 3, p. 228; KFC, vol. 2, p. 156.
24. CFC, vol. 3, p. 232; KFC, vol. 2, p. 158.

ceremonies surrounding the unveiling of a bronze statue to Beethoven's memory, on the seventy-fifth anniversary of the composer's birth, and it had become the talk of Europe. He had underwritten most of the bills and had assumed the cost of the statue, which stands in Bonn to this day. The effort not only bankrupted him, but had worn him down and he had succumbed to a serious case of jaundice.[25] His present tour of the provinces was meant to repair some of the damage to his purse. Chopin had been invited to the unveiling, along with other prominent musicians, but had declined to attend. All he could find to say about the celebration itself was "Liszt is having himself acclaimed at Bonn."[26] Liszt could not have found Chopin a particularly genial host, given the growing distance between them and the general air of malaise that was hanging over the Square d'Orléans. The passing years had frayed whatever bonds of friendship remained. It was the last occasion on which the two composers met.

V

Chopin and Sand managed to maintain the semblance of a social life, and they dragged themselves to the ballet and the theater, joining their fellow sufferers in all the coughing and sneezing going on around them. On December 12 we find them at the ballet and shortly after that they went to see a new opera by Michael Balfe (*L'Étoile de Séville*), which Chopin found completely disappointing, although he was delighted by the singing. He could not get over the fact that Meyerbeer was sitting nearby in his box, with two vastly superior operas already in his portfolio—*Le Prophète* and *L'Africaine*—and had so far been unable to secure a performance of either. Sand and Chopin found more pleasure in seeing their friend the actress Marie Dorval in the title role of a new play by Adolphe Dennery, *Marie-Jeanne*, the story of a working-class woman whose shiftless husband abandons her, obliging her to take their starving infant to the Home for Waifs and Strays. "The scene is marvelously acted," wrote Chopin. "Everyone sobs and cries, and all over the theater you can hear people

---

25. The weight of responsibility that Liszt had been called upon to bear in connection with the Beethoven Anniversary Festival is described in WFL, vol. I, pp. 417–28.
26. CFC, vol. 3, p. 212; KFC, vol. 2, p. 145.

blowing their noses."[27] What with colds and melodramas such as this to contend with, there must have been a run on handkerchiefs during the drab winter of 1845. The New Year brought no improvement in Chopin's health, but this did not prevent him from attending two Polish balls arranged by Prince Czartoryski at the Hôtel Lambert, one in January and another in February. By March, with Chopin still battling a lingering cold, Sand decided to install a central-heating system at Nohant, and Maurice was charged with the task of drawing up plans of the house and finding a Paris firm to do the installation. It was a further drain on her financial resources but she probably reasoned that it would be well worth the effort, not only for Chopin's comfort but for her own.

The fact is, the winter of 1845–46 was a difficult one for Sand, too, and perhaps for the first time she began to chafe openly beneath the yoke of her "resident patient," with his continual bouts of ill health, his hypersensitivity to everything around him, his fits of irritability, and what she perceived to be his piques of jealousy, brought on whenever he saw her in the company of the coterie of males that always seemed to surround her—including Emmanuel Arago, Pierre Bocage, Louis Blanc, and the twenty-eight-year-old Victor Borie (with whom Sand almost certainly had an affair that began in 1846, although it was hidden from Chopin). "I did well to get angry one day," she told Marie de Rozières, "and had the courage to tell him some home truths and to threaten him with being at the end of my tether. Since that moment he has been reasonable."[28] Perhaps Adam Mickiewicz was right after all. The poet had long maintained that Sand's liaison with Chopin was slowly killing her. He went so far as to say, "Chopin is her evil genius, her moral vampire, her cross, who torments her and will perhaps end up being the death of her."[29] It is hardly surprising that the idea for a new novel began to form in Sand's mind at this time. She had only to look around her in order to see in every situation the possibility of a fictionalized scenario

---

27. CFC, vol. 3, p. 226; KFC, vol. 2, p. 155.
28. CGS, vol. VII, p. 430. Chopin's outbreaks of jealousy were of long standing and have been well documented. According to Georges Lubin, the letter that Sand wrote to Bocage on July 20, 1843, is open to no other interpretation than that she had told Chopin that Bocage had in earlier days been her lover, and for this outbreak of "sincerity" on her part she complained that Chopin had offered her nothing but jealousy. To which Lubin attaches the dry footnote "Sincerity, like crime, does not pay." CGS, vol. VI, p. 202, n. 1.
29. KGS, vol. 3, p. 189.

between her and Chopin. During the spring of 1846 she applied herself to the task of transforming herself from "Lélia" into "Lucrezia Floriani"—the character in a new novel whose chief purpose would be to present the world with a thinly disguised account of the long-suffering role she played in Chopin's life.

On May 2, Chopin gave a great party in his rooms, with music, flowers, and what Sand called "a grand spread." Prince and Princess Czartoryski came, and also Princess Sapieha. Among the other guests were Delacroix, Louis Blanc, Emmanuel Arago, and Louis and Pauline Viardot. Chopin played the piano and Pauline Viardot sang. He could not have provided a better send-off for Sand, who departed for Nohant three days later with the manuscript of the still-unfinished *Lucrezia Floriani* traveling with her. After winding down his teaching mill, Chopin followed her there on May 27, taking with him some unpublished manuscripts of his own.

VI

Among them was a work that had begun to cause him difficulties—the Cello Sonata in G minor, op. 65, which would take him another two years to finish. Chopin had brought the Sonata to Paris in the late autumn of 1845 and had started to rehearse it with Auguste Franchomme, but was unable to make much headway. In a letter to his family, dated December 12–26, 1845, he told them, "I've tried out my cello sonata with Franchomme—it is coming along nicely. But I don't know if I will have time to get it printed this year."[30] Ten months later the work was still creating problems, for he was forced to admit, "With my cello sonata I am now contented, now discontented. I throw it into a corner and then pick it up again."[31] The Sonata would not be ready until October 1847, spurred on by technical advice from Franchomme, the work's dedicatee ("À *mon ami chéri et bien chéri Aug. Franchomme, FF. Chopin*").[32] The more than two hundred pages of manuscript sketches that have come down to us are

30. CFC, vol. 3, p. 228; KFC, vol. 2, p. 157.
31. CFC, vol. 3, p. 251; KFC, vol. 2, p. 175.
32. "*To my beloved friend, my truly beloved Aug. Franchomme, FF Chopin.*" No other dedication of Chopin expresses such warmth of affection as this one.

sufficient evidence of the struggle that the work entailed. Until recent times it was routinely chastised as a "sonata for piano with cello accompaniment." It is true that the monumental first movement requires a virtuoso pianist to do it justice, and this may have held back a wider acceptance of the work. When played with a repeated exposition, it lasts for a full fifteen minutes, about the same length of time taken by the remaining movements combined. The Sonata is, however, well written for the instrument (for which we must thank Franchomme, who also provided the fingerings and bowings), and it now attracts attention as an important composition for the medium. Passages such as the following, from the first movement's development section, are typical, and they offer serious challenges for the pianist; but the ravishing tapestry of sound that emerges when those challenges are met produces a highly Chopinesque backdrop against which the cellist unfolds an impassioned reworking of the main theme.

This was the fifth and final composition in which Chopin had tried his hand at classical sonata form (we include the Piano Trio in G minor, op. 8, in this grouping), and the running order of its movements follows the path laid down by its four predecessors—Allegro, Scherzo, Largo, and Finale—with the slow movement coming between the Scherzo and the Finale, a sequence he obviously preferred because he had never deviated from it.

The Largo, a nocturne-like aria over which hovers a mood of autumnal beauty (it has been described as "Mahlerian"), invites some speculation. Was this spacious melody inspired by the sound of the Stradivarius cello that Franchomme had purchased two or three years earlier for the considerable sum of 25,000 francs? The "Dupont" Stradivarius of 1711 was later owned by Mstislav Rostropovich and may be heard in several of his recordings. We may allow ourselves a small license in thinking that the characteristic tone of this instrument was in Chopin's mind's ear when he wrote such phrases as the following.

All the qualities for which Franchomme was celebrated are present in this melody, including the long cantabile lines for which his elegant bowing technique was well suited. Written in the spacious time signature of 3/2 (unique in Chopin[33]), this Largo conveys the impression that it has been conceived on a vast time scale. Yet it consists of a mere twenty-seven bars—four minutes or so in performance—a paradox that reminds us yet again that musical time cannot be measured against the stopwatch.

---

33. Unless we admit the puzzling case of the F-sharp major Prelude, op. 28, whose original 6/4 was changed in the autograph by Chopin to 3/2 time, without modifying the notation of the piece—leaving the player to grapple with the strange result. The published Prelude is likely to show either time signature, depending on the edition.

VII

It is a familiar lament of the music historian that composers do not always live long enough to fulfill the expectations held out by their later works. Grillparzer's epitaph for Schubert comes to mind: "Music has here entombed a rich treasure, but still fairer hopes." These words are also true of Chopin, who, had he lived for another ten years, would almost certainly have left us with fresh marvels to contemplate. By this we do not mean a mere continuation of the music he was already writing, rewarding though that prospect would have been, but rather the perfecting of some tentative experiments with musical form that he had already begun and that his untimely death did not allow him to explore. It is in any case a difficult business to trace the development of Chopin's musical language. His voice is so distinctive that there are early works that have been mistaken for later ones, and vice versa. Unlike Beethoven, whose output has long been divided into three recognizable "periods," Chopin's music does not yield easily to such treatment. Even so, there is ample evidence to show that after 1841 he had entered a new phase as a composer and was writing works that were characterized by bold innovations having to do with large-scale musical form.

A turning point had come with the Polonaise in F-sharp minor, op. 44, which breaks new ground by incorporating a mazurka into its vast central episode, an event marked in the score with the words "Tempo di Mazurka"—an unlikely injunction to come across in the middle of a polonaise. It is as if the dancers in a stately ballroom had been abruptly swept into the village square. As early as August 1841 we find Chopin writing to the Viennese publisher Pietro Mechetti, "I have at this moment a manuscript to place at your disposal. It is a kind of Fantasia in the form of a Polonaise, and I shall call it a Polonaise." He enclosed this letter with one he wrote to Fontana: "I am offering [Mechetti] a new manuscript (a sort of Polonaise, but more of a Fantasia.)"[34] Chopin did indeed end up by calling the work a polonaise, but his initial hesitation in doing so must be seen as the beginning of what he himself realized was a new stage in his creative development. (The genre of a "Polonaise-Fantaisie"

---

34. CFC, vol. 3, p. 66; KFC, vol. 2, p. 32.

was obviously on his mind some years before he composed the work to which he eventually attached that title.) The main theme of the F-sharp minor Polonaise is cut from similar cloth to that of the "Heroic" Polonaise, op. 53, composed the following year, and it evinces the same high level of inspiration.

The shift from the ballroom to the village square, mentioned earlier, is a signature moment in Chopin's output, involving a telescoping of genres— an augury of things to come. There has latterly emerged an opinion that the central episode is not really a mazurka at all, but is simply a passage marked "Tempo di Mazurka."[35] This is surely a distinction without a difference. And the distinction itself disappears when we learn that this music began life as an independent piece in E-flat major, a mazurka in embryo, that survives as a thirty-bar sketch held by the Chopin National Institute in Warsaw, which Chopin eventually incorporated as a full-fledged mazurka within his ongoing polonaise.[36]

---

35. For a glancing reference to this matter, see Jeffrey Kallberg's pioneering commentary (KCLS, p. 269), where the passage is described as "functionally peculiar."
36. Transposed into A major, this sketch makes its first tentative appearance in bars 141–47 of the Polonaise, emerging in its totality between bars 161 and 184. The document was acquired by the Chopin National Institute in 2005 and is held under the call number F. 9904. I am grateful to Paweł Kamiński, co-editor of the Polish National Edition, for drawing my attention to this sketch and its appearance in the F-sharp minor Polonaise.

It is impossible to let this work go without drawing attention to the stark, warlike passage that precedes the "Tempo di Mazurka," because there are few precedents in Chopin to compare with it for unbridled ferocity—a military cavalcade trailing paths of glory in its wake.

Stripped of harmony, these naked octaves are hammered out with unremitting force for twenty bars, pausing only briefly for a retrospective glance at one of the earlier, subsidiary themes, before returning with unrelieved vigor for sixteen bars more. Remarkably, the passage is also stripped of song. For thirty-six bars the great melodist produces no melody. There is no parallel elsewhere in Chopin, where melody abounds.

The great Fantaisie in F minor, op. 49, composed about the same time, presents us with yet bolder combinations of genres, making the work a traitor to its class. Its title, "Fantaisie," belies the tightly organized structure that lies behind this phantasmagorical term—an abridged sonata form, with a slow introduction and a full-fledged allegro exposition thrown in. This composition contains another genre equally unexpected in a work titled "Fantaisie": namely, a march, or rather two marches—a slow march comprising the introduction (bars 1–43) and a quick march contained within the second subject (bars 127–42). The Fantaisie even closes with a recitative (bars 320–22), a reminder that there is an operatic connection here as well. This mingling of different forms and genres was Chopin's main preoccupation during his last years.[37]

By 1845 we find Chopin telling his family in Warsaw that he was working on a new composition "for which I have not yet found a name."[38] It was his first reference to a work that he would come to identify as the Polonaise-Fantaisie, op. 61. As its title implies, it telescopes into one composition two genres that he had hitherto kept separate. His bemused observation that the piece was as yet nameless allows us to suppose that he may have been taken unawares to discover two contrasting genres residing cheek by jowl on his manuscript paper. From a structural point of view, the Polonaise-Fantaisie remains Chopin's most complex work, unfettered by traditional models. It is also one of the great soundscapes of piano music.

The use of the qualifying term "fantaisie" allowed Chopin to detach the polonaise from its past. Gone are the typical cadential endings with their accents on the second beat of the bar, originating in the choreography of the ballroom. Gone, too, are the extended ternary designs that we find in every other polonaise by Chopin, with their predictable "back-to-the-beginning" recapitulations. Some basic elements of the polonaise remain, of course, including the characteristic pattern ♩♩♪ ♫♫♩♩, whose fleeting appearances are sufficient to tie the piece to its genre. Otherwise, the Polonaise-Fantaisie breaks new ground. The composition did not come easily to Chopin. There are more sketches for this piece than for any other that he wrote for solo piano. These working drafts, eight pages altogether,[39] show that the Polonaise-Fantaisie went through several stages before reaching its final form, and they contain some surprises. The work originally began in C minor, not A-flat minor—a later choice of key that darkens the character of the material and is an object lesson in how musical ideas may arrive with their own key imprinted on them, and Chopin eventually discovered what to do. As for the rising arpeggios, which are such a striking feature of the fantasia-like opening, they found their way into the composition as an afterthought. Yet it is this

---

37. Chopin's Polish biographer Mieczysław Tomaszewski released several hares for his readers to chase when he pointed to "a hidden allusion" in the Fantaisie to Karol Kurpiński's patriotic song "Litwinka," composed during the November Uprising and often sung by Polish émigrés in Paris, where it would have been familiar to Chopin. One or two of the thematic parallels are, in fact, quite striking and may be pursued in TCSZ, pp. 218–20.
38. CFC, vol. 3, p. 225; KFC, vol. 2, p. 155.
39. They are preserved in the Chopin National Institute, Warsaw, under the call number M/238.

"afterthought" that sets its stamp on the work, and features one of the most memorable pedal effects in Chopin. With the sustaining pedal depressed, Chopin releases the genie from the bottle.

As the harmonic series takes hold, the keyboard shimmers from one end to the other, the blended dissonances creating a dreamlike, futuristic effect. What follows is a Fantaisie in search of its Polonaise, giving us along the way some hints of the cavalcade of themes yet to come. This introduction is not unlike a miniature symphonic development, and the names of Richard Strauss and Wagner have been evoked in scholarly discussions about it. The Polonaise, when it arrives, is heralded by the dance rhythm.

It is left to the Polonaise to establish the home key of A-flat major, into which it does not settle until bar 27, a long-postponed arrival that occurs about two minutes into the performance of the work:

This is unlikely material for a polonaise. We search in vain for the pageantry, the heraldry, and those echoes of patriotism that characterized the earlier polonaises. Instead we are offered a theme that sounds as if it were smuggled in from a prelude or an impromptu. Perhaps it was this mixture of styles that confounded the work's first hearers and contradicted their expectations. It is the same with the theme in the slow central episode, whose languorous mood takes us into the world of the nocturne, and reposes uneasily within the body of a polonaise.

Yet it is precisely when he comes to recapitulate these themes that Chopin reveals a master's touch. Beneath their seemingly calm exterior lies explosive music, which is brought to the fore in the remarkable climax to this work, unparalleled in Chopin's output. By drawing in these themes from diverse corners of the Polonaise, and by recapitulating them as one unbroken utterance transformed through apotheosis, Chopin has done something new. It was not the first time that he had apotheosized an earlier theme, of course (reference has already been made to the memorable examples in the G minor Ballade and the C-sharp minor Scherzo), but it was the first time that he had brought them in from such widely distributed parts of a structure, unrolled them as a single utterance, and produced an effect that is greater than the sum of its parts. The Polonaise's opening theme ("*mezza voce*") is now clothed in grandeur and functions as the portal to the recapitulation. An iron fist has been inserted into the velvet glove.

It leads ineluctably to an apotheosized version of the theme from the middle episode (*"poco più lento"*), which here becomes its other self, assuming heroic proportions.

The distinguished Polish writer and painter Feliks Jabłczyński went so far as to say, "Neither the *Eroica* nor the *Appassionata* of Beethoven has a single section of such raging passion." While there is much hyperbole in those words, we have to admit that Chopin rarely surpassed the heights of emotion reached in these culminating pages. Completed in the summer of 1846, the work could well be regarded as a valedictory utterance made in the face of an encroaching illness that was bringing his career to a standstill. True, the incomparable Barcarolle, op. 60, and the last Two Nocturnes, op. 62, were still in Chopin's portfolio, awaiting their final form. But they did not involve him in such labor as the Polonaise-Fantaisie. In a celebrated aphorism Voltaire has reminded us that the perfect is the enemy of the good. As we look through the sketches of the Polonaise-Fantaisie and observe the signs of struggle on every page, we are actually witnessing the way in which Chopin sees the good and then goes on to render it perfect in this spotless composition.

The Polonaise-Fantaisie seemed poised to give birth to a new genre, but Chopin's early death ensured that would not happen. It took many years for the work to advance to the forefront of his oeuvre, and it would lead us far afield were we to track the confused "reception history" that the piece left in its wake. Liszt did some damage when he wrote that the work "brings the mind to a pitch of irritability bordering on delirium."[40] Niecks followed suit and placed the work beyond the pale by informing his readers that "the work stands, on account of its pathological contents, outside the sphere of art,"[41] a comment that defies comprehension. In fact, Niecks had unwittingly broken the Eleventh Commandment: "Never make a value-judgment against music you dislike"—for dislike is an indicator of misunderstanding, as the history of criticism shows. The tone was now set for a debate that lasted for half a century or more. There were the usual attempts to connect the Polonaise-Fantaisie to a literary program, notably to the celebrated scene of Jankiel's concert in Mickiewicz's poem *Pan Tadeusz* (Tarnowski) and selected episodes from Słowacki's *Lilla Weneda* (Jachimecki); but they turned out to be signposts to nowhere. Performers were always ahead of the scholars in their appreciation of this work, and they kept it alive in the concert hall when it had already been declared dead in the literature. For the biographer it remains a source of wonder that the piece was written at all, emerging as it did from what we have called Chopin's harvest of sorrows.

Aside from his ill health, which made every day a burden to be borne and often paralyzed his pen, these sorrows were compounded by the growing realization (as yet unspoken) that his relationship with George Sand was beginning to founder, and might fall apart. This crisis, long in the making, was about to come into plain sight. During the miserable winter of 1845–46, "Lélia" had been slowly transforming herself into "Lucrezia Floriani," with consequences that even she could hardly have foreseen. When Chopin rejoined her at Nohant on May 28 that transformation was all but complete, and he was soon to find himself a stranger in a strange land.

---

40. LC, p. 62. Liszt's later conversion to the Polonaise-Fantaisie is not generally known, but when it came it was total. Twenty-five years after he had written his derogatory words, he admitted that he was wrong and had failed to understand the intimate nature of Chopin's last works, the Polonaise-Fantaisie and the Barcarolle especially. "Now I admire them totally." LLB, vol. VII, p. 122.

41. NFC, vol. 2, p. 248. As late as 1965 we find Herbert Weinstock placing Chopin's Polonaise-Fantaisie "among his flawed works," lamenting the fact that it was not "twenty-four or thirty measures shorter," while at the same time failing to tell us which twenty-four or thirty measures he would exclude. (WCMM, p. 282.) Among more recent writers, Jim Samson helped to upturn this verdict by drawing attention to the unique merits of the piece, and especially to the interior details of its complex thematic construction. SMC, pp. 200–211.

VIII

The summer of 1846 was as hot as the previous one had been cold. In an effort to seek relief from the soaring temperature, Sand took dips in the Indre, and lay on the sandy bed of the river with the water lapping under her chin while smoking a cigarette. Solange and Augustine often joined her, splashing around like a couple of sylphs or ducks, as she put it. Chopin refused to take the plunge, preferring instead to bask in the unexpected heat, but was mortified when he began to sweat and even to *reek*, as Sand put it. "We laughed until the tears come to our eyes to see such an ethereal being refusing to sweat like everyone else; but don't breathe a word about this to him. It would only make him furious." Chopin discovered how to make ice cream with a little machine that Marie de Rozières had procured for him and he had brought down to Nohant. "My God!" cried Sand, after admiring this latest technological marvel and sampling its product. "One feels so wonderful in all respects in the countryside, so why the Devil torment oneself and kill oneself in Paris?"[42]

In July, Nohant was enlivened by a visit from Sand's old friend and music-loving neighbor Charles Duvernet, who lived in nearby La Châtre. He was accompanied by a young lady named Elisa Fournier, who left us one of the very best descriptions of the Nohant soirées. On this particular evening Chopin obliged the company by playing for hours, almost until midnight. "Never have I heard a talent such as his: prodigious in its simplicity, softness, kindness, and wit," wrote Fournier. "Chopin began by treating the audience to a parody of a Bellini opera, singing all the parts himself. His performance was so precise in its observations, and so true to the composer's character, that it had the audience in fits of laughter." He then played a prayer for Poles in distress, which moved them to tears. That was followed by a medley of his own pieces, including a Funeral March and an Etude "based on the sound of a tocsin." After a moment's rest and a reminder from Sand how the melody went (she hummed the opening notes), he launched into an improvisation on "the jolly airs of a dance called the *bourrée*, which is common in this part of the country." But what riveted the audience that night was an astonishing *tour de force*:

---

42. CGS, vol. VII, pp. 370–71 and 392.

an imitation on the piano of a defective music box. It was executed with such skill and close attention to detail that, as Fournier noted,

> had we not been in the same room, we could never have believed that it was a piano that was tinkling beneath his fingers. All the rippling finesse and rapidity of the little steel struts which cause the invisible cylinder to vibrate, were rendered with matchless delicacy, and then suddenly a faint, barely audible cadence was repeatedly heard, only to be interrupted by the machine which had something wrong with it. He played us one of those airs, a Tyrolean one I think, in which a note is missing from the cylinder, and which got stuck each time the moment came to play this note.[43]

Few of the visitors who witnessed that concert, and relaxed in what they fondly believed to be the warm family atmosphere of Nohant, realized that the household was quietly falling apart. It started in small ways, as such things often do. Grzymała arrived in the company of Countess Laura ("Lorka") Czosnowska, an old friend of the Chopin family. Chopin naturally thought the connection strong enough to invite Laura to stay at Nohant, and was upset by Sand's less than friendly reception of her. Sand was happy to welcome Grzymała, but Laura was a different proposition. She reeked of musk, Sand complained, and her dresses were covered in baubles, the sort of feminine trinkets that the plain-dressed Sand despised. Worse, she had brought her small pooch Lily with her, whose breath was so malodorous that it made everyone gasp. Laura inevitably became the butt of some unseemly humor, her musk perfume reminding some of the dog, and the dog's breath reminding others of Laura. Chopin fumed silently at such jokes against this family friend, which he found offensive.[44] The sympathy that he felt for Laura went back to the Warsaw days, when her husband had shot himself at her feet in a fit of lover's jealousy. Grzymała would have been the only other member of Sand's circle to know the full details of that tragedy, which Laura bore with grace. It was the same with Chopin's old compatriot Józef Nowakowski, a former composition student

---

43. LGSB, pp. 28–29.
44. Not long after her unfriendly reception at Nohant, Chopin made amends to Laura by dedicating to her his set of Three Mazurkas, op. 63, published the following year.

of Elsner's at the Warsaw High School for Music, who had planned to travel down to Nohant and be reunited with Chopin. Sand refused to extend her hospitality on the grounds that there were no spare bedrooms. Chopin, after having been forced to fire his Polish manservant earlier on, was now being robbed of companionship with his Polish friends as well, and he began to feel marginalized. And when, despite the "accommodation problem," Sand allowed Maurice to bring his young friend Eugène Lambert (a fellow art student in Delacroix's atelier) to spend the summer at Nohant, Chopin, hypersensitive in such matters, knew that he was being relegated to a subordinate position in the household. Nor were these the only signs that the relationship between Sand and Chopin had become frayed. Sand remarked in front of Laura that Chopin's sister was worth a hundred of him. "I am perfectly well aware of it," Chopin replied. "One has to be as sweet a soul as Ludwika to leave pleasant memories of *everyone* here."[45] It was a subtle response with a sting in the tail. Such dialogue was doubtless meant to be passed over as harmless banter. But when a love affair is in decline language matters, for it often reflects some deeper emotion swirling below the surface.

IX

Sand's way of dealing with her fretted feelings for Chopin might have been foreseen. Why not produce a novel out of the dying embers of their love affair? *Lucrezia Floriani* amounts to an old-fashioned roman à clef, a veiled account of her years with Chopin, slanted heavily in Sand's favor. Lucrezia, a famous and worldly actress, takes the young Prince Karol de Roswald, a sickly and somewhat unstable neurotic, under her wing and falls in love with him. Sand always denied that the story had anything to do with her and Chopin, but her denial demeans her, for the difference between fact and fiction is razor thin. Lucrezia is thirty years old and Prince Karol is twenty-four when they first meet—exactly the same six-year difference that separated Sand and Chopin. By the time she meets Prince Karol, Lucrezia has had numerous love affairs, has borne children by different fathers, and is already famous across Europe—a close parallel

45. CFC, vol. 3, p. 246; KFC, vol. 2, p. 171.

with Sand herself. Lucrezia offers Karol her unconditional love and allows him to live with her at the Villa Floriani, nursing him through sickness when he falls ill—a situation similar to Chopin's at Nohant—but in return for her total devotion she is treated to the daily torments of his unfounded jealousies from her long-ago love affairs ("he became intolerant and intolerable"). Worn out prematurely, Lucrezia eventually dies, unable to bear the emotional burden. Sand provides Lucrezia with all the virtues she herself most admires—adoration of her children, unconditional love for her partner, and contempt for prurient hypocrisy—sparing no effort to present her readers with an idealized version of herself. Prince Karol, by contrast, is glacial and reserved, and does not respond easily to Lucrezia's advances—the qualities that had so distressed Sand when Chopin had unwittingly aroused her passions ten years earlier. Finally, Prince Karol comes from somewhere in "Eastern Europe" and bears a Polish name, another persuasive link in the chain that connects Chopin to the story line in the novel. In one passage Sand even writes of Karol in a manner similar to the way she describes Chopin in her autobiography, but because she is now writing fiction there are no constraints on her prose.

> As he was extremely polite and reserved no one was ever able to understand what was going on in his mind. The more exasperated he became, the colder his manner; one could only judge the depth of his fury by the iciness of his polite behavior. He was flippant, stiff, affected and bored with everything. He had the air of one who bites gently for the pleasure of doing it, and his bite went deep. Everything seemed uninteresting to him. He held aloof from every opinion, every idea. When someone tried to offer him some distraction, one could be certain that he despised what was said to him, and all that could be said.[46]

Sand's depiction of Karol as a parasite who feeds off Lucrezia's boundless love and takes advantage of his privileged place in the Villa Floriani is particularly cruel. She would have been incapable of writing such a covert character assassination in 1840 or even in 1844; but in 1846 the words just tumbled off the page. Were this characterization of Chopin even

---

46. Sand, *Lucrezia Floriani*, Paris 1888, pp. 249–50.

remotely true, Sand must have been living a lie for several years. Since she could admit to no such thing, she went out of her way in her autobiography to deny any connection whatever between Prince Karol and Chopin. She reminds her readers:

> Prince Karol was not an artist. He was a dreamer and nothing more. Not being a genius, he did not have the prerogatives of genius. He was therefore a character who was so far from being the portrait of a great artist that Chopin, who read the manuscript on my desk daily, had not the least inclination to see himself in it, suspicious as he was.
>
> Nevertheless, people have told me that, later in reaction, he imagined himself Karol. Enemies—and I had some who were close to him and called themselves his friends, as though that gave them the right to make him suffer—enemies made him believe that this novel was an exposé of his character. By that point, his memory had no doubt begun to fail; he had forgotten the book. If only he had reread it![47]

Sand's words come threadbare from the loom. Liszt was in no doubt who Karol was. In his biography of Chopin he had no trouble at all in linking Chopin with Karol, Sand with Lucrezia, and Nohant with the Villa Floriani. He quotes Sand *in extenso* where she delineates Karol's character and he takes it at face value as a description of Chopin himself. Since his book on Chopin had already been published several years before Sand wrote her autobiography, this represented a problem for her and she knew that she would have to go out of her way to deal with it. Her response may be summed up in a single sentence: Liszt, she says, was simply misinformed. "Some have claimed, because they thought that they recognized a few of [Chopin's] characteristics, that in one of my novels I described him in great detail. They were wrong . . . Liszt himself was unwittingly led astray in his *Vie de Chopin*, overly exuberant in style, but also filled with some very good things and some very beautiful pages."[48]

To Sand's self-serving commentary we need only add that she put the finishing touches to *Lucrezia Floriani* at Nohant, in the early summer of 1846, with Chopin sitting in the next room working on his Barcarolle and

---

47. SHV, vol. 2, p. 444.
48. Ibid.

the Polonaise-Fantaisie. The novel was serialized and published by installments in *Le Courrier français*, from June to August 1846, before appearing in hardcover, a work for which Sand received the generous sum of
12,000 francs. The book does little to enhance her literary reputation, for
it barely rises above the level of a Harlequin romance. It contains the kind
of writing that led Flaubert to call her "a great cow full of ink"—a slur on
her reputation that has pursued her across the generations. But Henry
James admired the book at a time when the philosophy behind it—"life
turned into literature"—was becoming fashionable among the literati.[49]
Whatever the case, it is hard to avoid the conclusion that *Lucrezia* amounted
to a betrayal. Sand had put on public display her most intimate relationship with Chopin in exchange for a mess of pottage. In one respect her
account is truthful, although it is not much of a defense. She tells us that
as she came down from her room each morning she left her nightly quota
of ten or more pages on the table so that Chopin might read them. He
even praised them, she added, but utterly failed to recognize himself in
them, regarding the book as just another piece of random fiction. This was
confirmed by Delacroix, who found himself squirming with embarrassment while Sand read aloud from her manuscript in the presence of
several friends, including Chopin and Delacroix himself, while Chopin
remained oblivious to the fact that he was to be placed between hard covers and clothed in a thin veneer of fiction. He had always disliked reading
(he read almost nothing, save the newspapers) and certainly lacked the
patience to dissect a literary text. In the end it did not really matter whether
Chopin recognized himself in the novel, as Sand well knew. The only thing
that mattered was whether she had put him there, and she clearly had.

Lucrezia aroused widespread interest among Sand's friends and colleagues who eagerly scanned each issue of *Le Courrier* to find out what
might happen next. Liszt was particularly frustrated when he was unable to
secure the latest issues of the journal because his tours were taking him
through Transylvania, and he asked for copies to be sent on to him. Was
this novel Sand's way of telling the world that her famous relationship with
Chopin was starting to unravel? This question was on everyone's lips, but
it was soon to become redundant. The facts about to replace her fiction
were more dramatic than anything she might have wanted to put into a

---

49. See James's seminal article on George Sand in *The Times Literary Supplement*, December 8, 1913.

novel. Even as Sand's narrative was being published, the stage was being set for a real-life drama at Nohant that in terms of sheer spectacle would put *Lucrezia Floriani* to shame.

X

Ever since Solange had returned from boarding school, Sand had begun to experience the full force of Goethe's aphorism "Sowing is not so difficult as reaping." The family had endured one minor crisis after another because of the girl's unruly behavior and her sharp tongue. The only solution that Sand could think of regarding her disruptive daughter was the time-honored one that families usually employed in similar situations. The sooner Solange was married off, the better. Already one suitor had appeared on the scene, the young but impoverished Viscount Fernand de Preaulx. Twenty-five years old, Fernand enjoyed a distinguished lineage but few prospects. Both Chopin and Sand liked him, and as the relationship blossomed Sand wrote to Charlotte Marliani that she thought Solange would not be displeased to be called "Madame." In an attempt to move things along Sand broke with the usual conventions and allowed the young couple to spend entire evenings unsupervised in Solange's room, with consequences that Sand failed to anticipate. The more Solange saw of Fernand, the less she liked him. He was completely lacking in culture and could barely sustain an interesting conversation. Sand tried to remedy these defects by loaning him some essential reading from her library, which simply gave Solange, with unwonted cruelty, the opportunity to taunt the young man. He was sent home humiliated.

Not long afterward, Sand and Solange attended a party given by Mme Marliani in her apartment on the Square d'Orléans. Among the guests was a retired army captain, Stanislas d'Arpentigny, who was accompanied by a black-bearded man with a Mephisto-like face and burning eyes that alighted on Solange the moment she walked into the room. He was a thirty-three-year-old sculptor with a past, named Auguste Clésinger, who made it known that he wanted to be introduced to the famous author George Sand. The conversation was brief and to the point. Mother and daughter simply must pose for him in his atelier and allow him to create marble busts of them, which they would receive as gifts. Their vanity aroused, the two women fell into the trap. They visited his studio almost daily while

Clésinger chipped and chiseled at his marble and brought their images to life. Sand was so impressed with Clésinger's talent that when he began to show an interest in Solange, she saw no reason to stand in his way, despite the fifteen-year difference in their ages. Stanislas d'Arpentigny, who had brought about the introductions in the first place, became alarmed when he saw the direction in which things were heading and warned Sand of the dangers. Clésinger was a spendthrift, he was heavily in debt, he drank to excess, and he had beaten one of his earlier mistresses while she was pregnant before abandoning her. Sand gave little credence to such stories, assuming them to be spread by those who failed to perceive the hand of genius in Clésinger—as if genius was all that was required to sanction the sort of reckless behavior in which he had long indulged. She had in any case heard far too many similar tales about herself across the years not to know that gossip and innuendo was the price one paid if one was an artist brave enough to flout the social norms. So instead of confronting Clésinger, and stifling his ardor on the spot, Sand thought it expedient to take Solange back to her refuge in Nohant and let events take their course. That was a mistake, which she came to regret.

XI

Clésinger had formed the idea that Sand was "rolling in money," and decided to take Solange by storm. After bombarding the young girl with roses, which arrived daily from Paris and caused a lot of local chatter, the sculptor himself turned up at Nohant. He appeared "like Caesar," Sand wrote, and imperiously demanded an immediate yes or no to his proposal of marriage. He wanted a reply to his ultimatum "within twenty-four hours," or the proposal would be withdrawn. All Sand's misgivings were swept away in the face of such single-minded determination, a quality rarely found in the men of her circle, and which she failed to realize was put on for her benefit. "This Clésinger does everything that he wants, at the very hour, at the very minute that he wants it, without bothering to eat or sleep," she declared in amazement. And she went on to rhapsodize, "This tension of the will, without fatigue or letup, amazes and pleases me."[50] At last her

---

50. CGS, vol. VII, p. 660. Between March and May 1847, Sand wrote letters to more than a dozen correspondents extolling the virtues of Clésinger in similarly effusive language, words she later wished she could withdraw.

unmanageable daughter had attracted the attention of a man who might
be able to dominate her, and might even have some prospects in the world
of art. For a time Sand deluded herself into thinking that he might become a second Michelangelo, an important appendage to her artistic
family. But would Solange accept his proposal? To Sand's astonishment
and delight the girl said yes and Nohant was suddenly alive with the prospect of a hasty wedding. And there was good reason for the haste. Solange, fearing that she was already pregnant by Clésinger, had started to
take cold baths and had then plunged into an icy stream in an attempt to
bring on her monthly period, and Sand started to panic. Wishing to avoid
local gossip, she instructed Maurice (who was in Paris) to contact Casimir Dudevant and draw up a marriage contract without delay. "Our position is impossible," she wrote to Maurice. "Buy a special marriage license
and have it sent on."[51] Solange had not yet attained her majority, so Casimir's permission was required before the wedding could take place, but
it was quickly granted. The prospect of no longer having a problem child
in the house was a welcome one for Sand, and she looked forward to the
wedding with relief. It is important to remember this point because later
on, when the marriage fell apart, she blamed everyone but herself for
what had happened. There were the inevitable discussions about Solange's
dowry, during which Clésinger learned that Sand had set aside 50,000
francs for Solange with a promise of more to follow, and also to make her
the eventual beneficiary of a small property that she owned, the Hôtel de
Narbonne (situated on the rue de la Harpe, in the Latin Quarter), valued
at 200,000 francs. Clésinger left for Paris in a state of euphoria, filled
with generous plans to help his future mother-in-law spend her fortune.[52]

On May 20, Solange and Clésinger were married in the tiny chapel at
Nohant. An element of farce marked the occasion. On the eve of the wedding Sand pulled a tendon in one of her legs and had to be carried down
the aisle in severe pain to witness the nuptials. It was a harbinger of things
to come. The presence of her former husband, Casimir, who had been her
houseguest for the past three days, had done nothing to brighten her mood,
and at the wedding breakfast following the ceremony Maurice drank so
much champagne that he began to weep crocodile tears over the fact that

51. CGS, vol. VII, pp. 671 and 690.
52. CS, p. 553.

Auguste Clésinger; an
undated engraving.

his younger sister was now married while he remained single. From this melancholy condition his father tried to rouse him by telling him in front of the married couple and the wedding guests that he was fortunate to be a bachelor, a favorable situation for any young man in which to find himself, especially when he looked at those around him. There was much autobiography in Casimir's observation as well as some upset feelings. Either by accident or by design, his name had been omitted from the formal wedding announcement, which referred to the bride simply as "Solange Sand." Meanwhile, just to round things off, Clésinger's younger brother, who had acted as his best man, became seriously drunk and indulged in some boorish behavior. He was aided and abetted by Uncle Hippolyte, who normally spent his days in a state of inebriation and was not inclined to make an exception on the day of Solange's wedding. Sand herself might have lost whatever composure was left to her had she known that shortly before the wedding Clésinger, anticipating the windfall that was about to come his way, had indulged in a wild spending spree in Paris. Even as he walked Solange down the aisle he was already in debt to the tune of 24,000 francs. Much of the money had been spent on jewels for his new wife, on the hire of a carriage, and on the reckless engagement of two liveried servants to respond to her every beck and call. When Sand learned what had happened, the scales fell from her eyes, and for the first time she saw Clésinger for what he was: a common fortune seeker. The atmosphere at Nohant became toxic. Within two weeks of the wedding Sand had thrown the happy couple out of the house, but not before verbal abuse, physical violence, and even the threat of murder had been brought into play. Sand was later to write, "The scenes that followed were scarcely to be believed . . . We were within an ace of cutting one another's throat."[53]

XII

What had happened forms an essential part of the story. A day or two after the wedding Clésinger and Solange had departed on a brief honeymoon to Paris. Clésinger, who was being pressed for the repayment of his debts, had tried and failed to secure a loan against the Hôtel de Narbonne, which, even though it was part of Solange's dowry, could not be touched by her until she had reached the age of twenty-one. Thoroughly dismayed, he wrote a letter to Sand, announcing his intention of returning to Nohant to see if it might be possible to secure a mortgage on the old house as a down payment against that part of the dowry promised by Sand. On receiving this news Sand became volcanic. Only then did she grasp the full extent of Clésinger's debts and the unscrupulous nature of the man she must now call her son-in-law. When Clésinger and Solange got back to Nohant, they found an implacable Sand waiting for them. The pair had been preceded by dozens of trunks containing Clésinger's hand tools and half-finished sculptures, a sure sign that they intended to dig in until the problems surrounding the dowry had been sorted out. Sand received them with icy politeness, showed them to their rooms, and waited for the opening shots to be fired. They were not long in coming.

It started simply enough. Solange decided to go out riding and insisted in her imperious way that Cousin Augustine accompany her. (Augustine

---

53. ML, p. 314; CGS, vol. VIII, p. 77.

Brault, we recall, was the recently adopted daughter of Sand, in whom she had invested hopes of a marriage to Maurice.) Augustine declined the invitation, feigning a headache. All Solange's pent-up jealousy against the girl came boiling to the surface. Putting on the airs of a countess, Solange seized a riding whip, got into the cabriolet, and commanded one of the servants to fetch Augustine downstairs at once because she had no intention of being kept waiting. Again Augustine refused. When Sand heard the growing commotion in the courtyard outside, she opened a window and shouted down to Solange that Augustine would *not* be joining her. It was an innocent-enough beginning to what developed into a three-day battle. Sand had provided the gunpowder; but it was Clésinger who obliged her by striking the match. The resulting explosion occurred at dinner when a spiteful Solange took it into her head to accuse Augustine (whom she described as a slut) of sleeping with Maurice, and becoming pregnant by him.[54] While she was reveling in her belligerence toward the poor girl, Sand intervened and sharply upbraided Solange for her language. Clésinger then accused Sand of showing no respect for his wife, insisting on an apology. Sand replied that if they felt like that they could both leave the house for good. At this point the confrontation became violent. Clésinger and Maurice got into such an argument that the sculptor got up and threatened him with a mallet. Sand pushed herself between them and while trying to wrest the mallet out of his hand tore at his hair. Clésinger responded by punching her in the chest. At that Maurice lost his head and rushed off in search of a gun. He might have shot Clésinger there and then, had not the local curate (who had officiated at the wedding service just two weeks earlier and was now witnessing the whole concept of married bliss turn to dust before his very eyes) rallied the servants, who helped him to intervene. And while all this was happening Solange stood by, gloating over the mayhem that she had helped to create.

---

54. This accusation, which was calculated to bring down Augustine and Maurice with her, had first surfaced in an anonymous letter addressed to the painter Théodore Rousseau, to whom Augustine had been briefly engaged. When Rousseau read it, he demanded to know why he should be expected to marry damaged goods. He used the letter to demand from Sand an enlarged dowry, to make it worth his while to take the girl off Sand's hands. Sand sent the young man packing, calling his request "an act of delirium," and the wedding was canceled. When Solange hurled the epithet "slut" at Augustine, she knew that it would lacerate the poor girl, who had no idea as to the authorship of the anonymous letter. It has been conjectured that it was written by the Clésingers themselves.

To these graphic details, drawn from Sand's own account of the fiasco that she gave to Marie de Rozières barely seven weeks after the wedding, she added, "The diabolical couple left last night, up to their necks in debt, triumphantly impudent, and leaving behind them a scandal they can never outlive. And so, for three days in my own house, I endured the risk of *murder*. I don't want ever to see them again; they will never again cross my threshold. They have gone too far. My God, I have never done anything to deserve such a daughter!"[55] Sand ended her letter by asking de Rozières to take possession of the keys to her apartment in the Square d'Orléans so that the "diabolical couple" could not gain access to it.

XIII

Chopin was happily unaware of what had taken place. He had left Nohant the previous November and had remained in Paris for the past several months, without the remotest idea that he would never return. The debacle that forever barred him from the house had not yet begun to unfold. He had tried to set out for Paris in the company of Sand's lawyer friend Emmanuel Arago toward the end of October 1846, but the floods in the Loire region were so serious that they had breached the nearby Olivet Bridge, making it necessary to descend via a twenty-foot ladder to the banks of the Loire below. It is difficult to imagine how Chopin could have negotiated such a hazard, given his frail constitution. So he waited for the waters to subside and began his journey on November 11.[56] It is an interesting commentary on his declining relationship with Sand that for the first time she let him return to Paris alone.

Sand had kept Chopin in the dark about the wedding until the very last moment, when the banns were read. By then it was early May 1847, just two weeks prior to the ceremony. It has sometimes been argued that she

---

55. CGS, vol. VIII, pp. 11–13.
56. The catastrophic flooding of the Loire Valley in the late autumn of 1846 was captured in a series of fifteen drawings by Maurice Sand, which brings the drama to light far more vividly than a camera might have done, and presents the physical obstacles that Chopin wanted to avoid on his return to Paris. A diligence sets out on its journey but slowly disappears beneath the rising waters; a wheel breaks off the carriage as it seeks higher ground; a horse breaks loose from its harness and gallops away, leaving vehicle and driver stranded in a wasteland. A selection of these scenes was reproduced in S-DMS, pp. 102–105.

did this out of consideration for Chopin's latest bout of ill health, an attack of "asthma" that laid him low for several weeks, and which was of genuine concern to her. Since his illness would have prevented him from returning to Nohant for the wedding, she argued, why burden him with the details? It is more likely that Sand wished to avoid the problem of explaining to him her newfound admiration for Clésinger, which had led her to accept him as a son-in-law. Chopin had of course met Clésinger about the same time as Sand herself and had taken an instant dislike to him. He feared for Solange's happiness and had disapproved of the daily trips to the sculptor's studio that mother and daughter had made. He was put off by Clésinger's roughshod ways, and he objected to his latest creation, now on public display in Paris, of a naked woman in such an indecent posture that "in order to justify the figure's attitude, he had to coil a snake around her legs. The way she writhes is frightful. The statue is of a kept woman, very well known in Paris."[57] Chopin was not especially prudish when it came to depictions of the female form. But when those depictions amounted to an overt attempt to court notoriety, he found them offensive. In a letter to his family Chopin went on to disclose his feelings about the marriage although he had obviously not yet learned of the fiasco that was now in full swing at Nohant. His comments are interesting for the light they shed on Clésinger's family and that family's evident disinterest in their prodigal son.

> Paris, June 8, 1847
>
> The marriage took place in the country, during my illness—I can honestly say that I am not vexed that it did, for I don't know what sort of face I could have put on. As for the young husband, God only knows where he comes from . . . His father is a sculptor in Besançon, well known in the town but nowhere else. His labors have brought him a certain amount of money, which is now invested in property in the town. He has a huge family. The son was taken up as a boy and protected by the Cardinal de Rohan. He was supposed to enter the church but gave up after six months and took to drawing and sculpture. At this point his life story becomes obscure— various shady affairs—so much so that he was driven from one place

---

57. CFC, vol. 3, p. 284; KFC, vol. 2, p. 204.

to another, ending with a trip to Italy—then he had to clear out of Florence on account of his debts. His father refused to have anything to do with him, so he joined the cavalry, but he did not stay there long. Two years ago he made a small statue of a faun that was much talked of. This year he made that statue of a woman and a few excellent busts. He did a portrait bust of Aguado's children [a Spanish banking family] and then he married Solange! He has no friends or connections. His father was not at the wedding. He merely wrote a letter and Mme Sand never met him.[58]

Chopin did not know that within days of writing this letter he would be drawn into the maelstrom that had descended on Sand and her dysfunctional family. The first inkling that something was wrong was contained in an urgent message from Solange, requesting the use of his carriage so that she and Clésinger could get out of Nohant as quickly as possible. Sand had absolutely refused to let her have it. "I am ill," Solange told Chopin, "and the journey by stagecoach from Blois will wear me out." (She was pregnant.) "I left Nohant forever after my mother made the most frightful scenes. Please wait for me in Paris. I must see you at once."[59] Chopin, not knowing what he was getting into, naturally raised no objections to the use of his carriage, and wrote a genial note along those lines to Sand. Bearing in mind everything that Sand had recently endured, she could not regard his letter as anything but a slap in the face, as one biographer puts it. Her reply is unfortunately lost, but when Chopin showed it to Delacroix, the latter described it as "atrocious."[60] By now Sand was fearful of the slanders that Solange was pouring into Chopin's ears, including the story that the chief reason he had been kept away from Nohant that summer was because Sand was having an affair with the journalist Victor Borie, one of her houseguests. Sand felt that she had no alternative but to force Chopin to take sides, which he politely declined to do, as his reply to her letter shows.

---

58. CFC, vol. 3, p. 288; KFC, vol. 2, p. 207.
59. CFC, vol. 3, p. 294; KFC, vol. 2, p. 210.
60. DJ, p. 236. Delacroix went on to talk about the cruel passions and long-repressed irritations that had left their stamp on this letter. "The author occasionally takes the place of the woman (Solange) and launches into tirades that seem to have been borrowed from a novel or from a philosophical treatise."

Paris, July 24, 1847

I do not have to discuss Mr. C[lésinger] with you. The very name of Mr. C[lésinger] did not become familiar to me until you gave him your daughter.

As for her, I cannot remain indifferent to her. You will remember that I used to intercede with you in favor of your children, without preference, and I did this whenever the opportunity presented itself, certain that it is your destiny to love them *always*—for those are the only affections that are not subject to change. Misfortune may cast a shadow over them, but cannot alter their nature.

This misfortune must be very powerful today if it can forbid your heart to listen to any mention of your daughter, at the beginning of her real life as a woman, at the very moment when her physical condition calls more than ever for a mother's care. When faced with such grave realities involving your most sacred affections I must pass over in silence that which concerns me personally. Time will do its work. I shall wait—*always the same as ever.*

Your most devoted,

Ch

My regards to Maurice[61]

Chopin's letter makes plain that he considered Sand to have brought her misfortunes on herself. Its opening lines must have given her pause. To be reminded of the simple truth that they conveyed was more than Sand could bear. It was the last letter that Chopin ever wrote to Sand, and her reply to him explains why.

Nohant, July 28, 1847

. . . Very well, my friend, follow now the dictates of your heart and assume that it is the voice of your conscience. I understand perfectly. As for my daughter, her illness gives no more cause for anxiety than last year. Neither my zeal, my attentions, my orders, nor even my prayers have ever been able to persuade her to behave otherwise than as a person who *enjoys* making herself ill.

It would ill become her to say that she needs a mother's love—a

---

61. CFC, vol. 3, pp. 295–96.

mother whom she hates and slanders, whose most innocent actions and whose home she blackens by the most frightful calumnies. You choose to listen to it all and maybe believe what she says. I do not propose to wage a war of that kind. I prefer to see you pass over to the enemy rather than defend myself from a foe bred of my flesh and reared on my milk.

Look after her, then, since it is she to whom you think you must devote yourself. I shall not hold it against you, but you will understand that I am going to maintain my right to play the part of the outraged mother, and henceforth nothing will induce me to allow the authority and dignity of my role to be slighted. I have had enough of being a dupe and a victim. I forgive you, and from now on I shall not utter one word of reproach, for you have made a sincere confession. It surprises me somewhat, but if, having made it, you feel freer and easier in your mind, I shall not suffer from this strange *volte-face*.

Farewell, my friend. May you soon recover from all your ills; I hope you will now (I have my reasons for thinking so); and I shall thank God for this strange end to nine years of exclusive friendship. Let me hear now and then how you are.

There is no point in ever discussing the rest.[62]

It was an astonishing response. Chopin had left the door open, but Sand had closed it with a vengeance. Perhaps the most revealing sentence in her missive is not the novelist's extravagant language describing Solange as "a foe bred of my flesh and reared on my milk," but rather the line in which Chopin is accused of crossing over to the enemy. Sand's anger was ungovernable and for a long time she refused to allow the name of Solange to be uttered at Nohant. It was a melodramatic gesture but it put everyone on notice that her daughter no longer existed for her. She also set about dismantling every connection that Chopin ever had with Nohant. She knocked down the connecting wall that had separated their bedrooms, taking over his space for herself; she stripped the wallpaper from the walls of his room, replacing it with a different pattern, and she sent his piano back to Pleyel. The comments that she started to make about Chopin

---

62. CFC, vol. 3, pp. 296–97.

overflow with bile and make us wonder if she had temporarily lost her senses. To Grzymała, his closest Polish friend, she complained that "his heart was hermetically sealed." And in the longest letter that she ever wrote on this topic, consisting of seventy-one impassioned pages, she told Emmanuel Arago, "For nine years, although I was so full of life, I was bound to a corpse."[63]

63. CGS, vol. VIII, p. 48.

DEEPENING SHADOWS,
1847–1848

You have gained in suffering and poetry; the melancholy of your
compositions now penetrates still deeper into one's heart.
                            —*Marquis Alphonse de Custine*[1]

I

Chopin now entered the bleakest period of his life. His breach with Sand
had devastated him, but his friends rallied around and tried to uplift
him. Franchomme, Delacroix, and Grzymała were frequent visitors to
the Square d'Orléans; the Viardots, Marcelina Czartoryska, and members
of the Polish diaspora also made sure that he did not feel abandoned.
Sand, in a jaundiced frame of mind that now colored everything to do
with Solange and Chopin, simply concluded that they, too, like Chopin,
had "gone over to the enemy." Pauline Viardot was so concerned about
the rupture that she wrote to Sand, imploring her to reconsider what she
had done. "You say that Chopin belongs to Solange's clique, making her
out to be a victim and running you down. That is absolutely false, I swear
it, at least as far as he is concerned."[2] Louis Viardot may not have helped
matters when he chimed in with a postscript to his wife's letter. After

---

1. CFC, vol. 3, p. 325.
2. Ibid., p. 305.

reviewing the fiasco of Solange's wedding, he observed, "I fear the breath of evil lips has come between you," and in a sentence that must have roiled her, he added, "The mother, has *she* no share in the fault?" Sand not only ignored the question but broke off her connection with the Viardots as well.

Paris continued to offer Chopin its usual array of attractions, including dinner parties with Auguste Léo and the ever-faithful Delacroix, and an occasional visit to the opera. At this time, too, his friendship with Alkan deepened. Alkan still lived in the Square d'Orléans, and Chopin occasionally went over to his apartment in order to spend the remains of the day with him. In early October, Chopin even spent a few days as a guest of Baron James de Rothschild, whose palatial home, the Château de Ferrières, lay just outside Paris. On November 18 and 20, Chopin was invited to the Hôtel Lambert and played for the Czartoryskis and their circle of friends, reunions and the Polish atmosphere surrounding them, which helped to cheer him. And in December he was greeted with a positive review in the *Neue Zeitschrift für Musik* of his Three Mazurkas, op. 63, and his Three Waltzes, op. 64. The first of these waltzes, the "Minute" Waltz in D-flat major, he dedicated to Delfina Potocka, who had returned to Paris and had made a brief reappearance in his life. He dined with Delfina and her guests in mid-February and afterward played for them. For much of the rest of this difficult winter of 1847–48 he taught a few pupils whenever his visibly declining health allowed him to do so, and he managed to see his Cello Sonata, op. 65, through the press. From this time, too, Chopin began to suffer financial hardship.

Watching all this from the sidelines was Chopin's pupil Jane Stirling, who was only too ready to move into the space vacated by Sand. She and her wealthy elder sister Katherine Erskine had been part of Chopin's Paris circle for the past four years, and Stirling, his pupil since 1844, was now receiving up to three lessons a week. The sisters visited Chopin regularly, attempting to make life softer for him, and they gradually became central to his social activities, taking over many of the mundane chores that he himself found irksome. Stirling was already in love with him, and in the months ahead she offered Chopin much material support and almost certainly saved him from penury.

II

His friends finally persuaded him to give a concert. In a letter to Ludwika, dated February 10, 1848, Chopin explained how it all came about. One morning, Pleyel, Auguste Léo, Thomas Albrecht, and Count Léon de Perthuis (in his official role of music director to King Louis-Philippe) turned up at his apartment and began to exert some gentle pressure on him. They assured him that he would have to do nothing but sit down and play. Everything else would be taken care of. The Salle Pleyel would be reserved for the occasion on February 16. Supporting artists would be contacted and their assistance assured, because everyone knew that Chopin had neither the money nor the energy to give the necessary guarantees. Chopin found it impossible to resist their arguments and his initial opposition to the idea crumbled. Aside from Franchomme, on whose participation Chopin absolutely insisted, the other artists were selected by his "committee of friends." Invitations went out to the violinist Jean-Delphin Alard, an outstanding chamber player and a professor at the Conservatoire; the tenor Gustave-Hippolyte Roger, who had sung the leading role in Meyerbeer's opera Le Prophète; and the mezzo-soprano Antonia Molina de Mendi, the young niece of Pauline Viardot.

Chopin had not played in public for six years. When a tentative announcement appeared in the press to the effect that the Sylph might deign to break his silence, Pleyel's offices were flooded with inquiries. And when just two weeks prior to the concert the date was actually fixed, all three hundred seats were sold within hours, at 20 francs each. The Court ordered forty tickets. Six hundred people were placed on a waiting list and promised a second concert on March 10 by the ever-resourceful Pleyel, an idea that Chopin dismissed with the words "I am certain I shall not give it, for I am sick of this one already."[3] He was, in fact, deeply apprehensive about this concert. It contained premiere performances of three of his recently published compositions—the Barcarolle, the Berceuse, and the Sonata for Cello and Piano. The Sonata especially bothered him, for he had kept on revising it almost to the moment of its publication a few weeks earlier. Charles Hallé had heard Chopin and Franchomme rehearse the work privately and witnessed the effort that this difficult piece had

---

3. CFC, vol. 3, p. 320; KFC, vol. 2, p. 228.

cost the composer. Chopin was in discomfort, and Hallé observed that he walked toward the piano "like a half opened penknife," but once he started playing and warmed to his work, "the spirit mastered the flesh."[4] Now that the concert was almost upon him, Chopin was alarmed by the eager rush to buy tickets, because he knew that he would have to start practicing in earnest, "for I feel that I play worse than ever."[5] To add to his woes, he had once more succumbed to influenza, which was making its annual sweep across Paris. In an attempt to assuage his anxieties, Pleyel sent one of his best pianos over to Chopin's apartment, the one that he was to use at the concert, so that he could get used to it. Pleyel also promised to deck the stage with flowers, and he even carpeted the aisles and the platform in order to create the impression of an elegant drawing room, the sort of environment that put Chopin at ease. No artist could have asked for more.

On Wednesday, February 16, at 8:30 in the evening, Chopin walked onto the platform of the Salle Pleyel and was greeted with rapturous applause. He was weak and his face was ghastly pale, but he walked with an upright carriage. The audience was distinguished and laced with aristocracy. In high-flown language, the *Revue et Gazette musicale* wrote that it contained "a select flowering of the most distinguished aristocratic ladies dressed in their most elegant finery." The journal observed that a second aristocracy was also present, "that of artists and music lovers, who were overjoyed to catch the flight of this musical sylph who had promised to let himself be heard once more, if only for a few hours."[6] He was surrounded by friends who sat around the piano on the platform, including Grzymała, Custine, the Czartoryskis, Delacroix, and Jane Stirling.

---

4. HLL, p. 36.
5. CFC, vol. 3, p. 322; KFC, vol. 2, p. 229.
6. Issue of February 20, 1848.

CHOPIN'S CONCERT
in the
SALON PLEYEL
February 16, 1848

PART ONE

Trio by Mozart for piano, violin, and violoncello,
    played by MM. Chopin, Alard, and Franchomme
Aria sung by Mlle Antonia Molina de Mendi
Nocturne }
Barcarolle } composed and performed by M. Chopin
Aria sung by Mlle Antonia Molina de Mendi
Études }
Berceuse } composed and performed by M. Chopin

PART TWO

Scherzo, Adagio, and Finale from the Sonata in G minor
    for piano and violoncello, composed by M. Chopin
    and played by the composer and M. Franchomme
A new aria from *Robert le Diable,*
    composed by M. Meyerbeer and sung by M. Roger
Preludes }
Mazurkas } composed and performed by M. Chopin
Waltzes }
    Accompanists: MM. Alary and de Garaudé

The Mozart Trio with which the program began was probably the one in E major (K. 542), a favorite of Chopin's. According to the *Revue et Gazette musicale,* "it was executed in such a manner that one despairs of ever hearing it again so well performed."[7] But it was the Barcarolle that caught the ears of the aficionados. Charles Hallé was in the audience and was struck by the way in which Chopin negotiated its various difficulties.

7. Issue of February 20, 1848.

He played the latter part of his Barcarolle, from the point where it demands the utmost energy, in the opposite style, *pianissimo*, but with such wonderful *nuances* that one remained in doubt if this new reading were not preferable to the accustomed one.[8]

From Hallé's description we infer that he was drawing attention to the coda, which is ushered in via a crescendo at bar 92, and is marked *fortissimo* and *più mosso*. For eighteen bars thereafter the floodgates are opened, and the keyboard is inundated with a level of sound that Chopin at that moment did not have the energy to deliver.

The concluding bars of this coda, incidentally, are unrolled over one of the grand pedal points in piano literature.

In Part Two of the concert Chopin still had to rally to the challenge of the Cello Sonata. An inspection of the program reveals that the first movement was dropped, almost certainly out of consideration for his frail condition, and the audience heard only the Scherzo, Largo, and Finale. (Chopin's pupil Mme Camille Dubois told Niecks that the movement was abandoned because it had no success when he had rehearsed it before friends, an explanation we find implausible.[9]) The concert concluded with an assortment of Chopin's Preludes, Mazurkas, and Waltzes, ending with the newly published "Minute" Waltz in D-flat major, op. 64, no. 1, which was encored. When Chopin got to the artists' room, he almost fainted.

The praise that Chopin garnered in the columns of the *Gazette* for his playing that evening amounted to one long eulogy.

---

8. HLL, p. 36.
9. NFC, vol. 2, p. 207.

The sylph has kept his word, and with what success, with what enthusiasm! It is easier to tell of the reception that he received, of the delirium he aroused, than to describe, to analyze, and to reveal the mysteries of a performance that has no parallel in our terrestrial sphere . . . To know Chopin is to understand him. All those who attended Wednesday's performance are convinced of this.

After describing the various items that Chopin played, the article continued:

Do not ask how all these masterpieces, great and small, were performed. We said at the outset that we would not attempt to describe the infinite number of nuances of an exceptional genius who has such a technique at his disposal. We will only say that the charm never ceased for one moment to hold his audience entranced, and that the effect lingered long after the concert was over.[10]

Not to be outdone, *Le Ménestrel* followed suit with language that entered the sphere of poetry. It referred to Chopin as "the ineffable artist, attached to this mortal world by the merest touch of a finger" and went on to describe his playing as resembling "the sigh of a flower, the whisper of clouds, or the murmur of stars."[11]

One of the most heartfelt messages Chopin received after the concert was a brief note from his old admirer the Marquis de Custine, who spoke for many when he wrote, "You have transformed a public into a circle of friends," a sentence that could well serve as Chopin's epitaph.

One is alone with you in the midst of a crowd; it is not a piano that speaks but a soul. And what a soul! Preserve your life for your friends. It is a consolation to be able to listen to you sometimes, in the dark days that threaten us . . .

Always unchanged,
A. de Custine[12]

---

10. Issue of February 20, 1848.
11. Issue of February 20, 1848.
12. CFC, vol. 3, p. 325.

III

"The dark days that threaten us." Within a week Custine's prophesy came true. On February 22, revolution broke out in Paris. The citizens no longer wanted their "Citizen King," Louis-Philippe. This monarch had no genuine connections to the French throne, having been placed there almost by chance, after the insurrection of 1830 (the "Three Glorious Days") had failed to produce a republic. Louis-Philippe had meanwhile tried to be all things to all men. He liked to walk around the streets of Paris with an umbrella over his arm, call the workers "my friends" and the National Guardsmen "my comrades." But when mass unemployment and starvation began to stalk the land, the French could no longer stand the charade of a puppet monarch and decided to get rid of him. Street barricades were erected and fighting began. Crowds assembled outside the royal palace and remained there all night, singing the "Marseillaise" and clamoring for reforms. Fifty rebels were killed in a fusillade of bullets from Royalist troops, and many more were wounded. As the corpses were carried away in makeshift carts, segments of the National Guard that had been brought in to restore order and had witnessed the carnage joined the revolution. It was a turning point. More than a million cobblestones were torn up and four thousand trees chopped down to create a series of barricades running across the city. Within forty-eight hours a howling mob had surrounded the palace at Saint-Cloud, where the king had taken refuge. Confronted with the prospect of civil war, Louis-Philippe was forced to abdicate and he fled with his family to Britain.

Chopin had taken to his bed after the concert, and these disturbances virtually passed him by. He lay there for several days, suffering from the lingering effects of influenza, oblivious to the sound of gunfire and the hand-to-hand fighting that raged in the streets below. With blood on the boulevards, and still more about to be shed, a second concert for March 10 was out of the question. Artistic life in Paris had come to a standstill, for people were fleeing the city. "The shops are open," Chopin wrote, "but there are no customers. Foreigners with passports in hand are waiting to depart, but they can't go anywhere until the damage to the railway lines is repaired." In the midst of all this confusion Chopin heard that Solange had given birth to a daughter, and he sent her a note of congratulations. "As you may imagine," he told her, "the birth of your little girl has brought me greater joy than the arrival of the Republic."[13]

By March 4, Chopin felt well enough to respond to an invitation to visit Mme Charlotte Marliani and her circle of friends. Separated from her husband, who had developed a roving eye, she had moved from the Square d'Orléans to an apartment at 18 rue de la Ville-l'Évêque, two kilometers away; so Chopin's cabriolet had to meet the challenge of negotiating a route past the potholes and rubble left on the streets by the riots, which had kept people confined to their homes. One of his fellow guests was Edmond Combes, the French vice consul to Morocco. This larger-than-life character had explored the Red Sea coast and had lived for several years in Abyssinia. His book about that country had earned for him the affectionate nickname "the Abyssinian." Chopin took to Combes at once, and at the end of the evening they left Mme Marliani's drawing room together.

As they descended the stairs, they unexpectedly encountered George Sand in the foyer. It was an unpleasant moment that both Sand and Chopin would have preferred to avoid. Chopin greeted her, and asked whether she had heard from Solange recently—"a week ago, yesterday, the day before?" Sand said no. "Then allow me to inform you that you are a grandmother," replied Chopin. "Solange has a little girl, and I am glad to be the first to give you this news." He then raised his hat and continued downstairs. As he reached the bottom, he suddenly realized that he had forgotten to add the important information that mother and child were well. Too weak to climb back upstairs, he sent Combes to impart the message. Sand came down and pressed him for more details about the health of her daughter, so Chopin gave her what information he could. She then inquired about Chopin's own health. "I said that I was well, called for the concierge to open the door, and returned to the Square d'Orléans, accompanied by the Abyssinian." All this may be gleaned from a letter that Chopin wrote to Solange the very next day, March 5, and it is worth remembering its contents, which stand in stark contrast to the account that Sand was to offer the world seven years later. Sand and Chopin never saw each other again. Edmond Combes described the effect that this meeting had on Chopin: "I brought him home very sad and very depressed."[14]

---

13. CFC, vol. 3, p. 329.
14. Ibid., pp. 331–32. Just four months after his meeting with Chopin, Combes died in an

Sand's own version of this same scene, which was published in her *Histoire de ma vie*, was designed for public consumption. "I saw him for a moment in March 1848. I clasped his icy, trembling hand. I wanted to talk to him, but he took to his heels," she wrote. "It was my turn to say that he no longer loved me. I spared him the pain, and left everything to Providence and the future."[15] This was an embellishment she had carefully burnished over time and it never changed. Just fifteen months after this chance encounter with Chopin, when she learned that a passing acquaintance, Mme Grille de Beuzelin, wanted to bring about a reconciliation, she was ready with her narrative. "He hastened to avoid me. I sent someone after him, and he came back unwillingly, to speak neither of himself nor of me, but to show in his attitude and looks, anger and indeed almost hatred."[16] Sand's account was the only one available to us until the publication in modern times of Chopin's letter to Solange, and her words are best left to bear witness against her.

Solange's infant did not survive beyond the first week of life. She was lowered into the ground on March 7, bearing the name Jeanne-Gabrielle. Within days of writing his first letter of congratulation to Solange, Chopin found himself having to write some words of commiseration. "You must be brave and calm. Take care of yourself for those who remain."[17] Perhaps the only good thing to arise from this sorry affair was that it eventually led to a rapprochement between Solange and her mother, but that was still many months away.

---

incident worthy of a place in one of his travel books. He had no sooner taken up a new diplomatic posting in Syria than his daughter Augusta died of cholera in Maraba, near Damascus. As he and his wife were returning to the city, they were intercepted by a hostile crowd of religious fanatics ("musulmen"), and molested with such severity that Combes died of his injuries—ignominiously in a barnyard—although his wife survived. CGS, vol. IV, p. 899.

15. SHV, p. 448.

16. CFC, vol. 3, p. 427.

17. Ibid., p. 334. On May 14, 1849, Solange informed Chopin that she had given birth to another daughter "as big as the other was small." (CFC, vol, 3, p. 410.) She, too, bore the name Jeanne-Gabrielle, in memory of her sister. "Nini," as the child was known in the family circle, spent two years at Nohant in the company of her grandmother while Solange and Clésinger were at loggerheads. Sand became completely enamored of her grandchild and would have been happy to bring her up as her own. In the spring of 1854, Clésinger turned up at Nohant and snatched the girl from her care. It was a cruel move, calculated to cause pain. "Nini" died of scarlet fever at the age of six, by which time Solange and Clésinger had gone their separate ways.

IV

The moment that the revolution had broken out and Louis-Philippe was deposed, Sand traveled to Paris to celebrate the proclamation of a republic with her left-wing friends. She was ecstatic at the overthrow of the monarchy and now called herself a Communist. Some of her old colleagues were even appointed to serve in the provisional government headed by Lamartine. They included Louis Blanc, Emmanuel Arago, and her old lover Félicien Mallefille. "Imagine!" wrote Chopin incredulously. "Mallefille is the governor of Versailles! Louis Blanc is head of the Labor Commission! Barbès is governor of the Luxembourg Palace itself!"[18] Chopin's incredulity was justified. Not one of these people had any experience in running anything, let alone a country. Armand Barbès had only recently been released from jail, where he had languished for the past eighteen years as punishment for his part in the July Revolution of 1830. Mallefille's life as a minor poet had done nothing to prepare him for the role of governor of Versailles, not even to write a poem about it. He remained in this elevated office for just three days and left. As for Louis Blanc, the public works program that he organized was well described as a fiasco. Unemployment was rife, one of the main causes of the revolution. So Blanc came up with a novel solution. Fifty thousand workers were hired to dig trenches in the Champs de Mars, while another fifty thousand were hired to fill them in again. He was eventually driven out of office for incompetence by the very colleagues who had placed him there, was nearly killed by angry workers, and was forced to seek asylum in London. Needless to say, Chopin was no Republican. He regretted the overthrow of the monarchy. The court of Louis-Philippe had patronized him for years, and he felt close to those members of the royal entourage who had always supported him.

The year 1848 has been called "the Spring of Nations." Crowned heads in Berlin, Dresden, and Vienna looked on with alarm at the sequence of events that had toppled Louis-Philippe. As if to remind them that their turn was coming, Karl Marx produced his *Communist Manifesto*, with its famous imperative: "Workers of the World, Unite! You have nothing to lose but your chains!" As the conflagration swept across Europe, cities such as Berlin, Dresden, Vienna, Pest, and Milan experienced upheavals that

---

18. CFC, vol. 3, pp. 329–30.

Fryderyk Chopin; a daguerreotype by Louis-Auguste Bisson (1847).[19]

19. It used to be thought that this celebrated daguerreotype was taken in the summer of 1849, in the Paris offices of Chopin's publisher Maurice Schlesinger, and that date appears in many of the major iconographies of Chopin. We now know it to have been taken by Bisson in his atelier at 65 rue Saint-Germain l'Auxerrois toward the end of 1847, not long after Chopin's break with George Sand. During Chopin's lifetime it belonged to Schlesinger's private collection and subsequently to the firm of Breitkopf and Härtel in Leipzig. It was later acquired by the Chopin National Institute in Warsaw. The original daguerreotype was destroyed during World War II. What we have today is a photograph of that daguerreotype made sometime before 1939 by Benedykt Jerzy Dorys.

produced a combined total of tens of thousands of dead. Poland had been a graveyard since 1831, its fate sealed. Would the Poles rise up too? On March 15, the Polish diaspora was electrified by news of a civil insurgency in Prussian-ruled Poznań. Five days later a newly created Polish legion, made possible by the large-scale amnesty of Poles in Prussian jails, was poised to take the fight into Greater Poland. Volunteers rushed from all over Europe to swell the legion's ranks. Prince Czartoryski traveled from Paris to Kraków to direct the coming struggle. All the old aspirations for an independent Poland were suddenly revived, especially in Paris. On May 15, crowds of Polish sympathizers massed at the Place de la Bastille chanting the slogan *"Vive la Pologne!"* and marched to the National Assembly, demanding a formal declaration in support of Poland. Many thought that the socialistic ideas published in the left-wing journal *La Vraie République* (to which George Sand was a contributor) had instigated this demonstration. Sand joined the crowd, sensing that her dream of a lasting republic was within reach. She was there when the mob broke down the doors of the Assembly and swept into the debating chamber. Chaos reigned inside the building for two hours until the rabble-rousers encountered the bayonets of the National Guard. The leaders, including some of Sand's fellow agitators, ended up behind bars. It was a political humiliation for them and for her. In the midst of the turmoil she had seen a woman haranguing the crowd from an upstairs window, and on asking who it was had been told, "George Sand." She fled to Nohant, fearing to lose her liberty and possibly her life. As she mourned the fate of her colleagues, together with the loss of her dreams, she wrote, "What deplorable folly!"[20]

When Chopin heard that Julian Fontana, who was in New York, planned to return to Europe and join the insurgency, he cautioned his old friend against it: "However impatient we may be, let us wait until the cards have been well shuffled, so that we do not waste our strength, which will be sorely needed when the right moment comes. That moment is near, but it is not today. Perhaps in a month, perhaps in a year. Everybody here is convinced that our affairs will be decided before the autumn."[21] Chopin was obviously well informed about the political situation in Europe. He told Fontana that the newspapers were filled with lies; that no republic

---

20. CGS, vol. VIII, p. 457.
21. CFC, vol. 3, p. 337; KFC, vol. 2, p. 239.

had yet been set up in Poznań; and in a shrewd piece of foresight he added that the German population within Prussia would hardly allow it, and would prefer to shed their blood rather than allow themselves to be absorbed into a Greater Poland. "If you want to do the right thing," he told Fontana, "stay where you are."

While Chopin was able to offer sound counsel to his friend, he had no such counsel to offer himself. When the *Warsaw Courier* carried a report about the concert that he had given the previous month, it stirred the pot by adding the quite spurious information that he planned to leave France immediately. This raised false hopes among his family members that he might return to Poland, especially if the events in Poznań turned in the country's favor. Overjoyed at such a possibility, Justyna wrote to Chopin on March 5, his name day,

> Warsaw, March 5,
> You gave us a real Carnival treat by writing to us, for a few lines coming directly from you calm our fears far more than any indirect news such as often reaches us. It is all the more so when influenza is raging where you are, and you can imagine our anxiety. The *Courier* reported that you had given a concert and would be leaving Paris as soon as possible. Of course we wondered: "Where will he go?" Some said, "To Holland"; others, "To Germany"; and again others, "To Petersburg." While we, who were longing to see you, thought: "Perhaps he will come here." The family at once started arguing about where you would stay. The Barcińskis were ready to give up their apartment; Ludwika too. It was really rather like a childish game of soap bubbles . . .
> Your loving Mother[22]

And a game of "soap bubbles" it turned out to be. These false hopes, like soap bubbles adrift in the air, soon burst without leaving a trace. So Chopin preferred to do what he always did when life confronted him with momentous choices. He procrastinated and waited for fate itself to force his hand.

---

22. CFC, vol. 3, p. 330; KFC, vol. 2, p. 235.

TWILIGHT IN BRITAIN, 1848

He took the audience, as it were, into his confidence, and
whispered to them of zephyrs and moonlight rather than of
cataracts and thunder.
—from the diary of James Hedderwick[1]

I

With Paris in the grip of revolutionary turmoil, there was an inevitable exodus of wealthy families from the city who took many of Chopin's pupils with them. The composer now found himself with a depleted income, and no ready means of making good the loss. Cholera also stalked the capital, and both theater and opera house shut their doors against the disease. Chopin was persuaded to leave France for a time and accept a long-standing invitation from his Scottish pupil Jane Stirling to visit Britain. There was a promise of concerts with substantial fees, and a good prospect of acquiring pupils from the upper-class families to which Jane Stirling was attached and undertook to introduce him. Altogether Chopin was to live in Britain for seven months, a considerable period of time that has been richly documented. He gave important concerts in London, Manchester, Glasgow, and Edinburgh, and was "taken up" by high society, giving numerous private

1. HBG, p. 200.

performances in the homes of prominent English and Scottish aristocrats. He was introduced to Queen Victoria and Prince Albert, and he mingled with celebrities such as the Duke of Wellington, Count Alfred d'Orsay, William Makepeace Thackeray, Charles Dickens, Thomas Carlyle, George Hogarth, and Ralph Waldo Emerson (who was on an extended visit to London). While this trip to Britain may have come at the right time for Chopin, its artistic success was purchased at great cost to his health, and almost certainly hastened his death.

II

Chopin arrived in London during the early evening of Thursday, April 20, after a rough voyage across the English Channel, and moved into temporary lodgings at 10 Bentinck Street, near Cavendish Square, rented for him by Jane Stirling and her sister Katherine Erskine.[2] The Scottish ladies had done their best, even providing him with such luxuries as his own monogrammed writing paper and his favorite hot chocolate; but the rooms did not suit him. He did not even bother to unpack the Pleyel grand piano that had been shipped from Paris with him. It was Maundy Thursday and the social life of London had started to languish in anticipation of the long Easter weekend to come. So Chopin took advantage of the "dreary quiet," abandoned his lodgings, and drove down to Kingston-upon-Thames to visit members of the exiled French royal family, a trip about which tantalizingly few details have emerged.[3] Talk was all about politics, the revolution in Paris (which had meanwhile spread to Berlin and would soon threaten Vienna), and above all the "Polish question." The British government was sympathetic to the fate of Poland, and the national debate that had been triggered by the recent uprising in Poznań was in full flow. For weeks the press was filled with news of the military confrontations between the Poles and the Prussians, in a struggle for what had formerly been Polish territory. The Battle of Miłosław (April 30), which resulted in several hundred

---

2. Jane Stirling wrote to Franchomme, "The crossing was not smooth and it rained—he was on the bridge . . . Thank God he does not appear to have caught cold." MI, XL/13, pp. 36–37.
3. After Louis-Philippe had abdicated the French throne, and sought asylum for himself and his family in Britain, he had moved into Claremont, a magnificent house near Esher, Surrey, lent to him by Queen Victoria, where he lived in exile until his death on August 26, 1850.

dead and wounded, and a temporary Polish victory against Prussia, had provoked impassioned speeches in both houses of Parliament—most notably from Lord Dudley Stuart, the chief sponsor of the Polish cause in Britain. As this latest Polish uprising faltered and then failed, fresh waves of Polish émigrés swept across Western Europe to join the ones already there, and several hundred of them settled in Britain—at least temporarily. Once he had crossed Albion's shores, Chopin unexpectedly found himself borne aloft on a tide of Polish national sentiment.[4]

Meanwhile, he had found somewhere else to live. With the help of Major Karol Szulczewski (a veteran of the 1830 Uprising and a representative of Prince Adam Czartoryski in London), Chopin moved into more spacious apartments at 48 Dover Street, a fashionable address in the heart of London, where he resided for three months. It was here that his Pleyel piano was removed from its packing case and set up for him by workmen from Broadwood and Company, on whose instruments Chopin had agreed to perform at all his public appearances in Britain. One of his first calls, in fact, was to the Broadwood showrooms at 33 Great Pulteney Street, where he selected the pianos to be used during his forthcoming trips into the provinces and Scotland.[5] On May 2, Broadwood delivered a grand piano

---

4. While the British newspapers had started to grumble about the eternal "Polish question," and its cost to the national purse, it did not affect the warmth of the reception accorded to Chopin by the British public at large. Sympathy for Poland had been kept alive by Lord Dudley Stuart, the president and founder of the Literary Association of the Friends of Poland, and member of Parliament for Marylebone. In this latter capacity he had funneled tens of thousands of pounds from the British Treasury in support of Polish causes and had supervised hundreds of annual pensions granted to Poles living in Britain. Lord Stuart's speeches in the House of Commons on May 16 and August 23, 1848, contain an eloquent defense of the government's practice of handing out pensions to Polish émigrés, some of whom had lived in Britain since 1831. See also his important "Address to the Poles," in SALA.

5. It was on this occasion that Chopin made the acquaintance of the young tuner and piano technician A. J. Hipkins, who remained with the firm of Broadwood all his life and in later years enjoyed a wide celebrity as a historian of musical instruments. It was not until 1899, however, fifty-one years after his first (and only) encounter with Chopin, that Hipkins put pen to paper and tried to recall what he had heard. It must always be borne in mind that his surprisingly detailed impressions of Chopin's playing, made after such a long lapse of time, were based on the experience of hearing the dying composer in such a physically weakened condition that when Chopin appeared at the Broadwood showrooms he was so fatigued that he had to be carried up the stairs. Once seated at the keyboard, however, Chopin revealed many of the characteristics that have meanwhile found a special place for him in the history of piano pedagogy. "He kept his elbows close to his side," wrote Hipkins, "and played only with finger-touch, no weight from the arms. He used a simple, natural position of the hands as conditioned by scale and chord-playing, adopting the easiest fingering, although it might be against

to Dover Street and placed it in Chopin's drawing room. Within days of hearing about this, Pierre Érard also "hastened to offer his services," and Chopin had three fine grand pianos in his London dwelling, courtesy of the three greatest piano manufacturers in Europe.[6]

Thanks to the revolutionary situation on the Continent, London was flooded with musicians who had crossed the Channel in the hope of pursuing their profession in England. Jenny Lind and Pauline Viardot were paramount among the singers; among the pianists were Charles Hallé, George Osborne, Émile Prudent, Friedrich Kalkbrenner, and above all Sigismond Thalberg, who had secured no fewer than twelve appearances at Her Majesty's Theatre during the coming season. Berlioz was also in London. The fiery Frenchman had arrived four months earlier at the invitation of the conductor Louis Jullien and the prospect of large fees. And now he had to while away his time in England, unable to get either himself or his purse back to Paris, where the banking system had collapsed. For this enforced sojourn we must be grateful, because Berlioz left some of the wittiest descriptions of artistic life in the British capital. We cannot fail to be amused at the apprehension with which he greets the tidal wave of talent unexpectedly washing across the city—"hordes of singers," "a mere four or five thousand top-class pianists"—there to take bread from his table. But he was essentially correct. London at this moment offered the richest and most varied concert life in Europe. And it was the best place for Chopin to be.

On May 4, Chopin went to Her Majesty's Theatre in the Haymarket at the personal invitation of Jenny Lind, the "Swedish Nightingale," in order to hear her sing the role of Amina in Bellini's *La sonnambula*, a sold-out event at which Queen Victoria and the Duke of Wellington were present. He told Grzymała,

> I have just returned from the Italian Opera [in the Haymarket]. J. Lind sang for the first time this year, and the Queen showed herself in public for the first time since the Chartist demonstrations.[7]

---

the rules, that came to him. He changed fingers upon a key as often as an organ player." HHCP, p. 5.

6. CFC, vol. 3, p. 341; KFC, vol. 2, p. 243.

7. For a month or more Queen Victoria had not been seen in public because of the threatened mass demonstration outside the House of Commons by the Chartists—a powerful working-

Both made a great impression. But what also impressed me was old Wellington, sitting beneath the royal box like an old *monarchical* watchdog in his kennel. I have made the acquaintance of J. Lind, who was so courteous as to send me her visiting card with a most excellent stall ticket. I had a splendid seat and heard everything very well. She is the type of Swede without compare, illuminated not only by the usual sort of halo but by a kind of Aurora Borealis. She was enormously effective in *La sonnambula*. She sings with an assurance and purity, and her *piano* is as smooth and even as a thread of hair.[8]

Five days later, on May 9, Lind's rival Pauline Viardot made her appearance in London singing exactly the same role—Amina in *La sonnambula*—at Covent Garden Theatre. Chopin was not present, but he was pleased to learn that Viardot had brought to London her vocal arrangements of some of his mazurkas, and that she proposed to introduce them to the London public. On May 12 she sang a group of them at Covent Garden with such success that they were encored. Chopin was not present on that occasion either. He was dining with Jenny Lind "and afterwards she sang Swedish songs to me until midnight."[9]

---

class movement that for years had presented to Parliament through its People's Charter a set of demands for social reform, and had been repeatedly turned down. On April 10, shortly before Chopin's arrival in London, the leaders of the movement arranged to march on Parliament. Half a million protesters were expected to rally on Kennington Common and then converge on the seat of government. The government in turn had armed tens of thousands of "special constables" with wooden staffs, telling the Chartists that they would not be allowed to cross the bridges spanning the Thames and enter Westminster. In the event, it poured with rain and so few turned up that the march was called off. Nonetheless, the continued threat of social unrest, with the specter of violence being imported from the Continent, spread a great deal of fear through the British establishment and the royals had temporarily retreated from public view. Such was the adulation surrounding Jenny Lind, however, that Victoria and Albert considered her appearance the most propitious moment to reveal themselves once more to their subjects.

8. CFC, vol. 3, p. 342; KFC, vol. 2, p. 244. This letter is generally misdated "May 11" in the collections. Jenny Lind made her much heralded return to Her Majesty's Theatre (Haymarket) on May 4.

9. CFC, vol. 3, p. 344; KFC, vol. 2, p. 245.

III

On May 10, Chopin made his first London appearance as a pianist, in Kensington's Gore House. This was the home of Lady Margaret Blessington and Count Alfred d'Orsay, whose union flourished without benefit of clergy and was blissfully unaffected by the air of scandal and impropriety hovering over it.[10] Chopin had his Pleyel grand piano transported to Gore House, perhaps because he had not yet had time to adapt to the heavier action of the Broadwood. It was the only known occasion during his sojourn in Britain that he did not play in public on a Broadwood, although he continued to practice on the Pleyel.

A number of engagements in London's stately homes followed. Most of them were initiated by Jane Stirling, whose temporary residence in nearby Welbeck Street proved to be a useful base of operations as she pursued her unrelenting campaign to promote Chopin and his music. He was invited to play in the luxurious abodes of Lady Anne Antrobus in Piccadilly (May 12); the Duchess of Sutherland in Stafford House (May 15); the Countess of Gainsborough in Cavendish Square (May 24); Mrs. Adelaide Sartoris[11] in Eaton Place (June 23); Mrs. Hart Dyke in Park Lane (June 29); and the Earl of Falmouth in St. James's Square (July 7). Chopin's repertoire at these concerts generally featured the Andante Spianato as an opener, followed by the B-flat minor Scherzo, op. 31. Then came a random selection from the Studies; the Berceuse, op. 57; and several of the Preludes, Mazurkas, and Waltzes. These programs were substantial and give the lie to the idea that Chopin was obliged to play mere fragments of his compositions because of fatigue. Playing, in fact, often revived him.

The invitation from the Duchess of Sutherland to appear in her magnificent home, Stafford House, on May 15, stands out from the others. Stafford (now Lancaster) House was renowned for an opulence that was said to have outclassed the palace of the monarch herself. This glittering occasion had been arranged to celebrate the christening of the Duke and Duchess of Sutherland's infant daughter, and the cream of British

---

10. Lest the fact has slipped the reader's memory, Count d'Orsay lived openly with Lady Blessington after having married her fifteen-year-old stepdaughter.
11. This was the singer Adelaide Kemble, younger sister of the famous actress Fanny Kemble.

aristocracy turned up. Chopin was introduced to Queen Victoria, Prince Albert, and Lady Byron; and he also met the Duke of Wellington. His letters portray these encounters with dry solemnity. Lady Byron he described as "a curiosity—I can well believe that she bored Byron."[12] Victoria and Albert were dispatched in three brief sentences: "Her Majesty was gracious and spoke to me twice. Prince Albert moved closer to the piano. Everybody said that these are rare favors." The Iron Duke was dismissed as "Old Wellington" and was bundled together "with his peers—although his peers do not resemble him."[13] The influential *Illustrated London News* summed up Chopin's part in this brilliant gathering in a single sentence: "Chopin's pianoforte playing before her Majesty at Stafford House, on Monday, created a great sensation."[14] After the success of this concert Chopin was told to expect an invitation to play for the queen at Buckingham Palace, but it never came. A few days earlier he had rejected an invitation to play one of his piano concertos at a prestigious Philharmonic Society concert. Because these events were so jealously fought over, Chopin's refusal made a bad impression on certain musicians who had the ear of the Court music director, through whose office Chopin's invitation to the palace would normally have been issued, and this official used Chopin's refusal as a reason to block the invitation to Buckingham Palace. Chopin's excuse for declining to play at the Philharmonic Society concert was that he was not well. But the real reason was that he did not wish to perform with the society's orchestra after just one public rehearsal—"to which people are admitted with free tickets. How could one try over and repeat passages?"[15] Chopin preferred to sacrifice the concert, and with it his fee. Another concert

---

12. CFC, vol. 3, p. 370; KFC, vol. 2, p. 266.
13. CFC, vol. 3, p. 367; KFC, vol. 2, p. 264. It was entirely fitting that one of the earliest engagements offered to Chopin should come from the Duchess of Sutherland, whose husband the duke was vice president of the Literary Association of the Friends of Poland, and he worked with Lord Dudley Stuart to raise money for Polish émigrés. In Lord Stuart's aforementioned Address to the Poles, we read, "Of all the entertainments given through the instrumentality of the Association, none were more interesting or more successful than the *matinées musicales* of Stafford House, the princely residence of the Duke and Duchess of Sutherland. Her grace, whose generous interest in the cause of Poland has been displayed in many ways, and is never so happy as when relieving distress, spared no pains to make those *matinées* charming to her guests and profitable to those they were meant to assist; and her success was complete. Her noble mansion was thronged with persons of highest distinction, and the price of the tickets of admission being two guineas each, the gain to the funds of the Association was very great." SALA, p. 31.
14. Issue of May 20, 1848.
15. CFC, vol. 3, p. 368; KFC, vol. 2, p. 265.

that calls for special mention took place in the home of the Earl of Falmouth, in St. James's Square, on July 7. Unlike the others, this was a public
affair that attracted an audience of two hundred. The *Daily News* covered
the concert in detail.

> There was a numerous and fashionable assemblage, who were de-
> lighted with the entertainment provided for them. M. Chopin per-
> formed an *Andante Sostenuto* and a Scherzo from his Opus 31, a
> selection from his celebrated studies, a "Nocturne and Berceuse,"
> and several of his own Preludes, Mazurkas and Waltzes. In these
> various pieces he showed very strikingly his original genius as a
> composer and his transcendent powers as a performer. His music
> is as strongly marked with individual character as that of any mas-
> ter who has ever lived. It is highly finished, new in its harmonies,
> full of contrapuntal skill and ingenious contrivance; and yet we have
> never heard music which has so much of the air of unpremeditated
> effusion. The performer seems to abandon himself to the impulses
> of his fancy and feelings—to indulge in a reverie, and to pour out,
> unconsciously as it were, the thoughts and emotions which pass
> through his mind . . .
>
> M. Chopin does not seek to astonish by loudness of sound or
> mechanical dexterity. He accomplishes enormous difficulties, but
> so quietly, so smoothly, and with such constant delicacy and re-
> finement, that the listener is not sensible of their real magnitude. It
> is the exquisite delicacy, with the liquid mellowness of his tone,
> and the pearly roundness of his passages of rapid articulation,
> which are the peculiar features of his execution, while his music is
> characterized by freedom of thought, varied expression, and a kind
> of romantic melancholy which seems the natural mood of the artist's
> mind.[16]

At the last moment Chopin invited Pauline Viardot to appear at the
concert with him, and she again sang a group of her own arrangements of

---

16. Issue of July 10, 1848. This anonymous review was written by George Hogarth, a piece of
information that comes to us from Chopin himself. In a letter to his family he told them that
among the distinguished personalities he had recently met was Hogarth, "who was Walter
Scott's beloved friend. He wrote a very nice article about me in the 'Delinius' [*Daily News*!] in
connection with my second recital." CFC, vol. 3, p. 369; KFC, vol. 2, p. 265.

his mazurkas. He had hesitated before approaching her, their long friend-ship notwithstanding. Throughout the season, in fact, Viardot had featured these mazurka arrangements in several of her concerts, including the one at Covent Garden to an overflow audience, and always with great success, for they revealed her threefold skill as singer, pianist, and composer.[17] Chopin was somewhat taken aback, however, when he discovered that his name had subsequently been dropped from Viardot's performances of these pieces. He observed, "There is no longer the item 'Mazurkas of Chopin' but merely 'Mazurkas arranged by Mme Viardot'—it appears that it looks better." And he added shrewdly, "It is all the same to me; but there is a pettiness behind it. She wants to have success and is afraid of a certain newspaper which perhaps does not like me. It once wrote that she had sung music 'by a *certain* M. Chopin' whom no one knows, and that she ought to sing something else."[18]

We are now in a better position to understand Chopin's reticence in inviting Viardot to sing at his concert. The day after she had presented her mazurka arrangements at Covent Garden, J. W. Davison had come out with a blistering critique in the columns of his journal *The Musical World*, the burden of which ran,

> She sang them with great *esprit* and the utmost delicacy of senti-ment, and proved herself a ready and skilful pianist by the style in which she executed the accompaniments. But we cannot allow that the human voice can be the medium of making ugly and affected music pretty and engaging any more than the pianoforte, and while

---

17. These arrangements were made with Chopin's full approval, and their inclusion in his concert at the Earl of Falmouth's house gave them the stamp of his personal imprimatur. All of them were still in manuscript, but the first set of six that Viardot eventually published in 1864, long after Chopin's death, reveal them to be settings of texts she commissioned from Louis Pomey, a minor French poet of the day, and they bear the titles "Seize ans!" (op. 50, no. 2); "Aime-moi" (op. 33, no. 2); "Plainte d'amour" (op. 6, no. 1); "Coquette" (op. 7, no. 1); "L'Oiselet" (op. 68, no. 2); and "Séparation" (op. 24, no. 1). Six more were to follow in 1888. Viardot was not above transposing certain mazurkas to fit her vocal range, nor even above re-moving the names of Chopin's original dedicatees and replacing them with those of her own friends and acquaintances. A close inspection of Viardot's arrangements discloses that she had not lost her youthful competence at the keyboard, despite the rigors of an international singing career. The occasional cadenzas and coloratura passages with which she adorns the vocal line, while at the same time attending to the accompaniments, offers evidence of an all-around musicianship not generally found among opera singers.
18. HSCC, p. 322.

MONSIEUR CHOPIN'S
Second Matinee Musicale,

FRIDAY, JULY 7th, 1848,

AT THE RESIDENCE OF

THE EARL OF FALMOUTH,

No. 2, St. JAMES'S SQUARE;

TO COMMENCE AT FOUR O'CLOCK.

Programme.

ANDANTE SOSTENUTO ET SCHERZO (Op. 31)........Chopin

MAZOURKAS DE CHOPIN, arrangées par Madame Viardot Garcia
Madame VIARDOT GARCIA et Mlle. DE MENDI.

ETUDES (19, 13, et 14)..........................Chopin

AIR, "Ich denke dein"......, ...Beethoven.
Madame VIARDOT GARCIA.

NOCTURNE ET BERCEUSE........................Chopin.

RONDO, "Non più mesta"......(Cenerentola)......Rossini.
Madame VIARDOT GARCIA.

PRELUDES, MAZOURKAS, BALLADE, VALSES........Chopin

AIRS ESPAGNOLES, Madame VIARDOT GARCIA
et Mlle. DE MENDI

Chopin's concert at Lord Falmouth's house in St. James's Square, July 7, 1848.

admiring Mad. Viardot's cleverness in making anything out of such dull matters, we must arraign her taste for selecting them.[19]

By calling the mazurkas "ugly and affected," and arraigning Viardot's taste for singing them in public, Davison placed the famous diva in the difficult position of either abandoning them or removing Chopin's name from the billing. She removed his name. She rightly guessed that since Davison admired everything else that she did, he would be unlikely to attack her Chopin arrangements if Chopin's name was nowhere in evidence. And so it proved. When Viardot sang the same pieces at Buckingham Palace on June 27, before Queen Victoria, Prince Albert, and four hundred specially invited guests, they were billed as "Mazurkas, Madame Viardot, arranged by Madame Viardot."[20] It was this that prompted Chopin to call Viardot's

19. Issue of May 13, 1848, p. 312.
20. *The Times*, June 28, 1848.

desire to please *The Times* petty. At any rate, when she agreed to sing at his concert at Lord Falmouth's house on July 7, the composer's name was restored, as the copy of the handbill on page 565 makes clear.

The admission fee was one guinea. After deducting various expenses, Chopin was left with a handsome profit of about 100 guineas.

IV

J. W. Davison's opposition to Chopin cannot be passed over in silence, because it has earned a place of notoriety in the annals of music criticism. Two years before Chopin arrived in Britain, Davison had been appointed chief music critic to *The Times* of London (a position he retained for thirty-two years), and from this seat of power he had begun to pontificate on all matters musical. Since he also retained his position as editor of *The Musical World*, a journal that he had founded in 1836 and that came out weekly, he had begun to wield exceptional influence over the musical life of London. He had already "welcomed" Chopin to Britain in the form of a backhanded compliment in the columns of *The Musical World*, after the composer had played in the home of Adelaide Sartoris.

> M. Chopin has lately given two performances of his own pianoforte music, at the residence of Mrs. Sartoris (late Miss Adelaide Kemble) which seems to have given much pleasure to his admirers; among whom Mlle Lind, who was present at the first, seems to be the most enthusiastic. We were not present at either, and, therefore, have nothing to say on the subject. *Vivat Regina!*[21]

As early as 1841, Davison had dismissed Chopin as "a maker of sickly melodies,"[22] and he was in no hurry to change his mind. Faced with a

---

21. Issue of July 8, 1848. Davison's Latin imperative "*Vivat Regina!*" served a double function. It deferred first to Jenny Lind (the reigning "queen" among singers), whose opinion was not to be lightly set aside. But it was also meant to emulate Queen Victoria's regal silence when she surveyed matters within her kingdom of which she disapproved but over which she had no control.

22. *The Musical World*, October 28, 1841. Davison's dislike of Chopin's music reached an apogee of sorts when, years after Chopin's death, he wrote that compared with Berlioz, Cho-

growing body of newspaper coverage proclaiming Chopin's importance, Davison produced a unique response. He simply placed Chopin under a taboo. *The Times* does not carry a single word about Chopin during his entire stay in the British Isles. It is as if the composer never existed, and is an astonishing omission from England's leading newspaper.

Davison was notoriously conservative. He saw himself as the guardian of tradition. His self-appointed mission was to promote and protect the reputation of two musical gods in particular, Beethoven and Mendelssohn, composers against whom all others must be judged—and if necessary found wanting. (In this regard it is enough to remind the reader that Davison described Schubert as "an overrated bungler" and Verdi as "the greatest imposter that ever took pen in hand to write rubbish.") Mendelssohn especially could do no wrong. Ever since the composer's unexpected death the previous November, Davison had elevated him from the level of a mere mortal to that of a saint, and had then gone on to anoint himself high priest of the Mendelssohn cult in England. When it reached Davison's ears that Chopin had declined to sign a memorial tribute to Mendelssohn, circulated among prominent German musicians living in Paris and addressed to Mendelssohn's widow, Cécile, Davison exploded. He castigated Chopin for his refusal and denigrated him as a mere piano player who, so he was led to believe, had written some rondos and dance tunes for the instrument.[23] But as Chopin later explained, it was for him a matter of protocol. The tribute was meant to come from German musicians and would be read by the German people. "How can you expect me, a Pole, to sign it?" he asked. When Davison was criticized for his truculence and accused of bitterness toward Chopin, he defended himself in the next issue of *The Musical World* in the way that he knew best, by returning to the attack.

> I have been reproached by some persons for the *bitterness* which dictated my observations last week *apropos* of M. Chopin and the late Felix Mendelssohn-Bartholdy. The reproach is unjust. No

---

pin was "a morbidly sentimental flea by the side of a furiously roaring lion." Ibid., November 17, 1877.

23. Ibid., December 4, 1847. The Memorial Address was dated "Paris, 28th November, 1847," and signed by a group of German musicians resident in Paris, including Kalkbrenner, Heller, Hallé, and Pixis.

bitterness gave birth to those remarks, but respect for the departed master, in whose single person was the concentrated essence of all music, and whose death is as though from now to a century forward were to be a blank in the progress of art . . . If not to admire the music of M. Chopin be proof of a bitter spirit, let me for ever be called "bitter."[24]

Davison's tirade need not be quoted in full, but his final sally deserves a place in the Great Lexicon of Musical Invective: "When placed next to Chopin, Mendelssohn is like the sun compared to a spark flickering in a tinder-box."

These words were written in December 1847, and it is important to note the date, coming as they did just five weeks after the death of Mendelssohn. To give some idea of the vituperative nature of Davison's attitude toward Chopin, we need only consider the review he had written a few years earlier after Wessel, Chopin's English publisher, had sent him a copy of the Four Mazurkas, op. 41, under the generic name of "Souvenirs de la Pologne," which Davison described as a "motley surface of ranting hyperbole and excruciating cacophony." In an attempt to justify himself to his prudish Victorian readership, he stooped to a personal attack, which represents one of the low points of his output.

> There is an excuse at present for poor Chopin's delinquencies, he is entrammelled in the enthralling bonds of that arch-enchantress, Georges [sic] Sand, celebrated equally for the number *and excellence* of her romances and her lovers; not less we wonder how she who once swayed the heart of the sublime and terrible religious democrat, Lammenais, can be content to wanton away her dream-like existence with an artistical nonentity like Chopin.[25]

To attribute Chopin's "delinquencies" to the malign influence of an affair with George Sand was both irrelevant and foolish, and made it impossible for Chopin to defend himself. But to call him an "artistical nonentity" was absurd. Wessel rose to the occasion and produced a roll call of more than

---

24. *The Musical World*, December 11, 1847.
25. Ibid., October 28, 1841.

a score of prominent musicians convinced of Chopin's greatness—including Schumann, Liszt, Czerny, Berlioz, and Mendelssohn himself, the unwitting cause of all the brouhaha. Like the cuttlefish when pursued, all that Davison could do was to eject a cloud of ink. He produced a labored reply, the burden of which was "We cannot recognize M. Chopin in the rank where fashion has stilted him." After wishing the firm of Wessel and Stapleton well for all the good they were doing for the rest of the musical world, he craved their understanding for "bursting a few air-bubbles."[26] The situation represented the sort of comedy that critics so often create for the laughter of future generations. But what happened next lacked all precedent. Wessel commissioned Davison to write a laudatory pamphlet on the composer he had just damned, titled "Essay on the Works of Frédéric Chopin," which appeared in 1843. The stench of hypocrisy pervades every sentence of this anonymous publicity puff, whose fawning flatteries were meant to counter the very criticisms put into circulation by Davison himself! We do not have to go beyond the first sentence to know what we are in for. "The appearance of a great light in this age of musical quackery, is an event worthy of the attention of all reflecting followers of art—an incident not to be passed over by those whose task it may be to chronicle important matters ere they merge into oblivion." Chopin's compositions are now characterized by "a profoundly poetic feeling," his latest works transformed into "the offspring of a vigorous intellect," his concertos formerly damned as trivial are "only surpassed by those of the great Beethoven," and so on. Chopin's contemporaries Thalberg, Czerny, Herz, and Döhler, when set beside the Pole, are wasting their time composing "new forms of clap-trap, arpeggioed into fresh showers of triviality." And Davison's eighteen-page panegyric ends with a rhetorical question: "Beethoven and Mendelssohn excepted [is not Chopin] THE MOST ACCOMPLISHED PIANOFORTE COMPOSER THAT EVER EXISTED?"[27] What brought about Davison's astounding *volte-face*? The simple answer is money. He was paid to produce his weasel words. And

---

26. Ibid., November 4, 1841, pp. 293–95.
27. See DEC for these and other examples of Davison's hypocrisy, where he described Chopin's music as a "Koran for true believers." And lest the reader struggle with such a concept, as a "Talmud for the Infidels."

since his essay was published anonymously, he was saved from having to explain his strange "conversion" to his readers.[28]

Chopin was under no illusions about Davison, although we shall never know if he knew or even cared who had written Wessel's pamphlet. The idea is confirmed when we read what Chopin had to tell his family after his concert season in London had got under way and he had started to attract attention and make some money. "Concerning my matinées, many papers gave me good notices—with the exception of *The Times* [which carried no notices at all], whose critic is a certain Davison (a creature of the late Mendelssohn), who does not know me and who fancies I am an antagonist of Mendelssohn (so they tell me). It doesn't matter. But you will observe that people always have some motive in this world other than the desire to tell the truth."[29]

V

London was expensive. Chopin's Dover Street apartment cost him 10 guineas a week, and he had a valet and a coachman to pay for as well. He told his family that for a London engagement he was paid 20 pounds; in fact he was often paid much more, and since he was now acquiring English pupils and giving several private lessons at home each day for one guinea a lesson, he was able to pay his bills. Nonetheless, there were times when the attitude of the English aristocracy must have exasperated him. Old Lady Rothschild, after inquiring how much he cost, declared that although he played beautifully his fee was lacking in moderation. On another occasion he was approached by a lady whose daughter was taking lessons twice a week from another pianist at half a guinea a time, and had the idea that she might as well arrange some from Chopin as well. She demurred after discovering that he charged twice as much, and decided

---

28. From a scrutiny of his later career we know that Davison's opinions could be bought. After his death, his successor at *The Times*, Francis Hueffer, was besieged with gifts that arrived at the front door, having been diverted from that of the deceased Davison. Hueffer, according to the official history of *The Times*, had to hire a four-wheeler in order to carry back to the musicians all the presents that had meanwhile made their way to him. Davison's biographer describes him as "the music monster," a designation with which it is hard to disagree. RMM, pp. 3 and 75–77.
29. CFC, vol. 3, p. 368; KFC, vol. 2, p. 265.

that one lesson a week would be more than sufficient for the musical development of her offspring. One pupil, after taking a series of lessons from Chopin, simply disappeared without paying the bill. Chopin well understood the nature of his clientele, for most of whom having him as a teacher amounted to little more than a fashion statement. Some of his best stories about the English aristocracy he saved up for when he got back to Paris, and was able to tell them to friends who would appreciate them.

"Oh, Mr. Chopin, how much do you cost?"

"Madame, I take twenty-five guineas."

"Oh, but I only want a tiny little piece," she exclaimed, clasping her hands.

"It is always the same price."

"Oh, so you could play *a lot!*"

"Even for two hours, if you like."

"Well, that's agreed, then. Do I have to pay the twenty-five guineas in advance?"

"No, Madame, afterwards."

"Oh, that's very fair!"[30]

Because the moneyed classes traditionally departed London in July, whatever passed for the artistic life of the capital departed with them, and Chopin's fees began to dry up. He now prepared for his celebrated trip to Scotland, where the indefatigable Jane Stirling, who had traveled ahead, was busily preparing appearances for him in the homes of her influential Scottish friends.

VI

Jane Stirling was now a daily presence in Chopin's life and remained the driving force behind much of what was about to happen to him. She was the youngest of thirteen children whose father, John Stirling, was the laird of Kippendavie and Kippenross. She had been born at Kippenross House, Dunblane, in 1804, but by the time she was in her mid-teens both her parents were dead and the young girl had moved in with her

---

30. HFCZ, vol. 3, p. 183.

much older sister Katherine, the widow of James Erskine, who had died in 1816 after just five years of marriage. The Stirling clan had during the previous two centuries acquired an immense fortune while engaged in the East India trading boom. Some of Jane's immediate ancestors had become independently wealthy as owners of sugar plantations in Jamaica. After the death of James Erskine, his younger brother Thomas was placed in charge of the combined Erskine estates, and he handled the financial affairs of a number of extended family members, including Jane and Katherine.

Born into prosperity, the two sisters were inseparable; they traveled widely in pursuit of culture, and in the early 1840s they settled for a time in Paris, where Jane took piano lessons from the English pianist Lindsay Sloper, who was himself a pupil of Chopin's. It was through Sloper that Jane

Jane Stirling; a portrait by Achille Devéria (c. 1842).[31]

31. The small girl standing beside Jane Stirling often goes unremarked. She is Frances Anne Bruce, the youngest daughter of Lord Thomas Bruce, seventh Earl of Elgin, and therefore Jane's cousin. Lord Bruce had died in Paris, in 1841, and Jane had taken the girl into her temporary protection.

was introduced to Chopin, probably in 1843, and by the following year she had become Chopin's pupil. He thought enough of her playing to remark, "One day you will play very, very well."[32] Katherine sometimes accompanied Jane to the lessons, and it was on one such occasion that they encountered Solange, who left a pen sketch of the two sisters in her memoirs: "During lesson times at the master's house, one would often come across two long persons, of Scottish origin and size, thin, pale, ageless, solemn, dressed in black, never smiling. Under this rather lugubrious surface were concealed two lofty, generous, and devoted hearts. The one who took lessons was called Miss Stirling; the other lady accompanying her was her sister Mrs. Erskine."[33]

Within a few months Chopin had composed and dedicated to Jane the Two Nocturnes, op. 55, an event that may be said to have symbolized the beginning of their friendship. On Jane's side friendship soon developed into a deep and abiding love, a sentiment that Chopin was unable to reciprocate. As far as he was concerned, his connection with Jane was platonic, a position from which he never wavered. At first this caused him no particular worries. He was pleased enough to receive all the attentions his "Scottish ladies" showered on him, and he readily acknowledged their generosity and kindness toward him. Over time, however, he began to feel beleaguered by them, even though their chief concern was to make life softer for him. Finally, after he arrived in Scotland and rumors reached him that he was being romantically linked with Jane and was even considering matrimony, it was the last straw. His attitude to her changed dramatically, and his letters contained critical and even hostile remarks about her and her sister, of which they knew nothing and hardly deserved. As early as June, we catch a glimpse of his true feelings as he unburdened himself to Grzymała: "My good Scottish ladies show me great affection. I am always with them when I am not invited out. But they are used to roaming around and being shaken up in a carriage while rushing all over London to leave their visiting cards. They would like me to visit all their acquaintances although I am more dead than alive."[34]

By mid-July he had almost had enough: "My Scottish ladies are kind . . .

32. GSFC, p. 135.
33. CFCS, p. 238.
34. CFC, vol. 3, p. 348; KFC, vol. 2, p. 248.

Chopin Visits Britain: April–November 1848

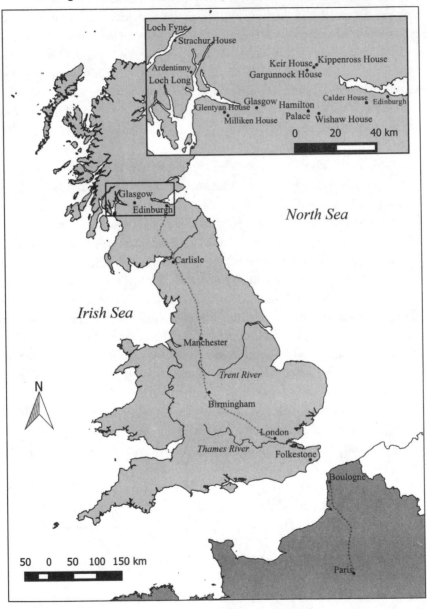

but they bore me so much that I don't know which way to turn."[35] As long as he remained in London, it was possible for him to stay in control of his affairs. But once he had arrived in Scotland he was totally at the mercy of the Stirling sisters, who seemed strangely unaware of the stress they were causing him. To no one did he express his conundrum more exquisitely than to Grzymała: "They will suffocate me out of politeness, and out of politeness I will let them."[36] This was the difficult background against which Chopin's sojourn in Scotland unfolded. But it was on the day before he departed Britain for Paris, on November 21, that he gave vent to his most cruel thoughts against Jane and Katherine: "One more day here and I shall not die but go mad. My Scottish ladies are so tiresome. May God protect them! They have got their grip on me and I can no longer tear myself away from them."[37]

Jane Stirling, especially, would have been devastated to learn of Chopin's true opinion of her; her boundless generosity toward him made her worthy of a warmer response. As our story unfolds, however, and we start to observe the vicissitudes of daily life that Chopin was called upon to endure in a country where he never felt at home and whose language he could not speak, we come to appreciate the dilemma in which he found himself, and which he was utterly incapable of resolving. If only his Scottish ladies had realized that what he most required was a warm room, a piano, plenty of rest, and little else, his stay in Scotland might have turned out better. But once he had crossed the northern border, Jane and Katherine were determined to show off their famous guest to as many people as possible, and by subjecting him to a life of unremitting activity may have shortened it.

VII

At 9:00 a.m. on Saturday, August 5, Chopin was seen off at Euston station by a representative of Henry Broadwood, who generously paid for three first-class seats—one for Chopin, another to enable him to put up his feet

---

35. CFC, vol. 3, p. 354; KFC, vol. 2, p. 255.
36. CFC, vol. 3, p. 390; KFC, vol. 2, p. 278.
37. CFC, vol. 3, p. 403; KFC, vol. 3, p. 289.

on the seat opposite, and a third for his new manservant, Daniel. Broadwood had asked Muir Wood, the concert promoter and owner of music shops in Glasgow and Edinburgh, to be Chopin's traveling companion and interpreter. The rail journey to Edinburgh, which covered a distance of 650 kilometers along the newly opened western route via Birmingham and Carlisle, took twelve hours. Broadwood had reserved rooms at the Douglas Hotel in St. Andrew's Square, then the best in Edinburgh, where Chopin was able to recover from his long journey. The following day, Sunday, he made a leisurely exploration of the city in a carriage provided by friends of the Stirlings, and was impressed by the views of the historic castle and the open vistas to the sea. He later sent pictures of the area to his family on printed notepaper. He also went to Muir Wood's music shop at 12 Waterloo Place, in order to make sure that the Broadwood grand piano shipped from London by steamer was safely unpacked.[38] At this time, too, there would have been a discussion about the two major concerts that Chopin was scheduled to give in Glasgow and Edinburgh under Muir Wood's management. While they were talking, Chopin overheard one of his mazurkas being played by a blind pianist who obviously knew the piece very well. He had hardly been on Scottish soil for twenty-four hours, and the first music he heard was his.

From Edinburgh he traveled to Calder House, which lay twenty kilometers outside the city, in a carriage provided by his host, Lord James Torphichen, the seventy-eight-year-old widowed brother-in-law of Jane Stirling. There he found not only a Broadwood grand waiting for him, but also Jane Stirling's Pleyel, which she had shipped from London especially for his use. Chopin was allotted his own room with a splendid view of the park, studded with trees and rolling hills in the background. The ancient dwelling was rich in history. Three hundred years earlier the room above Chopin's had been occupied by John Knox, the Scottish religious reformer, who had celebrated communion there in defiance of Rome and at risk to his life. The house was even reputed to have its own ghost, wearing a red hood, but this elusive spirit failed to put in an appearance during Chopin's stay there, somewhat to his disappointment. The walls of the

---

38. This was Broadwood Patent Repetition Grand no. 17001. It had been shipped from London's Leith and Glasgow Wharf on the steamer *Royal William* on Saturday morning, August 5, to be used for Chopin's concerts in Glasgow and Edinburgh. CCS, p. 25.

manor were eight feet thick in places, a fact that impressed Chopin as he wandered around the endless corridors "full of ancestral portraits, each one blacker and more Scottish-looking than the next."[39] He very much enjoyed the company of Lord Torphichen, a former sea captain with the East India Company, who somehow managed to carry on a conversation with his distinguished guest in broken French. Chopin's room was well away from the others, and he was able to play the piano undisturbed. He rarely showed himself before lunch, when he would join everyone at the dining table. In the afternoons he might go for a drive with the Stirling sisters, or if the weather was inclement stay indoors and write letters.

Dinner was served at seven o'clock, and it was not unusual for twenty or more guests to sit at the long table, enjoy Lord Torphichen's hospitality, and linger for as long or as little as they chose. Chopin could even be prevailed upon to play Scottish melodies for his host, who would hum along with him. He remained at Calder House for most of the rest of August. Despite the constant attentions heaped on him by Jane Stirling and her sister ("I am unable to think of anything that isn't realized immediately"), he complained to Franchomme that he felt out of place, unable to compose for lack of a single decent idea, and his nerves were frayed. "I am out of my rut—I am like a donkey at a fancy-dress ball—a violin E-string on a double-bass,"[40] he wrote. This bizarre imagery, a world in which nothing seemed to fit, symbolized his sense of disconnectedness and added to the shroud of gloom that often enveloped him. A letter from Julian Fontana, who was passing through London on his way back to America, only added to his feelings of emptiness. "If I were not so ill," he wrote despairingly, "I would travel to London tomorrow and embrace you. Without doubt we shall not meet again soon. We are a couple of old *cembalos*[41] on which time and circumstance have played out their miserable little trills." Fontana's letter reminded him that many of their compatriots were now dead, and he listed them: Jan Matuszyński, Antoni Wodziński, Stefan Witwicki, and Izydor Sobański. "Our soundboards are perfect," he wrote, continuing his earlier metaphor, "but the strings have snapped and a few pegs have jumped out. The real trouble is that we are the creation of some

39. CFC, vol. 3, p. 362; KFC, vol. 2, pp. 258–59.
40. CFC, vol. 3, p. 361; KFC, vol. 2, p. 257.
41. This is a pun on the Polish word *cymbały*, which can also mean "simpletons" or "numb-skulls."

Calder House near Edinburgh, the home of Jane Stirling's brother-in-law Lord Torphichen; a photograph (c. 1930).

famous maker, a kind of unique Stradivarius, who is no longer there to mend us."[42]

During his three-week stay at Calder House, Chopin gathered strength to prepare for what was to be a major highlight of his British tour: his concert in Manchester on August 28. Whatever reluctance he may have felt about accepting this engagement was overcome by the generous fee of 60 pounds attached to it. While the guiding hand of Henry Broadwood lay behind this invitation, the actual sponsor was the wealthy industrialist Salis Schwabe, and it was in the Schwabe family's luxurious home, Crumpsall House in the Manchester suburb of Middleton, that Chopin was received as a guest for the duration of his stay. Early on the morning of Friday, August 25, Chopin and Daniel set out by diligence from Calder House and caught the 10:30 train from Edinburgh. They arrived at Salford station in New Bailey Street after a journey of eight hours. It was early evening by the time they got to Crumpsall House and Chopin, com-

---

42. CFC, vol. 3, pp. 363–64; KFC, vol. 2, pp. 259–60.

pletely exhausted, was carried upstairs by Daniel, where he took to his bed and rested for the next twenty-four hours.

VIII

Salis Schwabe was a leading philanthropist and the money raised from Chopin's concert was destined to support the Manchester Royal Infirmary, of which Schwabe was a director.[43] The Gentlemen's Concert Hall was filled to overflowing for the event, in part because three well-known Italian singers also shared the platform with Chopin—Marietta Alboni, Amalia Corbari, and Lorenzo Salvi—performing popular operatic arias by Rossini, Verdi, and Bellini. More than twelve hundred people were in attendance, the largest audience before which Chopin ever appeared. The concert was one of the leading social events of the season, a point made clear by the injunction carried on the handbill: "No Gentleman will be admitted except in Evening Dress, with either White or Black Cravat." As the coachmen milled around the building to deposit the wealthy concertgoers at

---

43. Born in Oldenburg, Westphalia, Salis Schwabe (1800–1853) had formed his unusual first name by telescoping the two Hebraic ones with which he had been endowed at birth—Salomon ben Elias. When he was only seventeen, he had immigrated to Britain in order to escape the rampant anti-Semitism that prevailed in Germany, and arranged a new life for himself in a country whose freedoms offered him greater opportunity. His arrival in Britain coincided with the beginnings of the Industrial Revolution, and he saw an opportunity in northern England to open a business in the calico industry. He moved to Manchester in 1832, leased and renovated the derelict Daniel Burton Mill, which had been torched in the Luddite riots a few years earlier, and opened the Schwabe Calico Printing Works at Rhodes in the suburb of Middleton, which eventually covered more than eight acres and employed about 750 workers. In 1846, Schwabe added a crowning glory to his factory in the form of a chimney that rose to a height of 358 feet, was constructed from one and a half million bricks, and boasted a diameter of 22 feet at its base and 9 feet at its tip. This chimney (nicknamed "The Colossus of Rhodes" by the locals, because it was visible for many miles beyond Manchester's borders) was the highest in Europe, took eight months to erect, and cost Schwabe 5,000 pounds to build—a fortune in those days. These figures are worth recalling, because when the chimney was finally demolished in the 1980s, it took a team of skilled workers four years to dismantle—brick by painful brick. To attempt to bring down the "Colossus" in one piece was deemed to be too great a hazard to the neighborhood.

Chopin was impressed with this chimney, and wrote about it to Grzymała. "I was staying with my good friend Schwabe," he added. "You may have seen him at Léo's . . . He is a Jew, or rather a Protestant convert like Léo. His wife is particularly kind." (CFC, vol. 3, pp. 382–83; KFC, vol. 2, p. 273.) From this casual observation it is clear that Chopin was already acquainted with the Schwabe family in Paris, where they had a second home on the Champs-Élysées.

CONCERT HALL, MANCHESTER.

MONDAY EVENING, AUGUST TWENTY-EIGHTH, 1848.

DRESS CONCERT.
MISCELLANEOUS.

Part First.

OVERTURE............................" Ruler of Spirits"..............................*Weber.*
TERZETTINO......Signora ALBONI, Signora CORBARI, and Signor SALVI......" Io t'amava"......(Nabuco)......*Verdi*
RECIT. è CAVATINA......Signora CORBARI......" Come provar"......(La Cantatrice Villane)......*Pacini.*
ROMANZA.........Signor SALVI........." Ciel pietoso".........(Uberto).........*Verdi.*
NOCTURNE et BERCEUSE—PIANO-FORTE.................Mons. CHOPIN.................*Chopin.*
CAVATINA è FINALE...........Signora ALBONI............" Non più mesta"...........(Cenerentola)...........*Rossini*
DUETTO......Signora CORBARI and Signor SALVI......" Vieni in Roma"......(Norma)......*Bellini.*

An Interval of Twenty Minutes.

It is particularly requested that Parties in promenading round the Hall will keep to the right.

Part Second.

OVERTURE ...." Prometheus"...................................*Beethoven.*
DUETTO...............Signora ALBONI and Signora CORBARI..............." La Regatta Veneziano".............*Rossini.*
ROMANZA..........Signor SALVI........." Una furtiva lagrima".........(L'Elisir d'Amore).........*Donizetti.*
MAZOURKA, BALLADE, et VALSE—PIANO-FORTE.........Mons. CHOPIN.........*Chopin.*
DUETTO..........Signora ALBONI and Signor SALVI........" Un soave non so che ".........(Cenerentola).........*Rossini*
ARIA...........Signora CORBARI..........." Oh, dischiuso ".........(Nino).........*Verdi.*
TYROLIENNE..............Signora ALBONI..............." In questo semplice "................(Betly)............*Donizetti.*
TRIO...Signora ALBONI, Signora CORBARI, and Signor SALVI..." Cruda sorte "...(Ricciardo è Zoraide)...*Rossini.*
OVERTURE................." Il Barbiere di Siviglia".................*Rossini.*

Leader of the Orchestra...Mr. SEYMOUR.

TO COMMENCE AT SEVEN O'CLOCK PRECISELY.

The Committee earnestly request the co-operation of the Subscribers in maintaining silence during the Performances

Subscribers are informed that the 15th Rule will be strictly enforced :—" That no gentleman residing in or within six miles of Manchester is considered as a stranger, or admissible to either Public or Private Concerts without being previously elected a Subscriber ; and the gentlemen who have permanent places of business in Manchester are considered as residents."

No Gentleman will be admitted except in Evening Dress, with either White or Black Cravat.

Carriages, in setting down and taking up Company, are to have their horses' heads towards Oxford-street.

Cave and Sever, Printers, 18, St. Ann's-street, Manchester.

Chopin performs in the Gentlemen's Concert Hall, Manchester, August 28, 1848; a concert bill.

the main entrance, they were enjoined to line up the carriages "to have their horses' heads towards Oxford-street" while the concert was in progress. It was exactly the kind of public appearance that Chopin disliked.

The playbill shows him playing in the first half a Nocturne (unidentified) and the Berceuse, op. 57; and in the second half a Mazurka, a Waltz, and a Ballade (unidentified). He was obliged to make some changes to this program, for reasons we will come to presently.[44]

The Manchester Guardian captured the essence of the evening for its readers.

> Chopin appears to be about thirty years of age [he was, in fact, thirty-eight]. He is very spare in frame, and there is an almost painful air of feebleness in his appearance and gait. This vanishes when he seats himself at the instrument, in which he seems for the time perfectly absorbed. Chopin's music and his style of performance partake of the same leading characteristics—refinement rather than vigour—subtle elaboration rather than simple comprehensiveness in composition—an elegant, rapid touch, rather than a firm, nervous grasp of the instrument.
>
> Both his compositions and his playing appear to be the perfection of chamber music—fit to be associated with the most refined instrumental quartets and quartet-playing—but wanting in breadth and obviousness of design and executive power to be effective in a large concert hall. These are our impressions from hearing Mons. Chopin for the first time on Monday evening. He was warmly applauded by many of the most accomplished amateurs in the town, and he received an encore in his last piece, a compliment thus accorded to each of the four London artists who appeared at this concert.[45]

---

44. What Chopin actually played in the first half was the Andante Spianato and a Scherzo (possibly a modified version of no. 2, in B-flat minor); and in the second half a Nocturne, a group of his Studies (unidentified), and the Berceuse, op. 57. In brief, he dropped the Ballade, the Mazurka, and the Waltz. See BCM, pp. 22 and 25, where the substitute program is printed in full.

45. Issue of August 30, 1848. Chopin played on a Broadwood Repetition Grand (no. 17047), which he had selected from the Broadwood showrooms the previous month and which had

Despite these favorable comments it was obvious to Chopin's friends that he was ill and his playing lacked strength. Charles Hallé later wrote of Chopin's playing that "it was painfully evident that his end was drawing near."[46] An old acquaintance, the Irish pianist George Osborne, unexpectedly turned up in the role of accompanist to the singers. When Chopin learned of this, he begged Osborne to leave the hall while he played. "My playing will be lost in such a large room, and my compositions will be ineffective. Your presence at the concert will be painful both to you and to me." Osborne nonetheless sat in a remote corner at the back of the hall, where Chopin would not see him. "I helped to cheer and applaud him . . . but his playing was too delicate to create enthusiasm, and I felt truly sorry for him."[47]

The Musical World offered a review that echoed some of Osborne's reservations. Its generally negative tone will surprise no one who has followed Chopin's poor connections with that journal. It was not written by Davison, the editor, but was certainly designed to please him. The high priest of the Mendelssohn cult in Britain would not have been disappointed to see Chopin reduced in stature. After patronizing Chopin as "the French-celebrated pianist and composer, who is a novelty in these parts," the article ignored him until the very end, and then damned him with faint praise.

> You must pardon me if I venture to say very little of Mons. Chopin's pianoforte playing. He neither surprised me, nor pleased me entirely. He certainly played with great finish—too much so, perhaps, and might have deserved the name of *finesse* rather—and his delicacy and expression are unmistakable; but I missed the astonishing power of Leopold de Meyer, the vigour of Thalberg, the dash of Herz, or the grace of Sterndale Bennett. Notwithstanding,

---

been specially shipped out from London. There are comprehensive accounts of the events surrounding Chopin's appearance in Manchester in BCM and WCMM.

46. HLL, p. 37.

47. ORFC, p. 101. Charles Hallé shared Osborne's disappointment. Doubtless reflecting on the magnificent performances he had heard Chopin give in earlier times, Hallé dispatched the event in a single, cryptic sentence: "During the . . . month of August Chopin came, played, but was little understood." HLL, p. 111.

Mons. Chopin is assuredly a great pianist, and no one can hear him without receiving some amount of delectation.[48]

Of Chopin's compositions the review said not a word. *The Lancashire General Advertiser* was more positive and conceded that his works were "perfectly original." More generous still was *The Manchester Courier*, which told its readers that while Chopin was no Thalberg, he possessed both "chasteness and purity of style," and "for brilliancy of touch and a delicate sensibility of expression" his execution remained unsurpassed. The *Courier* went on to say that his Nocturnes, Etudes, and Berceuse elicited some "rapturous applause" from the audience and an unnamed encore possessed "great beauty."[49]

Few people in that Manchester audience would have known it, but a few days prior to the concert Chopin had been involved in an accident that, in his own words, nearly cost him his life. He had been a passenger in a coupé, drawn by a couple of young English Thoroughbred horses, traveling with Daniel in the vicinity of Calder House. Suddenly one of the horses reared, caught its foot, and bolted, taking the other horse with it. As the animals galloped out of control down the slope, the reins broke and the coachman was thrown to the ground and badly bruised. Daniel managed to leap clear, but Chopin did not have the strength to jump. The driverless coach headed helter-skelter toward a cliff and might have fallen over the edge had it not been flung against a tree. The horses were trapped beneath the wreckage and wounded. "Luckily I was unhurt," wrote Chopin, "apart from having my legs bruised from the jolting I had received." But he added: "The thought of broken legs and hands appalls me. To be a cripple would put the finishing touch to me."[50]

Did Chopin play twice in Manchester? We ask the question because Chopin's biographer Bernard Gavoty came forward in 1974 claiming to

48. Issue of September 9, 1848.
49. Issues of August 30, 1848.
50. CFC, vol. 3, p. 386; KFC, vol. 2, p. 275. *The Manchester Guardian* published an account of this mishap, following its review of the concert. In explaining to its readers why Chopin had departed from the printed program, it described the accident in detail and observed, "Chopin had a wonderful escape from injury except for a few bruises. He was nevertheless too shaken to prepare the new works he had at first intended to play in Manchester (we hear of him being in a 'highly nervous state'). Hence the alteration in 'the scheme.'"

have in his possession a letter that Chopin wrote to Solange in which the composer reported an unusual incident.

> A strange thing happened to me while I was playing my Sonata in B-flat minor for some British friends. I had played the allegro and the scherzo successfully, and I was going to attack the march when, suddenly, I saw the cursed creatures that one lugubrious night appeared to me at the monastery rising from the case of the piano. I had to go out for a moment to collect myself, after which I resumed playing without saying a word to anyone.[51]

The whereabouts of this letter remain unknown. Gavoty tells us that he purchased it in London and it is dated "September 9, 1848," which means that it was written at Johnstone Castle after Chopin had returned to Scotland. We are led to believe that this performance of the "Funeral March" Sonata took place "on August 29 . . . in a salon in Manchester" in the presence of the critic of *The Manchester Guardian*, who "wrote in astonishment at this brief interruption."[52] Several writers have come forward to suggest that the most likely venue would have been Crumpsall House, where Chopin was staying and where Salis Schwabe liked to put on private concerts. Whatever the case, some troubling inconsistencies emerge from this letter. *The Manchester Guardian* makes no mention of the performance, yet this newspaper's critic is supposed to have written about it. Nor do any of the other Manchester-based journals report it. More troubling still is the fact that Chopin was able to summon the strength to play one of his most physically demanding works at a time when he was in such a gravely weakened state that his manservant had to carry him from one part of the house to another. (Some reports state that he had been carried on and off the stage during his appearance in the Gentlemen's Concert Hall the previous day.) Chopin was moreover still badly bruised from the accident he had suffered in Scotland less than two weeks earlier. This had forced him to modify and even abandon other pieces to suit his parlous state of health; but we are asked to accept that he was still able to play this long and taxing sonata in its entirety. Finally, what are we to

---

51. GC, p. 283.
52. Ibid.

make of those "cursed creatures" that had tormented him in Valldemosa ten years earlier and now rose up in Manchester to force him to withdraw from the room and calm himself before playing the Funeral March? It was George Sand, not Chopin, who first introduced these apparitions into the literature when she published her account of the Majorca episode in her *Histoire de ma vie*; but that account did not appear until five years after Chopin's death. Despite these inconsistencies the impression has been allowed to form, and even to coagulate, that Chopin played his B-flat minor Sonata in Manchester. Unless there is more evidence than a missing letter of uncertain provenance, we cannot be sure that such a performance took place.

IX

After resting for a day or two at Crumpsall House, Chopin returned to Edinburgh on September 1. He spent one night there in the home of the Polish-born Dr. Adam Łyszczyński, the Calder House family physician, who treated him with numerous homeopathic remedies and became Chopin's main source of medical advice during the Scottish sojourn. On September 2, Chopin moved on to Glasgow and took up residence at Johnstone Castle, the home of Jane Stirling's widowed sister Mrs. Anne Houston.[53] Jane's family showered him with attention and tried to satisfy his every whim (even importing French newspapers for him every day), but he felt lonely and dejected. And when after the first few days the weather changed from bright sunshine to damp fog, which swirled around the old house, obliterating the fine vistas of the surrounding countryside, he became gloomy. "I am unwell, depressed, and the people weary me with their excessive attentions. I can neither breathe nor work," he told Grzymała. Later in that same letter there was an outbreak of humor that still makes the modern reader smile. After expressing astonishment that a Scottish lady to whom he had spoken claimed to be the thirteenth cousin of Mary Stuart—a connection vouchsafed in all seriousness by her

---

53. By coincidence Johnstone Castle was used to billet Polish soldiers during World War II, expatriates from a more modern Poland whose blood-soaked history was once more repeating itself. The castle was demolished in 1956 to make way for a housing development, and only the main tower remains.

husband, who was standing next to her—he went on, "They all seem to be cousins here, male and female, belonging to great families with great names nobody on the Continent ever heard of. The whole conversation is conducted on genealogical lines, like the Gospels: such a one begat so-and-so, and he begat another, who begat still another, and so on for two full pages up to Jesus Christ."[54]

Jane Stirling had arranged appearances for Chopin in a variety of stately homes with whose families she had connections—Milliken House, Strachur House, Keir House, Wishaw House, Gargunnock House, and Hamilton Palace among them—which meant that he was forever on the move, being "carted" from one location to another, as he put it. There was, in fact, an unusual air of excitement hovering over the social season in Scotland at this time because early in September Queen Victoria and Prince Albert arrived with their three children for a three-week holiday on their newly acquired estate at Balmoral Castle in Perthshire. The presence of the royal family in Scotland had attracted a larger than usual contingent of dukes, lords, and their ladies, who had come up from London in the wake of the royals, and had taken up residence in the various aristocratic homes where Chopin was scheduled to play. Chopin observed that "whenever members of English society are visiting Scotland . . . there are usually about thirty people to lunch." He then went on to provide some commentary about Victoria and Albert themselves.

> Various celebrated beauties are also here just now (Mrs. Norton left a few days ago), and dukes and lords. They were more numerous than usual this year as the Queen was in Scotland and passed this way unexpectedly yesterday by train. She has to be in London by a certain date, but the fog was so bad that she did not sail back, as she had come; and while the sailors and the usual escorts-in-attendance were awaiting her she took the night train at Aberdeen in the most prosaic manner. They say Prince Albert must have been very glad; he is always seasick, whereas the Queen, like a true Ruler of the Sea, is not afraid of it.[55]

---

54. CFC, vol. 3, p. 384; KFC, vol. 2, p. 274.
55. CFC, vol. 3, pp. 388–89; KFC, vol. 2, p. 277.

Johnstone Castle was well situated for the indefatigable Jane Stirling to put Chopin on display at other houses connected to her family, including nearby Milliken House, which was owned by Admiral Napier and his wife, Elizabeth, Jane's sister. There was also an excursion to Glentyan House, owned by Jane's brother Captain James Stirling. Her dearest wish was to exhibit Chopin at her birthplace, Kippenross House near Dunblane, but the composer was spared from embarking on such an excursion. In early September he received an invitation to visit Strachur House in Argyllshire, the residence of Lord John and Lady Mary Murray. Lord Murray was the advocate general of Scotland, whose wife, Mary, had taken lessons from Chopin in London. When Chopin referred to her as "one of my sixty-year-old pupils," he may have marginalized her, but she was clearly devoted to his welfare. A glance at the map (page 574) reveals the difficult journey that Chopin had to undertake in order to reach the remote village of Strachur, which in 1848 boasted fewer than a hundred dwellings and a population of barely five hundred people. The weather was rainy and unsettled and he had to sail across Loch Long via steamer to Ardentinny before disembarking and completing the rest of the journey by horse and carriage along rough, unmarked roads. The route could not be accomplished in less than four hours. Strachur House, which stands on the banks of Loch Fyne and commands wonderful views of the Scottish landscape beyond, was as far north as Chopin ever traveled. He stayed there for one week. Lady Murray, aside from her musical talents, was an excellent Greek and Latin scholar, and something of a specialist in English literature as well. Her French would certainly have been fluent enough to allow her to converse with Chopin and come to his rescue during much of the small talk that passed for dinner conversation at Strachur House.[56]

---

56. Lady Murray imparted some useful information about Chopin's teaching methods to the Polish pianist Cecylia Dzialyńska (1836–99), who had studied with Francis Planté in Paris and traveled to Strachur in 1859 in order to capture some recollections about Chopin from Lady Murray, who was already seventy-one years old. They are among the observations that Dzialyńska published in a booklet in 1882, together with others she gleaned from Marcelina Czartoryska. *The Glasgow Herald* published an informative obituary notice of Lady Murray on October 5, 1861.

X

Looming over everything else was Chopin's forthcoming concert in Merchants' Hall, Glasgow, which had been announced by Muir Wood for September 27. Billed as a "matinée concert," it was poorly attended. *The Glasgow Herald* informed its readers that the audience "while not large was extremely distinguished." Both observations may be explained by the fact that the organizers, the "Ladies of the Nobility and Gentry of the West of Scotland," had possessed the whimsy to charge an exorbitant entrance fee of half a guinea. Money and title often go together like a horse and carriage, but such a pairing often creates empty seats in the concert hall—a lesson that was not lost on Jane Stirling.

Prince Aleksander and Princess Marcelina Czartoryski turned up for the concert with their young son, Marcel. They had unexpectedly arrived in Edinburgh a day or two earlier, and on hearing the news Chopin had rushed by train from Glasgow to greet them. Their presence in Merchants' Hall revived his drooping spirits, although it could equally be said that his playing revived theirs. They had been forced to abandon their residence in Vienna because of the revolutionary upheavals there. Some set-piece military battles were already being fought between the Austrian and Hungarian armies, and Vienna itself was in turmoil, having been taken over by insurgents, albeit temporarily. A street mob had hunted down Count Latour, the minister for war, and hanged him from a lamppost, while Emperor Ferdinand V and his entourage had fled the city, which was in danger of being occupied by General Artúr Görgey and his Hungarian army. Aristocrats of whatever stripe were hardly safe in the Imperial City. To listen to Chopin playing in Glasgow was balm to the Czartoryskis' ears, and they were to repay him tenfold. From this point until the end, Princess Marcelina was a constant, reassuring presence in Chopin's life, and a chief caregiver.

To assist him with his Glasgow concert Chopin brought in a singer, the soprano Giulietta Adelasio de Marguerittes.[57]

---

57. "Giulietta," otherwise known as Julia Granville, was the daughter of an eminent émigré Italian physician based in London (Augustus Bozzi Granville, FRS), and she acquired her stage name through her marriage to Count Adelasio de Marguerittes, who had fled France in the wake of the 1848 revolution and was now almost entirely dependent on his wife for support. After a short stay in England, the impoverished couple settled in America, where once

PROGRAMME

of

M. CHOPIN'S MATINEE MUSICALE

MERCHANTS' HALL

September 27, 1848

CHOPIN	Andante et Impromptu
GUGLIELMI	Romanza: "La Camelia"
	Giulietta Adelasio de Marguerittes (soprano)
CHOPIN	Études
NIEDERMEYER	Mélodie et Romance: "Le Lac," poem by Lamartine
	Mme Adelasio
CHOPIN	Nocturnes et Berceuse
GUGLIELMI	Barcaruola: "La notte è bella"
	Mme Adelasio
CHOPIN	Prélude, Ballade, Mazurkas, Valses

To commence at half past two o'clock

TICKETS: Limited in number. Half-a-guinea each.

Mr. Muir Wood, 42 Buchanan Street

The contents of this program are tantalizingly vague. Muir Wood had spent the past two weeks vainly trying to extract from Chopin the repertoire for his concert, pursuing him across the Scottish countryside in what turned out to be a fruitless mission to pin him down. Chopin simply refused to make up his mind. So Wood had to make do with mere hints, which is basically what the printed program amounts to. From an annotated copy that had belonged to one Mr. D. C. Parker we are able to identify at least some of the pieces that Chopin actually played. They included the Andante Spianato, op. 22, followed by the Impromptu in F-sharp major, op. 36; two Studies from op. 25; the Nocturnes op. 27 and op. 55 (the latter dedicated to Jane Stirling); a group of Mazurkas,

---

more she propped up her husband through his appearances on the stage and her work as a journalist. When the Second Empire was established in 1852 and the count was recalled to France by Napoléon III, he abandoned Julia, who divorced him. Chopin appears to have known the couple in Paris, and it was almost certainly his idea that "Giulietta," one of the legions of refugees wandering around Britain at that time, should share the concert with him.

op. 7; and a group of Waltzes, op. 64. The most demanding piece in the concert was the Ballade in F major, op. 38—although whenever Chopin played this work in later years he tended to omit the tempestuous episodes.

Baffled by the music that he heard that afternoon, the critic of *The Glasgow Herald* was ready to share his bewilderment with his readers. After referring to Chopin as "the great French pianist," a description that must have perplexed the Polish contingent in the audience, the article continued,

> Of M. Chopin's performances, and of the style of his compositions, it is not easy to speak so as to be intelligible to unscientific musicians. His style is unique, and his compositions are very frequently unintelligible from the strange and novel harmonies he introduces. In the pieces he gave us on Wednesday, we were particularly struck with the eccentric and original manner in which he chose to adorn the subject. He frequently took for a theme a few notes which were little else than the common notes of the scale. Those who were present at the entertainment would observe this in the *Nocturnes et Berceuse*. This simple theme ran through the whole piece, and he heaped on it the strangest series of harmonies, discords and modulations that can well be imagined. Again, in another subject, one simple note of the key was heard with its monotonous pulsations moving through just as peculiar a series of musical embellishments. One thing must have been apparent to everyone of the audience, namely, the melancholy and plaintive sentiment which pervaded his music. Indeed, if we would choose to characterize his pieces in three words, we would call them novel, pathetic and difficult to be understood. M. Chopin is evidently a man of weak constitution, and seems to be labouring under physical debility and ill health. Perhaps his constitutional delicacy may account for the fact that his musical compositions have all that melancholy sentiment which we have spoken of. We incline to the belief that this master's compositions will always have a far greater charm when heard *en famille*, than in the concert room; at the same time we know that they possess certain technical peculiarities, which must render them

sealed treasures to by far the greatest number of amateur piano-forte performers.[58]

"Giulietta" was given short shrift, alas. The *Herald* concluded its review by telling its readers that she evinced a certain lack of enthusiasm "with which we were not at all charmed."

A more intimate description of the concert has been left to us by the Scottish diarist and traveler James Hedderwick, who rounds out our picture of Chopin the man. At two o'clock on the afternoon of Chopin's concert, Hedderwick found himself outside the entrance of Merchants' Hall. An elegant-looking carriage-and-four had just pulled up outside the hall in Hutcheson Street. It was such an unusual sight for that time and place that Hedderwick approached the policeman on duty to inquire what was going on. He was told that "a Mr. Chopin is giving a concert." The policeman's pronunciation of the name Chopin was so peculiar to Hedderwick's Scottish ear that he tells us the sound was suggestive of a quart measure.[59] He went in.

> On entering the hall, I found it about one third full. The audience was aristocratic, Prince Czartoryski, a man whose name was patriotically associated with the Polish struggle for independence, was present; so likewise were some representatives of the ducal house of Hamilton; while sitting near were Lord and Lady Blantyre, the latter a perfectly beautiful woman, and worthy of her lineage as one of the daughters of the Queen's favourite Duchess of Sutherland. Others of the neighboring nobility and gentry were observable; and I fancied that many of the ladies might have had finishing lessons in music from the great and fashionable pianist in Paris.
>
> It was obvious indeed that a number of the audience were personal friends of M. Chopin. No portrait of that gentleman had I seen; no description of him had I ever read or heard; but my attention was soon attracted to a little fragile looking man, in pale grey suit, including

---

58. Issue of September 28. Other reviews appeared in *The Glasgow Courier* (September 28) and *The Glasgow Constitutional* (September 28).
59. In Scotland a "chopin" is a liquid measurement of volume, the equivalent of a half pint.

frock-coat of identical tint and texture, moving about the company, and occasionally consulting his watch, which seemed to be

"In shape no bigger than an agate stone,
on the forefinger of an alderman."[60]

In this small grey individual I did not hesitate to recognize the musical genius we had all come to see. Whiskerless, beardless, fair of hair, and pale and thin of face, his appearance was interesting and conspicuous; and when, after a final glance at his miniature horologe, he ascended the platform and placed himself at the instrument of which he was so renowned a master, he at once commanded attention.

After comparing Chopin's nuanced playing with the noisy performances of Thalberg, Döhler, and Liszt ("tearing the wild soul of music from the ecstatic keys"), Hedderwick observed the "consummate sweetness and ease" of his interpretations. Out of "the whirl of liquid notes he wove garlands of pearls."[61]

After the concert (from which Chopin cleared 90 pounds) he was taken back to Johnstone Castle by Jane Stirling and Mrs. Houston, where they were joined for dinner by the Czartoryskis, Lord Torphichen, Lord and Lady Murray, Muir Wood, and Dr. Adam Łyszczyński and his wife. The Murrays had traveled more than 150 kilometers from their place in Strachur to be with Chopin, while the septuagenarian Lord Torphichen had come all the way from Calder House. Perhaps for the first time since arriving in Britain, Chopin felt supported by loyal friends who loved him. The dinner was a glittering affair, and Chopin lingered at the table for a change, conversing in both Polish and French. It was a perfect way to end the day, and he later told Grzymała that the occasion had done him a world of good and had given him new life.

Chopin then moved for a few days to Keir House in Perthshire, the splendid ancestral home of the Stirling family in the vicinity of Bridge of Allan, which was now the principal residence of Jane's cousin the

---

60. Hedderwick is quoting from Shakespeare's *Romeo and Juliet*, Act I, Scene 4. It is Mercutio's description of Queen Mab, the fairies' midwife, who reputedly brings sleep to dreaming humans.
61. HBG, pp. 199–202.

thirty-year-old bachelor William Stirling, who, when he later succeeded to the baronetcy, became Sir William Stirling-Maxwell and the titular head of the family. Chopin spoke warmly of Stirling, an avid art collector who loved to show his guests his priceless collection of Murillos and other Spanish masters.

William Stirling's library was all-encompassing, as befitted a cultured and learned scholar. Just a few months earlier, he had published a book on which his reputation still rests, *Annals of the Artists of Spain,* in three volumes. An amateur pianist, Stirling was drawn to Chopin's music and, according to Jane, worked hard to master the F major Ballade, modeling his performance on that of Chopin. At Keir House we find Chopin's mordant wit breaking out now and again. It was from this isolated location that he delivered himself of his famous observation about the Scottish Sabbath. "Sunday—no post, no trains, no carriages (even to take the air), not a boat, not even a dog to whistle to."[62]

> I am not fit for anything during the whole morning until two o'clock [he told Grzymała], and after that, when I have dressed, everything irritates me and I go on gasping until dinnertime. Dinner over, I have to remain at table with the menfolk, *watching* them talk and *listening* to them drinking. Bored to death (thinking of quite different things from them, in spite of all their politeness and explanatory remarks in French around the table), I must call up all my strength of mind, for they are by that time curious to hear me. Afterwards my good Daniel *carries* me off upstairs to my bedroom (as you know, bedrooms are usually upstairs in English houses), helps me to undress, puts me to bed, leaves a candle, and then I am free to gasp and dream until morning, when it starts all over again . . .[63]

XI

Chopin gave his last public concert in Scotland on October 4, in the Hopetoun Rooms, Queen Street, Edinburgh. Because Jane Stirling feared that

62. CFC, vol. 3, pp. 386–87; KFC, vol. 2, p. 276.
63. CFC, vol. 3, p. 389; KFC, vol. 2, p. 278.

the event might be just as poorly attended as the one in Glasgow the previous week, she is said to have bought one hundred tickets for distribution
among her friends. In consequence the hall was full. The concert coincided
with the annual Caledonian Rout, a social fixture in the Scottish calendar, in which the aristocracy indulged a weeklong passion for race meetings, hunting and shooting during the day, and dinners, hunt balls, and
entertainments in the evening. Jane Stirling's complimentary tickets were
distributed as part of the "entertainments" and were meant to ensure that
the "best people" came to Chopin's concert. Because he had so little energy to prepare a new program, some of the pieces he had recently played
in Glasgow were carried over into the Edinburgh recital.

HOPETOUN ROOMS, QUEEN STREET
M. CHOPIN'S SOIRÉE MUSICALE
October 4, 1848

1. Andante and Impromptu
2. Études
3. Nocturne and Berceuse, op. 57
4. Grande Valse Brillante
5. Andante, preceded by a Largo
6. Préludes, Ballade, Mazurkas, and Valses

To commence at half-past eight o'clock.
TICKETS: Limited in number. Half-a-guinea each.
Mr. Muir Wood, 12 Waterloo Place

A special distinction is attached to this concert. It was the only one in Chopin's entire career in which there were no supporting artists. The event
lasted for two hours and he performed at least fifteen pieces, as well as
encores. It would have been a notable achievement for a pianist in the
prime of health. But for Chopin, in his gravely weakened condition, it may
be described as heroic. Earlier that day he had written in his diary the
words "*au diable,*" indicative of the anxiety he felt before walking on stage.
    According to the *Edinburgh Advertiser* most of the elite of Edinburgh
society was present, "as well as a considerable sprinkling of strangers." The
newspaper commented on the refinement of Chopin's playing, "which fell
most deliciously on the ear accustomed to the 'hammer and tongs' work of
the modern school." And it selected for special praise Chopin's performance

of the Berceuse. The *Edinburgh Courant* went further, and after praising Chopin's compositions as "among the best specimens of classical excellence in Pianoforte music," it told its readers that Chopin's playing "is the most finished we have ever heard." While Chopin obviously lacked the power of Mendelssohn, Thalberg, and Liszt, it continued, "as a chamber pianist he stands unrivalled."[64]

It was left to *The Scotsman* to crown these reviews with a eulogy that was not surpassed throughout Chopin's entire tour of Britain.

On Wednesday evening the Hopetoun Rooms were filled with company to hear this celebrated performer. Any pianist who undertakes to play alone to an audience for two hours, must nowadays be a very remarkable one to succeed in sustaining attention and satisfying expectation. M. Chopin succeeded perfectly in both. He played his own music which is that of a genius. His manner of playing it was quite masterly in every respect . . . The Donner und Blitzen school of pianists—originating, we believe, in France—has thrown most European young ladies into fits of ecstatic admiration, and into a career of insanely ambitious imitation. The result of such amateur attempts to play this music has been a lamentable failure, and the almost total destruction of good rational pianoforte playing among the rising generation . . . M. Chopin's compositions have a peculiar charm, which, however, is only brought out by his own exquisite manner of playing them. We suspect that many of the salient points of melody in his compositions are reminiscences of the popular airs of Poland—of his own ill-fated land, and that the touching expression he gives to these arises from "feelings too deep for tears." The infinite delicacy and finish of his playing, combined with great occasional energy never overdone, is very striking when we contemplate the man—a slender and delicate-looking person, with a marked profile, indicating much intellectual energy.[65]

---

64. Issue of October 7, 1848. For both this concert and the earlier one in Glasgow, Chopin played on Broadwood Patent Repetition Grand no. 17001, which we recall had been sent from London in the care of Muir Wood's company in Edinburgh as early as August 5. The instrument was retained by Muir Wood until March 1849, when it was sold to a Scottish client for 30 pounds above its normal price. CCS, p. 34.
65. Issue of October 7, 1848.

XII

Chopin had now been in Scotland for eleven weeks, had given three public concerts during this period (if we include Manchester), and had played
in at least ten country houses—some of them several times. He was exhausted, and as the cold autumn weather advanced across the Scottish
landscape his symptoms grew worse—coughing, blood-flecked sputum,
and unremitting tiredness. The day after his concert in Edinburgh he was
taken back to Calder House, where he resumed the dull routine of his
earlier stay. He told Adolf Gutmann,

> I drag myself from one lord to another, from one duke to another. I
> find everywhere, besides extreme kindness and hospitality without
> limit, excellent pianos, beautiful pictures, choice libraries; there are
> also hunts, horses, dogs, interminable dinners, and cellars of which
> I avail myself less. It is impossible to form an idea of the refined
> luxury and comfort that one finds in English mansions.[66]

His recent concert he described with mock solemnity: "I played in Edinburgh. All the local aristocracy gathered to hear me. They say it went
well—a little success and a little money." He was, in fact, at his wits' end.
His "Scottish ladies" had once more taken over his life and insisted that
he accompany them first to visit the Duchess of Argyll at Inverary, then to
Lady Belhaven at Wishaw, and finally to the Duke of Hamilton, whose
magnificent home at Hamilton Palace in Lanarkshire was probably the
most luxurious abode he had yet seen in Scotland. Hamilton Palace not
only was the grandest stately house in Scotland by far, but was said to have
been the fifth-largest nonroyal residence in the Western world.[67] There
was even talk of Chopin making the journey to the Duke of Hamilton's
residence on the Isle of Arran (the family owned the island) but nothing
came of this plan.

While he was a guest at Hamilton Palace, Chopin put pen to paper
and relieved himself of a further volley of satirical comments about the

---

66. CFC, vol. 3, p. 393; KFC, vol. 2, p. 281.
67. The palace was demolished in the early part of the twentieth century because it was feared
that the underground tunnels from nearby coal mines had rendered the foundations unsafe.

dukes and duchesses whose presence he was obliged to endure, the mind-less dinner conversations that he vainly attempted to follow, and the low regard in which music itself seemed to be held by the moneyed classes with whom he was rubbing shoulders. He could not get over the fact that in Britain music was not regarded as an art form at all, but simply as a profession—that is, as a job of work not unlike carpentry or bricklaying, rather than a vocation. He was astounded when, after he had played some of his pieces to the other guests, an "important lady," a *grande dame*, pro-duced a concertina and with the utmost gravity began to play on it the most dreadful tunes. On another occasion a lady whistled to the accom-paniment of a guitar. "But what can you expect?" he concluded. "It seems to me that every one of these creatures has a screw loose." He cringed when they came forward with a request that he play his "Second Sigh" (the Noc turne in G major, op. 37, no. 2),[68] or observed of his playing, "I love your bells." And every encounter would end with the words "like water." "I have never yet played to an Englishwoman without her saying: '*Leik water!*'" And he added, "They all look at their hands and play wrong notes with feeling—God help them!"[69] To this letter he attached two caricatures, "one of a lord in a collar and gaiters—he stutters—and the other of a duke in red leather boots and spurs, with a dressing gown over the lot."

There were some precious moments when the devout Katherine Er-skine produced her Bible and tried to convert him to Protestantism. The wells of humor ran so deep within her that they were rarely able to find their way to the surface. She marked certain psalms for him to read and spoke to him earnestly about his soul and the afterlife.[70] Chopin, a lapsed

---

68. His English publisher Wessel had given the Two Nocturnes, op. 37, the French subtitle *Les Soupirs*—"The Sighs."

69. CFC, vol. 2, p. 395; KFC, vol. 2, p. 283.

70. Katherine Erskine is often dismissed in the Chopin literature as a quaint Bible-carrying missionary, aiding and abetting her younger sister Jane in her pursuit of Chopin. Our attitude toward her is softened by the knowledge that during her short-lived marriage to James Er-skine, Katherine had borne him four children, each one of whom had died within days of birth. And James himself had died when Katherine was only twenty-five years old, leaving her to endure an unusually long widowhood. Katherine and James are buried in the churchyard at Linlathan, near Dundee, with two of their children, Ann and James. The other two children, Mary and Katherine, are buried in Greyfriars Churchyard, Edinburgh.

It was for Katherine Erskine that Chopin wrote his last waltz, in B major, the manuscript of which bore the inscription "*Valse pour Madame Erskine / F. Chopin*," together with the date "*12 Octobre 1848*." This allows us to surmise that Chopin probably composed the piece in Calder House, a few days after giving his Edinburgh recital, and before moving on to Lady Belhaven's

Catholic, could handle such conversations; but he hardly knew how to deal with what happened next. The constant presence of Jane Stirling by his side (who by now had introduced him to practically every member of her extended family) led to rumors that they were going to be married. That Jane was in love with Chopin can hardly be doubted, but her feelings were not reciprocated. Tales of a possible romance must have crossed the Channel, because when Grzymała made some discreet inquiries of his old friend, Chopin replied bluntly:

> There must be some sort of physical *attraction*; and the unmarried one [Jane] is far too much like me. How can one kiss oneself? . . . Friendship is friendship, I have said so distinctly, but it gives no right to anything else. And even if I fell in love with someone who loved me in return, as I would desire, even then I would not marry, for we should have nothing to eat and nowhere to live. But a rich woman looks for a rich husband—and if she does choose a poor man he must not be infirm, but young and vigorous. One has the right to be poor alone, but when there are two it is the greatest misfortune. I may give up the ghost in a hospital, but I won't leave a wife in misery.[71]

And to make sure that Grzymała grasped the point, Chopin added, "I am nearer to a coffin than a bridal bed." After Chopin's death, Stirling was to devote herself to the cult of his memory almost to the extent of turning him into a religion. Jane Welsh Carlyle once caught sight of her in London, pale and dressed in deepest mourning, and described her as "like Chopin's widow," and for the remaining ten years of her life that was the role she created for herself.

During his stay at Hamilton Palace, Chopin caught a cold and needed medical attention. This led him to spend the last week of his Scottish sojourn in the home of his Polish compatriot Dr. Adam Łyszczyński, who lived at 10 Warriston Crescent, Edinburgh, with his Scottish-born wife, Elizabeth. Łyszczyński, the Calder House family doctor, was able to help Chopin with some homeopathic remedies. The Warsaw Uprising had

---

residence, Wishaw House. The manuscript of this unpublished waltz was discovered by Arthur Hedley in the late 1950s, in a private collection in London, but has meanwhile disappeared. A summary description of the piece may be found in the Kobylańska Catalogue, no. 1245.
71. CFC, vol. 3, p. 397; KFC, vol. 2, p. 284.

driven Łyszczyński from his homeland and he had come to Britain as an émigré, eventually settling in Edinburgh, where he had acquired his medical degree. After opening his practice in Edinburgh, Łyszczyński changed the spelling of his name to the somewhat more manageable "Lischinski," doubtless out of consideration for his Scottish friends, neighbors, and patients. Chopin cherished the Polish atmosphere that prevailed in the Łyszczyński household and enjoyed being able to converse with the doctor in Polish. In order to make Chopin's stay tolerable, the Łyszczyńskis turned the children's nursery into a bedroom for their illustrious guest, while an adjoining bedroom was prepared for Daniel; the children were meanwhile looked after by a friend in the neighborhood. Elizabeth Łyszczyński later recalled, "Chopin rose very late in the day, and in the morning he had soup in his room. His hair was curled daily by the servant, and his shirt, boots, and other things were of the neatest—in fact he was a *petit-maître*, more vain in dress than any woman." In the evenings after dinner he would sit shivering with cold in front of the fire. He would then go over to the piano and "play himself warm."[72] Dr. Łyszczyński's homeopathic treatments seemed to help Chopin, and within a few days he felt strong enough to embark on the long train journey back to London.

XIII

Arrived in the British capital on October 31, Chopin sought refuge in rooms that Major Szulczewski had found for him at 4 St. James's Place. He liked to open the windows in order to breathe more easily, but since that made him cold he would sit close to the fire that Daniel had lit for him, wearing an overcoat. As for going out of doors, that was virtually impossible. He had begun to dread the London fogs, laced as they were with the noxious fumes of thousands of chimneys, which brought on uncontrollable bouts of coughing. Princess Marcelina Czartoryska had taken over his old rooms in nearby Dover Street and assumed the role of caregiver. She brought in a local homeopath, Dr. Henry Malan, who was married to the niece of Lady Gainsborough, and he helped alleviate the worst of Chopin's symptoms. She also arranged for Chopin to be seen by Sir James Clark, the court physician and

---

72. NFC, vol. 2, p. 293.

a leading expert on tuberculosis in Britain.[73] But these worthies were unable to do much more than make the obvious recommendations: to leave the country and seek a warmer climate. This was the grim background against which Chopin accepted an invitation to play at the annual Polish Charity Concert and Fancy Dress Ball at the Guild Hall, on November 16.

The purpose of the event, held under the patronage of Lord Dudley Stuart, was to raise money for Polish exiles. Chopin knew that he must support his compatriots, come what may. Here he was, Poland's most famous musician and one of its most prominent emigrés, presently living in London thanks in part to the benefaction of Polish friends. How could he refuse? One of the chief supporters of the charity ball was Marcelina Czartoryska, whose daily ministrations placed Chopin under a special obligation to her. And so, with the help of Dr. Malan, "who pulled me into shape so that I could play,"[74] he roused himself from his sickbed, was carried to his waiting carriage, and was driven across London to the Guild Hall, there to display what remained of his talents to whoever was interested in listening to him.

It was an unfortunate decision. It seems that many people did not even know that Chopin was there. He played in the Old Council Chamber, with dancing, eating, and drinking going on next door, and crowds of people milling about in fancy dress. Broadwood had provided a grand piano for him,[75] and Chopin did his best, despite his weakened state. After he had finished playing, he did not stay for the ball, but called for his carriage and went home. *The Times* carried a brief notice of the event, but did not mention Chopin. No printed program has survived, but from the scattered references of friends who were present and from one further newspaper

---

73. Sir James Clark had been the personal physician to Queen Victoria since her adolescence. When she ascended the throne in 1837, at the age of eighteen, she had given him the title of baronet. Sir James examined Chopin, probably on November 22, 1848, although no medical records of the consultation have survived. We know, however, that the queen's physician held the quite erroneous view that tuberculosis was not contagious but was "constitutional," a disease passed on from one's forebears and confined to the individual sufferer, harmless to those in contact with him. When in earlier years, during his travels in Italy, Sir James had come across the isolation wards for tuberculosis patients in the hospitals of Rome, he actually condemned the practice. (LHT, p. 27.) According to Chopin, all he got from his consultation with Sir James was a "benediction."

74. CFC, vol. 3, p. 399; KFC, vol. 2, p. 286.

75. This was the same Broadwood Patent Repetition Grand, no. 17047, that Chopin had used for his recitals in London earlier in the year and that had also been shipped to Manchester for him. The instrument is today part of the Cobbe Collection. CCS, pp. 20 and 56.

report, it seems that he played, among other things, a group of Studies. Lindsay Sloper, who conducted a small ensemble of players and singers at this same concert, distinctly recalled that Chopin performed the Studies in A-flat major and F minor, from op. 25. It was *The Sun* that drew attention to the abysmal conditions under which Chopin was expected to play.

> We did not hear the performance under any circumstances of comfort, owing to the pressure that prevailed at the entrances . . . M. Chopin played a series of Etudes upon the pianoforte, with all his graceful skill and exquisite refinement of style. We should, however, have listened to him with more satisfaction in the retirement of the drawing room than amid such a disturbed and unreflecting multitude as this. The qualities which give him his special charm are too delicate and intellectual to challenge the favour of a crowd bent chiefly on physical enjoyment.[76]

Princess Czartoryska glossed over the negative aspects of the concert and reported to her uncle Prince Adam in Paris that Chopin had "played like an angel," but she went on to admonish the revelers by adding that their "artistic education is a little problematic."[77] It was left to Francis Hueffer, the London-based music critic, to provide us with a suitable epitaph. Long after the event, but with the benefit of having interviewed a number of people who were present, he wrote of this sad occasion that "his playing at such a place was a well-intentioned mistake."[78]

XIV

On November 23, Henry Broadwood drove Chopin and Daniel to the railway station to bid the composer farewell. They were joined on the platform by Marcelina Czartoryska, together with her husband, Prince Aleksander,

---

76. Issue of November 17, 1848. The only other newspaper to mention the event was the *Illustrated London News*, which simply said, "M. Chopin, the celebrated *pianiste* [sic], was also present, and performed some of his beautiful compositions with much applause" (November 18).
77. CB. Unpublished letter from Marcelina to Prince Adam Czartoryski dated November 17, 1848.
78. HMS, p. 64.

and their young son, Marcel. Princess Marcelina had brought with her Leonard Niedźwiedzki (another of Adam Czartoryski's agents) as Chopin's traveling companion, who boarded the train and seated himself next to Chopin.[79] Just as the train was pulling away Chopin suffered a seizure, a cramp below the ribs on the right side. Niedźwiedzki looked on with alarm, thinking that Chopin was about to expire in his presence. Chopin unbuttoned his waistcoat and trousers and began to massage himself. Such attacks happened frequently, he explained, and by the time the group arrived at Folkestone he appeared to have recovered. At Folkestone they had lunch, consisting of soup, roast beef, and wine, which was "taken away" during the channel crossing to Boulogne.[80] Following a restless night at Boulogne, Chopin and his two companions caught the train to Paris. From the Gare du Nord they took a cab to the Square d'Orléans, where they were greeted by Grzymała, Franchomme, and Marie de Rozières. Chopin had not seen his apartment for seven months. At his insistence Grzymała had kept a fire burning there night and day for a week, in order to dry out the damp rooms, for Chopin was apprehensive about spending another winter there. Grzymała had also placed a large bouquet of violets in the drawing room so that, in Chopin's words, he might experience a breath of poetry as he passed through the parlor en route to the bedroom, "where I know I am going to lie a long, long time."[81]

---

79. Leonard Niedźwiedzki, formerly an officer in the Polish army, had settled in London as an émigré before moving to Paris. He later became the head librarian at the Polish Library in Paris and left an account of this journey with Chopin in his unpublished diary. Polish Academy of Sciences, Kórnik, call number 2416.

80. The channel crossing from Folkestone to Boulogne took one and three-quarters hours in 1848. Because the railways had reached Boulogne earlier that same year, the entire journey between London and Paris could be accomplished in just over twelve hours, as opposed to the eighteen hours it had taken Chopin on his earlier visit to England. Three paddle steamers plied their cargoes of mail and passengers daily between the French and English ports: they were the *William Wallace* and the *Emerald* from Folkestone, and the 190-ton *City of Boulogne* from Boulogne. (BC-C, p. 110.) Chopin would have had sparse cover during the channel crossing; and the chill month of November, together with the pitching and rolling so typical of the early generation of paddle steamers, would have represented hazards that he was ill-prepared to face.

81. CFC, vol. 3, p. 403; KFC, vol. 3, p. 289.

THE DEATH OF CHOPIN, 1849

His life did not withdraw slowly, it fled from him.
—*Wojciech Grzymała*[1]

I

Chopin had hardly unpacked when news was brought to him of the death of his Paris homeopath Dr. Jean Molin, who had succumbed to the cholera epidemic that had broken out earlier in the year and had driven Chopin himself to Britain. It was an unexpected blow. Molin had been Chopin's doctor since 1843, and he was one of the last people that the composer had seen on the eve of his departure for Britain in April. At that time Molin had given Chopin a thorough medical examination, advising him on how to care for himself with various homeopathic remedies during his forthcoming journey. Chopin trusted Molin and had enjoyed a rare intimacy with him to an extent that few other doctors had been allowed.

During the last few months of his life Chopin was attended by three physicians of national repute. After the death of Molin he turned to one of the leading authorities on tuberculosis. Dr. Pierre Louis was a distinguished medical practitioner in Paris, and his book *Recherches sur la phthisie* remains a foundation work on the disease. The treatment he there

1. CFC, vol. 3, p. 442; KFC, vol. 2, p. 462.

recommends was the one that he now prescribed for Chopin: an infusion of moss (an herbal tea), syrup of gum (to ease chronic coughing), opiates (to dull pain and induce a feeling of well-being), and plenty of rest. Many of Dr. Louis's contemporaries were opposed to such benign treatment. Influenced by Dr. François Broussais and his followers, they recommended a more radical course of therapy, which included bleeding, leeches, blisters, and a rigorous diet almost amounting to starvation. Broussais bled his patients mercilessly. "Gallons of blood were let in Paris hospitals daily."[2]

The second doctor who attended Chopin during these final months was brought in by Dr. Louis as a consultant. Dr. Jean Blache was an attending physician at the Cochin Hospital in Paris, well known for his published articles on tuberculosis. Blache was actually a pediatrician, and when this fact was made known to Chopin it brought out a touch of humor that the gravity of his condition could not suppress, for he saw himself as an ideal patient for Blache. "There is something of the child in me," he observed, tongue in cheek.[3]

Chopin's medical team included a third doctor, the only one present at his death. This was Dr. Jean-Baptiste Cruveilhier, who held the distinguished position of professor of pathology at the University of Paris. He has been described as one of the great pathological anatomists of all time. His patients had included Talleyrand and Chateaubriand, and his atlas of pathology remains one of the outstanding works on the subject.

II

After his return from Britain the state of Chopin's health was so grave that he had to give up teaching entirely. Several pupils who had hoped to re-

---

2. LHT, p. 29. It is worth pointing out that the tubercle bacillus, the source of all this misery, was not discovered until 1882, by Dr. Robert Koch. Even then it took several years for Koch to develop his "tuberculin" vaccine, which was designed to attack the bacillus directly. In Dr. Louis's benign treatment of Chopin's symptoms we recognize the origins of the modern sanatorium movement, founded in Germany during the second half of the century by Dr. Hermann Brehmer and his pupil Peter Dettweiler, which soon spread across Europe and even reached the United States. When Chopin's medical alternatives in 1849 are considered, grim as they were, it must be acknowledged that the treatment he received was the most humane that could be obtained.
3. Ibid., p. 30.

sume their lessons with him were sent to his former student Mme Vera de Kologrivoff (now the wife of the painter Luigi Rubio), an advanced pianist who had studied with him since 1842 and had actively assisted him once before, in 1846. Jane Stirling was among their number, but she continued to see Chopin on a weekly basis. His friends rallied around, however, and regularly called on him at the Square d'Orléans. Grzymała remained a frequent visitor, and so did Franchomme. On March 30, Delacroix turned up in the company of Delfina Potocka and Maria Kalergis, and the trio brought much joy into a world that was slowly closing down for Chopin.

Charles-Valentin Alkan, his neighbor in the Square d'Orléans, also came over to pay his respects. Chopin valued their quiet conversations about music and it may have been on one such occasion that he resolved to bequeath his unfinished Piano Method to his old friend, hoping perhaps that Alkan might be able to make use of it. Chopin would certainly have been brought up to date with the conspiracy that had robbed Alkan of his professorship at the Conservatoire the previous year, together with his storied quarrel over this matter with Daniel Auber, the director, a dispute that had taken such a psychological toll that Alkan was about to raise the drawbridge and enter his legendary forty-year seclusion from the world.[4] Delacroix sometimes joined Chopin for dinner, tête-à-tête, and left several entries in his diary that disclose the desperate state of the composer's health. On April 14, for example, Delacroix wrote, "An evening at Chopin's. I found him on the verge of collapse, he was scarcely breathing."[5] Because Chopin could no longer teach, his main source of income dried up. The money he had earned in Britain was dwindling away, and since he was unable to compose he faced the prospect of a slow descent into poverty, a fate from which his friends were determined to save him, as we shall see. On one or two rare occasions he ventured out of doors to make a few purchases, but he remained in his carriage, wrapped in a warm mantle, making the tradesmen come to him. The slightest exertion caused him breathlessness,

---

4. Delacroix alludes to this quarrel in a journal entry dated April 7, 1848. (DJ, vol. 1, p. 283.) After the death of Pierre Zimmerman, who had headed the piano faculty for more than thirty years, Alkan was dropped from consideration as his replacement in favor of Antoine-François Marmontel, widely considered to be a mediocrity. Alkan described it as "the most incredible, the most shameful nomination" in a letter he wrote to George Sand on August 23, 1848, when he tried to enlist her support and have the nomination overturned. "Come to my aid, Madame . . ." FCA, p. 17.
5. DJ, vol. 1, p. 288.

and his manservant was obliged to carry him whenever he had to contend with a flight of stairs.

In March 1849 cholera again made its annual pilgrimage into Paris and began to reap an unusually grim harvest. The disease announced its arrival with 568 deaths that month. The dark, narrow streets of Paris, unchanged since medieval times, were breeding grounds for disease and pestilence. Excrement from animals and humans formed cesspools when it rained, and the cholera bacillus had no difficulty in finding its way into the drinking water. In April, a further 1,896 people succumbed to the disease. For the month of May that figure rose to 4,488; while in the month of June the roll call of the dead peaked at 9,149.[6] Its most famous victim that month was Kalkbrenner, notwithstanding his flight to the nearby spa of Enghien-les-Bains to avoid such a fate. Two days later the singer Angelica Catalani was swept away by the contagion.[7]

Chopin decided to close down his apartment at the Square d'Orléans and by mid-June had moved for the summer to Chaillot, an outlying suburb of the city overlooking the Seine, where he rented rooms on the second floor of an attractive villa, 74 rue de Chaillot, with magnificent views of the distant city. From his windows he could see Notre Dame, the Invalides, and the Tuileries. The rent was high—400 francs a month—and he was now desperately short of funds. Princess Natalia Obreskoff, who helped to arrange the move, kept the true cost of the rent from him, and paid half of it herself.[8] Chopin could hardly believe his good fortune, living in such an attractive place at a mere 200 francs a month. When his closest friends learned of his plight, they loaned him money. Franchomme sent him 1,000 francs; a similar sum came from the Rothschilds. Princess Marcelina Czartoryska, who had been so helpful to him in London, even found a Polish nurse for him, Katarzyna Matusz-ewska, and paid her salary. News of Chopin's dire situation also reached the ears of the elderly Justyna Chopin in Warsaw, for in June she sent her

---

6. The final body count in Paris between the months of March and October was 19,615. These figures come from *Recherches statistiques sur la ville de Paris et le département de la Seine*, published in Paris, 1860.

7. This was the same Angelica Catalani who had given the boy Chopin a gold watch during her visit to Warsaw in 1819. She had meanwhile married a French diplomat and lived in Paris.

8. Princess Obreskoff was the mother of one of Chopin's pupils, the Princess Catherine de Souzzo, the dedicatee of his Fantaisie in F minor, op. 49.

famous son 1,000 francs with instructions for how to secure further funds from Poland, as and when he needed the money.[9]

But all this benefaction was eclipsed by the extraordinary gift of 25,000 francs sent anonymously by Jane Stirling and her sister Mrs. Erskine. The banknotes had been delivered to Chopin's apartment in Paris the previous March in a sealed package, but had failed to reach him. When Stirling visited Chopin at Chaillot and discovered that he was still impoverished, she was astonished, and began some discreet inquiries as to what had happened to the money.[10] She discovered that the package had been intercepted and then "misplaced" by Chopin's concierge, Mme Étienne. The story of how the package was finally traced is one of the strangest in the Chopin literature. Mme Étienne was first asked to search her memory and come up with an explanation as to why she had not handed the package to Chopin. When she replied that she had no recollection of ever having received it, Jane Stirling consulted the fashionable clairvoyant Alexis, who enjoyed a high reputation among his wealthy Parisian clientele for his psychic powers.[11] Alexis assured Stirling that he would be

---

9. KFC, vol. 2, p. 298.

10. The conversion rate between the English pound and the French franc in 1848 puts this gift into perspective. One pound sterling equaled 25 francs. Therefore the gift of 25,000 francs that Jane made available to Chopin was the equivalent of 1,000 pounds sterling. These figures, provided by the Bank of England, help to rebut some recent claims that Jane Stirling could not possibly have given Chopin the massive financial support that has always been attributed to her because, so the argument runs, she did not have access to such large amounts of money. It is claimed that Jenny Lind was the real source of this benefaction and used Jane Stirling as her "cover," though no good evidence has ever been deduced to support such a claim. (The reader who wishes to pursue this strange business is referred to JCSN, pp. 68–80.) Jane Stirling's last will and testament proves that she was more than capable of mustering the sum in question. Her financial portfolio included shares in the Scottish North Eastern Railway Company, the Great Western Railway Company, the Western Bank of Scotland, and considerable cash reserves. She was also paid interest on substantial amounts of money owed to her by Lord Belhaven and the Earl of Elgin, secured through liens against their properties. Jane's sole executrix was her sister Katherine Erskine, who, after numerous generous bequests made by Jane to her relatives and friends, inherited everything. The will may be consulted in the National Archives of Scotland, under the call number NASC70/4/63, folder 5. As for Katherine Erskine, she was wealthier even than Jane, and her last will and testament is also deposited in the National Archives of Scotland, under the call number NASC70/4/116.

11. Alexis Didier (1826–86) had been a practicing clairvoyant from the age of sixteen. Born into a large but impoverished family of ten children, his extraordinary psychic gifts had manifested themselves early but they leaped into national prominence in 1847, just two years before Jane Stirling consulted him. That was when the Marquis de Mirville had determined to unmask Alexis as a fraudster. What followed created a sensation. De Mirville engaged the

able to reveal the mystery, but he first needed to touch some personal object belonging to Mme Étienne—a piece of clothing, perhaps, or a lock of hair. Through a mild piece of deception, Chopin procured a lock of Mme Étienne's hair, which was then conveyed to Alexis. The clairvoyant more than earned his fee that day. He declared that the sealed envelope containing the money had been hidden behind a wall clock next to Mme Étienne's bed, and was still intact. Mme Étienne, he added, was waiting for some "imminent occurrence" before deciding what to do with the envelope—euphemistic language to describe Chopin's approaching death, after which he would have no need of it. The same messenger who had delivered the package to Mme Étienne a few weeks earlier was now sent back with instructions to confront her, and she was prevailed upon to produce it because he told her exactly where she might find it. The package had remained sealed, the money untouched. These last points were in Mme Étienne's favor, and Chopin appears to have been indignant that she was ever a suspect, refusing to believe that the incident demonstrated anything more than a fragile memory. When Mrs. Erskine rather shamefacedly turned up and confessed her own role in the deception, the composer rounded on her and, in his words, told her a few home truths. "From no one but the Queen of England or Miss Coutts [the banking heiress to millions] would I consent to receive such lavish gifts, etc."[12] He also thought that both Stirling and Erskine had acted foolishly by entrusting such a large sum of money to a messenger they did not know, and who was not even instructed to get a receipt from Mme Étienne. At such stupidity "I let my hands drop in amazement," Chopin remarked. He at first refused to accept such a generous gift but was eventually prevailed upon to keep a part of it.[13] On the day of his confrontation with Mrs. Erskine, July 28, 1849, his

---

services of the celebrated magician Jean Eugène Robert-Houdin ("the father of modern magic"), who set various traps for Alexis, involving complex card games, descriptions of faraway houses he had never seen, and the identification of texts in unknown books while blindfolded. What finally convinced Robert-Houdin was the moment when Alexis correctly foretold what cards the former would deal him before they had even been placed on the table. Contemporary reports inform us that "Robert-Houdin turned pale."

12. CFC, vol. 3, pp. 429–30; KFC, vol. 2, pp. 309–10.
13. Chopin's detailed account of the affair may be found in his letter to Grzymała, dated July 28, 1849. (CFC, vol. 3, pp. 429–32, and KFC, vol. 2, pp. 309–10.) Solange subsequently provided some independent corroboration of the story in her memoir of Chopin. CFCS, pp. 237–38.

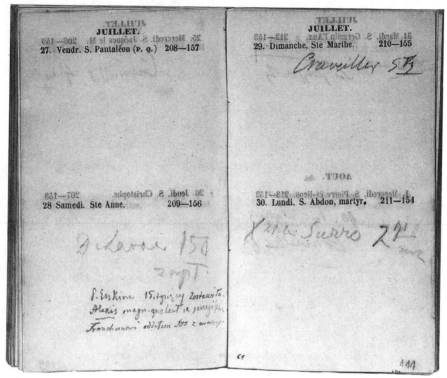

"Mrs. Erskine left 15,000 francs." Chopin's diary entry for July 28, 1849.

laconic diary entry reads, "Mrs. Erskine left 15,000 francs. Alexis the medium found the money in a remarkable manner."[14]

III

On June 21, Chopin had two serious hemorrhages and his legs began to swell with dropsy. Dr. Cruveilhier was summoned to Chaillot and his diagnosis left no doubt that Chopin had entered the final stages of consumption, and the condition was irreversible. From that point until his death less than four months later, Chopin was under Cruveilhier's constant care.

---

14. Chopin's diary for 1848–49 is in the possession of the Fryderyk Chopin Museum, Warsaw, under the call number M/380.

This latest crisis frightened him and in a self-revealing letter he begged his sister Ludwika to come and visit him.

June 25, 1849

My Life,

If you [and Kalasanty] can come, please do so. I am ill and no doctors will do me so much good as you. If you are short of money, borrow some. When I am better I shall easily make enough to pay back whoever will have lent it to you.[15]

Kalasanty's reluctance to make the journey to France created many problems for Ludwika, although she hid them from Chopin. When the Russian visas were finally approved, more than a month later, Kalasanty obliged her to borrow money from Chopin's mother to pay for the journey. We have reserved for a later page the telling of this painful saga, containing as it does some barely believable twists and turns in the Chopin narrative.

On August 9, after a delay of six weeks, Ludwika, Kalasanty, and their fourteen-year-old daughter, Ludka, finally arrived at Chaillot and moved in with Chopin. His joy was boundless, and for the first few days Ludwika hardly left his side, conversing with him in Polish and relaying all the important news from home. Chopin had now started to suffer from insomnia, so Ludwika sat with him through the night. "He liked to talk at night," Ludwika observed, "to tell me his sorrows and to pour into my loving and understanding heart all his most personal thoughts . . . I swallowed my tears so that he should not know his suffering was hurting me, too."[16] Kalasanty for his part soon lost patience with what he saw as the inordinate demands being made on his wife's time, and finding little to occupy him in Chaillot and its environs, he tried to persuade her to return with him to Warsaw. Ludwika made it clear that she wanted to stay with Chopin to the end; so Kalasanty left his wife and daughter at Chaillot and returned to Poland alone.

Chopin received a steady stream of visitors at Chaillot. The twenty-three-year-old diplomat Charles Gavard made the journey from Paris several times, and later recalled spending hours at Chopin's bedside reading

---

15. CFC, vol. 3, p. 417; KFC, vol. 2, p. 301.
16. Kobylańska: *Ruch Muzyczny*, no. 20, Warsaw, 1968.

to him. He was impressed by Chopin's refusal to share any sense of desperation with his friends.

> The invalid avoided everything that could make me sad, and, to shorten the hours which we passed together, generally begged me to take a book from his library and to read to him. For the most part he chose some pages out of Voltaire's *Dictionnaire Philosophique*. He valued very highly the finished form of that clear and concise language, and that so sure judgment on questions of taste. Thus, for instance, I remember that the article on taste was one of the last I read to him.[17]

Gutmann and Franchomme visited Chaillot, too, and their appearance cheered the composer. Another welcome visitor was Jenny Lind, who turned up unexpectedly during a brief trip to Paris and sang for him and an intimate gathering of friends. The loyal Grzymała appeared less frequently than either he or Chopin might have desired because he was at that moment being watched by the police as a result of his political allegiances and had to move about with caution, fearing arrest. The Polish Democratic Society, of which he was a founding member, was under suspicion because it wanted to see the government of the newly installed King Louis-Napoléon overthrown in the forthcoming elections, and he was forced to go underground. To compound his problems, Grzymała had recently lost a fortune on the Bourse (the place where he had first acquired it) and was now living in straitened circumstances. A grand piano had been loaned to Chopin and sent out to Chaillot by Pleyel, and both Gutmann and Franchomme are said to have played for Chopin. He himself was by now so weak that he could barely walk without support. But was he still able to compose? Scholars are divided on when, exactly, Chopin composed his last known work—the Mazurka in G minor, op. posth. 67, no. 2—but

---

17. JJ, vol. I, p. 601. We recall that Voltaire had been one of Mikołaj Chopin's favorite authors, and it is interesting to find his son expressing a similar preference for the writings of the great agnostic. Charles Gavard, incidentally, had become acquainted with Chopin through his sister Élise, Chopin's pupil and the dedicatee of the Berceuse, op. 57. After his appointment as first secretary to the French embassy in London, he jotted down some useful *Souvenirs de Chopin*. He loaned his unpublished manuscript first to Moritz Karasowski, who made generous use of it in Chapter Twelve of his biography of the composer. Later on the document came into the possession of Frederick Niecks, who also quoted extensively from it.

there is general agreement that it was completed at Chaillot no later than the early summer of 1849.

As for the Mazurka in F minor, op. posth. 68, no. 4, which for a long time enjoyed the sentimental distinction of being "Chopin's last mazurka" and indeed his very last composition (a position assigned to it by Fontana), it was actually "reconstructed" by Auguste Franchomme no later than June 1852 from sketches going back to 1846.[18]

IV

By mid-August, the cholera outbreak in Paris had subsided and Chopin moved back to the Square d'Orléans. He was visited by the Polish poet Cyprian Norwid, who recorded some impressions of the dying composer and was later to write a moving obituary of him.

> I found him lying on his bed fully dressed, his swollen legs encased in stockings and pumps. The artist's sister, whose profile was strangely similar to his, was sitting next to him . . . He looked remarkably beautiful, propped up against the cushions in the shadows of the deep curtained bed, wrapped in a shawl. He had, as always, something in even the most commonplace of his movements that was so accomplished, so monumental . . . something the Athenian aristocracy might have made into a cult at the height of the

18. On June 18, 1852, Jane Stirling wrote to Chopin's sister Ludwika, "I am sending you . . . what Franchomme was able to untangle from the last Mazurka written at rue de Chaillot, and which everyone thought to be indecipherable." An inspection of Chopin's abandoned sketch (preserved in the Chopin Museum under the call number M. 236-1958) reveals the difficulties that Franchomme faced in "untangling" Chopin's notation.

Hellenic civilization . . . In a voice interrupted by coughing and choking, he began to berate me for not having called on him recently. Then he teased me in the most childlike way for my mystical tendencies, to which, as it evidently gave him pleasure, I readily lent myself. After that I talked with his sister. There were more fits of coughing. Finally the moment came to leave him in peace, so I started taking my leave. Pressing my hand, he threw the hair back from his forehead and said: "I'm leaving this . . ." and was interrupted by coughing. Hearing this, and feeling that it was good for him to be contradicted, I assumed the usual false tone, and, embracing him, said, as one does to a healthy man: "Every year you say you're leaving this world, and yet, thank God, you're still alive!" But Chopin, finishing the sentence interrupted by his coughing, said: "I'm leaving this apartment and moving to another in the Place Vendôme."[19]

The decision to move Chopin to yet another apartment was not taken lightly. On August 30, 1849 (according to Chopin's diary), Cruveilhier and two of his colleagues assembled in Chopin's rooms at the Square d'Orléans and gave the composer a thorough medical examination. Its purpose was to decide whether his wish to leave Paris in search of a warmer climate was a realistic one. They were unanimous in declaring that it was not. Chopin could hardly move from room to room, and could not sit upright in bed without support. It was recommended instead that he find an apartment with a southern exposure. Several friends took a hand in selecting the new abode, an expensive five-room apartment on the first floor of one of the most fashionable addresses in Paris, 12 Place Vendôme, a building that had earlier housed the Russian embassy. They were helped in their quest by Chopin's friend Thomas Albrecht, a wine merchant who was also the Saxon consul in Paris with an office in the same building. Jane Stirling supervised the transfer of Chopin's belongings from the Square d'Orléans, and she even brought in the mahogany grand piano on loan from Pleyel that had remained behind in Chaillot; there is circumstantial evidence that she may have paid the rent on the new apartment as well. Chopin moved there on September 9, took to his bed, and never left it.

---

19. GNCK, vol. V, pp. 37–39.

V

It is difficult to reconstruct the traumatic events during the days leading up to Chopin's death, not because there are too few witnesses but because there are too many. Ludwika, Grzymała, Solange, Adolf Gutmann, Princess Marcelina Czartoryska, Pauline Viardot, Delfina Potocka, and Jane Stirling are among those whose "eyewitness accounts" of Chopin's final days and the death struggle have burdened posterity with so many contradictions that the biographer proceeds at his peril. Some accounts—particularly those of Ludwika, Grzymała, Solange, and Czartoryska, all of whom we know to have been present at the moment of Chopin's death—have stood the test of time and are trustworthy. The others have to be treated with caution, because while they remain useful they are sometimes based on hearsay. Some things can be said with reasonable certainty, however.

Once Chopin was installed at the Place Vendôme, word spread that the end was near. Pauline Viardot describes some disgraceful scenes as the antechamber leading to Chopin's bedroom was filled to overflowing with hordes of curiosity seekers clamoring for a final glimpse of the composer, wanting to catch his last words and perhaps pick up an occasional souvenir on their way out. "All the great ladies of society felt duty-bound to come and swoon in his bedroom, while his room was crammed with artists making hasty sketches of him," she recalled cynically.[20] Jules Janin was equally critical. "He had in his anteroom I know not how many princesses, countesses, marchionesses, and even a few bourgeoises, who, on their knees, awaited the hour of his last agony."[21] We even hear of a photographer who wanted to push Chopin's bed nearer the window in order to secure better lighting for his daguerreotype. Gutmann finally threw these people out.[22]

Delfina Potocka was in Nice when she heard of Chopin's imminent demise and hurried back to Paris and the Place Vendôme on October 15, two days before Chopin expired. Tradition has it that after a tearful re-

20. CFC, vol. 3, pp. 450–51; KFC, vol. 2, pp. 325–26.
21. JJ, vol. I, p. 476.
22. Grzymała added his own criticisms to those of Viardot and Janin, and wrote caustically of "Chopin worshippers in ermine and rags who during four consecutive days and nights recited prayers on their knees." CFC, vol. 3, p. 443; KFC, vol. 2, p. 462.

union Chopin requested that Delfina sing for him. He had always loved her voice. Confusion surrounds this deathbed scene, which has been much romanticized. Both Liszt and Karasowski (neither of whom was present) say that Delfina sang Stradella's "Hymn"[23] and the Marcello "Psalm." Gutmann recalled that it was the Marcello "Psalm" and an aria by Pergolesi. Franchomme was sure that it was an aria from Bellini's *Beatrice di Tenda*, and nothing else. Grzymała added to the muddle and claimed that Chopin was treated to melodies by Bellini and Rossini. One wonders just how much the dying composer cared, as he lapsed in and out of consciousness, choking for breath.

Among the many visitors to crowd into Chopin's bedroom, the most important from our point of view was the artist Teofil Kwiatkowski, who had already set up his easel several days before Chopin died and had begun to sketch that wonderful series of drawings of the composer's last hours. These remarkable images adorn every iconography of the composer, and they communicate the solemnity of the deathbed drama far more vividly than do the words of others. When Jane Stirling caught sight of them after Chopin's death, she commissioned Kwiatkowski to execute an oil painting depicting some of the people gathered around his bed. It was, of course, painted from the artist's memory of the event, and he exercised some license. Chopin, Ludwika, Marcelina, Grzymała, and even Kwiatkowski himself are all captured on this canvas. We know that Jane Stirling was disappointed not to find herself among their number.[24]

A far less welcome visitor to Chopin's bedside was a Polish friend of his youth, Aleksander Jełowicki, who had meanwhile become a priest. Jełowicki sat for hours next to Chopin, urging him to confess and receive the Last Sacraments, which Chopin declined to do. For many years he had neglected his Catholic faith and thought it hypocritical to return to its final rituals in his hour of desperation. This is not a familiar view of Chopin,

23. Stradella's famous "Hymn to the Virgin" was said to possess miraculous properties, having saved the life of its composer after a failed attempt to assassinate him, in 1677.
24. GSFC, p. 129. She confessed to Ludwika, "I regret not being represented in it." Stirling never wanted this painting exhibited, contrary to the wishes of Kwiatkowski, for she added, "I do not like the crowds to contemplate his last moments." And she went on to say that had the picture still been in her possession, "I would have burnt [it] at my death." Incidentally, Kwiatkowski painted a somewhat earlier version of this picture, which included the figure of Abbé Jełowicki standing behind Ludwika. We surmise that he was brushed out of the scene at Jane Stirling's request. Both pictures are shown in BFC, p. 331.

Chopin's last hours; an oil painting by Teofil Kwiatkowski (October 1849). Next to the bed stands Princess Marcelina, to her right sits Grzymała, and behind him stands Kwiatkowski. Ludwika sits to the far left, next to a table containing religious relics.

but his indifference towards organized religion cannot go unremarked. After his arrival in Paris he never attended mass, never joined a Catholic congregation, never went to confession, never owned a Bible, and is not known to have read one. It is not difficult to assume that he was by now an agnostic. Chopin would not have recognized the term, which was not introduced into the English language until after his death (in 1861 by Thomas Huxley), but he possessed all the requirements of a nonbeliever. Jełowicki persisted, believing it to be his mission to save his illustrious kinsman from eternal damnation. Four days before the end, and weakened by illness, Chopin allowed Jełowicki to administer the last rites and press the relics to his lips. In his self-serving account of the matter, Jełowicki goes on to claim that Chopin was so grateful for these ministrations that he tried to express his gratitude in the form of a large sum of money, which Jełowicki refused to accept. Chopin is then supposed to have replied, "It is not too much, because what I have received is priceless! Without you, my friend, I would have died like a pig."[25] When Pauline Viardot heard what had happened, she waxed indignant and later wrote, "He died a martyr at the hands of priests who forced him to kiss relics for six whole hours until his last breath."[26]

There were infinitely more secular matters than sacred ones pressing on Chopin's mind. He had frequently expressed the wish that all his unpublished manuscripts be burned after his death. A few hours before he expired he charged his compatriot Grzymała with this difficult task, who reported his heavy responsibility to their friend Auguste Léo.

"There will be found many compositions more or less sketched," he told me. "In the name of the friendship you bear me I ask that they should all be burnt, with the exception of the beginning of a [piano] method which I bequeath to Alkan and Reber to see whether any use can be made of it. The rest without exception must be consigned to the flames, for I have always had a great respect for the public and whatever I have published has always been as perfect as I could make it. I do not wish that under the cover of my name works that are unworthy of the public should be spread abroad."[27]

Fortunately, it was not up to Grzymała or to any of Chopin's friends to assume such a responsibility. As his nearest relative, the decision lay with Chopin's sister Ludwika, and she refused to comply. Had she gone along with Chopin's wishes we would have lost among other things the Fantaisie-Impromptu; eight of the Mazurkas; five of the Waltzes; the E minor Nocturne; the Rondo for two pianos; and most of the Seventeen Polish Songs. Chopin was a perfectionist, of course; but it is hard to find imperfections in music such as this. In the end, the manuscripts were entrusted

---

25. At this point Chopin had no money to give. See the exhaustive letter that Jełowicki wrote to Mme Xavier Grocholska of Warsaw, on October 21, 1849, from which the above quotation is taken (CFC, vol. 3, pp. 445–50; KFC, vol. 2, pp. 318–21). The text of this letter provided the basis for Jełowicki's much later article "Chopin's Tod," published in the *Deutschen Hausschatz* in 1877, the year of Jełowicki's own death. Jełowicki's boast that he had obtained an audience with the Pope in Rome, not long after taking holy orders, was later shown to be false, a claim that further undermines his general credibility.
26. CFC, vol. 3, p. 450; KFC, vol. 2, p. 325.
27. CFC, vol. 3, p. 443; KFC, vol. 2, p. 324.

by the Chopin family to the composer's amanuensis Julian Fontana, who brought them out over the next few years in his own edition.

VI

Chopin died on October 17, 1849, at two o'clock in the morning. He was thirty-nine years old. Gathered at his bedside were Ludwika, Solange, Kwiatkowski, Jełowicki, Gutmann,[28] and Dr. Cruveilhier. As the end drew near, Dr. Cruveilhier took a candle and, holding it up to Chopin's face, which had darkened with suffocation, remarked that he had become unresponsive. He gently asked Chopin if he was suffering, to which Chopin whispered, *"Non plus"*—No more. They were the last words he uttered. Solange was looking at him at the moment of his death and later wrote, "He passed away with his gaze fixed on me. He was hideous. I could see the tarnishing eyes in the darkness. Oh, the soul had died too."[29] A partial autopsy was carried out by Dr. Cruveilhier, who, in accordance with Chopin's own wishes, removed the heart, which was placed in a crystal jar, preserved in alcohol, and eventually taken to Warsaw by Ludwika, where it was to find a permanent resting place in the Church of the Holy Cross. It resides there to this day, having survived not only the uprising of 1863 but also the devastation of World War II. Dr. Cruveilhier's autopsy report was placed in the archives of the Hôtel de Ville, but perished with other records during the upheavals of the Paris Commune of 1870–71.

---

28. The much later assertion by Chopin's niece, Ludka Jędrzejewicz, that Gutmann was not present at Chopin's death must be discarded. Solange, who remained with Chopin until the end and witnessed his passing, contradicts her. Ludka was only fourteen at the time and would hardly have been allowed to stand vigil all night in the death chamber and watch her uncle's unpleasant death. Her reminiscence was published in the *Warsaw Courier* on August 9, 1882, thirty-three years after the event it purports to describe, and the loss of memory had taken its toll. One wonders how she could have forgotten that Gutmann was one of the pallbearers at her uncle's funeral. Gutmann himself passed away just two months after the article was published and was unable to rebut it. For some years he had lived in Florence, had abandoned the piano, and had taken up painting as his chief vocation.

29. "Sur la mort de Chopin." An autograph text dated 1852, preserved in the Bibliothèque Nationale under the call number Res.Vmc. ms. 23. (See also George Sand, *Visages du romantisme*, no. 349, p. 83.) Years later Solange elaborated on her recollections of Chopin's final moments. She not only repeated the phrase about Chopin's "tarnishing eyes" as he left this world, but confirmed that the composer died in Gutmann's arms. (CFCS, p. 231.) Hanna Wróblewska-Straus adds some useful commentary on this document in *Chopin Studies* 6, p. 72.

The sequence of events during the hours immediately following Chopin's death has been chronicled many times by his biographers. Even so, they generally neglect to ask the question: Where did Cruveilhier carry out the autopsy? We know with certainty that Chopin's body was removed from his bedroom by noon on the day of his death. At that time two officials from the Department of Justice in City Hall (Judge Eugène Lauveau and his secretary Charles-Antoine Barries) arrived and took an inventory of Chopin's possessions before placing seals on the doors in accordance with French law. The process took them more than seven hours. When they entered Chopin's bedroom, they were able to make a careful list of the contents, which included a description of the furniture, the curtains, the linen, and the deathbed itself, a task that would have been difficult in the presence of a corpse.[30] It used to be thought that Cruveilhier had already moved the body to his own institute in the Académie Nationale de Médecine, where the autopsy was carried out on October 18, the heart removed, and the remains embalmed, there to await transfer to the Madeleine Church.[31] A more persuasive argument has recently been advanced that the autopsy and embalming by Cruveilhier took place in Chopin's own apartment, on the early morning of his death, before Judge Lauveau arrived and started taking the inventory. Cruveilhier was a skilled pathologist who had carried out many autopsies in the past, and the removal of a heart was a relatively minor procedure. His institute was in the sixth arrondissement, more than two miles from Chopin's apartment, and the logistics involved in transporting Chopin's body there for the autopsy and back again to the Place Vendôme for viewing would have represented an unnecessary burden. Cruveilhier would moreover have wanted to begin the embalming process without delay to avoid the inevitable coagulation of the blood. This simple procedure involved injecting embalming fluid into an artery while draining blood from a nearby vein, a routine operation that Cruveilhier would most likely have delegated to an assistant. We know that by the third day (October 19) Chopin's body was already "embalmed and fully dressed, was laid out, covered in flowers, and friends and casual visitors were free to take a last look at the Great Master."[32] These words

---

30. MDD, Part I, p. 5.
31. SHC, pp. 147–48.
32. CFC, vol. 3, p. 444.

come to us from Grzymała, who was present at the Place Vendôme, and was responding to Auguste Léo's request for information about Chopin's last days.

Before this grim ritual had even begun, Clésinger gained access to the death chamber and, working by candlelight, had taken casts of the face and hands. Ludwika was horrified by the contorted features of the first impression and she insisted the sculptor try again. A further layer of wet plaster was applied to Chopin's face, from which Clésinger managed to smooth away signs of the death struggle. This beautified "death mask," which has been reproduced many times in the Chopin iconographies, had little to do with reality.[33] Meanwhile, the floral tributes began to arrive. Chopin's fondness for flowers was well known, and they were delivered in such quantities that, in Liszt's poetic reconstruction of the scene, "the bed on which he lay and the very room itself vanished beneath their different colours. He seemed to rest in a garden."[34]

Chopin had requested that Mozart's *Requiem* be performed at his funeral service. This led to a delay of almost two weeks because permission had to be obtained from the archbishop of Paris, Abbé Gaspard Deguerry, to allow the participation of female singers. It was not until October 30 that the funeral service was held. Chopin's body had meanwhile lain in the crypt below the church. It was the first time that Mozart's *Requiem* had been heard in Paris since Napoléon's remains had been returned from Saint Helena in 1840, and this fact helped to attract the crowds. It was a warm, almost cloudless Tuesday morning, and by eleven o'clock there were throngs of sightseers milling around the church. Almost three thousand people gathered inside to pay homage to Chopin's life and work, and much of the artistic life of Paris was represented. Admission was by printed invitation only, a carefully monitored process supervised by Ludwika herself.

At noon the great doors of the Madeleine Church swung open, and Chopin's coffin was borne along the nave toward the altar, with the pallbearers Prince Aleksander Czartoryski, Auguste Franchomme, Adolf Gutmann, and Eugène Delacroix[35] each holding a *cordon* of the pall. Walk-

---

33. A photograph of the first death mask, rejected by Ludwika, will be found in ECF, p. 199.
34. LC, p. 180.
35. Delacroix was in Rouen when Chopin died, and he did not hear of the composer's death until three days later. In his *Journal* for Saturday, October 20, he wrote, "After lunch I learned

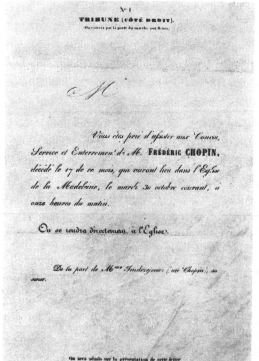

An invitation to Chopin's funeral service.

ing directly behind the coffin were Prince Adam Czartoryski and Giacomo Meyerbeer, followed by the chief family mourners, Ludwika and her daughter, Ludka; close friends of the composer's brought up the rear of the cortège. The coffin was placed on an elevated, specially built catafalque from which hung black shrouds, and occupied the semicircular area between the nave and the altar. All this took place to the accompaniment of the Funeral March from the B-flat minor Sonata, in an orchestral arrangement by Henri Reber. Later in the ceremony the resident organist Lefébure-Wély played the E minor and B minor Preludes on the organ. Meanwhile, the large chorus and orchestra that had been assembled to perform the Mozart *Requiem* wrestled with a peculiar problem. They had been placed at the far end of the church and hidden from view behind

of the death of poor Chopin. Strangely enough, I had a presentiment of it before I got up this morning. This is one of several such premonitions I have had. What a loss! What miserable rogues fill the place, while that beautiful soul is extinguished!" DJ, vol. 1, p. 325.

dark curtains. At the commencement of the *Requiem*, the drapes were partially withdrawn, exposing the male singers to view but concealing the female ones, whose presence in the vast church was considered to be so "uncanonical" that they were allowed only to be heard, not seen, a strange compromise with which only the archbishop could have been happy. The four distinguished soloists were Jeanne Castellan (soprano), Pauline Viardot (contralto), Alexis Dupont (tenor), and Luigi Lablache (bass), the last of whom had the distinction of being one of the soloists in the same work at Beethoven's funeral in Vienna, twenty-two years earlier. The orchestra and chorus, provided by the Conservatoire, were conducted by Narcisse Girard, and they did not come cheap; they arrived with a bill attached to their services for 2,000 francs. The total cost of the funeral came to more than double that, and was paid for by Jane Stirling and Mrs. Erskine.

As he gazed around the vast interior, the poet Théophile Gautier was struck by the haunting beauty of the scene. Outside the church, he remarked, the whole of nature was basking in some unexpectedly fine autumn weather. Suddenly, through the wide-open doors of the Madeleine "a golden shaft of light swept joyfully through the nave, blissfully unaware that it had gone astray in the middle of a funeral service."[36] The catafalque was temporarily illuminated, as if by a glow of elation.

J. W. Davison, the London music critic and Chopin's old nemesis, was there, representing the *The Musical World*, and adds detail to the scene.

> On our entry we found the vast area of the modern Parthenon entirely crowded. The nave and aisles, the choir, the galleries above the magnificent porticos that adorn the walls, the interstices behind and between the columns of the porticos, the organ gallery, and the gallery that runs round the choir, immediately under the windows, were alive with human beings, who had come to see the last of Frédéric Chopin . . . There could not have been less than 4,000 persons present. In the space that separates the nave from the choir, a lofty mausoleum had been erected, hung with black and silver drapery, with the initials "F.C." emblazoned on the pall.[37]

36. *La Presse*, November 5, 1849.
37. *The Musical World*, November 10, 1849, pp. 705–706.

At the conclusion of the service, the congregation emerged into brilliant sunshine, and the cortège began its long, five-kilometer journey from the Madeleine to the cemetery of Père Lachaise, where Chopin's body was to be laid to rest. Prince Adam Czartoryski and Meyerbeer walked behind the hearse; the pallbearers once again were Prince Aleksander Czartoryski, Delacroix, Franchomme, and Gutmann, joined now by Camille Pleyel. Some of the aristocrats had sent their carriages ahead, and they and their wives walked in solemn procession along with everybody else, as a mark of the universal respect in which Chopin was held. At Chopin's request no ceremony took place at the graveside, no music was played, and no speeches were delivered. And it is not true that as the coffin was lowered into the ground an urn of Polish soil brought to France by Chopin in 1831 was sprinkled over his grave.[38] This fictional scene was retrospectively derived from the factual one that was to take place the following year.

Shortly after the funeral a committee was formed to raise money for a monument to Chopin's memory. Headed by Pleyel, Grzymała, and Delacroix, its work suffered from internal dissent and the unfettered expression of conflicting ideas as to what Chopin himself might have desired. Clésinger had begun work on the design even before the money had been raised and before he had been formally commissioned, raising serious questions about his motives.[39] The final cost estimate came to 4,500 francs, a very

---

38. Why would Chopin take an urn of Polish soil with him at the moment of his departure from Warsaw in November 1830? He had every intention of returning home, and he is not known to have taken samples of Polish earth with him on his earlier forays abroad. It was only after the Warsaw Uprising broke out, in November 1830, that Chopin unexpectedly found himself an exile. That appears to have been sufficient reason for some of his early biographers to send him on his way with a sample of Polish earth, and enough foresight to keep it in his possession for nineteen years, with frequent moves from one part of Paris to another, until the purpose for which it had been retained was fulfilled.

39. Clésinger had arrived in Paris in the summer of 1849 in the middle of the cholera epidemic, together with Solange and their second child. This willful behavior, which exposed the family to high risk, had provoked Chopin. But the impoverished Clésinger had come to Paris with one purpose in mind, and that was to earn money. The prospect of making Chopin's death mask, as well as models of the hands that already enjoyed a European reputation, was too tempting to forgo. Alone among the many writers who have dealt with Chopin's last days, only the distinguished Polish poet and essayist Jarosław Iwaszkiewicz had the courage to state quite openly what others preferred to keep to themselves: namely, that "Clésinger was looking forward to the death of Chopin." So impatient was Clésinger for the arrival of the final moment that even while Chopin was still alive he had sculpted the model of his tombstone. He then exhibited this mediocre creation to Delacroix, who, while highly critical of its design,

The Madeleine Church, where Chopin's funeral took place on October 30, 1849.

large sum that might have doomed the project. Jane Stirling once more came to the rescue and provided the money. The funeral monument, a surprisingly modest structure, was finally unveiled at Père Lachaise Cemetery on October 17, 1850, the first anniversary of Chopin's death. During the ceremony a handful of Polish earth was sprinkled over the grave, sent by his family to mark the occasion. Ludwika was not there. She had returned to Warsaw in January 1850, worn out after a stay of five difficult months in Paris.

---

allowed himself to be persuaded by Solange that it would, indeed, result in a monument worthy of the composer's memory. Clésinger saw his business through to the end, remarks Iwaszkiewicz, shrewdly adding the Polish proverb "He baked his pie with the deathbed candles!" (IC, p. 344.) After having paid Clésinger 4,500 francs on completion of the monument, and then bought the death mask from him as well, Jane Stirling allowed herself the luxury of observing that far from being motivated by the highest ideals, Clésinger hated Chopin. This was not an idle sentiment on Stirling's part. During the months following Chopin's death, she had visited Clésinger's studio regularly in order to see for herself how work on the monument was progressing, and she had ample time to assess Clésinger's character and form some personal impressions. As for Chopin, he would surely have abhorred the thought that Clésinger, whom he had come to detest, was reaping such a handsome profit from his demise.

VII

The question has often been asked: How was it possible that Chopin's valuable possessions were dispersed so soon after his death? At first sight it is a complete mystery. When George Sand died at Nohant, for example, every chair, rug, curtain, saucer, bucket, and picture was preserved as she left them, and these mundane objects became part of an instant shrine to her memory. The situation was the same with Balzac, who died less than one year after Chopin. His apartment in Paris was transformed overnight into a museum, and it has remained like that ever since. But that was not the case with Chopin, who at the time of his death was already more famous than either of these artists. Our search for answers reveals an unexpected and highly unpleasant family drama that had for weeks been simmering in the background and now came boiling to the surface.

Chopin died intestate. Under French law a complete inventory of the estate had to be drawn up within twenty-four hours, and the dwelling sealed by an official from the Department of Justice. Only when the necessary taxes had been collected and outstanding debts paid could the items be released to the next of kin—which in this case happened to be Chopin's mother. Ludwika, acting as her mother's plenipotentiary, listened to Chopin's many friends who urged her to keep everything intact and create a Chopin museum. This plan, which was dear to her heart, she was prevented from carrying out. It was only in the year 1968, nearly 120 years after Chopin's death, that we learned why. That was the year in which an important document now known as "Ludwika's Confession" came to light. It takes the form of an accusatory thirty-two-page letter that Ludwika addressed to her husband, Kalasanty Jędrzejewicz, whom she excoriates for his behavior toward Chopin at the end of the composer's life and for his role in the events surrounding the liquidation of his estate. This letter throws sensational light on the tensions that existed between the pair, and the effect that it had on Ludwika's difficult decisions about what to do with her brother's personal belongings.[40]

---

40. The manuscript is preserved in the Chopin National Institute, Warsaw, under the call number M. 327.

VIII

Kalasanty, we recall, had at first been disinclined to leave Warsaw. He had moreover been unwilling to pay anything toward the cost of the family's travel, so Mme Justyna Chopin gave him 5,000 złotys toward it, and she neither asked for nor received any accounting of the money. There had been difficulties about obtaining passports, too, and Kalasanty had used the delay to torment Ludwika with the uncertainty about whom he would, or would not, allow to travel to France with her should he himself be denied permission to leave the country. In the end Kalasanty received his visa but then insisted that Chopin's younger sister, Izabella Barcińska, stay behind with Mme Chopin and look after their three youngest children. To the end of her days, Ludwika regretted not being allowed to take Izabella, who had not seen her brother since he left Poland in 1830, who wanted to be at his bedside during his last days, and who would have eased Ludwika's own burdens. Once in Paris, Kalasanty became bored and began to resent what he thought were the inordinate amounts of time Ludwika spent at her brother's bedside. Ludwika takes up the story.

> During our stay with Fr[yderyk], he seemed to have taken on a new lease on life. Yet I noticed how many incidents annoyed you, how little sympathy you showed for his idiosyncrasies and habits. Do you recall how angry you were when I spent long evenings sitting by his bed, and how you reproached me because he prevented me from getting enough sleep? Perhaps you were motivated by concern for me—yet it was painful to him, and an ordeal for me. I had come to take care of him, to nurse him, to console him, to endure any hardship as long as I could bring him one moment of relief. He liked to chat late at night and tell me of his sorrows, pouring his troubles into a loving and understanding heart. Until the very end I harbored illusions of hope.

Kalasanty was sustained neither by hope nor by illusion. There is little doubt that he was envious of Chopin's fame, and could not abide the atmosphere of adulation with which the composer was surrounded. Within a short time he had lost patience with the situation he found in Paris, abandoned his wife and daughter, and went back to Warsaw, from where he continued to exert a controlling influence over Ludwika. The "Confession" makes it clear that Kalasanty thought Chopin was heavily in debt. He had become familiar with the story of Mme Étienne, and the gift of 25,000 francs from Jane Stirling, and he wrongly feared that Ludwika would be prevailed upon by Stirling to pay back what remained unspent. He spread rumors in Warsaw that Chopin had enormous debts, which was untrue. Ludwika continues,

> I know he did not have the debts you thought he had: the money had been repaid. There was one loan outstanding, which could easily be repaid. F[ryderyk] mentioned it on more than one occasion. He worried about it and I had to plead with him not to worry. It was a sum that could easily be raised. After his death I told his devoted friends that I considered it my most sacred duty to repay this sum. They first denied that he owed anything at all and then begged me not to give it a second thought, not to mention it at all.

But it was over the disposition of Chopin's possessions that Kalasanty was shown at his unpleasant worst. When he heard of Ludwika's wish to establish a Chopin museum, he forbade her to go forward with the idea. A museum to the memory of his brother-in-law was evidently more than he could contemplate. So Ludwika told him that she had decided to assume the cost of shipping Chopin's possessions back to Warsaw, in order that the family might have them. At that Kalasanty exploded. In Ludwika's words,

> To this I received the most painful letter of my life. You commanded me to sell everything, absolutely everything, and you sent me an authorization signed by all of you. You added: "*Do not keep anything, not one rag will I let into my house.*" Oh—I shed tears of blood.

She pleaded with him to change his mind, but the only reply that she received in return was a further instruction to sell. In the midst of these confrontations with Kalasanty, Ludwika showed a flash of independence. On the night that Chopin died she and Marcelina Czartoryska went into the death chamber and filled a suitcase with his manuscripts and letters, taking them back to Ludwika's own room before the French authorities could put seals on the doors. She wanted to be sure that nothing

of a confidential nature fell into the hands of the police or, more especially, into the hands of the Russian diplomats, who might have been
eager to learn more about Chopin's contacts with Polish expatriates in
Paris. When she revealed her "misdemeanor" to Kalasanty, he accused
her of being naïve and selfish.[41]

At Ludwika's request the sale of Chopin's effects was held anonymously and took place at 42 rue des Jeûneurs, on November 30, a full six
weeks after his death. It would have been easier for this auction to have
been held in Chopin's own rooms, but Ludwika could not bear the prospect of having hordes of strangers poring over everything, and she herself
refused to be present. Only Chopin's close friends were told about it. A
surviving press advertisement mentions "fine furniture, silver, crystal,
rugs, linen, a gold watch, male clothing, curtains, etc." but makes no mention
of the famous person to whom these relics had belonged. That omission
affected the proceeds of the sale. More money would have been raised had
Chopin's name been attached to it. In the event, Ludwika received the
modest sum of 6,142.40 francs after the expenses had been paid and
the accounts settled. She signed the receipt with her maiden name,
"Louise Chopin."[42] Jane Stirling bought many items, including a portrait by
Ary Scheffer, a Sèvres porcelain service, a precious casket presented to
Chopin by Baron de Rothschild, and some valuable tapestries; and she
generously arranged to have these and other objects transported to Chopin's

---

41. Ludwika knew that the Place Vendôme, where Chopin had died, had earlier housed the
Russian embassy. She also knew that Chopin's close association with Adam Czartoryski, his
appearances at the Hôtel Lambert across the years, his recent contacts with Polish émigrés in
Britain, and his earlier rejection of a Russian passport were acts that would not have gone un-
noticed by those who wanted the Polish government in exile brought to its knees. Her removal
of Chopin's papers before the French authorities could secure them was motivated by the
native caution of one who had lived under Russian domination all her adult life and was soon
to go back to it. Ludwika provided no list of documents she removed from the death chamber,
but she was shrewd enough to know that letters from Grzymała, Fontana, and other Polish
émigrés left lying around might have compromised not only them but her family in Warsaw as
well. And this was the conduct that Kalasanty—a Polish lawyer who was mired in Russian
bureaucracy on a daily basis—dismissed as "naïve." Of more immediate interest to Chopin
scholars were two other sets of documents that Ludwika discovered and removed into safekeeping: the famous bundle of old letters from Maria Wodzińska wrapped in paper and
marked "My misfortune," and a unique run of letters from George Sand.
42. MDD, Part 3, p. 16. This same source gives a detailed inventory of Chopin's belongings,
together with the price fetched for each item. It also traces the dispersal of Chopin's property
after his death. It is obvious that Chopin's apartment at the Place Vendôme had been lavishly
furnished with some fine furniture and tapestries.

mother in Warsaw. A separate consignment of souvenirs was shipped to Scotland. (After Stirling's death in 1859 these items, too, were dispatched to Mme Chopin.) In a further act of kindness Stirling purchased Chopin's piano, which had been on loan from Pleyel, for the sum of 1,500 francs, and sent it as a gift to Ludwika in Warsaw, bearing the inscription "*Pour Louise.*"[43] When Mme Chopin died in 1861, these precious objects passed to Chopin's younger sister, Izabella Barcińska, who had meanwhile inherited the valuable run of letters between Chopin and Ludwika when the latter passed away in 1855. Izabella was now the owner of one of the most valuable collections of Chopiniana ever assembled in private hands. This priceless legacy was destroyed during the uprising of 1863, when Russian soldiers ransacked Izabella's apartment.

The dramatic details of how this came about reveal once again how Chopin's posthumous legacy has always hung by the merest thread. On September 19, 1863, the Russian governor of Warsaw, General Fyodor Berg, was riding in a carriage with an escort of soldiers past the Zamoyski Palace, where the Barcińskis lived. A bomb was thrown out of one of the upper windows; an aide to the general was hurt and two of the horses were wounded. In reprisal General Berg ordered everyone into the street, arrested all the males, and then allowed his soldiers to plunder the building. Chopin's sixty-year-old brother-in-law, Antoni Barciński, was among those taken to jail and badly beaten. When the soldiers got to the Barcińskis' apartment, they opened the windows and threw everything onto the street below—family letters, manuscripts, furniture, and the Buchholtz piano on which the teenage Chopin used to practice—and put them to the torch. There was an entire Chopin museum in Izabella's apartment, and it simply went up in flames. Only the Pleyel piano, which was fortunately at that moment in the possession of Chopin's niece, Ludka (then Mme Ciechomska), escaped harm and now belongs to the Chopin Museum in Warsaw.[44]

---

43. This was Pleyel no. 14810, which had earlier been sent out to Chaillot. The instrument was purchased by Jane Stirling directly from Pleyel himself on December 11, 1849. It was never put up for public auction.

44. Years later, Chopin's nephew Antoni Jędrzejewicz told Ferdynand Hoesick, "Among the various boxes, I recall that there were two or three cartons of music containing manuscripts of Chopin's compositions that he had neither revised nor corrected, mere drafts that were not—in his opinion—worth publishing. All this material that was stored in the Barcińskis' apartment after my mother's death . . . fell prey to the conflagration in 1863." (HSC, pp. 254–55.)

IX

When Kalasanty received details of the auction, and the practical way in which Ludwika had handled it, he demanded a full accounting. She told him that from the modest proceeds of the sale she had to pay the tradesmen and the contractor who had decorated Chopin's apartment on the Place Vendôme; she also had to pay for the printing and mailing of the invitation cards to Chopin's funeral. After these and other incidental expenses had been met, there was not a great deal of money left. Ludwika had wanted to bring back with her to Warsaw the Polish nurse Katarzyna Matuszewska, who had looked after Chopin in Chaillot and whom she thought might make a suitable governess for her own children and perhaps teach them French. But Kalasanty refused to have the woman in the house, so Ludwika asked her mother to employ her instead, an idea to which Mme Chopin readily agreed, even though there was little work to be done there. In an act of spite, Kalasanty then fired the German maid who had been employed by him for years, knowing that it would add to Ludwika's domestic burdens. All Ludwika could say about that in her "Confession" was "You became more and more petty. From a friend you became a tyrant. And I, from your friend, became a slave." And in a devastating afterthought, she added, "The slightest mention of him angered you—being with you I had to give up my memories."

Worn out with the stress of it all, Ludwika now wanted nothing more than to return to Warsaw. Her anguish was compounded by news that Kalasanty had virtually severed his ties to her family. He instructed her to meet him at the Polish border, and she set out in early January 1850. This was a nightmare journey for her; it was the depths of winter, and there was snow and ice everywhere. She had in her possession a number of things that had belonged to Chopin, and she also carried with her the crystal jar containing his heart. Fearing that it might be impounded at one of several customs checkpoints through which she had to pass along the way, she hid it under her skirts, assuming that she would be unlikely to be searched. Accompanied only by Ludka and Mme Matuszewska, she traveled on a

---

As for the Buchholtz piano, the recipient of all the young Chopin's musical thoughts, its destruction was memorialized in Cyprian Norwid's celebrated poem "Chopin's Piano." For an account of the inferno, "whose flames reached as high as the bell tower of the Holy Cross Church," see MCW, pp. 190–91.

Russian visa. Delayed by bad weather, the little party arrived at the Polish border only to discover that the ever-impatient Kalasanty had gone back to Warsaw alone. This turned out to be a blessing in disguise. It enabled Ludwika to make a detour to the home of the Barcińskis, where she was joyfully reunited with her three sons, with Izabella, and with her mother, Justyna. The hour was late, but the family stayed up until the small hours, eager to hear from Ludwika's own lips a description of the tragic events of the past several weeks. Mme Matuszewska was left there with Justyna, since Kalasanty had made it clear that he would not employ the woman. We have no doubt that Ludwika also left in the care of the Barcińskis a number of Chopin relics, including the urn containing his heart, which she would hardly have dared to bring into her own home. Given Kalasanty's intransigence, the last thing he would have wanted in his house was a relic both he and Ludwika must have known was going to command widespread veneration. So Chopin's heart was left in the temporary care of Izabella and Justyna, and was returned to Ludwika only after her husband's death.[45] Kalasanty, in fact, was angry that this unexpected visit to the Barcińskis had taken place at all, regarding it as devious, and left him feeling that he himself had been marginalized—as indeed he had.

Ludwika did not begin to write her "Confession" until after Kalasanty had passed away, so he never saw it. The marriage, such as it now was, could hardly have survived had he come into possession of the document's blistering contents. Kalasanty died in 1853, while Ludwika followed her husband to the grave two years after that.[46] We do not believe that she wished Kalasanty harm. We think that she was driven to put pen to paper—addressing her husband across the Great Divide, so to say—because of the abiding love she bore her genius brother. The writing of this narrative was for her a moral imperative. Setting out the facts in this essentially private way may have helped her to preserve some sanity as she reflected on what had happened. Nonetheless, Kalasanty's posthumous reputation as an upright, iconic member of the Chopin family collapses in the face of

---

45. Antoni Jędrzejewicz (b. 1843), recalled seeing the heart in the family home on Podwale Street during his childhood there.
46. She succumbed to the cholera epidemic that swept through the population of Warsaw in October 1855. Within a few days of her death some lavish tributes began to appear in the Warsaw press. Ludwika's virtues as a scholar, patriot, and mother were particular topics of praise. *Warsaw Gazette*, November 3, 1855, and *Gazeta Codzienna*, November 8, 1855.

Ludwika's devastating language. He is revealed as a difficult personality who brought grief into Ludwika's life and by association into the lives of Izabella and Justyna, too.

X

And what of the letters of George Sand that Ludwika had retrieved from the death chamber and brought with her on her arduous journey back to Poland? When the train on which her little party was traveling paused at the Polish border town of Mysłowice, she delivered them for safekeeping into the hands of a family acquaintance who lived there, one S. Kuźnicki, a partner in an export company, fearing that they might be confiscated by the Russian police and she herself detained while they were being translated. Kuźnicki delayed taking the letters to Warsaw because he, too, feared being searched by the Russian police, and wanted to avoid having his next consignment stopped. It was an unfortunate situation. Alexandre Dumas *fils*, who by chance happened to be staying in Mysłowice, was shown the letters by Kuźnicki and gleefully reported their contents to his father, Alexandre Dumas *père*, who in turn reported their whereabouts to George Sand. After reading the letters, the younger Dumas knew that he had struck gold. He told his father,

> Mysłowice
> May 15, 1851
>
> Just imagine! I have here in my hands the whole of her correspondence with Chopin, covering a period of ten years! I let you guess whether I copied those letters, which are a lot more interesting than those now proverbially famous letters by Mme de Sévigné! I send you a notebook full of them, because, unfortunately these letters have only been lent to me. How comes it, you will ask, that here in Mysłowice, in the depths of Silesia, I should have found a collection of letters that had their origin in Berry?[47]

Sand became frantic in her attempts to have the letters returned to her, as her correspondence with Dumas *père* makes clear. She had revealed

---

47. KGS, vol. 3, pp. 627–28.

too much of herself in them, and the intimate details of her long relationship with Chopin must at all costs be kept from the prying eyes of the world. Within a year, Dumas *fils*, under pressure from his father, filched them from their temporary guardian and arranged to bring them to Sand herself, at her urgent request. On June 3, 1851, young Alexandre was able to tell her brashly, "Within a few days I shall be in France and shall bring you personally, whether Madame Jędrzejewicz authorizes me or not, the letters that you wish to have."[48] There was a further crisis when Sand learned that Alexandre had been detained by Solange en route to Nohant. By now Sand was thoroughly frightened because she did not want Solange to read the letters, and she urged Alexandre to entrust the package to a lawyer, one Gabriel Falampin, who would forward it to her. Falampin was derelict in his duty, neglected his commission, and simply set the package aside, unaware of its importance. Dumas *fils* finally had to retrieve the box in which he had wrapped the letters and take it to Nohant in person. What passed through Sand's mind as she read her old correspondence with Chopin? We shall never know, but in her ongoing attempts to rearrange her past she must have been relieved that here was evidence with which she would no longer have to deal. She threw the correspondence on the fire and watched it turn to ashes.[49]

---

48. Ibid., p. 629.
49. The unpublished letter that Alexandre *fils* wrote to Sand in August 1851 confirms this sequence of events. Bibliothèque Nationale, n.a.fr. 24812, fol. 13. See also George Sand's *Visages du romantisme*, p. 83.

EPILOGUE

Truth is the daughter of time, not of authority.
—*Francis Bacon*[1]

I

Of pressing concern to Ludwika during her final, difficult years was the fate of Chopin's unpublished manuscripts. It was a considerable body of work, which she wanted to see published, despite Chopin's own wishes to the contrary. Ludwika played the piano and she was an amateur composer whose musical gifts were admired by her brother. As she turned the pages of these manuscripts, some of which had remained in Chopin's portfolio for many years, her attention would have been captured by the gleaming veins of genius shining through them, which clamored for an audience.

But whom to entrust with the task of sorting through everything, and seeing the best of these pieces through the press? It was to Julian Fontana that the Chopin family turned in their desire to have Chopin's unpublished compositions brought out in a posthumous edition under the best possible conditions. No one was more intimately acquainted with the composer's creative process than Fontana, and even today there are Chopin experts who have difficulty in distinguishing Chopin's calligraphy from

---

1. *Novum Organum*, Book I, Aphorism 84.

Fontana's. He also had a business background and was versed in the law. He could be trusted to take care of any financial arrangements in his dealings with publishers.

Ludwika's concerns were well grounded. Shortly after Chopin's death, unauthorized versions of his unpublished works had begun to appear. In 1851 the family came across two mazurkas (in G major and B-flat major) hitherto unknown to them, which had been published without permission by the firm of Rudolf Friedlein in Warsaw. The following year the Waltz in B minor (op. 69, no. 2) and the Waltz in F minor (op. 70, no. 2) had surfaced in Kraków, and had likewise been published without authorization by the firm of J. Wildt, under the specious title "Deux Valses mélancoliques." These same waltzes were pirated not long afterward by J. J. Ewer of London. "When our collection is published," Fontana wrote to Ludwika, "we will have to threaten these people with legal action."[2] Ludwika feared that worse might follow. She knew that there were any number of Chopin's manuscripts in private circulation. Across the years he had been prodigal in providing friends, pupils, and acquaintances with musical entries in their autograph albums and visiting books, even leaving entire manuscripts with them as souvenirs of a cherished visit. There was a ready market for such material.

This was the situation that prompted the Chopin family to draw up a letter giving Fontana legal authority to proceed with an authorized edition.

To Mr. Julian Fontana in Paris:

In giving you permission to publish the manuscripts of the deceased Frédéric Chopin in our possession, we the members of his family, namely his mother and his two sisters, are anxious to ensure that these works appear with the care and perfection they deserve, and to prevent forgery. We request that Mr. Julian Fontana, as a competent judge and friend of the composer, make a selection of the unpublished works with the goal of publishing everything worthy of the memory of the deceased, that in our name he will take care of all the work and transactions with publishers that he considers relevant in connection with this matter, and that he will collect royalties and acknowledge the receipt of them. Finally,

---

2. EJF, p. 41.

À Monsieur Jules Fontana, à Paris.

Voulant nous prêter au désir à nous manifesté de publier les manuscrits restés entre nos mains de la composition de feu Frédéric Chopin, nous, les membres de sa famille, nommément sa mère et ses deux soeurs, afin que ces oeuvres paraissent avec tout le soin et la perfection dont ils sont susceptibles, et pour éviter toute contre façon, nous prions par cet écrit Mr. Jules Fontana, comme juge compétant et ami du dit auteur, et nous l'autorisons par la présente, de faire le choix des morceaux inédits et d'en faire imprimer tout ce qui sera digne de la mémoire du défunt; — de faire en notre nom, tous les arrangements, et de passer avec les éditeurs toutes les transactions qu'il ju-
gera

Above, and following page: The letter authorizing Julian Fontana to be the sole editor of Chopin's posthumous works, signed by Chopin's mother, Justyna, and his two sisters, Ludwika and Izabella.

gera les plus convenables relativement à cette affaire, de toucher les recettes et d'en donner quittance, — enfin, tout ce qui se ra fait par lui à cette occasion, nous le reconnaîtrons comme valable et obligatoire. —

Comme la famille ne pense faire publier les œuvres de feu Frédéric Chopin que par l'intermédiaire de M. Fontana elle le prie de vouloir bien mettre au bas de l'intitulation de chaque cahier ou pièce, qu'elle provient du recueil dont il a fait choix par autorisation de la famille; de cette manière tout ce qui pour rait paraître comme œuvre posthume sans être revêtu de cette garantie au thentique, sera regardé comme contrefaçon.

Justine Chopin

Louise Iedrzejewicz
née Chopin.

Isabelle Barcinska
née Chopin

Varsovie ce 16 Juillet
1853. —

everything that has been done by him up to now is recognized by us as legally valid and binding.

Since the family intends to publish the works of the deceased Frédéric Chopin exclusively through the intermediary of Mr. Fontana, it requests of him that he place at the bottom of the title page of every fascicle or work, that it is part of the collection from which he made his selection with the legal permission of the family; in this way, everything that might appear as a posthumous work, but not carrying his authentic guarantee, would be regarded as unauthorized.

Justyna Chopin
Ludwika Jędrzejewicz *née* Chopin
Izabella Barcińska *née* Chopin
Warsaw, July 16, 1853[3]

II

A word or two about Fontana himself is called for at this juncture. Fontana had withdrawn from Chopin's life as early as 1844. His work as Chopin's amanuensis until then had been of incalculable value to the composer. It has been estimated that between the years 1837 and 1844, Fontana prepared copies of approximately fifty of Chopin's works, ranging from the Studies, op. 25, to the F minor Fantaisie, op. 49, which served as the basis for the French, German, and English editions. For this labor of love Fontana evidently received no remuneration. It was done out of the friendship he bore Chopin and the veneration he felt for his genius.

We remarked that Fontana had "withdrawn" from Chopin's life. Fontana was well aware that he was destined to remain under Chopin's shadow, and he eventually began to find his subordinate position untenable. The worm that began to eat at the heart of their friendship was Chopin's increasingly imperious demands, which made deep inroads into Fontana's life, to the point of psychological exhaustion. For it was not just as a copyist that Chopin pressed Fontana into service. The composer's letters are filled with myriad requests to search for apartments, to choose the right kind of

---

3. BC, plates 109 and 110.

wallpaper, to select for him a hat and a waistcoat, to negotiate with his publishers, to oversee the transport of his Pleyel piano from Paris to Palma, and so on *ad infinitum*.

In a revealing letter that Fontana wrote to his cousin in Poland, he confessed, "I have always relied on a good friend, who could have opened up a career for me, but who was always insincere, false and unfriendly. In order to escape his influence, I left Paris for a while, and that caused me great harm; only since my return have I set about composing."[4] This "friend" could only have been Chopin himself. Fontana had already confided as much to his old colleague Stanisław Egbert Koźmian in London, a month or so earlier. "The moral sway that Chopin held over me all these years was the reason why I wrote nothing until now. Seeing him always false and ill-disposed, I broke with him and have begun to write."[5] These are harsh words and they must have been forced from Fontana in a moment of personal anguish. After years of placing Chopin's interests above his own, he had hoped for something more from Chopin than open indifference toward his own career. Unable to establish himself in Paris as a pianist and sinking further into debt, Fontana announced his intention of emigrating to the New World. His unexpected departure from France in 1844 came as an unpleasant surprise to Chopin, who, from his own vantage point, may have felt abandoned. It is a fact that Fontana was shut out of Chopin's correspondence for four years.

Fontana went first to Cuba, where he enjoyed a modest celebrity in Havana, becoming the director of the Havana Philharmonic Society for a time. Later he settled in New York and went on tour with the violinist Sivori, the pupil of Paganini. He made several appearances as a soloist in New York, including one at a concert in New York's Apollo Rooms, where, on October 15, 1846, he gave the American premiere of Chopin's Fantaisie in F minor, op. 49. During his sojourn in Cuba he became acquainted with the wealthy Dalcour family, who owned vast estates on the island, and it was there that he met their twenty-six-year-old daughter, Camila. At that time Camila was married to an English businessman, Stephen Cattley Tennant, by whom she already had four young children. Two or three years

---

4. OFCL, pp. 94–95. Fontana's letter is dated "Paris, May 7, 1842." His cousin was Viscountess Kornelia de Verny, to whom he vainly appealed for financial help.
5. Ibid., p. 91.

after Fontana had departed for New York, however, she reentered his life in dramatic circumstances.

III

On November 3, 1848, Camila's husband, Stephen Tennant, was fatally injured in an accident at Farnborough railway station. He had raced onto the platform after visiting his English relatives, and had tried to open a carriage door before the train had come to a standstill. He slipped and fell between the narrow space separating the wheels and the edge of the platform. One of the wheels passed over him and he was killed on the spot.[6]

Camila was left with five children, a widow at the age of thirty. Independently wealthy, and heiress to a fortune, she traveled from Havana to New York, where she sought out Fontana, who was surprised by her unexpected visit. We are now in a better position to understand what motivated her. During Fontana's residence in Cuba, in 1844, the pair had conducted a clandestine love affair and in May 1845 Camila had given birth to Fontana's illegitimate daughter, Fernanda Leokadia, who was brought up as Stephen Tennant's own child, probably in the belief that she was. With Tennant's sudden demise everything changed. Within a few short weeks Fontana and Camila were married in St. Patrick's Old Cathedral (on Manhattan's Mulberry Street) and they moved to Paris, acquiring a comfortable home in Montgeron, not far from Poland's poet laureate, Adam Mickiewicz. In July 1853, Camila bore Fontana a son, Julian Camillo Adam. Mickiewicz acted as godfather. It was probably the happiest time of Fontana's life, but his bliss was short-lived. Within two years Camila had become pregnant again but she died of pneumonia while delivering their daughter Zofia, who also died. A grieving Fontana buried his wife and infant in Père Lachaise Cemetery and then made a sad journey to England, where he handed over custody of his stepchildren to the Tennant family. The unwelcome reality for Fontana was that Camila's income dried up with her death. He made several trips to the United States and to Cuba in order to gain access to Camila's estate, but without success. She had left no will

---

6. The accident was reported in the *Observer* newspaper (London) on November 6, 1848.

and her brothers in Havana had taken control of her properties, leaving Fontana almost penniless. He returned to Paris, where he took on some occasional teaching and lapsed into a life of genteel poverty.

This was the unsettling background against which Fontana completed his posthumous edition of Chopin's works, published in two parts. Part One appeared in May 1855, just two months after the death of his wife, and contained the solo piano music. Part Two appeared in 1859, and was devoted to the Sixteen Polish Songs.

Julian Fontana's posthumous edition of Chopin's works with opus numbers assigned by him

I: Compositions for piano (published by Schlesinger in Berlin, and by J. Meissonnier Fils in Paris, in May 1855)

Op. 66 Fantaisie-Impromptu in C-sharp minor (1834)
Op. 67 Four Mazurkas
    no. 1 in G major (1835)
    no. 2 in G minor (1848–49)
    no. 3 in C major (1835)
    no. 4 in A minor (1846)
Op. 68 Four Mazurkas
    no. 1 in C major (c. 1830)
    no. 2 in A minor (c. 1827)
    no. 3 in F major (c. 1830)
    no. 4 in F minor (c. 1846)
Op. 69 Two Waltzes
    no. 1 in A-flat major (1835)
    no. 2 in B minor (1829)
Op. 70 Three Waltzes
    no. 1 in G-flat major (1832)
    no. 2 in F minor (1842)
    no. 3 D-flat major (1828)
Op. 71 Three Polonaises
    no. 1 in D minor (1827–28)
    no. 2 in B-flat major (1828)
    no. 3 in F minor (1828)

Op. 72 Nocturne in E minor (c. 1828)

    Funeral March in C minor (1826)

    Three Écossaises (1826)

Op. 73 Rondo in C major for two pianos (1828)

II: Sixteen Polish Songs, op. 74 (published by Schlesinger in 1859)

no. 1 "Życzenie" (The Wish) (1829)

no. 2 "Wiosna" (Spring) (1838)

no. 3 "Smutna rzeka" (Sad River) (1831)

no. 4 "Hulanka" (Drinking Song) (1830)

no. 5 "Gdzie lubi" (What She Likes) (1829)

no. 6 "Precz z moich oczu!" (Out of My Sight!) (1827)

no. 7 "Poseł" (The Messenger) (1831)

no. 8 "Śliczny chłopiec" (Handsome Lad) (1841)

no. 9 "Melodya" (Melody) (1847)

no. 10 "Wojak" (The Warrior) (1831)

no. 11 "Dwojaki koneic" (Double Ending) (1845)

no. 12 "Moja pieszczotka" (My Darling) (1837)

no. 13 "Nie ma czego trzeba" (There Is No Need) (1845)

no. 14 "Pierścień" (The Ring) (1836)

no. 15 "Narzeczony" (The Bridegroom) (1831)

no. 16 "Piosnka litewska" (Lithuanian Song) (1831)

A seventeenth song, "Śpiew grobowy" (Hymn from the Tomb) (1836), was added in 1872.

In his preface to Part One, Fontana makes some interesting disclosures: "Not only did I hear [Chopin] play almost all the works from this period many times, but I also performed them in his presence and since then I have preserved them in my memory the way he created them, and that is how I now present them." He goes on to reveal that he had access to more manuscripts than he published, selecting only the ones he thought worthy.[7]

---

7. Ludwika compiled her own catalogue of Chopin's unpublished compositions, to which she attached a separate set of provisional dates, which do not always agree with the ones provided by Fontana. Known as "Ludwika's list," it was first published in 1904 by Mieczysław Karłowicz: KSFC, pp. 210–12.

IV

Fontana refused remuneration for his work.[8] The substantial body of twenty-three pieces for piano includes the famous Fantaisie-Impromptu, op. 66; the Nocturne in E minor, op. 72, no. 1; and the evergreen Waltz in G-flat major, op. 70, no. 1. It is not too much to say that these pieces were retrieved from oblivion by Fontana. The point is worth bearing in mind when we consider Niecks's jaundiced description of them as "insignificant and imperfect such as most of those presented to the world by his ill-advised friend are."[9]

Ludwika had the satisfaction of seeing the first volume published in May 1855, just four months before she died. Fontana, true to his mandate, added at the foot of each piece the declaration: "Since the family of Fryderyk Chopin has decided to print his unpublished compositions exclusively through the intermediary of and according to the selection of Mr. J. Fontana, any publication of Chopin's posthumous works appearing beyond this collection will be treated and *prosecuted* as forgeries."

On January 14, 1856, in an attempt to foster a wider interest in these pieces, Fontana gave a recital in the Salle Pleyel in which he played four Mazurkas, two Waltzes (none were identified), and the Fantaisie-Impromptu. All were world premieres, with the exception of the Fantaisie-Impromptu. That honor had fallen to Chopin's pupil Princess Czartoryska, who had already performed it in Paris, in March 1855. The concert, which also included a group of the unpublished Polish Songs sung by the German tenor Herr Lindau (in Polish), was reviewed in the *Revue et Gazette musicale* by Henri Blanchard: "A talented and conscientious interpreter of Chopin, M. Fontana in his delightful performance revealed to us not only the inspired and brilliant composer of piano music, but also the composer of songs of national elegies."[10]

Fontana gave two more recitals in the next few months, presenting some of the remaining pieces. At the last one, on February 11, 1857, he gave the first public performance of the Rondo in C major for Two Pianos, with Mlle Louise Scheibel. Pauline Viardot also took part, lending her name and

---

8. "I refused the payment from Berlin and Paris, part of which was offered me by the family, not expecting and not accepting any other reward than having the pleasure of seeing my name next to that of the immortal artist, and the honor of contributing to the rescue of the dispersed riches left by my friend and master." HFC, p. 442.

9. NFC, vol. 2, p. 271.

10. Issue of January 20, 1856.

fame to the memory of her departed friend and mentor. She, too, sang some of the Polish Songs in their original tongue, which, according to Henri Blanchard, "bore the imprint of both joy and sorrow, and were preceded by a familiar aria from *l'italiana in Algeri*."[11]

Fontana's final years were marked by economic hardship and a series of illnesses that amounted to a foretaste of death. But he kept working. He produced a translation of *Don Quixote* from Spanish into Polish, and he went on to write a book on popular astronomy and a treatise on Polish orthography. He eventually became deaf, losing the one faculty that had continued to give life its meaning. In the midst of mounting financial problems and unable to function as a musician, he committed suicide by carbon monoxide poisoning, on December 23, 1869.[12] Prior to his death he set his affairs in order and placed sixteen-year-old Julian in the care of a guardian, his old friend Auguste de Barthélemy, together with the provision of what little money had been set aside from Camila's estate for his son's welfare. The young man eventually found his way to New Orleans, where he lived with one of Camila's sisters, his aunt Lolita Olivier. Fontana was laid to rest in a tomb in Montmartre Cemetery containing the remains of other Polish expatriates.

Modern musicologists have tended to place Fontana beyond the pale, claiming that his work hardly meets the requirements of current scholarship. Can it really be the case that they would prefer that he had never attempted it? At the best of times editing can become problematic, the distance between sound and symbol all too often creating an unbridgeable abyss into which both player and editor can topple into free fall. True, Fontana added dynamic, tempo, metronome, and pedal markings to Chopin's scores with no other authority than the enviable one of his own intimate knowledge of the composer's working methods. But millions have heard and accepted these pieces, including some of the most illustrious Chopin players both past and present, embracing them with heart and soul, and including them in their recitals without discrimination. More than forty years have passed since the distinguished Polish scholar Jan Ekier, chief editor of the Polish National Edition, informed us that it is time for Fontana to be rehabilitated.[13] We are happy to answer the call.

---

11. Issue of February 15, 1857.
12. Fontana's method of suicide was carefully considered. "I have the utmost loathing of blood and smashed brains," he wrote. "No noise and no commotion. Why frighten the neighbors? Two vessels of coal await me." Fontana's letter is given in full in OFCL, p. 194.
13. Ekier wrote, "Regardless of its defects, Fontana's edition of Chopin's posthumous works is of fundamental value to contemporary editorial practice." EJF, p. 58.

V

The publication of Chopin's posthumous compositions was not the only concern facing Ludwika. Within two weeks of Chopin's funeral she received a letter from Liszt, in which he expressed his desire to publish "a few pages" in honor of the composer's memory. To this letter he attached a twelve-point questionnaire, inviting Ludwika to provide the answers.

> Madame,
>
> My long friendship with your brother, the sincere and deep admiration I always held for him as for one of the noblest glories of our art, force upon me, as it were, the obligation of issuing a few pages to honor his memory. They will probably form a brochure of 3 to 4 folios. In order to give this work all desirable accuracy, allow me to affirm to you my intimate relations with the illustrious deceased, and to submit several questions relating to his biography. I should be infinitely grateful if you will kindly put the answers in the margin.
>
> My secretary M. Belloni, who has the honor of bearing these lines to you, is likewise charged to bring me your response as quickly as possible.
>
> Please accept, Madame, my most respectful and devoted greetings.
>
> F. Liszt
>
> Pilsen, November 14, 1849.[14]

Ludwika did not acknowledge this letter. She probably regarded it as intrusive, coming only two weeks after Chopin's funeral. The questionnaire contained, moreover, some questions about Chopin's relationship with George Sand that Ludwika found tactless. Her native intuition told her that Liszt would not make a good biographer, a suspicion that was amply borne out. She was in any case besieged at that moment with problems arising from the impending auction of Chopin's estate, so she passed the letter and its attached questionnaire to Jane Stirling, who did her best to respond.[15] Did Liszt ever see Stirling's replies? If so, he made hardly any use

---

14. KSFC, p. 200.
15. In view of its biographical interest we have reproduced Liszt's questionnaire, together with Stirling's replies, as an Appendix.

of them. His "few pages" in honor of Chopin soon became a grossly in
flated book, filled with flowery prose that borders on the unreadable and
tells us more about Liszt than about Chopin. For this we must blame Liszt's
new companion, the Polish princess Carolyne von Sayn-Wittgenstein,
who wrote parts of the biography herself. The book has been memorably
excoriated as "a literary Tower of Babel."[16]

Liszt's biography, *F. Chopin*, was first published in 1852 by the firm of
M. Escudier. The text had already made its debut the previous year, having
appeared in seventeen installments in the journal *La France musicale* (February 9 to August 17, 1851). When Stirling read it, she was dismayed and
uttered some harsh words. She told Ludwika, "You will be very displeased
with the recent publication. A very reliable person evaluated it using a well-
known expression: 'he spat on the plate to spoil the others' appetite.'" Stirling
was especially critical of the fact that Liszt made no mention of Chopin's
unique piano playing: "As for the beautiful and inventive philosophy of piano playing that transformed it into a new instrument, there is not even a
word about it, which amazes me no end. Did he not understand it? Maybe
he intentionally kept silent about it." She ended her tirade against Liszt with
the words, "He is vain and petty, because he thinks only of himself."[17]

Grzymała or Fontana would have made better biographers, and in the
weeks following Chopin's death both men expressed a desire to enter the
field. Not only had they known Chopin for years, but they had the advantage of speaking and writing in Polish to him. Fontana became discour-
aged when he heard that he would be competing against Liszt, and simply
gave up. "Liszt is signing his piece and his name carries authority. If I venture to criticize and evaluate [Chopin], every reader will feel the right to
ask: Who are you? And even if I sign my name, he will say '*connais pas*' [I
don't know him]!" Fontana tells us that after he had searched through his
papers he discovered no fewer than fifty-eight letters addressed to him by
Chopin. Such an important cache of documents would surely have formed
the basis of an excellent biography, but Liszt had "spat on the plate" and
Fontana lost his appetite.

---

16. MAL, p. 179. For a fuller discussion of Liszt as an author, and for the genesis of this particular book, see the second volume of my life of Franz Liszt (the chapter titled "The Scribe
of Weimar"), with special reference to pp. 379–80.
17. W-SC, p. 140.

Also, I would have as much to say about the man, as about the artist. His tact, combined with an unusual sense of humour, hid from
the world what was not a secret to me, who knew him for almost
thirty years. If I remove the curtain and show him not quite the
way public opinion wants him, they will say that I am motivated by
jealousy, by self-interest. Anyway, how do you show an intimate side
of a man, without providing the reader with some proof? Thus, when
I sign my name, I may be placing myself in a negative light, yet when
I remove myself entirely, I would discredit the seriousness and
responsibility of the whole thing.[18]

As for Grzymała, he started to produce some detailed drafts of a biography
in French, and was making good progress. He possessed a rich treasury of
memories, had been a confidant of both Chopin and George Sand, and
was in a unique position to throw light on their complex relationship;
he was, moreover, the recipient of the largest body of letters that Chopin
wrote to any of his friends. We shall never know whether he might have
fulfilled his self-professed aim of writing "a detailed biography more factual than anything reported in the newspapers since his death."[19] His
mistake was to have shown his text to Jane Stirling, who was not only critical of his literary style but reported her misgivings to Ludwika. Grzymała
soldiered on, but he had to do so without the encouragement of either of
the two ladies who might have done most to help him. His difficulties were
compounded by loss of vision and he was never able to complete his work.
He took his drafts to Switzerland when he settled there in 1854, and the
manuscript is now presumed lost. We owe so much to Jane Stirling that it
is difficult to criticize her. Yet in the matter of finding the best biographer
for Chopin she proved to be a hindrance. Grzymała's thwarted biography
could have become a solid foundation on which subsequent books about
the composer might have rested their narrative. In the event, Chopin's biographers lost their way for the next twenty-five years. The fact is, Stirling's idealized view of Chopin the pianist colored her view of Chopin the
man, in whom she could see no fault. She wished him to be "cast in bronze."

---

18. OFCL, pp. 147–54. This letter, dated June 6, 1861, was written to Fontana's Polish
compatriot Stanisław Egbert Koźmian. It provides many poignant and intimate glimpses into
Fontana's close relationship with Chopin.
19. CFC, vol. 3, p. 454.

Any biography that failed to venerate his memory at every touch and turn was suspect.

With the death of Grzymała in 1871, the field of Chopin biography was wide open. Since his only "rival" for this honor, Julian Fontana, had passed away two years earlier, there were no obvious candidates waiting in the wings. The lacuna was unexpectedly filled by the Warsaw-born cellist Moritz Karasowski, who, while he never met Chopin, got to know Chopin's family (the Jędrzejewicz children and the Barcińskis), who gave him unfettered access to all the unpublished letters and documents in their possession. Karasowski seemed well qualified to write a definitive book about Chopin. He had already composed a short biography of George Onslow (1856) followed by a book on Polish opera (1859), and his knowledge of the Polish language gave him a great advantage over other possible contenders as Chopin's chronicler. We do not know exactly when Karasowski began work on his monograph, which was published in German, in 1877, bearing the title *Friedrich Chopin: Sein Leben, seine Werke und Briefe*. It probably started life as an offshoot of a brief article that he wrote about Chopin's younger years, and published in the Warsaw periodical *Biblioteka Warszawska* in October 1862. But with the uprising of 1863, and the political repressions that followed, Karasowski left Warsaw and settled in Dresden, where he secured a position as cellist in the court orchestra. It was there that he began serious work on his book. We know that he remained in touch with Chopin's younger sister, Izabella, for she continued to lend him materials and provide information. As it happened, Karasowski squandered a wonderful opportunity. His book is today generally regarded as a disappointment, and he himself has been disparaged as a "weaver of legends." This is a charge that is easy to justify, because as we turn the pages of his narrative we recognize the starting point for many of the myths and legends still to be found in the literature—material that was obviously handed down across the years by members of Chopin's own family until it was placed by Karasowski between hard covers.

It is Karasowski's cavalier approach to Chopin's letters that buries his reputation as a biographer. Mistranslations abound and they have been vigorously dealt with elsewhere.[20] Karasowski is not above inserting his own material into Chopin's letters if in his opinion that makes them more

---

20. HSLC, pp. 67–77.

interesting. To quote but one example: in Chopin's letter to his parents dated "Berlin, September 16, 1828," Karasowski decides to add a physical description of the German scientist Alexander von Humboldt, who was the president of the scientific conference in Berlin that Chopin was attending at that time. He writes: "[Humboldt] is not above middle height, and his features cannot be called handsome, but the prominent, broad brow, and the deep penetrating eyes reveal the searching intellect of the scholar, who is as great a student of human nature as he is a traveler."[21] Not a word of this can be found in Chopin's original letter. It was presumably inserted because Karasowski's book was to be published in Germany for German readers, and some surplus promotion of a prominent German intellect would be welcome, especially if it came from a Pole. It is, however, incomprehensible that Karasowski did not make copies of the many letters loaned to him by Izabella before he left Warsaw in 1863. This material perished when the Russians sacked the Barciński apartment in 1863. Karasowski's weak explanation of what happened runs, "When I gave back to his family the original letters, I did not dream that in a few months they would be destroyed . . . The loss is a great and irreparable one, for the number of letters from Paris, during a most brilliant epoch, was by no means inconsiderable." These despairing words, taken from the preface of the first edition of Karasowski's book, were suppressed when the second one appeared four years later, in 1881.

With the arrival of Frederick Niecks on the scene, Chopin's biography was removed from the realm of imagination and fantasy and placed firmly in the field of musicology. Niecks, who was born in Düsseldorf in 1845, came from a family of professional musicians. He studied the violin under Leopold Auer and piano under Julius Tausch. In addition he was a polyglot, speaking several European languages. Being simultaneously at home in the fields of practical music making and musicology were obvious advantages for anyone writing the story of Chopin's life. When in 1868 Sir Alexander Mackenzie invited him to play the viola in the Edinburgh Quartet, Niecks moved to Scotland and became a naturalized British citizen. At that time he also became organist at the Greyfriars Church in Dumfries. In 1891 he was elevated to the position of Reid Professor of Music at Edinburgh University. By then he had already published his two-volume biography of

---

21. KFC, p. 44.

Chopin, and for a number of years he was regarded as the leading authority in the field. That book, *Frederick Chopin as Man and Musician*, first issued in 1888, set new standards generally and went through three editions. This does not mean that it has stood the test of time, for modern scholars have not been slow to aim their slings and arrows in Niecks's direction. But he did his best to go where the evidence led him, and his book was not effectively displaced from its preeminent position in the English-speaking world until the beginning of World War II. He had the great advantage of interviewing numerous people who had known Chopin personally, including among others Ferdinand Hiller, Adolf Gutmann, Eduard Wolff, Camille Dubois, Sir Charles Hallé, Auguste Franchomme, and Chopin's Scottish doctor Adam Łyszczyński, who had treated the composer in Edinburgh. Above all, Niecks made personal contact with Franz Liszt, which gave him unparalleled access to the Hungarian composer's memories, going back to the 1830s. While some of these individuals gave Niecks misleading information, albeit in good faith, his method was scrupulously fair and thoroughly professional for its time.

No one could fault Niecks for not knowing anything about the obscure origins of Mikołaj Chopin in France, which only came to light much later (and which Mikołaj himself had buried so successfully that even his famous son knew nothing about them). Nor could he readily be blamed for misdating several important letters of Chopin, which occasionally misaligns the chronology of his narrative, because the task of publishing them and putting them into proper chronological order did not get under way until the 1950s. Still, he was not well informed about the reasons for Chopin's breakup with George Sand, and might have done better to remain silent rather than indulge in general speculation about it, which was corrected only when Wladimir Karénine's imposing four-volume biography of Sand reached completion in 1926.

Few Chopin scholars beyond Poland's borders had heard the name of Ferdynand Hoesick before World War II. Yet at the time of his death, in 1941, he had amassed a body of research that placed him in the forefront of the field. His two major books, *Chopin: Życie i twórczość* (Chopin: His Life and Works, in three volumes) and *Chopiniana* (Chopin's Correspondence—comprising letters to his family and friends), reflected a lifelong commitment to the composer's memory. Hoesick was a publisher and journalist by profession and from 1928 was the chief editor of the

Warsaw Courier, Poland's leading daily newspaper. Despite a busy schedule that in later years kept him nailed to his editorial desk, he devoted an astounding amount of time to the accumulation of detail about his musical hero. Published in 1910, to coincide with the centenary celebrations of the composer's birth, Hoesick's biography can only be described as monumental. Hoesick himself tells us that it was Niecks's biography of Chopin that compelled him to write his own. As he explains in his preface, he was ashamed that it had been left to a foreigner to produce what was at the time the best biography of the composer, and he felt it to be his duty to correct the various errors in Niecks's work, especially the ones concerning Chopin's earlier years in Poland.[22] Hoesick never succeeded in getting his work translated, which held back its wider reception, although shortly after the appearance of the first volume there were serious attempts to render it in Italian and German. With the arrival of World War I the effort was abandoned and never renewed.

Across the years, admiration for Hoesick's work has been tempered by criticism that his book is not just exhaustive but exhausting. The term "garrulous" has been used to describe the unstoppable torrent of words that issued from his pen. It is strange that the newspaper editor in him did not come to his rescue and stanch the flow. His all-inclusive approach to the topic, which allowed him to admit every conceivable scrap of information about Chopin, irrespective of its true worth, led one of Chopin's recent biographers to describe him as "one of the most famous of all Polish historical gossips."[23] Still, no researcher can afford to bypass Hoesick. Of some disquiet to scholars today is Hoesick's role in drawing attention to what he then thought were the unpublished letters between Chopin and Countess Delfina Potocka, which a later generation has come to regard as spurious. Hoesick tells us that he was unable to gain access to these letters despite many attempts to do so. He wrote, "A large number of Chopin's letters to Delfina Potocka written at various times between the years 1833 and 1840 are said to have been preserved."[24] He believed, like many others at the time, that there had been a passionate love affair between Chopin and Delfina, which the correspondence would prove. He did not

22. HFCZ, vol. 1, pp. 14–15.
23. ZCPR, p. 304.
24. HFC, Preface, p. iv.

live long enough to discover that these letters never existed, and what we now recognize as the notorious "Chopin-Potocka correspondence," first presented to an unsuspecting public in 1945, was nothing more than an elaborate hoax that was to torment two generations of biographers.

VI

We must open a parenthesis at this point in order to explain how such a situation could have arisen. Delfina had married Count Mieczysław Potocki in 1825, at the tender age of eighteen, an unhappy union that produced two daughters who died young. She fled the marriage and moved to Paris in 1829, where her beauty attracted the attention of a string of prominent suitors. Her lovers during the 1830s were said to have included Count Auguste Flahault; the Duke of Orléans (son of King Louis-Philippe); and the Duke de Montfort (nephew of Napoléon Bonaparte). Her licentious behavior earned her the sobriquet "Don Juan in Skirts." As if to cement Delfina's reputation for promiscuity, Balzac wrote to his Polish mistress Ewelina Hańska, "Mme Delfina P . . . went into a maternity hospital on Sunday and had a baby on Monday."[25] While no one came forward to claim the honors of paternity, they could not have fallen on Count Potocki, who had by then been separated from his wife for several years and was living on his estate in Tulczyn. When the Potocki family attempted to bring about a reconciliation between the mismatched pair, and Delfina briefly rejoined her husband in Tulczyn, the encounter broke up in disarray. She began divorce proceedings and left Poland for good.

Chopin met Delfina for the first time during his trip to Dresden, in 1830. Her family was one of the first that he visited shortly after he arrived in Paris, in 1831. "Today I dined with the Komars. Yesterday I dined with Mme [Delfina] Potocka, Mieczysław's beautiful wife," he wrote on November 18.[26] There is no question, then, that Chopin was well acquainted with Delfina and her family by the early 1830s. That he felt affection for her and admired her singing voice cannot be doubted, and he accepted her as an occasional pupil. He also socialized with her at the

---

25. Letter dated March 11, 1835. BLH, vol. 1, p. 236.
26. CFC, vol. 2, p. 15; KFC, vol. 1, p. 187.

very time that she was negotiating the terms of her generous divorce settlement. As far as a sexual liaison is concerned, the evidence appears to be against it. Their names were never linked romantically at the time, for Delfina was too busy with her other lovers. Still, it was not for nothing that Chopin changed the dedication of his F minor Piano Concerto, originally intended for Konstancja Gładkowska, to Countess Delfina Potocka when the work was eventually published in 1836. A year earlier Mikołaj Chopin had written to Fryderyk in oblique language, wondering why he was unable to "associate the fruit with its tree."

April 11, 1835

Owing, I think, to certain intrigues, the dedication was not given to the first person intended, so whom are you keeping it for? It surprises me that so far you have not had a chance to associate the fruit with its tree. There must be some living obstacle in the way. Can't you overcome it? Although you attach little importance to it, such a thing always calls attention to a publication.[27]

Mikołaj had clearly embarked on a fishing trip when he referred to some "living obstacle" standing in the way of the dedication, and obviously knew that the original recipient was to have been Konstancja Gładkowska. Some scholars have speculated that he may have got wind of Chopin's friendship with Delfina, which the actual dedication later confirmed. In any case, Chopin made no response to his father's question.

The great love of Delfina's life was not Chopin, but the Polish national poet Zygmunt Krasiński, whom she met after going to Naples in 1838 to visit her mother and her two sisters, Ludmila and Natalia. It drew from Hoesick a caustic observation that can hardly be bettered: "Krasiński soon became the fortunate successor of his fortunate predecessors."[28] Krasiński, six years her junior, regarded Delfina as his Beatrice, was deeply in love with her, and would have married her but for the fierce opposition of his father, who had plans of a different kind for his gifted son—a marriage to the unprepossessing Countess Eliza Branicka, whose great advantage over Delfina was that she lacked notoriety.

27. CFC, vol. 2, p. 142; KFC, vol. 1, pp. 256–57.
28. HFC, Preface, p. v.

Fifty years after Chopin's death the tongues started to wag, and the legend grew that Chopin had been one of Delfina's lovers. This story began in an unlikely place. The young widow of Dr. Aleksander Hoffman (the Polish physician who had lodged with Chopin in Paris during the period 1833–34) "remembered" long after her husband's death that he had once told her that Chopin and Delfina had had an affair, and that he had witnessed Delfina spending the occasional night with Chopin in the apartment he shared with the composer at 5 rue de la Chaussée d'Antin. We must not forget that Mme Emilia Borzęcka Hoffman was an infant when these trysts between Chopin and Delfina were supposed to have taken place, and although time only served to deepen her memory nobody was ever able to corroborate her story. Nonetheless, she reported it to Ferdynand Hoesick when he interviewed her half a century after the event, and he included it in his biography of Chopin, where it gained currency. The only thing lacking, of course, was some documentation, without which the story foundered. And that is where an obscure Polish music teacher named Paulina Czernicka came in, providing material in abundance.

The texts of the Chopin-Potocka letters all came from her, and she alone was responsible for what turned into a hue and cry. The story can be said to have begun in 1945 when Mme Czernicka approached Polish Radio in Poznań with a script in which she mentioned the existence of an unknown correspondence between Chopin and Delfina. The broadcast created a stir and the Chopin Society in Warsaw asked to see the originals, with a view to purchasing them. Czernicka explained that the autographs were in possession of one of her relatives, a member of a distant branch of the Komar family to which Delfina herself was related,[29] and she prevaricated. What followed was the release of some typescript fragments purporting to have been copied from original letters, the contents of which were nothing short of sensational. Some of the fragments were openly scatological, containing erotic passages and sexual innuendos of a kind that cannot be found elsewhere in Chopin's published correspondence. There are likewise critical references to some of Chopin's contemporaries—Liszt, Schumann, and Mendelssohn among them—which are impossible to reconcile with views he expressed about these

---

29. No genealogical link has ever been found to connect Czernicka with the Komar family.

same musicians during his lifetime. Of uncommon interest was Chopin's link between the creative process and sexual intercourse. The following passage can stand for the others.

> I intend to bore you yet again with matters concerning my inspiration and musical creation; but you will see that they are deeply connected to you. I have slowly come to the important realization that ideas and inspiration only come to me when I have not had a woman for a long time . . . The prescription is simple. Let the creator, no matter who he is, get women out of his life, and the strength that builds up in his body will not go into his prick and balls, but will find its way to his brain and perhaps inspire him to create the most elevated works of art.
>
> Think, my sweetest Findeleczko [a Polish diminutive of Delfina, with reversed syllables], how much of that precious fluid and strength I have lost, ramming you to no purpose. Since I have not given you a baby, God only knows how many of my finest inspirations have been lost forever . . . Perhaps Ballades and Polonaises, even a whole Concerto had vanished forever down . . . [30]

It is not necessary to finish such a sentence. With the release of texts such as these Paulina Czernicka became an overnight celebrity, and other quotations emerged from time to time in order to silence the Doubting Thomases. In her article "Chopin i poeci" (Chopin and the Poets), published a few months after her broadcast, Czernicka issued eleven more fragments of the Potocka texts.[31] It is important to note that there were never any letters in the usual sense of the word, just some scattered passages that Czernicka claimed to have culled from unpublished autographs that no one ever saw. It seems that Czernicka also had the gift of prophecy. Long before anybody in Robert Schumann's inner circle suspected that he might attempt suicide and end his days in the Endenich asylum, in 1854, we find her putting these words into Chopin's mouth: "That Schumann will go crazy. I predict and guarantee it." Chopin encountered Schumann just twice in his life, both times while passing through Leipzig. The first

---

30. SSCDP, p. 187.
31. They appeared in *Nauka i sztuka* (Science and Art), May–June 1946.

occasion was in October 1835 and the second was in September 1836. These meetings lasted no more than a few hours. That was eighteen years before Schumann was incarcerated, during which time the two composers had no further contact with each other.

VII

Not everyone remembers that Mme Czernicka was a struggling out-of-work musician, who had given birth to a mentally handicapped son, was now widowed, and was coping with poverty and encroaching insanity. Her family had a history of emotional instability. Two of her brothers as well as her mother had all committed suicide. These facts must be borne in mind when considering her motivations. Aside from craving attention it seems that she also wanted to reap some financial reward from her activities. Faced with an unprecedented clamor to produce the original correspondence, and after many evasions, Czernicka finally responded to a request from the Chopin Society and agreed to bring all the Potocka materials in her possession to Warsaw. Her account of what happened next beggars belief but it is the only one she gave. While she was waiting at the railway station to catch her train, she says, the precious parcel was snatched from her grasp by a member of Delfina's family who did not wish to see anything published. With nothing more to lose but her reputation, Czernicka committed suicide in September 1949, just in time to mark the centennial of Chopin's own death, and took many secrets to the grave. To this day no one knows where the "originals" are because Czernicka never produced them. All she ever revealed were typescripts containing fragments alleged to have come from a larger correspondence.

After her death, a virtual shrine to the composer's memory was discovered at her home, which was described at that time as "a Chopin Chapel." It was also revealed that her claim to have studied musicology in Paris was false. A search through her library brought to light numerous volumes devoted to Chopin containing underlined sentences from his authentic correspondence that she had embroidered for inclusion within her forged texts. The discovery of her "ledger book," in which she tried her hand at imitating Chopin's linguistic style, in different-colored inks, was the most damaging piece of evidence against her. The pages of this ledger contained

104 fragments of letters, a few of them already released by Czernicka in her typescripts, but many of them new and apparently destined for a more ambitious publication.[32] Since the world was waiting for the originals, they must perforce be created. Czernicka's home at this time must have resembled a veritable manufactory for the production and assembly of fabricated texts, with generous recourse to scissors and paste, as later inquiries were to establish. Philological evidence suggested that the most likely period for the creation of this counterfeit material was between the years 1926 and 1945. There was language in the fragments not in use in the Poland of the 1830s that only came into circulation later and helped to date the forgeries.

The experts were not slow to take sides. During the 1960s the world of Chopin scholarship was riven by a Great Schism in which the parties on each side of the divide argued their case in a most public and often personal manner. The main protagonist in the debate was Mateusz Gliński, who believed that the texts were genuine. His book *Chopin: Listy do Delfiny* (Chopin: Letters to Delfina) argues the pros and cons of the matter at length. The burden of his argument, which attracted supporters and still does, was that the crude, sexual references in the correspondence did not rule out Chopin as their author. Mozart was an obvious example of someone whose musical genius resided within the same personality as the one who enjoyed using four-letter words and delighted in sending them with lavatorial accompaniments of the basest kind to his cousin Maria Anna Thekla and other members of his family. So why should Chopin be an exception? If the letters to Delfina contradicted our received picture of Chopin as a refined, sensitive being who abhorred coarseness of all kinds, who placed women on a pedestal, and who wrote to no other woman in such a way, then it was the received picture that would have to change. This argument was countered by the obvious one. It was up to those who promoted this correspondence to prove that it was authentic, not up to the rest of the world to prove that it was false.

This was the position taken by Arthur Hedley, Gliński's nemesis. His impassioned assault on the Potocka correspondence may be read in the Appendix to his *Selected Correspondence of Fryderyk Chopin* (1962). For

---

32. Czernicka's ledger book, a stout volume of 262 pages, may be consulted at the Chopin Museum, Warsaw, under the call number M. 418-1960.

years the two scholars opposed each other. Hedley took his case directly to Poland and at an international conference convened in Nieborów (October 1961) specifically to consider the authenticity of the letters, he secured an official endorsement of the view that they were spurious. That endorsement was published in his aforementioned book, and drew widespread attention.[33] The issue might have ended there, but to Hedley's dismay the endorsement was withdrawn at the insistence of certain scholars who wished to "keep an open mind" and the conflict grew in intensity. One of their number was the distinguished editor of Chopin's correspondence Bronisław E. Sydow, who was the secretary-general of the Chopin Society at that time, and during the anniversary year of 1949 had come out with a comprehensive selection of the Potocka letters to which he was clearly prepared to attach his reputation.[34] The problem was that he was also the editor in chief of the forthcoming *Correspondance de Frédéric Chopin*, a comprehensive project in three volumes. The question now arose: Would he include the disputed Potocka letters in what was planned to be a definitive work? That it was his intention to do so is evident from his Preamble to volume one, in which he dealt with their discovery and provenance. He also revealed a rift in the editorial team when he let drop that his co-editors, Suzanne and Denise Chainaye, did not share his views. Sydow's untimely death while the project was still in progress meant that the task of continuing his work passed to these two collaborators. They declined to include the Potocka letters, but hid their reasons in a place that is peculiarly hard to find. The reader with time on his hands is directed to their five-hundred-word exposition in the index to volume two, in small print, tucked away beneath the entry on Delfina Potocka.

Meanwhile, what of Chopin's biographers? One would have hoped that they might have taken their cue from workers in the field, but there were notable exceptions. Casimir Wierzyński, in his widely read biography of

33. HSCC, p. 386. The minutes of the Nieborów conference were never published, despite repeated promises to do so. They may be consulted at the Chopin National Institute under the call number Pr. 5660-64.
34. MFC, pp. 49–73: "Excerpts from the unpublished letters of Chopin." The only authentic letter that Delfina is known to have written to Chopin (dated July 16, 1849, and sent from Aix-la-Chapelle shortly before she visited him in Paris), while showing concern for his health, is couched in formal terms and lacks the sort of language that one lover might address to another in the wake of an intimate affair. It begins "Cher Monsieur Chopin" and is signed "D. Potocka." CFC, vol. 3, pp. 423–24; KFC, vol. 2, p. 306.

Chopin, quotes generously from the Potocka letters without once revealing that their authenticity was suspect—save on the last page of his book where, after briefly acknowledging the tortured history of the topic, he accepted "at their face value the fragments to which he has had access."[35] It is difficult to avoid the conclusion that he did not want the facts to get in the way of a good story. Wierzyński was one of Poland's better-known poets, his book was widely read, was translated into several languages, was reprinted as a paperback in 1971, and was endorsed by Arthur Rubinstein. Ruth Jordan, too, quotes extensively from the Potocka letters in her *Nocturne: A Life of Chopin* (1978), making her book, like that of Wierzyński, a captive of the past. After considering the pros and cons of the matter in her foreword, she nails her colors firmly to the mast by declaring that "the ayes have it,"[36] as if all that had ever been required to solve this problem was to vote on it.

With Hedley's death in 1969 the torch was handed to the Polish scholar Jerzy Maria Smoter, whose book *Spór o'listy' Chopina do Delfiny Potockiej* (Controversy over Chopin's "Letters" to Delfina Potocka), which had been published in 1967 and soon came out in an expanded second edition, now made him the chief spokesman for the opposition, and Gliński's main adversary. Smoter spent years gathering materials related to this problem, and his various writings on it were unequivocal. He considered the Delfina letters to be apocryphal. A kind of stalemate now settled over the field and the various protagonists retired to their respective corners.

In 1973 all that changed when six photocopies of what were claimed to be manuscript fragments of the Potocka letters were published for the first time. The informed public could now see with its own eyes what these materials actually looked like, instead of having to rely on the descriptions of scholars who had only seen typescripts. These images had turned up among the papers of the deceased Polish composer Tadeusz Szeligowski, whose family claimed that Czernicka herself had given them to him in 1947. Who manufactured them and why they were passed to Szeligowski remains unknown, but the implication was that they had all issued from Czernicka's deceptive pen. They were reproduced in *Musical Opinion*[37]

35. WLDC, p. 422.
36. JN, p. 12.
37. Issue of May 1973, in an article titled "Fact or Forgery?"

by Adam Harasowski (a relative of Szeligowski's), who concluded that "they may be authentic," and once again the old enmities flared up. Matters were not helped when newspaper reports in Poland began to circulate, asserting that these images were in Chopin's handwriting. The prospect of a looming press war caused further disquiet. In a last-ditch effort to quell it, Jan Ekier asked the criminology division of the Warsaw Police to conduct a forensic investigation of the photographs. It was carried out by Captain Ryszard Soszalski and Colonel Władysław Wójcik, and their independent conclusions were marked by concision and clarity. They reported that after the images had been enlarged and subjected to microscopic examination, the retouching of individual characters could clearly be observed, together with tell-tale traces of scissor cuts. "It must be assumed that the disputed letters are the results of photomontage," they declared. In brief, they were fabricated.[38]

There were several attempts to reexamine this verdict, including one by the prominent American graphologist Ordway Hilton, who was invited to conduct an independent investigation in the mid-1970s by Chopin's biographers George Marek and Maria Gordon-Smith.[39] Hilton, who could not read Polish, declared that one or two of the photocopies left open the possibility that they might be genuine, without going so far as to say that they actually were; but this cautious view is today discounted in light of the conclusive findings in Warsaw, which have never been upturned. It remains a dreary business to go over ground that has been tilled so thoroughly by three generations of scholars. But such is the fascination exerted by the "Chopin-Potocka affair" that it continues to cast a spell over the literature. But what of the liaison that Chopin and Delfina were supposed to have pursued in the early 1830s, to which Hoesick attached importance, and which may be said to have begun the hue and cry? The chief advantage of this tale to those who cling to it is that it cannot be disproved. In any case, such a scenario does no real harm to the story of Chopin's life— providing we accept that the fabricated "correspondence" that it engendered belongs to a much later time and comes to us to from a perverted hand.

---

38. A judicious summary of the matter was provided by the Polish scholar Wojciech Nowik in his article "The 'Chopin' Letters to Delfina: Meanders of the Controversy Revisited" (Warsaw, 2001), where he writes, "It is possible to declare once and for all that the 'Letters to Delfina' were apocryphal." NCL, p. 189.
39. See "The Hilton Report," in MC, pp. 264–67.

There were always a lot of moving parts to this puzzle, and one still encounters scholars who would like to keep them in motion. But the conclusion today seems clear enough. The material was forged in its entirety by the mythomaniac Paulina Czernicka, and her letters should be described for what they are: a sordid deception.

VIII

As if Chopin's spurious letters to Delfina were not enough for his biographers to contend with, the composer's alleged "Journal" provided plenty of additional material with which to torment them. This matter, too, has a convoluted history, which began more than a hundred years ago. On January 8, 1907, the *Neue Musik-Zeitung* (Leipzig-Stuttgart) published extracts from a document purporting to be Chopin's personal diary, which ought to have sounded the alarm. Its promising German title ran, *Chopins Tagebuchblätter autorisierte Uebersetzung von Helene Wiesenthal*, which may be translated as "Pages from Chopin's Diary: An Authorized Translation by Helene Wiesenthal." Such trivial questions as what was the original language from which Frau Wiesenthal had translated the text, or who had "authorized" her to do it, or even how the document had come into her possession in the first place were swept aside on a tide of euphoria, the search for answers happily postponed for a later day. Here was a text of inestimable value, or so it seemed, one that might afford a glimpse into Chopin's private life with George Sand hitherto closed to us.

The journal made the rounds of the international press and within a few short months it had provoked a full-blown essay by one Gaston Knosp in *Le Guide musical* (September 8–15, 1907), with the diary extracts translated into French and bearing the unambiguous title "Le Journal de Chopin." "The sheets of this handwritten Journal have just been found," the article proclaimed. "Written in Polish, these sheets shed an entirely new light on certain questions that, until now, were part of legend and fantasy." Skeptics had already pointed out when the journal first appeared in its German version that there were things in it, such as dates and names, that did not chime with reality. The confusion of times, persons, and places was too great. Against these charges M. Knosp mounted a stout defense, the burden of which appeared to be that all one had to do was to modify one or two facts and the journal could be made to come true. He sought to have its authenticity endorsed by leading Chopin scholars—including Hugo Leichtentritt, who, so we were told, pronounced the document genuine. And by informing his readers in advance that the text of the journal was written in Polish, Chopin's mother tongue, a statement that later turned out to be false, Knosp was able to remove the sharpest arrow from his opponents' quiver, at least for a time.

One of the first entries, dated "Paris, October 10, 1837," shows us what we are in for:

> I have had three further meetings with her. It seems like only yesterday. She gazed deep into my eyes while I played. I had chosen some rather sad music . . . She leaned on the piano. Her eyes were like a fiery flood . . . My heart was captured! . . . She loves me . . . Aurore [George Sand], what a lovely name! Like the dawn it banishes the darkness.

The banality of the language aside, Chopin had no meetings with Sand in 1837, despite her repeated invitations for him to join her in Nohant. Save for seven days in early January, Sand was not even in Paris that year.

> Majorca, November 16, 1838
> Our two souls are alone on this island in the middle of the sea. At night, I lie down and listen to the sound of the waves over the pebbles. Rebecca Stirling came to visit us. She brought some violets, some large English violets. Their perfume overwhelms me day and night in this humid monastic cell. The convent is cold and dark, the wind blows in through the cracks in the doors which creak all night long. It is freezing.

Miss Stirling never visited Majorca. And the spectacle of her doing so while Chopin and Sand were in the middle of their "island honeymoon" does not bear contemplation. Chopin and Stirling were not to meet until 1843, and just how she managed to convey a bunch of English violets all the way from Britain to Majorca without having them wilt in her hands is a question best left unaddressed. And why would Chopin call Miss Stirling "Rebecca" when everyone knew that her name was Jane? M. Knosp conceded that this was rather odd but assumed that there must be some symbolic significance to the name Rebecca that scholarship would require time to sort out. One other small point also escaped notice. Chopin and Sand did not arrive at the Valldemosa monastery until December 15. Yet here we find Chopin complaining about his drafty cell one month before he had actually seen it.

The last extract, perhaps the most bizarre of them all, was dispatched from a place called "Castle Stirling."

> Castle Stirling, June 16, 1848
>
> Cruelly, my soul curses you, repulses you! Aurore, your kisses burn me like fire. What uneasiness seizes me! Shall I ever have rest? Earth from Poland will soon cover me. This silver urn contains a handful of it. I can take it in my hands! Dear country with the musical soul! This handful of earth from thy fertile fields is always near me. They are to throw it into my grave, on my breast—on that dead and tormented burden. But the burning, beating heart, they must take from me nerve by nerve, and send it back to the land from whence it came—dear Poland!

On June 16, Chopin was in London, not in Scotland, a country in which he had not yet set foot. And when he got there, during the first week of August, he stayed in Calder House, not "Castle Stirling," an odd description of the medieval fortress that dominates Stirling, a city Chopin never visited. As for the silver urn containing a handful of Polish earth destined to be buried along with him, the idea never came up for discussion during his lifetime, but only presented itself one year after Chopin's funeral when, as we have seen, it was thought fitting that some Polish earth should be sent from Warsaw and scattered over his grave when his memorial statue was unveiled at Père Lachaise Cemetery, on October 17, 1850, an event still more than two years away.

It would also have come as a surprise to Chopin to learn, in June 1848, that his heart was to be removed and sent to Warsaw. He took that decision shortly before his demise more than a year later—another proof that the journal was written by a strange hand, long after the events it purports to describe. As for the invocation to "Aurore," Sand would surely have recoiled from this use of her first name. Neither Chopin nor any of her lovers were known to have addressed her in this way. Whoever wrote the journal knew enough about the main facts of Chopin's life to make it believable to the general reader, but not enough to avoid getting themselves into difficulties when the text was put under scrutiny. But who had manufactured the document?

Attention turned to Frau Helene Wiesenthal, who, when pressed to identify the person who had supplied her with Chopin's "Journal," replied that she had translated it from an English text given to her by an American novelist, Miss Jeanette Lee from Northampton, Massachusetts. This explained much, for the journal entries did indeed read like a Harlequin romance. Frau Wiesenthal cheerfully informed her interlocutors that it was one of many similar articles she had translated from English into German for this particular author. What no one had told her, evidently, was that Chopin could hardly speak a word of English, and it was this revelation that set the alarm bells ringing. When asked to provide further information about "Jeanette Lee," there was a prolonged delay before Frau Wiesenthal came back with the unfortunate news that she had lost touch with Miss Lee and could not find her address—the same writer for whom she had been the "authorized translator" of not one but several articles. That led Nicolas Slonimsky, who wrote an entertaining exposé of the whole business, to describe Chopin's "Journal" as "Frau Wiesenthal's little invention."[40] Among the first to cast doubt on the document following its appearance in the *Musik-Zeitung* had been the Polish pianist Moriz Rosenthal. He had drawn attention to certain similarities between the text of the journal and the German edition of Karasowski's *Life of Chopin*— that same "weaver of legends" we considered earlier—which prompted the editor of the magazine *Die Musik* to invite Ferdynand Hoesick to enter the dispute. Hoesick prosecuted the case with such vigor, in an essay that extended to six thousand words, that no other conclusion was possible than that the document had been manufactured.[41] Gaston Knosp finally did his duty, donned the required sackcloth and ashes, and made a public recantation. His retraction was published in *Le Mercure musical* (April 15, 1909). "*Eh bien, et malgré tout, ce 'Journal' est apocryphe,*" he lamented ("Well, despite everything, this 'Journal' is apocryphal").

None of this would be of more than passing interest today were it not

---

40. *The Musical Quarterly*, October 1948.
41. "Ein angebliches Tagebuch Chopin's," *Die Musik*, Band XXIX, 1908–1909.

for the fact that passages from the journal continue to find their way into the literature long after it was exposed as a forgery. Some distinguished names in the fields of Chopin and Sand biography have fallen victim to it. André Maurois and Louise Vincent, irreplaceable Sand scholars both, are among the prominent casualties; and Tad Szulc's *Chopin in Paris* (published just in time to usher in the twenty-first century) also succumbed to the spell of its siren song. As long as their work continues to be read and cited, the deception will enjoy an afterlife. The lovelorn language of the journal will always find a home in those romantic biographies that see in Chopin little more than a perfumed dreamer. Chopin's "Journal" should be allowed to come to rest where it belongs: among the common rubble of banalities.

IX

In language both eloquent and poetic, Samuel Taylor Coleridge reminds us that history is "a lantern on the stern, which shines only on the waves behind us," even as the vessel continues its journey into the darkness. It is a compelling image, for it implies that the voyage of discovery is never ending. That is especially true for the biographer of Chopin who has always been plagued with contradictions and ambiguities, as the foregoing Epilogue has amply demonstrated. Still, we would not readily forgo a retrospective survey such as this, for it shows that the events in Chopin's posthumous life often exceeded in sheer fascination anything that he experienced in the life that he actually lived.

Few more dramatic scenes could have been illuminated by that "lantern on the stern" than the one that unfolded near midnight on April 14, 2014, in Warsaw's Church of the Holy Cross. After the last of the worshippers had left, a small group of specially selected witnesses gathered to observe the exhumation of Chopin's heart from its resting place behind one of the stone pillars inside the church. They included the archbishop of Warsaw, the minister of culture, the director of the Chopin National Institute, and two forensic scientists. It was a closely guarded ceremony from which the press was excluded. Many photographs were taken and hot wax was applied to the seals of the jar containing the heart to prevent possible evaporation of the contents. Those taking part in the ceremony were sworn to secrecy, and the fact that it had taken place at all was not revealed to the media until the following September—a delay of five months. There was a predictable outcry from those who felt that the exhumation should have been witnessed by international observers, and the heart inspected by independent forensic experts. The Associated Press was given selective photographs of the heart, which showed an enlarged white organ floating in a crystal jar of amber fluid, thought to be cognac. A visual inspection of the contents revealed the presence of membrane vesicles associated with tuberculosis. Dr. Tadeusz Dobosz, one of the forensic scientists present at the exhumation, confirmed this observation and described the occasion as more spiritual than scientific. "The spirit of the night was sublime!" he told the Associated Press.[42] Before the heart was returned to its resting place, the archbishop said prayers over it and blessed it. By the following morning all traces of the exhumation had been removed and visitors to the church were unaware that anything had happened.

But why had this exhumation taken place at all? For some years the Polish government had resisted requests to allow samples of Chopin's heart to be removed for genetic testing, which might determine the exact cause of his death. Several medical experts had come forward with the idea that it was cystic fibrosis and not tuberculosis that had ravaged Chopin's health and killed him. Cystic fibrosis was not identified as an illness in Chopin's time, and its symptoms were often masked by those of tuberculosis. A tissue sample might settle the matter one way or the other. But to tamper with Chopin's heart risked destroying it. The powerful emotions that the Poles have always felt for Chopin steered public sentiment away from the idea of disturbing this iconic object, an act that for many would have amounted to a desecration. Chopin's body might be in France, but his heart was now in Poland and it had found a sanctuary in the Church of the Holy Cross, where, with one or two interruptions, it had remained undisturbed since its consecration there in February 1880.

These "one or two interruptions" cannot be glossed over, because they form an essential part of the story and continue to provoke strong passions. After Ludwika had brought the heart to Warsaw from Paris, it remained in the joint custody of Chopin's mother and Ludwika herself, before being

42. Associated Press release, November 17, 2014.

placed in the catacombs of the Church of the Holy Cross, probably at the instigation of Ludwika shortly before her death in 1855, with neither plaque nor inscription to identify it. A journalist named Adam Pług came across it there in a box, in 1878, and drew attention to it in an article in a Warsaw journal.[43] His piece aroused widespread interest and stirred the national conscience. On Sunday, February 29, 1880, the heart was brought into the main church and formally consecrated. It was placed within a main pillar of the church, behind an imposing marble tablet dedicated to Chopin's memory, unveiled one week later on March 5, his name day. But it did not remain there.

During World War II, at the height of the fighting in Poland and with much of Warsaw facing destruction in reprisal for the September Rising of 1944, the heart was taken into safekeeping by a music-loving German officer, General Erich von dem Bach-Zelewski, who even as he sheltered the relic was busily engaged in the slaughter of 200,000 Poles. It was yet another bizarre twist to the story. The man who saved Chopin's heart from destruction was the man responsible for that destruction. Shortly before the demolition of the Holy Cross Church began, General Bach-Zelewski arranged that the heart be given for safekeeping to the archbishop of Warsaw, Antoni Szlagowski, who in turn entrusted it to the clerics of St. Hedwig's Church in Milanówek, a country suburb of Warsaw; it was escorted there by a contingent of German soldiers, an event captured on a Nazi propaganda film, and it remained there until war's end. Milanówek happened to be the place where Bronisław Sydow, the future editor of Chopin's letters, lived, and it is to him that we owe one of the best descriptions of the heart to come down to us. He requested that this national relic be inspected and that he be allowed to see the urn for himself. Within a smooth, dark-stained outer oak casket, wrote Sydow, was contained a second, polished ebony casket decorated with marquetry. "On the lid was a heart-shaped silver plate inscribed with Fryderyk Chopin's name and his birth and death dates. Inside that casket was a large crystal jar, hermetically sealed, containing Chopin's heart, perfectly preserved in clear alcohol. One is struck by the size of the heart, inordi-

---

43. In the illustrated magazine *Kłosy*, January 1, 1879, p. 62. "Adam Pług" was the pseudonym of the magazine's editor, the well-known writer Antoni Pietkiewicz. His curiosity had been aroused by an article published two months earlier in the *Warsaw Gazette*, on November 7, 1878, that stated the heart remained somewhere "in one of the Warsaw churches."

The Reverend Leopold Petrzyk carries Chopin's heart past a guard of honor toward the birth house at Żelazowa Wola, October 17, 1945.

nately large for a person of medium height, presumably due to the heart disease that was the chief contributing factor in Chopin's premature death, alongside tuberculosis."[44] With the war now ended, Sydow, in his capacity as the secretary-general of the Fryderyk Chopin Society, approached the newly installed Communist government in Warsaw for permission to arrange a ceremonial return of the heart to its original home in the Church of the Holy Cross, which was just then in the process of being restored from the pile of rubble left behind after the defeat of the Nazis. The new government saw a political advantage in this idea and indulged in an outbreak of patriotic pride by planning a route from Milanówek to the Church of the Holy Cross in Warsaw that was fit for a head of state.

On October 17, 1945, a day that marked the ninety-sixth anniversary of Chopin's death, the heart was brought back to the Polish capital via Żelazowa Wola, a circuitous route of more than ninety kilometers, with crowds lining the roads and national flags adorning every house. Hundreds of people converged on Żelazowa Wola itself to celebrate the event. In the

---

44. Sydow's report, part of a larger document compiled by Mieczysław Idzikowski and dated February 9, 1946, is preserved in the Chopin National Institute under the call number 6559.

absence of public transport many of them walked, some used bicycles, while others arrived on the backs of farming trucks. Many photographs were taken showing crowds milling around the place of Chopin's birth, and it is difficult to avoid the conclusion that the event was stage-managed. At seven o'clock on the morning of the solemnities, a mass was conducted in Milanówek by Archbishop Szlagowski, who made a brief speech before handing the casket to the Reverend Leopold Petrzyk, a rector of the Church of the Holy Cross. "A year ago I removed this great Pole's heart from the flames of Warsaw . . . Restore it to its place . . . may it be a symbol of the indomitable spirit of our nation. *Dixi*."[45] Reverend Petrzyk then carried the casket to a waiting car for the journey to Żelazowa Wola. Along the way something unusual happened. The car carrying the casket was passed by a faster-moving column of cars bearing leading members of the government. After continuing for a short distance the column stopped, letting Chopin's heart pass to the front and lead the way to Żelazowa Wola. There a Polish military guard of honor had been mustered, and stood to attention as the cars came to a standstill. A photograph taken at that moment shows Reverend Petrzyk carrying the casket along the driveway leading up to the house, accompanied by Bronisław Sydow (left) and the Polish pianist Bolesław Woytowicz (page 669).

Various delegates from the government and foreign embassies were waiting in the small dwelling to witness the ceremony that followed. The casket was set on a plinth covered in flowers with a portrait of the composer in the background. Father Leopold Petrzyk, speaking on behalf of Archbishop Szlagowski, presented the heart to President Bolesław Bierut of the National People's Council, who, after making a brief speech, passed the relic to the mayor of Warsaw. The dignitaries then moved to the next room, where a short piano recital had been prepared by the noted Polish pianist Henryk Sztompka, who had earlier been a pupil of Paderewski's, and who played among other things the A-flat major Polonaise, op. 53, and the *Lento con gran espressione* (the "Reminiscence" Nocturne).

Later that day the convoy bearing Chopin's heart set out for Warsaw and the Church of the Holy Cross, where a commemorative service was held in the afternoon and broadcast to the nation. The packed congregation included both the president and the prime minister of Poland, together

---

45. "*Dixi*—I have spoken." MDT.

with representatives from several countries, among them the British and American ambassadors. The service was conducted by Reverend Petrzyk and included a memorable eulogy by the cleric and musicologist Father Hieronim Feicht. "Chopin's heart is not an object of liturgical devotion," he noted, "but an object of national devotion, comparable with the remains of kings, whom the musical maestro rivaled and even surpassed in greatness."[46] The heart was then returned to its original resting place within the same stone pillar, which now bore a newly restored marble plaque, where it remained undisturbed until the aforementioned exhumation on April 14, 2014. In retrospect these celebrations represented a crowning moment in Chopin's posthumous career. The church, the state, the military, and the population at large all paid homage to him that day. These events still exert their patriotic influence whenever permission to take tissue samples from the heart is sought and denied. The minister of culture, Bogdan Zdrojewski, spoke for the majority when he uttered words on which it is hard to improve: "Additional information that might possibly be gained about his death would not be a reason to disturb Chopin's heart."[47]

Another inspection of the heart was promised to take place fifty years after the most recent one—that is, in 2064—by which time all the actors in the drama will have passed away. Of one thing we may be certain: as that date approaches, Coleridge's "lantern on the stern" will have brought to light many more of those Chopin cameos that seem to shine only in history's wake. The composer's posthumous Odyssey will meanwhile continue on its journey into the boundless realms of the future, while his music brings pleasure and solace to generations as yet unborn.

---

46. *Wolna Polska*, October 30, 1945.
47. Associated Press release, November 17, 2014.

APPENDIX:
LISZT'S QUESTIONNAIRE
CONCERNING HIS LIFE
OF CHOPIN

ADDRESSED TO MME JĘDRZEJEWICZ,
NÉE LUDWIKA CHOPIN
DATED NOVEMBER 14, 1849

Jane Stirling was placed in an awkward position when Chopin's sister Ludwika passed along to her the unwelcome task of replying to the questionnaire that Liszt had sent in connection with the composer's death. Stirling did her best to reply and the document has attracted some interest across the years. It was the first time that anyone had attempted to gain so much information about Chopin from a primary source.

The questions that Liszt asked about Chopin's liaison with George Sand were indiscreet, coming as they did only two weeks after Chopin's funeral and with Sand herself still very much alive. Liszt clearly thought that he had a right to ask them (he says as much in the questionnaire) because he had introduced Chopin and Sand to each other in the first place, and had watched the affair flourish before witnessing its demise. As we read through the document, it is difficult to avoid the conclusion that Liszt and Stirling were playing a game of cat and mouse on some of the issues. Liszt had read Sand's novel *Lucrezia Floriani* from cover to cover and knew full well that it was an account of her declining relationship with Chopin dressed as fiction. Yet this did not prevent him from asking, "Can one believe that the romance of Lucrezia Floriani with the Prince, which is supposed to be the story of their intimate relations, is true?" Stirling, who had also read the book and knew it to be true in all the essential details, was not about to endorse its veracity for Liszt. Instead she fell back on some weasel words: "[Chopin] exercised so much delicacy and integrity in all his relations that it would be very difficult to see him in these intimate pages."

Stirling's replies to some of Liszt's questions are reserved, others are sanitized, while one or two of the rest are laced with hostility. When Liszt idly wonders, for example, if the rumor was true that Chopin had asked to be buried in his concert dress, her response could hardly mask the sarcasm that lay behind it. She replied that anybody who had met Chopin just once would know that he would not waste time fretting about what to wear in the coffin as he went to meet his Maker. And when she reminded Liszt, who had inquired about the nature and number of Chopin's public concerts, that Chopin preferred to avoid the "salons of spectacle," it is not hard to see it as a reprimand to the great pianist himself, who was very much at home in them.

Liszt appears to have made scant use of Stirling's responses, as an inspection of his Chopin biography shows. But the questionnaire remains valuable because of the nature of the interrogations. The original document is missing. Fortunately, Stirling made a copy and sent it back to Ludwika in Poland, probably for her seal of approval. The manuscript was discovered in Warsaw by Mieczysław Karłowicz, who published it in 1904, together with Jane Stirling's answers,[1] and it is today in the collection of the Chopin Museum under the call number M/328.

Question 1
The date and place of his birth.

Question 2
What was his childhood like? Is there any anecdote or circumstance attached to it that might characterize his tastes and habits during that period?

Answers 1 and 2
The first and second questions can only be answered by the memories of his mother, who is still living. The recollections of Chopin's contemporaries are not enough to satisfy fully these two requests.

Question 3
When did his musical gifts first appear, and what were his first studies? Were they difficult for him? Was he accustomed to improvise from an early age?

Answer 3
His first piano studies already revealed his extraordinary musical gifts. In approaching the principles of harmony, one could say that he was recalling a forgotten skill rather than learning it for the first time. Perhaps because of his physical weakness improvisation fatigued him less than written composition, the perfecting of which never met the demands of his exquisite taste.

Question 4
In what college or school was he placed? Do we know the names of those of his classmates he liked most? Was not his musical talent already very well known and appreciated at that time? Was he not often invited by his friends' parents, whom he charmed with his talent and his mind? And did he not, around 1824, frequent the home of Princess [Ludwika] Czetwertyńska, among others, whose sons were his schoolmates? And was he at Princess [Joanna] Łowicka's residence, and the other great salons of Warsaw?

---

1. KFSC, pp. 200–203.

Answer 4

His father, a very learned man, was connected to the University of Warsaw, which, at the time of Chopin's education, had professors of high distinction. The training he received at home had already developed his aptitudes in a remarkable manner. He was greatly loved by all his schoolmates. Throughout his life he retained a lasting memory of them, and all who met him again in Paris were able to testify to the eagerness with which he sought to renew their former intimacy and to recall the memories of youth. His precocious talent opened the great salons of Warsaw for him. The Grand Duke Constantine himself and his wife took a keen pleasure in following the astonishing development of the marvelous child.

Question 5

Was he interested in any way in the Revolution of 1830? Where was he in November 1830 and during the following year? For what reason did he then depart from Poland? Did he leave his father and mother there? Did he maintain relations with them thereafter? Where did he then go upon leaving the country and what were his plans? How many concerts did he give in Vienna and Munich, and what was his purpose in giving them? Was this the first time he was heard in public or the first time that he gave concerts?

Answer 5

He was never involved in any of his country's political events. He had already left Poland in November 1830, and he never returned. He was too good a Pole to separate himself from his outlawed brothers. As a devoted son, however, the separation from his family caused him suffering. Death snatched his father away four years ago [five, in fact], and he never ceased to mourn him, in tender memory of the domestic hearth, with tears that flowed from the inexhaustible spring of his heart. Then, just as today, his sister Ludwika rushed hundreds of miles in order to lavish on him, with sublime affection, the solicitude that no weariness could weaken.

Before leaving Warsaw, Chopin gave several concerts and he did the same while traveling from Vienna to Paris. But even the greatest success of his concerts never allowed him to overcome his aversion to exploiting his talent in this way. His genius needed more independence than a nondescript public usually allows, which comes with vague demands and preconceived preferences. It understands with difficulty whatever lies off the beaten track, and it makes the artist or the poet descend to its level rather than have it rise to his. Moreover, the kind of effect produced not only by the intimate nature of his creative work but also by his marvelous playing, could not bear the glaring light of the salons of spectacle.

Question 6

What Polish families did he cultivate the most during his stay in Paris? Of what friends was he most fond in his last days?

My intimate association with Chopin gives me the right, perhaps, to ask you a few questions about his relations with Mme Sand? I should also like to have some details about his trip to the island of Majorca and the impression he retained from it. What time of life left him the sweetest memory? And what persons remained dearest to him during his final moments?

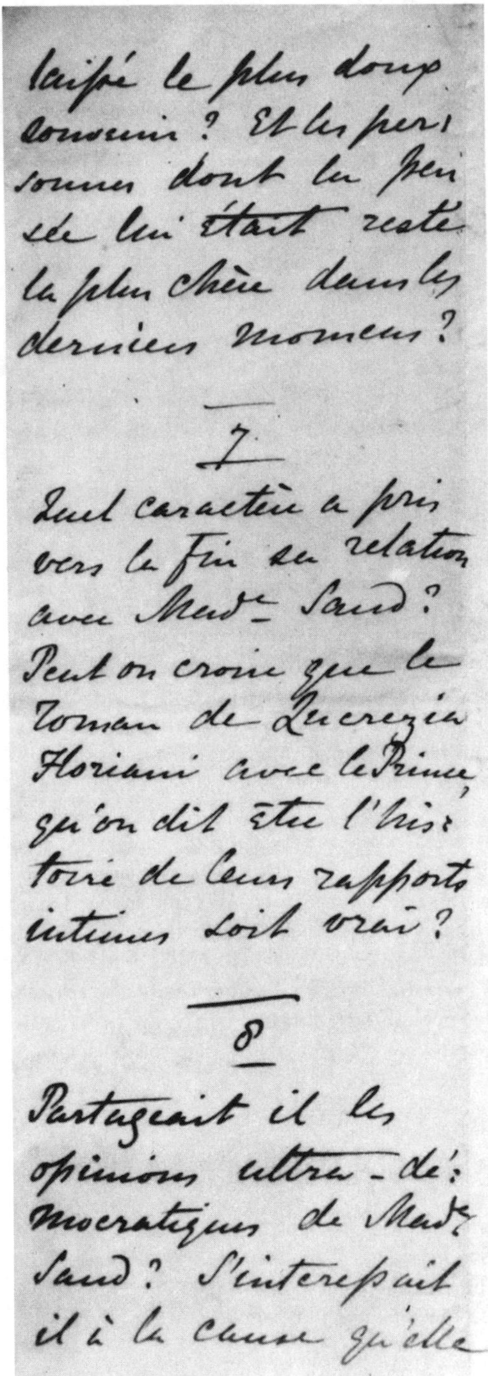

laissé le plus doux
souvenir? Et les per=
sonnes dont la pen=
sée lui était restée
la plus chère dans les
derniers momens?

—

7

Quel caractère a pris
vers la fin sa relation
avec Made Sand?
Peut on croire que le
roman de Lucrezia
Floriani avec le Prince
qu'on dit être l'his=
toire de leurs rapports
intimes soit vrai?

—

8

Partageait il les
opinions ultra – dé=
mocratiques de Made
Sand? S'interessait
il à la cause qu'elle

A page of Jane Stirling's copy
of Liszt's questionnaire.

Answer 6

All the Polish families living in Paris cherished him. He was welcome everywhere, from the Hôtel Lambert to the most modest abode. And during the three days of sacred agony all these families knelt at the foot of his bed, sharing their tears and their sorrows. Nothing better forms an opinion on the value of a life than such a death as this.

Question 7

What was the nature of his connection with Mme Sand toward the end? Can one believe that the romance of Lucrezia Floriani with the Prince, which is said to be the story of their intimate relations, is true?

Answer 7

Chopin's intimate life was a sanctuary that for him was equally intimate. He was too sparing of details for them to find a place in his biography. He fell gravely ill during his journey to the island of Majorca, and his strength was never able to return to normal. Inevitably his spirits, formerly so buoyant, succumbed to this situation more and more day by day. He was too elevated and too refined to willingly acknowledge the allusions to himself as the prince-hero of the novel *Lucrezia Floriani*, for he exercised so much delicacy and integrity in all his relations that it would be very difficult to see him in those intimate pages.

Question 8

Did he share Mme Sand's ultrademocratic opinions? Was he interested in the causes she supported? What were his relations with Louis Blanc, Ledru-Rollin, and other celebrities in Mme Sand's circle?

Answer 8

His political opinions had nothing in common with the exaggerated views of the persons mentioned. He made no propaganda and none was brought to bear on him—it would have made no difference anyway. He had too clear a mind not to sense the evils of the time, too great a heart to remain indifferent to them, and too much judgment to entangle himself in this kind of political unrest.

Question 9

Had he already broken off his liaison with her [Sand] in February 1848? And is it possible to determine the causes of this rupture? Was it violent or was it amicable? Did he suffer from it or was it easy for him? Did he often stay at Nohant, and was this particular visit agreeable for him?

When did he see Mme Sand for the last time? Did he request to see her?

Did he speak about her and with what sort of feelings before dying?

Answer 9

It appears that the marriage of Mme Sand's daughter [Solange] made this period rather difficult for the mother, so that Chopin's stay at Nohant could not continue without grave consequences. The daughter was dutifully present at his death. The mother was not in Paris. He did not speak of her in his last hours.

Question 10
Why did he go to London in 1848? How long did he stay there? Why did he return? Is the anecdote authentic that was reported to me by M. Schlesinger, about the lessons he gave to Queen Victoria, who took them in Chopin's quarters since he was too ill to go out?

Answer 10
Drawn to England by some friends, he stayed there for eight months; but the climate became fatal for him. He never reported anything extraordinary about his relations with the high personages of that country, except that they were extremely kind to him.

Question 11
From what year did his chest ailment date? How were his spirits in his final moments? Did he regret life? Did he watch the approach of death with terror? When did he stop composing? Did he express the desire to go on writing when he could no longer do so? Did he leave any unfinished works, and of what kind?

Answer 11
The autopsy revealed nothing about the basic cause of his death. The chest seemed to be less involved than the heart. It was the death of a pure soul, resigned and believing. Not the slightest cloud from beyond the tomb came to darken his final moments. All his features rested confident in faith and love. He left precise instructions that consigned his unpublished compositions to the flames.

Question 12
How were his last moments? It was reported by the music journals that he asked to be dressed in his concert clothes when he felt death approaching. Is that true?
　　　Did he receive the last rites? Did he ask for them or refuse them? And what priest came to his bed as he lay dying?

Answer 12
It is enough to have seen Chopin only once in his lifetime in order to believe him incapable of such pettiness of mind as to worry about his choice of apparel while awaiting death. He received it like a good Catholic, having made all his devotions under the guidance and ministrations of his old friend, the Abbé Jełowicki.

GENERAL CATALOGUE
OF CHOPIN'S WORKS
(LISTED IN ALPHABETICAL ORDER)

The compilation of a complete catalogue of Chopin's compositions is still a work in progress, with questionable dates not yet settled and lacunae not yet filled. The two most reliable thematic catalogues are by Krystyna Kobylańska (German edition of 1979) and by Chomiński and Turło (Polish edition of 1990). I have followed the Chomiński-Turło chronology in the main, but have made some minor changes where more recent research has superseded theirs. Maurice Brown's pioneering *Chopin: An Index of His Works in Chronological Order* has also been included in this survey. While it must give ground where the later catalogues contradict it, it happens to be the only publication of its kind in the English language, contains information that cannot be found elsewhere, and is still widely consulted today. I have brought all three catalogues into concordance with one another, which may be helpful to those readers who require more information than a simple alphabetical list of titles can offer.

CT = Chomiński-Turło[1]
KK = Kobylańska[2]
MB = Brown[3]

---

1. Józef Michał Chomiński and Teresa Dalila Turło. *Katalogue dzieł Fryderyka Chopina* (A Catalogue of the Works of Fryderyk Chopin). Warsaw, 1990.
2. Krystyna Kobylańska. *Frédéric Chopin. Thematisch-Bibliographisches Werkverzeichnis.* Translated from the original Polish edition (1977) by Helmut Stolze. Munich, 1979.
3. Maurice J. E. Brown. *Chopin: An Index of His Works in Chronological Order.* London, 1972.

TITLE	OP. NO.	DATE OF COMPOSITION	DATE OF FIRST PUBLICATION	DEDICATION	CT	KK	MB
			Pianoforte Solo				
Allegro de Concert in A major	46	1834–41	1841	Friederike Müller	1	673–78	72
Andante Spianato in G major	22	1830–35	1836	Baroness Frances Sarah d'Este	149	268–72	88
Andantino in G minor (arr. of Chopin's song "Wiosna" [Spring])	74:2	1838–48 (five versions)	1968		130	1101	117
Ballades							
in G minor	23	1835 (sketched 1831)	1836	Baron Nathaniel von Stockhausen	2	273–79	66
in F major	38	1839	1840	Robert Schumann	3	601–609	102
in A-flat major	47	1841	1841	Mlle Pauline de Noailles	4	679–87	136
in F minor	52	1842	1843	Baroness Charlotte de Rothschild	5	732–38	146
Barcarolle in F-sharp major	60	1845–46	1846	Baroness Stockhausen	6	807–14	158
Berceuse in D-flat major	57	1844	1845	Mlle Élise Gavard	7	774–82	154
Bolero	19	1833	1834	Countess Émilie de Flahault	8	246–49	81
Bourrées (two arrangements)	—	1846	1968		—	1403–1404	160B
Canon at the octave in F minor	—	1839	Unpublished		—	1241	129B
Cantabile in B-flat major	—	1834	1931		9	1230	84
Contrabass Part (to a three-part Canon in B minor by Mendelssohn)	—		1930 (facsimile)			1411	69

Pianoforte Solo

TITLE	OP. NO.	DATE OF COMPOSITION	DATE OF FIRST PUBLICATION	DEDICATION	CT	KK	MB
Contredanse in G-flat major	–	1827	1934 (facsimile)		–	1391	17
Écossaises	72:3	1829	1855		11–13	1069–85	12
in D major							
in G major							
in D-flat major							
Fantaisie in F minor	49	1841	1841	Princess Catherine de Souzzo	42	702–707	137
Fantaisie-Impromptu in C-sharp minor	66	1834	1855	Baroness Frances Sarah d'Est	46	932–39	87
Fugue in A minor	–	1841	1898		(p. 238)	1408	144
Impromptus							
in A-flat major	29	1837	1838	Countess Caroline de Lobau	43	479–84	110
in F-sharp major	36	1839	1840		44	581–87	129
in G-flat major	51	1842	1843	Countess Joanne Esterházy	45	723–31	149
Largo in E-flat major	–	1847	1938		49	1229	109
Marches							
Military March	–	1817	1817		–	890	2
Funeral March	72:2	1826	1855		50	1059–68	20
Funeral March from the Sonata in B-flat minor	–	1837	1840		202	570–80	114

Pianoforte Solo

Mazurkas

TITLE	OP. NO.	DATE OF COMPOSITION	DATE OF FIRST PUBLICATION	DEDICATION	CT	KK	MB
Two Mazurkas in G major in B-flat major	–	1826	1826		100–101	891–900	16
in G major	–	1829	1879		102	1201–1202	39
in A minor	70:2	1829	1902				
Four Mazurkas in F-sharp minor in C-sharp minor in E major in E-flat minor	6	1830	1832	Countess Pauline Plater	51–54	26–46	60
Five Mazurkas in B-flat major in A minor (second version) in F minor in A-flat major (composed in 1824; rev.) in C major	7	1830–31	1832	Paul Emile Johns of New Orleans	55–60	47–79	61
in D major (second version)	–	1832	1880		–	1224	71
in B-flat major	–	1832	1909	Mlle Alexandrine Wolowska	103	1223	73
Four Mazurkas in B-flat major in E minor	17	1832–33	1834	Mme Lina Freppa	60–63	220–36	77

TITLE	OP. NO.	DATE OF COMPOSITION	DATE OF FIRST PUBLICATION	DEDICATION	CT	KK	ME
in A-flat major							
in A minor							
			Pianoforte Solo				
in C major	–	1833	1870		–	1225–26	82
in A-flat major	–	1834	1930		–	1227–28	85
Four Mazurkas	24	1833	1836	Count Léon-Amable de Perthuis	64–67	280–96	89
in G minor							
in C major							
in A-flat major							
in B-flat minor							
Four Mazurkas	30	1837	1838	Princess Maria de Württemberg	68–71	485–504	105
in C minor							
in B minor							
in D-flat major							
in C-sharp minor							
Four Mazurkas	33	1838	1838	Countess Róża Mostowska	72–75	520–48	115
in G-sharp minor							
in D major							
in C major							
in B minor							
Four Mazurkas	41	1838–39	1840	Stefan Witwicki	76–79	626–45	122
in E minor							126
in B major							126
in A-flat major							

TITLE	OP. NO.	DATE OF COMPOSITION	DATE OF FIRST PUBLICATION Pianoforte Solo	DEDICATION	CT	KK	MB
in C-sharp minor							126
in A minor ("Notre temps")	–	1840	1842		106	918	134
in A minor	–	1840	1841		105	919–24	140
Three Mazurkas	50	1842	1842	Émile Gaillard	80–82	708–22	145
in G major				Léon Szmitkowski			
in A-flat major							
in C-sharp minor							
Three Mazurkas	56	1843	1844	Catherine Maberly	83–85	761–73	153
in B major							
in C major							
in C minor							
Three Mazurkas	59	1845	1845		86–88	791–806	157
in A minor							
in A-flat major							
in F-sharp minor							
Three Mazurkas	63	1846	1847	Countess Laura Czosnowska	89–91	836–48	162
in B major							
in F minor							
in C-sharp minor							
Four Mazurkas	67	c. 1835	1855	Mlle Anna Mlokosiewicz	92–95	940–65	93
in G major		1848–49		Mme Klementyna Hoffman			167
in G minor		1835					93
in C major		1846					163
in A minor							

TITLE	OP. NO.	DATE OF COMPOSITION	DATE OF FIRST PUBLICATION	DEDICATION	CT	KK	MB
			Pianoforte Solo				
Four Mazurkas	68		1855		96–99	966–87	
in C major		c. 1830					38
in A minor		c. 1827					18
in F major		c. 1830					34
in F minor		c. 1846					168
Moderato in E major ("Album Leaf")	—	1843–44	1910	Countess Anna Szeremetieff	107	1240	151
Nocturnes							
in E minor	72:1	1827–30	1855		126	1055–58	19
in C-sharp minor (*Lento con gran espressione*)	—	1830	1875	Ludwika Chopin	127	1215–22	49
Three Nocturnes	9	1830–31	1832	Mme Camille Pleyel	108–10	87–108	54
in B-flat minor							
in E-flat major							
in B major							
Three Nocturnes	15	1830–33	1833	Ferdinand Hiller	111–13	198–215	55
in F major							55
in F-sharp major							55
in G minor		1833	1833				79
Two Nocturnes	27	1835	1836	Countess Thérèse d'Apponyi	114–15	357–69	
in C-sharp minor							91
in D-flat major							96
Two Nocturnes	32	1836–37	1837	Baroness Camille de Billing	116–17	510–19	106
in B major							
in A-flat major							106
in C minor	—	1847	1938		128	1233–35	108

Pianoforte Solo

TITLE	OP. NO.	DATE OF COMPOSITION	DATE OF FIRST PUBLICATION	DEDICATION	CT	KK	MB
Two Nocturnes	37				118–19	588–600	
in G minor		1838	1840				119
in G major		1839	1840				127
Two Nocturnes	48	1841	1841	Mlle Laure Duperré	120–21	688–701	142
in C minor							
in F-sharp minor							
Two Nocturnes	55	1843	1844	Jane Stirling	122–23	749–60	152
in F minor							
in E-flat major							
Two Nocturnes	62	1846	1846	Mlle de Könneritz	124–25	822–35	161
in B major							
in E major							
Polonaises							
in G minor	–	1817	1817	Countess Wiktoria Skarbek	161	889	1
in B-flat major	–	1817	1934 (facsimile)		160	1182–83	3
in A-flat major	–	1821	1902	Wojciech Żywny	162	1184	5
in G-sharp minor	–	1822	1864	Mme Ludwika Dupont	163	1185–87	6
in B-flat minor	–	1826	1881	Wilhelm Kolberg	164	1188–89	13
in D minor	71:1	1825	1855	Count Michał Skarbek	157	1034–54	11
in B-flat major	71:2	1828	1855		158	1034–54	24
in F minor	71:3	1828	1855		159	1034–54	30
in G-flat major	–	1829	1870		165	1197–1200	36

TITLE	OP. NO.	DATE OF COMPOSITION	DATE OF FIRST PUBLICATION	DEDICATION	CT	KK	MB
Pianoforte Solo							
Grand Polonaise in E-flat major (also issued with orchestral accompaniment)	22	1830–35	1836	Baroness Frances Sarah d'Est	149	268–72	58
Two Polonaises in C-sharp minor in E-flat minor	26	1834–35	1836	Josef Dessauer	150–51	345–56	90
Two Polonaises in A major ("Military") in C minor	40	1838–39	1840	Julian Fontana	152–53	615–25	120 121
in F-sharp minor ("Tragic")	44	1840–41	1841	Princess Charles de Beauvau	154	663–67	135
in A-flat major ("Heroic")	53	1842–43	1843	Auguste Léo	155	739–43	147
Polonaise-Fantaisie in A-flat major	61	1845–46	1846	Mme Anne Veyret	156	815–21	159
Preludes							
(set of twenty-four)	28	1836–39	1839	Camille Pleyel (French Edition); J. C. Kessler (German Edition)	166–89	370–478	
in C major							124
in A minor							123
in G major							107
in E minor							123
in D major							107
in B minor							107
in A major							100
in F-sharp minor							107
in E major							107
in C-sharp minor							123
in B major							107

Pianoforte Solo

TITLE	OP. NO.	DATE OF COMPOSITION	DATE OF FIRST PUBLICATION	DEDICATION	CT	KK	MB
in G-sharp minor							107
in F-sharp major							107
in E-flat minor							107
in D-flat major ("Raindrop")							107
in B-flat minor							107
in A-flat major							100
in F minor							107
in E-flat major							107
in C minor							107
in B-flat major							123
in G minor							107
in F major							107
in D minor							107
in A-flat major	—	1834	1918	Pierre Wolff	191	1231–32	86
in C-sharp minor	45	1841	1841	Princess Elisabeth Czernicheff	190	668–72	141
Rondos							
in C minor (see also Pianoforte Duet)	1	1825	1825	Mme Bogumil Linde	192	1–5	10
Rondo à la Mazur	5	1826	1828	Countess Alexandrine de Moriolles	193	22–25	15
in C major (see also Pianoforte Duet)	73	1828	1954		196	1086–91	26
in E-flat major	16	1833	1833	Mlle Caroline Hartmann	195	216–19	76
Scherzos							
in B minor	20	1831–32	1835	Thomas Albrecht	197	250–54	65

TITLE	OP. NO.	DATE OF COMPOSITION	DATE OF FIRST PUBLICATION	DEDICATION	CT	KK	MB
Pianoforte Solo							
in B-flat minor	31	1837	1837	Countess Adèle de Fürstenstein	198	505–509	111
in C-sharp minor	39	1839	1840	Adolf Gutmann	199	610–14	125
in E major	54	1842	1843	Mlle Jeanne de Caraman (German edition); Mlle Clothilde de Caraman (French edition)	200	744–48	148
Sonatas							
in C minor	4	1827–28	1851	Józef Elsner	201	928–31	23
in B-flat minor	35	1839	1840		202	570–80	128
in B minor	58	1844	1845	Countess Émilie de Perthuis	203	783–90	155
Studies (Vol. I: set of twelve)	10	1829–33	1833	Franz Liszt	14–25	109–63	
in C major							59
in A minor							59
in E major							74
in C-sharp minor							75
in G-flat major ("Black Keys")							57
in E-flat minor							57
in C major							68
in F major							42
in F minor							42
in A-flat major							42
in E-flat major ("Arpeggio")							42

Pianoforte Solo

TITLE	OP. NO.	DATE OF COMPOSITION	DATE OF FIRST PUBLICATION	DEDICATION	CT	KK	MB
in C minor ("Revolutionary")							67
Studies (Vol. II: set of twelve)	25	1832–36	1837	Countess Marie d'Agoult	26–37	297–344	104
in A-flat major ("Aeolian Harp")							97
in F minor							99
in F major							78
in A minor							78
in E minor							78
in G-sharp minor ("Thirds")							78
in C-sharp minor							98
in D-flat major ("Sixths")							78
in G-flat major ("Butterfly")							78
in B minor ("Octaves")							78
in A minor ("Winter Wind")							83
in C minor ("Ocean")							99
"Trois Nouvelles Etudes"	–	1839–40	1840		38–40	905–17	130
in F minor							
in A-flat major							
in D-flat major							
Tarantella in A-flat major	43	1841	1841		205	654–62	139
Variations							
on *Der Schweizerbub* (German national air)	–	1824	1851	Katarzyna Sowińska	227	925–27	14
on a theme of Paganini ("Souvenir de Paganini")	–	1829	1881		229	1203	37

TITLE	OP. NO.	DATE OF COMPOSITION	DATE OF FIRST PUBLICATION	DEDICATION	CT	KK	MB
Pianoforte Solo							
on a theme by Hérold ("Ronde" from *Ludovic*)	12	1833	1833	Emma Horsford	226	178–80	80
for *Hexaméron* (a set of six variations by different composers on the March from Bellini's *I puritani*)	–	1837	1839	Princess Cristina Belgiojoso	230	903–904	113
Waltzes							
in A minor (sketch)	–	1829	1955		224	1238–39	40(B)
in E-flat major	–	1829–30	1902		–	1212	46
in E-flat major	18	1831	1834	Laura Horsford	207	237–45	62
Three Waltzes	34				208–10	549–69	
in A-flat major		1835	1838	Mlle Thun-Hohenstein			94
in A minor		1831	1838	Baroness C. d'Ivry			64
in F major		1838	1838	Mlle A. d'Eichthal			118
in A-flat major	42	1840	1840		211	646–52	131
Three Waltzes	64	1846–47	1847		212–14	849–69	164
in D-flat major ("Minute")				Delfina Potocka			
in C-sharp minor				Baroness Rothschild			
in A-flat major				Countess Katarzyna Branicka			
Two Waltzes	69				215–16	988–1006	
in A-flat major ("L'Adieu")		1835	1855	Maria Wodzińska			95
in B minor		1829	1852	Wilhelm Kolberg			35

Pianoforte Solo

TITLE	OP. NO.	DATE OF COMPOSITION	DATE OF FIRST PUBLICATION	DEDICATION	CT	KK	MB
Three Waltzes	70				217–19	1007–33	
in G-flat major		1832	1855				92
in F minor		1842	1855				138
in D-flat major		1829	1855				40
in E-flat major ("Sostenuto")	—	1847	1955		223	1237	133
Two Waltzes	—	c. 1829			220–21		
in E major			1867			1207	44
in A-flat major			1902			1209–11	46
in E minor	—	1830	1868		222	1213–14	21
in A minor	—	1847	1955		224	1238–39	150

Songs

TITLE	OP. NO.	DATE OF COMPOSITION	DATE OF FIRST PUBLICATION	DEDICATION	CT	KK	MB
Seventeen Polish Songs	74		1859		129–45	1092–381	
"Życzenie" (The Wish)		1829					33
"Wiosna" (Spring)		1838					116
"Smutna rzeka" (Sad River)		1831					63
"Hulanka" (Drinking Song)		1830					50
"Gdzie lubi" (What She Likes)		1829					32
"Precz z moich oczu!" (Out of My Sight!)		1827					48
"Poseł" (The Messenger)		1831					50
"Śliczny chłopiec" (Handsome Lad)		1841					143
"Melodya" (Melody)		1847					165
"Wojak" (The Warrior)		1831					47

Songs / Pianoforte Duet

TITLE	OP. NO.	DATE OF COMPOSITION	DATE OF FIRST PUBLICATION	DEDICATION	CT	KK	MB
Songs							
"Dwojaki koniec" (Double Ending)		1845					156
"Moja pieszczotka" (My Darling)		1837					112
"Nie ma czego trzeba" (There Is No Need)		1845					156
"Pierścień" (The Ring)		1836					103
"Narzeczony" (The Bridegroom)		1831					63
"Piosnka litewska" (Lithuanian Song)		1831					63
"Śpiew grobowy" (Hymn from the Tomb)		1836	1872				101
Two Songs							
"Czary" (Spells)	—	1830	1910		146	1204–1206	51
"Dumka" (Elegy)	—	1840	1910		147	1236	132
Pianoforte Duet							
Variations on a Theme of Thomas Moore—1 piano	—	1826	1965		228	1190–92	
Rondo in C minor (arr. of the Rondo in C minor for Solo Piano)—1 piano	1	1825	1834		192	1–5	10
Rondo in C major (arr. of the Rondo in C major for Solo Piano)—2 pianos	73	1828	1855		196	1086–91	27

Chamber Music

TITLE	OP. NO.	DATE OF COMPOSITION	DATE OF FIRST PUBLICATION	DEDICATION	CT	KK	MB
Trio in G minor, for Piano, Violin, and Cello	8	1828–29	1832	Prince Antoni Radziwiłł	206	80–86	25
Introduction and Polonaise in C major, for Piano and Cello	3	1829–30	1831	Josef Merk	148	16–21	41/52
Grand Duo in E major, on themes from Meyerbeer's *Robert le Diable*, for Piano and Cello	–	(1831)	1833	Mlle Adèle Forest	10	901–902	70
Sonata in G minor, for Piano and Cello	65	1845–46	1847	Auguste Franchomme	204	870–88	160
Variations in E major, for Flute and Piano, on a theme from Rossini's *La Cenerentola*	–	1824	1955 (facsimile)			1392	9

Pianoforte and Orchestra

TITLE	OP. NO.	DATE OF COMPOSITION	DATE OF FIRST PUBLICATION	DEDICATION	CT	KK	MB
Variations on "Là ci darem la mano" from Mozart's *Don Giovanni*	2	1827	1830	Tytus Woyciechowski	225	6–15	22
Grand Fantasia in A major, on Polish Airs	13	1828	1834	Johann Pixis	41	181–87	28
Krakowiak: Grand Concert Rondo in F major	14	1828	1834	Princess Anna Czartoryska	194	188–97	29
Concerto in F minor	21	1829–30	1836	Countess Delfina Potocka	48	255–67	43
Concerto in E minor	11	1830	1833	Friedrich Kalkbrenner	47	164–77	53
Grand Polonaise in E-flat major (the "Andante Spianato" for solo piano was prefixed to this polonaise and both were published together)	22	1830–31	1836	Baroness Frances Sarah d'Est	149	268–72	58

LIST OF SOURCES

ACC   Azoury, Pierre. *Chopin Through His Contemporaries: Friends, Lovers, and Rivals.* London, 1999.

ACLA   Agoult, Marie d'. *Correspondance de Liszt et de la Comtesse d'Agoult.* Edited by Daniel Ollivier. 2 vols. Paris, 1933–34.

ACMS   Abraham, Gerald. *Chopin's Musical Style.* Revised ed. London, 1960.

AM   Agoult, Marie d' ("Daniel Stern"). *Mémoires, 1833–54.* Edited by Daniel Ollivier. Paris, 1927.

AmZ   *Allgemeine musikalische Zeitung*, Leipzig. Cited by issue.

AWC   The Alan Walker Collection. Archival Letters and Documents, 1956–2007. Special Collections, McMaster University, Canada.

BAS   Bülow, Hans von. *Ausgewählte Schriften, 1850–1892.* 2nd ed. Herausgegeben von Marie von Bülow. Leipzig, 1911.

BC   Binental, Leopold. *Chopin: Dokumente und Erinnerungen aus seiner Heimatstadt.* Translated from the Polish by A. von Guttry. Leipzig, 1932.

BC-C   Burtt, Frank. *Cross-Channel and Coastal Paddle Steamers.* London, 1934.

BCM   Brookshaw, Susanna. *Concerning Chopin in Manchester.* Private publication, 1951.

BCS   Bülow, Hans von (ed.). *Sämmtliche Klavier-Etuden von Fr. Chopin.* Munich, 1889.

BFC   Burger, Ernst. *Frédéric Chopin. Eine Lebenschronik in Bildern und Dokumenten.* Munich, 1990.

BJT   Brzowski, Józef. Travelogue: "Artistic Impressions of a Journey Through Germany and France, 1836–37," collated and translated by Marie-Paule Rambeau and Ewa Talma-Davous in *Chopin e il suono di Pleyel.* Villa Medici Giulini, Italy, 2010.

BLH   Balzac, Honoré de. *Lettres à Madame Hańska.* 2 vols. Paris, 1990.

BM   Berlioz, Hector. *Mémoires.* Paris, 1870. Translated by David Cairns. London, 1969.

BRRS   Bory, Robert. *Une retraite romantique en Suisse. Liszt et la Comtesse d'Agoult.* Lausanne, 1930.

BSH   Barbedette, H. *Stephen Heller: His Life and Works*. Translated by Robert Brown-Borthwick. London, 1877.

BWF   Boetticher, Wolfgang. "Weitere Forschungen an Dokumenten zum Leben und Schaffen Robert Schumanns." *Robert Schumann: Ein romantisches Erbe in neuer Forschung*. Mainz, 1984.

CB   Czartoryski Bibliothèque, Paris. Unpublished documents cited by date.

CCPLS   *Chopiniana in the Collections of the Polish Historical and Literary Society. The Polish Library in Paris*. Edited by Arkadiusz Roszkowski. Paris, 2010.

CCS   Cobbe, Alec. *Chopin's Swansong: The Paris and London Pianos of His Last Performances Now in the Cobbe Collection*. London, 2010.

CEC   Clavier, André. *Emilia Chopin*. Liège, 1974.

CFC   *Correspondance de Frédéric Chopin*. 3 vols. Edited, revised, and annotated by Bronisław Edward Sydow, with Suzanne and Denise Chainaye. Paris, 1953–60.

CFCS   Clésinger, Solange. "Frédéric Chopin, souvenirs inédits." *Revue musicale de Suisse romande*. Winter 1978, no. 5.

CGS   *Correspondance de George Sand*. Collected, arranged, and annotated by Georges Lubin. 26 vols. Paris, 1964–91.

CHS   Choussat, Hélène. *Souvenirs*. Palma, 2010.

CJFC   Czartkowski, Adam, and Zofia Jeżewska. *Fryderyk Chopin*. Warsaw, 1970.

CKS   *Fryderyk Chopin: Kurier Szafarski*. Edited with an introduction and notes by Hanna Wróblewska-Straus. Warsaw, 1999.

CM   Czartoryski, Prince Adam. *Memoirs of Prince Adam Czartoryski and His Correspondence with Alexander I*. Edited by Adam Gielgud. 2 vols. London, 1888.

CPG   Courcey, Geraldine de. *Paganini the Genoese*. 2 vols. Oklahoma, 1957.

CS   Cate, Curtis. *George Sand*. Boston, 1975.

CSP   *Chopin e il suono di Pleyel* (Chopin and the Pleyel Sound). Villa Medici Giulini, Italy, 2010.

CTP   Coxe, William. *Travels into Poland, Russia, Sweden, and Denmark*. 2 vols. London, 1784.

DCSN   Delaigue-Moins, Sylvie. *Chopin chez George Sand à Nohant. Chronique de sept étés*. Châteauroux, 1986.

DDEP   Dembowski, Karol. *Deux ans en Espagne et en Portugal, pendant la guerre civile, 1838–1840*. Paris, 1841.

DEC   Davison, James William. *An Essay on the Works of Frédéric Chopin*. London, 1843 [published anonymously].

DGP   Davies, Norman. *God's Playground: A History of Poland*. 2nd ed. 2 vols. New York, 2005.

DJ   Delacroix, Eugène. *Journal de Eugène Delacroix*. With Introduction and Notes by André Joubin. Paris, 1932.

ECE   Eigeldinger, Jean-Jacques. *Chopin vu par ses élèves*. 2nd ed. Neuchâtel, 1979. Translated as *Chopin: Pianist and Teacher, as Seen by His Pupils*, by Naomi Shoher with Krysia Osostowicz and Roy Howat. Cambridge, 1986.

ECF   Eisler, Benita. *Chopin's Funeral*. New York, 2003.

ECIB   Ekiert, Janusz. *Fryderyk Chopin: An Illustrated Biography*. Warsaw, 2009.

EJF   Ekier, Jan. *Julian Fontana as the Editor of Chopin's Posthumous Works*. Chopin Studies 7. Warsaw, 2000.

FCA   François-Sappey, Brigitte (ed.). *Charles-Valentin Alkan*. Paris, 1991.

FLSL   *Franz Liszt Selected Letters*. Translated and edited by Adrian Williams. Oxford, 1998.

GC   Gavoty, Bernard. *Frédéric Chopin*. Translated by Martin Sokolinsky. New York, 1977.

GCW   Goldberg, Halina. *Music in Chopin's Warsaw*. New York, 2008.

GFF   Grattan Flood, William. *John Field of Dublin: Inventor of the Nocturne*. Dublin, 1920.

GJK   Gajewski, Ferdinand. "The Apotheosis of the Dąbrowski Mazurka"— Appendix I: Extract from the unpublished diary of Józef Krasiński (1838). *Studi Musicali*. Accademia nazionale di Santa Cecilia. Florence, 1990.

GMB   *Giacomo Meyerbeer, Briefwechsel und Tagebücher*. Edited by Heinz and Gudrun Becker. Berlin, 1960–85.

GNCF   Gajewski, Ferdinand. "New Chopiniana from the Papers of Carl Filtsch." *Studi Musicali* XI, 1982.

GNCK   Gomulicki, J. W. (ed.). "Czarne Kwiaty" (Black Flowers), in *Pisma Wybrane*, Warsaw, 1968.

GNP   Gottschalk, Louis Moreau. *Notes of a Pianist*. Edited with a Prelude, a Postlude, and Explanatory Notes by Jeanne Behrend. New York, 1964.

GSFC   Ganche, Édouard. "Dans le souvenir de Frédéric Chopin." *Mercure de France*. Paris, 1925.

GVM   Godeau, Marcel. *Le Voyage à Majorque de George Sand et Frédéric Chopin*. Paris, 1959.

HAC   Hanslick, Eduard. *Aus dem Concertsaal. Kritiken und Schilderungen aus den letzten 20 Jahren des Wiener Musiklebens*. Vienna, 1870.

HBG   Hedderwick, James. *Backward Glances, or Some Personal Recollections*. Edinburgh and London, 1891.

H-BZW   Hugo-Bader, Kazimierz. *O dawnej i nowej Żelazowej Woli* (On the Old and the New Żelazowa Wola). Warsaw, 1937.

HC   Hedley, Arthur. *Chopin*. London, 1947.

HCM   Huneker, James. *Chopin: The Man and His Music*. London, 1910.

HCV   Hugo, Victor. *Choses vues: souvenirs, journaux, cahiers, 1830–1885*. Texte présenté, établi et annoté par Hubert Juin. Paris, 2002.

HFC   Hoesick, Ferdynand. *Chopiniana*. (Chopin's correspondence, etc.). Warsaw, 1912.

HFCZ   Hoesick, Ferdynand. *Chopin: Życie i twórczość* (Chopin: His Life and Works). 4 vols. Kraków (reprint), 1962–68.

HHCP   Hipkins, Edith J. *How Chopin Played. From Contemporary Impressions Collected from the Diaries and Notebooks of the Late A. J. Hipkins, F.S.A.* London, 1937.

HLL   Hallé, Sir Charles. *Life and Letters*. London, 1896.

HMB   Heine, Heinrich. *Musikalische Berichte aus Paris*. 1841. In *Sämtliche Werke*, vol. 9, edited by Fritz Strich. Munich, 1925.

HMBE   Hiller, Ferdinand. *Felix Mendelssohn-Bartholdy: Briefe und Erinnerungen von Ferdinand Hiller*. Cologne, 1874.

HMS   Hueffer, Francis. *Musical Studies*. Edinburgh, 1880.

HMVA   Herz, Henri. *Mes voyages en Amérique.* Paris, 1866.
HRP   Hube, Romuald. *Romualda Hubego Pisma* (The Writings of Romuald Hube),
            edited by Karol Dunin. Warsaw, 1906.
HSC   Hoesick, Ferdynand. *Słowacki i Chopin. Z zagadnień twórczości* (Słowacki
            and Chopin: Some Problems Arising from Their Work). Warsaw, 1932.
HSCC   Hedley, Arthur. *Selected Correspondence of Fryderyk Chopin.* Abridged and
            translated from Bronisław Sydow's three-volume collected edition. London,
            1962.
HSLC   Harasowski, Adam. *The Skein of Legends Around Chopin.* Glasgow, 1967.
HW-S   Helman, Zofia, and Hanna Wróblewska-Straus. "The Date of Chopin's Ar-
            rival in Paris." *Musicology Today,* 95–103. Warsaw, 2007.
IC   Iwaszkiewicz, Jarosław. *Chopin.* Warsaw, 1938.
JCSN   Jorgensen, Cecilia and Jens. *Chopin and the Swedish Nightingale.* Brussels,
            2003.
JJ   Janin, Jules. *735 Lettres à sa femme.* Textes décryptes, classés et annotés par
            Mergier-Bourdeix. 3 vols. Paris, 1973–79.
JN   Jordan, Ruth. *Nocturne: A Life of Chopin.* London, 1978.
KCLB   Karasowski, Moritz. *Friedrich Chopin. Sein Leben und seine Briefe.* 3rd ed.
            Dresden, 1881.
KCLS   Kallberg, Jeffrey. "Chopin's Last Style." *Journal of the American Musicological
            Society* 38, no. 2, Summer 1985.
KCM   Kallberg, Jeffrey. "Chopin's March, Chopin's Death." *19th-century Music* 25,
            no. 1.
KCOL   Kobylańska, Krystyna. *Chopin in His Own Land: Documents and Souvenirs.*
            Collected and edited by K. Kobylańska. (Translated by Claire Grece-
            Dąbrowska and Mary Filippi. Editor, Janina Wierzbicka.) Kraków, 1956.
KFC   *Korespondencja Fryderyka Chopina.* 2 vols. Edited by Bronisław Edward Sydow.
            Warsaw, 1955. Cited whenever Chopin's correspondence is written in Polish.
KGS   Karénine, Wladimir (pseudonym of Mme V. D. Komarova). *George Sand,
            sa vie et ses œuvres.* 4 vols. Paris, 1899–1926.
KK   Kolberg, Oskar. *Korespondencja* (Complete Works, vol. 62). Wrocław-Poznań-
            Kraków-Warsaw, 1965.
KSFC   Karłowicz, Mieczysław. *Souvenirs inédits de Frédéric Chopin.* Translated
            from the Polish by Laure Disière. Paris, 1904.
LACK   Leichtentritt, Hugo. *Analyse von Chopin'schen Klavierwerke.* 2 vols. Berlin,
            1921–22.
LC   Liszt, Franz. *F. Chopin.* Paris, 1852. Translated with an Introduction by Ed-
            ward N. Waters. New York, 1963.
LCS   Litzmann, Berthold. *Clara Schumann: Ein Künstlerleben.* 3 vols. Leipzig,
            1902–1908.
LED   *Lettres de Eugène Delacroix (1815–1863),* recueillies et publiée par
            M. Philippe Burty. Paris, 1878.
LGSB   Lubin, Georges. *George Sand en Berry.* Brussels, 1992.
LHT   Long, Esmond R. *A History of the Therapy of Tuberculosis and the Case of
            Frédéric Chopin.* University of Kansas Press, Lawrence, 1956.
LL   *Living with Liszt: The Diary of Carl Lachmund, an American Pupil of Liszt,
            1882–1884.* Edited, annotated, and introduced by Alan Walker. Stuyvesant,
            N.Y., 1995.

LLB	La Mara (ed.). *Franz Liszts Briefe*. 8 vols. Leipzig, 1893–1905.
LLF	La Mara. *Liszt und die Frauen*. 2nd ed. Leipzig, 1919.
LM	Lamond, Frederic. *The Memoirs of Frederic Lamond*. Glasgow, 1949.
LPZ	Lenz, Wilhem von. *Die grossen Pianoforte-Virtuosen unserer Zeit*. Berlin, 1872.
LRC	Leikin, Anatole. "Repeat with Caution: A Dilemma of the First Movement of Chopin's Sonata, Op. 35." *The Musical Quarterly* 85, no. 3, 568–82.
LSS	Legouvé, Ernest. *Soixante ans de souvenirs*. 4 vols. Paris, 1887.
MAL	Melagari, Dora. "Une Amie de Liszt, la Princesse de Sayn-Wittgenstein." *La Revue de Paris*, September 1, 1897.
MAML	Moscheles, Ignaz. *Aus Moscheles' Leben, nach Briefen und Tagebüchern, herausgegeben von seiner Frau*. 2 vols. Leipzig, 1872–73.
MC	Marek, George R., and Maria Gordon-Smith. *Chopin*. New York, 1978.
MCPW	Mikuli, Carl. *Foreword to Frederick Chopin's Pianoforte Works*, edited by Mikuli. Leipzig, 1880.
MCW	Mysłakowski, Piotr. *The Chopins' Warsaw*. Translated by John Comber. Warsaw, 2013.
MDD	Musielak, Henri. "Dokumenty dotyczace spadku po Chopinie" (Documents Regarding Chopin's Estate). *Ruch Muzyczny*, nos. 14 (July 2), 15 (July 16), and 16 (July 30), Warsaw, 1978. This three-part article traces the disposition of Chopin's property after his death.
MDT	Mysłakowski, Piotr, and Krzysztof Dorcz. *Tułacze serce Chopina* (Chopin's Wandering Heart). Warsaw, 2014. Unpublished manuscript in the Chopin National Institute, Warsaw.
MFC	Mizwa, Stephen P. (ed.). *Frédéric Chopin, 1810–1849*. New York, 1949.
MFPC	Mysłakowski, Piotr. "Finding the Place Where Chopin's Talent First Manifested Itself." *Journal of the International Federation of Chopin Societies*, no. 23, 19–26. Warsaw, 2013.
MI	Chopin, Fryderyk. "Miscellania Inedita." Edited by Krystyna Kobylańska. *Ruch Muzyczny*, XL/4. Warsaw, 1996.
ML	Maurois, André. *Lélia: The Life of George Sand*. Translated by Gerard Hopkins. New York, 1953.
MMML	Mason, William. *Memories of a Musical Life*. New York, 1901.
MPC	Marmontel, Antoine. *Les Pianistes célèbres. Silhouettes & Médaillons*. 2nd ed. Paris, 1887.
MRCG	Madariaga, Isabel de. *Russia in the Age of Catherine the Great*. London, 1981.
MSFC	Mysłakowski, Piotr, and Andrzej Sikorski. *Fryderyk Chopin: The Origins*. Translated by John Comber, with a Preface by Jim Samson. Warsaw, 2010.
MWRS	*The Musical World of Robert Schumann: A Selection from Schumann's Own Writings*. Translated, edited, and annotated by Henry Pleasants. London, 1965.
MZM	Mickiewicz, Adam Bernard. *Żywot Adama Mickiewicza* (The Life of Adam Mickiewicz). 3 vols. Poznań, 1894.
NAP	Neuhaus, Heinrich. *The Art of Piano Playing*. Translated by K. A. Leibovitch. London, 1973.
NCGB	Nowaczyk, Henryk F. *Chopin w podróży. Glosy do biografi*. Warsaw, 2013.
NCL	Nowik, Wojciech. "The Chopin Letters to Delfina: Meanders of the Controversy Re-visited." Published in *Falsifications in Polish Collections and Abroad*, edited by Jerzy Miziołek in collaboration with Peter Martyn. Institute of Archaeology, Warsaw University, 2001.

NFC   Niecks, Frederick. *Frederick Chopin as Man and Musician*. 3rd ed. 2 vols. London, 1902.

NZfM   *Neue Zeitschrift für Musik*. Edited by Robert Schumann. Leipzig, 1834–44. Cited by issue.

OAAL   Ollivier, Daniel (ed.). *Autour de Mme d'Agoult et de Liszt (Alfred de Vigny, Emile Ollivier, Princesse de Belgiojoso). Lettres publiées avec introduction et notes*. Paris, 1941.

OFCL   Oliferko, Magdalena (ed.). *Fontana and Chopin in Letters*. Translated by John Comber. Warsaw, 2013.

ORFC   Osborne, G. A. *Reminiscences of Frederick Chopin*, from the "Proceedings of the Musical Association," Sixth Session. London, April 5, 1880.

PDM   Ponce, José de Vargas. *Descripctión de la Isla de Mallorca*. Madrid, 1778.

PPS   Przybyszewski, Stanisław. *No drogach duszy* (On the Paths of the Soul). Kraków, 1900.

P-SCB   Pereświet-Sołtan, Stanisław. *Listy Fryderyka Chopina do Jana Białoblockiego* (Letters of Fryderyk Chopin to Jan Białobłocki). Warsaw, 1926.

RGS   Ramann, Lina (ed.). *Franz Liszt's Gesammelte Schriften*. 6 vols. Leipzig, 1880–83.

RGSF   Rocheblave, Samuel. *George Sand et sa fille, d'après leur correspondance inédite*. Paris, 1905.

RLKM   Ramann, Lina. *Franz Liszt als Künstler und Mensch*. 3 vols. Leipzig, 1880–94.

RMM   Reid, Charles. *The Music Monster: A Biography of James William Davison, Music Critic of* The Times *of London, 1846–78*. London, 1984.

RRG   Rosen, Charles. *The Romantic Generation*. Cambridge, 1995.

SAC   Smoter, Jerzy Maria. *Album Chopina (L'Album de Chopin), 1829–1831*. Kraków, 1975.

SALA   Stuart, Lord Dudley Coutts. *Address of the Literary Association of the Friends of Poland to the Poles*. London, 1850.

SBNF   *Robert Schumann's Briefe. Neue Folge*. Herausgegeben von F. Gustav Jansen. Leipzig, 1904.

SCD   Sellards, John. *Dans le sillage du romantisme: Charles Didier*. Paris, 1933.

SCP   Szulc, Tad. *Chopin in Paris. The Life and Times of the Romantic Composer*. New York, 1998.

S-DMS   Sand, Christiane and Delaigue-Moins. *Maurice Sand, fils de George*. Tours, 2010.

SDNL   Saffle, Michael, and James Deaville (eds.). *New Light on Liszt and His Music: Essays in Honor of Alan Walker's 65th Birthday*. Stuyvesant, N.Y., 1997.

SHC   Sielużycki, Czesław. *On the Health of Chopin: Truth, Suppositions, Legends*. Chopin Studies 6. Warsaw, 1999.

SHM   Sand, George. *Un hiver à Majorque* (A Winter in Majorca). Translated and annotated by Robert Graves from the Paris edition of 1869. Majorca, 1956.

SHV   Sand, George. *Histoire de ma vie*. Œuvres autobiographiques, 2 vols. Texte établi, présenté et annoté par Georges Lubin. Paris, 1971.

SJI   Sand, George. *Journal intime*. Published posthumously by Aurore Sand. Paris, 1926.

SLV   Sand, George. *Lettres d'un voyageur*. Paris, 1869.

SMC   Samson, Jim. *The Music of Chopin*. London, 1985.

SPFS	*Pamiętniki Fryderyka hrabiego Skarbka* (The Memoirs of Count Fryderyk Skarbek). Edited by Piotr Mysłakowski. Warsaw, 2009.
SRCY	Skrodzki, Eugeniusz (writing under the pseudonym "Wielisław"). "Kilka wspomnień o Szopenie z Mojej Młodości" (Some Recollections of Chopin from My Youth), published in *Bluszcz* (Ivy), nos. 32–36, August–September, Warsaw, 1882.
SSCDP	Smoter, Jerzy Maria. *Spór o 'listy' Chopina do Delfiny Potockiej* (Controversy over Chopin's "Letters" to Delfina Potocka). Kraków, 1976.
TCM	Tovey, Donald Francis. *Essays in Musical Analysis: Chamber Music.* London, 1956.
TCSZ	Tomaszewski, Mieczysław. *Frédéric Chopin und seine Zeit.* Translated from the Polish by Małgorzata Kozłowska. Laaber, Germany, 1999.
VCA	Vier, Jacques. *La Comtesse d'Agoult et son temps, avec des documents inédits,* 6 vols. Paris, 1955–63.
VGS	Vincent, Marie-Louise. *George Sand et le Berry.* Paris, 1919.
WCB	Willis, Peter. *Chopin in Britain.* New York, 2017.
WCMM	Weinstock, Herbert. *Chopin, the Man and His Music.* New York, 1965.
WFC	Walker, Alan (ed.). *Frédéric Chopin: Profiles of the Man and the Musician.* New York, 1967.
WFL	Walker, Alan. *Franz Liszt.* 3 vols. New York, 1983–96. Vol. 1: *The Virtuoso Years, 1811–1847.* Vol. 2: *The Weimar Years, 1848–1861.* Vol. 3: *The Final Years, 1861–1886.*
WLDC	Wierzyński, Casimir. *The Life and Death of Chopin.* Translated by Norbert Guterman. New York, 1949.
W-SC	Wróblewska-Straus, Hanna. "Listy Jane Wilhelmine Stirling do Ludwiki Jędrzejewiczowej" (Letters from Jane Stirling to Ludwika Jędrzejewicz). *Rocznik chopinowski* 12 (1980), 140.
WVB	Weinstock, Herbert. *Vincenzo Bellini: His Life and His Operas.* New York, 1971.
WZW	Wojtkiewicz, Mariola. *Żelazowa Wola: The History of Chopin's Birthplace.* Translated by John Comber. Warsaw, 2012.
ZCPR	Zamoyski, Adam. *Chopin, Prince of the Romantics.* London, 2010.
ZFC	Zieliński, Tadeusz A. *Frédéric Chopin.* Translated from the Polish by Marie Bouvard, Laurence Dyèvre, Blaise and Krystyna de Obaldia. Paris, 1995.

INDEX

Page numbers in italics refer to main entries.

Abend Zeitung (Dresden), 442*n.*
Adelasio de Marguerittes, Giulietta
    (*née* Granville) (1814–1866),
    588 and *n.*, 591
Agoult, Countess Marie-Sophie-
    Catherine d' (1805–1876), 302,
    321–22 and *n.*, 348, 351, 352,
    430–32
Ajasson de Grandsagne, Stéphane
    (1802–1845), 359–62
Alard, Jean-Delphin (1815–1888), 544
Alboni, Marietta (1826–1894), 579
Albrecht, Thomas (1803–1865), 613
Albrechtsberger, Johann Georg
    (1736–1809), 123
Alexander I, Tsar of Russia (1777–1825),
    57, 60*n.*, 82–84, 93*n.*, 199
Alkan, Charles-Valentin Morhange
    (1813–1888), 243*n.*, 277, 344, 458,
    543, 605 and *n.*
    Napoléon-Alexandre (brother)
        (1826–1906), 344
Allgemeine musikalische Zeitung (Leipzig),
    84, 151, 482
Almanach populaire (Paris), 298*n.*
Antrobus, Lady Anne (c. 1800–1885),
    561

Apponyi, Countess Thérèse d'
    (1790–1874), 343, 422
Arago, Emmanuel (1812–1896), 536, 541,
    552
Arenys de Mar (Spain), 391
Arles (France), 397
Arpentigny, Stanislas d' (1791–1864),
    530–31
Arundel (England), 313
Ashdown, Edwin (1826–1912), 317
Auber, Daniel-François-Esprit
    (1782–1871), 605
    Fra Diavolo, 182
    Le Maçon, 203
    La Muette de Portici, 182
Auer, Leopold (1845–1930), 650
Ault-Dumesnil, Édouard d' (1796–1870),
    437
Azoury, Pierre (1930–2014), 158*n.*

Bach, Johann Sebastian (1685–1750), 16,
    465
    48 Preludes and Fugues, 16, 48, 405,
    423, 425, 438
Bach-Zelewski, General Erich von dem
    (1899–1972), 668
Bacon, Francis (1561–1626), 635

Balakirev, Mily Alexeyevich (1837–1910), 64, 197
Balfe, Michael William (1808–1870), 487, 511
  L'Étoile de Seville, 511
  Les Quatre Fils Aymon, 487
Ball, Edward Hughes (1798–1863), 304
Ballanche, Pierre-Simon (1776–1847), 293, 433
Balzac, Honoré de (1799–1850), 421, 625
  Beatrix, 432
  La Comédie humaine, 432
  description of George Sand, 432–33
Barbès, Armand (1809–1870), 552
Barcelona (Spain), 372–73, 391–92
Barciński, Antoni Feliks (1803–1878), 67, 472–75, 629
  marriage to Izabella Chopin (*q.v.*)
Barthélemy, Auguste de (1807–1893), 645
Bartók, Béla (1881–1945), 82
Bascans, Ferdinand (1801–1861), 499
Batta, Alexandre (1816–1902), 344
Batthyány, Lajos (1807–1849), 453
Bayer, Konstancja, 185–86
Bayzat, Beverly, xxviii
Beethoven, Ludwig van (1770–1827), 145, 323, 465
  Chopin and, 16, 328
  Monument of (1845), 511 and *n.*
  WORKS
  Missa solemnis, op. 123, 166
  Overture: "Fidelio," op. 72, 143
  Piano Concerto no. 5, in E-flat major, op. 73, ("Emperor"), 313
  Sonatas:
    no. 12, in A-flat major, op. 26 ("Funeral March"), 425
    no. 14, in C-sharp minor, op. 27, no. 2 ("Moonlight"), 425
    no. 18, in E-flat major, op. 31, no. 3, 16
    no. 23 in F minor, op. 57 ("Appassionata"), 522
    no. 29, in B-flat major, op. 106 ("Hammerklavier"), 293
    no. 32, in C minor, op. 111, 328

Symphonies:
  no. 3, in E-flat major, op. 55 ("Eroica"), 416, 522
  no. 9, in D minor, op. 125 ("Choral"), 143, 166, 274, 313*n.*
Belgiojoso-Trivulzio, Princess Cristina (1808–1871), 337–40, 341
  Hexaméron Variations, 338–41
Belhaven, Lady Hamilton (c. 1790–1873), 596
Belleville, Anna-Caroline de (1808–1880), 167, 463
Bellini, Vincenzo (1801–1835), 245, 341, 411
  death and funeral of, 342 and *n.*
  Heine on, 342
  WORKS
  Beatrice di Tenda, 615
  I Capuleti e i Montecchi, 313
  Norma, 341
  Il pirate, 341
  I puritani, 339, 341
  La sonnambula, 341, 559
Belloni, Gaëtano (1810–1887), 646
Bełza, Prof. Józef (1805–1888), 473–74
Bem, General Józef Zachariasz (1795–1850), 216
Benedict, Sir Julius (1804–1885), 428
Bentkowski, Feliks (1781–1852), 105
Berg, General Fyodor (1793–1874), 629
Berlin (Germany):
  Friedrichstrasse, 127
  Königstadt Theatre, 128
  Kronprinz Inn, 127
  Spree River, 127
  Staatsbibliothek, 127
  University, 126
Berlioz, Hector (1803–1869), 4 and *n.*, 10, 13, 236*n.*, 293, 343, 462, 559
  Harriet (wife, *née* Smithson) (1800–1854), 236*n.*
  Les Francs-juges, 281
  Harold en Italie, 281, 293
Bertrand, General Henri-Gratien (1773–1844), 434
Białobłocki, Jan ("Jasio") (1805–1828), 4, 46, 71, 87, 112, 121

Bianchi, Eliodoro (1773–1848), 84n.
  Carolina Crespi (wife), 84n.
Bierut, President Bolesław (1892–1956),
  670
Bischofswerda (Germany), 89
Bisson, Louis-Auguste (1814–1876), 553
Blache, Dr. Jean (1798–1871), 604
Blackwall (England), 313
Blahetka, Joseph (1782–1857), 142
  Anne-Marie Leopoldine (daughter)
    (1809–1885), 142, 144–45
Blake, William (1757–1827), 483
Blanc, Louis (1811–1882), 552
Blanchard, Henri-Louis (1778–1858),
  468n., 644
Blanche, Dr. Esprit (1796–1852), 421
Blessington, Lady Marguerite
  (1789–1849), 561
Blois (France), 538
Blumenfeld, Felix (1863–1931), 18
Bocage, Pierre (1799–1862), 450, 470n.,
  512n.
Boieldieu, François-Adrien (1775–1834),
  143
  La Dame blanche, 143
Bonn (Germany), 16, 510
Borie, Victor (1818–1880), 512, 538
Borodino, Battle of (September 7, 1812), 26
Bourges, Michel de (1797–1853), 352
Brahms, Johannes (1833–1897):
  as Chopin's editor, 411–12 and n.
  Rhapsody in E-flat major, op. 119,
    no. 4, 246
Branicka, Countess Eliza (1820–1876),
  654
Brault, Augustine (1824–1905), 501,
  534–35
  Adèle (mother), 501
  Joseph (father), 501, 503n.
Brehmer, Dr. Hermann (1826–1899),
  604n.
Breithaupt, Rudolf Maria (1873–1945),
  254
Breitkopf and Härtel (Leipzig), 16, 422n.
Brighton Pavilion (England), 317
Broadwood & Co. (London), 558–59,
  576n., 581n., 595, 600n.

Broadwood, James Shudi (1772–1851),
  314, 315
  Henry Fowler (son) (1811–1893),
    575–76, 600
Brochów (Poland), 32
Brodziński, Kazimierz (1791–1835), 46, 105
Bronic, Adam (1765–1830), 59
Broussais, Dr. François-Joseph-Victor
  (1772–1838), 604
Brown, Maurice John Edwin
  (1906–1975), 152n., 382n.
Bruce, Lord Thomas (1776–1841), 572n.
  Frances Anne (daughter) (1831–1894),
    572n.
Brünn (Brno, Czech Republic), 106
Brunner, August Fidelis (1787–after
  1832), 83
Brzezina, Andrzej (d. 1831), 110–11
Brzezińska, Katarzyna, 178
Brzowski, Józef (1805–1888), 272, 309,
  351, 365
  on Chopin's playing, 303–304
Buchholtz, Fryderyk (1792–1837), 47, 117,
  124, 630n.
Bukowski, Andrzej, 116
Bülow, Hans Guido von (1830–1894), 244
  as Chopin's editor, 325, 327, 330
Buloz, François (1803–1877), 408,
  420–21
Busoni, Ferruccio (1866–1924), 258

Calamatta, Luigi (1801–1869), 432
Canut, Bazile (1793–1844), 390n.
Canut, Mme Hélène Choussat de
  (1810–1896), 375
Caplier, Dominique (b. 1965), xxvii
Carafa, Michele (1787–1872), 342
Carlisle (England), 576
Carlsbad (Karlovy Vary, Czech Republic),
  45, 282–84
Carlyle, Thomas (1795–1881), 557
Carlyle, Jane Welsh (1801–1866), 598
Castellan, Jeanne Anaïs (1819–after
  1858), 622
Catalani, Angelica (1780–1849), 61, 243,
  606 and n.
Catania (Sicily), 342

Cate, Curtis Wilson (1924–2006), 8, 368, 402, 503
Catelin, Adolphe-Étienne (1806–1875), 386n.
Catherine the Great, Empress of Russia (1729–1796), 24–25, 57–58 and n.
Cauvière, Dr. François (1780–1858), 392, 397
Celiński, Marceli (1809–1842), 139, 144, 208
Cervantes, Miguel de (1547–1616), 645
    Don Quixote, 645
Chainaye, Denise (1898–1970), 12, 659
Chainaye, Suzanne (1897–1960), 12, 659
Chateaubriand, François-Réne de (1768–1848), 604
Châteauroux (France), 418
Chatiron, Hippolyte (Sand's half brother) (1799–1848), 355, 405, 496, 509
    Émilie (wife), 405
    Léontine (daughter), 361
Chenonceau (France), 509
Cherbourg (France), 435
Cherubini, Luigi Carlo Zanobi Salvadore Maria (1760–1842), 237, 342, 508
    Medea, 313
Chichester (England), 313
Cholera outbreaks:
    Vienna (1829), 202
    Paris (1832), 228
    Paris (1848–49), 606
    Warsaw (1855), 631n.
Chomiński, Józef Michal (1906–1994), 679
Chopin family members:
    Mikołaj (father) (1771–1844), 4, 5, 21–25, 70, 97, 126–27, 151, 170, 178, 199, 202, 221, 227, 236, 239, 282–85, 291–92, 654
        boarding school of, 44–45
        character of, 46–47
        death of, 4, 469–75
    Tekla Justyna (mother, née Krzyżanowska) (1782–1861), 31–32, 170, 282–85, 302, 470–71, 555, 626

Ludwika Marianna (sister) (1807–1855), 5, 35–37, 47, 476–78, 487, 526, 610, 643n.
    marriage to Józef Jędrzejewicz (q.v.), 282n.
    Józio's Journey, 307–308n.
    "Ludwika's Confession," 625–28
Justyna Izabella (sister) (1811–1881), 5, 37–39, 177, 626
    marriage to Antoni Barciński (q.v.), 38
Emilia (sister) (1812–1827), 39–40, 44
    death of, 4, 5, 112–14
Anne (paternal aunt) (1769–1845), 22
Marguerite (paternal aunt) (1775–1845), 22
François (paternal grandfather) (1738–1814), 21
Chopin, Fryderyk Franciszek (1810–1849):
    accidents to:
        (1826), 96
        (1848), 583 and n.
    application for travel funds denied, 131–33
    anti-Semitic language of, 385–86, 444
    autopsy of, 619
    Bach and, 48, 405
    Beethoven and, 16, 328
    Bellini and, 341–42
    Berlioz and, 16
    birth and baptism of, 32–35
    correspondence of, 11
    death and funeral of, 618–25
    descriptions of his piano playing:
        (1829), 144, 146
        (1832), 226
        (1836), 294–95
        (1841), 443
        (1842), 449
        (1848), 595
    diary of, 594, 609
    Elsner and, 105, 108, 115, 139, 147, 237–38
    Field and, 111, 220, 231–35
    funeral and burial of, 618–23
    Hallé and, 336–37, 546–47
    Heine on, 241

"hallucinations" of, 383–84, 584–85
improvisations of, 60, 64, 82, 83, 88,
    129, 143–44, 149, 163, 343, 525
"journal" of, 662–66
Kalkbrenner and, 219–24
Konstancja Gładkowska and, 153–79,
    184, 189–90, 207, 209
Liszt and, 15–16, 62–63, 194, 226–27,
    441–42 and n., 449, 510–11
Maria Wodzińska and, 279–308
Mendelssohn and, 290, 506 and n.
Moscheles and, 426–30
Mozart and, 53–54, 163, 175
metronome and, 323–24 and n.
mimicry, talent for, 68, 199, 401
money and, 199, 202, 203, 224, 227, 229
    and n., 236, 385–86, 395–96, 606
as organist, 87–89, 255, 395
pupils of, 422–26, 448
religion and, 31–32, 615–17
Rellstab and, 333–36
Schumann and, 14–15, 416
sea-sickness and, 310, 602
as teacher, 230–31, 422–25
Thalberg and, 186
tuberculosis and, 5–6
CHOPIN AND THE PIANO
fingerings, 242, 249–52, 255–62
pedalings, 242, 265–67
"Piano Method" of, 242, 248–51,
    253–54, 605
pianos, preferences for, 142, 219
tempo rubato, 462–63 and n.
COMPOSING TECHNIQUES
"apotheosis of themes," 274–75, 389,
    521–22
atonality, 387
"developing variation," 275–76
harmonic innovations, 272–74
WORKS
SOLO PIANO
Allegro de Concert, op. 46, 423, 444
Andante Spianato, op. 22, 247, 561
Ballades:
    in G minor, op. 23, 238, 274, 294
    in F major, op. 38, 291, 303
    in A-flat major. op. 47, 444, 447

Barcarolle, op. 60, 246–47, 547
Berceuse, op. 57, 259–60, 489–92, 581
Bourrées, in G and A major, 477
Fantaisie in F minor, op. 49, 270–71,
    640
Funeral March in C minor, op. posth.,
    95n.
Hexaméron variation, 340
Impromptus:
    in A-flat major, op. 29, 262, 345–46
    in G-flat major, op. 51, 466
Lento con gran espressione, op. posth.,
    195–98, 299, 670
Largo (Hexaméron), 340–41
Largo in E-flat major, 268n.
Mazurkas:
    in F-sharp minor, op. 6, no. 1, 193
    in B-flat major, op. 7, no. 1, 194–95,
      460n.
    in A-flat major, op. 7, no. 4, 80–81
    in A minor, op. 17, no. 4, 77–78 and n.
    in C-sharp minor, op. 30, no. 4, 272
    in C major, op. 33, no. 2, 461–62
    4 Mazurkas, op. 41, 568
    in C-sharp minor, op. 50, no, 3, 508
    3 Mazurkas, op. 59, 498, 503–508
    3 Mazurkas, op. 63, 525n.
    in G minor, op. posth. 67, no. 2,
      611–12
    in F minor, op. posth. 68, no. 4, 612
"The Moon Has Risen," 31
Nocturnes:
    in B-flat minor, op. 9, no. 1, 261
    in E-flat major, op. 9, no. 2, 23,
      256–57, 286
    in B major, op. 9, no. 3, 275–76
    in F-sharp major, op. 15, no. 2, 244
    in C-sharp minor, op. 27, no. 1, 247
    in D-flat major, op. 27, no. 2, 266–67
    in B major, op. 32, no. 1, 245–46
    in G minor, op. 37, no. 1, 256, 316,
      597
    in C minor, op. 48, no. 1, 256, 259,
      466, 468
    in B major, op. 62, no. 1, 245
    in E minor, op. posth. 72, no. 1, 109,
      111–12

Chopin, Fryderyk Franciszek (*cont.*)
  Polonaise-Fantaisie, op. 61, 498, *519–23*
  Polonaises:
    in G minor (1817), op. posth., 50–52
    in A-flat major (1821) op. posth., 63
    in B-flat minor, op. posth., 98–99
    in A major, op. 40, no. 1, 386*n.*
    in C minor, op. 40, no. 2, 386*n.*
    in F-sharp minor, op. 44, *516–18*
    in A-flat major, op. 53 ("Heroic"),
      451–55
  24 Preludes, op. 28, 4, *381–86*
    no. 2, in A minor, 384–85
    no. 3, in G major, 255
    no. 6, in B minor, 255–56
    no. 8, in F-sharp minor, 384
    no. 13, in F-sharp major, 515*n.*
    no. 15, in D-flat major ("Raindrop"),
      383–84
    no. 17, in A-flat major, 382*n.*
    no. 23, in F major, 266
  Rondo à la Mazur, op. 5, 61, 109, 319
  Rondo in C minor, op. 1, 84, 319
  Rondo in C major, op. 73 (op. posth.),
    110, 124
  Scherzos:
    in B minor, op. 20, *187–91*, 238, 319
    in B-flat minor, op. 31, 271–72, 316,
      319, 461
    in C-sharp minor, op. 39, 270,
      387–89, 426
    in E major, op. 54, 450
  Sonatas:
    in C minor, op. 4, 122, 141
    in B-flat minor, op. 35 ("Funeral
      March"), 259, *409–18*, 423–24,
      436, 584–85, 621
    in B minor, op. 58, 267, *478–86*
  "Souvenir de Paganini," *134–35*
  12 Studies, op. 10, 50, 151, 238, *319–22*
    no. 1, in C major, 151, *262–63*
    no. 2, in A minor, 151, *263–64*
    no. 3, in E major, *322–23*
    no. 4, in C-sharp minor, 324
    no. 5, in G-flat major ("Black Keys"),
      257
    no. 6, in E-flat minor, 325

    no. 10, in A-flat major, *325–26*
    no. 11, in E-flat major, *326*
    no. 12, in C minor ("Revolutionary"),
      209, *326–28*
  12 Studies, op. 25, *319–22*
    no. 1, in A-flat major ("Aeolian
      Harp"), 247, *294*, 303, *328*
    no. 3, in F major, *328–29*
    no. 5, in E minor, 258
    no. 6, in G-sharp minor ("Thirds"), 329
    no. 8, in D-flat major ("Sixths"),
      329–30
    no. 10, in B minor ("Octaves"), *330*
    no. 11, in A minor ("Winter Wind"),
      330–31
    no. 12, in C minor ("Ocean"), *332*
  Trois Nouvelles Études, *428–29*
  Waltzes:
    in E-flat major, op. 18, *200–201*,
      279–80
    in A-flat major, op. 34, no. 1, 285
    in A minor, op. 34. no. 2, 259
    in D-flat major, op. 64, no. 3
      ("Minute"), 543, 547
    in A-flat major ("L'Adieu"),
      op. posth. 69, no. 1, 286, 288
    in F minor, op. posth. 70, no. 2, 463
    in D-flat major, op. posth. 70, no. 3,
      155
  SONGS
  "Czary" (Enchantment), 164–65
  "Precz z moich oczu!" (Out of my
    Sight!) 164–65
  "Wiosna" (Spring), 487
  "Życzenie" (The Wish), 110, 164–65,
    190
  PIANO AND ORCHESTRA
  Concerto in E minor, op. 11, 110,
    172–76, 185, 203, 224, 236, 281,
    345, 466, 467
  Concerto in F minor, op. 21, 110,
    162–64, 171, 319
  Grand Fantasia on Polish Airs, op. 13,
    82*n.*, 110, 129, 148, 172, 203
  Krakowiak: Grand Concert Rondo in
    F major, op. 14, 61, 110, 143, 146,
    151

Variations on Mozart's "Là ci darem la
mano," op. 2, 14–15, 109, *118–20*,
141, 168, 198, 224, 319
CHAMBER MUSIC
Introduction and Polonaise in C major
for Cello and Piano, op. 3, 161
Piano Trio in G minor, op. 8, 110, 130–31
Sonata in G minor for Cello and Piano,
op. 65, 218, 414, *513–15*, 543,
544–45, 547
Chorley, Henry Fothergill (1808–1872),
252
Ciampi, Sebastiano (1769–1847), 65
Cicero (107 B.C.–43 B.C.), 66
Ciechomska, Ludwika Marianna (*née*
Jędrzejewicz) (1835–1890), 474
Cimarosa, Domenico (1749–1801), 128
Il matrimonio segreto, 128
Cinti-Damoreau, Laure (1801–1863), 438
City of Boulogne (paddle steamer), 602*n*.
Clark, Sir James (1788–1870), 5, 599–600
and *n*.
Clary-Aldringen, Prince Karl von
(1777–1831), 149
Clavier, André, 40
Clementi, Muzio (1752–1832), 232*n*.,
320, 425
Gradus ad Parnassum, 320, 425
Clésinger, Jean-Baptiste-Auguste
(1814–1883), *530–36*, 537, 551*n*.
620, 623 and *n*.
Solange (wife, *née* Sand) (1828–1899)
(*q.v.*)
Jeanne-Gabrielle (daughter)
(1848–1848), 550
Jeanne-Gabrielle (daughter)
(1849–1855), 551*n*.
Coleridge, Samuel Taylor (1771–1834),
666, 671
Combes, Edmond (1812–1848), 550–51
and *n*.
commedia dell'arte, 401
Conrad, Joseph (1857–1924), 205–206
Constantine Pavlovich, Grand Duke
(1779–1831), 46, 55–59, 92, 171,
180
Juliane (first wife) (1781–1860), 58–59

Joanna Grudzińska (second wife)
(1791–1831), 59–60, 92, 180
Josephine Friedrichs (mistress)
(1778–1824), 60
Paul (illegitimate son) (1808–1857), 60
Constantinople (Turkey), 57
Cooper, James Fennimore (1789–1851),
493
Copernicus, Nicolaus (1473–1543),
85–86, 272
Corbari, Amalia (singer), 579
Correspondents' Gazette, 55
Cortot, Alfred-Denis (1877–1962), 278,
327
Coste, Dr. Jacques-Hubert, 391*n*.
Courrier français, Le (Paris), 16, 529
Coutts, Baroness Angela (1815–1907),
608
Coxe, Reverend William (1748–1828),
23–24
Cresy, Edward (1792–1858), 458
Cristina, Queen Regent of Spain
(1806–1878), 373, 447
Cromwell, Oliver (1599–1658), 356
Cruveilhier, Dr. Jean-Baptiste
(1791–1874), 604, 609, 613, 619
Custine, Marquis Astolphe-Louis-Léonor
de (1790–1857), 302–303, 309,
365, 542, 548
Cybulski, Izydor Józef, 51
Czapek, Leopold Eustachius
(1792–1840), 91
Czartoryska, Princess Marcelina (*née*
Radziwiłł) (1817–1894), 218, 243,
588, 601, 606, 627
Aleksander Romuald (husband)
(1811–1886), 588
Marcel (son) (1841–1909), 588
Czartoryski, Prince Adam Jerzy
(1770–1861), 58, 92, 180, 192,
206–207 and *n*., 218, 601, 620
Anna Sophia (*née* Sapieha) (wife)
(1799–1864), 207*n*.
Czaykowski, Adjutant Alfons, 171
Czernicka, Paulina (1897–1949), 655–58
Czerny, Carl (1791–1857), 144, 320, 422
School of Velocity, 320

Czetwertyńska, Princess Idalia
(1782–1846), 54
Borys (son) (1808–1863), 54
Kalikst (son) (1809–1888), 54
Czosnowska, Countess Laura
(1778–1846), 525
Count Janusz (husband) (d. 1831), 525

Dagestan (Russia), 205
Daily News (London), 563 and n.
Dalcour, Camila (1818–1855), 640–42
Dalmas, Dr. Adolphe (1799–1844), 342n.
Damascus (Syria), 551n.
Dąmbska, Justyna (c. 1765–1808), 28
Dantan, Jean-Pierre (1800–1869), 458
Davies, Norman (b. 1939), 25
Davison, James William (1813–1885),
466, 564
description of Chopin's funeral service,
622
"Essay on the Works of Frédéric
Chopin," 569
opposition to Chopin's music, 566–70
and n.
Debussy, Claude-Achille (1862–1918), 16,
176, 480
Decazes, Duke Élie (1780–1860), 292
Deflin, Marguerite (1736–1794), 22
Deguerry, Abbé Gaspard (1797–1871),
620
Dekert, Bishop Jan (1786–1861), 23, 469
and n.
Delaborde, Sophie-Victoire (Sand's
mother) (1773–1837), 353–54, 355
Delacroix, Eugène (1799–1863), 343, 369,
419, 444, 450, 456, 492, 503, 529,
538 and n., 605, 620 and n.
description of Nohant, 457
Delaroche, Paul (1797–1856), 447
Dembiński, General Henryk (1791–1864),
216
Dembowski, Karol (1808–1863), 378n.
Dennery, Adolphe-Philippe (1811–1899),
511
Deschartres, "Abbé" Jean-François-Louis
(1761–1828), 355, 359
Dettweiler, Dr. Peter (1837–1904), 604n.

Diakow, General Piotr Nikolayevich
(1788–1847), 163
Dickens, Charles John Huffam
(1812–1870), 314, 557
The Pickwick Papers, 314
Didier, Alexis (1826–1886), 607n.
Didier, Charles Emmanuel (1805–1864),
431n.
Diebitsch, General Hans von
(1785–1831), 191–92
Dieffenbach, Johann Friedrich
(1792–1847), 333
Dietrichstein, Prince Moritz (1775–1864),
144
Długosz, Józef (1778–1853), 83
Dmuszewski, Ludwik Adam (1777–1847),
179n.
Dobosz, Dr. Tadeusz (b. 1948), xxv, 667
Dobrzyński, Ignacy Feliks (1807–1867),
108–109
Döhler, Theodor (1814–1856), 320, 428
Donizetti, Domenico Gaetano Maria
(1797–1848), 245
Dorval, Marie (1798–1849), 365, 420,
433, 511
Dover (England), 317n.
Dresden (Germany), 150, 285, 288
Dreyschock, Alexander (1818–1869), 254
Heine on, 240
Dubois, Camille (née O'Meara)
(1830–1907), 547, 651
Duchâtel, Count Charles-Marie-
Tanneguy (1803–1867), 420
Duchnowski, Father Jan, 34
Dudevant, Baron Jean-François
(1754–1826)
Baroness Gabrielle-Louise (wife)
(1772–1837), 362
François-Casimir (illegitimate son)
(1795–1871), 357–59, 362–63,
370
Duffus & Co. (shipbuilders), 373
Dumas, Alexandre, père (1802–1870),
458, 632
Dumas, Alexandre, fils (1824–1895), 632
Dumfries (Scotland), 650
Dunblane (Scotland), 571, 587

Duperré, Laure, 461
   Victor Guy, Admiral Duperré (father)
      (1775–1846), 461
Dupin de Francueil, Mme Marie-Aurora
      (1748–1821), 353, 354, 357
Dupin, Maurice-François-Élisabeth
      (1778–1808), 353–55, 398
   Sophie-Victoire (wife) (1773–1837), 355
"Dupont" Stradivarius (1711), 515
Duport, Louis (1781–1853), 201–202
Duprez, Gilbert-Louis (1806–1896), 394
Dupuytren, Baron Guillaume
      (1777–1835), 234
Dussek, Jan Ladislav (1760–1812), 478
Duteil, Alexis (1796–1852), 359
Dorval, Marie (actress), 365, 420
Duvernet, Charles-Benoist (1807–1874),
      524
Dwernicki, General Józef (1799–1857),
      191
Dzialyńska, Cecylia (1836–1899), 587
Dziekoński, Tomasz Sylwester
      (1790–1875), 65
Dziewanowski, Dominik ("Domuś")
      (1811–1881), 9, 27, 46, 69–70,
      178, 231, 235
   Juliusz (father) (1779–1854), 70, 72
      and n.
   Wiktoria (mother) (1789–1869), 71n.
   Honorata (stepmother) (1803–1868),
      71 and n., 86
   Ludwika (aunt) (1775–1880), 70, 71

East India Company, 577
Echo Muzyczne, 100, 135
Edinburgh (Scotland):
   Calder House, 576–77
   Castle, 576
   Douglas Hotel, 576
   Hopetoun Rooms, 593–94
   St. Andrew's Square, 576
   University, 650
   Waterloo Place, 576
Edinburgh Advertiser, 594
Edinburgh Courant, 595
Eichthal, Baron Adolphe d' (1805–1895),
      343

Eigeldinger, Jean Jacques (b. 1940),
      242–43n.
Ekier, Jan (1913–2014), 95n., 112n., 645
      and n., 661
El Mallorquin (paddle steamer), 373–74
      and n., 389, 391
Elba (Italy), 26n.
Elbe River (Germany), 285
Elsner, Józef Antoni Franciszek
      (1769–1854), 9, 83, 100, 103n.,
      104–108, 122, 126, 141, 151,
      153–54, 201, 221, 237–38
   Klara Abt (first wife) (d. 1797), 106
   Karolina Drozdowska (second wife)
      (1785–1852), 106
   Emilia (daughter) (c. 1811–1864), 109
   Coronation Mass, 136
   High School for Music, 9, 104–106, 139
   maxims of, 107–108
Emerson, Ralph Waldo (1803–1882), 557
Emerald (paddle steamer), 602n.
Énault, Louis (1824–1900), 458
Enghien-les-Bains (France), 305, 309, 477
Érard, Pierre (1796–1855), 460, 559
   Sébastien (father) (1752–1831), 268
Ernemann, Maurycy (1800–1866), 124
Ernst, Heinrich Wilhelm (1814–1865),
      344, 438
Erskine, Katherine (née Stirling)
      (1791–1868), xxviii, 543, 572–73,
      597n., 622
   James (husband) (1787–1816), 572, 597n.
   children of, 597n.
Escudier, Léon (1821–1881), 420, 443
Étienne, Mme, 607–608, 627
Ewer & Co. (London publisher), 636

Falampin, Jean-Gabriel (1803–1860), 633
Falkenstein, Karl (1801–1855), 128
Falmouth, Lord George Henry Boscawen
      (1812–1897), 498, 563, 565
Farnborough (England), 641
Fauré, Gabriel-Urbain (1845–1924), 17
Feicht, Father Hieronim (1894–1967), 671
Fenger, Jakub (1729–1798), 27, 28
Ferrà, Bartolomeu Juan (1893–1946),
      390n.

Festetics, Count Leó (1800–1884), 441n.
Fétis, François-Joseph (1784–1871), 33n.,
    226, 232, 428
  Biographical Dictionary of Musicians,
    319
  description of Chopin, 226
Field, John (1782–1837), 111, 220, 231–35
  Romance in E-flat major (1814), 234
Filtsch, Károly (Carl) (1830–1845), 5, 243,
    461, 466, 463–68
  Josef (brother) (b. 1813), 464, 466
  death in Venice, 468, 493
  Impromptu in G-flat major, 467
  Konzertstück, 467n., 468
  Liszt and, 466
Flahault de Billarderie, Count Auguste-
    Charles (1785–1870), 653
Flaubert, Gustave (1821–1880), 529
Flora journal (Munich), 203
Flury, Pierre-Hippolyte, 375
Folkestone (England), 602
Fontana, Julian Ignacy (1810–1869), 9,
    46, 122, 178, 216, 297, 312, 371,
    380, 386n., 554–55, 635–38,
    639–45
  Camila (née Dalcour) (wife)
    (1818–1855), 640–42
  Julian Camillo Adam (son) (b. 1853),
    641, 645
  Zofia (daughter) (1855–1855), 641
  Fernanda Leokadia (illegitimate
    daughter) (b. 1845), 641
  Chopin's letters to, 375, 376, 380–81,
    395, 410, 444, 516, 555, 577
  as editor of Chopin's posthumous
    works, 642–43, 644
  Havana Philharmonic Society and, 640
  projected Chopin biography, 647–48
  suicide of, 645 and n.
Fournier, Elisa, 524
  description of Chopin, 525
France musicale, La (Paris), 443, 447
Franchomme, Auguste-Joseph
    (1808–1884), 218–19, 470, 487,
    513–15 and n., 606, 612 and n., 620
  Amélie Paillot (wife), 219
Freppa, Mme Lina, 341

Friedlein, Rudolf Fryderyk (1811–1873),
    636
Friedman, Ignaz (1882–1948), 429, 453
Friedrich Wilhelm III, King of Prussia
    (1770–1840), 126
Gainsborough, Countess Adelaide Harriet
    Augusta (1821–1867), 561
Gajewski, Ferdynand Jan (b. 1941), 467n.
Gallenberg, Count Wenzel Robert
    (1783–1839), 142, 201
Ganche, Édouard (1880–1945), 22n.,
    390n.
García, Manuel Patricio Rodriguez
    (1805–1906), 424, 501
  Joaquína Sitchez (wife) (1780–1864),
    424
  Pauline Viardot-García (daughter) (q.v.)
García-Vestris (1797–1856), 201
Gargunnock House (Scotland), 586
Garibaldi, Giuseppe (1807–1882), 337
Gautier, Théophile (1811–1872), 252, 622
Gavard, Charles (1826–1893), 610
  Élise (sister) (1824–1900), 490
  description of Chopin, 610–11
Gavoty, Bernard (1908–1981), 583
Gdańsk (Danzig, Poland), 115–17, 125,
    299
Gendre, Major-General Alexander
    Andreyevich (1776–1830), 180
Genoa (Italy), 396
Gide, André (1869–1951), 246
Gilels, Emil (1916–1985), 248
Girard, Narcisse (1797–1860), 236, 281,
    622
Girardot, Baron (Dr.) François
    (1773–1831), 69, 72
Gładkowska, Konstancja Salomea
    (1810–1889), 118, 153–79, 184,
    189–90, 207, 209
  Andrzej (father) (c. 1763–c. 1828), 154
  Salomea (mother) (1790–1865), 154
  Aleksander Józef Grabowski (husband),
    (1803–1878), 177, 209
Glasgow (Scotland):
  Glasgow Constitutional, The, 591n.
  Glasgow Courier, The, 591n.

Glasgow Herald, The, 587*n*., 590–91
  Merchants' Hall, 588
Glentyan House (Scotland), 587
Glinka, Mikhail Ivanovich (1804–1857), 231
Gliński, Mateusz (1892–1976), 658
  Chopin Listy do Delfiny, 658
Gloger, Zygmunt (1845–1910), 144*n*.
Goethe, Johann Wolfgang von
    (1749–1832), 150, 161, 530
  Faust, 150
Goldberg, Halina (b. 1961), 54*n*.
Gómez, Señor, 375–76
Görgey, General Artúr (1818–1916), 588
Goszczyński, Seweryn (1801–1876), 437
Gottschalk, Louis Moreau (1829–1869), 223, 277
Gounod, Charles (1818–1893), 219
Gourgaud, General Gaspard (1783–1852), 434
Gow, Andrew Carrick (1848–1920), 68*n*.
Grabowski, Count Stanisław
    (1780–1845), 131–32
Graf, Conrad (1782–1851), 142, 183, 200
Gräfe, Karl Ferdinand von (1787–1840), 333
Granville, Dr. Augustus Bozzi
    (1783–1872), 588*n*.
Graves, Robert Ranke (1895–1985), 384*n*., 391*n*.
Gregory XVI, Pope (1765–1846), 205*n*.
Grembecki, Franciszek (c. 1747–1827), 34
Grieg, Edvard Hagerup (1843–1907), 175
Grillparzer, Franz (1791–1872), 516
Grisi, Giulia (1811–1869), 447
Grosskurth, Emma (1862–1935), 330*n*.
Grzymała, Wojciech (Albert)
    (1793–1870), 161, *216–17*, 351,
    365, 368, *406–408*, 489, 525, 579,
    602, 603, 617
  Michelina Krüger (wife), 217
  Wincenty (son) (b. 1820), 217
  accident to, 477
  projected Chopin biography, 648–49
Guicciardi, Giulietta (1782–1856), 142
Gunsberg, Paul (d. 1845?), 5

Gutowski, Count Ignacy (1812–1888), 304
Gutmann, Adolf (1819–1882), 218, 243,
    254, 291, 322, 344, 387, 412*n*.,
    424, 426, 596, 611, 618 and *n*.,
    620
Gyrowetz, Adalbert (1763–1850), 53

Habeneck, François-Antoine (1781–1849), 435, 467
Halévy, Jacques-Fromental (1799–1862), 447
Hamilton, Duke William Alexander
    Archibald (1811–1863), 596
Hallé, Sir Charles (1819–1895), 318, 582
  on Chopin's playing, 16, 318, 544–45, 546–47
Hamilton Palace (Scotland), 586, 596–97
Handel, George Frideric (1685–1759),
    128, 438
  Deborah, 280
  Ode for Saint Cecilia's Day, 128
Hanka, Václav (1791–1861), 147
Hańska, Ewelina (1801–1882), 653
Harasowski, Adam Jerzy (1904–1996), 661
Hart Dyke, Mrs. Elizabeth (1802–1893), 561
Haslinger, Tobias (1787–1842), 120, 141,
    146, 198–99
  Karl (son) (1816–1868), 122, 141
Havana (Cuba), 640, 641
Haweis, Reverend Hugh Reginald
    (1838–1901), 418
Haydn, Franz Joseph (1732–1809), 53
  The Creation (oratorio), 492
Hedderwick, James (1814–1897), 556, 591–92
Hedley, Arthur (1905–1969), 158*n*., 324*n*.,
    416*n*., 467*n*., 598*n*., 658–59
  *Selected Correspondence of Fryderyk
    Chopin*, 467*n*., 658
Heidelberg (Germany), 291
Heine, Heinrich (1799–1856), 228,
    240–41, 254, 277, 342
  and Chopin, 15, 241
  Musikalische Berichte aus Paris, 228, 240

Heinefetter, Sabine (1809–1872), 183
Helman, Zofia, 12, 208n.
Heller, Stephen (1814–1888), 133, 221n.,
    253
Héreau, Mme Michelle (b. 1793), 499
Herz, Henri (1803–1888), 219, 277
    criticism of Chopin, 346
    Heine on, 240
    voyage to America, 277n.
Hiller, Ferdinand (1811–1885), 68, 223,
    277, 280, 350
    Régine (mother), 280–81
Hilton, Ordway (1914–1998), 661
Hipkins, Alfred James (1826–1903), 255,
    558n.
Hoesick, Ferdynand (1867–1941), 11–12,
    65, 300–301, 317n., 331n., 629n.,
    651–53, 661, 665
Hoffman, Dr. Aleksander Julian
    (1805–1867), 236–37, 296, 331, 655
    Emilia (wife, née Borzęcka)
    (1832–1911), 331 and n., 655
Hoffmann, Jakub Fryderyk (1758–1830),
    82, 121
Hogarth, George (1783–1870), 563n.
Horowitz, Vladimir (1903–1989), 18
Houston, Mrs. Ludovic (née Ann Stirling)
    (1783–1851), 585
Hube, Romuald (1803–1890), 139, 144,
    184–85
Hueffer, Francis (1845–1889), 601
Huesca, Battle of (May 24, 1837), 306
Hugo, Victor Marie (1802–1885), 365
    description of Napoléon's re-burial, 435
Humboldt, Alexander von (1769–1859),
    126–27, 130, 650
Hummel, Johann Nepomuk (1778–1837),
    50, 119, 122–23, 175, 184, 198,
    238, 478
Humnicki, Ignatius (1798–1864), 39
Huneker, James Gibbons (1860–1921),
    329, 504, 505
Hünten, Franz (1793–1878), 239

Illustrated London News, 562, 601n.
Indre River (France), 399, 496
Indyk family, 140–41

Idzikowski, Mieczysław, 669n.
Iwaszkiewicz, Jarosław (1894–1980), 348

Jabłczyński, Feliks (1865–1928), 522
James, Henry (1843–1916), 529
Janin, Jules-Gabriel (1804–1874), 365
Januszkiewicz, Eustachy (1805–1874), 437
Jarocki, Feliks Paweł (1790–1865),
    126–27, 130
Jasiński, Władysław Piotr (1790–1856), 65
Jawurek, Józef (1756–1840), 62, 90
Jędrzejewicz, Józef Kalasanty
    (1803–1853), 36–37, 472, 476, 610
    marriage to Ludwika Chopin (q.v.),
    36–37
    Henryk Bronisław (son) (1833–1899),
    282
    Ludwika Magdalena (daughter)
    (1835–1890), 610, 618n.
    Antoni Żelisław (son) (1843–1922),
    305, 629n.
Jefferson, Thomas (1743–1826), 25n.
Jełowicki, Abbé Aleksander (1804–1877),
    615–17 and n.
Joachim, Joseph (1831–1907), 136
Johnson, Dr. Samuel (1709–1784), 325
Johnstone Castle (Scotland), 587
Jolicki, Dr. Feliks, 125–30
Jordan, Ruth (1926–1994), 660
Journal de Rouen, 345
Journal des débats (Paris), 4n.
Jullien, Louis-Antoine (1812–1860), 559

Kähler, Friedrich (1781–1834), 129
Kalisz (Poland), 27, 179
Kalergis, Countess Maria (née
    Nesselrode) (1822–1874), 605
Kalkbrenner, Friedrich Wilhelm Michael
    (1788–1849), 75, 142, 219–24,
    250–51, 277, 336, 458, 559, 606
    Arthur (son) (1828–1869), 223–24n.
    Heine on, 240
Kallberg, Jeffrey (b. 1954), 409n., 517n.
Kamiński, Paweł (b. 1958), xxv, 517n.
Karasowski, Moritz (1823–1892), 53n.,
    130n., 230n., 327, 479, 611n.,
    649–50

Karénine, Wladimir (pseud. of Mme V. D.
Komarova) (1862–1943), 651
Karłowicz, Mieczysław (1876–1909),
474n., 674
Keir House (Scotland), 586, 592–93
Kemble, Frances Anne ("Fanny")
(1809–1893), 561n.
Kessler, Joseph Christoph (1800–1872),
386n.
Kikół (Poland), 115
Kingston-upon-Thames (England), 557
Klengel, August Alexander (1783–1852),
148–49 and n.
48 Canons and Fugues, 148
Klindworth, Carl (1830–1916), 110
Kniaziewicz, General Karol (1762–1842),
216, 292
Knosp, Gaston (1874–1942), 662, 663, 665
Knox, John (1514–1572), 576
Kobylańska, Krystyna (1925–2009),
598n., 610n., 679
Koch, Dr. Robert (1843–1910), 604n.
Kodály, Zoltán (1882–1967), 82
Kolberg, Wilhelm Karol Adolf ("Wiluś")
(1807–1877), 70, 71, 79–80, 98,
208
Juliusz (father) (1776–1831), 46
Henryk Oskar (brother) (1814–1890),
80n., 144n.
Köller (Koehler), Dr. Ludwik (1799–1871),
178
Kościuszko, General Tadeusz
(1746–1817), 25 and n., 52, 127
Kossecki, General Franciszek
(1778–1857), 133
Koźmian, Stanisław Egbert (1811–1885),
312–13, 314, 640, 648n.
Kraków (Poland), 140–41, 554
Krasiński, Zygmunt (1812–1859), 216, 654
Krasiński, Józef Wawrzyniec (1783–1845),
287
Kreutzer, Conradin (1780–1849), 144
Krysiak, Antoni (c. 1810–c. 1900), 64–65
Kulig, Magdalena, xxv
Kullak, Theodor (1818–1882), 327
Kumelski, Norbert Alfons (1802–1853),
203, 213

Kurpiński, Karol Kazimierz (1785–1857),
106, 109, 172, 519n.
Kuźnicki, S., 632
Kwiatkowski, Teofil Antoni (1809–1891),
615 and n.

La Châtre (France), 354, 370, 524
Lablache, Luigi (1794–1858), 243, 447,
467, 622
Lachmann, Thérèse, 240
Lachmund, Carl Valentine (1853–1928),
454
Lachner, Franz Paul (1803–1890), 145
Lach-Szyrma, Prof. Krystyn
(1790–1866), 138
Lamartine, Alphonse-Marie-Louis de
Prat de (1790–1869), 552
Lambert, Louis-Eugène (1825–1900), 526
Lamond, Frederic Archibald
(1868–1948), 452
Lancashire General Advertiser, The, 583
Landré-Beauvais, Augustin-Jacob
(1772–1840), 360
Lanner, Joseph (1801–1843), 199
Las Cases, Count Emmanuel de
(1766–1842), 467
Lassailly, Charles (1806–1843), 421
Latouche, Henri de (1785–1851), 352
Latour, Count Theodor (1780–1848), 588
Lausanne (Switzerland), 436
La Vraie République (Paris), 554
Lefébure-Wély, Louis James Alfred
(1817–1869), 621
Legouvé, Ernest (1807–1903), 229, 439
description of Chopin, 229, 346
Le Havre (France), 367, 435
Leichtentritt, Hugo (1874–1951), 18, 328,
479–80, 663
Leikin, Anatole (b. 1946), 412n.
Leiser, General, 149–50
Lelewel, Joachim (1786–1861), 12
Łempicki, Ludwik (1791–1871), 149
Lenormand, Mlle Marie (1772–1843),
301–302
Lenormand, René (1882–1951), 273
Lenz, Wilhelm von (1809–1883), 322n.
first meeting with Chopin, 460–62

Léo, Auguste (1793–1859), 292, 343, 371, 455, 496, 544, 617
Leroux, Pierre-Henri (1797–1871), 457
Leschetizky, Theodore (1830–1915), 254
Le Sueur, Jean-François (1760–1837), 219, 237
Lichnowsky, Count Moritz (1771–1837), 144
Lichtenstein, Prof. Martin Karl Heinrich (1780–1857), 127
Lind, Johanna Maria ("Jenny") (1820–1887), 245, 559–60, 566n., 611
Linde, Samuel Bogumił (1771–1847), 8, 29, 45–46, 65–67, 68–69, 83, 116
    Ludwika (first wife, née Bürger) (1786–1823), 46
    Luiza Aleksandra (second wife, née Nussbaum) (1800–1836), 69
    Johann Wilhelm (brother), 116
Lipiński, Karol Józef (1790–1861), 134–38
Liszt, Franz (1811–1886), 13, 62 and n., 292–93, 348, 364, 399, 448, 454, 506, 522 and n.
    Beethoven Monument (1845), 510–11
    biography of Chopin, 194, 226, 351, 528, 646–47, 673–78
    letter concerning Ludwig Rellstab, 335–36n.
    "Lisztomania," 441–42n.
    review of Chopin's concert (1841), 439–43
    WORKS
    "Ab irato," 428
    Funérailles, 453
    Lucia di Lammermoor Paraphrase, 468
    Nuages gris, 78
    "Paganini" Study, in E-flat major, 268–69
    Rákóczy March, 441n.
    Reminiscences on Meyerbeer's Robert le Diable, 442n.
    Rhapsody no. 14, in F minor, 247
    "Venezia e Napoli" Suite, 268
Literary Association of the Friends of Poland, 558n.
Lives of the Saints, 356
Loch Fyne (Scotland), 587
Loch Long (Scotland), 587

Lockroy, Joseph-Philippe (1803–1891), 420
London (England):
    Bentinck Street, 557
    Bryanston Square, 314
    Buckingham Palace, 562, 565
    Covent Garden, 560, 564
    Dover Street, 558
    Eaton Place, 561
    Euston Station, 575
    Gore House, 561
    Great Pulteney Street, 558
    Guild Hall, 600
    Her Majesty's Theatre, 438, 463
    House of Commons, 559n.
    Sablonnière Hotel, 312
    Stafford (now Lancaster) House, 562
    Welbeck Street, 561
Long, Dr. Esmond (1890–1979), 4
Louis, Dr. Pierre-Charles-Alexandre (1787–1872), 603
Louis-Philippe I (1773–1850), King of the French, 170, 214, 344, 426
    Queen Marie-Amélie (wife) (1782–1866), 344, 426–27, 447
    Princess Adélaïde (sister) (1777–1847), 344
    abdication of, 549
Lovelace, Richard (1617–1657), 270n.
Lubecki-Drucki, Prince Xavier (1778–1846), 192
Lubin, Georges (1904–2000), 8, 368n., 378n., 470n., 512n.
Lubomirski, Prince Casimir (1813–1871), 216
Lubowidzki, Major Mateusz (1789–1874), 180
Łyszczyński, Dr. Adam (1806–1893), 585, 592, 598–99
    Elizabeth (wife) (1821–1908), 598–99

Maciejowice, Battle of (October 10, 1794), 25
Maciejowski, Wacław Aleksander (1793–1883), 9, 65
    Ignacy (son), 139
Mackenzie, Sir Alexander Campbell (1847–1935), 650

Macready, William Charles (1793–1873), 493

Madrid (Spain), 71

Maella, Battle of (October 1, 1838), 373n.

Maelzel, Johann Nepomuk (1772–1838), 323

Magnuszewski, Dominik Alojzy Gonzaga (1810–1845), 65

Mahé, Charles (d. 1810), 42

Malan, Dr. Henry (c. 1815–c. 1890), 599–600

Malcz, Dr. Jan Fryderyk Wilhelm (1795–1852), 98, 112–13

Malfatti, Dr. Johann (1776–1859), 198, 219
  Helena (wife, née Ostrowska) (1794–1826), 198

Malibran-García, Maria Felicità (1808–1836), 243, 424

Mallefille, Jean-Pierre-Félicien (1813–1868), 352, 366–68, 552

Mallet, Adolphe-Jacques (1787–1868), 343

Mallet, Louis-Jules (1789–1866), 336, 343

Manchester (England):
  Crumpsall House, 578
  Gentlemen's Concert Hall, 579, 584
  Royal Infirmary, 579
  Salford railway station, 578

Manchester Courier, 583

Manchester Guardian, 581, 583n., 584

Marainville (France), 21–22

Marcello, Benedetto (1686–1739), 615

Marchand, Count Louis-Joseph-Narcisse (1791–1876), 434

Marek, George (1902–1987), 661

Marienbad (Mariánské Lázně, Czech Republic), 293

Marliani, Charlotte (1790–1850), 365, 371, 419, 430, 431, 458, 509, 530
  Emmanuel (husband) (1795–1873), 371

Marmontel, Antoine-François (1816–1898), 233–34, 369–70, 605n.
  on Chopin, 265–66

Mars, Mme (pseud. of Jeanne-Marguerite Salvetat) (1748–1838), 458

Marseilles (France), 89
  Hôtel de Beauvau, 393
  Notre-Dame-du-Mont, 89

Marx, Karl (1818–1883), 552

Marylski, Eustachy (1804–1871), 11, 46

Mathias, Georges-Amédée Saint-Clair (1826–1910), 424, 425

Matthay, Tobias Augustus (1858–1945), 254

Matuszewska, Katarzyna, 606, 630

Matuszyński, Dr. Jan Edward Aleksander (1809–1842), 4, 9, 186, 189, 208, 296–97, 351, 478
  Thérèse-Charlotte-Clothilde (wife, née Boquet) (1796–1878), 296–97, 449
  death and burial of, 449, 458
  description of Chopin, 296

Maugham, William Somerset (1874–1965), 18

Maurois, André (pseud. of Emile Herzog) (1885–1967), 8, 359, 666

Mazzini, Giuseppe (1805–1872), 337

Mechetti, Pietro (publisher) (1775–1850), 183, 516

Medina, Captain Gabriel, 391

Méléagre (French brig-of-war), 391

Mendelssohn-Bartholdy, Felix (1809–1847), 13, 16, 128, 223, 247, 280, 290, 481, 567–68
  Cécile Charlotte (wife) (1817–1853), 505 and n., 506, 567
  St. Paul oratorio, 290, 295

Mendi, Antonia Molina de (b. 1827), 544

Ménestrel, Le (Paris), 277, 548

Mercadante, Saverio (1795–1870), 447

Mercure musical, Le (Paris), 665

Merk, Josef (1795–1852), 161

Metternich, Prince Klemens Wenzel von (1773–1859), 187, 283

Meyer, Leopold de (1816–1883), 582

Meyerbeer, Giacomo (1791–1864), 310, 337, 461–62, 621
  Heine on, 240
  WORKS
  L'Africaine, 462
  Il crociato in Egitto, 145
  Les Huguenots, 462, 487
  Le Prophète, 544
  Robert le Diable, 442n.

Mickiewicz, Adam Bernard (1798–1855), 12, 13, 105, 216, 351, 433, 450, 495, 512, 641
  lectures at the Collège de France (1840–44), 436–37, 451
  Messianism and, 455–56
  Pan Tadeusz, 436, 523
Mieroszewski, Ambroży (1800–1879), 35, 37, 38, 49
Mikuli, Karol (1819–1897), 243
  on Chopin, 252–53, 261, 263, 423
Milanówek (Poland), 668
Milliken House (Scotland), 586, 587
Miloradovich, Count Mikhail (1771–1825), 93
Miłosław, Battle of (April 30, 1848), 557
Mittag, August, (1795–1867), 464
Mochnacki, Maurycy (1803–1834), 122, 169
Moke, Marie-Félicité-Denise (1811–1875), 309–10, 314
Molin, Dr. Jean-Jacques (1797–1848), 492, 510, 602
Montfort, Duke Napoléon-Karol (1814–1847), 653
Moriolles, Alexandrine de (1801–1842), 60–61
  Count Alexandre-Nicolas de (father) (1760–1845), 60
Moscheles, Ignaz (1794–1870), 142, 175, 238, 313–15, 506
  Charlotte (wife, *née* Embden) (1805–1889), 426
  "Alexander" Variations, 167
  Méthode des Méthodes, 427–28
  descriptions of Chopin, 426–27, 430
  Piano Concerto in E-flat major, 181
  Piano Concerto in G minor, 83
  Sonata in E-flat major (four hands), 351
Mostowski, Count Tadeusz (1766–1842), 132–33
  Róza (daughter) (1809–1864), 133n.
Mozart, Wolfgang Amadeus (1756–1791), 50, 54, 123, 129, 248, 276, 341
  Don Giovanni, 17, 118
  Piano Concerto in C major, K. 467, 175

Piano Trio in E major, K. 542, 17, 546
Requiem, 17, 350, 436–37, 492, 620, 621–22
Rondo in A minor, K. 511, 276n.
Müller-Streicher, Friederike (1816–1895), 260–61, 262, 422–24, 436, 461
  Johann Baptiste Streicher (husband) (1761–1833), 174, 424
Munich (Germany), 202–203
Muravyov, Governor-General Mikhail (1796–1866), 205
Murray, Lord John Archibald (1778–1859), 587
  Mary (wife, *née* Rigby) (1788–1861), 587 and n.
Musical World, The (London), 315, 566, 567, 582, 622
Musset, Alfred-Louis-Charles de (1810–1857), 352, 396, 425n.
Mysłakowski, Piotr (b. 1944), *xxvi*, 9
Mysłowice (Poland), 632

Naples (Italy), 341, 394
  Hôtel Barbaie, 394
  San Carlo opera house, 394
Napoléon Bonaparte, Emperor of France (1769–1821), 17, 214, 216
  description of his re-burial, 433–36
Napoléon III, Emperor of the French (1808–1873), 589n.
Neue Zeitschrift für Musik (Leipzig), 290, 294, 543
Neuhaus, Heinrich Gustavovich (1888–1964), 18, 248–49 and n., 417, 478
Neva River (Russia), 93
Newhaven (England), 317n.
Newsom, Jon, 274n.
New York (United States):
  Apollo Rooms, 640
  Morgan Library, 120n., 242n., 453n.
  St. Patrick's Old Cathedral, 641
Nicholas I, Tsar of Russia (1796–1855), 93, 133, 191–92, 207 and n., 305
  coronation of (1829), 133, 134, 136

Nidecki, Ludwik (1810–1840), 109
  Emilia (wife, *née* Elsner) (*q.v.*)
Nidecki, Tomasz Napoléon (1800–1852),
  12, 108, 109, 146, 185
Nieborów conference (Poland), 659 and *n.*
Niecks, Frederick Maternus (1845–1924),
  68, 254, 273, 330, 423*n.*, 480,
  523, 547, 650–51
  Frederick Chopin as Man and Musician,
  651
Niedźwiedzki, Leonard (1810–1892), 218,
  602 and *n.*
Niemcewicz, Julian Ursyn (1757–1841),
  53, 292, 351
Nohant (France), xxvii, 355, 357, 398–99
Norwid, Cyprian Kamil (1821–1883), 216,
  612
  description of Chopin, 612–13
Nowik, Wojciech (b. 1940), 661*n.*
Nourrit, Adolphe (1802–1839), 89, 243,
  351, 364
  suicide and funeral of, 394–95
Novara, Battle of (March 22, 1849), 215*n.*
Novosiltsev, Count Nikolai (1761–1836), 94
Nowaczyk, Henryk (b. 1941), 103*n.*
Nowakowski, Józef (1800–1865), 125*n.*,
  525–26

Obreskoff, Princess Natalia (1795–1862),
  510, 606 and *n.*
Obrowo (Poland), 86
Observer, The (London), 641*n.*
Ogiński, Prince Michał Kleofas
  (1765–1833), 51–52
  "Farewell to the Fatherland," 52
Ojców (Poland), 140
Oldenburg (Germany), 579*n.*
Oliver y Suau (Spanish piano makers),
  390*n.*
Onslow, André-George-Louis
  (1784–1853), 128, 236*n.*, 649
Orléans (France), 418
Orłowski, Antoni (1811–1861), 229,
  345
Orsay, Count Alfred-Guillaume-Gabriel-
  Grimod d' (1801–1852), 557, 561
  and *n.*

Osborn, Emma (1816–1906), 314 and *n.*
Osborne, George Alexander (1806–1893),
  582
Ostrowski, Count Władysław
  (1790–1869), 216
Oury, Antonio James (1800–1883), 463
Oxford (England):
  Bodleian Library, 505*n.*

Pac, Count Michał Jan (1730–1787), 22–23
Paderewski, Ignacy Jan (1860–1941), 188,
  670
Paër, Ferdinando (1771–1839), 169,
  219–20, 342
Paganini, Niccolò (1782–1840), 84*n.*,
  134–39, 148, 151, 171
  Achille Ciro Alessandro (son) (b. 1825),
  137*n.*
Pagello, Dr. Pietro (1807–1898), 352
Palma (Majorca), 373–77
Palmerston, Lord Henry John Temple
  (1784–1865), 207*n.*
Pape, Jean-Henri (1789–1875), 232–33,
  344
Papet, Dr. Gustave (1812–1892), 400,
  450, 498, 509
Paris (France):
  Boulevard Poissonnière, 212, 213, 215,
  228
  Chaillot (suburb), 606, 609–10
  Champs de Mars, 552
  Champs Élysées, 435
  Chapel of St. Jérôme, 435
  Cité Bergère, 212, 229, 236
  Collège de France, 436, 451, 455
  Comédie-Française, 420, 487
  Conservatoire, 231, 237, 338, 435, 501
  Hôtel de France, 350
  Hôtel de Narbonne, 532
  Hôtel de Ville, 236
  Hôtel Lambert, 218, 493, 512, 543
  Les Invalides, 436
  Île Saint-Louis, 218
  Luxembourg Palace, 456, 552
  Madeleine Church, 409, 415, 619–24
  Montmartre cemetery, 449, 476, 645
  Palais-Royal Theatre, 344

Paris (*cont.*)
　Panthéon, 215
　Père Lachaise Cemetery, 228, 342,
　　623, 641, 664
　Place Vendôme, 218, 613, 619, 630
　rue de la Chaussée d'Antin, 216, 236,
　　292, 296, 309, 322, 331, 351, 368,
　　655
　Rue des Messageries, 212
　Rue Pigalle, 420, 432
　Saint-Cloud, 426–27
　Salle Érard, 442n.
　Salle Pleyel, 222, 224, 438, 544
　Square d'Orléans, 458–59, 464, 470,
　　476, 488, 492, 494, 509, 602
　Théâtre-Italien, 281, 425, 493
　Tuileries Palace, 447
Parish, George (1807–1881), 310
Parker, Douglas Charles, 589
Parys, Dr. Józef, 154
Paskevich, General Ivan Fyodorovich
　　(1782–1856), 192, 204–205
Pasta, Giuditta Negri (1797–1865), 313
Paul I, Tsar of Russia (1754–1801), 57
　Tsarina Maria Feodorovna
　　(1759–1828), 55, 57
Pereświet-Soltan, Stanisław (b. 1866),
　　22n., 133n.
Pergolesi, Giovanni Battista (1710–1736),
　　615
Périer, Jean Casimir (1777–1832), 228
Perpignan (France), 371, 372
Persiani, Fanny (1818–1867), 447
Perthuis, Count Léon-Amable de
　　(1795–1877), 382n., 544
　Émilie (wife) (1795–1877), 486
Peruzzi, Mme Élise, 260
Petrzyk, Reverend Leopold (1889–1960),
　　670, 671
Phénicien, Le (passenger ship), 391
Philharmonic Society (London), 562
Philipp, Isidor Edmond (1863–1958), 264
Philippeus, Colonel Teodor Friedrich,
　　165
Pieskowa Skała (Poland), 140
Pixis, Friedrich Wilhelm (1786–1842),
　　148

Pixis, Johann Peter (1788–1874), 148
Planté, Francis (1839–1934), 587n.
Plater, Count Ludwik (1774–1846), 216
　Countess Pauline (daughter)
　　(1813–1889), 343
Pleasants, Henry (1910–2000), 15n.
Pleyel, Joseph-Étienne-Camille
　　(1788–1855), 222, 309–10, 382,
　　623
　Marie (wife, *née* Moke) (*q.v.*), 309–10,
　　314
　Salle Pleyel, 222, 224, 438–39, 544–45
Ług, Adam (pseud. of Antoni
　　Pietkiewicz) (1823–1903), 668
　　and n.
Plutarch (45 A.D.–120 A.D.), 3
Polish Constitution (May 3, 1791), 24
Polish Literary Society (Paris), 235–36
Pomey, Louis (1831–1891), 564n.
Ponce, José de Vargas (1760–1821), 377n.
Poniatowski, Prince Józef (1763–1813),
　　295
Porpora, Nicola Antonio (1686–1768), 457
Posillipo (Italy), 276
Potocka, Countess Delfina (*née* Komar)
　　(1807–1877), 182, 382n., 463, 543,
　　605, 614–15, 653–54
　Count Mieczysław (husband)
　　(1799–1878), 182, 653
　Chopin's spurious letters to, 652–62
Potocki, Count Bernard (1800–1874), 351
Poturzyn (Poland), 156
Poznań (Poland), 129, 554
Pozzo di Borgo, Count Carlo (1764–1842),
　　305
Prądnik River (Poland), 140
Prague (Czech Republic), 147–48
　National Museum, 147
　Saint Vitus Cathedral, 148
　Vltava River, 148
Preaulx, Viscount Fernand de, 530
Prémord, Abbé Charles-Léonard de
　　(1760–1837), 356
Probst, Heinrich Albert (1791–1846), 385
Prokofiev, Sergei (1891–1953), 17
Prudent, Émile-Racine-Gauthier
　　(1817–1863), 559

Pruszak, Aleksander (1777–1847), 123
Marianna (wife) (1789–1853), 124–25
Konstanty ("Kostuś") (son)
(1808–1852), 123
Weronika Alexandra ("Olesia")
(daughter) (1814–1868), 123
Przybyszewski, Stanisław (1868–1927),
190

Quetglas family (Majorca):
Gabriel Quetglas Amengual
(1892–1971), 390n.
Gabriel Quetglas Olin (b. 1968), xxvi
Quodrado, Don José María (1819–1896),
393n.

Rachel (pseud. of Mlle Élisa Félix)
(1821–1858), 487
Radom (Poland), 154
Raducz (Poland), 177
Radziwiłł, Prince Antoni Henryk
(1775–1833), 54, 130–31, 166
Ludwika (wife) (1770–1836), 161
Andrzej Walenty (brother) (1778–1838),
229
Eliza Fryderyka (daughter)
(1803–1834), 102–103, 130, 159,
161
Wanda Augusta Wilhelmina (daughter)
(1808–1845), 130, 159
Antonin hunting lodge, 54, 159–62
Faust (opera), 161
Ramorino, General Girolamo
(1792–1849), 214–15 and n.
Ravel, Maurice (1875–1937), 17, 245
Miroirs, 176
Rawsthorne, Alan (1905–1971), 387
Reber, Napoléon-Henri (1807–1880), 415,
621
Reinerz (Duszniki-Zdrój, Poland), 45,
98–101
Reinschmidt, Józef Marceli (1809–1873),
178
Rellstab, Ludwig (1799–1860), 81n., 120,
318
Chopin and, 333–36
Iris im Gebiete der Tonkunst, 333

Rembieliński, Alexander (1800–1828),
89–90
Revue des deux mondes (Paris), 393
Revue et Gazette musicale, La (Paris),
281, 344, 348, 368, 439, 449,
547–48
Revue indépendante, La (Paris), 457
Rey, Alexandre (1812–1904), 368
Rhône River (France), 397
Richmond (England), 313
Richter, Sviatoslav Teofilovich
(1915–1997), 248
Ries, Ferdinand (1784–1838), 50, 62,
73n., 345
Robert-Houdin, Jean-Eugène
(1805–1871), 608n.
Rochefoucauld, Duke de la, 464
Roemer, Dr. Fryderyk (1770–1829), 95
Roger, Gustave-Hippolyte (1815–1879),
544
Rogerson, Dr. John (1740–1828), 58n.
Rogoziński, Antoni (1797–1835), 96
Rosen, Charles Welles (1927–2012),
247–48, 412n.
Rosenthal, Moriz (1862–1946), 429, 665
Rossini, Gioacchino Antonio
(1792–1868), 219, 342, 438
Il barbiere di Siviglia, 89, 178n., 489
La cenerentola, 145
La donna del lago, 182
La gazza ladra, 98
l'italiana in Algeri, 645
Mosè in Egitto, 149
Otello, 184, 424
Il turco in Italia, 165
Rostropovich, Mstislav Leopoldovich
(1927–2007), 515
Rothschild, Baron James Mayer de
(1792–1868), 230, 467, 543, 606,
628
Betty (wife) (1805–1886), 467, 509
Rouen (France), 345
Chopin's concert (1838), 345–46
Rousseau, Jean-Jacques (1712–1778),
170
Rousseau, Théodore (1812–1867), 535n.
Royal William (steamer), 576n.

Rozières, Marie-Élisabeth-Épicharis de
    (1805–1865), 445–46, 450,
    487–88, 512, 524, 536, 602
Rubini, Giovanni Battista (1794–1854), 341
Rubinstein, Anton Grigorevich
    (1829–1894), 266, 438
Rubinstein, Arthur (1887–1982), 18, 660
Rubio, Luigi (1795–1882), 605
    Vera (wife, née de Kologrivoff)
        (1816–1880), 322n., 605
Rudorff, Ernst (1840–1916), 322n.
Rzymski, Father (priest), 114

Saint Helena (Great Britain), 433–34, 620
Saint Petersburg (Russia), 92–93, 192,
    466, 496
Sainte-Barbe, Édouard de (1794–1858), 304
Sainte-Beuve, Charles-Augustin
    (1804–1869), 421
Saint-Gratien (France), 309
Saint-Saëns, Charles-Camille
    (1835–1921), 329
Salvi, Lorenzo (1810–1879), 579
Salzmann, Christian Gotthilf
    (1744–1811), 39
Samson, Jim (b. 1946), 523n.
Sand, George (pseud. of Amantine-
    Lucile-Aurore Dupin)
    (1804–1876), 5, 6, 343, 348,
    353–59, 632–33
    Maurice Dupin (father) (q.v.)
    Sophie-Victoire (mother) (née
        Delaborde) (q.v.)
    François-Casimir Dudevant (husband)
        (q.v.)
    Maurice (son) (1823–1889), 358, 371,
        375, 399, 419, 450, 497, 500–503
    Solange (daughter) (1828–1899),
        359–62, 371, 399, 498–503,
        530–36, 573, 618 and n.
    affairs of, 352, 512 and n.
    descriptions of Chopin, 54–55, 68,
        404–405, 438, 444, 445–46, 470,
        527
    judicial separation of, 370–71
    money problems of, 407–408, 421
    political activities of, 552, 554

    rupture with Chopin, 538–41
    WORKS
        Consuelo, 358n., 457, 493
        Cosima, or Hatred Within Love, 408,
            420–21
        François le Champi, 477
        Histoire de ma vie, 353, 361, 551, 585
        Un hiver à Majorque, 392–93 and n.
        Horace, 430
        Lélia, 352, 393
        Lucrezia Floriani, 446, 513, 523,
            526–30, 673
        La Mare au diable, 502
        Le Meunier d'Angibault, 493
        "Relation d'un voyage chez les sauvages
            de Paris," 493
        Spiridion, 393
        Teverino, 494
Sandeau, Jules (1811–1883), 352, 363–64
    Rose et Blanche, 363
Sanguszko, Prince Roman Adam
    Stanisław (1800–1881), 205
Sanniki (Poland), 123–24
Sapieha, Prince Kazimierz Nestor
    (1757–1798), 47
Sartoris, Mrs. Adelaide (Kemble)
    (1814–1879), 561, 566
Sayn-Wittgenstein, Princess Carolyne
    Elisabeth Jeanne von (1819–1887),
    647
Scheffer, Ary (1795–1858), 447
Scheibel, Louise (b. 1836), 644
Schinkel, Karl Friedrich (1781–1841), 159
Schlesinger, Maurice Adolf (1797–1871),
    346 and n., 385, 487, 553n.
Schmidt, Hans (1854–1923), 485
Schnabel, Joseph Ignaz (1767–1831), 181
Schoenberg, Arnold (1874–1951), 108
Schönche, Carl (1785–1861), 203
Schröder-Devrient, Wilhelmine
    (1804–1860), 243, 313
Schubert, Franz Peter (1797–1828), 145,
    478, 516
    Erlkönig, 143, 351
    Die Gestirne, 395
    Impromptu in E-flat major, op. 90,
        no. 2, 246

Schumann, Robert Alexander
(1810–1856), 10, 13, 14, 175, 188,
254, 290, 305n., 410
Clara (wife, née Wieck) (1819–1896),
14–15, 224, 291
description of Chopin, 294
Endenich asylum, 656
review of Chopin's "Là ci darem"
Variations, 14
WORKS
Carnaval, op. 9, 295n.
Kinderszenen, op. 15, 78
Kreisleriana, op. 16, 291
Sonata no. 1, in F-sharp minor, op. 11,
291
Schuppanzigh, Ignaz (1776–1830), 142,
145, 147
Schwabe, Salis (Salomon ben Elias)
(1800–1853), 578–79 and n.
Scotland, National Archives of, 607n.
Scotsman, The (Edinburgh), 595
Scott, Sir Walter (1771–1832), 563n.
Scriabin, Alexander (1871–1915), 17
Seine River (France), 215, 435, 510
Sèvres (France), 448
Seyfried, Ignaz Xaver von (1776–1841),
145
Sèze, Aurélien de (1799–1870), 361
Shakespeare, William (1564–1616),
592n.
Sielużycki, Czesław (1921–2006), 101
Siemiradzki, Henryk (1843–1902),
130–31
Sierakowski, Count Antoni (1783–1842),
116
Sikorski, Andrzej (b. 1955), 9
Sikorski, Józef (1815–1896), 11
Sivori, Ernesto Camillo (1815–1894), 640
Skarbek, Count Fryderyk Florian
(1792–1866), 11, 29–30, 34, 42,
94, 98, 121, 147
Kacper Melchior Baltazar (father)
(1763–1823), 27–28, 102n.
Ludwika (mother, née Fenger)
(1765–1827), 4, 27–31, 98, 121
Prakseda (wife), 98
Józef (son) (1819–1900), 98

Anna Emilia (sister) (1793–1873), 34
Michał (brother) (1796–1834), 45
suicide of, 45, 282
Skarbek, Wiktoria (1791–1828), 51 and n.
Skowron, Zbigniew, 12
Skrodzki, Józef Karol (1789–1832), 9, 11,
46,
Eugeniusz (son) (1821–1896), 11, 46,
48, 88, 96–98, 114
Slavík, Josef (1806–1833), 185
Slonimsky, Nicolas (1894–1995), 665
Sloper, Edward Hugh Lindsay
(1826–1887), 572–73, 601
Słowacki, Juliusz (1809–1849), 4, 12, 216,
279, 285 and n., 523
Służewo (Poland), 279, 298–99
Smart, Sir George (1776–1867), 313
Smoter, Jerzy Maria (1937–1975), 660
Sobański, Izydor (1791–1847), 577
Sochaczew (Poland), 171
Sokołowo (Poland), 72, 89
Soliva, Carlo Evasio (1792–1853),
104–105, 137 and n., 153–54, 165,
167, 172, 261
Anna Marianna (wife, née Kralewska
(b. 1801), 154
Somosierra Pass (Spain), 71
Sontag, Henriette (1806–1854), 166–67,
243, 333
Carlo Rossi (husband), 166
Sophocles (496 B.C.–406 B.C.), 470n.
Antigone, 470n.
Sowiński, General Józef (1777–1831), 27,
204–205, 208
Katarzyna Antonina (wife, née
Schröder) (1776–1860), 36
Sowiński, Wojciech (1805–1880), 230n.
Spohr, Ludwig (1784–1859), 136
Piano Quintet, 154, 295
Spontini, Gaspare Luigi Pacifico
(1774–1851), 128
Stamaty, Camille-Marie (1811–1870), 224
Stapleton, Frederick (1817–c. 1870), 316n.
Stanisław August II, King of Poland
(1732–1798), 49
Staszic, Stanisław Wawrzyniec
(1755–1826), 94–95

Stefani, Józef (1802–1876), 109
Stein, Mattäus Andreas (1776–1842), 142
Stiepanek, Johann Nepomuk
    (1783–1844), 148
Stirling, Jane Wilhelmina (1804–1859),
    xxviii, 33*n*., 270*n*., 543, 545, 556,
    557 and *n*., 571–75, 586, 598,
    607–608 and *n*., 613, 622, 628–29,
    647
    John (father) (1742–1816), Laird of
        Kippendavie and Kippenross, 571
Stirling-Maxwell, Sir William
    (1818–1878), 593
Stoepel, François (1794–1836), 281
Strachur House (Scotland), 586
Stradella, Alessandro (1639–1682), 615
    and *n*.
Strasbourg (France), 211, 212
Strauss, Johann (1804–1849), 199–200
Strauss, Richard Georg (1864–1949), 520
Strzyżewo (Poland), 102, 159
Stuart, Lord Dudley Coutts (1803–1854),
    313, 558 and *n*., 600
    "Address to the Poles," 558*n*., 562*n*.
Stuart, Mary (1542–1587), 585
Stuttgart (Germany), 203
    Chopin's "Stuttgart Diary," 27, 207–11
Sue, Joseph-Marie-Eugène (1804–1857), 351
Suez, Mlle Caroline, 499
Sumner, George (1817–1863), 493
Sun, The (London), 601
Sutherland, Duchess Harriet Leveson-
    Gower (1806–1868), 561–62
Suvorov, General Alexander (1729–1800),
    25, 94
Sydow, Bronisław Edward (1886–1952),
    12, 659, 668
    Correspondance de Frédéric Chopin, 659
Szafarnia (Poland), 11, 27, 71–82
    Szafarnia Courier, 11, 74–79
Szászebes (Transylvania), 464
Szeligowski, Tadeusz (1896–1963),
    660–61
Szembek, General Piotr (1788–1866), 171
Szklener, Dr. Artur (b. 1972), xxv
Szlagowski, Archbishop Antoni
    Władysław (1864–1956), 668, 670

Sztompka, Henryk (1901–1964), 670
Szulc, Marceli Antoni (1818–1898), 195
Szulc, Tad (1926–2001), 666
Szulczewski, Major Karol (1813–1884),
    218, 558, 599
Szwencki, Dr. Fryderyk (1774–1860), 96
Szymanowska, Maria (1789–1831), 134, 221

Taganrog (Russia), 92
Taglioni, Marie-Sophie (1804–1884), 458
Talleyrand-Périgord, Charles-Maurice de
    (1754–1838), 604
Tańska, Klementyna (1798–1845), 54*n*.,
    140*n*., 492
    Aleksandra (sister) (1793–1850), 53–54
    and *n*.
Tarnowski, Count Stanisław (1837–1917),
    210
Taubert, Wilhelm (1811–1891), 428
Tausch, Julius (1827–1895), 650
Tausig, Carl (1841–1871), 110
Tetschen (Děčín, Czech Republic), 284
Tellefsen, Thomas Dyke Acland
    (1823–1874), 424
Tennant, Stephen Cattley (1800–1848),
    640–41
Teplitz (Teplice, Czech Republic), 149
Thackeray, William Makepeace
    (1811–1863), 557
Thalberg, Sigismond (1812–1871), 144,
    233, 276, 559
    Chopin and, 16, 186
    Don Giovanni Fantaisie, op. 14, 464
    Liszt and, 338–39
Thames River (England), 560*n*.
Thekla, Maria Anna (1758–1841), 658
Thiers, Adolphe (1797–1877), 447
Thomas, Ambroise (1811–1896), 219
Thun-Hohenstein, Count Franciszek, 284
    Josefina (daughter) (1815–1895), 284–85
Times, The (London), 565*n*., 570 and *n*.,
    600
Tomaszewski, Mieczysław (b. 1921), 416,
    519*n*.
Torphichen, Lord James Sandilands
    (1770–1862), 576–78, 592
Toruń (Poland), 27, 45, 85–86, 279

Tovey, Sir Donald Francis (1875–1940), 332, 429

Towiański, Andrzej Tomasz (1799–1878), 455

Troupenas, Eugène (1798–1850), 412n.

Turło, Teresa Dalila, (1931–2017), 679

Urhan, Chrétien (1790–1845), 338

Vaccai, Nicola (1790–1848), 143

Valldemosa (Majorca), 376–81, 585

Vaughan Williams, Ralph (1872–1958), 82

Veltheim, Charlotte (1799–1873), 143

Verdi, Giuseppe (1813–1901), 567

Verny, Viscountess Kornelia de, 640n.

Versailles, Treaty of (1919), 25

Viardot-García, Pauline (1821–1910),
    424–25, 435–36, 438, 444–45,
    489–90, 497, 502–503, 614
  Louis Viardot (husband) (1800–1883),
    425 and n., 496, 542–43
  Louise (daughter) (1841–1918), 445,
    489
  arrangements of Chopin's mazurkas,
    564, 497–98, 563–66

Victoria, Queen of England (1819–1901),
    557, 559 and n., 586, 600n.
  Albert, Prince Consort (1819–1861),
    557, 586

Vierzon (France), 418

Vienna (Austria):
  Conservatory of Music, 485
  Hietzing, 198
  Kärntnertor Theatre, 142, 201
  Prater, 199
  St. Stephen's Cathedral, 186
  Währing Cemetery, 145

Villèle, Abbé Guillaume-Aubin de
    (1770–1841), 356

Villeneuve, René de (1777–1863), 509

Vincent, Marie-Louise (1867–1929), 666

Vogel, Zygmunt (1764–1826), 8, 65

Voigt, Henrietta (1808–1839), 295
  description of Chopin, 295

Voltaire (François-Marie Arouet)
    (1694–1778), 22, 29, 611n.
  Dictionnaire philosophique, 611

Wagner, Wilhelm Richard (1813–1883),
    247, 442n., 520
  Tristan, 273, 325

Walewska, Countess Marie (née Łączyńska
    (1786–1817), 27

Wallenstein, Albrecht von (1583–1634), 149

Waplewo (Poland), 116

Warsaw (Poland):
  Belvedere Palace, 59–60, 171, 180
  Brühl Palace, 55
  Brzezina's music shop, 110
  Casimir (Kazimierz) Palace, 46, 47, 65,
    93, 114
  Charitable Society, 38, 53, 113
  Church of the Capuchins, 469
  Church of the Holy Cross, xxv, 39, 96,
    618, 666, 667
  Church of the Visitation, 87
  Coffee houses:
    Dziurka (Little Hole), 168
    Kopciuszek (Cinderella), 168
    Suchy Las (Dry Forest), 168
  Conservatory of Music, 83, 104–105,
    142, 331
  Dzielna Street, 178
  Evangelical Church, 83
  Freemasons, 94
  High School for Music, 131
  Jan Böhm House, 44
  Krakowskie Przedmieście, 32, 44, 47
  Krasiński Palace, 114, 117–18, 121, 177
  Lyceum, 29–30, 42, 44
  Miodowa Street, 110, 469
  National Theater, 133, 172–73
  Nowy Świat Street, 472
  Oboźna Street, 96
  Powązki Cemetery, xxv, 469
  Radziwiłł Palace, 52
  Royal Castle, 83, 136
  Saxon (Saski) Palace, 42, 44, 55
  Tepper Palace, 177
  Town Hall, 94
  University, 87, 96
  Vistula River, 171, 191
  Zamoyski Palace, 629

Warsaw Courier, 83, 100 and n., 119, 169,
    179n., 291, 469, 555, 618n., 652

Warsaw Daily, 122
Warsaw Gazette, 53*n*., 118, 138*n*., 631*n*.
Waterloo, Battle of (June 18, 1815), 433
Weber, Carl Maria von (1786–1826), 128, 478
    Euryanthe, 143, 166
    Der Freischütz, 128
Weinstock, Herbert (1905–1971), 523*n*.
Weiss, Colonel Gustav, 60
Wellington, Duke Arthur Wellesley (1769–1852), 301, 557, 559–60, 562
Wessel, Christian Rudolph (1797–1885), 316, 385, 409, 463, 568–69, 570
Weydlich, Adam (1742–d. before 1815), 22–23
    Françoise (wife), 23
    Franciszek (brother), 23
Whittle, Bridget, xxviii
Wieck, Friedrich (1785–1873), 14–15, 290, 464
Wieniawski, Henryk (1835–1880), 136
Wierzyński, Casimir (1894–1969), 70, 659–60
Wiesenthal, Frau Helene, 662
    Chopin's spurious "Journal," 662
Wiesiołowska, Anna (*née* Skarbek) (*q.v.*), 102 and *n*., 159
    Stefan (husband) (1791–1861), 102
Wildt, J. (Kraków publisher), 636
William Wallace (paddle steamer), 602*n*.
Windsor (England), 313
Wishaw House (Scotland), 586
Witwicki, Stefan (1801–1847), 44, 110, 178, 433, 443*n*., 455*n*., 492
Wodzińska, Maria (1819–1896), 197, 279–308, 352, 365
    Wincenty Szymon (father) (1784–1849), 279
    Teresa (mother) (1784–1849), 289
        letters to Chopin, 297–300, 306, 317
    Antoni (brother) (1812–1847), 279, 286, 289, 306, 445–46
        borrows money from Chopin, 45, 306, 396
    Feliks Edmund (brother) (1815–1870), 279

Józefa (sister) (1824–1905), 65
Kazimierz (brother) (1816–1875), 67, 279
Antoni (nephew) (1849–1930), 286*n*.
Maciej (uncle) (1781–1848), 281, 285
Józef Skarbek (first husband) (1819–1900), 98, 101, 307 and *n*.
Władysław Orpiszewski (second husband) (1822–1881), 308
Wojtkiewicz, Mariola (b. 1974), xxv, 35*n*., 283
Wolff, Eduard (1814–1880), 428, 651
Wolicki, Archbishop Teofil (1767–1829), 129, 130
Wolicki, Konstanty Leon (1792–1860?), 61
Wołków, Anna (1811–1845), 167, 169, 172
Wood, John Muir (1805–1892), 576, 589
Wordsworth, William (1770–1850), 21, 42, 194
Wörlitzer, Sigismund 167
Wóycicki, Kazimierz (1807–1879), 39
Woyciechowski, Tytus Sylwester (1808–1879), 14, 46, 124, 151, 155–58, 165, 168–69, 172, 174, 178, 179, 182–83
    Aloysia Marcjanna Poletyło (wife) (c. 1815–1903), 158
    Fryderyk (son) (b. 1839), 158
Woytowicz, Bolesław (1899–1980), 670
Wright, William, xxix
Wróblewska-Straus, Hanna, 12, 208*n*., 618*n*.
Wrocław (Breslau, Poland), 181
Würfel, Wilhelm (1790–1832), 4, 87*n*., 142

Yui, Dr. Lisa, xxvii

Zaleski, Józef Bohdan (1802–1886), 492
Zamoyska, Countess Zofia, (*née* Czartoryska) (1778–1837), 52–53, 62
Zarzycki, Aleksander (1834–1895), 486 and *n*.
Zboiński, Count Ksawery (1795–1853), 115–16

Zdrojewski, Bogdan Andrzej (b. 1957),
   671
Żelazowa Wola (Poland), 4, 27, 29, 42,
   63–65, 90, 170, 198, 282, 669–70
Zelter, Carl Friedrich (1758–1832), 128
Zieliński, Faustyn (1796–1867), 173 and
   n., 292
Zieliński, Tadeusz Andrzej (1931–2012),
   111

Zimmerman, Pierre-Joseph-Guillaume
   (1785–1853), 344, 605n.
Zoilus, Greek grammarian (c. 400–320 B.C.),
   335n.
Züllichau (Sulechów, Poland), 129
Żywny, Wojciech (Adalbert) (1756–1842),
   17, 63, 121, 207
   as Chopin's teacher, 47–50
   death of, 449